MILLER'S
INTERNATIONAL
ANTIQUES
PRICE GUIDE

1988 AMERICAN EDITION

MILLER'S
INTERNATIONAL
ANTIQUES
PRICE GUIDE

1988 AMERICAN EDITION

COMPILED AND EDITED BY
JUDITH AND MARTIN MILLER

VIKING

HOW TO USE THE BOOK

Miller's uniquely practical *International Antiques Price Guide* has been compiled to make detailed information immediately available to the consumer.

The book is organized by category of antique: e.g. Pottery, Porcelain, Furniture, etc. (see Contents List on page 6); within each major category there are sub-categories of items in alphabetical order: e.g. basket, bowl, candlestick, etc., and these in turn are ordered by date. There are around 10,000 photographs of antiques and collectibles, each with a detailed description and price range. There is also a fully cross-referenced index at the back of the book.

In addition to individual entries there are special features throughout the book, giving pointers for the collector – likely condition, definitions of specialist terms, history, etc. – together with general articles, chapter introductions, glossaries, bibliographies where further reading is important, tables of marks etc. As all the pictures and captions are new every year the selection of items included quickly builds into an enormously impressive and uniquely useful reference set.

PRICES

All the price ranges are based on actual prices of items bought and sold during the year prior to going to press. Thus the guide is fully up-to-date.

Prices are *not* estimates: because the value of an antique is what a willing buyer will pay to a willing seller, we have given not just one price per item but a range of prices to take into account regional differences and freak results.

This is the best way to give an idea of what an antique will *cost*, but should you wish to *sell* remember that the price you receive could be 25-30% less – antique dealers have to live too!!

Condition
All items were in good merchantable condition when last sold unless damage is noted.

ACKNOWLEDGEMENTS

Judith and Martin Miller wish to thank a large number of International auctioneers, dealers and museums who have helped in the production of this edition. The auctioneers can be found in our specialist directory towards the back of this edition.

Copyright © Millers Publications 1987

**Viking Penguin Inc.,
40 West 23rd Street, New York,
New York 10010, U.S.A.
Penguin Books Canada Ltd.,
2801 John Street, Markham,
Ontario, Canada L3R 1B4**

Designed and created by
**Millers Publications
Sissinghurst Court
Sissinghurst
Cranbrook
Kent, England**
in association with
**A.G.W. International Ltd.,
Chicago, Illinois.**

All rights reserved.
First published in 1987 by Viking Penguin Inc.
Published simultaneously in Canada
ISBN: 0-670-81870-4

Typeset in England by Ardek Photosetters,
St. Leonards-on-Sea, England.
Origination by David Bruce Graphics, London.
Printed and bound in England by
William Clowes Ltd, Beccles

Editors' Introduction

by

Martin and Judith Miller

We started *Miller's Antiques Price Guide* in 1979 as a small cottage industry. We believed that there was a great need for a guide that illustrated photographically a very large number of antiques and collectibles that had recently actually been on the market, and that gave good precise descriptions and realistic prices. We wanted to produce the book, because it was the book we wanted to buy and could not find. Obviously we were not alone, because the 1987 Edition of the guide, which we produced – as we did the previous seven mainly for the British market, sold well over 100,000 copies and is now used daily not only by huge numbers of consumers but by major antique dealers and auction houses around the world as a standard reference work.

Three years ago we decided to produce a new edition especially for the US market. We have both travelled extensively and have always been convinced that, although there are obviously regional differences in the world of antiques, it is very much an *international* world and an *international* market – a fact borne out by the fact that the major auction houses in New York and London are the same companies. Dealers and collectors buy from all over the world directly or indirectly, and this makes a real impact upon the choice available everywhere. It really is a world without national barriers.

The first US edition followed the tradition of the original book. What we have produced was, we believe, by far the most comprehensive and practical book on the subject. Good, clear photographs of over 10,000 antiques and collectibles accompanied by detailed descriptions, masses of background detail, and researched price ranges made the book a standard reference for collector and professional alike.

The first three US editions of Miller's proved so successful in meeting the growing needs of the collector, dealer and enthusiast alike, that we have continued with this 1988 edition. The 1988 Guide has the added advantage of 120 pages of colour photographs.

We constantly stress that *Miller's International Antiques Price Guide* is a GUIDE and not a LIST. There is no set price for an antique but *Miller's* will give you the best pictorial and descriptive guide there is, and a realistic price *range*.
(See *How To Use the Book,* opposite).

We believe in a visual approach to the subject – how can you possibly judge the likely value of the item you wish to assess on the basis of comparative descriptions alone, except in the case of a few numbered collectibles? – so we change every photograph every year. This means that if you buy *Miller's* for a few years you will build up a fully comprehensive visual encyclopedia of every major category of antique and collectible with no repetitions from edition to edition.

We never use the standard photographs of museum pieces you will see in some guides. In any case these pieces are well covered in standard thematic reference books. All the items in *Miller's* are 'available' – they have actually been bought and sold during the past year. So we really do give a guide to the market, not just a theoretical survey.

Many people have helped us to compile the guide. However we could not possibly list everyone who has helped to make this book what it is, but their help has been invaluable. Because it is impossible for two people to have all the expertise to compile a general international price guide, we are in constant touch with salerooms and dealers all over the world to check and recheck our facts. Catalogues from all over the world pour into our headquarters here in Kent, England, for assessment and sorting. Trends are predicted, anomalies resolved, final selections made. *Miller's* is a never ending task – but one which we find fascinating and personally rewarding.

We hope to show you something of the inside world of antiques and that you enjoy the book and find it a profitable companion throughout 1988 and beyond.

CONTENTS

A rare early 20th century English bronze
statuette of Iris Ascending, the female figure
rising gracefully in front of a rocky crag.
Inscribed 'Executed in bronze by H.J. Hatfield
for the Art-Union of London 1902 from the
original by W.B. Kirk', this cast appears to have
been made from a subsequent edition of the
statuette which was originally produced in
1847. It is the only cast of the model at present
known. 21½in (54.5cm) high.
$4,000-5,500

INTRODUCTION

Recent trends continue to suggest that collectors are concentrating on the best possible examples they can afford within their collecting sphere. As a result lesser quality pieces either remain in the dealers' stock for long periods or at auction are unsold unless given realistic reserves.

As knowledge of English pottery increases due to the academic interest of some collectors and expert dealers the price levels rise. This aspect of rising prices tends to be associated with pottery of the late 17th and early 18th century but it is possible that judicious purchases within the presently anonymous group of Staffordshire wares will prove beneficial as scholarship within this field improves.

Price levels are also stimulated by interesting pieces appearing on the market. The impetus provided by the Rous Lench sale of July 1986 continued throughout 1987. This has been most strongly felt in the case of rare, perhaps dated, pieces of delft, Whieldon, slipware and saltglaze but this interest has also been reflected in the enthusiasm to buy rare survivors of what must have been fairly common domestic wares – small mugs, coffee cups, small jugs and the like.

Watch out for a continued rise in the price of 18th century black basalt wares with Wedgwood marked pieces continuing to lead the way.

English delftware remains a popular collecting field with a wide variety of price ranges to suit all pockets. An interesting selection of English tiles from the Liverpool, Lambeth and Bristol factories can still be built up relatively cheaply. Badly damaged tiles should fall into the $ 8-36 range, unless featuring Chinese figures or animals ($53-120). Biblical tiles of the more common type (perfect or minor damage only) $38-70 . Landscapes $38-90 Floral $30-80 . A perfect tile with Chinese figures $120+ . Tiles depicting animals $150+ .

The excitement generated by majolica over the past few years has not yet abated though there are signs that the prices of wares from unidentified factories may drop. Minton, Wedgwood and George Jones continue to be market leaders.

Baskets

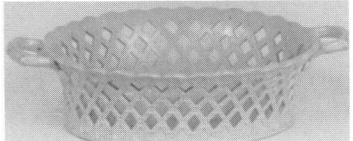

A saltglaze basket, 1765-70, 8in (20cm) wide.
$300-400

A Prattware basket, c1800, 3in (8cm) wide.
$400-500

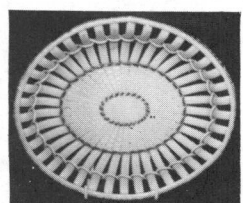

A pierced pearlware basket, with blue feather edge moulding, impressed Leeds Pottery.
$150-250

A Holics basket with rope twist handles, the rim moulded and painted with sprays of flowers between puce rims, manganese H2 mark, c1770, 11in (28cm) wide.
$1,300-1,800

A Dutch Delft polychrome fire basket, painted in yellow and manganese with lattice work top, 18thC, 4½in (12cm).
$600-900

Bellarmine

A Frechen stoneware bellarmine, with unusual twisted handle, early 17thC, 8in (20.5cm).
$1,000-1,400

Bottles

A London delft inscribed and dated sack bottle, inscribed in blue, cracks to body, glaze flaking to handle and rims, minor chips, 1648, 6in (15cm).
$3,000-4,500

Cf. Louis L. Lipski and Michael Archer, Dated English Delftware, No. 1359, possibly this example.

A Bunzlau brown stoneware glazed hexagonal bottle with pewter screw top, with double dolphin-shaped handle, 16thC, 12½in (31cm).
$5,500-7,000

A Castel Durante baluster armorial pharmacy bottle, the contents A.ED. Scabios a., named on a ribboned scroll beneath a yellow panel, the reverse painted with military trophies in brown and manganese reserved on a blue ground, minor chips, 17thC, 8½in (22cm).
$3,000-4,500

Bowls

A Liverpool delft char dish, the raised rim painted on the outside in polychrome, 10½in (27.5cm) wide.
$1,300-1,800

An English delft blue and white bowl, painted with Oriental figures within a shaped rim, hairline crack, 12in (31cm) diam.
$1,000-1,400

CREAMWARE

★ a low fired earthenware first produced c1740
★ Josiah Wedgwood perfected the body in the mid-1760's. This perfected body he named Queen's Ware in honour of Queen Charlotte
★ Wedgwood sold Queen's Ware in the white and with overglaze enamel decoration
★ the body was well suited to overglaze transfer printing
★ other potteries also produced creamware in large quantities, notably Leeds, Melbourne, Cockpit Hill (Derby) and Liverpool

A Herculaneum creamware bowl, with black transfer printed galleon, impressed mark, c1810, 10in (25.5cm) diam.
$150-250

A George Jones comport, the border with a rim of Gothic inspiration, the stem modelled as a tree trunk draped with ivy and with a doe seated at its base, naturalistic polychrome colouring, with impressed registration mark for 1878, 10in (25.5cm) and another smaller version of the same without the doe, with indistinct registration mark, 5½in (13.5cm).
$900-1,300

A blue and white Brameld broth bowl, with Castle of Rochefort pattern, some damage.
$60-100

Two Dutch Delft blue and white dishes, painted with flowers and scrolling foliage, one hair crack, 18thC, 15in (38.5cm) diam.
$400-500

A Dutch Delft shallow bowl, the cavetto painted with flowers in Chinese vases, in yellow enamel and underglaze blue, 13in (33cm).
$1,000-1,400

A pearlware inscribed and dated blue and white deep bowl, restoration to rim, cracks, 1784, 12½in (31.5cm) diam.
$1,500-2,600

Blagill was a lead mine at Tynehead in the Alston area in operation until the mid-19thC. The Logh-vein was primarily known as the Thorngill Vein.
Documentary pieces always command higher prices. This is especially true if the piece has local interest.

A Wedgwood salad bowl with electroplated rim, the feet modelled as cucumbers, impressed Wedgwood Rd 12072, 9½in (24.5cm) diam, and a Wedgwood electroplate and ceramic salad bowl and servers, naturalistic polychrome colouring, impressed Wedgwood, 9in (23cm) diam.
$750-1,000

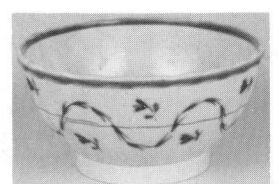

A Prattware bowl, c1790, 4in (10cm) diam.
$60-100

An Enoch Wood bust of Rousseau, c1800, 7in (18cm).
$400-500

An Enoch Wood bust of Voltaire, c1800, 6½in (16.5cm).
$450-700

A bust of gentleman, possibly Portobello, c1825, 8in (20cm).
$300-400

A Victorian pottery bust of a boy, on circular plinth, 18in (46cm).
$250-350

A Wedgwood 'Fairyland' lustre bowl of inverted bell shape, the exterior decorated with pixies playing amongst toadstools and cobwebs on a blue ground, pattern Z.5444, printed urn mark, 10in (25.5cm) diam.
$1,300-1,800

Busts

A bust of the Madonna, probably by Ralph Wood the younger, 15in (38cm).
$700-900

A Wedgwood black basalt bust, 'Democrates', on circular base, impressed mark, 14½in (36.5cm).
$750-1,000

A bust of Admiral de Winter, Continental pattern, c1840, 9in (23cm).
$250-350

A pair of German pottery busts of a bearded negro and his companion, each wearing earrings and colourful Eastern costume, set on a mottled socle base, late 19thC, 16in (41cm).
$600-900

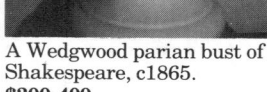

A Wedgwood parian bust of Shakespeare, c1865.
$300-400

Commemorative

A Staffordshire copper lustre oviform jug, printed with Cornwallis surrendering to Washington at York Town, October 19th, 1781, the reverse with the head and shoulders of General La Fayette, 5in (12cm).
$250-350

A Staffordshire plate in support of Queen Caroline, the ghost of Princess Charlotte appearing above crying 'Protect my Mother', c1819.
$300-400

A blue and white pottery deep dish, printed with King George IV sitting in his ermine trimmed robes, handing a bible to a child, inscribed 'I hope the time will come when every poor child in my dominions will be able to read the bible', early 19thC, 10in (25cm).
$450-600

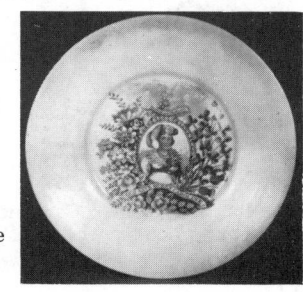

A Liverpool creamware mug, printed and coloured with 'an east view of Liverpool light house and signals, on Bidton Hill', above a numbered plan explaining the various flags, hair crack to base, c1788, 6½in (17cm).
$300-400

It is important to remember with commemorative wares that rarity does not always mean a high price. Desirability does.

A Liverpool creamware oviform jug, printed and painted with the American eagle above inscription and date 1804 and flanked by an oval panel, the reserve with bust portraits below the inscription 'in Memory of Washington and Patriots of America', the reverse with a soldier before a cannon and flag with ship in the background and inscribed 'Success to America Who's Militia Is Better Than Standing Armies', star cracked to body, rim chips, cracks, 10in (26cm).
$1,300-1,800

A jug, supporting Queen Caroline, sepia transfer and copper lustre, c1819.
$300-500

A Staffordshire jug, moulded in white with 2 bust portraits entitled 'Success to Queen Caroline' within oval beaded borders on solid pink lustre grounds, the rim with trailing foliage painted in enamels, c1820, 6½in (16cm).
$450-700

A commemorative plate of George IV, in coloured enamels heightened with lustre, c1822, 8in (20cm).
$450-600

A commemorative jug in purple lustre, with Princess Charlotte and Prince Leopold on the reverse, c1825, 7in (18cm).
$250-350

A Staffordshire jug, commemorating the coronation of William IV and Queen Adelaide in September 1831, printed in black with bust portraits, on a splashed pink lustre ground, c1831, 5½in (14cm).
$150-250

A Staffordshire plate for Queen Victoria's Coronation, 1838.
$300-400

A mug of Queen Victoria's Coronation, 1838.
$1,000-1,400

A white smear glaze stoneware jug, with relief decoration, commemorating the wedding of Edward, Prince of Wales and Princess Alexandra in 1863, marked W.B. ALBION COBRIDGE, 6½in (16.5cm).
$150-250

A Sunderland lustre jug, printed in black with sailing vessels entitled 'William IV' and flanked by The Mariners Compass and Prose, with sparse enamel decoration and within borders of broad pink lustre bands, c1830, 9½in (24cm).
$450-700

A Staffordshire mug for the wedding of Victoria and Albert, 1840.
$450-600

A Prattwate plate, for the wedding of Albert Edward, Prince of Wales and Princess Alexandra, c1863.
$250-350

A Castle Headingham Essex jug, the dark brown body moulded with 3 oval panels of figures and applied with shield-shaped crests of various Essex families, moulded mark and inscription and dated 1867, 12½in (31.5cm).
$250-350

Five stoneware jugs of Victoria's Diamond Jubilee, by Copeland Spode, 1897.
Smallest $75-150
Largest $150-250

A plate for Victoria's Golden Jubilee celebrations at Birmingham, Wallis Gimson, 1887.
$150-200

A Doulton mug for the wedding of the Duke of York and Princess May, showing the bride's mother, the Duchess of Teck, 1893.
$250-350

A German porcelain pink lustre mug for Victoria's Diamond Jubilee, hand-coloured on a white panel, 1897.
$60-100

A Staffordshire mug for Queen Victoria's Diamond Jubilee, 1897.
$60-100

A Doulton Lambeth blue green glazed beaker, decorated with applied moulded young and old portraits, 1897 Jubilee, 5in (12cm).
$75-150

A bone china mug for Victoria's Diamond Jubilee, by Hammersley, 1897.
$100-150

A Doulton Lambeth brown glazed stoneware jug, printed in brown with young and old portraits and inscription, 1897 Jubilee, 7in (18cm).
$100-200

A large Doulton stoneware jug, commemorating the Empire at Victoria's Diamond Jubilee, 1897.
$250-350

A Doulton Lambeth blue green glazed jug, with inscription 'She wrought her people lasting good', handle and lip restored, 9in (23cm).
$75-150

A Doulton bone china cup and saucer, heavily gilded, with colour portraits of King Edward VII and Queen Alexandra for their Coronation, 1911.
$150-250

A Doulton bone china beaker for the coronation of Edward VII, heavily gilded, 1902.
$250-350

A Royal Doulton brown glazed stoneware jug, printed in brown with portraits and inscription, hairline crack to lower handle, 1902 Coronation, 8in (20cm).
$45-70

A German biscuit porcelain grotesque match-striker, in the form of a caricature of Lloyd George, Chancellor of the Exchequer, c1909.
$75-150

A Royal Doulton brown blue glazed stoneware mug, printed in brown with portraits, 1911 Coronation, 4in (10cm).
$75-150

A Toby jug of George V, last of a series of 11 leaders of the Allies, in the Great War, 1914-18, designed by F. Carruthers Gould, made by Wilkinson for Soane & Smith, London.
$600-900

A plate made to commemorate the visit of Edward, Prince of Wales, to Canada, 1919.
$60-100

A Staffordshire mug for the Wedding of Mary, the Princess Royal to Viscount Lascelles, 1922.
$250-350

A pair of blue and white pottery plates, printed with views and scenes for North East Coast Industries Exhibition, Newcastle upon Tyne, May 1929-Oct., 11½in (29cm).
$100-200

A plate, In Memoriam, George V, 1936.
$150-200

Cottages

A pastille burner, modelled as a two-tiered building with pierced gilt edged windows and an iron red doorway, the shaped rectangular base modelled with an arbour and flowers, outlined in gilt, slight chips, c1840, 7in (18cm).
$600-900

l. A large two-handled loving cup bearing: The Smokers, 405, and Jolly Topers, 406, on a malachite ground with gold line decoration.
$300-500

c. A large two-handled loving cup of waisted form, bearing: Balaclava, Inkerman, Alma, 166, and The Redoubt, 216, on a maroon ground with gold line decoration.
$750-1,000

r. A two-handled loving cup, bearing: Passing the Pipe, 404, and The Smokers, 405, on a malachite ground with gold line decoration.
$300-400

A Copeland Spode pottery three-handled loving cup, Edward VIII, printed in black and decorated in colours and gilt with portrait and trophies, royal arms and Britannia, and inscription, edition No.10, 5½in (14cm).
$600-900

An unusual Mintons pottery vase, moulded in relief and decorated in colours with profile portraits and inscription, 1937 Coronation, 8½in (21.5cm).
$150-250

l. A Staffordshire cottage money box of double-fronted form, 19thC, 3½in (9cm).
$75-150

r. A Staffordshire cottage ornament in the form of a double-turreted chapel, 19thC, 9in (23cm).
$60-100

A Staffordshire cottage ornament, modelled as a large double-fronted house with 3 entrance doors, the sides clad in ivy, 19thC, 10in (25.5cm).
$75-150

A Prattware cow creamer, sponged in yellow, blue and ochre, c1790, 5in (13cm).
$1,000-1,400

A Yorkshire cow creamer, with brown markings, the shaped rectangular base modelled with blue and yellow leaves outlined in brown, c1790, 6in (15cm).
$1,200-1,600

> ### POTTERY: COW CREAMERS
> ★ the price of cow creamers depends upon age, type and complexity
> ★ Whieldon cow creamers are probably the most expensive
> ★ they are thinly potted and readily damaged and consequently few survive
> ★ they are to be distinguished by their rich tortoiseshell lead glaze coloured by the inclusion of different metallic oxides
> ★ these early cow creamers have a glassy appearance, the later Staffordshire and North of England products have a more primitive look, the potters relying on sponging simple high fixed oxides for decorative effect
> ★ generally speaking neatness of potting and a harmonious colouring make a piece expensive
> ★ other considerations are the presence of a milkmaid – 'hobbled' legs also add to value.

Cow Creamers

An early Staffordshire Whieldon type cow creamer, c1770, 5in (13cm).
$3,000-4,500

A Pratt cow creamer, a milkmaid kneeling beside a cow, with brown spotted markings, on green glazed base, c1780, 5in (12cm).
$4,000-5,500

Cow creamers have continued to increase in value. The early Pratt colours and milkmaid add to this desirability.

A Scottish cow creamer, the body sponged in black, puce and ochre, on a base sponged in green, black and puce, ears chipped, horns restored, c1790, 7½in (18.5cm) long.
$900-1,300

A Yorkshire style cow creamer and cover, modelled as a cow with dark brown and ochre markings, a calf at its side, the green glazed base modelled with stiff leaves, c1790, 5½in (14cm).
$4,000-5,500

Again the good colours, additional calf, good modelling and perfect condition add to this price.

A Staffordshire cow creamer and cover, with iron red and black sponged trefoils, standing on a green base, tail and ears restored, c1800, 7in (17cm) wide.
$450-700

A pair of cow creamers, Yorkshire or Staffordshire, c1800, 5½in (14cm).
$1,500-2,600

A rare Don Pottery group, modelled as a standing cow with brown and black markings, a gentleman wearing a black top hat, blue jacket and breeches, and a dog, on sponged base, c1800, 6in (15cm).
$2,250-3,000

Although not a creamer, this group is a delightful example of cow groups which are naturally associated with the creamers.

A brown treacle glaze cow creamer and milkmaid, c1820, 5in (13cm).
$400-500

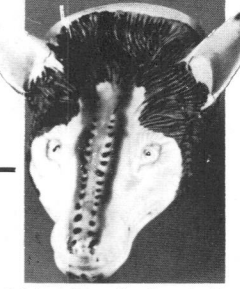

Cups

A Whieldon type fox head stirrup cup, naturalistically modelled, enriched in brown, green and yellow, small firing cracks, c1765, 5in (13cm) long.
$3,000-4,500

A Leeds creamware fox head stirrup cup, naturalistically modelled, enriched in iron red and black, the rim moulded with a band of foliage, repair to ears, c1765, 6½in (16.5cm) long.
$2,250-3,000

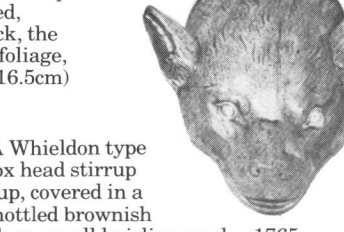

A Whieldon type fox head stirrup cup, covered in a mottled brownish glaze, small hairline crack, c1765, 5½in (14cm) long.
$1,500-2,600

A Whieldon type fox head stirrup cup, enriched in manganese and yellow, minor chips to ears and rim, c1765, 6in (15.5cm) long.
$2,250-3,000

A Prattware stag's head stirrup cup, enriched in ochre and brown, the antlers in yellow, minor repair to rim and tip of antlers, c1770, 5in (12.5cm) long.
$2,250-3,000

A Portobello cow creamer, with sponged decoration typically in raspberry, black and green, c1810, 5½in (14cm).
$800-1,200

A rare Pratt-type cow creamer, with black and ochre markings, the oval green mound base modelled with blue flowers, c1790, 8in (20cm).
$2,500-3,500

A Whieldon type green glazed fox head stirrup cup, entirely covered in a green glaze, repairs to ears, c1770, 5in (13cm) long.
$1,000-1,400

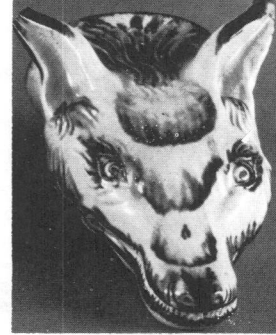

A Staffordshire fox head stirrup cup, the fleece enriched in blue, the interior rim inscribed TALEO (sic), one ear chipped, minor chips to rim, c1770, 5½in (14cm) long.
$1,200-1,600

A Staffordshire creamware fox head stirrup cup, repairs to ears, c1775, 5½in (14cm) long.
$750-1,000

A pottery cow creamer group, repair to hind leg, 19thC.
$150-250

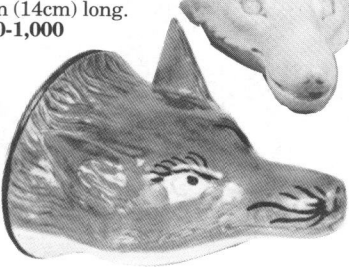

An early Staffordshire pottery stirrup cup, with some restoration, c1790, 3in (7.5cm).
$450-600

Stirrup Cups

Stirrup cups, sometimes known as hunting cups were, as their name suggests, cups used by huntsmen from which to quaff hot toddies or wine before the hunt commenced.

The act of drinking to the success of the hunt goes back through the ages and a number of types of drinking vessel are associated with such rituals. During the late 17th and early 18thC the most popular blood sports were fowling and hare hunting. Both gentry and countryfolk took part and numerous brown-glazed stoneware mugs decorated with hunting scenes in relief have survived to testify to the sport's popularity.

Fox-hunting became increasingly popular during the mid-18thC. Silver stirrup cups used by the mounted gentry rather than the foot-followers and dating from 1760 onwards, though uncommon, appear on the market from time to time. See *Miller's 1985* for an English example and *Miller's 1984* for a Russian example.

Pottery and porcelain examples from the 18thC are rare but 19thC examples, though still relatively scarce, do appear fairly regularly at auction.

Most often available are pottery examples produced in Staffordshire between 1820 and 1860 when the popularity of fox-hunting was at its peak. These are usually modelled in the form of fox or hound heads and measure between 3 and 6in (7.5-15cm) in length. Prices range between $600 and $1,200 for attractive examples. Particularly well decorated examples or those depicting unusual dogs command a premium and would range in price between $1,200 and $2,100 .

Top of the range are the superbly modelled black basalt examples from the Wedgwood and Bentley factory. Hound, fox and hare heads were produced and might fetch in the region of $7,500 in today's market. A particularly fine hare's head, marked 'Wedgwood and Bentley' in the left ear fetched $12,750 at Sotheby's in 1986. This was considered an exceptionally high price.

Any form of damage affects the price of stirrup cups considerably and it is well worth scrutinising pieces very carefully to ensure that the presence of chips, hair cracks or restoration is reflected in the price.

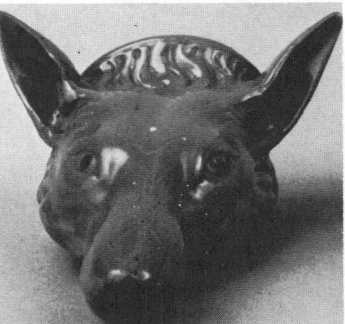

A Leeds fox head stirrup cup, entirely covered in an even brown glaze, the eyes enriched in black, c1770, 5in (13cm) long.
$600-900

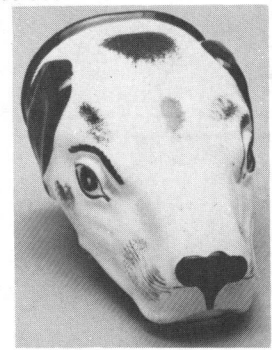

A Staffordshire pottery hound's head stirrup cup, the moulded head picked out in black and brown on a white enamel ground, late 18thC, 4½in (11.5cm) long.
$750-1,000

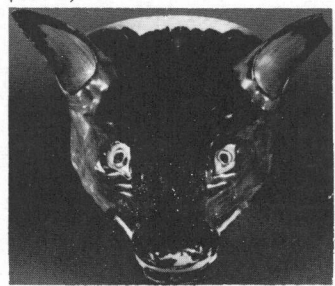

An English creamware fox head stirrup cup, enriched in brown and black tones, the mouth slightly open revealing its tongue, the reverse with the initials JD and the date 1778, hairline crack, one ear chipped, 5in (12.5cm) long.
$3,000-4,000

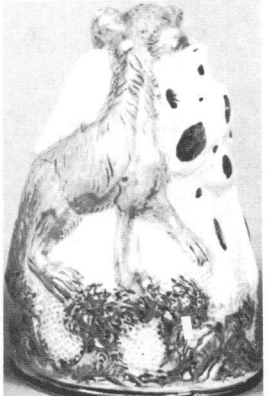

A Prattware stirrup cup, modelled as a hound, a fox and a goose on circular mount base enriched in ochre, brown and green, the rim with a blue band, hairline crack, small chip to rim, c1770, 4½in (11.5cm) long.
$2,500-3,500
Unusual subjects will always command a top price.

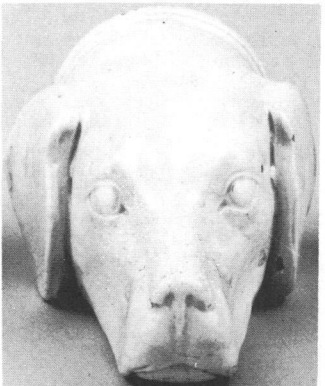

A Staffordshire hound's head stirrup cup, covered in an even cream glaze, c1780, 5½in (13.5cm) long.
$1,200-1,600

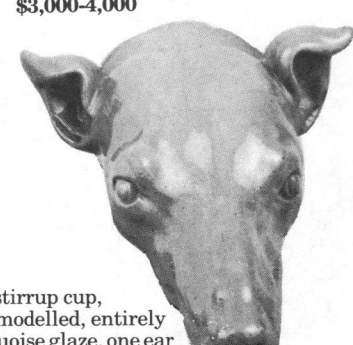

A hound's head stirrup cup, naturalistically modelled, entirely covered in a turquoise glaze, one ear repaired, c1800, 7in (17cm) long, wood stand.
$1,500-2,600

A creamware teabowl and saucer, c1775.
$100-200

A Somerset cider loving cup, together with 3 other pieces of cottage pottery.
$100-200

A Sunderland commemorative loving cup, from a seaman to his wife, showing the Eclyps out of Hull, 6in (15cm).
$250-350

A creamware feeding cup, with curving spout and feather moulded terminal to the loop handle, the back of the bowl with separate reservoir for hot water, small chip to rim, c1770, 7in (18cm) wide.
$300-400

Ewers

A pair of Wedgwood and Bentley black basalt ewers with dolphin handles, both handles repaired, one with neck restuck, some chipping to relief, unmarked, c1775, 16in (41.5cm) and 17in (42.5cm).
$6,000-8,000

An Italian majolica ewer, decorated with an oval reserve, inscribed Battaglia F., the blue ground decorated with flowers, the handle as a female caryatid and grotesque mask, raised on a blade knop stem and circular foot, restored, 19thC, 26in (66cm).
$250-350

A Minton helmet-shaped ewer, glazed in predominantly green, brown, blue and yellow, restoration to rim, impressed Minton 474 S and date mark for 1862, 12½in (31cm).
$1,300-1,800

A Dutch Delft blue and white ewer and cover, chips, early 18thC, 7in (18cm), and two Delft blue and white plates with flowers, chips, 18thC, 9in (23cm) diam.
$400-500

A Frankfurt blue and white enghalskrug, the handle with foliage scrolls with contemporary foot rim and hinged cover with shell thumbpiece, the cover inscribed MVD and dated 1695, hair crack to neck, minor rim chips, blue H mark, late 17thC, 9½in (24cm).
$1,500-2,600

Make the most of Miller's

Miller's is completely different each year. Each edition contains completely NEW photographs. This is not an updated publication. We never repeat the same photograph.

A German faience enghalskrug, painted in colours, with contemporary pewter foot rim and hinge, domed cover and ball thumbpiece, manganese Z mark of probably Zerbst, late 18thC, 10½in (27cm).
$3,000-4,000

A Staffordshire figure of a sheep, moulded with foliage, the base with sponged black and yellow decoration, horns restored, c1780, 6in (15cm) wide.
$450-700

An early Staffordshire solid agateware cat, in brown and cream clays, heightened with cobalt blue, c1760, 5in (12.5cm).
$3,000-4,000

A Staffordshire figure of a cat, lightly enriched with manganese scrolls and green patches, one ear repaired, minor chip to base and other ear, c1760, 4½in (11.5cm).
$750-1,000

A creamware model of a recumbent sheep, with brown markings, on oval-shaped base, c1780, 3in (8cm).
$400-500

A Staffordshire pottery figure of a creamware cat, c1800, 4in (10cm).
$600-900

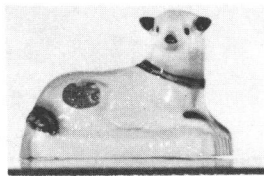

A creamware model of a recumbent sheep, with brown markings, on oval base, c1780, 3in (8cm).
$250-350

A rare model of a horse with black markings, wearing a yellow and blue saddle, on blue lined canted cornered base, c1800, 6in (15.5cm).
$1,300-1,800

A Staffordshire pottery figure of a lion, his head turned to the left and his left paw resting on a yellow ball, the lion with brown fur markings, the base enriched in green, repair to tail, c1770, 8in (20.5cm) long.
$3,000-4,000

A Staffordshire pottery figure of a lion, with beige hair markings, his left front paw resting on a yellow ball, the base with yellow line border, damage to tongue, c1780, 12½in (32cm) long.
$1,300-1,800

The growing number of American collectors of English pottery has increased the number of pieces sold in New York.

A Yorkshire figure of a horse, on a green sponged base, its coat sponged in black and with striped red and green saddle cloth with blue girdle, one ear repaired, minor chips to base and ears, c1790, 6½in (16cm).
$4,000-5,500

Cf John and Griselda Lewis, Prattware, p. 277, No. 64, for the type.

A Staffordshire saltglaze solid agateware cat, with blue lined ears and sparse blue patches, its coat with brown striations, c1750, 5in (12.5cm).
$4,000-5,500

A Rockingham glazed lion, attributed to the United States Pottery Company, Bennington Vermont, restored, c1850, 7½in (19cm).
$550-650

An early Staffordshire pottery figure of a leopard, c1800, 2½in (6cm).
$750-1,000

A rare Walton type model of a camel standing before a flowering tree, on shaped green mound base, 7½in (19cm).
$2,250-3,000

This price is dependent on the rareness of the animal and the good condition of the piece. It is also an early figure compared to the following late 19thC examples.

Two early Staffordshire greyhounds.
$150-250

A Staffordshire Whieldon type figure of a cockerel, c1785, 4in (10cm).
$450-600

A Victorian Staffordshire dalmatian, c1855, 5in (13cm).
$100-200

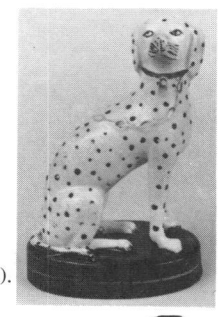

A hen on nest with baby chicks, c1850, 6½in (16cm).
$100-200

A pair of rare figures of camels, with water bottles at their feet, on coloured pink lustre lined bases, c1880, 6in (15cm).
$750-1,000

Cf. Antony Oliver, The Victorian Staffordshire Figure, *pl. 180.*

A pair of Staffordshire pottery elephants, 1860-70, 8½in (22cm).
$1,000-1,400

A rare figure of a spaniel with brown markings, wearing a gilt collar, the base modelled with leaves on a pink ground, c1855, 10in (25.5cm).
$1,000-1,400

A pair of Victorian Staffordshire greyhounds with hares at their feet, c1850, 10½in (26.5cm).
$250-350

A rare pair of rabbits with black markings, enamels with slight wear, c1850, 5½in (14cm).
$3,000-4,500

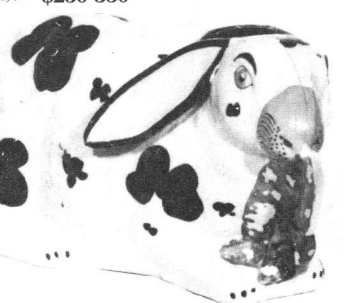

A George Jones figure of a camel, laden with panniers, pale blue, brown and cream highlighted with gilding, impressed with monogram CJ and Kumassie, 9½in (23cm).
$1,500-2,600

English Majolica

As reported in last year's guide, the market for English majolica is exceptionally strong. High prices at auction have, as is so often the case, stimulated the market and a steady supply of good-quality pieces has appeared for sale.

The market is not yet sufficiently established to be certain of what will and what will not hold its value. Suffice to say that most pieces sell well, including good pieces with minor damage. Watch out though! Damage can be difficult to spot and it does affect value. I was offered a pleasant Wedgwood jug in Chelsea for $352 though a hairline crack, visible only from the inside, should have reduced the value of the piece by a third or more. Take care too not to pay too high a price for unmarked wares from lesser factories. These have not held their value in recent years.

Minton, Wedgwood, George Jones and marked pieces from the minor factories should prove good buys in the forthcoming year.

A German figure of a monkey, with an iron red and yellow belt about its waist, decorated in grey and yellow glazes, fingers and toes chipped, late 19thC, 18in (46cm).
$750-1,000

A pair of Luneville figures of recumbent lions, with manganese face and body markings and with yellow manes and tails and sponged green bases, inscribed on the fronts Luneville, one figure with extensive glaze damage, late 18thC, 18½in (47.5cm) long.
$2,500-3,500

A Brown, Westhead, Moore & Co jardiniere, modelled as a rectangular plate holder of wooden slats draped with oak branches, above which an owl is perched on a log, the owl with glass eyes, naturalistic polychrome colouring, one ear restored, impressed Brown, Westhead Moore, 13in (33cm).
$3,000-4,000

A Continental pottery faience figure of a cat, decorated with medallion to neck, and green and black glass eyes, 14in (35.5cm).
$2,250-3,000

Figures – People

A Staffordshire figure of a peasant, by Ralph Wood, wearing pale blue jacket and green breeches, standing on a tree stump base, on square plinth, c1770, 7in (18cm).
$1,500-2,600

THE WOOD FAMILY	
Ralph Wood senior	1715-72
Ralph Wood junior	1748-95
Aaron Wood (brother of R. Wood snr)	1717-85
Enoch Wood (son of A. Wood)	1759-1840

A figure entitled 'The Lost Sheep' by Ralph Wood, decorated with coloured glazes on an unglazed base, c1775, 9in (23cm).
$1,500-2,600

Make the Most of Miller's

We do not repeat photographs in Miller's. However, the same item may appear in a subsequent year's edition if our consultants feel it is of interest to collectors and dealers. Ralph Wood's famous figures such as 'The Lost Sheep' and 'St George and the Dragon' have appeared in various editions, but as important period pieces it is of interest to see how prices have altered.

A figure of St Paul by Ralph Wood Jnr, with under and overglazed enamel, c1790, 14in (35.5cm).
$600-900

A Staffordshire pearlware figure of a girl in a blue dress and mob cap, on rockwork, above a square base moulded with garlands of flowers, chip to coat, c1790, 6½in (17cm).
$400-500

A Ralph Wood figure of Admiral Rodney, enriched in mottled green glazes, with blue breeches and brown shoes, the word 'Rodney' moulded beside his right leg, on rockwork moulded with naval trophies and square base moulded with flutes, minute chips to hat and base, c1780, 6½in (17.5cm).
$2,500-3,500

A Staffordshire hunting group, minor chips and repairs, the reverse impressed Titlenson (?), c1790, 6½in (16.5cm).
$2,500-3,500

A Staffordshire figure of a boy leaning against a tree stump with a dog at his side, in yellow spotted blue cloak and black shoes, on a rockwork base, chip to staff, c1790, 6½in (16.5cm).
$450-600

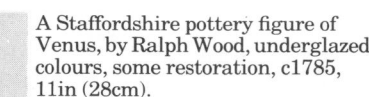

A figure of a huntsman, wearing a black plumed hat and holding a hunting horn, on square brown-lined based, c1795, 9in (23cm).
$300-400

A Ralph Wood figure of George and the Dragon, 1780-90, 11½in (29cm).
$1,500-2,600

A Staffordshire pottery figure of Venus, by Ralph Wood, underglazed colours, some restoration, c1785, 11in (28cm).
$600-900

A Prattware figure of a gaunt young man, late 18thC, 7in (18cm).
$400-500

A Staffordshire figure of The Good Shepherd by Enoch Wood, 8in (20.5cm).
$450-600

A square-based Staffordshire group of musicians, small repair, c1800.
$400-500

A Staffordshire pottery figure of Bacchus, by Ralph Wood, with coloured glaze, c1785, 13in (33cm).
$600-900

A Staffordshire figure of The Harvester by Ralph Wood the younger, c1800, 8in (20.5cm).
$450-700

A Staffordshire New Marriage Act group, c1823, 7in (18cm).
$1,500-2,600

A Staffordshire pottery village group, probably Walton, c1820, 8in (20.5cm).
$800-1,200

A Walton type group of Flight into Egypt, on shaped green rockwork base modelled with flowers, donkey with part ear missing, and other minor damages, c1815, 9½in (24cm).
$1,000-1,400

A Walton bocage group of a putto holding a basket of flowers, another basket at his feet, 5½in (14cm).
$150-200

Make the Most of Miller's

The pottery section is ordered by item and then by date. English pottery precedes Continental pottery.

A pair of Walton pottery bocage groups, of a barefoot boy and girl standing on a grassy mound, he with a dog, she with a lamb, slight damage, impressed Walton, 5½in (14cm).
$400-500

A Walton tythe pig group, c1815, 6in (15cm).
$450-600

An Obadiah Sherratt figure of St Peter, painted in enamel colours, with typical Sherratt bocage, c1820.
$750-1,000

JOHN WALTON

★ John Walton worked from c1805-50
★ is known mainly for sentimental figures with bocage backgrounds
★ bocage tended to support the figures in the kiln
★ uses some excellent vivid colours
★ work is often marked with an impressed name on a scroll at the rear
★ any animal groups with amusing lions are very desirable

A circus bear group of Savoyard and the Dancing Bear, probably by Obadiah Sherratt, c1830, 9in (23cm).
$1,500-2,600

An unusual Staffordshire figure of The Sailor's Return, possibly by Obadiah Sherratt, in under and overglazed enamel, c1820, 9½in (24cm).
$750-1,000

An Obadiah Sherratt group of Venus, c1820, 10in (25.5cm).
$450-600

OBADIAH SHERRATT
(1755-1845)

★ Sherratt worked at Hot Lane, Burslem, from c1815-28 and then moved to Waterloo Road

★ Sherratt specialised in 'social comment' groups

★ some Derby copies were tried at the factory but they tend to be crude and not of high value

★ highly collected are the 'Teetotal' groups (the word teetotal was not coined until 1833)

★ these groups are very detailed and hence some damage and restoration is acceptable

★ it used to be thought that the footed groups were early – but the teetotal groups are usually footed and they are certainly late

★ Sherratt's 'bull baiting' and 'Red Barn Murder' groups have great appeal

★ after Sherratt's death the factory was continued by his wife and son Hamlet until the late 1850's

★ many models were produced at this time using old moulds – these tend not to have the same detail and can have less vivid colours

A Staffordshire figure of 'The Poor Soldieer' (sic), depicting a Sergeant of the Staffs Regt, brightly coloured in enamels, c1830, 6in (15cm).
$750-1,000

A Wedgwood black basalt figure, 'Voltaire', impressed mark, 11in (28cm).
$450-700

A Wedgwood black basalt figure, 'Rousseau', impressed mark, 10½in (26.5cm).
$450-700

A pair of Staffordshire figures of William Shakespeare and Robbie Burns, 19thC, 13½in (34cm).
$300-400

A Dutch Delft blue and white seated magot, his robe panelled with flowers, some repair to his pipe and cup and saucer, minor glaze chips, early 18thC, 7in (18cm).
$1,500-2,600

An Obadiah Sherratt group of a lady, on a rearing horse, wearing orange hat and mauve habit, the horse mottled in brown with an orange ribbon about its tail, on an oval green mound base, she lacks crop, restoration to ears, reins, left foreleg of horse, minor glaze flaking, c1830, 8½in (22cm).
$2,500-3,500

A pair of figures of a milkmaid and boy, on oval coloured gilt lined bases, one horn chipped, c1860, 7in (18cm).
$600-900

A Victorian Staffordshire group, 'The Rival', c1850, 13in (33cm).
$100-200

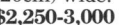

An Obadiah Sherratt group of lovers, she in large feathered yellow hat and puce bodice, holding a handbag, her companion in top hat and green jacket, both seated on a yellow garden seat, the base moulded with foliage scrolls and stiff leaves, damage to tree, restoration to arms and her hat, some flaking to enamels, c1830, 8in (20cm) wide.
$2,250-3,000

A Victorian Staffordshire figure of St George and the Dragon, 11½in (29cm).
$300-400

An elephant with Rajah and dead tiger, c1850, 9in (23cm).
$450-700

A Dutch Delft polychrome figure of a child seated in a wheeled high chair with scrolled back and marbelised sides, chips, 18thC, 5½in (13.5cm).
$2,250-3,000

A pair of Staffordshire figures of Victoria and Albert, slight restoration, 1845-50, 4in (10cm).
$150-250

A rare group of Victoria standing wearing a blue bodice and tartan skirt, her right arm around The Princess Royal standing above a goat, on oval gilt-lined base, c1842, 10in (25.5cm), (A,57/178).
$250-350

A Dutch Delft equestrian figure of Prince William of Orange, in manganese hat, orange jacket and brown breeches, base inscribed on the side 'Vivat Oranje', repaired through Prince William's right leg and coat tail, minor chips, blue script mark of De Lampetkan, mid-18thC, 6in (15cm).
$600-900

In the Ceramics section if there is only one measurement it usually refers to the height of the piece

A pair of Sicilian figures of Adam and Eve, with vine leaves around their waists, on leaf mound bases with yellow borders of gadroons, chips to edges of base and to the bird, minor glaze losses, late 17thC, 10½in (26cm).
$1,500-2,600

A Staffordshire figure group, 'Princess Royal and Prince Frederick William of Prussia', mid-19thC, 15in (38cm), (A,70, 217).
$250-350

STAFFORDSHIRE FIGURES

★ made as chimney ornaments
★ figures characteristic of the Victorian era became established in the 1840's
★ body actually whiter than earlier Staffordshire figures
★ made in 3 part moulds
★ base typically flat and oval
★ 1840-60 – strong colours, note particularly cobalt blue
★ early pieces well moulded and decorated to imitate porcelain
★ later flat-back figures much simplified
★ c1860's there was a development away from the strong colours to a lighter, more sparse colouring with more gilt decoration
★ 1870's virtual disappearance of underglaze blue
★ Victorian Staffordshire figures show immense interest in:–
  a. Royalty
  b. great interest in war
  c. politically most figures tend to be left-wing
  d. religious tend to be nonconformist (possibly caused by northern cottage interest – way of expressing dissatisfaction with ruling classes)
★ up to 1880 mercuric gold used on figures – tended to rub off
★ in the 1880's 'Bright Gold' used – much harsher in appearance
★ reproductions have none of the spontaneity of the Victorian figures
★ late figures modelling not sharp
★ most desirable figures tend to be the highly coloured prior to 1860!
★ the Crimean war period (1854-56) was probably the high point – both of production and quality
★ theatre, crime and sport seem to be the three collecting areas which hold their price and frequently astound estimators with some record prices
★ collectors should beware of description in sale catalogues which state 'rare' as this is frequently incorrect

A Staffordshire figure, Garibaldi, with horse, c1860, 10in (25.5cm), (C,97,282).
$300-400

A rare figure of George Parr, wearing a green flat cap, holding a cricket ball in his right hand, before a jacket, stumps and wicket, on gilt-lined base, c1865, 14in (35.5cm), (F,7/13).
$900-1,300

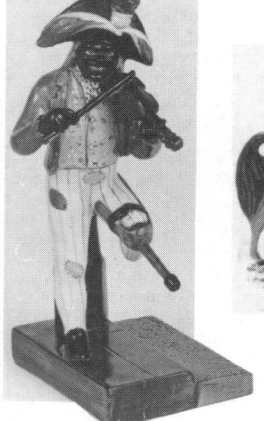

A Victorian Staffordshire figure of Billy Waters, negro busker, peg-leg, c1830, 8½in (21.5cm), (E,36).
$750-1,000

A late figure modelled as Jumbo the elephant, on raised oval base, named in impressed capitals, c1890, 6in (15cm), (E,104,212).
$150-200

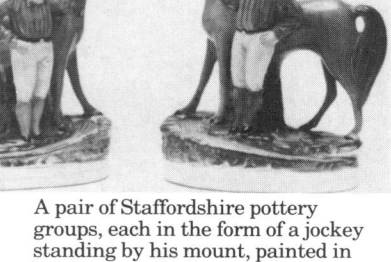

A pair of Staffordshire pottery groups, each in the form of a jockey standing by his mount, painted in bright enamel colours and gold, slight damage, 8½in (21.5cm).
$750-1,000

A Staffordshire Portrait figure of Sir R Tichborne 'The Tichborne Claimant', 19thC, (G,16,34).
$900-1,300

A very rare figure of Robert Evans standing wearing a black jacket, the base entitled 'Mr Robert Evans' in gilt moulded capitals, c1856, 11½in (29cm), (D,24,49).
$900-1,300

Two Staffordshire figure ornaments, 'Scottish Highlanders', mid-19thC, 14½in (36.5cm). (E).
$250-350

STAFFORDSHIRE FIGURES – VALUE POINTS

Condition The effect this has on the price varies with the rarity of the figure: on common figures damage substantially affects the price, on rare figures this effect diminishes proportionally with rarity and desirability.

Modelling Crisp, well-defined figures always fetch more than their 'last-out-of-the-mould' counterparts.

Colour Most Staffordshire collectors favour the brightly coloured examples (mostly early before the 1860's). These tend to be more expensive than sparsely coloured and white and gilt examples.

Subject Theatrical groups tend to command high prices. Many are untitled but tend to have great visual interest. The circus groups in particular are full of life.

Title In almost all cases a titled figure is worth more than its untitled counterpart.

Unascribed pieces An interesting aspect of the collecting of these figure groups is the rise in value if an unrecorded or unascribed piece can be found to have an authenticated source. If a piece can be identified from either a contemporary print or a theatrical handbill the value can rise as much as ten times. So research is worth while!

Decorative This is an extremely difficult point as so much depends on individual taste. It is important to note, however, that some pieces, although basically quite common, always fetch good prices because they are decorative and hence a large number of collectors enjoy their visual appeal.

Rarity and desirability These are extremely important areas when discussing the pricing of Staffordshire figures. As with all areas of antiques rarity tends to increase value. These figures were, in general, produced in large quantities, although for some strange reason, some figures turn up very rarely indeed. The desire for crisp figures also cuts down the number of figures which attract high prices. Some figures are very popular because they attract collectors from more than one specialist area.

Flatware

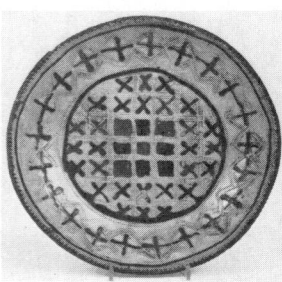

A Staffordshire slipware dish, the centre press-moulded with a criss-cross design of coloured squares in ochre and brown, surrounded by crosses on a cream slip ground, the well with a band of crosses within rouletted zig-zag pattern, the reverse with areas of chipping and flaking, minor flaking to design, early 18thC, 14in (36cm) diam.
$15,000-21,000

A pair of delft plates, painted in manganese with cracked ice border, possibly Bristol, c1750, 9in (23cm) diam.
$700-900

A London delft blue-dash oak leaf charger, painted in ochre, green, yellow and underglaze blue, with a blue-dash rim, slight crack at 11-o-clock, c1675, 13in (33.5cm) diam.
$4,500-7,000

Cf Louis L Lipski and Michael Archer, Dated English Delftware, no. 59, for a charger with the arms of Northampton dated 1671 with similar diaper-pattern panels to the border.

A Bristol delft blue-dash Adam and Eve charger, painted and sponged in blue, the couple standing on turquoise grass, with a blue and yellow line and blue-dash rim, chips and cracks to rim, c1710, 13in (30.5cm) diam.
$1,500-2,600

A Bristol delft blue and white small salver, on 3 shaped feet, enriched with whorl-pattern, chips to rim and feet, c1740, 5½in (13.5cm) diam.
$900-1,300

A Bristol delft dish, decorated with a mimosa pattern, c1740, 14in (35cm).
$300-400

A Liverpool delft plate, with bianco-sopra-bianco, decorated in Fazackerley palette, c1760, 9in (23cm) diam.
$450-600

A large delft dish decorated in colours, probably Liverpool, minor crack, c1760, 13in (33cm).
$400-500

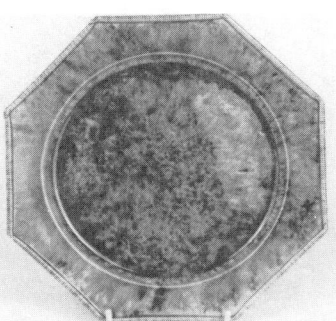

A Whieldon octagonal manganese plate, c1770, 9in (23cm) diam.
$300-400

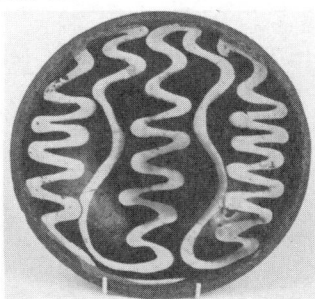

A slipware dish, late 18thC, 10in (26cm) diam.
$750-1,000

A Leeds creamware plate, decorated in black with the baptism of Samuel, 18thC, 9½in (25cm) diam.
$450-700

A Staffordshire dish, moulded with a swan or a goose, late 18thC, 4½in (11.5cm) diam.
$600-900

A Masons Ironstone plate, silver shape with peony decoration, impressed mark, c1820, 8in (20cm).
$100-150

A London delft blue-dash tulip charger, the centre painted in turquoise, blue, yellow and iron red, the border with stylised leaves and fruits and with a blue-dash rim, cracked and chips restored to rim, late 17thC, 13½in (34cm) diam.
$1,500-2,600

A large spongeware Scottish pottery dish, printed in red and green with repetitive stylised foliate bands and painted in blue and red with large flowersprays within blue lines, 16in (41cm) diam.
$150-250

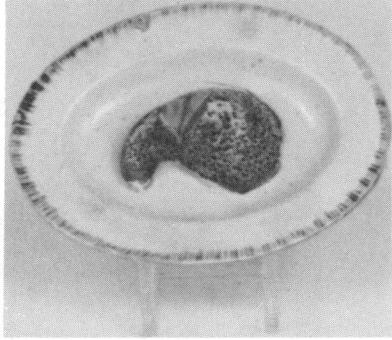

A Don pottery child's pearlware plate, with a transfer print in black of children with spinning top.
$60-100

A blue and white oval ashet liner, pierced and decorated with a sphinx to the centre, with key pattern border, early 19thC, 17in (43cm) wide.
$150-250

A Staffordshire dish, moulded with a joint of meat, late 18thC, 3½in (9cm) wide.
$400-500

A Glamorgan child's plate, 1815-20, 6in (15cm) diam.
$30-50

A child's plate, c1820, 5in (12.5cm) diam.
$30-50

A dish with a lobster, late 18thC, 4½in (11.5cm) wide.
$600-900

A pearlware plate with chinoiserie decoration in blue, with feather edge moulding, possibly Leeds.
$60-100

c. A large Bristol delft dish decorated in blue, some chips, c1760, 13in (33cm).
$450-600

l. and r. A pair of Bristol delft plates, decorated in blue, some chips, c1760, 9in (23cm).
$450-600

A Bassano dish, rim chips, late 18thC, 13½in (34cm) diam.
$1,500-2,600

A transfer printed blue and white pottery platter, by Bathwell & Goodfellow, marked Rural Scenery, some damage, c1820, 19in (48cm) wide.
$150-250

This pattern appears to be unrecorded.

A blue and white transfer printed plate, Pastoral Scene by Edward and George Phillips, c1825, 10in (25cm).
$75-150

A Bayreuth blue and white dish, painted with a border of foliage lappets, minor rim glaze chips, c1730, 8½in (22cm).
$1,500-2,600

A blue and white transfer printed plate, with a Chinese Temple pattern, impressed Leeds Pottery.
$60-100

A George Jones sweetmeat dish, with moulded decoration of oak leaves and acorns, moulded maker's monogram GJ and Stoke-on-Trent and impressed registration lozenge for 1868, 12in (30cm) diam.
$1,200-1,600

A Dutch Delft blue and white saucer dish, the centre painted with chinoiserie figures with an elephant, the reverse with panelled circles, rim ground and cracks repaired, blue SVE mark of Samuel Van Eenhorn, c1680, 17½in (44cm).
$1,500-2,600

A blue and white transfer printed plate, in the Castle of Rochefort pattern, impressed Brameld.
$60-100

A Delft plate decorated in blue, 1698, 10in (25cm).
$450-700

A fourteen piece Deldare earthenware service, consisting of a large pitcher, a large platter and 6 mugs, designed by A Roch, entitled 'An Evening at Ye Lion Inn', and 6 plates designed by A Delaney, entitled 'Ye Town Crier', printed Made at Ye Buffalo Pottery 1908, Deldare Ware underglaze, pitcher 12in (31cm).
$1,300-1,700

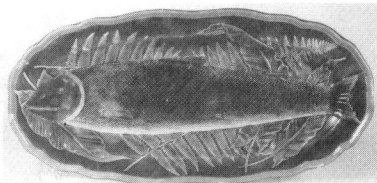

A Wedgwood salmon platter, with relief moulded decoration of a salmon on a bed of fern and leaves, naturalistic polychrome colouring on a brown ground, impressed Wedgwood, 25in (64cm) long.
$1,500-2,600

A pair of Creil pottery plates, printed in black and brightly painted, each border decoration with birds and scrolling foliage, 8in (21cm).
$400-500

A blue and white transfer printed plate, depicting the Scene after Claude Lorraine pattern, impressed Leeds Pottery.
$60-100

A Delft plate decorated in blue, 1714, 8½in (21.5cm).
$400-500

A Dutch Delft blue and white plate, the centre with S + B above the date 1740, the border with a pagoda, trelliswork and flowers, rim chips and glaze flaking, 9in (23cm).
$400-500

A Dutch Delft polychrome plate, painted with a parrot and rockwork, 9in (23cm).
$150-250

Five Dutch Delft blue and white plates, painted with mythological scenes, with chocolate rims, one repaired, rim chips, blue CB and star marks, mid-18thC, 9in (23cm) diam, and a polychrome bowl with a bird in a landscape, chips, 7½in (18.5cm) diam.
$1,500-2,600

A large French faience plate, c1830.
$150-250

A pair of Dutch Delft blue and white dishes, mid-18thC, 9½in (24cm) wide.
$2,250-3,000

A French faience plate applied with apples, painted in colours with stylised foliage swags and yellow panels, the centre with yellowish-green apples, firing crack to plate, 9in (23cm) diam.
$800-1,200

A Savona blue and white pierced tazza, minor rim chips, blue lighthouse mark, c1700, 14in (35.5cm) diam.
$1,300-1,800

A Strasbourg hexafoil plate, the centre with a tulip and the border with 3 other flowers and with brown rim, c1750, 9½in (24cm).
$1,500-2,600

Jars

A Lodi faience plate, brightly painted, the rim painted with insects and sprigs, late 18thC, 9in (23cm).
$600-900

Two English delft miniature drug jars, early 18thC, 1½in (4cm) high.
Left **$250-350**

Right (due to damage).
$150-250

Delescot is the name of the apothecary.

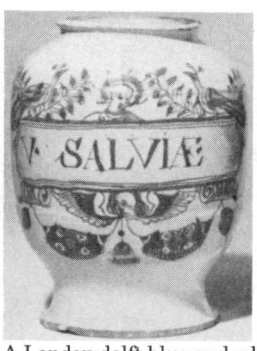

A London delft blue and white Apollo drug jar, named for 'V. SALVIAE', slight rim chips, c1680, 7½in (19cm).
$1,000-1,400

A London delft blue and white drug jar for 'C. ANTHOS', named on a cartouche, chip to rim, cracked, some minor glaze flaking, c1680, 6½in (16.5cm).
$800-1,200

A London delft dry drug jar, inscribed 'U. PERPET', c1720, 6in (15cm).
$600-900

A pair of London delft blue and white wet drug jars named for 'S.E.SPIN.CERU' and 'S. PAPAU.ERR' on ribbon cartouches, one cracked, both with chips to rims, c1740, 6½in (17cm).
$750-1,000

A pair of Donovan pottery jars and covers, in ochre and blue, c1810.
$1,000-1,400

A pair of Venetian albarelli, the contents named in blue and manganese gothic script for 'Argiento vino' and 'Elle eletrof', reserved on blue grounds, scraffito and painted with scrolling flowering foliage in colours, one with rim crack, rim chips, c1500, 7in (17.5cm).
$3,000-4,000

Jugs

An inscribed Liverpool delft puzzle jug, decorated in blue, c1750, 8in (20cm).
$4,000-5,500

A Staffordshire saltglaze cream jug and cover, painted in a bright 'famille rose' palette with a bird perched on pierced blue rockwork, the cover with 2 flowersprays within a green and black scroll border, c1750, 5in (12.5cm).
$1,500-2,600

A Staffordshire saltglaze bear jug and cover, covered in chippings of frit, with a chain through its nose and with long fangs, its neck with a band of dark brown slipware dots forming a collar, left leg re-stuck, damage to chain, neck and cover and pieces lacking, c1755, 9½in (24cm) long.
$3,000-4,500

A Whieldon type creamware jug, moulded in the form of a fish, the fins painted green, the scaly body yellow, 6in (15cm) long.
$450-600

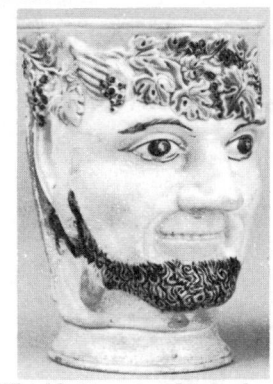

A Whieldon type mask jug, the smiling Bacchanalian mask with brown curly beard and yellow horns, enriched in blue and green, his eyes enriched in blue, small chip below the chin, c1755, 5in (13cm).
$600-900

A Prattware puzzle jug, with figures inside wheel, c1790, 9in (23cm).
$750-1,000

A pearlware inscribed jug, painted in colours in the manner of Absolon of Yarmouth, inscribed 'Mr. & Mrs. Binsteed – taking the Air', the reverse inscribed 'Success to the Toll Dish', and with a carnation spray beneath the spout, with blue diaper and ochre line rim, crack to body, minute chip to foot rim, stained, c1790, 7½in (18.5cm).
$3,000-4,500

A toll dish was a bowl of stated dimensions for measuring the toll of grain exacted by the miller in payment for grinding. It would seem, therefore, that Mr and Mrs Binsteed were millers, although their names do not appear to be recorded in the local parish records.

An unusual Leeds creamer, with a pair of fowl in a cage, possibly Dutch decorated, slight chip, 18thC, 4½in (11cm).
$600-900

A deeply moulded Prattware jug, depicting a resting traveller and horse, c1795, 8½in (21.5cm).
$600-900

A rare blue and white Brameld jug, marked Brameld.
$150-250

Four pieces of Turner marked stoneware, 18thC:
l. A water jug.
$750-1,000
l.c. A sugar box with restored lid.
$400-500
r.c. A moulded jug.
$450-600
r. A silver mounted mug, with crack.
$150-250

A silver lustre jug, with rural scenes in purple, c1820, 6in (15cm).
$300-400

A Staffordshire mask jug, early 19thC.
$150-200

SUNDERLAND LUSTRE

In the 1950's Sunderland lustre jugs used to be priced roughly £1 to an inch. This has certainly changed. Lustre now is valued on historical interest of subject; rarity of shape, quality of print or painting, and of course condition. A great deal of lustre ware has been damaged and repaired.

An early Prattware jug, the Duke of York, c1790, 6½in (16.5cm).
$250-350

An ironstone footbath and jug, with Chinese decoration, c1820.
$1,000-1,400

A creamware inscribed jug, with the inscription 'Jane Strickelton Armley', probably Leeds, chips to spout, c1800, 5in (13cm).
$400-500

A pink lustre jug, c1820.
$450-700

A copper lustre jug, with sheep on one side and a greyhound on the reverse, c1830, 8in (20cm).
$300-400

A purple lustre jug, c1835, 6in (15cm).
$250-350

A Ridgway stoneware jug, c1840.
$400-500

A terracotta jug with enamel decoration, possibly Watcombe, c1870, 3½in (9cm).
$30-50

A Dutch Delft blue and white helmet-shaped jug, the fluted body painted with lappets of cell-pattern and flowers between bands of flowering foliage, on spreading circular foot, minor rim chips, c1700, 9in (22.5cm).
$1,500-2,600

A Westerwald armorial blue and grey stoneware baluster jug, moulded with the arms of the Holy Roman Empire, with the date 1688, the blue ground incised with scrolling flowerheads and foliage and with contemporary hinged pewter cover with shell thumbpiece, 10in (25cm).
$1,000-1,400

Toby Jugs

TOBY JUGS

There are many contradictory theories about the inspiration of this jug in the form of a drinking figure in a three cornered hat. Some claim the honour for Sir Toby Belch, of 'Twelfth Night', and others Uncle Toby in 'Tristram Shandy' by Sterne. It is more likely however that the character came from a print published in 1761 of Toby Philpot illustrating a popular song 'The Brown Jug'. By far the most desirable 'Tobys' were made by Ralph Wood but most of the pottery factories produced them in quite substantial quantities. For the collector there are many varieties: 'The Nightwatchman', 'The Drunken Parson', 'Prince Hal', 'Hearty Good Fellow', 'Admiral Jarvis', 'Martha Gunn' etc. On these early jugs, crisp modelling, good colouring and any unusual features all increase value. Many Toby jugs were produced depicting characters from the First World War and also later of Churchill. As most of these were limited editions, their rarity leads to reasonably high prices today.

A Dixon Austin and Co Sunderland creamware jug, decorated with an oval vignette of the cast iron bridge over the river Wear at Sunderland, the ground with pink lustre, 19thC, 8in (20.5cm).
$450-600

A collection of country pottery from provincial France.
$50-150 each

A large Sunderland lustre jug, c1850.
$600-900

A creamware Toby jug, decorated in blue, grey and yellow translucent glazes, possibly Leeds factory, c1775, 9½in (24cm).
$800-1,200

A Ralph Wood Toby jug of conventional type, the warty-faced man seated holding an overflowing jug of ale, with a pipe in his arms, in green jacket, beige waistcoat and ochre breeches, hat and right foot restored, c1770, 10in (25cm).
$3,000-4,500

A Ralph Wood Toby jug, with dark brown hat, translucent green waistcoat, mottled tortoiseshell coat, blue breeches and dark brown shoes, 10in (25cm).
$1,500-2,600

A rare 'Village Idiot' Toby jug, decorated in coloured enamels, 9in (23cm).
$1,000-1,400

A Staffordshire Toby jug, with brown face and hands, grey jacket and waistcoat and pale yellow breeches, a dog between his feet, minute chips to hat, slight crack to base, c1770, 8½in (23.5cm).
$2,500-3,500

A Ralph Wood Toby jug, in brown hat and jacket, grey waistcoat and yellow breeches, holding a jug with a pipe at his side, pipe repaired, small crack to base and minor glaze flaking, c1770, 10in (25cm).
$1,500-2,600

A Ralph Wood Toby jug, impressed 51, 10½in (26.5cm).
$2,250-3,000

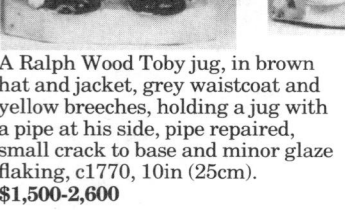

A rare Pratt type Toby jug modelled as a rotund gentleman, on brown lined canted cornered square base, the underside entitled 'Tobey', c1790, 10in (25cm).
$1,000-1,400

A Whieldon Toby jug, hat, shoes and chair with tortoiseshell glazes, wearing a blue waistcoat and apple green coat and breeches, a blue and white jug inscribed B.T. in his left hand, a glass in his right, on octagonal base, 10in (25cm).
$2,250-3,000

Any unusual feature such as the inscribed jug adds to the value of these collectable items.

A Ralph Wood 'Planter' Toby jug, in coloured translucent glazes, c1785, 12in (30cm).
$2,500-3,500

EMPEROR OF THE FRENCH, LEGAL REFORMER, MILITARY GENIUS AND OUR 1,643RD CLIENT.

When Napoleon had made his last charge, one Harry Phillips of London was charged with disposing of the emperor's assets.

Not that such an auction was particularly unusual for our founder.

Indeed, twenty-five years earlier, after the revolutionaries had brought down the blade on the head of Marie Antoinette, it was Mr Phillips who brought down the gavel on her collection of paintings.

However illustrious our past client list may be, Phillips today prides itself on being accessible to everyone, whether they bring us a fine work of art or a merely functional piece of furniture.

Everyone who comes to Phillips can have personal contact with any of one-hundred-and-twenty or so specialists, a decided advantage, as regular vendors at auction will know.

And with eighteen auction rooms throughout the country, by far the largest network in the UK, the specialists are always available for you to call upon.

If you would like any further information about Phillips, as well as a complimentary copy of our preview of forthcoming auctions, just ring Andrew Singleton on 01-629 6602.

You will find our service is as impressive as our heritage.

FINE ART
AUCTIONEERS
AND VALUERS
SINCE 1796

BLENSTOCK HOUSE, 7 BLENHEIM STREET, NEW BOND STREET, LONDON W1Y 0AS · Telephone: 01-629 6602
406 EAST 79TH STREET, NEW YORK, NY 10021, U.S.A. · Telephone: 0101 212 570 4830
LONDON (3 AUCTION ROOMS) · BATH · CAMBRIDGE · CARDIFF · CHESTER · COLWYN BAY · CORNWALL
EDINBURGH · EXETER · FOLKESTONE · GLASGOW · IPSWICH · KNOWLE · LEEDS · MELBOURNE · MORLEY
NORWICH · OXFORD · SHERBORNE · BRUSSELS · GENEVA · NEW YORK · PARIS · ZURICH
Members of the Society of Fine Art Auctioneers.

Pottery and Porcelain

A Staffordshire slipware inscribed and dated puzzle jug, spout lacking, chips and glaze flaking, c1709, 4½in (11cm).
$9,000-12,000

A blue dash charger, decorated with the Temptation, London, c1640, 14½in (37cm) diam.
$10,500-14,000

A Staffordshire saltglazed stoneware Dog of Fo, with incised zig-zag pattern cut with a wheel, c1730, 7in (18cm). **$10,500-14,000**

A pair of Staffordshire saltglaze polychrome swans, each with moulded plumage, with 2 cygnets beneath their breasts, on oval mound bases, c1750, 7in (17cm). **$75,000-90,000**

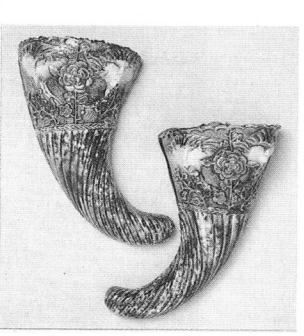

A large English delft dish, c1750, 13½in (34cm).
$300-400

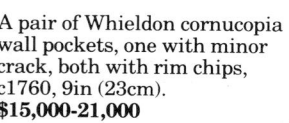

A pair of Whieldon cornucopia wall pockets, one with minor crack, both with rim chips, c1760, 9in (23cm).
$15,000-21,000

A Whieldon owl jug and cover, its head forming the cover, with loop handle, chips and other damage, c1760, 6in (15.5cm).
$60,000-75,000

A Ralph Wood Toby jug, with raised arm and translucent colour decoration, c1775, 9½in (24cm).
$1,500-2,600

Four delftware tea caddies, c1760, 3 to 4½in (7.5 to 12cm).
$1,000-1,400

Three Ralph Wood Toby jugs, c1775, 9½in (24cm).
$1,200-1,600

An intricately pierced creamware chestnut basket and cover, with double rope twist handles, Leeds, c1790, 9½in (24cm).
$2,250-3,000

A Masons footbath and jug, c1820.
$4,000-5,500

A rare Yorkshire cow creamer, with typical sponge decoration, the cow attended by a crinoline lady of the period, c1800.
$1,500-2,600

A Yorkshire money box in bright underglaze colours, impressed mark J Emery, Mexborough, c1838.
$1,500-2,600

Staffordshire Figures

Jenny Lind as Alice.
$450-700

Dick Turpin. **$150-250**

MacDonalds of Glencoe.
$400-500

Giulia Grisi & Guiseppe Mario.
$700-900

Prince Albert. **$150-250**

Protestantism & Popery.
$450-700

The British Lion and
Napoleon III. **$250-350**

Alexander II of Russia.
$400-500

Sexton. **$400-500**

Gladstone. **$400-500**

A non-portrait Crimean
figure. **$450-600**

Napoleon. **$150-250**

A garniture of Nevers vases, 17thC. **$9,000-12,000**

A Böttger stoneware teapot and cover, modelled by Johann Jacob Irminger, c1715. **$28,500-31,500**

A Minton plant trough, 14in (35.8cm). **$13,500-17,500**

A Gubbio lustre tondino and plate, rim chips, c1530, 8½ and 9½cm (22 and 25cm) diam. l. **$9,000-12,000** r. **$15,000-21,000**

A documentary Moustiers mythological polychrome plaque, inscribed J. Fouque on reverse, Olerys factory, c1740, 8in (21cm). **$45,000-52,000**

A Böttger glazed red stoneware teapot and cover, each side engraved with a crowned oval cartouche, c1715, 5½in (13.5cm) wide. **$27,000-30,000**

A Rookwood standard glaze pottery Indian portrait vase, decorated by Grace Young, impressed mark with date cypher for 1905, 12in (30.5cm). **$4,000-5,500**

A pair of polychrome pottery horses, early W Han Dynasty. **$48,000-52,500**

A Han stone horse head. **$13,500-17,500**

An early vessel, Han Dynasty, 16½in (41.5cm) long. **$9,000-12,000**

A glazed model of a watchtower with figures, Eastern Han Dynasty, 35in (89cm) high. **$30,000-34,500**

A Han pottery horse. **$30,000-34,500**

A Changsha stoneware ewer, Tang Dynasty, 9thC. **$18,000-22,500**

A Sancai pottery figure of a caparisoned horse, Tang Dynasty, 24in (61cm). **$21,000-24,000**

A Yuan blue and white dish, minor foot chip, c1360, 17½in (44cm) diam.
$150,000+

An early Ming heavily potted celadon garden seat, late 14th/15thC, 16½in (41.5cm).
$13,500-17,500

A celadon foliate bowl, under a translucent olive glaze covering the foot, 14thC, 12½in (32cm) diam. **$9,000-12,000**

A heavily potted celadon dish, 14thC, 17½in (44.5cm) diam.
$9,000-12,000

A blue and white vase, minor fritting, Yuan Dynasty, 7½in (19cm). **$18,000-22,500**

A Yingqing ewer and cover, under a pale bluish white glaze, Song Dynasty, 6½in (16cm) wide.
$6,000-9,000

A Wucai box and a cover, star crack and re-touched, Wanli 6-character mark and of the period, 7½in (19cm) diam. $19,500-24,000

A Ming blue and white vase, meiping, late 15thC, 12½in (31.5cm) high. $10,500-14,000

A rare blue and white jar, Wanli 6-character mark and of the period, 14in (36cm). $45,000-60,000

A heavily potted Ming blue and white jar, minor fritting, late 16thC, 14in (35cm). $10,000-13,000

A rare metal mounted Ming blue and white 'Magic Fountain' ewer, restoration to neck, the porcelain late 16thC, later mounts, 12in (30.5cm). $7,500-10,500

A rare Ming blue and white vase, guan, painted with Xi Wang Mu, 15thC, 14in (36cm) high, wood box. $75,000-90,000

A rare Ming blue and white ewer, the foot uncut and base unglazed, stretcher crack, spout frit chipped, late 15thC, 9½in (24.5cm). $18,000-22,500

A Ming blue and white baluster jar and a cover, guan, interior chip, finial made up, late 15th/early 16thC, 14½in (37cm). $10,500-14,000

A Ming blue and white dish, minor fritting, c1500, 20in (51cm) diam, fitted box. $16,500-22,500

A Ming Wucai box and cover, cover restored,
Wanli six-character mark within a horizontal
double square and of the period, 14in (35cm)
wide. **$9,000-12,000**

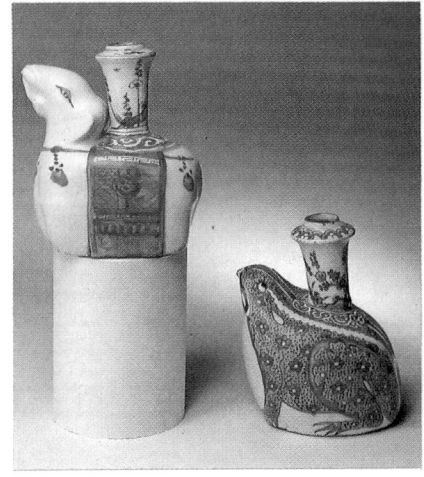

Ming blue and white kendi modelled as
an elephant and a frog, damaged, Wanli,
l. **$7,500-10,500** r. **$15,000-21,000**

Two Wucai dishes, chips,
Tianqi, 5½in (14cm) wide.
$2,250-3,000

A Wucai dish, warped, Tianqi/
Chongzheng, 8in (20cm) diam.
$5,500-7,000

A late Ming dish, fritted and
repairs, 5½in (14cm) diam.
$3,000-4,500

Two Transitional Wucai vases and
covers, fritted and restored,
late 17thC, 14½ and 15½in
(36.5 and 39cm) high.
l. **$1,500-2,600** r. **$7,500-10,500**

A pair of blue and white vases,
one neck cracked, mid-17thC, 19in
(48cm) high. **$6,000-9,000**

A garniture of blue and white jars
and domed covers, marked, Kangxi,
12½ to 13½in (31.5 to 34cm) high.
$10,500-14,000

41

A pair of blue and white garden seats,
Kangxi, 18½in (47cm) high.
$7,500-10,500

A Louis XV ormolu mounted glazed Chinese
porcelain brule parfum, modelled as a toad,
Kangxi, with later enamelled coat-of-arms,
10½in (26cm). **$39,000-42,000**

A moulded pale celadon deep bowl, Yongzheng
six-character seal mark and of the period,
13in (33.5cm) diam.
$15,000-21,000

A pair of 'famille rose' black
ground vases and covers, c1735.
$21,000-24,000

A pair of blue and white armorial dishes,
one cracked, c1752, 13in (35cm) diam.
$18,000-21,000

A brush pot, Kangxi mark
and of the period, 6in
(15.5cm) diam, box.
$13,500-17,500

A 'famille rose' and
Ducai vase, Qianlong mark
and of the period, 6in
(15.5cm). **$15,000-21,000**

A 'famille rose' tureen and cover, restored, Qianlong. **$16,500-19,500**

A 'famille rose' armorial ecuelle, cover and stand, gilding rubbed, early 19thC, stand 10in. **$30,000-36,000**

A 'famille rose' hunting punch bowl, chipped, Qianlong, 13in (32.5cm). **$6,000-8,000**

A 'famille rose' armorial garniture of vases and covers and 2 beaker vases, restoration, c1775, largest 14in (36cm). **$28,500-34,000**

A pair of 'famille verte' Buddhistic lions, damage and restoration, mid Qing Dynasty, 22½in (57cm) high. **$60,000-75,000**

A 'famille rose' figure of a Dutch merchant, restored, Qianlong, fixed wood base, 16½in (42.5cm). **$60,000-75,000**

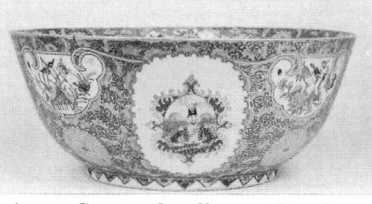

A rare Canton 'famille rose' Royal portrait bowl, rim chip restored, late Qing Dynasty. **$6,000-8,000**

A pair of blue and white baluster vases and covers, cover damaged, c1800, 25in (64cm). **$10,500-14,000**

A pair of 'famille rose' trays, with central inscription, Jiaqing seal marks and of the period, 6½in (16cm) wide, fitted box. **$6,000-8,000**

A 'famille rose' garniture, the beakers restored, drilled, early Qianlong, the vases 11½in (29cm), on wood stands. **$24,000-27,000**

A rare Doucai censer, the exterior carved with an inscription dated Qianlong 5th year, for AD 1740, and of the period, 12½in diam. **$21,000-27,000**

A pair of Canton 'famille rose' vases,
19thC, 128cm. **$15,000-21,000**

Kakiemon models of Bijin, late 17thC.
l. **$7,500-10,500**   r. **$15,000-21,000**

A Kakiemon bowl with moulded rim, c1680,
8½in (21.5cm) diam.
$18,000-21,000

A Kakiemon ewer of
Islamic form,
restored, Kanbun/
Empyo period, 13in
(33cm) high.
$15,000-21,000

A pair of 'famille rose' fish bowls,
late Qing Dynasty, 20in (51cm) diam.
$16,500-19,500

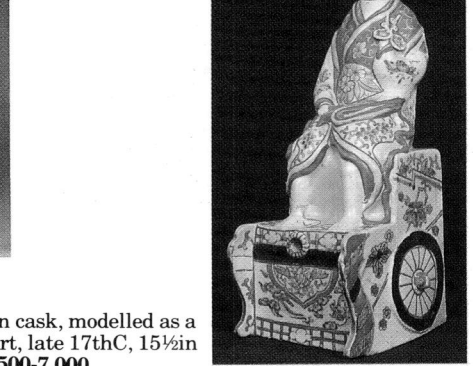

An Imari gin cask, modelled as a
bijin on a cart, late 17thC, 15½in
(40cm). **$4,500-7,000**

A large Satsuma vase, signed Satsuma Isshuin Chikusai ga, late 19thC, 19in (48cm) high. **$9,000-12,000**

A pair of Hirado dishes, in Kutani style, signed on bases Dai Nihon Hirado san Shiei Sei, late 19thC, 24in (61cm). **$6,000-9,000**

A Bow owl, petal missing, c1758, 8in (20cm). **$42,000-45,000**

A Genroku style Imari dish, late 19thC, 22½in (57cm) diam. **$13,500-17,500**

An Arita apothecary bottle, chips, c1680, 11in (28cm). **$6,000-9,000**

Chelsea teabowls and saucers in the Kakiemon palette, c1752. **$2,250-3,000 each**

A Bow leaf dish, red anchor and dagger mark, small chip, c1760. **$800-1,200**

A Chelsea sauceboat and dish, in Kakiemon palette, c1750. l. **$10,500-14,000** r. **$6,000-9,000**

Chelsea plates and a dish, in the Kakiemon palette, c1752. l. **$3,000-4,500** c. **$7,500-10,500** r. **$10,500-14,000**

A Chelsea salt, modelled as a crawfish, after a silver original by Nicholas Sprimont, damage to legs, c1745, 5in (12.5cm) wide. **$22,500-25,000**

Chelsea teabowls and saucers, c1752. l. **$3,000-4,500** r. **$7,500-10,500**

Chelsea peach shaped jugs with stalk handles, c1750, 4½in (11cm) wide. **$7,500-10,500 each**

A Chelsea cream jug, chips, crown and trident mark in blue, c1749. **$7,500-10,500**

A Chelsea cane handle, damage, c1745. **$3,000-4,000**

and a Chelsea goat and bee jug, damage, incised triangle mark, c1745. **$6,000-9,000**

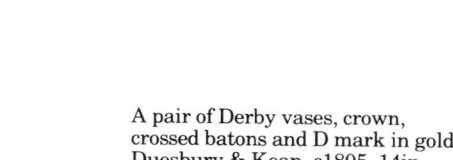

A Chelsea group of 2 goats, painted in the workshop of William Duesbury, restorations, raised red anchor mark, c1751, 6½in (16.5cm) wide. **$15,000-21,000**

A pair of Derby vases, crown, crossed batons and D mark in gold, Duesbury & Kean, c1805, 14in (35cm). **$9,000-12,000**

A pair of Chantilly cache pots, puce hunting horn marks, c1745, 5½in (13.5cm) high. **$27,000-30,000**

A pair of Derby figures of Leda and The Swan and Europa and the Bull, repairs, c1765, 11in (28cm) high. **$9,000-12,000**

A Worcester coffee cup and saucer from the Stormont service, chips, c1770. **$4,500-7,000**

A documentary Bristol white figure of Lu Tung-Pin, Benjamin Lund's factory, 1750. **$30,000-37,500**

A pair of Worcester baskets, covers and stands, some minor chipping, c1770, the stands 10½in (26.5cm) wide. **$10,500-14,000**

A Bloor Derby dinner service, comprising 116 pieces, circular Bloor Derby mark in red enclosing a crown. **$7,500-10,500**

A KPM teapot and domed cover, painted in the manner of J G Höroldt, c1730. **$75,000-90,000**

A Plymouth mug, in 'famille rose' palette, c1770. **$7,500-10,500**

47

A Fulda figure of Scaramouche, modelled by Wenzel Neu from the Commedia dell'Arte, chips, blue cross mark, c1770. **$33,000-37,000**

A pair of Frankenthal figures of a youth and a girl, by J F Lück, repairs, c1775. **$9,000-12,000**

A Frankenthal group of a youth unmasking a girl, by J W Lanz, chips, marked, c1757. **$6,000-9,000**

A pair of Fulda figures of fruit sellers, by Georg Ludwig Bartholome, chips and repairs, blue crowned FF marks, c1785, 6in (15cm). **$33,000-37,000**

A Höchst chinoiserie group, repairs and chips, iron red wheel mark, before 1753, 9½in (24cm). **$45,000-52,000**

A pair of Ludwigsburg figures of Chinese musicians, by Joseph Weinmüller, damage and restoration, blue crown interlaced Cs and incised marks, c1767, 11in (28cm) high. **$27,000-33,000**

A Fürstenberg figure of Columbine, from the Commedia dell'Arte, by Simon Feilner, repairs, c1753, 7½in (19.5cm). **$27,000-33,000**

A pair of Fulda figures of vintagers, by Georg Ludwig Bartholome, repairs, blue cross marks, c1770, 6in (15cm). **$30,000-36,000**

A Ludwigsburg figure of a cellist, from the Musik Soli series, by J C W Beyer, restoration, incised FN monogram, c1770, 7in (18cm) high. **$7,500-10,500**

A Fulda sporting group of a huntsman and companion, damage, blue crowned FF mark, c1780, 6in (15cm) high. **$52,000-60,000**

A Böttger porcelain Hausmalerei leaf shaped
pickle dish, painted by Ignaz Preissler,
damage, c1725, 4½in (11cm). **$10,500-14,000**

A pair of Meissen bottle vases, painted by J E
Stadler, repairs, marked, c1732. **$15,000-21,000**

A Meissen tureen and cover, blue
crossed swords mark, c1730, 12½in
(32.5cm). **$7,500-10,500**

A pair of Meissen Kakiemon sake bottles and covers
and a coffee pot and cover, c1730. **$7,500-10,500**   **each**

A Meissen tray and plate, blue cross swords mark,
c1730. l. **$7,500-10,500**
r. **$22,500-25,000**

A Meissen Augustus
Rex vase, painted
in the Kakiemon
palette, rim chips,
blue AR monogram
mark, 1731-36,
11in (27.5cm).
$15,000-21,000

l. A Meissen figure of a magot, c1743, 7½in
(19.5cm). **$6,000-9,000**; r. A Meissen teapot
and cover, c1738, 8in (21cm). **$9,000-12,000**

A Hausmalerei teabowl and saucer, painted by J P
Dannhöfer, damage, c1725. **$30,000-34,500**

A Meissen vase, painted in Böttger lustre by
J E Stadler, damage, blue AR monogram, c1734,
12in (30.5cm). **$10,500-14,000**

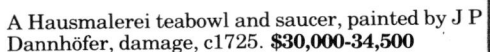

A Meissen group, by J J Kändler, c1740. **$49,500-54,000**

A pair of Louis XV ormolu, tôle and Meissen porcelain candelabra, 8½in (21.5cm). **$15,000-21,000**

A pair of Meissen figures of stags, modelled by J J Kändler, restoration, c1750. **$15,000-21,000**

A Meissen figure of Harlequin Alarmed, by J J Kändler, c1740. **$67,000-75,000**

A Meissen group of Mezzetin and Columbine, c1741. **$37,000-42,000**

A Meissen group of Die Polnische Verlobung, c1745. **$10,000-13,000**

A Louis XVI ormolu mounted Meissen covered bowl, cracked, c1745, 12in (30cm). **$10,500-14,000**

A pair of ormolu mounted Meissen porcelain pomade pots, c1745, 8½in (21.5cm). **$7,500-10,500**

A Meissen chinoiserie tankard and contemporary silver gilt cover, painted by J G Höroldt, c1745, 7½in (18.5cm). **$21,000-24,000**

A porcelain (part) dinner service from the Peterhof Palace comprising 22 pieces, c1860. **$10,500-14,000**

A Vincennes tray, rim chip, blue interlaced L marks and inscribed, c1750, 11in (27cm). **$1,500-2,600**

A pair of Paris vases, 8½in. **$18,000-21,000**

A pair of ormolu mounted Sèvres pots-a-oille with covers, c1830, 13½in (34cm) high. **$16,500-19,500**

A pair of Sèvres vases Hollandais, chips, inter-laced L marks and date letter G for 1759, painter's mark and CN incised, 7½in (18.5cm). **$19,500-24,000**

A pair of ormolu mounted Sèvres 'bleu celeste' porcelain Versailles tubs, the porcelain 18thC, possibly painted later, 9in (23cm). **$4,500-7,000**

A pair of documentary Vincennes white hunting groups, modelled by Jean Chabry, damage, c1752, 12½in (32cm) wide. **$150,000+**

A pair of Vincennes 'bleu lapis' vases. **$4,500-7,000**

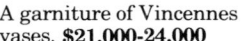

A pair of ormolu mounted Sèvres vases. **$6,000-9,000**

A garniture of Vincennes vases. **$21,000-24,000**

A Sèvres, Louis Philippe, Royal presentation botanical dessert service, comprising 83 pieces, damage, 1835-1842. **$375,000+**

A pair of Sèvres pattern gilt bronze mounted vases, the reverses with crowned LP monograms, late 19thC, 34in (86cm) high. **$9,000-12,000**

An ormolu mounted Sèvres porcelain seau a liqueurs, porcelain 1792, mounts c1820. **$6,000-9,000**

A Sèvres 'bleu nouveau' and Louis XVI ormolu jardinière, gilt crowned interlaced L's enclosing the date letters GG for 1784 and gilder's mark of Vincent, 20½in (52cm) wide. **$45,000-52,000**

A German oval porcelain plaque depicting Mary Magdalen, after Corregio, with inscription, early 19thC, the ormolu possibly Russian, 11½in (29cm) high. **$21,000-24,000**

A pair of Vienna figures, from the Commedia dell'Arte, repaired, impressed D on Columbine's base, c1755, 5½in (14.5cm) high. **$48,000-52,500**

A Sèvres ewer, cover and oval basin, minor chip to cover, blue interlaced L marks enclosing date letter P for 1768 and painter's mark of Buteux aîné, the ewer 7½in (19cm) high. **$27,000-30,000**

A Sèvres 'bleu Lapis' oval jardinière, minor repair to 2 feet, blue interlaced L marks enclosing date letter R for 1770, and painter's mark, incised, 9in (23cm) wide. **$19,500-24,000**

1. Goss Sulgrave Manor, 12.5cm long. **$1,200-1,600**
2. Goss Lloyd George's Early Home at Llanstymdwy, Criccieth, glazed, 6.2cm long. **$150-250**
3. Willow Art Shakespeare's House at Stratford, 6.5cm, **$15-30,** and Willow Art Old Maid's Cottage at Lee, Ilfracombe, 5.9cm. **$60-100**
4. Willow Art Whittington Inn with inscription to rear, 10cm long. **$100-200**
5. Alexandra, Bulldog, inscribed 'Duggie Haig', 6.3cm. **$150-200**
6. Goss two views of Rufus Stone, New Forest, Hampshire. **$15-30**
7. Carlton map of Blighty, with City of London arms, 11.5cm. **$45-70**
8. Goss Christchurch Court House, 7.6cm. **$450-600**
9. Goss Bottle Oven with orange chimney, 7.5cm. **$250-350**
10. Willow Art kitbags, 7.5cm. **$15-30 each**
11. Arcadian Black Boy playing banjo, 8.5cm. **$100-200**
12. Arcadian Trusty Servant of Winchester origins, 13.7cm. **$150-200**
13. Carlton Felix the Cat, on oval base, 7.5cm. **$60-100**
14. Goss Wordsworth's Birthplace, Cockermouth, 8.1cm. **$300-400**
15. Goss Old Market House, Ledbury, 6.8cm. **$400-500**

A club shaped decanter, with simulated wine label and gilt lozenge stopper, c1790, 7½in (19cm). **$250-350** and a green decanter, **$250-350**

A perfume bottle, with cut ball stopper, c1780, 6in (15cm). **$150-200**

A pair of spirit bottles, with gilt inscriptions, and gilt lozenge stoppers, c1810. **$400-500**

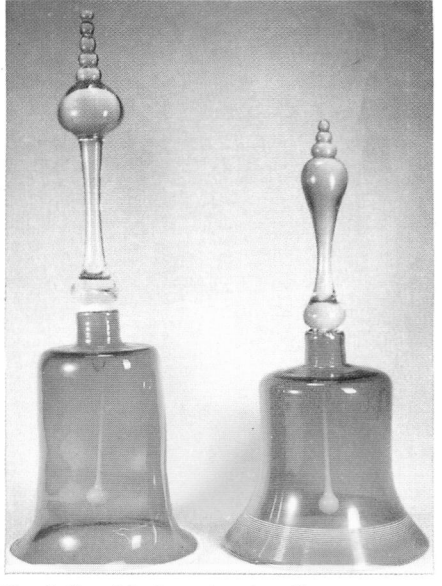

Two bells with clear glass handles, c1870. **$150-250 each**

Four double ended scent bottles with silver gilt mounts, c1860, 3½ to 5in (9 to 13cm). **$150-250 each**

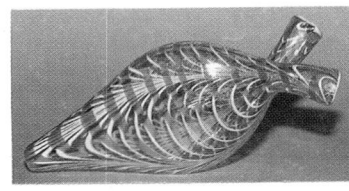

A Nailsea type gimmal flask, mid-19thC. **$150-250**

Two flasks, mid-19thC. **$150-200**

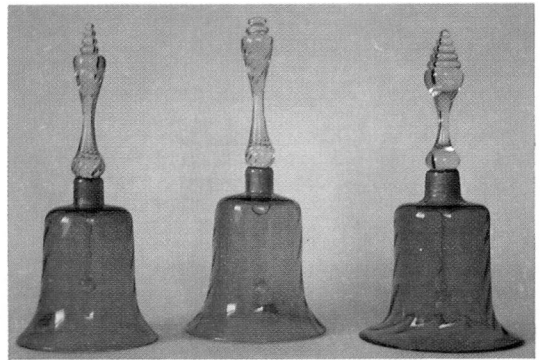

Three ruby bells with clear handles and clappers, mid-19thC, 12½in (32cm). **$150-200 each**

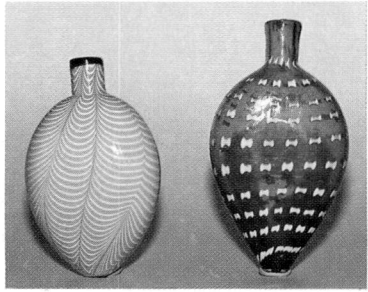

A decanter, c1810, 8in (20cm).
$300-400

A club shaped decanter, with
3 annulated neck rings, hollow
mushroom stopper, star cut on
top, c1800, 8in (20cm).
$400-500

A 'Bristol' tapered decanter,
with 3 bladed neck rings and
plain lozenge stopper, c1780,
7½in (19cm).
$250-350

Three ovoid rummers, 1810-40, 5in (13cm).
$150-250 each

A Nailsea jug, c1800, 8½in (22cm).
$400-500

Three spirit decanters, with simulated gilt
wine labels and gilt lozenge stoppers, c1790,
7 to 8in (17.5 to 20cm). **$250-350 each**

A set of 3 Bristol decanters, in
a papier mâché and brass frame,
c1780, 7½in (18.5cm).
$1,200-1,600

55

A set of 8 champagne glasses, with facet cut stems and cut overlay, c1870, 5in (13cm). **$300-400**

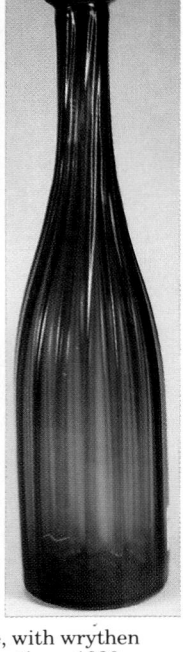

An engraved goblet, on hollow baluster stem and plain conical foot, c1860, 8in (20cm). **$150-200**

A wrythen moulded cream jug and sugar basin, with folded rims, North Country, c1800, 3½in (9cm). **$400-500**

A spirit bottle, with wrythen moulded decoration, c1830, 12½in (31.5cm). **$250-350**

Three spirit flasks with metal mounts, c1825, 7½in (19cm). **$150-250 each**

l. A set of 6 wine glasses, c1820. **$450-600** and r. A roemer type wine glass, c1810. **$75-150**

An opaque white flask, combed in pink, mid-19thC. **$150-200**

A Nailsea or Shropshire jug, c1810. **$450-600**

A pair of Bristol decanters, with gilt wine labels, c1790. **$1,500-2,600**

'Blanc de lait' pressed glass by Sowerby's of Gateshead, c1878. **$60-100 each**

A Prattware 'Hearty Good Fellow' type of Toby jug, late 18thC, 11in (28cm).
$1,200-1,600

A Neale & Co Toby jug in enamel colours, on a marble base, impressed mark on base, c1790, 9½in (24cm).
$800-1,200

A Staffordshire Toby jug, 'The Drunken Parson', 'The Sinner' or 'Doctor Johnson', c1810, 6½in (16cm).
$900-1,300

A rare Minton Toby jug depicting 'The Barrister', decorated in majolica colours, impressed and date mark, 11in (28cm).
$1,200-1,600

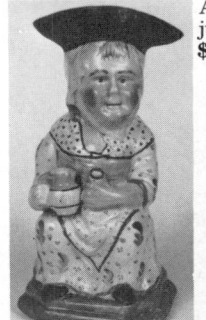

A Staffordshire 'Martha Gunn' Toby jug, c1820, 10in (25cm).
$1,500-2,600

A Pratt Toby jug wearing an ochre tricorn hat, and blue and ochre overcoat, holding a jug of ale on his lap, on canted cornered square shaped base, c1790, 9in (23cm).
$750-1,000

A Royal Doulton jug, 'Tom Bowling', a finely modelled and painted jug with hat by Charles Vyse, Chelsea, signed, hat damaged, 11½in (29cm).
$450-600

A Toby jug entitled 'Hearty Good Fellow', with enamel decoration, marked Walton, c1825, 11in (28cm).
$800-1,200

A Staffordshire Davenport Toby jug, 'The Gin Woman', c1845, 10in (25cm).
$600-900

A Wilkinsons pottery Toby jug from the First World War series by Sir F Carruthers Gould, depicting Admiral Beatty noted for modernising the fleet with dreadnoughts, submarines and torpedoes, c1917, 10½in (26.5cm).
$250-350

A Pratt Toby jug, predominantly decorated in yellow, blue and brown, holding a foaming jug of ale, on octagonal base, 10in (25cm).
$600-900

A Pratt Toby jug modelled as a rotund man, wearing a light brown and yellow tricorn hat, blue jacket and yellow breeches, holding a jug on his lap, on square canted cornered base, c1800, 10in (25cm).
$750-1,000

Mugs

A creamware mug, printed and enamelled, with sailing ship, c1770, 5in (13cm).
$750-1,000

A rare Liverpool pearlware mug, with illustration of the newly invented guillotine and inscription describing the execution of Louis XVI on Jan 21 1793.
$300-400

A mug in pink lustre, inscribed and dated 1817, 3in (8cm).
$150-200

A Staffordshire creamware mug with grooved loop handle, applied with a profile portrait of Admiral Rodney, inscribed 'Success to Admiral Rodney And Is Fleet', on a ground of marbled brown, yellow, black and cream glazes, with green ribbed bands to the rim and foot rim, chip to rim, c1782, 4½in (12cm).
$1,500-2,600

Two Masons mugs in mazarine blue, c1820.
Left **$250-350**
Right **$400-500**

A pink lustre mug, c1860, 2½in (6cm).
$60-100

A Staffordshire pearlware cylindrical mug with loop handle, applied with a bust length portrait of Lord Rodney, inscribed 'Success to G.B. Rodney' and with a rose and scattered flowersprays beneath a feuille-de-choux and blue line rim, chips to rims, c1782, 5in (12.5cm).
$600-900

Cf P D G Pugh, Naval Ceramics, *pl.23B.*

A pearlware coffee can, c1800, 2½in (6cm).
$60-100

A Staffordshire mug with flower painting, c1870, 4in (10cm).
$30-50

Plaques

A pottery quart mocha mug, 19thC.
$60-100

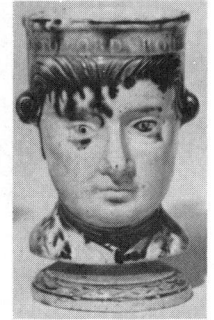

A Staffordshire mask mug modelled as the head of Lord Rodney, his hair en queue, with double scroll handle, enriched in mottled manganese and ochre, the rim moulded with 'Success to Lord Rodney', minor chips to base, c1785, 5in (12cm).
$1,500-2,600

A creamware inscribed and dated mug, inscribed in black within a flower and foliage cartouche, cracks to base and rim, chips to base, 1794, 6in (15cm).
$300-400

A pair of Yorkshire oval plaques, moulded with 'Patricia and her lover', their clothes enriched in blue and ochre, Patricia with a green umbrella, standing on green rockwork within self-moulded frames, enriched with an ochre line, c1800, 10½in (26cm) and 11in (27.5cm).
$4,000-5,500

These plaques are taken from a mezzotint published in 1780 by R Sayer and J Bennett from a series entitled 'Jack on a Cruise' and sub-titled 'Avast, there! Back your mainsail'.

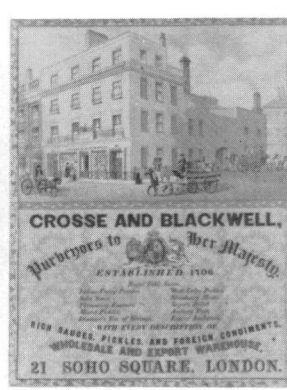

A Ralph Wood plaque of Patricia, c1780, 11½in (29cm).
$1,500-2,600

A Crosse and Blackwell's advertising plaque, the lower half with products advertised, on a blue and yellow patterned ground.
$1,300-1,800

A Sunderland pottery two-handled chamber pot, the exterior decorated with 2 verses 'Present' and 'Marriage' within pink lustre borders, damaged, 5½in (14cm).
$150-250

A Delft Doré small chamber pot, painted in the Kakiemon palette, the interior of the rim with Buddhistic symbols, minor chips, iron red AK monogram mark of Adriaenus Koeks, c1700, 6½in (16cm) wide.
$2,250-3,000

A Castelli plaque painted with Abraham sacrificing a lamb and kneeling before the flaming altar, rim chips, c1720, 10½ by 8in (27 by 20.5cm).
$1,500-2,600

A delft posset pot of typical form, decorated in blue, cracked, c1770, 5½in (14cm).
$400-500

A pair of Marseille semi-circular bough pots and covers, the finials modelled as sleeping putti, painted in colours, some restoration to both bases, Robert, c1765, 10in (25cm).
$1,000-1,400

A Dutch Delft polychrome plaque, the canopy painted in blue with a seated woman flanked by flowers on a brown ground, rim chips, mid-18thC, 13½ by 17in (34.5 by 42.5cm).
$4,500-7,000

A slipware honey pot and cover, 18thC, 7½in (19cm).
$2,250-3,000

> ### Make the Most of Miller's
> *The pottery section is ordered by item and then by date. English pottery precedes Continental pottery*

Pots

A Bristol delft posset pot and cover, decorated in Chinese style with flowers in blue, c1720, 8in (20cm).
$3,000-4,000

A Leeds blue and white spittoon, 18thC, 3½in (9cm).
$450-600

Pot Lids

Bears Reading Newspapers (7).
$900-1,300

The Attacking Bears (8), black
monochrome only.
$1,000-1,400

Rifle Contest, Wimbledon 1864
$60-100

Embarking for the East (206).
$75-150

Eastern Lady and Black Attendant
(100), small.
$6,000-9,000

Wimbledon July 1860 (224).
$60-100

Wellington (160A).
$150-250

Sebastopol (209).
$75-150

Gothic Archway (125), small,
without wording.
$1,500-2,600

Meeting of Garibaldi & Victor
Emmanuel (211).
$60-100

England's Pride (149).
$150-250

The Allied Generals (168).
$150-200

Mending the nets (70).
$150-200

Battle of the
Alma (75).
$150-250

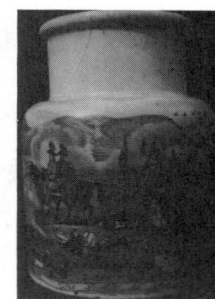

Balaklava, Inkerman, Alma (166).
$450-600

Constantinople – The Golden Horn
(80).
$100-200

Sauceboats

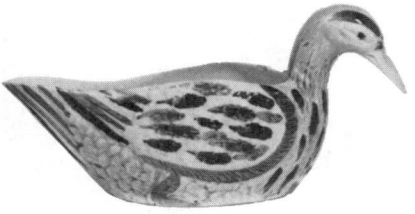

A large Prattware duck sauceboat, c1785, 7in (18cm) wide.
$1,000-1,400

A Whieldon type dolphin sauceboat, moulded with scale pattern, enriched in pale green and brown, star crack to base, c1755, 7in (17.5cm) long.
$450-600

A pottery sauceboat in the form of a duck with green head, yellow beak, blue and brown plumage, perhaps Yorkshire, c1785, 6½in (17cm) wide.
$900-1,300

A Yorkshire pearlware sauceboat in the form of a duck, its plumage enriched in ochre, green, blue and manganese and with green head, cracks and rim chip, c1790, 7½in (19cm) long.
$1,300-1,800

Tankards

A Bayreuth tankard, with contemporary hinged pewter cover, painted in blue with Chinese figures, between blue lines, the cover with ball thumbpiece, chips to foot, blue B.P.F mark of Pfeiffer and Fränkel, 1747-60, 10in (24.5cm).
$2,500-3,500

A Rhenish stoneware tankard, with crested English silver neck mount, chips to foot, hair cracks in neck, c1700, 7½in (19cm).
$750-1,000

A Prattware fox and swan sauceboat, painted in ochre, blue and green, c1790, 6in (15cm) wide.
$900-1,300

An Erfurt cylindrical tankard, with contemporary pewter mounts and hinged cover, painted in colour between blue lines, the cover with ball thumbpiece and inscribed No.8Z, iron red S mark of Georg Matthäus Schmidt, c1740, 11in (28cm).
$1,000-1,400

A Westerwald grey stoneware tankard, moulded with a medallion of William III on horseback, hair crack in base, late 17thC, 6in (15cm).
$750-1,000

Tea & Coffee Pots

A Staffordshire redware teapot, mid-18thC, 6in (15cm).
$300-500

A dated Siegburg pale grey stoneware schnelle, with contemporary hinged pewter cover, modelled in low relief with standing figures of Judith, Esther and Lucretia, the figures of Judith and Lucretia dated 1566, repair to base, 8½in (21cm).
$1,500-2,600

Provenance: A.ˢᵉ Maze.

A William Greatbatch creamware teapot and cover, transfer printed and coloured in puce, green, yellow and iron red with Juno seated in her chariot, the reverse with the Hebrew inscription 'the heavens' with a figure of Liberty, the cover with flowerhead finial flanked by winged angels' heads, minute chips to spout, cover and inside rim of teapot, c1775, 6in (15cm).
$4,500-7,000

Tea Caddies

A Staffordshire glazed redware globular teapot and cover of Astbury type, applied with cream slip bunches of grapes, chips to spout, rim and cover, c1750, 4½in (11cm).
$600-900

A Staffordshire saltglazed globular teapot, decorated in 'famille rose' coloured enamels, c1750, 4in (10cm).
$1,000-1,400

A Whieldon pattern square tea caddy, with tortoiseshell glaze and brass circular cover, late 18thC, 4in (10cm).
$400-500

A creamware globular teapot and cover, painted in iron red and black, the cover with knob finial, perhaps Leeds, crack to cover and base, chip to cover, spout and rims, c1770, 5in (12cm).
$1,500-2,600

A dated Dutch blue and white tea caddy, with contemporary pewter screw cover, the base inscribed in various initials and the date 1740, minor chips, 7in (18cm).
$1,000-1,400

A Leeds creamware teapot, decorated in the style of Robinson and Rhodes, in iron red and black, slightly damaged, c1780, 7in (18cm).
$300-500

A Staffordshire pearlware blue and white teapot and cover, painted with a bust portrait, inscribed below 'O: Brave Rodney 1780', the cover with flower finial, body and handle extensively riveted, spout, cover and finial chipped, 1780, 6in (14.5cm).
$600-900

A Staffordshire saltglaze large globular teapot and cover, painted in bright enamels, chips to spout, handle and rims, c1760, 6½in (17cm).
$2,250-3,500

Two Staffordshire marbled teapots, mid-18thC:—

l. 4in (10cm).
$1,500-2,600

r. with feet.
$1,500-2,600

A miniature Yorkshire teapot, printed in yellow on brown ground, late 18thC, 4in (11cm).
$250-350

A saltglaze solid agateware kettle on stand, small restoration to handle, 10½in (26.5cm).
$400-500

A miniature Wedgwood teapot, in black basalt, painted, c1860, 3in (8cm).
$250-350

A Leeds pottery coffee pot, with red and green flowers, c1800, 10in (25cm).
$900-1,300

A teapot, the cover with teapot finial, the dark brown body with moulded inscription dated 1904, 13½in (34cm) wide.
$150-200

A teapot and cover with ball finial, the dark brown body with moulded inscription dated 1872, 12in (30cm) wide.
$150-200

A blue and white teapot with scenes in reserve panels, Belle View pottery.
$150-250

A Staffordshire basalt coffee pot, with swan finial, c1840.
$600-900

Tiles

A pair of Minton tiles, blue background with white and yellow circle, 8in (20cm) square.
$25-35 each

A Victorian pink and brown floral tile. with registration mark.
$15-30

A green transfer tile, 6in (15cm) square.
$15-30

A Minton blue and white tile, 6in (15cm) square.
$30-50

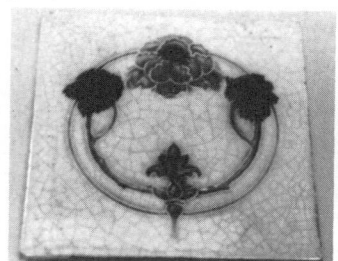

An Art Nouveau tile, in green and mauves, by Maw, 6in (15cm) square.
$25-35

A Victorian tile, designed and made by Maw, with pink trailing flower, green leaves and yellow daisies, 6in (15cm) square.
$15-30

A Victorian tile depicting birds in a flowered tree.
$15-30

A series of 12 sepia tiles, designed by Moyr Smith, depicting Walter Scott's novels, first produced at the Paris Exhibition, 1878, 8in (20cm) square.
$60-100

A Victorian hand-decorated tile, by Sherwin & Cotom, yellow background with green, blue and brown trim.
$30-50

A Royal Jubilee tile, reg. no. 63928, 1887, 6in (15cm) square.
$60-100

A Minton tile from Shakespearian series, depicting Othello, 6in (15cm) square.
$45-70

A rare picture made from a tile, of General Foch by George Cartridge, J. H. Barratt & Co., Stoke-on-Trent, after a photo by Elliot and Fry Ltd.
$75-150

A beige and black Minton and Hollins Shakespearian tile, from The Tempest, showing Caliban and his confederates punished, 8in (20cm) square.
$45-70

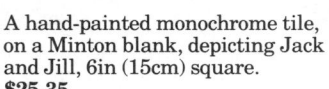

A hand-painted monochrome tile, on a Minton blank, depicting Jack and Jill, 6in (15cm) square.
$25-35

Two Minton brown and white tiles, designed by Thomas Allen, depicting Aesops Fables, c1875.
$45-70 each

A set of 10 Minton black and white tiles, depicting industrial scenes, designed by Moyr Smith.
$450-600

Make the most of Miller's

When a large specialist well-publicised collection comes on the market, it tends to increase prices. Immediately after this, prices can fall slightly due to the main buyers having large stocks and the market being 'flooded'. This is usually temporary and does not affect very high quality items.

A pair of Dutch Delft blue and white tile pictures, one inscribed 'DE HOOP KOMMZ WEERS' and the other 'VILPRO VINCIEN ADM. DE RUITER', in brown wood frames, 19thC, 15 by 10in (38 by 25cm).
$800-1,200

A pair of tiles, each with hand enamelled decoration depicting sporting subjects, each mounted in a glazed oak frame.
$750-1,000

Six Dutch Delft blue and white tile pictures, 5 consisting of 4 tiles and one of 6 tiles, some chips, one tile cracked, 18th/19thC, 10 by 10in (25 by 25cm), one 15 by 10in (38 by 25cm).
$1,200-1,600

Three Dutch Delft birdcage tile pictures, each painted with a yellow bird within a manganese cage, one extensively damaged, some repairs, 18thC, 15 by 10in (38 by 25cm), each consisting of 6 tiles.
$450-700

Two Dutch Delft tile pictures of cats, one painted in manganese, the other in blue, each consisting of 6 tiles, some damages, 18th/19thC, 15 by 10in (38 by 25cm).
$750-1,000

Tureens

A creamware oval tureen, cover and ladle, probably Leeds, small crack from rim, incised numeral to cover and tureen, c1775, 13½in (34cm) wide.
$1,000-1,400

A Staffordshire pigeon tureen in Pratt colours of blue, green and ochre, c1790, 6in (15cm) wide.
$1,000-1,400

A Wedgwood pie crust tureen, with minor restoration, 18thC, 9½in (24cm) wide.
$1,200-1,600

An ironstone tureen, decorated in blue and white.
$450-700

An early Staffordshire hen tureen, c1825, 6in (15cm).
$300-400

A creamware butter tub, c1780.
$400-500

A Mason's Caramanian Ironstone tureen with pink and blue decoration.
$1,200-1,600

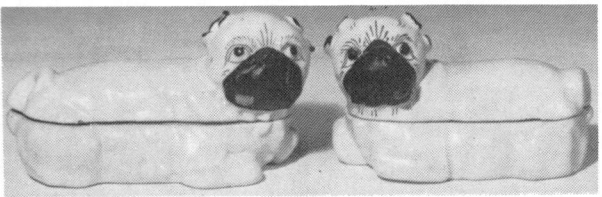

A pair of Erfurt pug dog tureens and covers, with black facial markings and yellow bodies, some restoration, one with blue 46 mark to each piece, the other with 23, c1755, 7½in (19cm) wide.
$6,000-8,000

An ironstone soup tureen, decorated in green and blue, c1830.
$450-700

A George Jones game pie dish and cover, naturalistic polychrome colouring on a cobalt blue ground, impressed maker's monogram GJ, George Jones within crescent moon and registration lozenge for 1873, 14½in (37cm) wide.
$3,000-4,500

Vases

A rare Obadiah Sherratt style spill vase, modelled as lady and gentleman musicians, centre vase repaired, boy's arm restored, c1800, 8in (20cm).
$1,000-1,400

A Liverpool delft vase, decorated in blue and white, with classical ruins, c1760, 8in (20cm).
$900-1,300

A small Lambeth delft bottle vase, c1740.
$700-900

A rare Bristol campana shaped vase with double rope twist handles, decorated in blue, c1750, 7in (18cm).
$4,000-5,500

A Wedgwood and Bentley black basalt two-handled vase and cover, the body applied with an oval medallion with Diomedes and the Palladium, on a circular fluted foot, with small domed cover, finial and base lacking, unmarked, c1775, 15½in (40cm).
$4,000-5,500

A pair of Wedgwood and Bentley black basalt urn shaped vases and covers, on a circular spreading foot and square base, Wedgwood & Bentley Etruria marks within a circle, c1775, 14½in (37cm).
$13,500-17,500

A pair of Wedgwood solid lilac jasper cylindrical vases, moulded in white relief with Corinthian columns, one vase cracked round top and with small hole, rims chipped, impressed lower case mark, c1785, 6in (15.5cm).
$1,000-1,400

A Wedgwood black basalt encaustic-decorated vase of campana form, painted in red and enriched in white with Apollo and Diana, the circular foot painted with berried foliage, unmarked, late 18thC, 9½in (24cm).
$2,500-3,500

A Staffordshire pearlware vase in the form of a castle, painted and incised to simulate brown brickwork and with castellated upper parts, one castellation lacking, another repaired, another chipped, crack to base and rim, c1790, 14in (35.5cm) wide.
$4,000-5,500

A Wedgwood jasper model of the Portland vase, 19thC, 10½in (26.5cm).
$900-1,300

A spill vase modelled as a leopardess recumbent with cubs, on coloured gilt lined base, c1850, 10in (25.5cm).
$450-600

An Obadiah Sherratt spill vase group of the marriage at Gretna Green, modelled as a blacksmith and a young couple, before a brightly coloured two-turretted building and trees, the oval green mound base painted in bright colours modelled with blue scrolls, c1820, 7½in (19cm).
$2,250-3,000

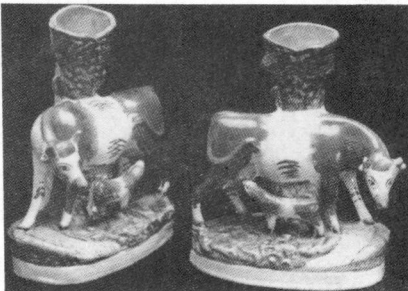

A pair of Staffordshire brown and white cow and calf pottery spill vases, each cow leaning on a tree, c1850.
$400-500

A pair of Bonn pottery cream, floral and gilt decorated vases, late 19thC, 15in (38cm).
$150-250

A pair of spill vases, modelled as hounds with brown markings, one with crack to back of base, c1845, 6in (15cm).
$600-900

A pair of Dutch Delft blue and white slender baluster bottle vases, rim chips, blue H10 marks, c1700, 10½in (26.5cm).
$1,000-1,400

A spill vase modelled as an elephant standing by a tree, on an oval shaped coloured gilt lined base, c1860, 7in (18cm).
$300-400

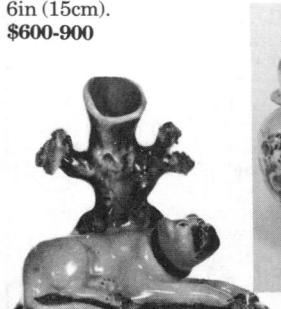

A spill vase modelled as a mastiff before a tree, on shaped coloured gilt lined base, c1845, 6in (15cm).
$300-400

A pair of Delft inverse baluster blue and white vases, 12½in (31.5cm).
$400-500

A rare pair of Wedgwood pot pourri pots, in crimson dipped jasperware, 20thC, 17in (43cm).
$1,500-2,600

A pair of Dutch Delft blue and white octagonal baluster vases, with garlic neck, painted with panels of deer and flowers, minor rim chips, blue marks, 12½in (32cm).
$1,200-1,600

A Palermo waisted albarello, painted with a figure of Christ within double scroll cartouche, the upper half repaired, late 16thC, 10½in (26.5cm).
$900-1,300

A pair of Sicilian vasi-a-palli, painted with portrait busts of a man and a woman, reserved on a blue ground with scrolling flowering foliage, rim chips, late 16thC, 12½in (32cm).
$5,500-7,000

A pair of Wemyss seated pigs painted with black markings, one with glazed chip, painted mark in yellow, 6in (15cm) wide.
$1,300-1,800

Wemyss

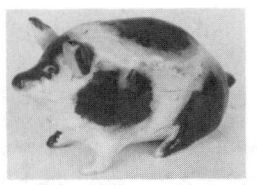

A Wemyss sponged black and white pig, 4in (10cm).
$150-250

A large Wemyss pig, decorated with roses from the Bovey Tracey period, 1930-40, 18in (46cm) wide.
$1,300-1,800

A large Wemyss black and white pig, the nose, ears, trotters and tail in pale pink, 17½in (44cm) long.
$900-1,300

A small Wemyss pig, self coloured green.
$300-400

A rare model of a cat, seated upright and facing to the right with an alert expression, painted all over with pink roses, green and ochre foliage, with glass eyes and whiskers, front legs repaired, impressed and painted marks, 12½in (31.5cm).
$3,000-4,500

WEMYSS WARE
c1883-1930

★ Robert Methven Heron introduced a group of continental artists into his Fife pottery in the 1880's. The very characteristic nature of Wemyss derives from their influence although roses, apples and cherries had been stiffly painted before

★ most of the artists returned home but Karel Nekola remained. Wemyss was always wanted by the rich and the ware was well supported by Scottish Lairds

★ Wemyss was fired at low temperatures to produce a biscuit body which would absorb the delicate brush strokes. Then it was dipped in a soft lead glaze and fired again at a low temperature. This accounts for the fragility of Wemyss and the relative rarity of exceptional quality pieces

★ Nekola trained James Sharp, David Grinton, John Brown, Hugh and Christina McKinnon and they were later joined by Nekola's sons Carl and Joseph

★ Karel Nekola tended to paint the large important pieces and also the commemorative pieces from Queen Victoria's Jubilee in 1897 until the Coronation of George V in 1911. He died in 1915

★ Edwin Sandiland became chief decorator in 1916. The change in public taste after the First World War, with the introduction of the Art Deco movement, saw a move away from the traditional Wemyss designs. Various new designs were tried but by the time Edwin Sandiland died in 1928, the end was in sight. The Fife Pottery closed in 1930

★ the Bovey Tracey pottery in Devon bought the rights and moulds of the Fife pottery and gave employment to Joseph Nekola, who continued the familiar decorations to a high standard until his death in 1952. Royal Doulton subsequently acquired the rights

A Wemyss ware jug and bowl set, with pink roses.
$600-900

A large Wemyss comb tray, painted with wild roses, 11½in (29cm) wide.
$150-250

A large Wemyss brush vase, painted with roses, 11½in (29cm).
$150-250

A large Wemyss coomb pot, painted with apples, 9½in (24cm).
$400-500

A Wemyss inkstand, decorated with roses, 6in (15cm) wide.
$300-500

A Wemyss bowl painted with thistles, 6in (15cm) diam.
$75-150

A Wemyss preserve pot, painted with plums, 5in (13cm).
$75-150

One of the commonest patterns.

A large Wemyss honey pot, painted with beehive and bees, 6in (15cm).
$150-250

A Wemyss plate, painted with oranges, 6½in (16.5cm) diam.
$100-200

A pair of Wemyss candlesticks, painted with oranges, 12in (30.5cm).
$400-500

A Wemyss plate, painted with raspberries, 6½in (16.5cm) diam.
$75-150

A Wemyss ring stand, painted with roses, 3½in (9cm).
$100-200

VALUE POINTS FOR WEMYSS

★ quality of painting – especially a large piece painted freely by Karel Nekola

★ condition – Wemyss is by nature fragile and since many of the pieces were made for nursery use, many have been damaged

★ other painters of note – James Sharp, David Grinton, John Brown, Hugh and Christina McKinnon, also Karel's two sons, Carl and Joseph

★ early pieces particularly with red border

★ unusual subject matters – nasturtiums, gorse, pink flamingoes

★ beware unmarked pieces – usually these were rejects or copies from another factory

★ for more information buy the book *Wemyss Ware, A Decorative Scottish Pottery*, presented by Victoria de Rin and David Macmillan written by Professor Peter Davis and Robert Rankine, published by the Scottish Academic Press

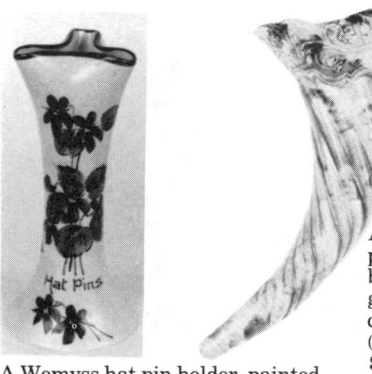

A Whieldon wall pocket of waisted form, moulded with a bearded mask beneath a mottled manganese glaze, rim chips, c1760, 8½in (22.5cm).
$1,500-2,600

A Whieldon spirally-moulded wall pocket, with a border of trailing vine beneath streaked manganese and grey glazes, small repair to one corner, slight chips, c1750, 9½in (24cm).
$2,500-3,500

A Wemyss hat pin holder, painted with violets, 6in (15cm).
$150-250

Miscellaneous

A Bristol delft candle recess or niche, recess painted in blue with a partially draped lady holding a goblet, the top painted to simulate a dome with flowerhead, diaper and scroll motifs suspending drapery, surrounded by a sponged manganese border, one corner repaired, c1750, 10in (25.5cm).
$7,500-10,500

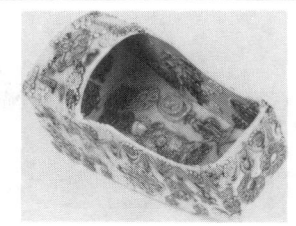

A Ralph Wood cradle, the interior applied with a figure covered with flowerheads, surrounded by applied portrait medallions, the exterior applied with drapery, urns, flowerheads and 2 medallions with the flagship 'Villa de Paris' (sic), enriched in green, manganese and blue, on 2 rockers, crack to rim and chipping to medallions, c1785, 9½in (24cm) long.
$16,500-26,000

Literature:
Sir Harold Mackintosh, Early English Figure Pottery, *No. 135, where it is suggested that this was made at the time of the death of Lord Rodney's daughter.*
No similar example would appear to be recorded.

An English delft blue and white model of a lady's shoe, probably Lambeth, inscribed under the instep with the initials 'S.C.' and dated 1718, 6½in (16.5cm) long.
$3,000-4,500

A Staffordshire shoe, early 19thC, 4in (10cm) long.
$250-350

An important Lambeth delft polychrome pill slab, painted in blue with the Arms of the Worshipful Society of Apothecaries with unicorn supporters, the inscription in manganese, purple, pierced for suspension, early 18thC, 10in high by 8½in wide (25.5 by 21.5cm).
$5,500-7,000

See Apothecary Jars *by Rudolph E A Drey, Illustration page 137, plate 70D.*

A Lambeth delftware blue and white shield shaped Apothecary's pill slab, decorated with the coat of arms of the Apothecaries Company, pierced for hanging, some damage, 13 by 10½in (33 by 24cm).
$4,000-5,500

A large Brannam pottery jardiniere, applied with swirling handles, boldly decorated with fish and pond weed in muted enamel colours, slight glaze chip, inscribed and dated 1896, 15in (38cm) diam.
$250-350

A large Wedgwood pottery jardiniere, decorated in turquoise, grey, green, pink and yellow, impressed mark, 12½in (31cm) diam.
$450-700

A large majolica jardiniere on stand, in royal blue ground with raised leaf and cabochon decoration in pink, green and tan, 49in (124cm).
$1,200-1,600

A large George Jones majolica jardiniere, decorated in high relief, on 3 leaf feet with naturalistic polychrome colouring on a cobalt blue ground, some damage, registration mark for 1876, 19in (48cm).
$1,000-1,400

An oval foot bath, decorated inside and out with blue and white transfer pattern, printed to base 'Swiss Villa', chipped, 19thC, 14in (35.5cm) diam.
$700-900

A polychrome floral design ironstone foot bath, 16½in (41.5cm) wide.
$1,000-1,400

A Prattware bird whistle, c1800, 6½in (16.5cm).
$1,200-1,600

An English delft flower brick, with chinoiserie decoration in blue and white, 18thC.
$750-1,000

A Lauder & Smith pottery jardiniere, boldly incised and painted with fish and pond weed in muted enamel colours, inscribed Lauder, Barum, late 19thC, 10in (25.5cm).
$450-600

A pair of Dutch Delft blue and white two-handled wine flask coolers, with central divider, some chips, one with hair cracks, blue VE monogram and IO mark of Lambertus van Eenhoorn at De Metale Pot Factory, c1700, 12½in (32cm) wide.
$6,000-8,000

A Bristol pottery marriage barrel in Pratt colours, initialled 'A.J. & B.P.', dated February 20th 1818, 4½in (11.5cm).
$250-350

A majolica cheese dish and cover, deep blue ground, the lid with a handle in the shape of a recumbent cow, some damage, late 19thC, 10½in (26cm) diam.
$75-150

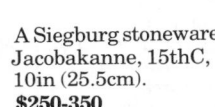

A Siegburg stoneware Jacobakanne, 15thC, 10in (25.5cm).
$250-350

A pair of French faience oval two-handled glass coolers, seaux crénelés, painted with bouquets of flowers between blue feuille-de-choux and puce C-scroll rims, probably Sceaux, one with rim repair, minor chips, c1760, 11in (28cm) wide.
$1,500-2,600

A Spode blue and white oval foot bath, with two loop end handles, with Italian tower transfer decoration, late 18thC, 18in (46cm) wide.
$1,500-2,600

A Staffordshire pottery blue and white toilet set, c1890.
$450-600

A Wedgwood biscuit barrel, in three-colour jasperware, with plated mounts, in pink, green and white, c1881, 9in (23cm).
$450-600

A collection of 3 wine labels, probably Lambeth delftware, late 18thC, 5in (13cm) wide.

Port. **$150-250**

J (Jamaican) Rum. **$150-250**

Canary. **$250-350**

A clock and figures in the form of a watch stand, unusually decorated in pink lustre, Dixon Austin & Co, 1820-26, 11in (28cm). **$1,000-1,400**

A Wedgwood garden seat, with moulded decoration in the Japanese manner, mottled green and white with a shaped carrying hole, impressed Wedgwood, 18in (46cm). **$1,500-2,600**

A Minton vase, with mermaids in moulded relief, naturalistic polychrome colouring on pale blue ground, impressed Minton and with date code for 1870, 16in (40.5cm). **$1,500-2,600**

Minton

MINTON MAJOLICA

★ Joseph-Léon-François Arnoux appointed art director of Minton c1848
★ before 1850 Arnoux introduced a ware imitating 16thC Italian maiolica
★ opaque white glaze over pottery body as surface for polychrome painting in opaque colours
★ in 1851 Mintons displayed wine coolers, flower pots and stands 'coloured in the majolica style'
★ transparent coloured glazes of green, yellow, brown and blue often used over patterns moulded in low relief. These are in imitation of wares produced by Bernard Palissy in the mid-16thC but are sometimes mis-named majolica
★ rival firms copied majolica wares but Minton examples usually bear the name Minton impressed
★ game dishes especially popular with collectors
★ other collectable factories include Wedgwood and George Jones

A Minton game pie dish, on 4 lion's paw feet, the body with moulded decoration imitating basket weave, the finial modelled as a gun dog lying on a bed of fern with a gun and shooting pouch beneath him, naturalistic polychrome colouring, impressed Minton 497, and with date code for 1862, 17in (43cm) wide. **$4,000-5,500**

A Minton majolica centrepiece, in the form of a long slim shell being supported by seaweed with 3 open shells below, painted in typical enamel colours, very slight chip, impressed marks and date code for 1864, 7½in (19.5cm). **$750-1,000**

A large Minton jardiniere with bearded ram's head handles, aubergine with naturalistic polychrome colouring, underdish with date code for 1851, 14in (36cm). **$1,500-2,600**

A Minton majolica game pie tureen and cover, date cypher triangle, ▶ slight chips, 14in (35cm) wide. **$800-1,200**

A Minton jug, with moulded decoration, lip restored, impressed Minton 474 and with date code for 1870, 12½in (32cm) high. **$900-1,300**

A pair of Minton wine coolers, with a moulded narrative frieze, the handles modelled as rams' heads, the feet decorated with vine, naturalistic polychrome colouring, each with impressed date code for 1859, 10in (25.5cm). **$1,500-2,600**

A Minton urn-shaped garden stool, decorated with the Norfolk pattern with blue floral and foliage sprays on yellow ground, with blue borders and circular foot, 17½in (44cm).
$900-1,300

A pair of Minton vases, with moulded decoration of male and female masks, brown with naturalistic polychrome decoration, impressed Minton 827 and 827A, 14in (35.5cm).
$2,500-3,500

A set of 7 Minton Hollins tiles, with moulded Pompeian style decoration of palmettes and florets, polychrome, impressed Minton Hollins & Co., Stoke on Trent, each tile 8in (20cm) square.
$1,000-1,400

A large Minton jardiniere and matching stand, naturalistic polychrome colouring on a pale blue ground, both pieces impressed Minton and with date code for 1862, 15½in (39.5cm).
$1,500-2,600

A pair of Minton majolica jugs, the form based on a 17thC bellarmine, a mask beneath the spout, blues and yellow, each one impressed Minton 596, one with date code for 1867, one for 1870, 9½in (24.5cm).
$400-500

A pair of Minton majolica candlesticks, the flared sockets over putti holding fish, rabbits and game birds, raised on circular fluted bases, restored, impressed mark, 19thC, 8½in (22cm).
$250-350

A Minton jardiniere with a moulded frieze, pale blue and white with a pink interior, impressed Minton 534, 11½in (29cm).
$1,000-1,400

A Minton oval wall plaque, ochre and cobalt blue on a turquoise ground, impressed Minton 1668, and with date code for 1873, 20in (51cm).
$1,000-1,400

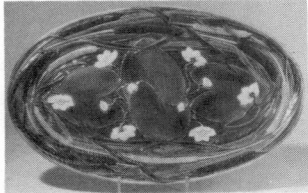

A large Minton platter, on 4 bracket feet, moulded in relief with white waterlilies among lily pads within border of intertwining bulrushes, glazed in green, yellow, brown and white, impressed Minton 927 0 and date mark for 1870, 24in (61cm) wide.
$1,500-2,600

A large Minton jardiniere, with moulded decoration in the aesthetic manner of fauna, dark and light blue and white, impressed Minton and with date code for 1882, 13in (33cm).
$1,500-2,600

A majolica teapot in the form of a monkey, wearing a peaked cap, eating an apple, his tail forming the handle, the spout moulded as a serpent issuing from between his legs, on naturalistic base, probably Minton, 10½in (26cm) long.
$750-1,000

ENGLISH PORCELAIN

18th century wares

Porcelain was first made in England about 1745. Between 1745 and 1755 some 10 factories started to manufacture wares using this new English porcelain body (soft paste as opposed to Chinese and European hard paste). These early wares, especially from short lived factories, continue to be scarce and much sought after whether blue and white or polychrome.

Buyers are more discriminating with regard to damaged wares produced after 1760 unless the wares are from factories with a specialist following. Unusual shapes remain popular with collectors and there is continuing evidence of specialisation within factories focusing on the earlier periods of production.

Dated pieces continue to command a high price.

There are still bargains to be found. Early blue and white printed wares from the Worcester factory can still be purchased for under $225 and wares from all factories circa 1760 to 1780 are surely undervalued in comparison with their slightly earlier counterparts.

Baskets

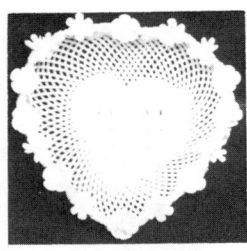

A Belleek First Period basket, the centre interlaced with 4 lattice strands, the rim applied with roses, shamrocks and other flowers, impressed Belleek Co, Fermanagh, 6½in (16.5cm) wide.
$400-500

A small Derby basket, painted by the cotton stalk painter, handles re-stuck, c1758, 5in (12.5cm) wide.
$600-900

A Derby basket, handles restored, c1758, 8in (20cm) wide.
$450-700

A Chelsea basket with flower decoration, red anchor period, c1755, 8in (20cm) wide.
$750-1,000

A Coalport white ground centre 'leaf' basket, gilded and decorated with colourful porcelain encrusted floral sprays, the centre with edge richly gilded and hand-painted central floral panel, c1860, 12in (30cm) diam.
$600-900

A Derby armorial basket on stand, the basket with lattice pierced gilt border, both painted with a coat-of-arms within a wreath of oak leaves and surround of gilt stars and roundels on a royal blue ground, basket damaged, gold mark on base and iron red mark on basket, 19in (48cm) long.
$1,500-2,600

A Belleek basket and cover, with 3 strand basket weave base, minor chips, impressed applied label mark, 1863-1891, 8½in (21.5cm) wide.
$1,500-2,600

18th CENTURY DERBY

★ some early white jugs incised with the letter D have been attributed to the Derby factory under the direction of John Heath and Andrew Planché, believed to start c1750

★ early Derby is soft paste and is generally lighter than Bow and Chelsea

★ very rare to find crazing on early Derby, the glaze was tight fitting and thinner than Chelsea

★ glaze often kept away from the bottom edge or edge was trimmed, hence the term 'dry-edge' (particularly applied to figures)

★ c1755, three (or more) pieces of clay put on bottom of figure to keep it clear of kiln furniture, giving 'patch' or 'pad' marks – which now have darker appearance

★ Duesbury had joined Heath and Planché in 1756

★ Duesbury's early works display quite restrained decoration, with much of the body left plain, following the Meissen style

★ Derby can be regarded as the English Meissen

★ the porcelain of this period has an excellent body, sometimes with faintly bluish appearance

★ 1770-84 known as the Chelsea-Derby period

★ Chelsea-Derby figures almost always made at Derby

★ 1770's saw the introduction of unglazed white biscuit Derby figures

★ this points to the move away from the academic Meissen style towards the more fashionable French taste

★ in 1770's leading exponent of the neo-classical style, and comparable to contemporary wares of Champion's Bristol

★ body of 1770's is frequently of silky appearance and of bluish-white tone

★ 1780's Derby body very smooth and glaze white, the painting on such pieces was superb, particularly landscapes, Jockey Hill and Zachariah Boreman

★ 1780's and 1790's noted for exceptional botanical painting of the period especially by 'Quaker' Pegg and John Brewer

★ around 1800 the body degenerated, was somewhat thicker, the glaze tended to crackle and allow discolouration

A Derby basket with early flower decoration, pale green with red and pink, 1758-60, 8½in (21.5cm) wide.
$900-1,300

A Rockingham basket, the centre painted with a vignette of Carisbrook Castle (sic) surrounded by gilt seaweed-pattern, within an irregular grey border and gilt line rim, puce griffin mark, partly erased, c1835, 6in (15cm) wide.
$750-1,000

A Derby inscribed basket, the interior painted with birds, the exterior with blue and yellow flowerheads and with pink and yellow rope-twist handles with flower terminals, one handle repaired, the base inscribed 'Thomas Moor', c1758, 8½in (21.5cm) wide.
$1,200-1,600

A small Lowestoft blue and white basket, c1770, 5in (12.5cm) diam.
$900-1,300

Two Worcester chestnut baskets, covers and stands, one stand painted with a flower spray, the other with fruit and butterflies, one basket repaired, chips to flowerheads and foliage, one cover with blue 5, the other with 4 mark, c1760, stands 11in (28cm) wide.
$7,500-10,500

A Rockingham primrose-leaf-moulded basket, with entwined gilt twig and blossom handle, the centre painted with Chain Pier Brighton, within a gilt cartouche, flanked by moulded gilt-veined primrose leaves within a gilt line rim, cracked across lower part of panel and above the foot, small crack to rim, puce griffin mark, c1835, 13½in (34cm) wide.
$1,500-2,600

A late Meissen pierced basket on 4 gilt scroll moulded feet, the interior painted with a flowerspray and scattered flowers, outlined in gilt, blue crossed swords mark, 10½in (26cm).
$1,000-1,400

A First Period Worcester dry blue basket, piece of trellis re-stuck, one flower restored, c1770.
$250-350

A Longton Hall conical footed bowl, painted in a vibrant palette with a bird strutting among shrubs beneath a tree with pendant branches issuing from pierced rockwork, the interior with a flower spray, c1755, 4in (10.5cm) diam.
$2,250-3,000

A Meissen punch bowl, painted in colours with an adaptation of William Hogarth's engraving 'A Modern Midnight Conversation' with ozier moulded rim painted with garlands of 'deutsche manier Blumen', the interior with a gilt rim, blue crossed swords mark, Pressnummer 61, c1755, 12½in (31cm) diam.
$7,500-10,500

Bowls

An Amstel bowl, painted with figures on a canal with rural buildings and a church, gilt dentil rim, blue script mark, c1785, 8½in (22cm) diam.
$900-1,300

A Royal Crown Derby porcelain bowl, the interior with a painted circular panel, the outer rim with a continuous seascape with boats, within gilt line borders on a pale turquoise ground, by W E J Dean, signed, printed marks in red, 9in (23cm) diam.
$300-400

A Frankenthal pipe bowl, modelled as the head of a pilgrim in black hat with a pink shell, with contemporary silver fittings and ivory stem, c1770, the pipe bowl 3in (8cm) high overall.
$1,500-2,600

A Meissen chinoiserie slop bowl, painted with Chinese figures, in gilt and lustre quatrefoil cartouches surrounded by puce and iron red foliage, the panels divided by rich sprays of 'indianische Blumen', the interior with a figure on a terrace, minute rim chip, blue enamel crossed swords mark and gilder's mark 55, c1725, 7in (17.5cm) diam.
$4,000-5,500

A Meissen Kakiemon ogival bowl, painted with flowering plants issuing from blue rockwork and purple ground, with chocolate rim, blue crossed swords mark and incised Dreher's mark, c1730, 8in (20cm) diam.
$2,500-3,500

A Meissen chinoiserie slop bowl, painted with Chinese figures, within purple lustre and gilt foliage scroll cartouches, divided by fenced 'indianische Blumen' and with gilt 'Laub-und-Bandelwerk' rim, blue crossed swords mark and star mark and numeral 4, gilder's number 96, Pressnummer 32, c1740, 7in (17.5cm) diam.
$4,000-5,500

Probably a replacement for a slightly earlier service.

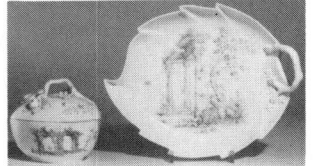

A Meissen peach-shaped bowl, cover and leaf-shaped stand, with branch finial and handle with flower terminals, decorated by Canon August Otto Ernst von dem Busch, with Italianate ruins and birds in garden landscapes, the cover with birds and insects, the stand repaired, the bowl and stand signed and dated Busch 1757, the stand signed twice, blue crossed swords mark, the bowl with Pressnummer 35, the stand 10in (26.5cm) wide.
$4,000-5,500

A Samson of Paris 'Chinese Lowestoft' punch bowl, hand painted in blue and gold with coat-of-arms, small chip to enamel on side, pseudo Chinese mark on base in iron red, 11in (28cm) diam.
$300-400

A 'Sèvres' porcelain bowl, set in an ornate gilt metal stand, moulded and applied with fruit and flowers, the exterior of the bowl brightly painted, the interior with sprays of flowers, reserved on a gold decorated deep blue ground, 10in (25cm).
$1,200-1,600

A Sèvres bleu nouveau quatrefoil basin, painted in colours within 'ciselé' gilt panels, on bleu nouveau ground and with gilt dentil rims, green interlaced L mark enclosing the date letter T for 1772, 11in (28cm) wide.
$1,200-1,600

A Tournai bowl, probably painted in colours by Joseph Duvivier with exotic birds in landscape vignettes and with brown rim, c1770, 8in (20cm) diam.
$1,000-1,400

Joseph Duvivier returned to the Tournai factory in 1763 after a successful career at the Chelsea factory in England.

A Worcester potted meat dish, of fluted oval form moulded with rococo scroll cartouches, painted in a delicate 'famille rose' palette, the interior with a flowering branch beneath a green diaper border reserved with flowers, crack down one pleat, c1753, 7in (18cm) wide.
$6,000-8,000

A Worcester blue and white bowl, printed on one side with garden flowers and on the reverse flowers, ferns and insects, late 18thC, 6½in (16cm).
$100-200

Above. A Royal Worcester 'Hadley-style' centre bowl, on white ground decorated with pheasants, signed 'R. Poole', black mark, pattern 254, c1960, 8½in (21.5cm) diam.
$750-1,000

Below. A Royal Worcester 'Hadley-style' centre bowl, on white ground decorated with Mallard ducks, signed 'R. Poole', black mark, pattern 254, c1960, 8½in (21.5cm) diam.
$750-1,000

Boxes

A Berlin armorial snuff box and cover with contemporary silver gilt mount, the cover with an elaborate coat-of-arms, the interior with a floral monogram, c1770, 3½in (9cm) wide.
$3,000-4,000

A Chelsea chicken box and a cover, its wing and tail feathers enriched in yellow, pink and puce, rim chip restored to base, c1756, 3½in (9cm) wide.
$1,500-2,600

A Doccia snuff box and cover, painted with scattered flower sprays and gilt insects, with copper gilt mount, c1770, 3½in (9cm) wide.
$600-900

A Worcester bowl, pencilled in black with an Oriental on a cow beneath a tree in a river landscape with two covered rafts, the interior with a flower spray, minute rim chip, painter's mark and incised X, c1754, 4½in (12cm) diam.
$750-1,000

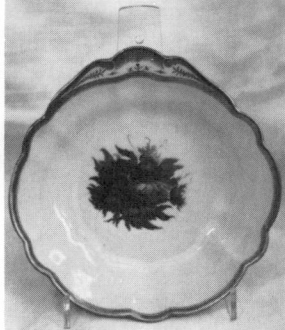

A Worcester shell-shaped bowl, by Billingsley.
$750-1,000

A Worcester bowl, painted in Giles's workshop, pink flower design, c1770, 6in (15cm) diam.
$300-400

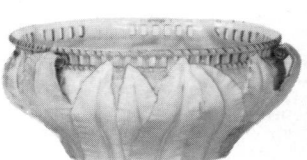

A Royal Worcester four-handled bowl, with pierced rim and leaf decoration, unsigned, pattern 1947, c1897, 9in (23cm) diam.
$300-400

Two Meissen rose boxes and covers, naturally modelled and edged in puce and with bud finials, one cover repaired, c1750, 3½in (9cm).
$1,500-2,600

A Fürstenberg snuff box and cover with silver mount, the interior of the cover with a family seated in a landscape, blue script F mark on base, the silver mounts marked with pseudo-Hamburg marks, the porcelain 18thC, 3½in (8.5cm) wide.
$2,500-3,500

A Meissen bombé large snuff box, painted all over, the fluted sides with symmetrical gilt 'Laub-und-Bandelwerk' divided by smoking trophies, with gilt metal mounts, perhaps 18thC, 5in (12cm) wide.
$4,000-5,500

A Meissen snuff box and cover, painted with 'deutsche Blumen' within shaped green scale borders, the interior of the cover with 2 couples in a garden landscape, with silver gilt mount, c1755, 3in (7cm) wide.
$2,500-3,500

A Rockingham butterfly box and cover, the sides applied with trailing coloured flowers between gilt line rims, the cover with the butterfly's wings marked in gilding, C12 in red, puce griffin mark, c1835.
$1,500-2,600

A Vienna pink ground snuff box and cover, the interior of the cover painted with cupids, the exterior with flowers in grey panels surrounded by gilt and pink bands with chain-pattern borders, with copper gilt mount, cover repaired, blue beehive mark, c1780, 3½in (8.5cm) wide.
$1,000-1,400

MEISSEN

★ in 1709 J F Böttger produced a white hard paste porcelain
★ wares often decorated by outside decorators (Hausmaler)
★ in 1720 kilnmaster Stozel came back to Meissen bringing with him J G Herold
★ from 1720-50 the enamelling on Meissen was unsurpassed – starting with the wares of *Lowenfink* – bold, flamboyant chinoiserie or Japonnaise subjects, often derived from the engravings of Petruschenk, particularly on Augustus Rex wares, *J G Herold* – specialised in elaborate miniature chinoiserie figure subjects, *C F Herold* – noted for European and Levantine quay scenes
★ crossed swords factory mark stated in 1723
★ marks, shapes and styles much copied
★ underside of wares on later body has somewhat greyish chalky appearance
★ in late 1720's a somewhat glassier, harder looking paste was introduced, different from the early ivory tones of the Böttger period
★ finest Meissen figures modelled by J J Kändler from 1731
★ best figures late 1730's and early 1740's – especially the great Commedia dell'Arte figures and groups
★ other distinguished modellers who often worked in association with Kändler were Paul Reinicke and J F Eberlein
★ cut-flower decoration (Schnittblumen) often associated with J G Klinger. The naturalistic flower subjects of the 1740's, epitomised by Klinger, gradually became less realistic and moved towards the so-called 'manier Blumen' of the 1750's and 1760's
★ early models had been mounted on simple flat pad bases, whereas from 1750's bases were lightly moulded rococo scrolls

A Mennecy double snuff box with contemporary silver gilt mounts, painted with trailing vines and bound with yellow cords, the hinged contemporary mounts with a dechargé of Antoine Leschaudel, fermier général, c1750, 2in (5.5cm).
$4,000-5,500

A Meissen snuff box and cover, painted with lovers, the interior of the cover with 2 putti in a cornfield in coloured cloths, with copper gilt mount, c1760, 2½in (6.5cm) diam.
$2,250-3,000

A Sèvres deep 'bleu celeste' hunting snuff box and cover, with contemporary Louis XVI hinged gold mount, with painted vignettes within 'ciselé' gilt quatrefoil panels on 'bleu celeste' ground and with gilt dentil rims, the interior entirely gilt, the mounts with bright-cut wave pattern and bracket thumbpiece, c1775, 4in (9.5cm) wide.
$2,250-3,500

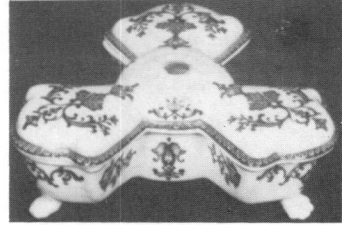

A St Cloud blue and white triple spice box and cover, painted with Berainesque foliate scrolls and flowerheads, the cover lacking finial, early 18thC, 5½in (14cm) wide.
$1,300-1,800

A French pink and white overlay casket and cover with gilt metal hinged mounts, enriched with gilt scrolling foliage and C-scrolls, 4in (10cm) wide.
$900-1,300

Caddies

A Frankenthal ornithological tea caddy and a cover, painted with birds perched on rockwork and flowering plants in landscape vignettes, blue lion rampant mark and incised marks, 1756-59, 5½in (13.5cm).
$2,250-3,000

A Fürstenburg tea caddy painted with figures in rural landscape vignettes, the shoulder with gilt foliage, chip to shoulder, impressed no. 2, c1770, silver cover, 4in (10.5cm).
$1,300-1,800

A Meissen chinoiserie oviform tea caddy and cover, painted with Chinese figures, the shoulder with the remains of gilt 'Laub-und-Bandelwerk', the cover with an iron red and gilt foliage medallion, gilder's marks 21 to each piece, c1730, 4in (10.5cm).
$4,000-5,500

A Böttger white porcelain tea caddy, moulded with sprays of grape and vine leaf between ribbing, c1720, 5in (12cm).
$2,250-3,000

A William Ball Liverpool tea caddy, c1756, 5in (13cm).
$3,000-4,500

A Meissen yellow ground tea caddy and cover, painted with the Quail pattern and flowersprays within puce quatrefoil panels reserved on the yellow ground, the shoulder with coloured flowersprays, the cover with pinecone finial, blue crossed swords mark, Pressnummer 28 and painter's mark I in iron red, c1740, 5in (12cm).
$10,500-14,000

A Meissen tea caddy and cover, painted with huntsmen with hounds pursuing a stag and a boar, on brown and gilt rococo supports, the cover with flower bud finial, minor repair to cover, blue crossed swords mark, c1750, 5in (12.5cm).
$1,300-1,800

A Meissen tea caddy and cover, with pinecone finial painted with 'indianische Blumen' and scattered insects and enriched with gilding, blue crossed swords mark, c1735, 5in (13cm).
$2,500-3,500

A pair of Samson tea caddies, decorated in pink and green, c1860.
$250-350

A Worcester fluted hop-trellis tea caddy and cover, painted with red berried foliage divided by puce and gilt trellis between turquoise scale-pattern borders, edged in gilding, finial repaired, c1770, 6½in (17cm).
$1,500-2,600

A Worcester tapering cylindrical tea caddy and cover, painted in the Kakiemon palette with the Quail pattern, the cover with flower finial, slight chip to foot rim, c1775, 5½in (14cm).
$1,500-2,600

A pair of Höchst candlesticks, moulded with spiral rococo scrolls edged in puce and painted in colours, the nozzles edged in puce and with stiff leaves, puce wheel marks and incised SI, c1760, 6in (15cm).
$1,300-1,800

Candelabra

A Coalport taperstick, hand-painted in reserves on mid-blue ground, some damage, c1820, 3in (8cm) diam.
$60-100

A Derby candlestick figure of a boy piper, pale period, c1758.
$750-1,000

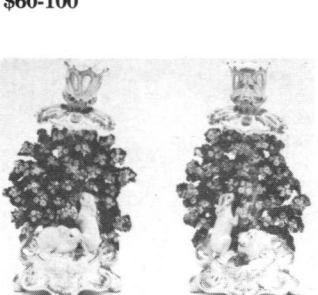

A pair of Chelsea-Derby candlesticks, modelled as 2 rabbits eating leaves from flowering trees which support the candle nozzles, pierced and gilt, with foliage in green, the pierced scroll bases outlined in puce and gold, 9½in (23.5cm).
$1,500-2,600

An English porcelain candlestick figure of 'Girl on a Horse' type, modelled as an exotic pheasant with puce and turquoise wing feathers with yellow breast and legs, the base picked out in iron red and painted with flowersprays, restoration to beak, some minor chipping, perhaps West Pans, c1765, 8½in (21cm).
$4,500-7,000

Cf Dennis G Rice, Derby Porcelain, pl. 42 for another example. See also the text Chapter 3, where figures of the 'Girl on a Horse' class are listed and the difficulties presented in their attribution are discussed.

HÖCHST

★ factory was founded in 1746 by the painter A F von Löwenfinck from Meissen
★ porcelain was produced from 1750
★ milk-white in colour, almost tin-glazed appearance
★ early wares tended to have poor translucency and be somewhat heavy
★ from 1758-65 the style reminiscent of the French 'Louis Seize' style came into fashion
★ this style was continued and developed by J P Melchior who was chief modeller 1767-79
★ the base of figures from 1765 tends to be in the form of a distinctive grassy mound, executed in dark café-au-lait and green stripes
★ the factory closed in 1796

A Longton Hall candleholder with a mauve parrot, c1755.
$1,500-2,600

A pair of ormolu-mounted Meissen figure candelabra, on rococo bases with 3 branches above with shaped salets, 19in (48cm) overall.
$2,250-3,500

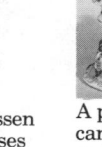

A pair of Sitzendorf porcelain candlesticks, decorated with putti and maidens, on circular bases, 12in (30cm).
$450-600

A pair of Royal Worcester figural three-light candelabra, modelled by Hadley in Kate Greenaway style, coloured overall in toned ivory heightened in gilt, tree stump repaired on male figure and chipped on the other, raised registration mark for 1883, impressed and printed factory marks and year code for 1886, impressed Hadley on reverse and 964 on base, 13in (33cm).
$1,300-1,800

A pair of Meissen candlesticks after European silver originals, painted with sprays of 'Holzschnitt Blumen', the stems with gilt gadroons, with gilt rims, blue crossed swords marks, c1740, 5in (13cm).
$10,500-14,000

This form of candlestick occurs on the toilet service made for Augustus III's mother-in-law, the Empress Dowager, in 1735, Cf Rückert, fig. 424.

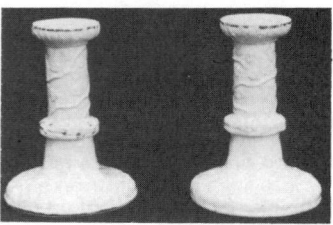

A pair of Rockingham candlesticks, of knopped tapering cylindrical form, moulded with overlapping leaves and trailing ivy, heightened in gilt, griffin mark in puce, 7in (18.5cm).
$300-400

A pair of Sèvres pattern royal blue ground and gilt bronze mounted three-light candelabra, the shield-shaped gilt cartouches enriched with turquoise beading, the gilt bronze finials terminating in porcelain vase-shaped nozzles, one vase lacks fixed ring handle, late 19thC, 18½in (47cm).
$2,250-3,000

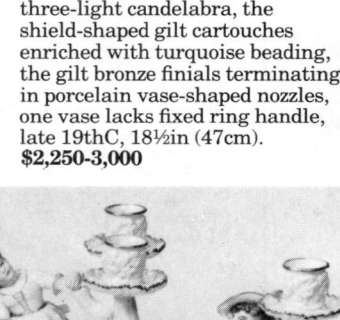

A pair of Royal Worcester double candelabra, white ground, signed to reverse of base 'Hadley', some gilding, puce mark, pattern 1124/1125, impressed mark to base 1886, 8in (20cm) diam.
$1,300-1,800

Centrepieces

A pair of Minton tazzas in the form of parian flamingoes holding up gilded bowls, c1860, 6in (15cm).
$1,200-1,600

A Copeland parian gold and turquoise side piece, impressed mark, 11½in (29cm).
$450-700

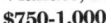

A Paris porcelain centrepiece, the basket printed with blue and pink ribbons, the circular base terminating in 4 Greek key scroll feet, the whole decorated in pastel shades, damaged, underglaze blue cross and star mark of Jules Viallate, 19thC, 25½in (65cm).
$750-1,000

A Royal Worcester table centre in white and gold, modelled as 4 lotus buds resting on leaves with gilt veining, printed mark in puce for 1883, 7in (18cm).
$750-1,000

A Worcester centrepiece, having floral panels, mask head handles and gilded decoration.
$450-700

A Royal Worcester footed centrepiece, white ground with blue and rich gilding, 2 centre bird panels, scroll feet, gilded mask handles, c1875, 13in (33cm) wide.
$1,200-1,600

Cups

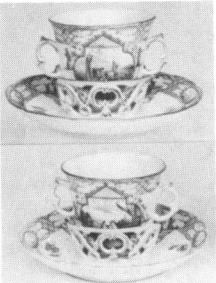

A pair of Berlin two-handled beakers and pierced trembleuse saucers, each painted within quatrefoil gilt and iron red foliage 'Laub-und-Bandelwerk' borders, underglaze blue sceptre marks and impressed I, 1765-70.
$1,000-1,400

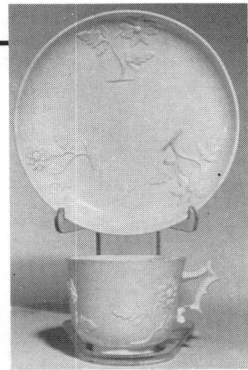

A Capodimonte, Carlo III, white teacup and saucer, each piece moulded with 3 sprays of flowers and with angular handle, rim chips to cup, blue fleur-de-lys mark, c1750.
$700-900

A Berlin iron red ground two-handled cup, cover and stand, reserved and painted with a portrait of Alexander I, named in gilt on the reverse, the cup with richly gilt interior and with gilt artichoke finial, blue sceptre mark, c1830.
$1,500-2,600

A Capodimonte coffee cup and saucer, painted by Giovanni Caselli, in colours with fruit in 'ciselé' gilt landscape vignettes within gilt borders with foliage scrolls, saucer broken in two and repaired, blue fleur-de-lys marks, c1750.
$5,500-7,000

A Caughley blue and white cup and saucer, c1785.
$75-150

A Caughley crested coffee cup and saucer, c1780.
$250-350

CAUGHLEY

★ factory ran from 1772-99, when it was purchased by the Coalport management
★ painted wares tend to be earlier than printed ones
★ Caughley body of the soapstone type
★ often shows orange to transmitted light, but in some cases can even show slightly greenish which adds to the confusion with Worcester
★ glaze is good and close fitting, although when gathered in pools may have greeny-blue tint
★ from 1780's many pieces heightened in gilding, some blue and white Chinese export wares were similarly gilded in England
★ main marks: impressed 'Salopian', 'S' was painted on hand-painted designs, 'S' was printed in blue printed designs, although an 'X' or an 'O' was sometimes hand-painted beside it, one of the most common marks was the capital C. Hatched crescents never appear on Caughley; they were purely a Worcester mark
★ Caughley is often confused with Worcester; they have many patterns in common, e.g. 'The Cormorant and Fisherman' and 'Fence' patterns

A Caughley blue and white miniature coffee cup, tea bowl and saucer.

Cup and saucer. **$150-250**

Tea bowl. **$60-100**

A Chelsea octagonal tea bowl and saucer, painted within chocolate line rims, c1752. **$900-1,300**

A Chelsea fluted sugar bowl, the lower part with a double iron red line, the interior with a chocolate line rim, the reverse cracked, c1752, 4in (10cm) diam. **$1,500-2,600**

A pair of Chelsea tea bowls and saucers, one saucer with minute chip to underside, red anchor marks, c1755. **$4,000-5,500**

A Chelsea two-handled cup, painted with figures standing on rockwork in an estuary with 2 boats at sail, the reverse with a loose bouquet, the interior with a pansy and flowerhead, 1750-52, 2½in (7cm). **$4,000-5,500**

A Chelsea tea bowl, with classical ruin decoration, raised anchor period, c1750. **$1,500-2,600**

A Derby botanical tea bowl and saucer, painted with specimen pink and yellow flowers within gilt dentil rims, minute chips to underside of saucer, red anchor marks, Wm Duesbury & Co, c1770. **$1,500-2,600**

CHELSEA
TRIANGLE PERIOD 1745-49

★ wares scarce and costly
★ many based on silver prototypes
★ many left undecorated
★ if decorated generally in Kakiemon or Chinese style
★ body comparatively thick, slightly chalky with 'glassy' glaze

RAISED ANCHOR PERIOD 1749-52

★ paste now improved
★ shapes still derived from silver, although Meissen influence noticeable
★ mostly restrained decoration either Kakiemon or sparse floral work (often to cover flaws)

RED ANCHOR PERIOD 1752-56

★ this period mainly influenced by Meissen
★ glaze now slightly opaque
★ paste smoother with few flaws
★ the figures unsurpassed by any other English factory
★ on useful wares, fine flower and botanical painting
★ Chelsea 'toys' are rare and very expensive
★ Chelsea is one of the few English factories to be collected by Continentals which has always kept the price buoyant
★ Continentals particularly like the 'toys' and all products of the 'Girl in a Swing' factory. This was probably a small factory closely associated with the Chelsea factory. It was possibly only in existence for a few years in the late 1740's/early 1750's. Very few useful pieces have yet been attributed to the factory whose products are extremely rare and always expensive
★ the most collectable ware of this period is fable decoration by J H O'Neale

GOLD ANCHOR PERIOD 1757-69

★ Chelsea's rococo period, with rich gilding and characteristic mazarine blue
★ quite florid in style, in comparison to earlier more restrained painting
★ influenced by Sèvres
★ elaborate bocage greatly favoured on figures
★ has thick glaze which tends to craze

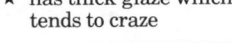

A Chelsea Derby tea bowl and
saucer, chipped, c1770.
$150-250

A Derby cup and saucer, with rare
Imari pattern, c1765.
$450-700

A Derby cup of London shape, with a
panel painted with shipping in
Plymouth Sound, the high loop
handle with mask thumbpiece, on
circular pedestal foot, with gilt line
borders.
$150-250

A Doccia tea cup and saucer, richly
painted with extensive landscapes,
with gilt rims, c1765.
$700-900

A Frankenthal cup and saucer,
painted in colours with mythological
figures, within green lined and gilt
Greek key pattern borders, minor
rim chip repair to saucer, blue
crowned CT marks and various
painter's and incised marks, c1775.
$1,300-1,800

A Fulda cup, cover and saucer,
painted in colours, with gilt borders,
blue crowned FF marks, the saucer
with incised 1K, c1790.
$1,500-2,600

Literature: George Savage, 18thC
German Porcelain, *pl. 123b.*

A Fulda cup and saucer, with double
scroll handle painted in colours,
with gilt rims, blue crowned FF
marks and impressed 1B and 3K,
c1780.
$4,000-5,500

Six Le Nove tea bowls and saucers,
painted in underglaze blue, iron red
enamel and gilt with Oriental
flowering plants issuing from
rockwork and with ovolo borders,
comet marks, c1770.
$1,000-1,400

A Christian's Liverpool polychrome
cup, with Chinese figures playing
games, c1765.
$150-250

A Christian's Liverpool polychrome
cup and saucer, c1768.
$150-250

A Longton Hall blue and white cup
with twig handle, Rous Lench
collection, c1756.
$1,300-1,800

A Lowestoft blue and white tea bowl and saucer, 1770-75.
$100-200

LOWESTOFT

★ late period blue and white tea bowls and saucers and other common tewares in painted or printed patterns should still be found at reasonable prices, particularly if damaged

★ coloured wares have been undervalued in recent years and it is still possible to form a collection of extremely interesting pieces without spending a fortune

★ many collectors are interested in unusual shapes – bottles, inkwells, eggcups, salts, eye baths and so on. Even damaged items can be very collectable but tend to be expensive

★ Lowestoft produced quite a large number of inscribed and dated pieces. These are highly collectable even if damaged. Beware of fakes produced by French factories earlier this century which are hard, rather than soft paste

★ early blue and white wares are of great interest to collectors. It is worth consulting a specialist book in order to help identify these pieces correctly as there is a growing tendency to give pieces an inaccurate early date

A Lowestoft blue and white coffee cup, c1790.
$75-150

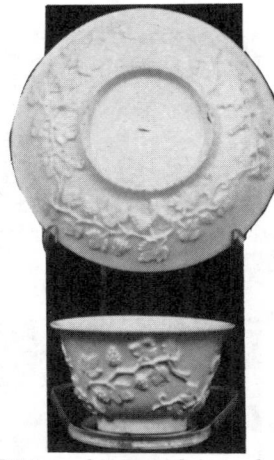

A Böttger white porcelain tea bowl and saucer applied with trailing vine, minute rim chips to underside of saucer and foot rim, underside of saucer incised with 3 fish, c1720.
$1,000-1,400

A Meissen purple ground tea cup and saucer, gilt rubbed, blue crossed swords and gilders No. 29 to each piece, c1740.
$2,250-3,500

A Meissen powdered purple ground octagonal cup and saucer, painted within ogival cartouches and with gilt rims, saucer cracked, blue crossed swords marks, incised marks and painter's marks, c1740.
$900-1,300

A Meissen tea bowl and saucer, painted in the manner of B G Haüer, the interior of the cup, the border and reverse to the saucer with sprays of 'indianische Blumen', blue crossed swords mark and gilder's mark D to each piece, c1735.
$3,000-4,500

A Meissen ornithological tea cup and saucer, and a similar saucer, blue crossed swords, cup impressed 4, mid-18thC.
$600-900

A rare Lowestoft cup and saucer, with chinoiserie print, chip on saucer, 1775-80.
$400-500

A Meissen two-handled beaker and saucer, painted with merchants, in continuous river landscape, within double iron red lines and with brown rim, the handles edged in puce, blue crossed swords marks, c1740.
$2,250-3,500

A Meissen tea cup and saucer, finely painted with lovers standing by a tree with a church and sailing vessel in the distance, in the manner of Horoldt, crossed swords mark, Pressnummer 45/46.
$1,500-2,600

A pair of Meissen Hausmalerei cups and saucers, painted by F J Ferner in enamel colours and underglaze blue enriched with gilding, on slightly moulded café-au-lait grounds, blue crossed swords marks and various painter's marks, c1750.
$2,250-3,000

A rare New Hall faceted sugar bowl, pattern 83, c1787.
$150-250

A Rockingham cabinet cup and stand, painted with flowers within gilt line rims, one handle repaired, crack to rim, the stand and cup with C13 in iron red, the stand with puce griffin mark, c1835.
$1,000-1,400

A pair of Meissen ogee cups and saucers, each painted with pastoral landscapes of country figures tending animals, within gilt foliate scrolls, blue crossed swords marks.
$450-700

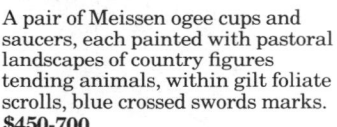

ROCKINGHAM

★ works had for a long time produced pottery
★ porcelain factory opened c1826 and closed in 1842
★ potters of the Brameld family
★ bone china appears softer than contemporaries
★ of a smoky ivory/oatmeal colour
★ glaze had a tendency to irregular fine crazing
★ factory known for rococo style of decoration, frequently with excellent quality flower painting
★ tended to use green, grey and puce
★ large number of erroneous attributions made to the Rockingham factory, especially pieces actually made at Minton and Coalport
★ pattern numbers over 2,000 are *not* Rockingham

A Rockingham cup and saucer, painted with a scene, puce griffin marked.
$150-200

A Marcolini Meissen cup, cover and stand, with burnished gold and lacquer border on a dark blue ground, the saucer with grapes in a shaded panel, crossed swords and star mark in underglaze blue.
$750-1,000

A Rockingham cup and saucer, painted with sprays of flowers, red griffin marked.
$150-250

A rare Vincennes trembleuse, in blue with puce cameos, date mark 1753, painting incorporating the date 1750, pot 6½in (16.5cm).
$4,500-7,000

Documentary pieces always command a high price and it is particularly so when the painting is also of high quality.

Three New Hall coffee cans, unusual or rare patterns, workmen's marks, c1800.
$60-100

A Sèvres hard paste cup and saucer, painted with rural figures, within gilt kidney-shaped panel and with borders of foliage scrolls, blue crowned interlaced L mark enclosing the date letter U for 1773, painter's mark in purple of a flower.
$750-1,000

A pair of Sèvres 'bleu celeste' tea cups and shallow saucers, painted in colours within gilt foliage cartouches reserved on the 'bleu celeste' ground and with gilt dentil rims, blue interlaced L marks and letter P, various incised marks, c1780.
$3,000-4,500

A St Cloud white beaker, cover and saucer, with silver gilt mounts, moulded with sprays of prunus in relief, replacement finial, minor chips, c1730.
$1,000-1,400

A Sèvres 'bleu nouveau' cup and saucer, painted within panels on the 'bleu nouveau' ground gilt with berried laurel, blue interlaced L marks enclosing the date letter Z for 1777 and painter's marks of Commelin and gilder's mark DR.
$400-500

A Venice, Cozzi, tea bowl and saucer, painted with a river landscape with boats and distant buildings and with gilt rims, iron red anchor marks, c1775.
$1,500-2,600

A Vienna gold ground baluster cup and saucer, the rims moulded with bands of grapes and vine leaf in burnished gilt, the handle with foliage, blue beehive marks and date coding for 1823, in fitted case.
$400-500

A St Cloud white beaker and trembleuse saucer, moulded with prunus blossom, slight rim chip to beaker, c1735.
$600-900

A pair of Vienna, Du Paquier, tea bowls and saucers, painted in colours with chinoiserie figures, impressed cross in a circle to the bases of the tea bowls and the terminals of the foliage, the saucers with scratch marks, c1725.
$4,500-7,000

A rare Worcester tea bowl, cup and saucer, with pencilled boy on buffalo, in mint condition, c1755.
$1,300-1,800

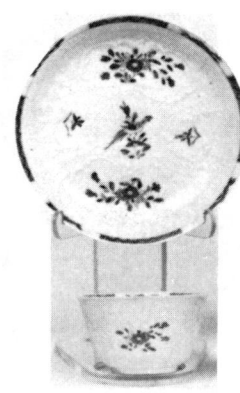

A Worcester pleated tea bowl and saucer, painted in the 'famille verte' palette, within green diaper borders reserved with half flowerheads, chip to saucer, tea bowl with minute rim chips restored, c1756.
$800-1,200

l. A Worcester First Period coffee cup, with hand painted exotic birds, scale blue ground, c1765, 2½in (6.5cm).
$150-250

r. A Worcester First Period coffee cup, with puce and gold decoration, c1765, 2½in (6cm).
$100-150

A Worcester cup and saucer, in the Jabberwocky pattern, c1770.
$800-1,200

A Worcester cup and saucer, with 'electric' pattern, c1768.
$250-350

Two Worcester First Period tea bowls, with printed underglaze blue decoration.
$60-100

18th CENTURY WORCESTER

★ founded in 1751
★ soft paste porcelain using soaprock (steatite)
★ c1751-53 a short experimental period. Sometimes difficult to differentiate between Lund's Bristol and Worcester
★ both blue and white and 'famille verte' polychrome wares produced
★ c1752-54 some wares marked with an incised cross or line
★ c1755-60 some finely painted and potted wares produced
★ painter's marks, resembling Chinese letters, appear on base of wares
★ the underglaze blue is well controlled and of a good pale colour
★ polychrome decoration is crisp and clean
★ almost all patterns are based on Chinese prototypes
★ transfer printed wares appear c1754
★ from 1760-76 a consistently high standard of potting and decorating achieved though lacking spontaneity of earlier wares
★ most blue and white pieces now marked with a crescent
★ 1776-93 the Davis/Flight period
★ often difficult to differentiate from Caughley where open crescent mark also used

---

A set of 6 Royal Worcester coffee cups and saucers, decorated in red and gold on a black ground, the insides of the cups gilt, and 6 silver tea spoons, in case.
$300-400

A Worcester coffee cup and saucer, printed in black with milkmaids, by Hancock, cup slightly damaged, c1765.
$150-250

A Chamberlain's Worcester lilac ground cabinet cup and saucer, painted with named views of Nuneham, the Seat of Earl Harcourt, and Cave Castle, the Seat of H. Barnard Esqr., within gilt cartouches, the borders with gilt quatrefoils between gilt line rims, minute chip to foot rim of cup, script mark, c1815.
$1,000-1,400

A very fine coffee/chocolate can, with a view of Warwick Castle, c1830.
$450-600

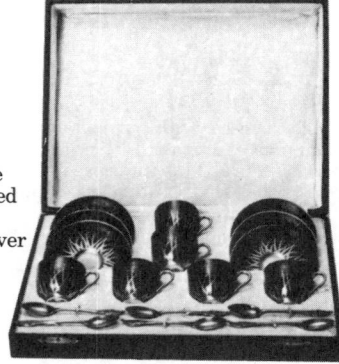

A rare armorial tea cup and saucer from the Giles Workshop, with coat-of-arms of the Plummers Company, in gilt, iron red, pink and blue enamels, inscribed with the motto 'Justitia Et Pax-In God Is All Our Hope', with gilt dentil rim, crossed swords mark and numeral 9 in underglaze blue.
$1,300-1,800

A rare Worcester ewer and basin, painted with 'Limoges Enamels' on cobalt ground by Thomas Bott, signed and dated 1866, gilding attributed to Josiah Davis, repair to cherub handle, ewer 11½in (29cm).
$4,500-7,000

A Royal Worcester Persian ewer on cream ground, gilt painted and polychrome enamelled decoration, date mark code for 1886, shape number 783, 15in (38cm).
$450-600

Ewers

A Paris yellow-ground ewer and oval basin, reserved and painted with a band of garden flowers, between gilt band borders and further gilt with berried foliage, the rims and handle enriched with gilding, c1820, the ewer 10½in (26.5cm).
$1,000-1,400

A Royal Worcester ewer, painted by John Stinton with Highland cattle, on bronze and green patinated grounds enriched with gilding, the bronze patinated flared neck with gilt trefoil rim and with green and bronzed foliage scroll handle, the lower part moulded with lappets and stiff leaves and on a shaped spreading foot, signed, puce printed mark and date code for 1911, pattern no. 1309, 16in (41cm).
$1,500-2,600

A pair of Royal Worcester ewers, with scroll handles terminating in satyr's masks, painted on buff ground, on circular socle, square base, No. 1144, 1904, 11in (28cm).
$750-1,000

A pair of small Rockingham ewers, with gilt scroll handles painted with Clock Tower, St Leonards and North Lodge, St Leonards named on the bases, one with restoration to handle, neck and foot, both with some chipping to flowers, puce griffin marks, c1835, 7in (17.5cm).
$750-1,000

Fairings

A Potschappel ewer, the body modelled with naked boys sporting amongst rushes on a river bank and riding on fish, supported by 3 figures of mermaids, 19thC, 17½in (44cm).
$450-600

'Can Can'. **$300-400**

A pair of Royal Worcester ewers, painted by Edward Salter, 1901, 16½in (42cm).
$4,000-5,500

An untitled match striker subject depicting a Turkish soldier and a woman beside a cannon and a pile of cannon balls.
$150-250

'English neutrality 1870 attending the sick and wounded'.
$450-600

'Every Vehicle driven by a Mule, Horse or Ass 2d', restored handlebar, arm and front wheel.
$450-600

An untitled fairing depicting a blacksmith repairing the hoop on a lady's dress.
$150-250

'The Convenience of Married Life'.
$450-700

'Infallible', chipped fingers.
$300-400

Figures – Animals

A Royal Dux group of 2 stone-coloured seated hounds, on a green and gilt oval mound base, pink triangular pad mark, late 19thC/early 20thC, 10½in (26.5cm) wide.
$450-600

A pair of Chelsea figures of a recumbent cow and bull, the cow with brown and purple markings, the bull with purple markings, their hoofs enriched in brown, some restoration to both, the cow with red anchor mark behind left foreleg, c1756, 5in (12.5cm) wide.
$6,000-8,000

CHELSEA FIGURES

★ triangle period (1745-49) figures are extremely rare
★ the raised anchor period (c1749-52) figures are again scarce – many were left in the white
★ the finest figures were made in the red anchor period (c1753-57). These figures are beautifully proportioned and exquisitely enamelled – the colours are always used sparingly. They were often direct copies of Meissen but due to the soft paste porcelain seem to have a 'softer' appearance. They lack the brilliant whiteness and brittleness of the German counterparts. Virtually no gilding appears until c1759
★ this heralded the beginning of the gold anchor period (c1758-70). The glaze was now thicker, gilding which appears in the early gold anchor period became less restrained following the current fashion at Sèvres. Figures were frequently backed by heavy bocages and stood on heavy scroll bases

A pair of Chelsea figures of great spotted cuckoos, their plumage in puce, brown, yellow and black, perched astride tree stumps applied with coloured flowers and lightly enriched in green, restorations, one with raised red anchor mark, c1750, 7½in (19cm).
$7,500-10,500

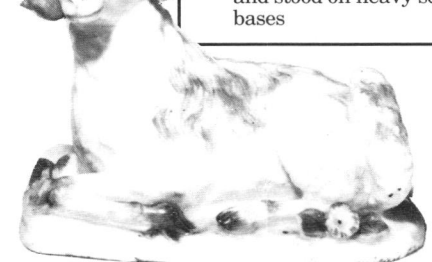

A Chelsea recumbent ram, his curly fleece with brown markings, on a base applied with coloured flowers, slight chips, red anchor mark, c1756, 4in (10cm) wide.
$900-1,300

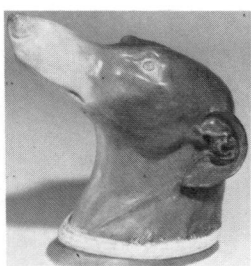

An English model of a whippet's head, with brown coat and white muzzle and collar, minute chip to rim, perhaps Copeland & Garret, c1830, 7in (17.5cm).
$1,500-2,600

A Derby cow, left horn chipped, c1745, 3½in (9cm).
$400-500

A Derby owl, its plumage in yellow, brown and pink perched astride a flowering tree stump, Wm Duesbury & Co, chips to flowers, c1765, 2½in (6.5cm).
$1,500-2,600

A Derby pug, c1770, 3in (8cm).
$400-500

A pair of Derby pugs, c1770, 2½in (6.5cm).
$600-900

A pair of Derby sheep, in mint condition, c1800, 5in (13cm).
$750-1,000

A Derby figure of a stag, in mint condition, c1800, 6½in (16.5cm).
$750-1,000

An English figure of a rabbit, probably Derby, c1800, 2in (5cm).
$300-500

A Chamberlain's Worcester white figure of a kingfisher, the base applied with foliage and a fish, beak and tail chipped, c1800, 4½in (12cm).
$1,000-1,400

A pair of Dresden figures of jays, with brown plumage, their tails and wing tips black and yellow, with a little white and iron red, 19thC, 9in (23cm).
$800-1,200

A Kloster Veilsdorf group of a leopard attacking a mule, modelled by Pfränger, the mule's ears repaired, tail missing, hair crack through base, c1775, 8½in (21.5cm) wide.
$1,000-1,400

A pair of English recumbent pugs, one with turquoise collar, the other with green collar with bright yellow bells, with black faces and streaked brown coats, on cushions with brilliant yellow tassels at the corners and edged in puce, one tail with minor restorations and one paw with minor chip, 1750-55, 2½in (6cm) wide.
$7,500-10,500

Cf George Savage, 18th Century English Porcelain, pl. 89b, where a similar example is attributed to Derby; however a dated example of the same model left in the white is in the Rous Lench Collection and illustrated by Bernard Watney, Longton Hall Porcelain, pl. 3c. On the evidence of paste and glaze and the use of vibrant yellow enamel a Longton Hall attribution would seem to be the most satisfactory.

LONGTON HALL

★ factory founded by William Jenkinson in c1749
★ in 1751 he was joined by Wm Littler and Wm Nicklin
★ earliest pieces the 'Snowman' figures and some blue and white wares
★ there has been a re-attribution of some Longton wares to the West Pans factory started by Wm Littler in the early 1760's
★ West Pans wares are usually decorated in a crude tone of blue, polychrome decoration is often badly rubbed
★ some West Pans wares are marked with 2 crossed L's with a tail of dots below
★ the figures, in particular, tend to have a stiff, lumpy appearance
★ the porcelain is of the glassy soft-paste type
★ the glaze can tend to have a greenish-grey appearance
★ pieces often thickly potted
★ Duesbury worked at Longton Hall before going to Derby
★ the 'middle period' of the factory from c1754-57 saw the best quality porcelain produced
★ specialised in wares of vegetable form, some of ungainly appearance, unlike the more sophisticated wares of Chelsea
★ much of the output of the middle period was moulded
★ two famous painters from the period are the 'Castle painter' and the 'trembly rose' painter
★ Sadler's black printed wares are extremely rare and sought after
★ the porcelain is generally unmarked
★ some Longton moulds purchased by Cookworthy for use at Plymouth
★ the factory closed in 1760 – all wares are now rare

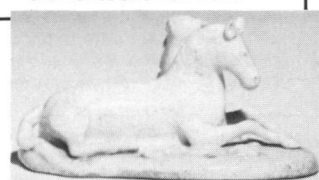

A Longton Hall white figure of a recumbent horse of Snowman type, its ill-defined features obscured by a thick bubbled glaze, recumbent before a tree stump, on an oval base with flowerheads and foliage, ears and left foreleg restored, c1750, 6½in (17cm) wide.
$1,500-2,600

A Meissen figure of a golden oriole, modelled by J J Kändler, with yellow body plumage and black and brown wings, perched on a tree stump with berried leafy branches and a beetle, restoration to beak, chips to foliage and base, blue crossed swords mark on bottom, 1735-40, 11in (27.5cm).
$5,500-7,000

A pair of Meissen seated figures of a pug dog and bitch with pup, modelled by J J Kändler, with black facial and hair markings and beige coats, repair to 3 legs and the bitch's right forepaw and her puppy's left, c1740, 7in (18cm).
$6,000-8,000

Two Meissen figures of guineafowl, modelled by J J Kändler, with iron red combs and wattles and black and grey spotted plumage, on tree stump mound bases with foliage and mushroom, one neck restored, minor chips to foliage, traces of blue crossed swords mark, c1745, 6½in (16cm).
$7,000-9,000

A Meissen figure of a pug on a paperweight, in turquoise with gilt, c1840, 7½in (19cm) wide.
$450-600

Two Meissen figures of camels, naturally modelled with brown hair markings, on rockwork supports and gilt edged scrolled bases, one neck repaired, blue crossed swords and dot marks, c1765, 6½in (16cm).
$3,000-4,500

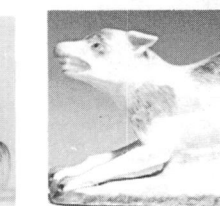

A Meissen miniature figure of a snarling dog, with brown fur markings on green edged mound base, restoration to tail and base, c1770, 2½in (6cm) wide.
$600-900

A Meissen figure of a Bolognese terrier, its rough coat splashed in brown, one ear restored, blue crossed swords and incised numeral marks, c1880, 9in (23cm).
$750-1,000

A Meissen figure of a squirrel, modelled by J J Kändler, with black fur markings and iron red collar with gilt chain, on mound base applied with coloured flowers, damage to ears, repair to base of tail, blue crossed swords mark at side, c1745, 8½in (21cm).
$6,000-9,000

A pair of Chelsea chinoiserie figures, modelled as an Oriental and companion, wearing green, pink and gilt flowered clothes, seated beside oviform pot pourri jars, on shaped scroll moulded bases enriched in gilding, he with restoration to back, hat and hands, she with minor repairs and chipping, gold anchor marks, c1765, 8in (20cm).
$5,500-7,000

An early Derby Ranelagh figure, c1758, 9in (23cm).
$1,000-1,400

Figures command a much higher price when there is no restoration, such as this example.

A Derby figure of a farmer holding a tithe pig, wearing a puce hat, green jacket, yellow breeches and purple shoes, Wm Duesbury & Co, damage to hat, some minor chipping, restoration to left wrist and pig's trotter, c1760, 6½in (17cm).
$750-1,000

A Derby white 'dry edge' figure of Winter, modelled as a putto seated on logs warming his hands before a fire, on an oval base, damaged, Andrew Planché's period, c1752, 4in (10.4cm).
$800-1,200

A Derby white figure of St Philip, with flowing cloak, standing beside an upturned basket of fruit on a circular scroll moulded base, Wm Duesbury & Co, hands lacking, c1760, 10in (25.5cm).
$1,000-1,400

A pair of Derby musicians, 1760-65, 9in (23cm).
$750-1,000

A pair of Derby musicians, c1765.
$1,300-1,800

A pair of Derby figures of a boy and a girl with cockerels, some restoration, c1765, 9½in (24cm).
$900-1,300

A pair of Derby figures of a map seller and companion, companion restored, c1765, 5½in (14cm).
$1,500-2,600

A Derby figure of Jupiter holding a thunderbolt, in flowered robes, with a pink cloak, an eagle at his side, base enriched in turquoise and gilding, Wm Duesbury & Co, thunderbolt and crown damaged, c1770, 11½in (29cm).
$800-1,200

Derby figures, all with restorations, c1770.

left to right:
Shepherdess with lamb, 7½in (19cm).
$450-600

One of the Continents, female with cape, holding garland of flowers, lion to base, 8in (20cm).
$600-900

Woman with black apron.
$450-600

King with eagle, 8½in (21.5cm).
$450-600

Queen with peacock, 8in (20cm).
$450-600

A Frankenthal Janus-headed figure in fur-lined white cloak and yellow dress on gilt scroll moulded base, head and hands restuck, restoration to cloak, blue crowned CT and AB monogram marks, incised S2, c1765, 6½in (17cm).
$1,500-2,600

Emblematic of January from a set of the months modelled by Konrad Link. Cf Hofmann, p. 84, no. 378.

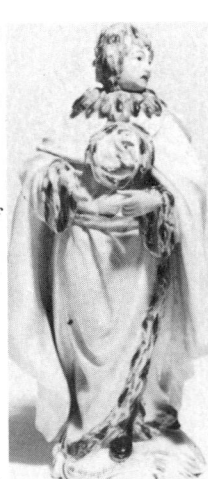

A Frankenthal group of a gallant and companion, modelled by J F Lück, the young man in flowered and gilt jacket with pink trim and puce breeches, his companion in maroon dress with green flowers, on gilt rococo scroll base, c1755, 8in (20.5cm).
$9,000-12,000

The model appears unrecorded in Hofmann.

A Frankenthal group of a young man and 2 young women, modelled by K G Lück, the man in black tricorn hat, white jacket, iron red cell pattern waistcoat and yellow breeches, his companions in predominantly yellow and pink, on a rococo scrolled base, some restoration to arms and extremities, blue crowned CT monogram mark and dating for 1778, 9in (23cm) wide.
$4,500-7,000

Apparently unrecorded by Hofmann.

FRANKENTHAL

★ Paul A Hannong started producing porcelain at Frankenthal in 1755, under the patronage of the Elector Karl Theodor
★ glaze has a quite distinctive quality as it tends to 'soak in' the enamel colours
★ high quality porcelain produced under Modellmeister J W Lanz
★ K G Lück and his brother or cousin J F Lück came to Frankenthal from Meissen in 1758
★ K G Lück's work tends to be quite fussy and often on grassy mounds, with rococo edges picked out in gilding
★ in the late 18thC a fine range of figures produced by J P Melchior and A Bauer
★ Melchior also worked at Höchst
★ Frankenthal utility ware is noted for the quality of the painting, particularly flower painting
★ factory closed in 1799
★ moulds from the factory were used in many 19thC German factories

A Fulda figure of a young man, in orange tunic with blue lining, iron red floral borders, blue floral waistcoat, the mound base with foliage in relief, some repair to his right thigh, blue cross mark, c1770, 4½in (12cm).
$7,500-10,500

A Frankenthal figure of a Chinaman, modelled by K G Lück, in yellow bib and striped dress and sash, the grasswork base edged with gilt scrolls, chips to jug and finger, blue crowned CT mark, c1770, 6in (15cm).
$2,250-3,500

A Fulda figure of a young girl emblematic of Winter from a set of the Four Seasons, in fur lined puce hat and jacket, holding a black muff, with white skirt with gilt hem and green lined iron red striped apron and green shoes on scrolled mound base, repaired through waist, blue cross mark, c1775, 5½in (14.5cm).
$4,000-5,500

This is from the series of children emblematic of the Seasons originally modelled by the sculptor Valenti. Later examples were reworked by Bartholome. All 4 figures are clearly inspired by the portraits of the children of the Fulda Hofmarschall Freihess stein zu Attenstein painted by Johann Andreas Herrlein, the Fulda Hofmaler in 1769.

A Frankenthal group, 'The Picnic', on naturalistic green base decorated in gilt scrolls, monogram of Elector Karl Theodor, 6in (15cm).
$4,000-5,500

A Fulda figure of a young man, modelled by George Ludwig Bartholome, standing in black hat with yellow ribbon band, flowered jacket with gilt edge, white shirt and purple striped breeches, on mound base with foliage, repaired through neck and legs, restoration to his hat and hands, blue crowned FF mark, c1785, 6½in (16.5cm).
$7,500-10,500

A Fürstenberg figure of a bird seller, modelled by Desoches, in brown hat, black jacket and puce breeches with a young girl at his side and a basket with various birds, another under his left arm and at his feet, 2 birds restuck, minor chips, blue script F mark, c1775, 6½in (16cm).
$2,250-3,000

A Fürstenberg figure of Harlequin, from the Italian Comedy series modelled by Simon Feilner, in black hat and harlequinade tunic, on tree stump mound base, repaired through neck, arms and body, chips, incised V on base, 1753-54, 7½in (19.5cm).
$3,000-4,500

FÜRSTENBERG

* ★ factory founded in 1747 but it was not until Johann Benckgraff arrived from Höchst in 1753 that porcelain was produced here
* ★ principal modeller at this period was Simon Feilner
* ★ enamelling technique was not perfected at this factory until the early 1760's, and underglaze blue remained of poor quality until the late 1760's
* ★ the body remained of a yellow tinge until the 1770's and the glaze tended to speck
* ★ it was these imperfections which encouraged the use of high-relief rococo scrollwork
* ★ other modellers of note are A C Luplau, J C Rombrich and Desoches
* ★ the factory passed into private ownership in 1859 and still exists today

A Fürstenberg group of Perseus slaying the monster, modelled by Desoches, in brown shirt, pink and yellow cape and iron red skirt, holding the Medusa shield and a sword, restoration to his right arm and his hat, chips, blue script F mark, c1780, 10½in (26.5cm).
$600-900

A Fürstenberg figure of a stonemason, in grey hat, puce jacket and black breeches, leaning over a block of stone with his various tools of trade, repaired through legs, restorations, blue script F mark, c1775, 4½in (11cm).
$450-700

A pair of Fürstenberg children at play, 19thC, 6in (15cm).
$450-700

A Höchst figure of a nymph emblematic of Intelligence, with tied hair, in a pink lined flowered robe, restoration to left arm, impressed 2H and iron red painter's mark IZ of Johannes Zeschinger, 1753-54, 6½in (16cm).
$750-1,000

A Höchst figure of a nude putto, with a purple ribbon in her hair and holding a green cloth above her head, seated on blue edged cloud scrolls modelled with a bird, repair to cloth, iron red wheel mark, c1760, 10in (20.5cm).
$750-1,000

A Le Nove white group of a dancing gallant and companion, on tree stump mound base, a chip to his hat and her left hand, c1780, 6½in (16cm).
$600-900

A Höchst figure of a young boy, modelled by J P Melchior, with a flower garland in his hand, black hat and pink chintz jacket and breeches, on a tree stump mound base, minor chip to hat and garland, blue wheel mark, c1770, 5½in (14cm).
$1,300-1,800

A Höchst group of The Garlanded Sleeper, Der bekrantze Schläfer, modelled by J P Melchior, a girl placing a garland on the head of a sleeping boy with a dog at his side, on grassy mound base before an urn on a pillar, minor restoration to the top of the urn, blue wheel mark and incised SX, c1770, 7½in (19cm) wide.
$4,500-7,000

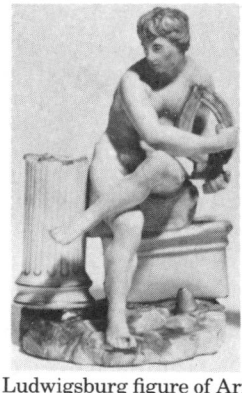

A Ludwigsburg figure of Arion, restoration to legs, left arm and instrument, blue interlaced L mark and impressed I.L.F.53, and with iron red painter's mark of Sausenhofer, c1765, 6in (15cm).
$450-700

A Ludwigsburg figure of Flora, with a cornucopia of fruit in puce and green edged white and yellow clothes, on fluted square plinth with swags, restoration to right arm, c1775, 10½in (26.5cm).
$300-400

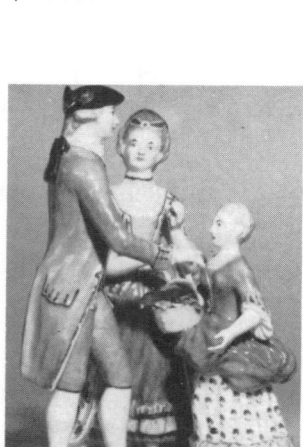

A rare Limbach figure of Winter, 1765-70, 6½in (16.5cm).
$700-900

A Ludwigsburg miniature group, in iron red, puce and green on rockwork base, damage to back of chair, blue interlaced C marks, c1770, 3in (7.5cm) wide.
$3,000-4,000

A pair of Mennecy white figures of a Sultan and Sultana, he repaired at neck, minor chips to both figures, incised D.V. marks on the mound bases, c1740, 9in (23cm).
$5,500-7,000

A pair of Mennecy figures of a young man and woman, in simulated pink lined straw hat, flowered jacket, bodice and apron, puce striped breeches and puce skirt, on square bases and tapered square plinths painted with sprays of flowers, minor chips to his hat and edge of his jacket, c1740, 7in (17.5cm).
$3,000-4,500

A Ludwigsburg chinoiserie group, modelled by J Weinmüller, of a woman standing in flowered Oriental costume, being embraced by a man in puce and yellow tunic, another figure playing a lute at her side, the rockwork base with a cushion, a vase and fruit, damages and repairs, incised Geer mark, c1770, 13½in (34cm).
$3,000-4,500

A Limbach group of a family, the man in black tricorn hat and puce tunic, his wife in puce flowered dress and orange skirt, their daughter in orange bodice and apron and puce flowered skirt, on grassy mound base, restoration to the father's right arm and to the daughter, puce LB monogram mark, c1775, 9in (23cm).
$600-900

A Meissen figure of Pantalone, modelled by J J Kändler, bearded, in black cap, green lined yellow cloak, blue shirt with lustre trim, yellow belt, iron red breeches and blue socks, on mound base with coloured foliage, minor chips to foliage, the porcelain c1740, the decoration probably later, 6in (15.5cm).
$3,000-4,500

A Meissen figure group of a child with a dog at her bedside, on a mound base with gilt arched border, blue crossed swords mark, c1880, 7in (18cm).
$450-700

A Meissen 'Pagoda' figure, with nodding head and moving hands and tongue, in a brightly painted floral dress and yellow shoes, painted mark and inscribed numerals, 19thC, 7in (18cm).
$1,000-1,400

A Meissen figure of a gardener, with a dog at his feet, on a scroll moulded mound base, leaf chipped, blue crossed swords mark and incised 61168, 7in (18cm).
$400-500

A pair of Meissen groups, some damage, 19thC, 9½in (24cm).
$2,250-3,000

A pair of Meissen figures, the man wearing a plumed cap and green coat, the woman contemplating a broken mirror, wearing a floral and green dress, on gilt scroll decorated circular bases, small faults, late 19thC, 6in (15cm).
$750-1,000

A Nymphenburg white figure of the Mater Dolorosa, modelled by Franz Anton Bustelli, her hands clasped in grief, in flowing robes, on square base, minor chips, impressed Bavarian shield mark at front of base, c1758, 12in (31cm).
$19,500-32,000

The Madonna with the companion St John with their associated Crucifix are among the earliest of Bustelli's works at Nymphenburg. Indeed their close relationship with contemporary Bavarian rococo wood carving prompted some authorities in the past to see in them the work of Ignaz Günther, the leading wood sculptor of the day and Bustelli's master. However, the pair in the Munich Stadtmuseum with the impressed mark FB makes the attribution to Bustelli beyond dispute.

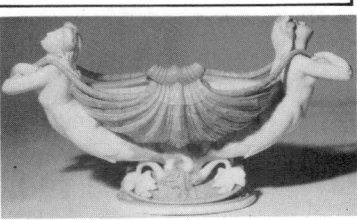

A Minton figural group, modelled as 2 long haired mermaids, supporting a large shell by foliate swags held in their crossed hands, sage green and white, impressed Minton and with date code for 1870, 17in (43cm) wide.
$2,250-3,000

A Meissen figure of a lady seated beside a birdcage, 6in (15cm) and another similar figure of a lady seated at a harmonium, 19thC, 4½in (10cm).
$750-1,000

A Minton figure of a putto seated on a conch shell, the shell resting on a rocky mound decorated with shells and algae, pale green and white, impressed Mintons 1539, and with date code for 1873, 17in (43.5cm).
$1,500-2,600

NYMPHENBURG

★ factory founded in the late 1740's but the main production started in 1753
★ J J Ringler was employed as arcanist
★ from 1757 a fine milky-white porcelain was produced
★ the porcelain is of great quality and virtually flawless
★ F A Bustelli modelled some excellent figures from 1754-63 which perfectly expressed the German rococo movement
★ the models are the epitome of movement and crispness and are invariably set on sparingly moulded rococo pad bases
★ note light construction of these slip-cast figures
★ J P Melchior, previously at Frankenthal and Höchst, was chief modeller from 1797-1810
★ on finest pieces the mark is often incorporated as part of the design
★ the factory still exists

A Nymphenburg 'Commedia dell'Arte' figure, after Bustelli, hand restored, 8in (20.5cm).
$600-900

A Plymouth group of 2 cherubs, supporting a garland of flowers, wearing loincloths and circlets of flowers, scroll base heightened with puce, the base impressed S.D., 6in (15cm).
$600-900

A rare Plymouth group, emblematic of Africa from the Continents, the white figure on a rococo base with a recumbent lion surmounted by a crocodile, tree riveted, 12½in (30.5cm).
$300-400

PLYMOUTH

- ★ factory ran from c1768-70
- ★ a hard-paste porcelain body patented by William Cookworthy
- ★ high proportion of kiln wastage
- ★ had a tendency to firing flaws and smokiness as a result of improper technique in kiln and many imperfections in the glaze
- ★ very black underglaze blue
- ★ most recognised products are the bell-shaped tankards painted with dishevelled birds in the manner of the mysterious Monsieur Soqui
- ★ the shell salt, also known at Worcester, Derby and Bow, most commonly found piece
- ★ Cookworthy transferred the factory to Bristol c1770

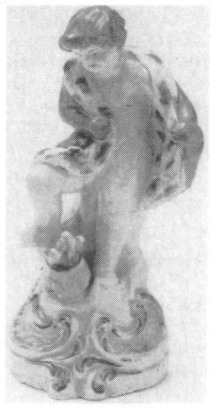

A Plymouth figure of a boy representing Winter, standing on a rocky outcrop by a brazier, in a fur trimmed purple cloak, on a high scroll base, late 18thC, 5½in (14cm).
$600-900

A pair of Rockingham figures of a Russian priest wearing a gilt and red hat, crimson and white robe with pink lower robe, an oval medallion painted with a crucifix pendant from his neck, and a priestess, wearing a red black dotted headdress, cream and white gilt dotted cloak and pink robe, restored, 10in (25.5cm).
$450-700

A Vienna white figure of St Paul, clutching the Sword of the Spirit, on rockwork mound base, right arm restuck through shoulder, some repair to right hand, sword hilt and left foot, blue beehive mark, c1760, 18½in (47cm).
$1,500-2,600

A Rockingham biscuit porcelain figure of 'Famme de L'Andalousie', a peasant girl, wearing a netted headdress and veil, carrying a basket of flowers, on a rocky flower encrusted base, slight damage, inscribed, impressed griffin mark and incised number No. 119, 7½in (19cm).
$750-1,000

A Rockingham biscuit porcelain figure of 'Paysanne de Sagran en Tirol', a peasant girl, wearing a dress with rouched neck, diapered waist band and ribbon tied apron, by a rustic water pump, on a rocky base encrusted with flowers, slight chips, inscribed, impressed griffin mark and incised No. 22, 7½in (18.5cm).
$1,000-1,400

A Vincennes white group of a water goddess, Baigneuse avec urne, recumbent and leaning on an urn of flowing water, before rockwork and waterweeds, minor chips, 1754-65, 8½in (21cm) wide.
$6,000-9,000

After the 1742 painting Vénus et l'Amour by François Boucher and perhaps modelled by Louis Fournier.

A Samson figure of Mars, in the Chelsea style, with plumed helmet and cape, carrying a sword and shield on a naturalistic base with tree stump, flaming torch and wreath, 11in (28cm).
$300-400

A pair of Worcester parian busts of Queen Victoria and Prince Albert, by E J Jones, W H Kerr & Co, impressed E.J. Jones Sculptor and printed marks, c1855, 13½in (34.5cm).
$600-900

A Sèvres group of a shepherd and shepherdess, Corydon et Lisette ou La Mangeuse de Raisins, modelled by Falconet after Boucher, minor chips, incised marks, perhaps DS and Ch, c1755, 9½in (24cm) wide.
$4,500-7,000

l. A Royal Worcester figure of 'Mischief', modelled by F G Doughty, pattern No. 2914, 3in (8cm).
$450-600

r. A Royal Worcester figure, 'Scotland', modelled by F G Doughty, pattern No. 3104, 5½in (14cm).
$300-400

A Tournai white group of a young girl, in a bonnet and long dress, an open cabinet by her side with drapery and a recumbent dog by her side, minor damages, c1775, 4½in (12cm).
$600-900

A pair of rare Royal Worcester figures of a youth and a girl, the boy fondling a dog seated on his knee, the girl shrinking from a lizard at her feet, the drapery and bases in pearl lustre, the figures in natural colours, the youth with Hadley impressed on the back of the tree trunk, 7in (18cm) and 7½in (19cm).
$700-900

Royal Worcester figures, from left to right:
Officer of the Third Dragoon Guards, Pattern No. 2675, c1969, 12½in (31.5cm).
'Queen Elizabeth I', Pattern No. 2648, c1970, 10in (25.5cm).
Charles II, Pattern No. 2672, c1969, 10½in (26.5cm).
Officer of the Coldstream Guards, Pattern No. 2676, c1969, 12½in (31.5cm).
Henry VIII, Pattern No. 2637, c1969, 9½in (24cm).
Officer of the 17th Light Dragoon Guards, Pattern No. 2677, c1969, 12in (30.5cm).
$250-350 each

A Vienna group of child musicians, after Marcolini, c1830, 11in (28cm).
$750-1,000

A pair of rare Royal Worcester chinoiserie coloured subjects holding parakeets, modelled by Miss Pinder Davis, no mark, shape 3446/3447, 14in (35.5cm).
$400-500

A Volkstedt group of a family seated round a rustic table with a dog beneath, 11½in (30cm) wide.
$450-700

A Royal Worcester parian bust of Queen Victoria, on tapering pedestal base and supported by 4 recumbent lions, the pedestal with a profile bust portrait of Prince Edward, c1887, 54in (137cm).
$1,500-2,600

A Royal Worcester figure, 'The Bather Surprised', a nude female figure leaning against a tree trunk, on gilt base, restored hand and hairline crack on base, signed T. Brock, London, No. 486, date code for 1906, 25½in (64.5cm).
$750-1,000

A Chelsea plate with fruit and insect decoration, some rubbing, gold anchor period, c1760, 8½in (21.5cm).
$400-500

A Chelsea dessert plate, with 2 fabulous birds in unusual posture, gold anchor period, 8½in (21.5cm).
$750-1,000

A shaped Coalport porcelain plate, well printed in blue with portrait of Lord Roberts within Victoria Cross, names of battles and 'Principal Commanding Officers' of 'South African War', inscription to reverse no. 647, 10½in (27cm).
$100-150

A Chelsea mottled claret ground dish, painted with gilt panels joined by gilt C-scrolls and garlands of roses within a gilt dentil rim, minute chip to rim, 13in (33cm), and a shaped oval dish en suite, ground scratched, 13½in (34cm), gold anchor marks, c1760.
$2,250-3,000

A Coalport Great Exhibition plate, reverse inscribed 'The Albion' and further inscribed 'Manufactured at Coalbrook Dale / By John Rose & Co / for J.&.T. Staples / for the Royal Table at the / Entertainment / given by the Corporation of the City of London / to Her Majesty Queen Victoria / at Guildhall / in Celebration of the / Great Exhibition / of the Industry of all Nations / July 9th 1851, 10½in (26cm) diam.
$1,300-1,800

A Copeland bone china ribbon display plate, centre finely painted and signed 'C.F. Hurton', pierced lattice border, gilded and with jewelled enamelling, impressed date mark for February 1885, 9in (23cm).
$750-1,000

The quality of painting and exceptional jewelled enamelling explain this high price.

A Copeland wall plate, painted and enclosed by turquoise and gilt border bearing 3 floral panels, printed green mark, late 19thC, 9½in (24cm).
$75-150

COALPORT (Rose & Co)

★ factory was founded in the early 1790's by John Rose when he left Caughley
★ early blue and white wares very close in style and feeling to Caughley products
★ note particularly the clear royal blue tone of the cobalt
★ Rose purchased the Caughley works in 1799 and ran them until he had them demolished in 1814
★ produced hard paste porcelain certainly after 1800, before then produced soapstone porcelain, quite similar to Caughley but does not have yellow-brown translucency
★ early wares heavy, with greyish appearance
★ in this period quite similar to Newhall and Chamberlains
★ the highly decorated Japan wares were of exceptional quality as are some of the flower painted examples
★ in around 1811 firm taken over by John Rose, William Clark and Charles Maddison
★ in 1820 a new leadless glaze was invented and they also began to use Billingsley's frit paste, whereas original Welsh plates were thinly potted. Coalport were much heavier and less crisp
★ in 1820 Rose also bought moulds from Nantgarw and Swansea and Billingsley came to work at Coalport
★ best period for the Coalport factory began in 1820 when the factory produced a brilliantly white hard felspar porcelain, with a high level of translucency
★ the rococo wares of the late 1820's and 30's are often confused with Rockingham
★ after 1820, CD, CD monogram, C.Dale, Coalbrookdale and Coalport were all marks used, before this date the marks tend to vary and much was unmarked
★ in 1840's and 1850's Coalport perfected many fine ground colours: maroon, green and pink
★ these often rivalled Sèvres especially in 1850's and 1860's and are close to the Minton of this period
★ Coalport also at this time produced some Chelsea copies, with fake marks – these are very rare
★ the Coalport factory is still in existence today

An oval dessert dish and a pair of plates, by H & R Daniel, the centres outlined with pale yellow bands with gilt beading, the green borders modelled in relief and gilt with foliage scrolls and petal ornament, all marked in puce script H. & R. Daniel, Stoke upon Trent, Staffordshire, the dish 11in (27.5cm), the plates 9in (22.5cm).
$450-700

A pair of Derby fluted dishes, the centres painted in the manner of Steele on a shaded brown ground, the matt gilt border burnished with trailing vine and reserved with anthemion, crown, crossed batons and D marks in iron red, Duesbury & Kean, c1810, 11in (28.5cm) wide.
$2,250-3,000

A Derby quatrefoil dish, painted in sepia by Boreman, within a gilt line and entwined foliage oval cartouche and gilt border, crown, crossed batons and D mark, pattern no. 66 in carmine, Duesbury & Kean, c1795, 10in (24.5cm) wide.
$800-1,200

A Derby plate in the Chelsea style, the centre painted in the manner of Duvivier within a gilt and puce feather-moulded rim, crown, crossed batons and D mark in puce, Duesbury & Kean, c1785, 8½in (21.5cm).
$750-1,000

A Doccia blue and white plate, printed with an artist seated before his easel, and a beggar child, the cell-pattern border with panels of flowers, the reverse with 2 flowersprays, star crack, minor rim chip, c1752, 9in (22.5cm).
$1,300-1,800

Doccia was the first continental factory to discover the process of transfer-printing. Whether this antedates the similar but independent discovery at Worcester is an open question.

A Crown Derby dessert dish, painted in the centre with an urn garlanded with flowers outlined with blue and gilt, the border with green husk festoons suspended from a rich blue and gilt border, crowned D mark in blue enamel, 8in (21cm).
$400-500

A Derby topographical plate, painted in the manner of Zachariah Boreman with South Front view at Chatsworth, Derbyshire, the spirally-moulded blue border similarly gilt, crown, crossed batons and D mark, pattern no. 50 in blue, Wm Duesbury & Co, c1790, 9in (22cm).
$700-900

Make the most of Miller's

CONDITION is absolutely vital when assessing the value of an antique. Damaged pieces on the whole appreciate much less than perfect examples. However a rare, desirable piece may command a high price even when damaged.

A Frankenthal plate painted 'en grisaille' with a simulated engraving pinned to the 'bois simulé' ground, the engraving inscribed 'Wills pinxit' and 'Hausman Sculp', blue crowned CT monogram mark, c1775, 9½in (23.5cm).
$1,500-2,600

A pair of Derby botanical plates, painted in the manner of John Brewer with Venus's Looking Glass and Tall Blue Aster, gilt line rims, named in blue script, Wm Duesbury & Co, c1790, 9in (23cm).
$750-1,000

A pair of Fürstenberg celadon green ground plates, with pierced borders of interlocking circles, the centres within quatrefoil gilt cartouches on the green ground, one with rim repair, blue script F marks and impressed MA and MI, c1760, 9½in (24cm).
$5,500-7,000

A Höchst plate painted in colours, blue wheel mark and incised NA, c1760, 9½in (23.5cm).
$900-1,300

A Lowestoft blue and white birth tablet inscribed and dated, within a dot and line pattern rim, the reverse with a trailing flowerspray, pierced for hanging, cracked across and re-stuck, 1777, 3in (7cm) diam.
$2,250-3,000

A Meissen Kakiemon plate painted in iron red and gilt with a tiger approaching green, iron red and gilt bamboo, 2 rim chips repaired, blue enamelled crossed swords mark and black incised Johanneum mark N = 73, c1730, 8½in (21.5cm).
$3,000-4,500

A Höchst plate in the Meissen style, painted with a bouquet of flowers, the border moulded with 4 flowersprays, the rim gilt with net pattern, blue wheel mark, incised NZ, c1760, 10in (24.5cm).
$450-700

A Meissen plate painted in underglaze blue and enamel colours, the well with a green band of flowerheads, the underglaze blue border with trelliswork enclosing red and puce flowers and reserved with 4 panels of insects and enriched with gilding, rim crack and chip, blue crossed swords mark within a double circle, c1725, 8½in (22cm).
$2,250-3,000

A large Meissen fluted saucer with scalloped rim, painted with a Chinaman and woman in iron red and yellow clothes in an iron red circle, the border enriched with gilding, blue crossed swords mark, c1735, 6in (15.5cm).
$2,250-3,000

A Liverpool lobed spoon tray, printed and coloured with bouquets, flowersprays and insects, attributed to Wm Ball's Factory, minute rim chip, c1758, 5in (13cm) wide.
$1,000-1,400

A Meissen chinoiserie plate, the centre painted with a circular iron red foliage or salami medallion with puce, green and yellow flowers, the reverse with 3 sprays of 'indianische Blumen', restored, blue crossed swords mark, c1728, 8½in (22cm).
$2,500-3,500

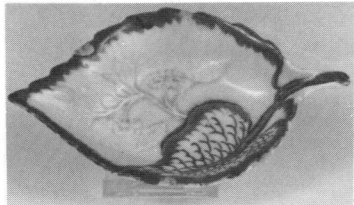

A Pennington's Liverpool blue and white pickle leaf, unglazed rim areas, c1790, 4½in (12cm) wide.
$100-200

A pair of Longton Hall plates, the centre painted in colours, the borders moulded with strawberry leaves, enriched in puce and green, minor chip to one, c1755, 8½in (21.5cm).
$6,000-8,000

A Meissen Hausmalerei shaped plate, painted by F F Mayer von Pressnitz with a mythological scene of Venus and Adonis, the well with gilt foliage scrolls, the border with 4 sprays of flowers, blue crossed swords mark and impressed Dreher's mark E, 1735-40, 9in (22.5cm).
$2,250-3,000

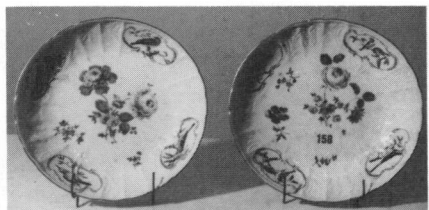

A pair of Meissen plates, late 18thC.
$900-1,300

l. and r. A pair of Nantgarw plates, in bright enamel colours with a serrated gold rim, impressed Nant-Garw C.W., early 19thC.
$1,500-2,600

c. A matching larger plate, impressed Nant-Garw C.W., 10in (25cm).
$1,300-1,800

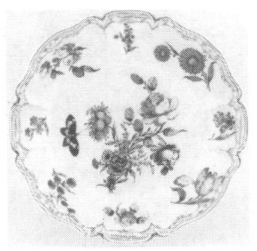

A Nymphenburg shaped octafoil saucer dish from the Hof service, painted with 'deutsche Blumen' and a butterfly, with gilt rocaille borders with blue lines, rim chip, impressed P2, c1760, 10½in (27cm).
$4,500-7,000

Five Paris botanical plates, each painted in colours reserved on blue and gilt 'oeil-de-perdrix' ground, with shaped gilt rims, green script, Boyer rue de la Paix, c1830, 9½in (24cm).
$2,250-3,000

A Rockingham plate, painted with a scene, with claret border, puce griffin marked.
$250-350

A Rockingham plate, with flower decoration, marked with a red griffin.
$100-150

A Rockingham plate, the centre painted by John Wager Brameld with Cole Titmouse and Gold-finch named on the reverse, the rim with cream and gilt C-scrolls, 2 rim restorations, puce griffin mark, c1835, 9in (23cm).
$900-1,300

A Plymouth pickle dish in blue and white, c1770, 3½in (9cm) wide.
$450-600

The same form and pattern was produced at Worcester.

A Rockingham plate, with a shark's tooth and S-scroll moulded border and gilt line rim, puce griffin mark and pattern no. 562, c1835, 9in (23.5cm).
$450-600

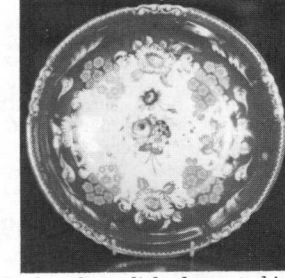

A Rockingham dish, decorated in claret and apricot, with shark's tooth moulding.
$250-350

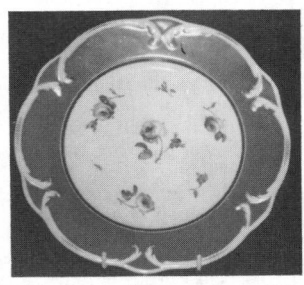

A Rockingham plate, painted with roses within a green border, marked with a puce griffin.
$150-200

A Rockingham plate, painted in colours within a sea green border moulded with acanthus leaves and heightened in gilt, griffin mark in puce, possibly decorated by John Randall, 9in (23cm).
$250-350

A Ridgway porcelain dessert plate, with flowers and insect painting, blue and gold relief border, c1820.
$400-500

A pair of Swansea porcelain plates, each painted with the Mandarin pattern in bright enamel colours and gold, the rim painted with reserves, printed mark in red, early 19thC, 8½in (21cm).
$2,250-3,500

SWANSEA PORCELAIN

★ factory produced high quality soft-paste porcelain from 1814-22
★ factory started by Dillwyn, Billingsley and Walker
★ superb translucent body, excellent glaze
★ in many ways one of the best porcelain bodies produced in the British Isles
★ also noted for delicacy of flower painting, usually attributed to Billingsley although much was obviously done by other decorators including Pollard and Morris
★ a close study of marked pieces will give one an idea of Billingsley's work but unless actually signed by him pieces should be marked 'possibly by Billingsley'
★ on pieces moulded with the floral cartouches the moulding can be detected on the other side of the rim, unlike the heavier Coalport wares which later utilised same moulds
★ especially notable are figure and bird paintings by T Baxter
★ the Swansea mark often faked, particularly on French porcelain at the end of the 19th, beginning of the 20thC
★ in 1816 Billingsley left to start up again at Nantgarw
★ many pieces were decorated in London studios

A collection of Vienna portrait plates, most signed Wagner.
$400-750 each

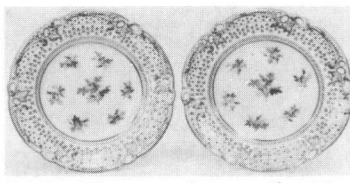

A pair of Swansea plates, each with a slightly scalloped rim, the centre painted with sprays of pink roses with a band of stylised flowers to the rim, moulded with acanthus leaves and highlighted in gilt, impressed mark, 9in (22.5cm).
$300-400

VIENNA

★ factory founded by C I du Paquier in 1719 with the help of Stolzel and Hunger from Meissen
★ the body of du Paquier wares has a distinctive smoky tone
★ decoration tends to cover much of the body and can be more elaborate than Meissen
★ extensive use of trellis work or 'gitterwerk'
★ the 'State' period of the factory ran from 1744-84
★ the style of this period was 'baroque', with scrollwork and lattice-like gilding
★ plain bases were used from mid-1760's
★ excellent figure modelling was undertaken by J J Niedermayer from 1747-84
★ Konrad von Sorgenthal became director from 1784-1804
★ the style became far less based on rococo and much simpler in taste, but with good strong colours and raised gilding
★ factory closed in 1864

A Vienna, du Paquier, lobed dish, painted with a two-leaf spray, one of the leaves painted with a Chinese figure in a landscape vignette, the other painted in iron red with pagodas, the underglaze blue border reserved with 4 symmetrical baroque panels divided by gilt and iron red flowering foliage, the reverse with 2 sprays of flowers, c1730, 13½in (34.5cm).
$7,500-10,500

A Wedgwood plate of the 1902 Coronation, printed in blue with a portrait of Edward VII, inscription to reverse, 10in (26cm).
$100-200

A Vienna, du Paquier, dish painted in 'Schwarzlot', the border with 4 sprays of flowers, minor chips, c1730, 8½in (22cm).
$2,250-3,500

A Worcester blue and white leaf dish of deep form, the underside moulded with veins, painter's mark, c1755, 6in (15.5cm) wide.
$1,200-1,600

A Worcester Blind Earl sweetmeat dish, moulded with rose buds and leaves and painted with pink swags of flowers, suspended from panels of green diaper pattern edged with gilt C-scrolls, the centre with a bird perched on a branch within a gilt line rim, c1770, 6in (15.5cm) wide. **$1,500-2,600**

A pair of Worcester scalloped edge plates, brightly painted with sprays of flowers, within scrolling gold reserves on a blue scale ground, crescent mark, c1770, 8½in (21.8cm). **$1,200-1,600**

Condition is vitally important to the value of blue scale wares.

A Worcester blue scale plate, blue square seal mark, c1770, 8in (21cm). **$900-1,300**

A Worcester plate painted in the 'famille rose' style, the border with trailing flowers within a gilt Van Dyck pattern rim, slight rubbing, c1770, 9½in (23.5cm). **$1,000-1,400**

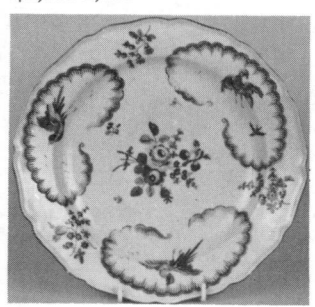

A Worcester plate, decorated with exotic birds and flowersprays in the James Giles atelier, 9in (23cm). **$600-900**

Note the direct influence of Sèvres style in the blue and gold 'feuille de choux' panels.

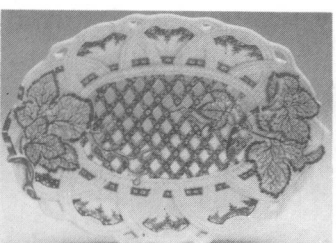

A pair of Worcester blue and white fruit dishes of two-handled basket form, with pierced base, firing and stress cracks, crescent mark, late 18thC, 11½in (29.5cm). **$800-1,200**

A Worcester plate with hop trellis pattern, with pink border, c1770, 8in (20cm). **$750-1,000**

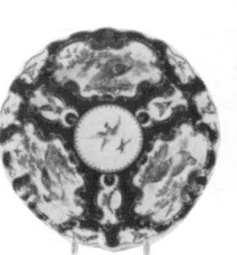

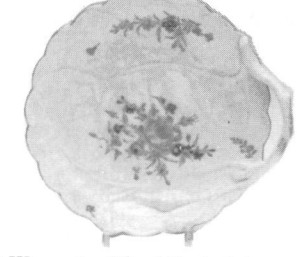

A Worcester Blind Earl plate, brightly painted with sprigs and sprays of flowers within a gold rim, late 18thC, 6in (15cm). **$600-900**

A pair of Worcester, Flight, Barr & Barr, dishes from the Stowe service, the borders richly gilt with lyres, urns and scrolling foliage, within gilt line rims, on a pale salmon pink ground, impressed marks, c1813, 12in (31cm) wide. **$4,500-7,000**

A Worcester square dessert dish, with shaped borders, painted by Giles, on a white panel, the rich blue ground gilt with fruiting vine, open crescent mark, 8in (19.5cm). **$400-500**

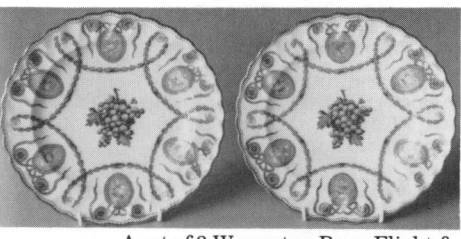

A set of 3 Worcester, Barr, Flight & Barr, dessert plates, the borders outlined in gilt, painted in tones of pink, divided by continuous green and yellow wheatear swags, the centre with a bunch of blue grapes and foliage, impressed mark B.F.B., printed mark Barr, Flight & Barr, Proprietors of the Royal Porcelain Works, Worcester, Established 1751, 9in (22cm). **$1,000-1,400**

A Worcester dessert dish, painted in the centre on a shaded brown panel with gold edge, on a gilt vermicular ground within a gold border, impressed mark BFB crowned and printed in brown with name in full and Worcester and London addresses, 11in (28.5cm). **$600-900**

A pair of Chamberlain's Worcester plates, the blue ground with gilded decoration, the centre panels depicting 'Frogmore' and 'Drayton' by George Sparks, c1845, 9½in (24cm).
$750-1,000

 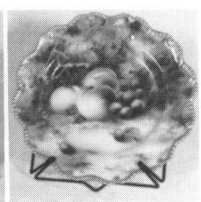

A Royal Worcester plate, with painted central reserve of Highland cattle by John Stinton, within ivory and gilt borders, 10in (26cm).
$450-700

A pair of Royal Worcester dessert plates, decorated within a gilt shaped border and signed 'F. Roberts', date mark for 1913, 9in (23cm).
$800-1,200

A Chamberlain's Worcester plate, with cobalt blue ground border, chip, printed mark, 9in (23cm).
$250-350

Three Russian botanical plates, each finely painted in colours with a named specimen rose, one with 'Rosier Rouille tres epineux', one with 'Rosier Des hayes (?)', the other with 'Rosier de Francfort', the rim with a band of gilt foliage, the reverse inscribed in gilt 'Archangelski 1827 Tome 2 p 29, 1827 Tome 1 p 51', the other '1826 Tome 2 p 47', 9in (23cm).
$3,000-4,500

A Viennese cabinet plate, painted with the Judgment of Paris mythological group, royal blue border with finely chased gilt arabesque and white enamel, 19thC, 9½in (24cm).
$600-900

A Chamberlain's Worcester armorial plate, decorated with the arms of Allan within cobalt blue ground border, printed mark, 9in (23cm).
$400-500

Ice Pails

A pair of Coalport ice pails with pineapple finials and moulded shell handles, painted in iron red, blue and gold, c1820, 10in (25.5cm) wide.
$2,250-3,500

A pair of Coalport yellow ground coolers, covers and liners, enriched in gilding with bands of foliage, with 2 scroll handles and scroll finials, one liner with hairline crack, some rubbing to gilding, c1800, 11in (28cm).
$2,250-3,000

A Flight, Barr & Barr Worcester ice pail, cover and liner, liner damaged, impressed mark, 14in (35.5cm).
$4,500-7,000

Inkwells

A pair of small Sèvres 'bleu celeste' two-handled seaux-à-bouteille, painted, one with chip to underside of footrim, blue interlaced L marks enclosing the date letter K for 1763 and the painter's mark of Levé, the decoration later, 4in (10.5cm).
$1,300-1,800

A Coalport inkwell, painted with shaped panels of flowering vines in iron red, blue and gilt, 9½in (24cm) wide.
$450-600

A Rockingham inkwell in the form of a scallop shell, with shell shaped pierced pen holders and loose cylindrical well, painted with anthemion and outlined in gilt, well cracked, griffin mark in red, number CL3 in gilt, 3½in (9cm) wide.
$600-900

An ormolu and Sèvres encrier of Louis XVI design, the stepped frieze with turquoise plaques with cherubs, flowerheads and musical trophies, with scrolling foliate angles and bun feet, inkwell lacking glass liner, the porcelain 18thC, redecorated, 11in (28cm) wide.
$4,000-5,500

A Staffordshire inkwell, with well modelled poodles, c1835, 4in (10cm).
$400-500

Jardinières

A pair of yellow ground miniature jardinières, probably Pinxton, 3½in (8.5cm).
$1,200-1,600

A Royal Worcester jardinière printed and painted with flowersprays in shaped oval panels, outlined in gilt on a peach and yellow ground, gilt slightly rubbed at rim, printed mark, 9in (23cm).
$450-600

A Sèvres gilt mounted garniture of 3 jardinières, all painted with putti in woodland landscapes, within gilded reserves on powder blue grounds, late 19thC, oval jardinière 10½in (26.5cm) and a pair of cache pots 6in (15cm) diam.
$1,000-1,400

A Coalport jug, c1805.
$300-500

A Frankenthal hot milk jug and cover in the Meissen style, on powdered purple ground, minute chip to spout, blue crowned CT monogram mark, incised HI and purple 6 and 11, c1765, 5½in (14.5cm).
$6,000-9,000

Jugs

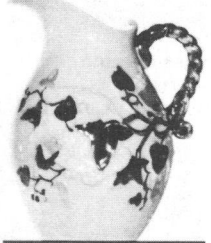

A Belleek jug modelled and painted with fruiting vines, small chip on outer rim, black printed mark, 6in (15cm).
$250-350

A Caughley blue and white jug, with gold trim, 1790-95, 3½in (7.5cm).
$100-200

A Caughley baluster shaped jug, printed in blue, C mark in blue, 7in (18cm).
$450-600

A Fulda cream jug and cover, with scroll spout and double scroll handle, minor chips to finial, blue crowned FF mark and incised 3K, c1785, 4½in (11.5cm).
$3,000-4,000

A Derby jug, painted with a river scene, and a gilt monogram below a gilt border, 19thC, 5½in (14cm).
$150-250

A Höchst hot milk jug and cover with artichoke finial, painted in the 'famille verte' style, the cover with a further landscape within cell pattern borders, chips to spout and foot, incised HI on base, c1760, 5½in (14.5cm).
$750-1,000

A Meissen jug and cover, of Swan service type, minor chip to underside of footrim, blue crossed swords mark, 18thC, 9½in (24cm).
$5,500-7,000

A Meissen Kakiemon baluster jug, with pewter hinged cover and spout cover on chain attachment, painted with birds and flowers, the pewter cover with ball thumbpiece and the engraved initials 'M.E.P.', minor chips to footrim, spout repaired, blue crossed swords mark, c1730, 8in (20cm).
$2,500-3,500

A porcelain pitcher, by The Union Porcelain Works, Greenpoint, N Y, designed by Karl Mueller, with walrus-head spout and polar bear handle, the pink ground body modelled on the obverse with a god presenting Uncle Sam with a beer centering a goat standing on a barrel, inscribed 'UPW', the reverse with a Chinese cardshark being attacked by a man, spout cracked, c1880, 10in (25cm).
$2,600-3,000

A Meissen pale powdered lilac ground hot milk jug and cover, with contemporary French silver gilt mount, painted with 4 panels of harbour scenes, the handle with 'indianische Blumen' and gilding, blue crossed swords mark, the mount with the décharge of Louis Robin, c1740, 4½in (12cm).
$3,000-4,000

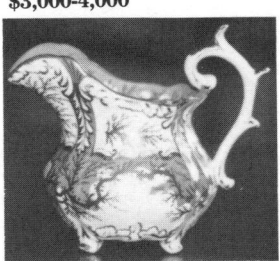

A Rockingham cream jug, with 3 spur handle and painted with green and gilt.
$150-200

A Sèvres cream jug, with 3 branch feet, painted beneath a gilt dentil rim, blue interlaced L marks enclosing the date letter N for 1788 and the painter's mark P.R., 5in (12.5cm).
$400-500

A Worcester blue and white jug, painted with Root pattern, restored, early painter's mark, c1755, 4in (10cm) wide.
$250-350

A Worcester blue and white creamer, with herringbone moulding, c1760, 4in (10cm).
$450-700

A Worcester sparrow beak jug, with chinoiserie scenes, in mint condition, unmarked, 3½in (9cm).
$800-1,200

A Worcester cream jug, embossed with leaves around the base, painted with Kakiemon-type flowers and prunus between vertical decorated blue panels, square mark, 1760-70, 3½in (9cm).
$1,000-1,400

A large Worcester blue and white cabbage leaf moulded vase jug, printed with pine cones and flowers, crescent mark, c1775, 12in (30.5cm).
$700-900

A pair of Tucker porcelain pitchers, enamelled in black on the obverse and reverse with landscapes, with gilt decoration on rim, handle and base, one cracked, Philadelphia, c1830, 9in (23cm).
$2,600-3,000

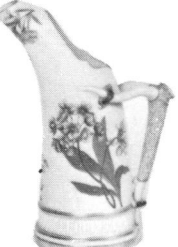

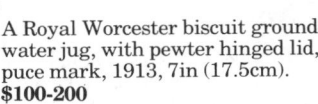

A Royal Worcester biscuit ground water jug, with pewter hinged lid, puce mark, 1913, 7in (17.5cm).
$100-200

A Chamberlain's Worcester spirally moulded jug, painted in sepia with a river landscape, the ground with alternate gilt, pink and yellow stripes, the neck with gilt star and dot pattern and with a blue band border, c1795, 5½in (13cm).
$450-600

A Royal Worcester 'tusk' ice jug, with painted and gilt botanic style floral spray decoration, year mark 1886.
$250-350

A Longton Hall mug with bird decoration, c1756, 3½in (8.5cm).
$1,300-1,800

Mugs

A Caughley mug, painted in sepia and pale colours with a lady and a dog beside an urn in an oval medallion, the border with trailing gilt foliage and blue dot pattern, c1790, 3½in (8.5cm).
$450-700

A rare Chelsea 'ho ho' bird beaker, triangle period, c1749, 3in (7.5cm).
$3,000-4,000

A Spode coffee can, with peony and clover pattern, c1820.
$60-100

A First Period Worcester mug, painted in underglaze blue and iron red with a Chinese landscape, with grooved strap handle, workman's mark in underglaze blue, 4½in (11.5cm).
$2,250-3,000

A Chelsea Derby mug with ribbed neck, painted with bouquets and sprays of flowers within dark blue and gilt borders, D and an anchor mark in gold, 5in (12.5cm).
$450-600

A First Period Worcester blue and white mug, c1760, 4in (10cm).
$750-1,000

A Worcester mug, with rare chinoiserie pattern, c1768, 4½in (11.5cm).
$800-1,200

A First Period Worcester blue and white coffee can, printed with the Fence pattern.
$75-150

A Worcester blue and white mug, with double strap handle, printed with the Parrot and Fruit pattern, c1755, 3½in (8.5cm).
$300-400

A Grainger's Worcester mug, painted with an extensive view of Elgin within a gilt mirror framed cartouche on a pink ground, scroll handle, G Grainger, Worcester script mark and named 'Elgin', 4in (10cm).
$300-400

A pair of Berlin convex plaques, each painted with a 'Gainsborough' lady holding a bouquet of flowers, 7 by 5in (17 by 12.5cm), with gilt frames.
$1,500-2,600

Plaques

A rare Belleek plaque, painted by Horatio H Calder, very slight hair crack to one edge, signed, black printed Belleek mark, First Period, 6½ by 4½in (17 by 11cm).
$4,000-5,500

A Berlin plaque, painted with a portrait of a girl holding a closed fan, wearing lace-edged white blouse and pale grey skirt, impressed KPM and sceptre marks, c1880, 12½ by 10½in (32 by 26cm).
$2,500-3,500

A Berlin plaque, painted with Venus and Cupid, impressed KPM mark and sceptre marks, c1880, 10 by 7½in (25.5 by 19cm).
$3,000-4,500

BERLIN PLAQUES

★ have seen tremendous increase in value over last 4 years
★ main value points: pretty subject; well painted; slightly risqué subjects; clear KPM mark
★ religious subjects are not the easiest to sell, unless of superb quality
★ to make top prices plaques must be absolutely perfect – no rubbing, no cracks, no restoration
★ the Japanese market is only interested in really top quality undamaged pieces

---

A Berlin plaque, painted after Holbein, with 'The so-called Darmstadt Madonna', the Virgin standing in a pillared recess holding the Infant Christ with kneeling figures at Her feet, impressed KPM and sceptre marks, c1865, 10 by 7½in (25 by 18.5cm), gilt wood frame.
$1,500-2,600

A Berlin plaque, painted after Carlo Dolci, with a portrait of Saint Cecilia, seated playing an organ, with a halo above her head, impressed sceptre and KPM marks, c1880, 12 by 9½in (30 by 24.5cm), with red plush and carved gilt wood frame.
$3,000-4,500

A porcelain plaque, hand enamelled with a portrait of a finely dressed woman in a jewelled silk court dress, some cracks, early 19thC, 7in (18cm) diam, in a gilt metal mount.
$600-900

Pots

A white Chelsea chocolate pot and replacement cover, the body crisply moulded with overlapping leaves, on 4 feet, restoration to base, spout, handle and rim, 1745-49, 9½in (24cm).
$1,500-2,600

A pair of Coalport iron red ground flared bucket-shaped flower pots and stands, with fixed gilt ring handles painted in sepia by Thomas Baxter, on a gilt striped iron red ground between gilt hatch pattern and foliage borders, one with crack to rim and chip to stand, one signed T. Baxter, c1805, 5in (13cm).
$4,500-7,000

A pair of Coalport documentary flared flower pots and stands, with fixed gilt ring handles, painted by Thomas Baxter, the altars inscribed 'T. Baxter 1801', between gilt bands, one stand with rim chips, c1801, 6in (15cm).
$6,000-9,000

For a detailed discussion of Baxter's career cf Geoffrey A Godden, Chamberlain-Worcester Porcelain 1788-1852, *pp. 184-6.*

Two St Cloud white cylindrical jars and covers, moulded with flower sprays and with silver mounts, one cover repaired, finials damaged, incised t S.C.T, marks to each piece, c1730, 6in (15cm).
$800-1,200

A garniture of 3 Davenport bulb pots with gilt ring handles, painted with fruit on tables, in the manner of Thomas Steel, impressed marks, c1805, 5in (13cm) to 6in (15cm).
$300-400

A pair of Derby bough pots and pierced covers, on a pale beige ground, on 4 scroll feet, the pierced covers with cauliflower finials, one cover repaired, the other cracked, c1840, 8in (20cm) wide.
$1,500-2,600

A pair of late Dresden vases, hand painted on yellow ground, Augustus Rex mark, A.R., 18½in (47cm).
$800-1,200

A pair of Meissen baluster pots and covers, with snail finials naturally decorated in colours, blue crossed swords marks, one with Pressnummer 37, c1740, 3½in
$4,500-7,000

A pair of Dresden covered jars, painted on a yellow ground, with gilt diaper borders, late 19thC, 14in (35.5cm).
$450-700

A Venice, Cozzi, white veilleuse, cover and stand, minor chips, 18thC, 10½in (27cm).
$1,500-2,600

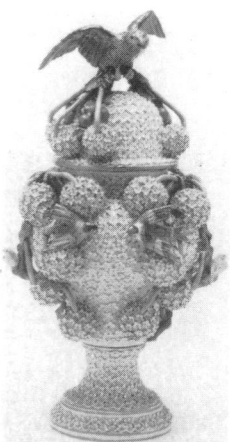

A large French 'Schneeballen' jar and cover, in the Meissen style, some damage, crossed swords mark in underglaze blue, 23½in (59.5cm).
$450-600

A set of 6 German storage jars, by Villeroy & Boche, early 20thC.
$75-150

A Worcester potted meat dish with Peony pattern, workman's mark.
$450-700

A pair of Vincennes 'bleu lapis' pots and covers, with flower and gilt foliage finials, painted in colours within gilt floral cartouches, reserved on the 'bleu lapis' grounds with gilt dentil rims, one cover repaired and chips, traces of blue interlaced L marks and painter's mark of Parpette, c1754, 2½in (7cm).
$1,000-1,400

A pair of French pot pourri jars and covers, set on scroll feet, painted with flowers and exotic birds, late 19thC, 14in (36cm).
$700-900

Sauceboats & Cream Jugs

Four Derby leaf moulded sauceboats, enriched in green and painted in colours with flowersprays, the stalk forming the handle, with bud terminal, one cracked, 2 repaired, c1760, 7in (18cm) long.
$600-900

A Chelsea sauceboat with scroll handle, printed with a bird perched on a fruiting branch and bird in flight, the interior with a butterfly and other insects, cracked, red anchor mark, c1755, 7in (18cm) wide.
$600-900

A Chelsea fluted oval salt or strawberry dish, painted with a pink flowered plant, the exterior with butterflies and insects, on fluted oval foot applied with foliage and strawberries, chips to foliage, the bowl with rim restorations, incised triangle mark, 1745-49, 5in (12.5cm) wide.
$3,000-4,000

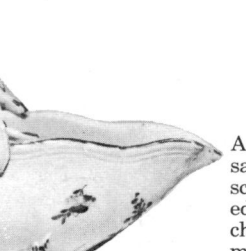

A Frankenthal double lipped sauceboat, with interlaced rococo scroll handles and scrolled feet edged in puce, painted in colours, chip to one lip, blue crowned CT monogram mark and dating for 1775, 10in (25cm) wide.
$1,000-1,400

A Derby butter boat, decorated in coloured enamels, c1760, 3½in (9cm).
$300-400

A Liverpool blue and white moulded sauceboat, the interior with an Oriental beneath a tree, attributed to William Ball's factory or Brownlow Hill, c1758, 6½in (16.5cm) wide.
$2,500-3,500

A Worcester cos lettuce leaf moulded sauceboat, the stalk handle with fruit and foliage terminal, modelled with overlapping leaves, within a brown line rim, rim chip, c1760, 7½in (18.5cm) wide.
$750-1,000

An early Worcester blue and white sauceboat, c1755, 8in (20.5cm) wide.
$600-900

As shown in Banyan, French and Sandon's 'Worcester blue and white Porcelain', *plate 1B19.*

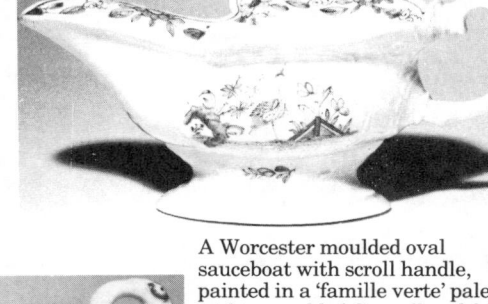

A Worcester moulded oval sauceboat with scroll handle, painted in a 'famille verte' palette, within moulded C-scroll and foliage cartouches, the interior with trailing flowers, on an oval foot, minute rim fritting, c1754, 6½in (16.5cm) wide.
$1,500-2,600

An early Worcester blue and white sauceboat, c1755.
$750-1,000

LIVERPOOL
Brownlow Hill (c1755-68)

(It is now thought that wares previously attributed to William Ball were manufactured at Brownlow Hill, Liverpool, by William Reid, c1755-61, by his successor William Ball c1761-64 and by James Pennington from 1764-68. Ball may have been Reid's factory manager and could have continued in that capacity under James Pennington.)

★ underglaze blue is often bright and the glaze 'wet' and 'sticky' in appearance
★ shapes and style of decoration influenced by the Bow factory
★ decoration often resembles delft
★ paste often shows small turning tears. These show up as lighter flecks when held up to the light
★ polychrome wares are rare and collectable
★ polychrome transfer prints overpainted with enamels are sought after
★ elaborate rococo sauceboats were a factory speciality

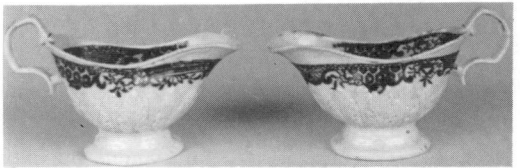

A pair of Pennington's Liverpool sauceboats, 6½in (16.5cm) long.
$250-350

Scent Bottles

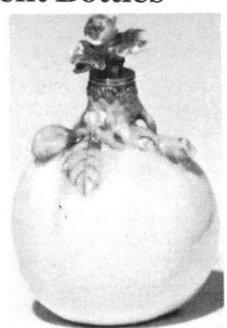

A Chelsea gold mounted scent bottle, naturally modelled as a peach marked in pink and yellow, the neck formed as the stalk, the stopper as blossom, stopper chipped, c1755, 2½in (6cm).
$3,000-4,000

A Chelsea gold mounted scent bottle and stopper, modelled as a flattened pear shaped flask, the lower part with pale yellow basketweave, the shoulder with a ticket inscribed 'Eau de Senteur' suspended from a moulded gilt chain, the stopper as a bird, minute chip to stopper, c1755, 3½in (8.5cm).
$800-1,200

l. A Chelsea Derby scent bottle, polychrome, c1765, 3in (7.5cm).
$900-1,300

r. A Chelsea Derby scent bottle in white, slight restoration, c1765, 3in (7.5cm).
$750-1,000

A Meissen scent bottle, formed as a galloping horse, the rider in turquoise suit and green saddlecloth on dappled piebald horse, his head forming the stopper and with gilt contemporary mounts and mirror base, c1755, 3½in (9cm).
$3,000-4,500

A Kloster Veilsdorf scent flask, modelled as a putto with a quiver of arrows, scantily clad in a red cloth, before a tree stump, with silver gilt cover, minor chip to his hands, c1775, 4½in (11cm).
$600-900

A Rockingham onion shaped table scent bottle and stopper, applied with garden flowers within gilt line rims, slight chipping, C12 in red, puce griffin mark, c1835, 6in (15cm).
$700-900

A pair of Rockingham scent ewers and stoppers, of acanthus sheathed slender baluster form, encrusted with foliage overall and raised upon beaded circular pedestal bases, painted in colours and gilt, slight chips, numbered Cl.3 in red, 9½in (24.5cm).
$750-1,000

A Meissen two-handled pilgrim flask scent bottle, with coloured and gilt female masks to the sides, restoration to neck and foot, blue crossed swords mark, gilt metal stopper, c1728, 3½in (9cm).
$1,200-1,600

l. A Worcester scent bottle, commemorating Queen Victoria's 1887 Jubilee, 2in (5cm).
$150-250

c. A Crown Derby back-to-back scent bottle, enamelled with flowers, birds and butterflies, c1875, 3½in (9cm).
$250-350

r. A white porcelain bird whistle, 18thC, 2in (5cm).
$75-150

Services

A Berlin dinner service, painted in iron red and enriched in gilding, comprising: sauce tureens and stands, serving dish, 83 dinner plates, some damage, with blue printed crowned WR marks, blue sceptre and iron red printed KPM marks, late 19thC/early 20thC.
$3,000-4,500

An Ansbach Jagd part service, painted with deer in landscape vignettes, the 2 covers with hares and the rims gilt, comprising a hot milk jug and cover, a cream jug on 3 feet, a sugar basin and cover and a cup and saucer, the sugar basin with A mark in blue, c1770.
$4,000-5,500

No comparable Ansbach wares would seem to be recorded.

An Aynsley dessert service, decorated with highland arcadian scenes including 'Stirling Castle, Loch Levern Castle, Bothwell Castle and Linlithgow', decorated in gilt with foliage on a 'gros bleu' ground, comprising 6 plates, 2 oval dishes and 2 fluted oval dishes, some damage, printed green mark and iron red inscribed titles.
$700-900

A Copeland Spode blue, red and gilt ▲ Derby style revolving tray on stand, with 6 matching cups and saucers.
$400-500

A Charles Bourne part tea service, painted with sprays of garden flowers on dark blue grounds, divided by gilt stylised leaves, comprising: a milk jug, a sugar bowl and cover, a slop bowl, a tea pot stand, a bread plate, 3 coffee cups, 5 tea cups and saucers, red mark, C.B./675.
$1,000-1,400

A blue and gilt decorated part tea service, with panels of flowers and fruit, comprising: tea pot and cover with stand, two-handled sugar bowl and cover, basin, jug, 2 plates 9½in (24cm), 7 cups, some tea and some coffee, 5 saucers, probably Coalport, 19thC.
$900-1,300

A Chelsea part dessert service, painted in colours, the borders enriched in gilding, comprising: 14 plates, 7 dishes, 2 sauce tureens, covers and one stand, and a diamond shaped dish, some damage, iron red and gilt anchor marks, c1758.
$2,500-3,500

A Coalport dinner service, decorated in underglaze blue, iron red and gold with a Japan pattern, with narrow dark blue and gold borders, comprising: soup tureen and cover, 2 vegetable dishes and covers, sauce tureen, cover and stand, 8 dishes, 41 plates.
$6,000-8,000

A Coalport dessert service, comprising 21 pieces, pattern no. 4/544.
$700-900

A Coalport, John Rose, part dessert service, painted in pink, iron red, pale apricot and gilt line borders, comprising: 12 pieces, c1810.
$2,250-3,500

A Coalport turquoise ground part dessert service in the Sèvres style, the turquoise borders reserved and painted within shaped gilt scroll cartouches, beneath waved gilt dentil rims, comprising: 5 stands, 16 plates, and a similar shallow dish, c1865, 9½in (24.5cm) diam.
$700-900

A Daniel's pink ground part tea service, painted with flower sprays within shaped gilt panels, comprising: a tea pot, cover and stand, 2 bowls, 2 bread plates, 15 cups and 7 saucers, patt. 4571.
$450-700

Cf M Berthoud, H R Daniel, pl. 49.

A Davenport Japan pattern dessert service, each piece of octagonal form, comprising: 2 tazzas, 4 comports and 12 plates, impressed marks.
$400-500

A Davenport Japan pattern tea service, decorated in Imari colours, comprising 37 pieces, pattern no. 3545, c1880.
$1,000-1,400

A Tucker porcelain part tea and coffee service, comprising a coffee pot, teapot, creamer, waste bowl, shallow bowl, 7 saucers, 7 dessert plates and 8 teacups, each enamelled with red and green flowers with yellow or blue centres on a white ground with gilt rim, crack to creamer's handle, Philadelphia, c1830, coffee pot 6in (15cm).
$6,000-9,000

A Meissen, Marcolini, tea and coffee service, painted with bouquets of flowers beneath shaped puce scale borders etched with gilt scrolls, comprising: a baluster coffee pot and cover, a hot milk jug and cover, a sugar bowl and cover, a slop bowl, an arched tea caddy and cover, a quatrefoil tea pot stand, a cover, 18 cups and saucers, minor chip to spout of milk jug, blue crossed sword and star marks, various Pressnummern, c1785.
$9,000-12,000

A Meissen part dessert service, each piece brightly painted with flowers and birds on branches within gold decorated pierced borders, comprising: 2 double comports with dolphin supports, 3 circular comports and an oval comport.
$1,000-1,400

A Meissen, Marcolini, part service, decorated with classical Egyptian subjects, within yellow and blue chequered borders, flanked by gilding, comprising: 23 pieces, inscribed on the reverse 'Vue de village de Luxor et de ses monuments, d'un autre aspect', blue crossed swords and star marks and various Pressnummern, c1790.
$7,500-10,500

A Spode part tea service, comprising: sucrier and cover, milk jug, 7 cups and 10 saucers, each piece painted with English, Welsh and Irish views, script mark 'Spode' and names of views in grey, the majority of the pieces with impressed cross and the milk jug with impressed numeral 24, 19thC.
$900-1,300

A Staffordshire dessert service, with pink borders outlined with gilding, comprising: centre footed dish, 4 comports, 3 dishes and 15 plates, impressed mark C.G. & Co.
$750-1,000

A Swansea part tea service, painted with iron red and gilt flowers divided by wide blue leaves, comprising: a milk jug, a slop bowl, 6 cups and 7 saucers, painted mark patt. 239.
$450- /00

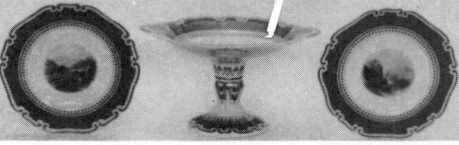

A Chamberlain's Worcester green ground part dessert service, comprising: a pair of ice pails, covers and liners, a sauce tureen, a centre dish, 3 dishes, 4 shell dishes and 20 plates, some damage and repairs, impressed marks and script marks in red, c1830.
$4,000-5,500

▶

A Grainger's Worcester dessert service, each centre painted with an extensive landscape, within a pink and gilt vermiculated ground, comprising: 3 comports, 3 dishes and 18 plates, one with hairline crack, impressed Grainger Worcester, Pattern No. 1014.
$1,000-1,400

A Grainger's Worcester dessert service, the biscuit ground gilded with pastel floral decoration, comprising: 4 plates and 2 dessert dishes, c1894.
$750-1,000

A Worcester dessert service, painted in polychrome enamels within border, on gold and turquoise gilt dentil rim, comprising: 12 plates and 4 comports, on scroll feet, impressed marks, 19thC.
$900-1,300

▼ A French dessert service with painted flowers on turquoise blue ground, comprising: 4 comports and 12 dessert plates.
$250-350

A dessert service, comprising: 4 comports, 12 plates, each with puce banded borders embellished in gilt with a crest, the centre of each hand-enamelled, some damage.
$700-900

DOCCIA

- ★ factory started by Carlo Ginori, near Florence in 1735
- ★ hybrid hard-paste porcelain of pronounced greyish-white appearance
- ★ body liable to firecracks
- ★ often decorated with mythological, religious and hunting subjects
- ★ glaze can have a 'smudgy' look
- ★ used strong enamel colours
- ★ from 1757-91 the factory was directed by Lorenzo Ginori, glaze and body improved considerably
- ★ figures often in the white and sometimes decorated with an iron red colour exclusive to the factory
- ★ porcelain often confused with Capodimonte, although Doccia is hard-paste and Capodimonte soft-paste
- ★ around 1770 figures covered in a white tin-glaze, often firecracked
- ★ factory still exists

A Christian's Liverpool tea pot, painted with a rare chinoiserie pattern, chips restored on lid, c1720, 6in (15cm).
$400-500

A Höchst coffee pot and cover, with gilt pear finial, double scroll handle and gilt edged scroll spout, painted in colours, repair to rim of cover and end of handle damaged, blue wheel mark and incised 1N, c1765, 7in (18cm).
$1,500-2,600

A Limbach coffee pot and domed cover, with lemon finial and scroll spout and handle edged in puce, painted with Jagd scenes of sportsmen, on puce scroll supports and with 'ozier' borders, chips to spout, blue crossed L's mark, c1780, 10½in (26cm).
$4,000-5,500

A Fulda tea pot and cover, with flower finial and scroll spout and handle, the rims, handle and spout enriched with gilding, minor chips to finial and spout, blue crowned FF mark, impressed 1A, c1785, 5½in (14.5cm) wide.
$2,250-3,500

▲ A Meissen tea pot and cover, with Böttger lustre knob finial, painted in underglaze blue, enamel colours, gilt and Böttger lustre, the border with 'Laub-und-Bandelwerk' in puce and iron red, blue crossed swords and dot mark, c1730, 6½in (16cm) wide.
$2,250-3,500

◄ A Meissen topographical oviform coffee pot and cover, painted with views in Dresden and Schandau, named in black script on the base, on richly gilt spreading foot, minor chip to spout, blue crossed swords and I marks, c1815, 7½in (19.5cm).
$800-1,200

A Meissen Hausmalerei tea pot and cover, painted 'en grisaille' with a shepherd and shepherdess in continuous rural landscape between iron red and gilt lines, the cover decorated with flowerheads and foliage, restoration to base and chip to cover, the porcelain c1728, the decoration later, 6½in (17cm) wide.
$1,300-1,800

A Sèvres tea pot and cover, the 'bleu celeste' ground with 'oeil-de-perdrix', painted with flowerheads and birds, with a gilt cherry finial, the spout and ear shaped handle with ornate gilding, blue interlaced L's and hh for 1785, painter's mark of Taillandier and gilder's mark of Sioux âiné, 4½in (11.5cm).
$2,250-3,500

A Böttger globular tea pot and domed cover, applied with sprays of roses and with traces of cold colour decoration and gilding, c1720, 6½in (16cm) wide.
$7,500-10,500

This applied decoration is generally described as 'Irmingerschen Belegen'.

A Worcester polychrome tea pot, with chinoiserie decoration, in mint condition, c1768, 7in (18cm).
$1,200-1,600

A Rockingham tea pot with crown finial and 3 spur handle, painted in reserve panels.
$400-500

A Sèvres tea pot and cover with flower bud and gilt foliage finial, with gilt dentil rims, minor chip to underside of cover and finial, c1765, 6½in (16cm) wide.
$600-900

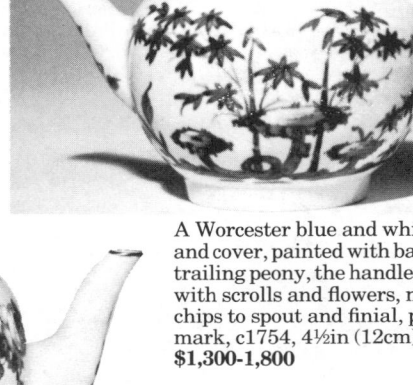

A Worcester blue and white tea pot and cover, painted with bamboo and trailing peony, the handle and spout with scrolls and flowers, minute chips to spout and finial, painter's mark, c1754, 4½in (12cm).
$1,300-1,800

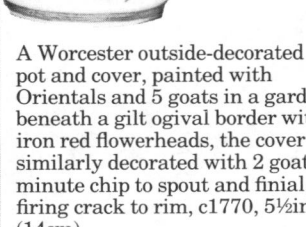

A Worcester outside-decorated tea pot and cover, painted with Orientals and 5 goats in a garden, beneath a gilt ogival border with iron red flowerheads, the cover similarly decorated with 2 goats, minute chip to spout and finial, firing crack to rim, c1770, 5½in (14cm).
$1,500-2,600

A Worcester blue and white tea pot, damaged, c1770.
$60-100

This common printed pattern and the damage account for this low price.

A Worcester blue and white herringbone moulded baluster coffee pot and cover, painted with trailing flowering branches, minute crack to spout, blue crescent mark, c1770, 9in (22.5cm).
$900-1,300

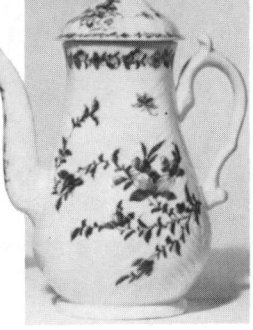

A First Period Worcester tea pot, painted with the Fan pattern, with chip and crack, lid and petals restored, c1770, 6½in (16.5cm).
$250-350

A rare Worcester blue and white tea pot and cover, printed on either side with The Man in the Pavillion pattern, the cover printed with a house and boughs of blossom, c1770, 5½in (14.5cm).
$1,200-1,600

A Worcester blue and white tea pot, painted with the Landslide pattern, early painter's mark on pot and lid, c1755, 5½in (14cm).
$1,300-1,800

The fact that this is a rare pattern associated with the early painter's mark on both tea pot and cover explains the high price.

A First Period Worcester blue and white tea pot, printed with Fence pattern, c1770.
$250-350

A Meissen, Marcolini, asparagus tureen and cover, naturally modelled and coloured in pink and green and tied with a pink ribbon, minor chip, cancelled blue crossed swords and star mark, late 18thC, 5in (12.5cm) wide.
$1,000-1,400

A Meissen écuelle, cover and stand, painted in colours after Teniers, on an allover basketwork moulded ground, the scroll handles enriched in gilding, tail of bird and tip of one leaf repaired, blue crossed swords marks, Pressnummer 21, c1742, the stand 9½in (24cm) diam.
$3,000-4,500

A Sèvres écuelle, cover and quatrefoil stand, with berried branch finial, painted within blue line and gilt dash borders and with gilt dentil rims, the stand with blue interlaced L marks enclosing the date letter M for 1765 and the painter's mark of Weydinger père, 9in (22.5cm) wide.
$1,300-1,800

Tureens & Butter Tubs

A Ludwigsburg rococo tureen and cover, the sides painted in colours, the white and gold handles with rococo scrolls and the cover surmounted by a nude female, her right arm repaired, chips to base, blue crowned interlaced C mark and impressed IP, c1765, 12½in (32cm) wide.
$4,500-7,000

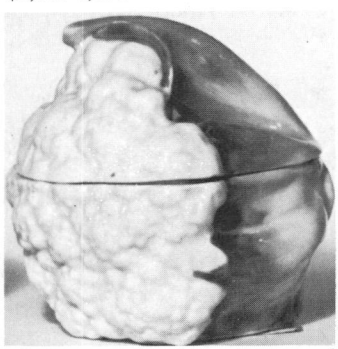

A Worcester cauliflower tureen and a cover, with naturally modelled shaded green leaves and white flowers, the cover with EX mark in black, the base with an encircled dot mark, c1758, 4½in (11cm) wide.
$1,300-1,800

A Sèvres yellow ground écuelle, cover and stand, painted in colours, the border divided by red bands and gilt dots and with yellow borders with gilt rims, blue interlaced L marks enclosing the date letters CC for 1780 and with the painter's and gilder's marks of Tandart and Vincent, the écuelle incised 4300 B9, the stand with fp, the stand 8in (20cm) diam.
$2,250-3,500

A pair of Meissen Imari tureens and ▲ covers, with pine cone finials, on blue grounds, blue crossed swords marks and K for Kretschmar, c1735, 9½in (24.5cm) diam.
$7,000-9,000

A Sèvres hard-paste green ground soup tureen and cover, Terrine Duplessis, with gilt artichoke and vegetable finial, painted with 'ciselé' gilt foliage cartouche reserved on the green ground, gilt interlaced L marks and HP mark of Prévost, c1785, 12in (30cm) wide.
$2,250-3,500

Vases

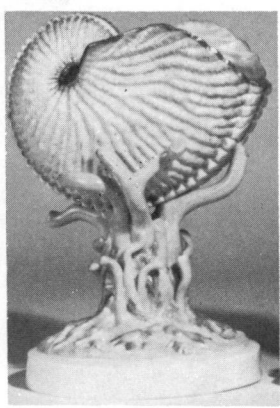

A pair of Belleek nautilus vases, heightened in pink, enriched with gilding, supported on pink coral above yellow and green foliage, bases moulded with pink shells, the rims to the bases left in the white, tip of one coral branch lacking, impressed Belleek, Co. Fermanagh and black printed Belleek marks, First mark, 8in (21cm).
$1,500-2,600

A pair of Derby pear-shaped vases and covers, entirely encrusted with yellow-centred pink blossom, the finials formed of red berries and foliage, one cover restored, slight chipping, Wm Duesbury & Co, c1760, 7in (18cm).
$1,300-1,800

A pair of Derby vases, each painted with summer flowers on a gilt ground, both with chips to base, c1810, 12½in (32cm).
$7,000-9,000

A Derby ▶ baluster pot pourri vase and pierced domed cover, finial restored, Wm Duesbury & Co, c1760, 7½in (19cm).
$750-1,000

A pair of Derby Crown Porcelain Co vases, each applied with 2 handles terminating in masks, the body decorated with a profuse overall design of birds and butterflies amongst foliage, in gold on a deep red ground, printed mark and date code for 1890, 6in (15.5cm).
$750-1,000

A Coalport, John Rose, vase, painted with a silhouette portrait of George III within a gilt shield inscribed 'An Honest Man's The Noblest Work of God', reserved on concentric bands of blue and gilt anthemion and yellow C-scrolls, the lower part with an orange band, between gilt line rims, c1810, 8in (20.5cm).
$450-700

A very rare and fine Derby vase, decorated with European figures and flowers, c1756, 10½in (26cm).
$1,500-2,600

A Derby campana shaped vase, decorated in the manner of John Brewer, c1810.
$1,500-2,600

A pair of Derby yellow ground vases, with floral decoration in blue, gilt and rust, 9½in (24cm).
$450-600

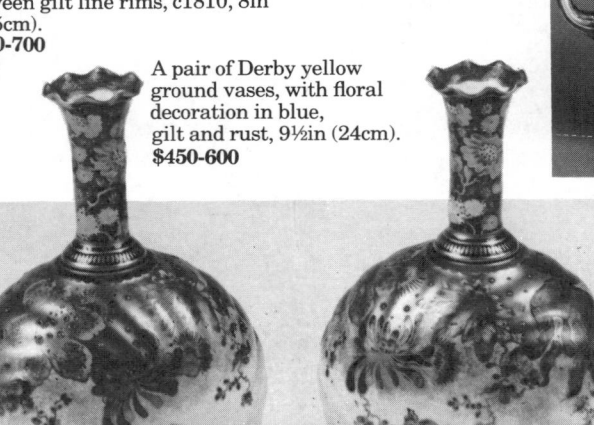

A Derby vase of flowers, painted with a fox in a fenced garden, the reverse with a bouquet between green and gilt line rims, the top formed as a conical display of pink, yellow and iron red flowers, flowers chipped, Wm Duesbury & Co, c1760, 6½in (17cm).
$750-1,000

A pair of Royal Crown Derby two-handled slender oviform vases and covers, painted by A Gregory, within borders of gilt leaf scrolls on blue and green grounds, printed marks, c1904, 18in (46cm).
$4,500-7,000

A Royal Crown Derby vase, painted with an oval landscape panel of 'Bettws-y-coed' by W E Dean, within gilt jewelled border on a blue and gilt striped ground, pattern no. 1651 and date code for 1914, 7in (17cm).
$450-600

A fine Royal Crown Derby pedestal vase and cover, the ovoid body finely painted by Richard Pilsbury, on a cream ground, under the base bearing the Royal Coat-of-Arms is inscribed 'First piece bearing Royal Arms, 1890', some damage and discolouration.
$600-900

A pair of Royal Crown Derby vases and covers, each painted with an oval floral medallion by A F Wood, within gilt jewelled border on a blue and gilt striped ground, one neck repaired, pattern no. 1505 and date code for 1914, 6in (16cm).
$450-600

A pair of Dresden vases and covers, on socle bases, each with twin ram's head handles, the domed covers with seated putto finial, pseudo crossed swords mark, 19½in (49.5cm).
$1,000-1,400

A Dresden classical vase on pedestal base, with applied female busts, on matching detachable platform base, mark of Carl Thieme, late 19thC, 18in (46cm).
$400-500

A Meissen Kakiemon baluster vase, painted with a yellow tiger creeping around bamboo, the reverse with prunus issuing from a tree stump, chip repair to foot, blue crossed swords mark, c1735, 4½in (11cm).
$1,500-2,600

A pair of Paris porcelain vases, with gilt metal mounts, one damaged, one in fragments.
$13,500-17,500

A pair of late Meissen pot pourri vases, with pierced necks and domed covers, painted with seashore landscapes on 3 gilt-edged lion mask raised feet, blue crossed swords marks, 7½in (19cm).
$1,300-1,800

A Meissen vase, with pate-sur-pate figure of Diana and a cupid on a grey-green ground, 19thC, 14in (36cm).
$1,500-2,600

A Mennecy white pot pourri vase, one duck's wing restored, chips, incised DV mark on base, c1740, 4½in (12cm).
$400-500

A pair of Sèvres pattern vases with domed covers, painted with lovers wearing 18thC dress, signed 'H. Foitevin', outlined in gilt on yellow grounds with gilt metal mounts, 16½in (42cm).
$900-1,300

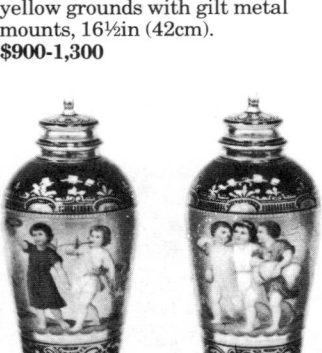

A pair of Staffordshire porcelain vases with high domed covers and branch handles, painted with Eastern temples and ruins, on grounds of large applied flowers, 17½in (45cm).
$300-400

A pair of Vienna vases and covers, painted with continuous bands of putti, in colours on a richly gilt ground, by A Ullmann, within 'gros bleu' borders richly gilt with foliage, shield mark in blue, indistinctly inscribed in red, signed, 8in (21cm).
$450-600

A pair of Viennese enamel brûle-parfums, the vases with polychrome decoration depicting Diana and Bacchantes in frivolous Arcadian pursuits, with twin champlévé handles and pierced lids, on spreading feet, 5½in (14cm).
$2,500-3,500

A Worcester, Flight, Barr & Barr, vase, 17in (43cm). ▶
$1,500-2,600

A Chamberlain's Worcester vase ▶ and pierced cover, c1805.
$2,250-3,000

A pair of Sèvres style vases of campanulate form, on a deep blue ground decorated in gold with a coral design, 7in (18cm).
$1,500-2,600

A Worcester, Flight, Barr & Barr, urn shaped two-handled vase and cover, the flat gilt loop handles with white flowerhead and bead pattern, the domed cover with gilt bud finial, finial repaired, slight chipping to rims and stem, impressed and script marks, c1820, 18in (46cm).
$3,000-4,000

A pair of Worcester, Flight, Barr & Barr, vases and covers, edged with beadwork, the white ground decorated with neo-classical gilding to the necks, painted in colours, each resting upon 3 winged female caryatid supports and inverted triangular plinths, mark in script, one foot cracked, 7½in (18.5cm).
$6,000-9,000

A Royal Worcester bulbous-shaped spiral vase, with wild flower decoration and gilding on biscuit ground, puce mark, pattern 1452, 1906, 11in (28cm).
$450-600

A pair of Royal Worcester bulbous vases, with circular domed dentil feet, with gilding on biscuit ground, puce mark, pattern 859, 1893, 11in (27cm).
$750-1,000

A pair of Royal Worcester two-handled bulbous vases on feet, with pierced rim, gilded with cabbage rose decoration, signed 'W.H. Austin', pattern 237, c1918, 10½in (26.5cm).
$1,000-1,400

A Royal Worcester globular vase and cover, painted by Baldwyn, on a pale blue ground, the shoulders relief moulded with feathery C-scrolls and applied with C-scroll handles, the low domed cover also moulded, enriched with gilt, signed, puce printed mark and no. 1515, date code for 1903, 8in (20cm).
$1,500-2,600

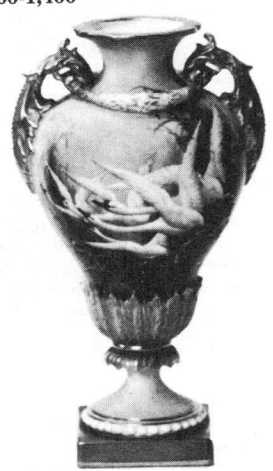

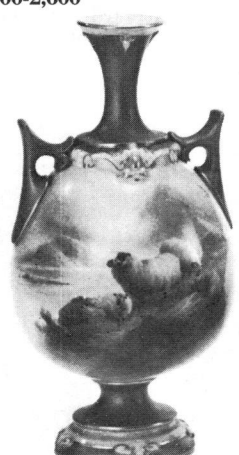

A pair of Royal Worcester vases, potted in the Persian style with handles in the form of dragons breathing smoke and flame, in naturalistic enamel colours on an ivory ground, the moulded neck and foot picked out in gold, shape no. 1117, signed under the base with the initials 'A.B.', printed mark and date code for 1888, 12in (30.5cm).
$1,300-1,800

A Royal Worcester vase, painted by Baldwyn, on a pale blue ground, the neck applied with foliate scroll handles joined by swags, the lower part with stiff leaves, on a waisted square pedestal foot, signed, green printed mark and no. 1937, date code probably for 1900, 8in (20cm).
$900-1,300

A pair of Royal Worcester oviform vases, painted by H Davis, with green patinated elongated neck, angular handles and mounted foot, signed, puce printed mark and no. 2440, date code for 1896, 8in (20cm).
$2,250-3,500

A Royal Worcester vase, heavily gilt and decorated with sheep, by H Davis, 12in (30cm). ▶
$1,200-1,600

A pair of Victorian Royal Worcester vases, decorated on a pale turquoise ground, with elephant head gilt simulated oval handles, one repaired, the necks with decorative gilt bands, date code for 1874, 11in (29cm).
$1,500-2,600

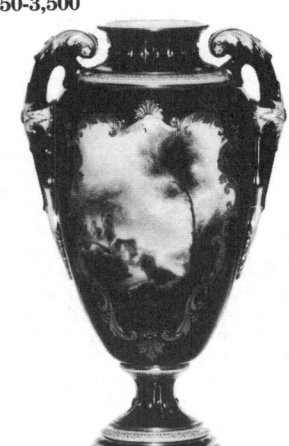

A Royal Worcester globular vase and cover, painted by C H Baldwyn, on a duck egg ground, the neck moulded in low relief with feathery C-scrolls and applied with C-scroll handles, the low domed cover also moulded, signed, puce printed mark and no. 1515, date code for 1902, 9in (23cm).
$2,250-3,000

A Royal Worcester vase, painted with ruins beside a river, by H Davis, within a border of gilt stylised foliage, on dark blue ground, printed mark, 13in (32cm).
$750-1,000

A Rockingham pastille burner, modelled as a pierced bulbous cover with flame finial, painted with flowers between moulded gilt foliage, finial chipped, the cover with C12 in iron red, the stand with red griffin mark, 1826-30, 4in (9.5cm).
$600-900

A large English porcelain pastille burner, in the form of a rambling thatched mansion, part of the house pulling out to reveal a drawer, drawer restored, early/mid-19thC, 9in (22.5cm) wide.
$6,000-8,000

An English porcelain lilac ground pastille burner, with separate base, c1835, 5in (13cm).
$600-900

An English porcelain triple pastille burner, probably Coalport, c1735, 7in (18cm).
$1,200-1,600

A rare Chamberlain's Worcester fort, c1830, 4½in (11.5cm).
$750-1,000

A Derby blue and white painted asparagus server, c1775, 3in (8cm) long.
$250-350

A Louis XV gold-mounted Sèvres rose pompadour knife handle, painted with pendant flowers suspended from rose pompadour gadroons and gilt leaves, the contemporary mount bearing the décharge of Eloy Brichard, fermier-general, 1756-62, c1759.
$6,000-9,000

The rose pompadour ground colour was invented by Hellot or Xhrouet in 1757 and was produced at the factory for the following 9 years until Hellot's death in 1766. A gold-mounted object such as this must surely have been destined for an important client.

A Royal Worcester oil lamp, with detachable reservoir, gilded and painted on a pale ivory ground and with formal Persian style moulded borders, on gilt brass base mount, date mark for 1890, 13½in (34cm).
$600-900

A rare Worcester blue and white knife handle, c1756.
$250-350

A pair of porcelain letter racks, painted with panels of birds and flowers on blue and gilt grounds, perhaps Coalport, c1820, 7½in (19cm).
$300-400

A Vincennes étui, with silver gilt mount painted with Diana attended by cupids, hair crack at back, minor repair, c1750, 5in (12.5cm).
$3,000-4,500

A Sitzendorf mirror, the frame encrusted with flowers and putti, with oval C-scroll surmount, with candle branches below, 32in (81cm).
$1,000-1,400

An English porcelain three-well pen and ink stand, probably Chamberlain's, the panels painted on a gold decorated deep blue ground, some damage, 6½in (17cm) long.
$450-700

Bow Porcelain

Brief History

1744 Thomas Frye, artist, and Edward Hewlyn, glass manufacturer, took out a patent to manufacture a 'material' of the same nature as china.

1745-47 Probable period of experimentation.

1748 Thomas Frye took out a new patent which makes it clear that he intended to manufacture and sell porcelain. A small factory was probably established at Bow.

1749-50 The New Canton Porcelain Manufactory built at Bow. Finance for the project probably from Alderman George Arnold. Two new partners are found on insurances – John Weatherby and John Crowther, porcelain dealers.

1749-60 Attractive coloured wares and blue and white wares produced. The factory became the largest in England.

1760-65 Gradual falling off in quality of products. The precise date of the factory's closure is unknown though it is thought that Crowther continued as sole proprietor from 1765 until the mid 1770's.

Early Polychrome Wares c1747-54

This is an extremely popular period with collectors. Wares are mainly decorated in 'famille rose' colours, most are unmarked though a few bear incised lines or an incised capital R c1750-52.

Patterns are mostly confined to chrysanthemum and peony amongst rocks. Early colours are vivid.

Wares from the pre-1750 period are scarce. Some damage is, therefore, acceptable and has less effect on value than with later coloured wares. Shapes c1747-50 include cylindrical mugs with flared bases, shell salts on rocky bases, fluted shell salts on dolphin bases, hexagonal sauceboats and oval sauceboats on lion-mask and paw feet.

After 1750, although still scarce, a wider range of shapes is found. These include tea wares, baluster mugs and octagonal dishes.

A German porcelain wine barrel, naturally modelled, enriched with gilding, with later gilt metal stopper, c1880, 18in (45cm) overall.
$1,500-2,600

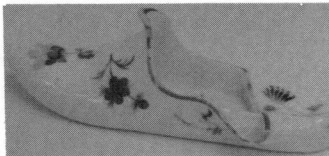

A Rockingham porcelain slipper, painted in colours with gilt line rims, griffin mark in puce and numbered CL.2, 4in (10cm) wide.
$1,000-1,400

A Bow flattened hexagonal sauceboat, with scroll handle painted in the 'famille rose' palette, the interior with a flowerspray within a green diaper border, minute rim chip, c1753, 8in (20.5cm) wide.
$800-1,200

Four Royal Worcester 'ivory' wall brackets, emblematic of the Seasons, decorated in pale tints, Summer with one leg repaired, one with impressed mark, c1880, 10½in (26cm).
$1,200-1,600

A rare early sauceboat of hexagonal form, decorated in a wet 'famille rose' palette with sprays of foliage, minor chips, c1750, 5½in (14cm) long.
$750-1,000

A cylindrical mug, decorated in a wet 'famille rose' palette with pink chrysanthemum stemming from rocks, beneath a green diaper border reserved with flowerheads in puce, c1752, 5in (13cm).
$900-1,300

A globular tea pot, decorated with Chinese figures and swooping birds, c1754, 5in (13cm).
$600-900

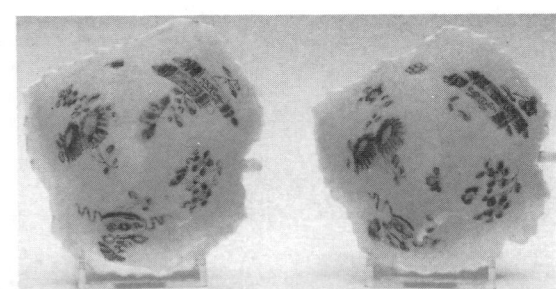

A pair of Bow polychrome pickle dishes, each in the form of a deeply moulded leaf, the exterior moulded with veins, the interior brightly painted with flowers, Chinese scrolls and a vase, one with faint interior crack, mid-18thC, 4½in (11cm) wide.
$1,300-1,800

WARES IN THE WHITE
c1747-65

★ a wide range of undecorated white porcelain, much of it moulded with prunus blossom, was produced. Early examples are popular with collectors

★ influences on shape derive mainly from Chinese forms

★ early pieces tend to be of a grey white colour whilst late wares are creamy and tend to be less crisply moulded

A baluster shape mug, with double scroll handle and applied moulded prunus blossom beneath a soft glaze, otherwise undecorated, scratch R mark, c1752, 6in (15cm).
$1,000-1,400

A rare vase, stylishly decorated in underglaze blue with a flowering tree peony amongst rocks, incised R mark, c1750, 7in (18cm).
$1,500-2,600

◄ A globular tea pot, decorated in polychrome with loose bouquets of garden flowers, pristine condition, c1758, 5in (13cm).
$750-1,000

POLYCHROME WARES
c1754-65

★ as output expanded so the range of shapes increased dramatically. Decoration was also influenced by fashionable taste

★ Japanese influenced Kakiemon designs, including the well-known 'Partridge' pattern, were in production by 1754

★ the taste for European decoration in the style of Meissen influenced Bow from the mid-1750's. Of particular note are the 'botanical' dishes produced c1756-58

★ a more common form of decoration included bouquets of budding roses and an open chrysanthemum

A group of Bow miniature wares, each decorated with bouquets in bright tones of puce, yellow, pale blue and green, c1760.
Sucrier, rare but chipped. **$600-900**
Coffee cup and saucer. **$450-600**
Tea pot, cracks. **$600-900**
Jug, chips. **$400-500**

A Bow plate, painted in Kakiemon palette with Quail pattern, c1760, 9in (23cm).
$250-350

A sparrow beak cream jug, boldly painted with Chinese figures in coloured enamels, rim chip, c1765, 3in (7.5cm).
$250-350

127

A Bow butter boat, decorated in enamel colours, c1760, 4in (10cm) wide.
$400-500

A tea pot lid, c1754.
$25-35

Illustrated to show that attractive pieces can be purchased cheaply.

BLUE AND WHITE WARES
c1750-55

★ vast quantities of blue and white were produced from c1750

★ wares c1750-54 are decorated in a bright blue peculiar to the factory. These pieces are often heavily potted and thickly glazed

★ most of these early pieces are decorated with simple Chinese landscapes or flowers among rocks

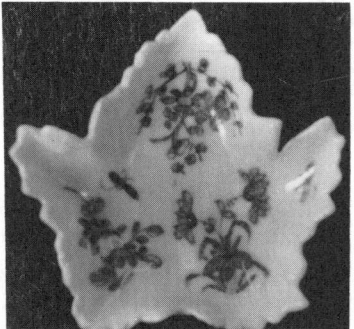

An unusual blue and white pickle dish, c1754, 4½in (11cm) wide.
$300-400

A Bow blue and white bell-shaped mug, painter's numeral 21, c1755, 3½in (9cm).
$300-400

A sauceboat, after a silver original, the squat body raised on lion's mask and paw feet, decorated in bright underglaze blue with a stylised Chinese garden, c1752, 9in (23cm) wide.
$1,200-1,600

A blue and white sparrow beak jug, decorated in pale grey blue, with simplified houses and plants, hair crack, c1754, 3½in (9cm).
$450-600

BLUE AND WHITE WARES
c1755-70

★ by 1756 wares are decorated in a darker, almost inky blue and patterns include Chinese landscape and floral designs as well as European flowers

★ early wares are sometimes marked with incised lines or a scratch R. In the mid-1750's painters numerals were sometimes used

★ collectors have a more discriminating attitude towards later blue and white. The value of the most common pieces is severely affected by damage and it is possible to buy them relatively cheaply

An early blue and white cream jug, painted with a scarce pattern depicting 2 deer and a pine tree, c1753, 3in (7.5cm).
$600-900

A Bow sauceboat with fluted sides, in underglaze blue with Desirable Residence pattern, c1755, 6in (15cm) wide.
$150-250

A Bow coffee cup, decorated in underglaze blue with a pine tree and plants, c1754, 2½in (6cm).
Perfect **$150-250**
Slight Damage **$100-150**

A blue and white Golfer and Caddy pattern cream jug, minor chips, c1756, 3½in (9cm).
$450-700

A popular and scarce pattern more usually found on flatware.

l. A Bow blue and pickle dish, small chip restoration, c1760, 3½in (9cm) wide.
$150-250

r. A Bow blue and white pickle leaf dish, stalk missing, c1765, 4in (11cm) wide.
$150-250

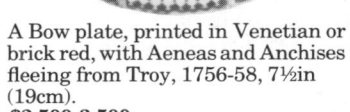

A Bow plate, printed in Venetian or brick red, with Aeneas and Anchises fleeing from Troy, 1756-58, 7½in (19cm).
$2,500-3,500

A Bow plate, printed in Venetian or brick red, with a combined scene of the Tea Party and the Wheeling Chair, with printed 'R. Hancock fecit', c1755, 7½in (19cm).
$1,500-2,600

A Bow octagonal plate, printed in Venetian or brick red, with Young Archers, 7in (18cm).
$2,500-3,500

A mug and finger bowl, with underglaze blue and overglaze iron red and gilt decoration, c1756.
Mug. **$600**
Finger Bowl – a rare shape.
$750-1,000

Both pieces in excellent condition. Any damage would affect the value quite considerably.

TRANSFER-PRINTED WARES

★ transfer-printing enabled the 18thC porcelain factories to produce cheap goods in large quantities
★ transfer-printed wares were produced at Bow but the method of manufacture was not successful for the factory
★ in the mid 1750's overglaze prints in black, red, brown, purple or lilac were marketed. These are more collectable than later printed wares
★ coloured-in outline prints were produced in the 1760's as were some underglaze blue and white wares

FIGURES

★ the Bow factory produced a large range of figures, animals and birds throughout the 1750's and 60's
★ amongst the most popular today are those left in the white. Some of the earliest of these white figures are strongly modelled and have a dramatic quality not often found in later figures

A Bow blue and white butter boat and stand, moulded as overlapping vine leaves and painted with bunches of grapes and leaves, within blue 'feuille-de-choux' borders, rim chips restored, c1770, the butter boat 4in (10cm) wide.
$1,000-1,400

A Bow figure of a recumbent lion, painted in Muses style, with streaked and washed brown fur, his forepaw resting on a marbled ball, on a green washed base, minute chip to mane, c1750, 3½in (9.5cm) wide.
$6,000-9,000

A Bow white figure of a toper, drinking from a bottle, holding a dead duck in his hand, some minor chipping, incised arrow mark, c1750, 5in (13cm).
$1,500-2,600

W H Goss China

Goss porcelain has recently attracted much attention and has featured in several television programmes on antiques. The newly published book *William Henry Goss: The Story Of The Staffordshire Family of Potters Who Invented Heraldic Porcelain* by Lynda and Nicholas Pine (Milestone Publications) has also furthered its fame.

Produced between 1858 and 1939, the range of Goss china is enormous and encompasses the early days (First Period 1858-87) when white parian busts, statuettes and ornamental ware was produced in small quantities, and ranges through to the heraldic boom of 1881-1934 (Second Period), when souvenir hunting was at its height, to the Third Period with the later, more colourful ware and domestic pottery.

Collecting Goss is made easier as almost every piece has a factory mark, with the exception of the earliest prototype pieces. Each artefact or named model has its name printed on the base, so identifying the shape is simple.

Collectors can look out for coloured cottages, white glazed buildings, crested and transfer shapes, animals and brown crosses as well as a marvellous array of tea sets and ornamental ware. For further information, collectors are recommended to *The Price Guide to Goss China* by Nicholas Pine (Milestone Publications) and the monthly sales catalogue (annual subscription $18) available from Goss & Crested China Ltd, 62 Murray Road, Horndean, Hants PO8 9JL.

A Goss china figure of The Boot-Black, coloured.
$750-1,000

A Goss brown parian St Ives Cross, 5½in (14cm).
$300-400

A Goss brown parian Hexham Abbey Frid Stol.
$60-100

The Allies on a Folkestone Ewer, with colourful decoration of the 7 flags.
$30

A coloured version of an early parian figurine, known as the Lady with the Kid (1), 17in (43.5cm), if perfect
$2,250

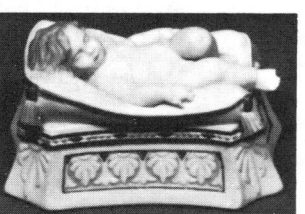

A Goss parian Evangeline sleeping on a cushion, coloured on casket, slight chips.
$300-500

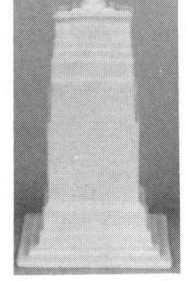

A Goss white parian Cenotaph.
$75-150

A Goss Kirk Braddan Cross.
$300-400

A Goss Hereford Cathedral Font, 4in (10cm).
$150-250

A Goss white parian figure of Shakespeare.
$400-500

A Goss white glazed chimney sweep, 11½in (29cm).
$1,200-1,600

Usually coloured, rare to be white.

A Goss parian figure of a Season, holding sheaf of corn on her head, 13½in (34.5cm).
$250-350

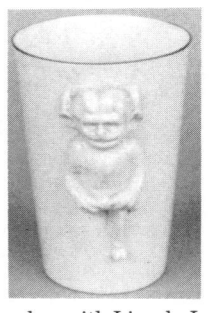

A Goss beaker with Lincoln Imp.
$100-150

Ellen Terry's Farm (462).
$300-400

Thomas Hardy's House (435).
$450-600

An unglazed parian bust of William Henry Goss.
$250

A Goss angel's head wall vase, thought to be modelled on his daughter, Florence.
$250-350

A Goss coloured hand ring tree.
$150-200

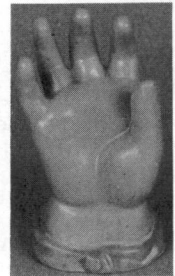

A Goss bust of Scott in suit.
$150-200

Miniature forget-me-not tea service on a square tray.
$250

Portman Lodge, Bournemouth (452), open door.
$450-700

A white parian bust of Wordsworth.
$150-200

GOSS AND CRESTED WARE

Damage certainly affects the value of porcelain. Hair cracks, chips and faded enamelling on the crests can more than halve the value recorded here. Minor firing flaws can be ignored. Goss china shrank up to 10% in the firing processes so manufacturing flaws and minor differences in size are common.

A bust of Southey, on square base.
$250-350

A Brown Carew Cross, 6in (15cm).
$150

St Nicholas Chapel, Ilfracombe (456), unglazed.
$150-250

A coloured bust of Ann Hathaway.
$300-400

Robert Burns house, Dumfries, coloured.
$150-250

Cat and Fiddle Inn, Buxton (425).
$250-350

A coloured model of Mowcop Castle.
$150-250

131

Crested China

In the mid 1880's there were some 300 potteries in Staffordshire who were in the midst of a depression in the potting industry, when the collecting of crested china caught the imagination of the nation. By 1913, before the outbreak of war, the craze was at its height, and patriotic collectors progressed to the military guns, tanks, aeroplanes and shells which were to become so popular during the next decade.

Later shapes which included figures, busts, animals, cottages and household objects had additional hand painted colouring. Almost every piece has a coat-of-arms or crest as it is now generally but incorrectly known, but about only half are factory marked. The major firms of Arcadian, Carlton, Willow Art and Savoy also owned other potteries who used the same moulds but a complete list of what was made and by who, together with current market prices can be found in *The Price Guide to Crested China* by Nicholas Pine (Milestone Publications).

The quality of the different makes varies and the standards of perfection applied to Goss to determine value cannot be applied to crested china generally, as most pieces tend to have firing flaws, inaccuracies of proportion and rubbed gilding. Yet there is something irresistible and appealing about these delightful porcelain mementoes of a bygone era.

For further reading see *Crested China* by Sandy Andrews (Milestone Publications) and the monthly sales catalogue of Goss & Crested China Ltd available from 62 Murray Road, Horndean, Hants PO8 9JL.

Arcadian fully coloured birthplace of Dean Goodman.
$250-350

Yorkshire cartoon decoration on an Arcadian vase.
$15

Arcadian, Grafton and Willow Art white glazed buildings and castles.
$45-70

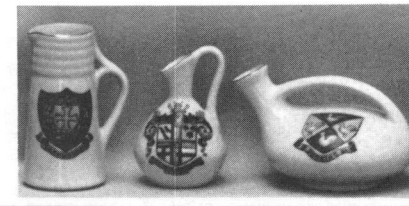

Carlton artefacts, all named on the base.
$10each

Lucky black cat transfers on Willow Art shapes.
$5-10

A pierced ribbon plate of German manufacture.
$15

Welsh hats by Gemma, Willow, Arcadian and Carlton.
$15each

Pillar boxes, less than 3in (8cm).
l. **$12**
c. **$18**
r. **$9**

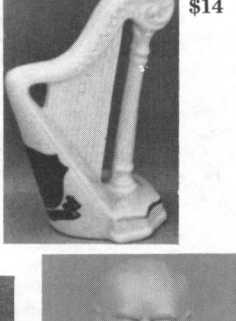

A Willow Art Irish harp.
$14

l. A Grafton bust of Lloyd George.
$75-150
r. A Grafton bust of Kitchener.
$60-100

Shelley and Podmore gramophones.
l. **$36**
r. **$30**

H & L bust of Kitchener.
$100-150

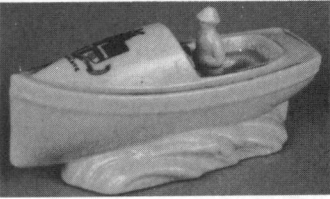

A Shelley speed boat.
$45-70

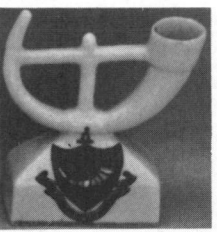

A Carlton Ripon horn
with Arms of Ripon.
$30

An Arcadian bust of a Territorial.
$45-70

HMS Humber and HMS Tiger by
Carlton.
$60 and $150

A Savoy battleship, HMS Queen
Elizabeth, 6½in (16.5cm).
$100-200

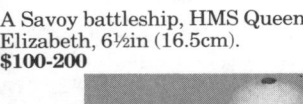

A Shelley armoured car.
$45-70

A Shelley Welsh lady, 9.5cm.
$100

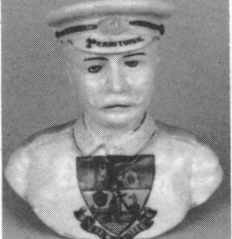

An Arcadian tank.
$30-50

A Carlton E9 submarine, blunt nose
version.
$45

A Carlton large saloon car.
$100-200

A Carlton whippet tank.
$150-200

A Carlton double decker bus.
$250-350

A Daintyware charabanc with
driver.
$75-150

Oriental Pottery & Porcelain

Bowls

A Northern celadon bowl, the interior carved with peony heads, the exterior carved with simple petals, the glaze stopping above the shallowly-cut grey foot, rim crack, Song Dynasty, 4½in (11cm) diam.
$1,200-1,600

A Longquan celadon broad globular bowl and shallow domed cover, carved with lotus petals, under a semi-translucent bluish-green glaze firing to an olive colour on parts of the body, slightly chipped, Southern Song Dynasty, 5½in (14.5cm) diam.
$1,500-2,600

A Ming celadon bowl, the interior freely carved and incised below a diaper band, the exterior with 6 flowerheads below a wavy band, all under a fine even glaze, 15thC, 10½in (26cm) diam.
$2,500-3,500

A Ming blue and white bowl, painted in deep colour with meandering chrysanthemum, 15thC, 12½in (31.5cm) diam.
$1,500-2,600

A Ming blue and white bowl, painted on the exterior in a washy blue with 4 winged dragons, the centre of the interior with a roundel of a similar winged dragon within breaking waves, short crack at the centre, small rim chip, glaze scratched, Chenghua, 8½in (22cm) diam.
$7,000-9,000

A Ming blue and white bowl, delicately painted with monkeys climbing trees, the interior with a scholar and his attendant, chip, encircled Wanli six-character mark and of the period, 5½in (13.5cm) diam.
$1,500-2,600

A Ming blue and white bowl, painted with fishermen on their boats in a rocky river landscape, minor fritting, Wanli, 8½in (22cm) diam.
$1,500-2,600

A rare large Dehua blue and white bowl, painted in a rich deep colour of violet hue with a mountainous landscape, the foot steeply cut and the base unglazed, minor fritting, late 16th/17thC, 13½in (35cm) diam.
$2,500-3,500

A provincial late Ming blue and white deep bowl, Wanli, 8½in (21.5cm) diam.
$450-600

A blue and white bowl painted in violet blue, the base with a six-character inscription and collector's mark, Kangxi, 8in (20.5cm) diam.
$1,200-1,600

The six-character mark reads 'Wen Run Hin Gu Zhen Shang' meaning 'The warm lustre will be a treasured pleasure for all time'.

A pair of Ming blue and white shallow bowls, with the seal mark 'de hua chang chun', surrounded by the four-character mark 'Wanli nian zao', and of the period, minute fritting, 5in (12cm) diam.
$3,000-4,500

The mark is illustrated by Hobson, The Wares of the Ming Dynasty, p. 222. Comparable dishes with the same mark are in the catalogue of the Percival David Foundation, no. 663, sec. 3, and in the catalogue of the Seligman Collection, no. D254, vol. II, pl. LXXVI.

A blue and white bulb bowl, painted with the character 'Fu', happiness, between 4 seated scholars, frit chips, Kangxi, 8½in (22.5cm).
$1,000-1,400

A rare white porcelain bowl, the exterior finely incised with 2 five-clawed dragons pursuing flaming pearls amongst cloud and fire, the interior and base glazed, encircled Kangxi six-character mark and of the period, 4½in (11cm) diam.
$1,500-2,600

A blue and white bowl, painted with 3 boys at play in the interior, and panels of a scholar and a lady on pavilion terraces on the exterior, encircled Kangxi six-character mark and of the period, 6½in (16cm) diam, fitted box.
$1,500-2,600

A blue and white bowl, painted with a romantic scene on the exterior and the interior with a boy holding a toy windmill, minor frit chips, early 18thC, 6in (15.5cm) diam.
$1,300-1,700

A blue and white tripod broad globular bulb bowl, painted with 4 roundels of cranes in flight, Kangxi/Yongzheng, 10½in (26cm) diam.
$800-1,200

A 'famille rose' bowl, painted on the exterior with flowering peony and chrysanthemum, Qianlong, 8in (20cm) diam.
$600-900

A pair of 'famille rose' bowls, painted with a cockerel, hen and 3 chicks between daisy and peony issuing from rockwork, encircled Yongzheng mark and of the period, 4½in (11cm).
$1,500-2,600

A 'famille rose' hunting punch bowl, painted on one side with 'the chase', the other side with a hunt scene, the interior with a roundel of a man with a gun and hounds in a landscape, cracked, riveted, Qianlong, 11½in (29cm) diam.
$1,300-1,800

A rare 'famille rose' erotic moulded punch bowl, painted with 2 shaped panels, reserved on a dense cell-pattern ground in underglaze blue, the interior with 2 figures on a terrace, the base with a most unusual painting of an erotic scene with a couple making love, mirrored by dogs in a doorway, restored, Qianlong, 10½in (26.5cm) diam.
$2,250-3,500

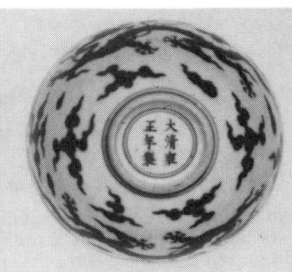

A pair of small blue and white dragon bowls, Yongzheng six-character marks and of the period, 4in (10cm) diam.
$6,000-9,000

A Chinese blue and white porcelain pouring bowl, Qianlong, c1750.
$1,300-1,800

These bowls, with handles and spouts, were possibly used to separate cream from milk.

This piece came from the 'Nanking Cargo'.

A pair of Chinese 'famille verte' bowls, decorated in bright enamels, 18thC.
$450-700

Make the most of Miller's

Every care has been taken to ensure the accuracy of descriptions and estimated valuations. Price ranges in this book reflect what one should expect to pay for a similar example. When selling one can obviously expect a figure below. This will fluctuate according to a dealer's stock, saleability at a particular time, etc. It is always advisable to approach a reputable specialist dealer or an auction house which has specialist sales.

An export coin collector's punch bowl for the Scandinavian market, decorated round the sides in sepia and gilt with a series of dated coins of Swedish origin, including 10 representations of classical gods, allegories and royalist significance, below a band of European shell scroll, restored, c1760, 10½in (26.5cm).
$1,300-1,800

Cf Howard and Ayers, op. cit., no. 233a; Hervoüet, p. 227. The coins are all examples of the emergency Swedish copper daler coinage minted and issued between 1715-19 to cope with the exigencies of a current Nordic War; Howard and Ayers, ibid.

A 'famille rose' punch bowl, painted with an unusual design of ladies playing a version of polo, crack restored, Qianlong, 15½in (40cm) diam.
$3,000-4,000

A large 'famille rose' deep bowl, painted with peony and pomegranate on one side and small lotus clusters on the other, the interior with central peony sprays, c1800, 15½in (40cm) diam.
$1,500-2,600

A Cantonese 'famille verte' bowl, painted on the exterior with figures at leisure below panels of birds reserved on a band of cell pattern, the interior with similar band and panels, Daoguang, 10½in (26.5cm) diam.
$900-1,300

A coral red ground bowl with lotus decoration, Jiajing, 5in (13cm) diam.
$5,500-7,000

A Chinese blue and white pierced flared oval basket and stand, painted with pagodas in river landscapes, c1810, the stand 9in (23cm) wide.
$750-1,000

A pair of Cantonese rounded square bowls, painted with continuous bands of figures at leisure, reserved on a green scroll gold ground, 9in (23cm) wide.
$1,500-2,600

A large Cantonese 'famille rose' bowl, densely and elaborately decorated in rose medallion style, all reserved on gilt grounds enriched with foliage and butterflies, the exterior similarly decorated, 19thC, 18½in (46.5cm) diam.
$1,500-2,600

A large Cantonese bowl, enamelled all over in 'famille rose' palette with groups of figures, with alternate panels of birds, butterflies, flowers and fruit on a green and gold ground, 16in (41cm).
$1,000-1,400

A 'famille verte' and powder blue ground fish bowl, painted with 2 large quatrefoil panels, divided by smaller cartouches of Buddhistic lions and birds on branches, 19thC, 14in (36cm) diam.
$1,300-1,800

A 'famille rose' lime green ground relief-moulded fish bowl, late Qing Dynasty, 16in (41cm) diam.
$2,250-3,000

A green and yellow dragon bowl, incised and painted in green enamel on a mustard yellow ground with 2 five-clawed dragons, unencircled Guangxu six-character mark and of the period, 6in (15cm) diam.
$900-1,300

A Chinese bowl, the exterior painted in brightly coloured enamels within red, brown, black and gilt lattice grounds, arrowhead decorative footrim, the interior also decorated with a figure scene, 19thC, 11in (29cm).
$1,200-1,600

A blue and white bowl, vividly painted in a strong deep colour with exotic animals, between borders of key pattern and tooth pattern on the exterior, and with a similar dragon in a central roundel in the interior, unencircled Xuantong six-character mark and of the period, 8½in (21cm) diam.
$2,250-3,500

A Chinese porcelain bowl on a stem base with liner and cover, painted in iron red, between formal blue and enamelled borders at neck and foot, late 19th/early 20thC, 7in (18cm) diam.
$150-200

A Satsuma type bowl, painted all over predominantly in iron red and enriched in gilt, signed on a red lacquer ground, 9½in (24cm) diam.
$900-1,300

An Imari barber's bowl, painted in typical colours, the reverse with 2 sprays of plum blossom, rim chip, Genroku period, 10½in (26.5cm) diam.
$800-1,200

An earthenware bowl, the interior finely painted in coloured enamels and gilt, the exterior with insects amongst scrolling foliate tendrils on a stippled ground above chrysanthemum clusters and a band of swimming fish all below a keyfret border, unsigned, Meiji period, 5in (12cm) diam.
$1,500-2,600

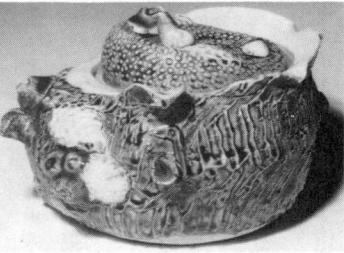

A rare bowl and cover, modelled as a seashell with smaller shells, including clams, in high relief, the details painted in iron oxide and underglaze cobalt blue, small rim chip, late 18thC, probably Hirado, 5½in (14cm) wide.
$800-1,200

A Kyoto bowl, decorated in various coloured enamels and gilt on underglaze blue, the exterior with scattered cherry and plum blossom, signed on the base, Nanbe, 8½in (21.5cm) diam.
$450-700

Bottles

A Ming celadon pear-shaped bottle, yuhuchun, freely carved and combed with peony above a band of slender petals, all under a translucent olive glaze, base cracked, minor fritting, 15th/16thC, 9in (22.5cm).
$1,000-1,400

A Ming blue and white pear-shaped bottle, yuhuchun, chipped, 16thC, 9in (22.5cm).
$2,250-3,000

Two late Ming blue and white bottles, one painted with landscapes, the other with 2 geese on a river bank, edge frits and chips, one neck cracked, Wanli, 10in (25.5cm).
$1,500-2,600

A rare Swatow blue and white bottle, painted with 2 deer amongst bamboo, birds and foliage, late 16th/17thC, 8in (21cm).
$1,300-1,800

TRANSITIONAL WARES

★ these wares are readily identifiable both by their form and by their style of decoration

★ forms: sleeve vases, oviform jars with domed lids, cylindrical brushpots and bottle vases are particularly common

★ the cobalt used is a brilliant purplish blue, rarely misfired

★ the ground colour is of a definite bluish tone, probably because the glaze is slightly thicker than that of the wares produced in the subsequent reigns of Kangxi and Yongzheng

★ the decoration is executed in a rather formal academic style, often with scholars and sages with attendants in idyllic cloud-lapped mountain landscapes

★ other characteristics include the horizontal 'contoured' clouds, banana plantain used to interrupt scenes, and the method of drawing grass by means of short 'V' shaped brush strokes

★ in addition, borders are decorated with narrow bands of scrolling foliage, so lightly incised as to be almost invisible or secret (anhua)

★ these pieces were rarely marked although they sometimes copied earlier Ming marks

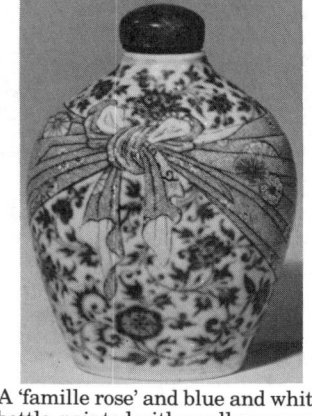

A 'famille rose' and blue and white bottle, painted with a yellow ground brocade cloth, on a ground of blue floral scrolls in the Ming style, Yongzheng six-character mark, Qing Dynasty, 4in (10cm), fitted with an aventurine stopper, fitted box.
$3,000-4,500

A large 'famille rose' yellow ground pilgrim bottle, the reverse painted with a battle scene surrounded by stylised peonies, fruit and scrolling foliage, gilt dragon handles, foot cracked and chipped, 19in (49cm).
$450-700

A late Ming blue and white kraak pear-shaped bottle, fritted early 17thC, 7in (18cm).
$300-400

Two Chinese pear-shaped bottles, each painted in underglaze blue and copper red, and later Dutch-decorated in iron red, green enamel and gilt, the porcelain Kangxi, 7½in (19cm).
$1,200-1,600

A Chinese blue and white tapering bottle, painted below a band of leaves on the shoulder, the neck with a 'guei' dragon and scrolling lotus, Transitional, c1640, 15½in (39cm).
$1,500-2,600

A 'famille verte' bottle, painted on each face with clusters of peony and chrysanthemum within underglaze blue borders, reserved with iron red flowerheads, Kangxi, 8in (21cm), fitted as a lamp.
$1,000-1,400

A pair of blue and white pilgrim bottles, the neck with flying bat handles, rim and handle chips, 19thC, 15½in (39cm).
$3,000-4,500

A pair of Satsuma bottles, painted in colours and richly gilt on the sides alternately with figures in interiors, on dark blue grounds richly reserved with gilt prunus and 'ho-o' medallions, 10in (25cm).
$1,300-1,800

Cups

A Ko-Imari apothecary bottle, with double lipped rim, decorated in iron red, turquoise green, black and gilt, the neck applied with scattered flowers below a band of stiff leaves, chip to lower lip, late 17thC, 9in (23cm).
$1,500-2,600

A pair of unusual Arita blue and white bottle vases, each painted and decorated in gold and black 'hiramakie, takamakie and heidatsu', with matching lacquer stoppers, 19thC, 24½in (62cm).
$19,500-32,000

A Ming celadon stem cup, moulded with an incused chrysanthemum spray, under a semi-translucent thick bluish-olive glaze, crack, 15thC, 5in (12cm) diam.
$700-900

Censers

A celadon tripod censer, the centre of the interior and the foot base unglazed, Song/Yuan Dynasty, 4in (10cm) diam.
$750-1,000

A celadon tripod censer, 14th/15thC, 3½in (9cm).
$1,200-1,600

A rare Ming white-glazed stem cup, with a stylised chrysanthemum meander above a band of chrysanthemum petals, 15th/16thC, 6½in (16.5cm) diam.
$1,500-2,600

A celadon tripod deep globular censer, boldly carved, under a rich translucent deep olive glaze, pooling on the 3 short splayed feet, cracked, 14th/15thC, 10in (25cm) diam.
$3,000-4,500

A massive green and ochre glazed pottery tripod censer, moulded in high relief with 2 dragons pursuing a flaming pearl, some restoration, Ming Dynasty, 24in (61cm), with metal liner.
$2,250-3,500 ·

A blanc-de-chine tripod censer, 17th/18thC, 5in (13cm) diam.
$1,300-1,800

A Ming blue and white stem cup, painted with a carp leaping from waves below a border of trellis pattern in the interior, with plain exterior, 16th/early 17thC, 5in (13cm) diam.
$1,000-1,400

Make the most of Miller's

When a large specialist well-publicised collection comes on the market, it tends to increase prices. Immediately after this, prices can fall slightly due to the main buyers having large stocks and the market being 'flooded'. This is usually temporary and does not affect very high quality items.

A cup and saucer from the Nanking Cargo, Qianlong.
$250-350

A Transitional blue and white pear-shaped ewer, painted in strong tones with a scholar and his assistants on a rocky garden terrace, below stylised tulip at the neck, c1650, 8½in (22cm).
$2,250-3,000

An Arita blue and white oviform ewer, with loop handle, painted with 3 panels of flowering shrubs on a ground of scrolling foliage, late 17thC, 11in (27cm).
$1,300-1,800

A pair of rare 'famille rose' covered loving cups, restoration and damages, Qianlong, c1780, 11in (28.5cm).
$900-1,300

Ewers

A Ming blue and white pear-shaped ewer, with garlic top, damaged, encircled Xuande six-character mark, early 16thC, the porcelain 9½in (24cm) high, mounted in metal with replacement handle, stretcher, rim and chained cover, 11in (29cm) overall height.
$1,500-2,600

A pair of blue and white Kendi for the Middle Eastern market, painted with small birds perched amongst scrolling asters, rim hair cracks over-painted, Kangxi, 6½in (17cm).
$800-1,200

A blue and white ewer, painted with peony, camellia, chrysanthemum and lotus, chipped, minor rim damage, Kangxi, 8½in (22cm).
$800-1,200

A Chinese blue and white ewer, without lid, c1600.
$3,000-4,500

Figures – Animals

A grey pottery figure of a rhinoceros, the legs knife-cut and trimmed, one horn restored, third horn missing, Western Jin Dynasty, late 3rd Century AD, 11in (28cm) wide.
$2,250-3,500

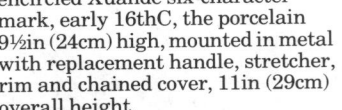

A small green glazed pottery figure of a dog, covered with a dark green glaze, now with an overall iridescence, Han Dynasty, 6in (15cm) wide.
$1,300-1,800

A large red-painted grey pottery horse head, with extensive maroon-red pigment remaining, with orange nostrils, sharp teeth with white pigments, lower jaw repaired, Han Dynasty, 10½in (26cm).
$2,250-3,000

A pair of Ming green, straw and brown glazed equestrian figures, some restoration, 16th/17thC, 12½in (32cm).
$1,500-2,600

An unusual grey pottery dragon head finial, with 2 apertures for its ears, now missing, covered with white slip, its neck, mouth and nostrils painted in red, other details in black, Han Dynasty, 5in (12.5cm) wide, on wood stand.
$3,000-4,500

An export glazed model of a monkey, lightly incised with hair markings and washed overall with an aubergine brown glaze, holding a yellow and green leafy peach in the right hand, old restoration, 17th/18thC, 9½in (24cm).
$1,500-2,600

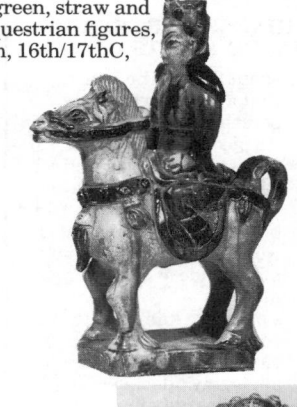

A 'famille verte' group formed as a large Buddhistic lion and a small cub, the larger body green with an aubergine mane and the cub with the colours reversed, on a high plinth enriched with trellis pattern, 19thC, 12½in (31.5cm).
$800-1,200

An unusual 'famille rose' group modelled as a monkey, with sepia hair markings, all on a mottled pink and blue base, finger chipped, Qianlong, 5½in (13.5cm).
$1,500-2,600

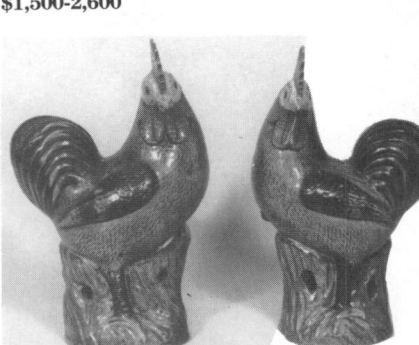

A pair of turquoise glazed parrots, the glaze pooling in places, Qing Dynasty, 7½in (19cm), fitted box, wood stands.
$900-1,300

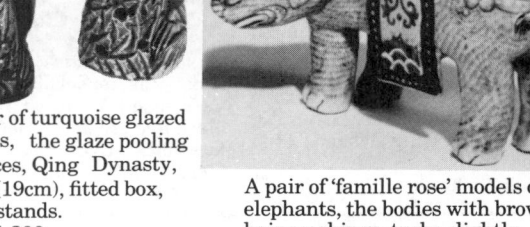

A pair of 'famille rose' models of elephants, the bodies with brown hair markings, tusks slightly chipped, late Qing Dynasty, 9½in (24cm).
$2,250-3,000

A pair of Chinese porcelain cockerels, late 19thC.
$4,000-5,500

A pair of Chinese earthenware cockerels, in bright blue, aubergine and yellow/green glazes, late 19thC, 9½in (24cm).
$400-500

A red-painted pottery figure of a camel, with deep red pigment remaining over a white ground on the exterior, chipped, Tang Dynasty, 4½in (12cm) wide.
$1,000-1,400

A pale pottery bust of a lady, slight traces of pigment remaining, small chip to base, Tang Dynasty, 5in (13cm), wood stand.
$1,300-1,800

A pair of polychrome mythical beasts, with their bodies brightly enamelled and gilt, some restoration, late 19thC, 9½in (25cm).
$1,500-2,600

A Tang Dynasty figure.
$1,200-1,600

A tilemaker's green, buff and brown glazed figure, chips, Ming Dynasty, 17½in (45cm).
$1,200-1,600

A pair of Arita polychrome groups, depicting carp painted in green and aubergine enamels, iron red, black and gilt, late 17thC, 8½in (21.5cm).
$2,500-3,500

A pair of export models of Manchurian cranes, with iron red crests, black beaks, legs and wing feathers, and creamy plumage densely incised, astride ribbed turquoise tree stumps, extremities restored, late Qing Dynasty, 11in (28.5cm).
$2,250-3,500

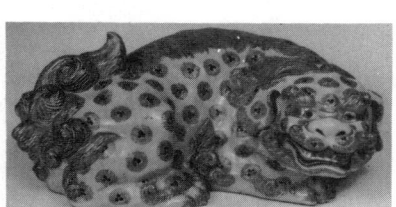

A Satsuma model of a recumbent karashishi, decorated in iron red, black and green enamels and gilt, late 19thC, 13½in (34cm) wide.
$2,250-3,500

A Chinese Ming tileworks figure of a warrior, decorated in green, white and yellow glazes, 18½in (47cm).
$3,000-4,500

Figures – People

A Cizhou figure of Xuanwu, wearing flowing robes belted around the chest, supported on a rockwork base with a snake entwined around a tortoise, 16th/17thC, 8½in (21cm).
$1,200-1,600

Cf the example in the Franks Collection at the British Museum no. OAF 2241 (45) where the figure is described as Lord of the Dark Heavens.

A glazed pottery figure of Guanyin, with splashed turquoise, aubergine and ochre glazes, face, hands and feet reserved in the biscuit and with specks of gilding remaining, base chips, 17thC, 16in (40.5cm).
$1,500-2,600

A blanc-de-chine figure of Guanyin wearing flowing robes and a floral pectoral, with the glaze pooling to blue in areas, small chips, 17thC, 11½in (29cm).
$3,000-4,500

A large Dehua blanc-de-chine figure of Buddha, seated in 'dhyanasana', some restoration to lotus leaves, minor chip to robe, with double gourd and square seal mark on the reverse, c1800, 24½in (62cm).
$4,500-7,000

The double gourd seal mark reads 'Dehua', the seal mark reads 'Xu Yunlin'. Donnelly dates the 'Xu' family production to 1770-1800 or later.

A large 'famille rose' figure of Guanyin, painted with iron red cloud scrolls and gilt floral roundels, hands missing, minor damage to extremities, Qianlong/Jiaqing, 19½in (50cm).
$1,500-2,600

A 'famille jaune' figure of a seated dignitary, the robes reserved with aubergine dragons and a green floral undergarment on a rectangular turquoise ground plinth enriched with butterflies, restored, late Qing Dynasty, 14in (35cm).
$900-1,300

A pair of 'famille verte' laughing twins, Hehe Erxian, one cracked, Kangxi, 7½in (19cm).
$1,200-1,600

A 'famille rose' group of Guanyin, holding a basket of flowers, with a spotted deer at her side, Qianlong, 7in (18cm).
$400-500

A large Arita polychrome model of Buddha, seated in 'dhyanasana', decorated in iron red, yellow, aubergine, green, turquoise and dark blue enamels, his hands, arms, feet, chest, hair and ears silvered, Meiji period, 18in (46cm).
$800-1,200

A pair of 'famille rose' figures of Shoulao, wearing green floral robes and iron red trousers, some restoration and chips, 18th/early 19thC, 10½in (25cm).
$750-1,000

A seated figure of Kuan Yin, her robes decorated in underglaze blue with flowersprays, 19thC, 14in (36cm).
$600-900

A pair of almost life-sized stoneware models of a courtier and a courtesan, dressed in kimono, covered in a finely crackled off-white glaze, both damaged and restored, probably Kyoto ware, late 19thC, 59in (149cm).
$13,500-17,500

Flasks

A pair of Kaga moon flasks with lizard handles, 11½in (29cm).
$1,500-2,600

A blue and white moon flask with ogival handles, painted in violet tones in the early Ming taste, rim chip restored, 18thC, 12in (31cm), wood stand.
$3,000-4,500

An Imari figure, in traditional Japanese costume, standing and holding a basket of eggs, damaged base, c1900, 13in (33cm).
$300-400

Flatware

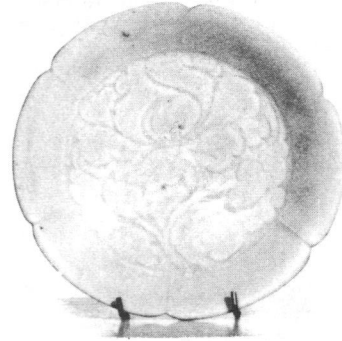

A large Ming blue and white dish, painted with peony heads amongst leafy scrolls, the exterior similarly decorated above a band of formal scrolls, minutely fritted, c1500, 20in (51cm) diam.
$3,000-4,000

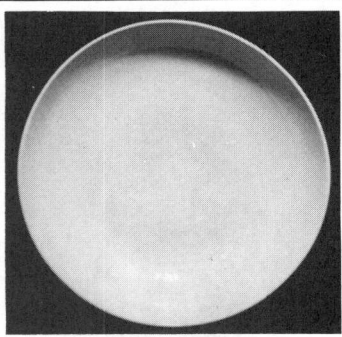

A Ming white glazed circular saucer dish, Jiajing six-character mark within a double circle in underglaze blue, and of the period, 13in (33cm).
$2,250-3,500

The interior of the foot showing the bluish tinge characteristic of the period.

A Yingqing foliate dish, carved to the centre with scrolling peony under a bluish white glaze, 12thC, 6in (15cm) diam.
$750-1,000

A Ming Swatow polychrome dish, painted in iron red and green enamel, 16th/early 17thC, 14in (36cm) diam.
$1,500-2,600

A celadon dish, with shiny olive glaze, rim chipped on the underside, Yuan/early Ming Dynasty, incised Arabic collector's inventory mark within the foot, 17½in (44.5cm) diam.
$1,500-2,600

An Annamese blue and white dish, the rim unglazed, 15thC, 15in (38cm) diam.
$1,500-2,600

A Ming copper red, blue and white dish painted with a dragon, the reverse painted with stylised chrysanthemum and flowers, cracked and chipped, late 15th/early 16thC, 15in (38cm) diam.
$450-700

A late Ming blue and white Kraak porselein dish, with a border of peony and chrysanthemum alternating with Daoist Immortals' attributes in 8 lappet panels, minor fritting, Wanli, 14in (36cm).
$1,500-2,600

A late Ming blue and white saucer dish, painted with scrolling pencilled lotus washed in greyish blue, Wanli six-character mark and of the period, 6in (15cm) diam.
$3,000-4,500

A Ming blue and white dish, restored, late 16thC, 17½in (43.5cm) diam.
  $1,000-1,400

A 'famille verte' shell-shaped dish, painted with scholars' utensils and an archaistic censer, above 2 Buddhist emblems within a border of lotus on a seeded green band, frit chips, Kangxi, 7½in (19cm) wide.
$750-1,000

A rare blue and white 'ship' plate, the European three-masted merchant vessel flying flags of Chinese type, the stern with a large ceremonial façade in late mediaeval Western taste, fritted, Kangxi, 10in (26.5cm) diam.
$2,250-3,500

A 'famille verte' dish, boldly painted with 3 Buddhistic lions around a central ribboned brocaded ball in the interior, the foot grooved, crack, rim fritting polished, encircled Hua mark, Kangxi, 13½in (34.5cm) diam.
$1,200-1,600

Two blue and white 'peacock' dishes, the reverse with emblems, rim chips, Kangxi, 16½in (42cm) diam.
$6,000-8,000

A 'famille verte' dish decorated in 'famille verte' and iron red, rim chips, Kangxi, 10½in (25.5cm) diam.
$400-500

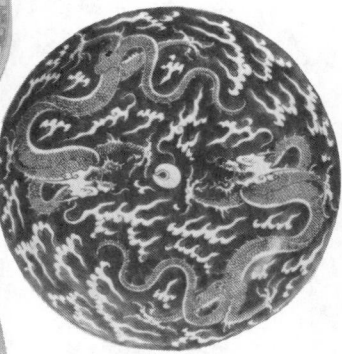

A blue and white dragon dish, with 4 precious emblems on the exterior above the grooved foot, underside chip, encircled lotus mark, Kangxi, 15in (38.5cm) diam.
$1,200-1,600

A blue and white European subject 'Rotterdam Riot' plate, painted with a central design depicting the good burghers of Amsterdam demolishing the canal-side house of the City Bailiff, hair cracks, c1720, 8in (20cm) diam.
$800-1,200

Cf A du Boulay, op. cit. p. 201; Hervouët, op. cit., p. 204. This, according to the latter authorities, is the first known example of export porcelain relating a social event (in specific detail).

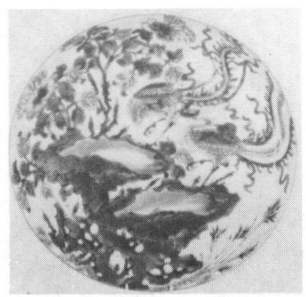

A Chinese blue and white deep saucer dish, Kangxi, 13in (33cm) diam.
$750-1,000

A large blue and white dish, painted with a basket of peony and exotic flowers, Yongzheng, 19in (48.5cm) diam.
$1,500-2,600

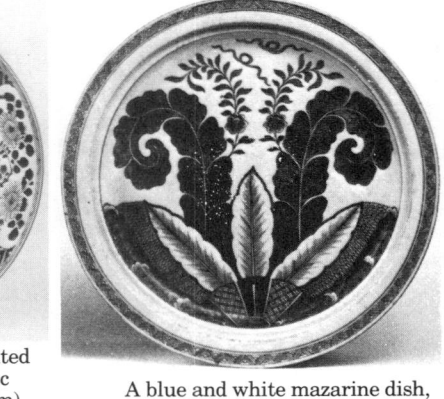

A blue and white mazarine dish, chipped, early Qianlong, 16½in (42cm) diam.
$1,300-1,800

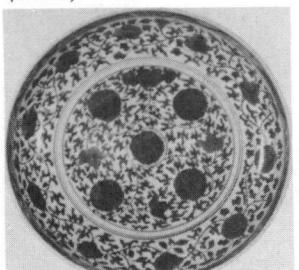

A large Chinese blue and white deep saucer dish, painted with Ming-style formal scrolling flowers and leaves within a border of breaking waves, Kangxi, 14½in (36.5cm) diam.
$600-900

A 'famille verte' crested dish, with a crest at the moulded rim, fritted, Kangxi, 12in (30.5cm) wide.
$2,500-3,500

A 'famille rose' dish, painted with peony, rose and exotic cabbage within an iron red trellis pattern border, chipped, Yongzheng/early Qianlong, 15in (38cm) wide.
$800-1,200

Two red, blue and white saucer dishes, freely drawn, Qianlong six-character seal marks and late in the period, 7½in (19.5cm) diam.
$1,500-2,600

A large export armorial dish, boldly painted primarily in shades of blue, yellow, iron red, green and gilt with a central coat-of-arms and coronet, the border with gilt interlaced initials dividing gilt ground floral panels, border restored, c1740, 17in (43cm) diam.
$5,500-7,000

The arms are those of Marini of Italy or Atäide of Portugal.

A 'famille verte' dish painted with an exotic bird flying above clusters of chrysanthemum and prunus, butterflies and lotus sprays, the border reserved with fish panels on a seeded green floral ground, fritted, Kangxi, 12½in (31.5cm) wide.
$3,000-4,500

An export armorial soup plate, painted at the centre in blue, grey and gilt, the border with 3 'bianco-sopra-bianco' flower sprays, c1740, 9in (23cm) diam.
$1,000-1,400

A pale blue glazed dish, painted in underglaze linear white slip infilled in darker underglaze blue, within the octafoil rim, fritted, Qianlong six-character seal mark and of the period, 10in (26cm) diam.
$1,000-1,400

An export armorial plate, slightly rubbed, c1745, 9in (23cm) diam.
$1,300-1,800

A 'famille rose' European subject 'Valentine Pattern' plate, painted with a design known as the 'Altar of Love', Qianlong, 9in (23cm).
$1,000-1,400

A grisaille European subject soup plate, delicately painted at the centre with a scene derived from Classical sources, cracked, mid-Qianlong, 9in (23cm) diam.
$900-1,300

A 'famille rose' European subject plate, brightly painted with a pattern derived from the travels of Don Quixote, the border with 4 grisaille landscapes, crack restored, c1750, 9in (23cm) diam.
$3,000-4,500

A 'famille rose' dish, painted in a bright palette within a gilt line rim, Qianlong, 14in (35.5cm) diam.
$2,250-3,000

A pair of 'famille rose' 'double peacock' dished salts, with a peacock and hen standing on sepia rockwork beside tree peony, below a border of linked ingot-pattern, Qianlong, 3in (7cm)
$1,300-1,800

Another service of this pattern was in the Brazilian Royal collection in the 18thC.

A Chinese armorial plate, the centre blazoned with the arms of John Papworth, the rim painted with reserves of foliage within a diaper band, Qianlong, 9in (23cm).
$800-1,200

A Chinese blue and white saucer, c1750.
$150-200

From the famous 'Nanking Cargo'.

A 'famille rose' armorial plate, painted at the centre with a coat-of-arms, the puce scale pattern border reserved in 4 floral cartouches, some regilding, c1750, 8½in (22.5cm) diam.
$1,300-1,800

A 'famille rose' armorial dish, with a stag-head crest above the arms, slightly rubbed, chipped, c1750, 15in (39cm) wide.
$3,000-4,000

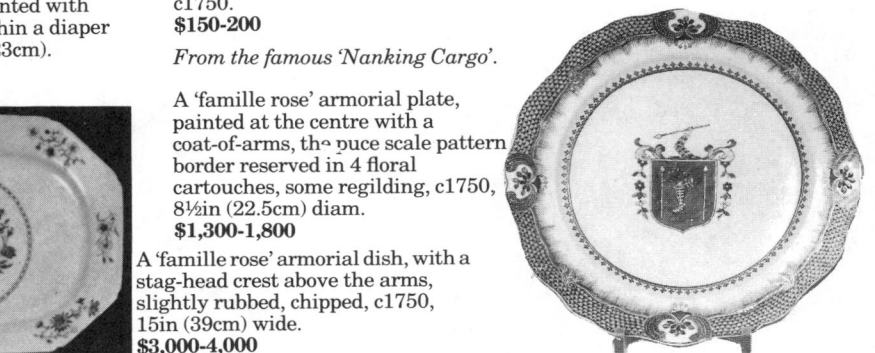

A 'famille rose' armorial octagonal plate, painted with coat-of-arms, crest and motto, with puce feather scroll at the rim, small rim chips restored, c1785, 9½in (24cm) wide.
$800-1,200

A large Chinese 'famille rose' plate, the centre brightly painted with flowers, the rim similar within a spearhead border, Qianlong, 15in (38cm) diam.
$750-1,000

A 'famille rose' dish, painted with a central cartouche of 2 ladies in a garden with 2 boys and an ox, Qianlong, 12in (30cm) wide.
$1,000-1,400

A 'famille rose' meat dish, painted with figures in a riverside garden, Jiaqing, 13in (33cm) wide.
$750-1,000

A grisaille European subject plate, painted at the centre, the border with rococo cartouches and neo-classical allusions, mid-Qianlong, 9in (23cm) diam.
$1,000-1,400

A large Ao-Kutani dish, decorated in iron red, coloured enamels and gilt with Jo and Uba, 'The Spirits of the Pine Trees', marked on the base in a square reserve, Kutani, 19thC, 18in (45.5cm).
$1,300-1,800

A pair of Imari oval dishes, in the form of a flowerhead decorated with radiating petals, each painted in typical palette, 13in (33cm) diam.
$700-900

A large Chinese 'famille rose' meat dish, Qianlong, 17in (43cm) wide.
$2,250-3,000

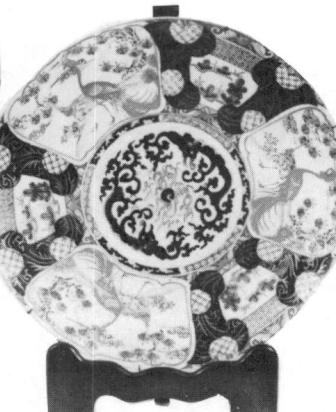

An Imari plaque, rim damaged, 22in (56cm).
$450-700

A group of 4 various sized octagonal Imari dishes, decorated in iron red, enamel and gilt on underglaze blue, all late 17th/early 18thC, 7 to 10in (18 to 25cm) wide.
$2,250-3,000

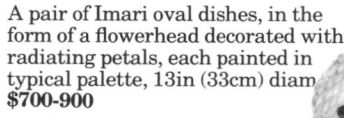

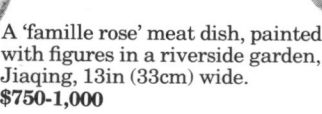

l. & r. A pair of Imari shallow dishes, decorated in iron red, enamels and gilt on underglaze blue, the reverse with peony flowerheads, 19thC, 18½in (47.5cm) diam.
$3,000-4,000

c. A large Imari shallow dish, decorated in iron red, enamel and gilt on underglaze blue with 2 large fan-shaped panels, late 19thC, 24½in (62cm) diam.
$3,000-4,000

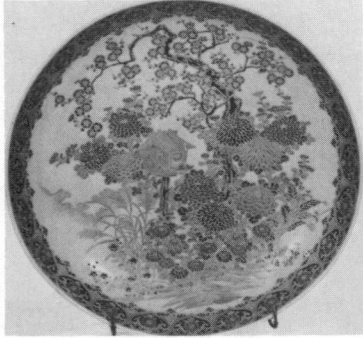

A Satsuma thickly potted saucer dish, painted in iron red, green and dark blue enamel, and richly gilt, the base with a blue enamel 'shimazu mon', 14in (35.5cm) diam.
$1,300-1,800

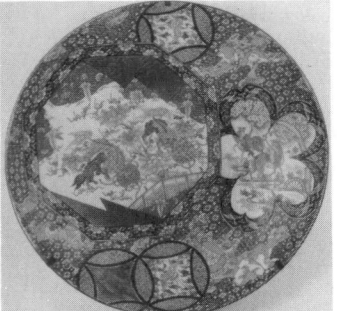

An unusually large Imari dish, painted in underglaze blue, iron red, coloured enamels and gilt within shaped panels, the reverse with a wide band of peony and scrolling foliage in underglaze blue, late 19thC, 31in (78.6cm) diam.
$5,500-7,000

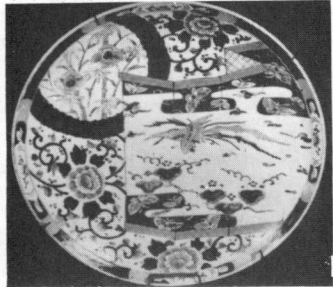

An Imari fluted dish, painted with radiating panels of flowers and geometric designs, around a central medallion painted with a fierce dragon, 19thC, 18½in (47cm) diam.
$450-600

An Imari charger, decorated with a peacock in a garden setting, early 20thC, 18in (45.5cm) diam.
$750-1,000

A set of 6 Nabeshima porcelain saucer dishes, each cavetto painted in underglaze blue with an overall design, the underneath with tassels and comb patterns, 4 with slight damage, 19thC, 9in (22.5cm).
$450-600

A Japanese charger, white ground and decorated in blue enamel with carp and flowers, 19thC, 21in (53cm) diam.
$400-500

A large Imari saucer dish, with reserves of insects, flowers and exotic birds, 18in (45.5cm) diam.
$150-250

A large Imari dish, the centre painted, the wide everted rim painted with chrysanthemum, birds and geometric designs, 18in (46cm) diam.
$1,000-1,400

A Seifu blue and white plate, the design continuing onto the reverse, signed Seifu, late 19thC, 8½in (21cm) diam.
$800-1,200

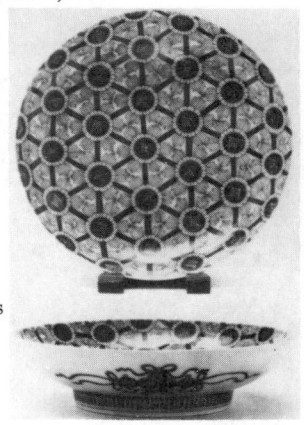

Make the most of Miller's

Every care has been taken to ensure the accuracy of descriptions and estimated valuations. Price ranges in this book reflect what one should expect to pay for a similar example. When selling one can obviously expect a figure below. This will fluctuate according to a dealer's stock, saleability at a particular time, etc. It is always advisable to approach a reputable specialist dealer or an auction house which has specialist sales.

Garden Seats

A pair of 'famille rose' puce ground jardinières, painted in the Qianlong taste, 8in (20.5cm) wide, elaborately pierced wood stands.
$1,300-1,800

An unusual miniature 'famille rose' barrel-form garden seat, Jiaqing, 9in (23cm).
$1,500-2,600

A porcelain garden seat, early 20thC.
$300-400

Jardinières

A 'famille rose' jardinière, painted with 4 panels, reserved on a black ground, decorated with a flower scroll design between diaper bands, interior crack, 13½in (34cm).
$1,000-1,400

A Canton 'famille rose' barrel-shaped garden seat, enamels slightly rubbed, 19thC, 18in (46cm).
$1,500-2,600

A Transitional Wucai oviform jardinière, painted with a yellow dragon and a phoenix in flight amongst precious emblems above waves breaking, minor frit chips, late 17thC, 9in (23cm) diam.
$3,000-4,500

A Chinese 'famille rose' jardinière, the exterior painted with peonies below a band of flowers and butterflies, 12in (30cm).
$1,000-1,400

A pair of Canton 'famille rose' barrel-shaped garden seats, one cracked, 19in (48cm).
$4,000-5,500

A large blue and white jardinière, delicately painted in strong tones with a pair of scaly-bodied horned four-clawed dragons contesting a flaming pearl, 19thC, 24in (61cm) diam.
$5,500-7,000

An Imari jardinière, painted in typical colours, the interior painted with carp, 18½in (47cm) diam, on elaborately carved wood stand.
$1,300-1,800

A pair of large Cantonese garden seats pierced with cash roundels, both cracked, 18in (46cm).
$3,000-4,000

A 'famille rose' lemon yellow ground jardinière, painted with panels of children and rustic figures, glaze rubbed, slightly chipped, late Qing Dynasty, 16in (40cm).
$2,250-3,000

Jars

A large phosphatic-splashed oviform jar, the pale slightly streaked glaze with irregular darker areas in brown and lavender stopping above the buff stoneware uncut foot, Tang Dynasty, 18in (46cm).
$7,500-10,500

A large Cizhou jar, with thickened rim covered overall in a pale ivory glaze decorated in brown, Ming Dynasty, 21½in (54.5cm).
$2,500-3,500

A heavily potted celadon broad oviform jar, with a translucent olive glaze, base drilled, associated cracks extending through the body, 14th/15thC, 13in (33cm).
$2,250-3,000

A late Ming blue and white hexagonal jar and shallow cover, cracked, the mark polished out, Wanli, 5½in (14cm) wide.
$1,500-2,600

A late Ming blue and white hexagonal baluster jar, Wanli, 8in (20.5cm).
$600-900

A late Ming blue and white hexagonal jar, painted in strong tones, foot chip, neck crack and restoration, late 16thC, 12½in (31.5cm).
$1,300-1,800

A large blue and white oviform jar and domed cover, the body painted all around with a dignitary accompanied by servants, finial old damage, cover inner rim repair, 17thC, 25in (63cm).
$3,000-4,500

A Ming blue and white oval jar and cover, painted with lotus and other flowers, fritted, 15thC, 7½in (19cm) wide.
$1,500-2,600

A Chinese blue and white jar, painted with 4 ducks, the neck with stiff leaves, Transitional, 9in (23cm).
$900-1,300

A Transitional blue and white broad oviform jar, painted with a demon-like 'Guixing', c1655, 9in (23cm).
$750-1,000

A Transitional blue and white oviform jar, painted with a goose and another bird in flight above a frog seated between lotus clusters, the shoulder with a band of 'anhua' waves, encircled Jiajing six-character mark, c1645, 7½in (19cm).
$1,300-1,800

A large Chinese blue and white broad jar, painted with flowering shrubs issuing from rockwork beside bamboo and 2 birds in flight, Transitional/early Kangxi, 13in (33cm), wood cover and stand.
$1,200-1,600

A large blue and white jar, painted with large headed lotus in a wide leafy meander band around the body, between borders of 'ruyi' lappets and stiff leaves at the foot, Qianlong, 19½in (50cm).
$2,250-3,000

A pair of large Imari jars and domed covers, with grounds of underglaze blue scrolling flowers and leaves heightened in gilt, late 17th/early 18thC, 19½in (50cm), replacement wood finials.
$4,500-7,000

A Chinese blue and white jar, painted with 2 deer and 2 cranes, Kangxi, 9in (23cm).
$900-1,300

A Chinese blue and white jar, painted with 3 qilin among widely breaking waves and rockwork, Kangxi, 8in (20.5cm).
$450-700

A Satsuma globular koro and pierced domed cover, painted in colours on a dark blue ground enriched with gilt flowers and waves, 5in (12.5cm) diam.
$600-900

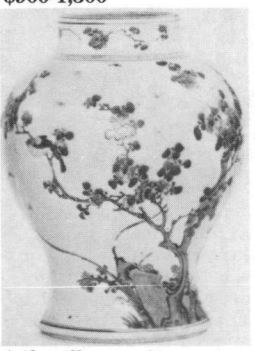

A 'famille verte' jar, painted with 2 birds in flight and perched among the branches of a flowering plum tree issuing from green rockwork, Kangxi, 12½in (31.5cm).
$1,200-1,600

A pair of 'famille verte' baluster jars and covers, painted with a plump long-tailed bird perched on a hawthorn branch beside bamboo, below 'ruyi' bands, late Qing Dynasty, 16in (41cm).
$1,300-1,800

A Satsuma reticulated oviform jar, 6½in (16.5cm).
$1,000-1,400

A pair of Oriental blue and white ginger jars with lids, 9½in (24.5cm).
$250-350

A Chinese blue and white jar and cover, painted with 2 panels of mythical beasts on a ground of prunus heads and cracked-ice pattern, hairline crack to cover, Kangxi, 8in (20.5cm).
$400-500

A Komai tea jar and shallow domed cover with ivory finial, with inner cover, some pieces of inlay missing, unsigned, late 19thC, 8½in (21.5cm).
$3,000-4,000

Tea & Coffee Pots

A pair of 'famille rose' European subject coffee pots and covers, probably for the Portuguese market, each decorated on both sides with figures in colours, covers chipped, one finial replaced, c1730, 6½in (17cm).
$7,500-10,500

Almost certainly made for the Portuguese market, the decoration is related to the European figures appearing around the border of 'clarinettist' plates, frequently found also in Portugal.

A pair of 'famille rose' black ground teapots, covers and stands, one stand cracked, small finial frits, minor rim chips, Yongzheng, the stands 6in (15.5cm) diam.
$3,000-4,500

VALUE POINTS FOR CHINESE PORCELAIN

★ condition – this is always an important factor when dealing with porcelain. Some collectors will only buy perfect pieces – this is particularly the case with Far Eastern buyers. They will pay high prices for excellent condition. This affects the price considerably as a very good piece with a hairline crack or small chip can reduce the value by up to two thirds

★ rarity – as with most aspects of antiques, rare items fetch substantially more than common counterparts. This is also important when thinking of damage, as damage to a common piece is much more likely to affect the price dramatically than a similar damage to a rare piece

★ imperial v. export – most of the high prices for Chinese porcelain seem to come from the Hong Kong salerooms. The Far Eastern buyers tend to collect the pieces made by the Chinese potters for their own market rather than exportware. Hence prices are higher

A Chinese export grisaille and gilt decorated European subject globular teapot and domed cover, painted on each side with a mythological scene, glaze cracks to base, Qianlong, 7in (18cm) wide.
$1,000-1,400

An Imari conical coffee pot, on 3 lappet-shaped feet, decorated in iron red, green, mauve, black enamels, and gilt, with detachable brass tap, late 17thC, 13½in (34cm).
$2,250-3,000

A 'famille rose' armorial barrel-shaped chocolate pot and cover, with seated Buddhistic lion finial, crack from rim and cover rim, c1780, 9in (22.5cm`.
$1,000-1,400

An Imari moulded pear-shaped coffee pot and cover, decorated in typical colours and gilt on underglaze blue, the fluted body with applied handle, decorated with a continuous landscape, the tripod feet formed as bijin holding fans, minor chips, the bijin and finial restored, late 17th/early 18thC, 13in (33cm).
$1,200-1,600

An Imari coffee pot and deep cylindrical cover, painted on each side with buildings in a river landscape, early 18thC, 10in (25.5cm).
$1,000-1,400

A pair of soup tureens and covers, decorated in 'famille rose' enamels, Qianlong, 9in (23cm).
$4,500-7,000

A pair of Chinese export sauce tureens, covers and stands, painted in vibrant blue enamel on white, with 4 soup plates and 10 dinner plates, minor damages, Jiaqing.
$450-700

Tureens

A 'famille rose' oblong tureen and cover, with iron red hare head handles and pomegranate finial, chipped, Qianlong, 13½in (34cm) wide.
$2,500-3,500

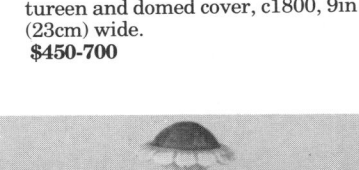

A Chinese blue and white vegetable tureen and domed cover, c1800, 9in (23cm) wide.
$450-700

A tobacco leaf covered sauce tureen, the lid with gilt decorated and iron red finial, the oval bombé body with gilt intertwined strap handles and decorated in bright colours, minor fritting to handle, late Qianlong, 5½in (14cm) diam.
$2,250-3,500

A pair of export polychrome 'Quail' pattern octagonal tureens and stands, painted in iron red and greyish blue, within iron red and gilt floral borders, old damage, Qianlong, the stands 7½in (19cm) wide.
$2,500-3,500

A rare crested sepia Fitzhugh pattern tureen and cover, the domed cover with an artichoke finial, both decorated in strong sepia tones with a lion head crest beneath the motto 'Essayez', finial restored, c1790, 13½in (35cm) wide.
$4,000-5,500

The motto and crest is that of Dundas.

A 'famille rose' tobacco leaf pomegranate-shaped tureen, domed cover and stand, the stand cracked, Qianlong, the stand 9½in (24.5cm) wide.
$9,000-12,000

Vases

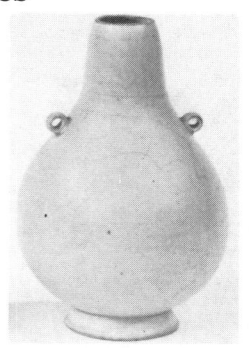

A rare Yingqing pear-shaped vase with simple tubular handles, under a translucent pale bluish-white glaze pooling at the top of the short conical foot, chip restored, Song Dynasty, 8in (20.5cm).
$1,500-2,600

A Hunan vase, painted in iron brown with a stylised peony spray and an inscription, under a pale olive-white glaze spreading over a broad iron brown band at the foot, body crack, Song Dynasty, 14in (36.5cm).
$3,000-4,500

The inscription reads:
'wei jun san cun qi, bai liao shao nian tou,' which may be translated literally as: 'To gain three inches of air whitens the young man's head.' This suggests that young men should not strain themselves to further their careers at the expense of their health.

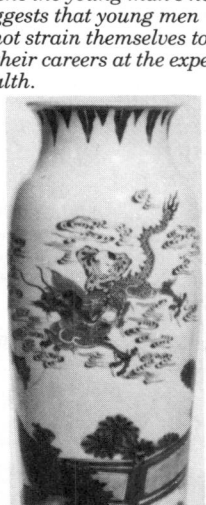

A Transitional blue and white sleeve vase, rim polished, c1645, 18in (46cm).
$700-900

A Transitional blue and white sleeve vase, painted with a boy astride a four-clawed dragon, minor restoration to rim chips, c1640, 17½in (44cm).
$1,200-1,600

A Transitional blue and white double gourd vase, painted in a vivid blue with 2 scholars, below upright tulips dividing Buddhist emblems on the upper section and neck, firing cracks to foot rim, fritted, c1650, 10in (25cm), fitted box.
$1,500-2,600

A Ming blue and white vase, 'meiping', 16thC, 8½in (22cm).
$1,200-1,600

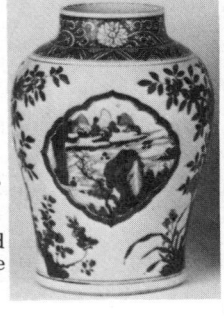

Two blue and white baluster vases, boldly and vividly painted, with a washed blue band at the shoulder and scrolling lotus on a similar band at the short neck, minor fritting, one neck crack, Kangxi, 13in (33cm).
$6,000-9,000

A Wucai baluster vase and cover, enamelled in yellow, red and green on an underglaze blue ground, chip to cover and neck rim, mid-17thC, 15½in (39.5cm).
$1,500-2,600

A Chinese blue and white vase, Kangxi, 7½in (19cm).
$450-700

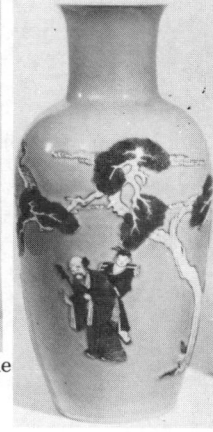

A pair of 'famille verte' vases, one damaged, the other cracked and fritted, Kangxi, 12½in (32cm).
$1,500-2,600

A Chinese blue and white vase, painted with scattered flowers and fruit sprays, Transitional, 10in (25.5cm), wood stand.
$600-900

A 'famille verte' hexagonal double gourd vase, fritting, Kangxi, 12½in (31.5cm).
$1,300-1,800

A celadon ground vase, painted in blue, copper-red and white with relief-moulded figures, deer and birds, glaze bubbles, rim cracks, Kangxi, 17½in (45cm).
$3,000-4,500

A Chinese Imari baluster vase and cover, painted with 2 pairs of iron brown and gilt peacocks, below 'ruyi' lappets reserved with iron red scrolling foliage and lotus, cover drilled and wood finial, crack to body and neck, c1730, 22in (56cm).
$2,500-3,500

A pair of 'famille verte' baluster vases and domed covers, painted on green seeded grounds, below further panels and lotus meanders on iron red grounds, the necks with precious emblems, the covers divided into similar panels, fritted, one vase and the finials damaged, Kangxi, 10½in (27cm).
$1,500-2,600

A pair of blue and white yanyan vases, boldly and densely decorated, one rim slightly chipped, Kangxi, 18in (45.5cm).
$3,000-4,500

A 'famille rose' eggshell vase, delicately painted on both sides with figures, on a ground of gilt flower scrolls, rim chipped, Yongzheng, 10½in (27cm).
$600-900

A baluster vase decorated in manganese and 'verte', late 17thC.
$1,500-2,600

A pair of Chinese 'famille verte' vases, enamelled with continuous scenes of Noblemen, underglaze blue double circle mark to base, Kangxi, 10in (25.5cm).
$600-900

A massive Chinese blue and white vase and cover, the finial moulded as a seated female figure, the hexagonal body decorated all over with trailing flowers and Greek key bands, 39½in (100cm).
$4,500-7,000

A pair of Chinese porcelain vases of bold baluster form, painted in 'famille rose', blue, green and yellow-green, one repaired and both ground down lips, four-character marks, 18thC, 8in (20cm), hardwood covers and stands.
$400-500

A flambe-glazed pear-shaped vase, thinning to celadon at the rim, under a thick rich glaze with lavender splashes on the neck and lower half, 18thC, 15in (38cm).
$1,300-1,800

A blue and white hexagonal baluster vase, Qianlong seal mark, 17in (43.5cm).
$1,300-1,800

A large Chinese blue and white pottery baluster shaped vase and cover, decorated with flowers, butterflies and various utensils, 24in (61cm).
$1,200-1,600

A blue and white pear-shaped vase, painted with a procession and warriors at play, fixed lion mask and ring handles, 20½in (52cm).
$750-1,000

A pair of 'famille rose' beaker vases, brightly painted on both sides with a tall panel of figures, within blue bat and butterfly borders, reserved on gilt scrolling grounds enriched with scattered flowersprays, some restoration, late Qianlong, 15½in (39cm).
$6,000-9,000

A pair of 'famille verte' powder blue ground vases, minor fritting, late Qing Dynasty, 15in (38cm).
$2,250-3,500

A Cantonese enamelled vase, with a gilded brocade pattern ground, and applied with gilded lizards and chi-chi to the neck and shoulders, 19thC, 18in (46cm).
$800-1,200

A pair of Cantonese vases, 19thC.
$1,000-1,400

A flambe-glazed bottle vase, under a vivid splashed red and lavender blue glaze, 19thC, 18in (45.5cm).
$1,500-2,600

A large Chinese bottle-shaped porcelain vase, decorated in brightly coloured enamels, 25in (63.5cm).
$600-900

A large Canton 'famille rose' vase, applied with 2 gilt lion and cub handles divided by 'chilong' at the shoulder, 19thC, 35in (89cm).
$2,500-3,500

A pair of 'famille verte' and powder blue ground rouleau vases, painted with panels of warriors on blue grounds with gilt flowersprays and ribboned emblems, late Qing Dynasty, 23½in (60cm).
$2,250-3,000

A large baluster vase, decorated with 'famille verte' panels of figures, 19thC, 24in (61cm).
$700-900

A Chinese 'famille verte' vase, painted on each facet with a dignitary seated at a table surrounded by attendants, 19thC, 23in (58cm).
$600-900

A Cantonese enamelled rouleau vase, with decorated panels all on gilded brocade pattern ground, mid-19thC, 14in (35.5cm).
$400-500

A pair of 'famille verte' rouleau vases, one neck restored, late Qing Dynasty, 18½in (47.5cm).
$1,200-1,600

A pair of large Canton vases, with elephant head handles, painted with figures in palace interiors on a ground scattered with household objects, flowers and insects, one damaged, 19thC, 23½in (60cm).
$1,000-1,400

An Imari vase and cover, painted in typical colours in rectangular and heart-shaped panels, on a powder blue ground scattered with gilt chrysanthemum and foliage, cracked and restored, early 18thC, 29in (73.5cm).
$4,000-5,500

A pair of Imari vases, each painted and gilt with shaped panels of kirin and deer, 21½in (54.5cm).
$2,500-3,500

A large Kyoto Satsuma oviform vase, decorated in iron red, coloured enamels and gilt, rim damaged and repaired, signed Nihon Kyoto Kinkozan zo, 19thC, 32½in (83cm).
$4,000-5,500

A pair of Japanese Satsuma earthenware vases, painted with panels of warriors and geishas on brocade ground, 19thC, 12in (30cm).
$300-400

A Japanese Imari porcelain vase and cover in traditional colours, 17in (43cm).
$300-400

An Imari porcelain baluster vase, reeded and painted with opposing panels of flower baskets alternating with brocade pattern panels, mid-19thC, 9½in (24cm).
$300-400

An Imari vase, the body moulded with hexagons and painted with panels of birds, fish, animals, boats and pagodas, below a waisted neck, 18in (46cm).
$600-900

A Satsuma baluster vase and domed cover, decorated in various coloured enamels and gilt with floral roundels, on a brown and gilt striped ground, the flared foot with bands of gilt key pattern, 10in (25.5cm).
$2,250-3,000

A Japanese Satsuma pottery pot pourri vase and cover, decorated with polychrome enamels and gilt, on a pierced ground, the domed cover decorated with river scenes and flowers, surmounted by a fluted knop, raised on 3 lobed feet, damaged, 7in (17.5cm).
$400-500

A pair of Satsuma vases and covers, the cream ground painted in colours with swimming fish and flowering peonies, 18in (46cm), wood stands.
$600-900

A Japanese Satsuma pottery pot pourri vase and cover, decorated in polychrome enamels and gilt, 8in (20cm).
$2,250-3,000

A pair of Imari porcelain vases and covers, decorated with opposing panels of flowering prunus trees, alternating with stylised flower vase panels, late 19thC, 9in (23cm).
$250-350

A pair of Satsuma vases, painted with panels of children at play and flowering plants with birds and insects amongst the blossom, one with star crack, 9½in (24cm).
$750-1,000

A pair of tall tapering Kyoto Satsuma bottle vases, decorated in various coloured enamels and gilt on an orange ground, signed Dai Nihon taizan sei, late 19thC, 12½in (31cm).
$1,000-1,400

A pair of large Japanese porcelain vases, damaged, 19thC, 37½in (95cm), on ebonised hardwood stands.
$1,200-1,600

A pair of Kutani ware vases, gilded and polychrome enamelled with 2 groups of scholars and boy attendants in a continuous frieze below bamboo leaves, on a matt black ground, early 20thC, 10in (25.5cm).
$450-700

Two Imari cylindrical vases, early 20thC, 9½in (24cm).
$150-250

159

A Shofu oviform vase, decorated in underglaze green, yellow and pink on a pale pink ground blending into a pale green, signed in underglaze blue, Shofu, late 19thC, 8½in (22cm).
$450-600

A Ming blue and white kendi, painted with scrolling 'lingzhi' on the body, triangular leaves on the neck, foliage at the shoulder, minor fritting, early 17thC, 6½in (17cm).
$750-1,000

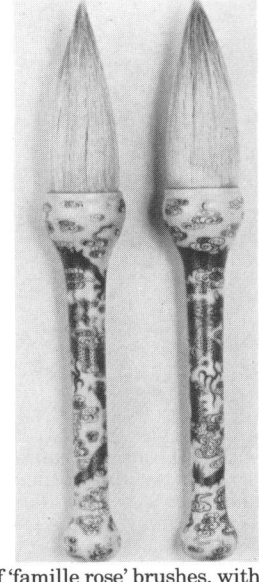

A pair of 'famille rose' brushes, with iron red and gilt coiling five-clawed dragons amongst wisps of turquoise, yellow and pink clouds set with natural bristles, minor cracks, the head of each handle with an iron red Qianlong six-character seal mark, 10in (25.5cm).
$4,000-5,500

A pair of Satsuma vases, 20thC, 7½in (19cm).
$450-600

These are water gilt, not fire gilt.

A Chinese blue and white candlestick, painted with flowerheads, with a triple knop stem, set on an octagonal base, Kangxi, 5½in (14.5cm).
$1,300-1,800

A rare metal-mounted 'famille rose' European subject circular bombé snuff box and flat cover, the interior painted, the base with small sepia and iron red bird and landscape roundels, repaired, the porcelain Qianlong, the mounts probably contemporaneous, 2½in (7cm) diam.
$1,000-1,400

Miscellaneous

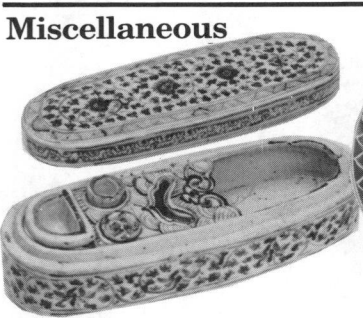

A rare Ming slender oval pen box and cover, chipped, 15thC, 9in (23cm) long.
$6,000-9,000

A massive blue and white shallow cistern, painted with a large landscape, the flat rim with wave pattern above a wide band of diaper and rain cloud in the vertical well, c1800, 27½in (70cm) diam, high folding six-legged wood stand.
$9,000-12,000

A 'famille rose' gilt-mounted snuff box, the unusual interior painted with a scene of boatmen by a lake building with a pagoda in underglaze blue, base rubbed, Qianlong, 2½in (7cm) diam, cloth pouch.
$2,250-3,000

A pair of clobbered blue and white candlesticks of European silver shape, painted with a landscape scene, over-decorated with lime green and iron red enamels, fritting, one repaired, the porcelain 18thC, the enamels early 19thC, 8½in (21cm).
$1,500-2,600

Chinese dynasties and marks

Earlier Dynasties

Shang Yin, c.1532-1027 B.C.
Western Zhou (Chou) 1027-770 B.C.
Spring and Autumn Annals 770-480 B.C.
Warring States 484-221 B.C.
Qin (Ch'in) 221-206 B.C.
Western Han 206 BC-24 AD
Eastern Han 25-220
Three Kingdoms 221-265
Six Dynasties 265-589
Wei 386-557

Sui 589-617
Tang (T'ang) 618-906
Five Dynasties 907-960
Liao 907-1125
Sung 960-1280
Chin 1115-1260
Yüan 1280-1368

Ming Dynasty

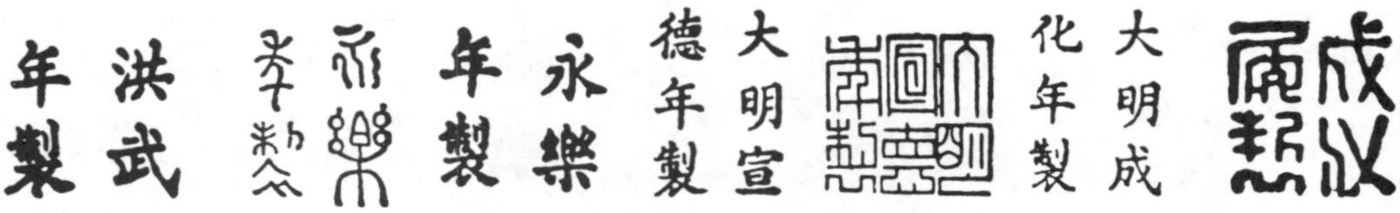

Hongwu (Hung Wu)
1368-1398

Yongle (Yung Lo)
1403-1424

Xuande (Hsüan Té)
1426-1435

Chenghua (Ch'éng Hua)
1465-1487

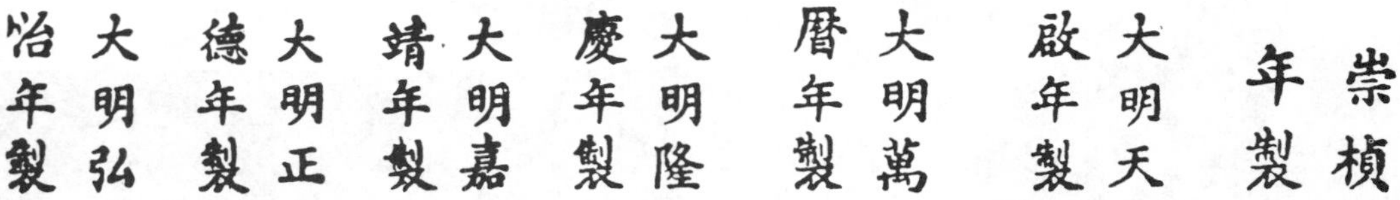

Hongzhi
(Hung Chih)
1488-1505)

Zhengde
(Chéng Té)
1506-1521

Jiajing
(Chia Ching)
1522-1566

Longqing
(Lung Ching)
1567-1572

Wanli (Wan Li)
1573-1620

Tianqi
(Tien Chi)
1621-1627

Chongzhen
(Ch'ung Chêng)
1628-1644

Qing (Ch'ing) Dynasty

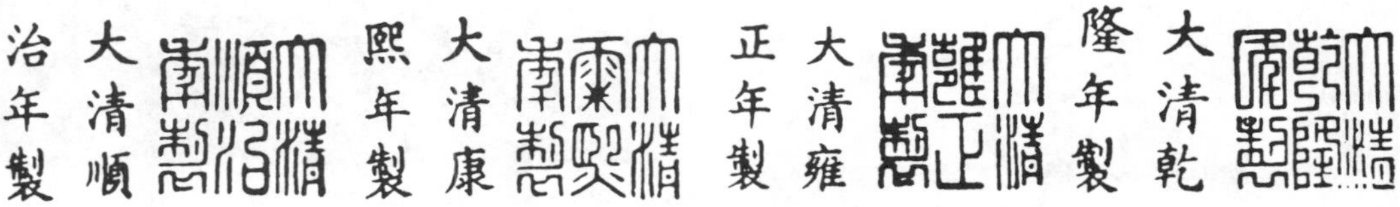

Shunzhi
(Shun Chih)
1644-1661

Kangxi (K'ang Hsi)
1662-1722

Yongzheng (Yung Chêng)
1723-1735

Qianlong (Ch'ien Lung)
1736-1795'

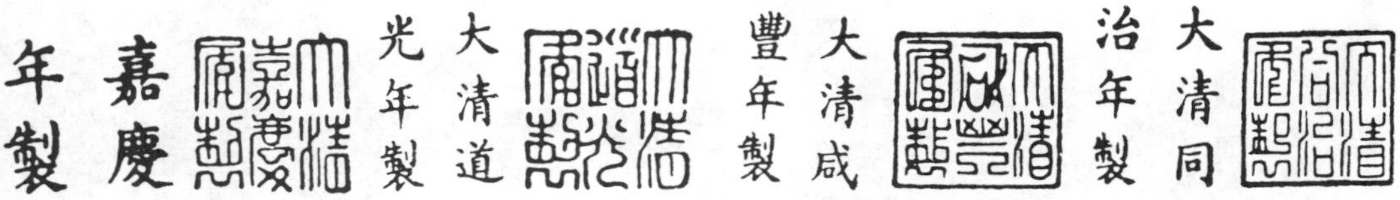

Jiaqing (Chia Ch'ing)
1796-1820

Daoguang (Tao Kuang)
1821-1850

Xianfeng (Hsien Féng)
1851-1861

Tongzhi (T'ung Chih)
1862-1874

Guangxu (Kuang Hsu)
1875-1908

Xuantong
(Hsuan T'ung)
1909-1911

Hongxian
(Hung Hsien)
1916

Beakers

A Bohemian beaker, in green and blue marbelised glass cut with drapes, ovals and diamonds, with gilt lined rim, 5in (12.5cm).
$400-500

A Bohemian amethyst overlay beaker, painted with panels, the foot cut with ovals outlined in gilt, 4½in (11.5cm).
$250-350

A Bohemian amber-flash beaker, cut with oval panels engraved with named buildings, the base applied with amber prunts, 5in (13cm).
$300-400

Bottles

A set of 4 Bristol blue sauce bottles and stoppers, with gilt labels for Kyan, Ketchup, Soy and Anchovy, one stopper damaged, the bases incised W.R. & Co., and one with a date 1788 (?), 4½in (11cm).
$250-350

A set of 3 cruet bottles, 2 oil/vinegar and one dry mustard, on square lemon squeezer bases, c1800, 6 and 6½in (15 and 16cm).
$150-200

A mallet shaped wine bottle with string rim, chipped, seal with inscription 'I. Buck 1732', c1732, 7in (18cm).
$450-700

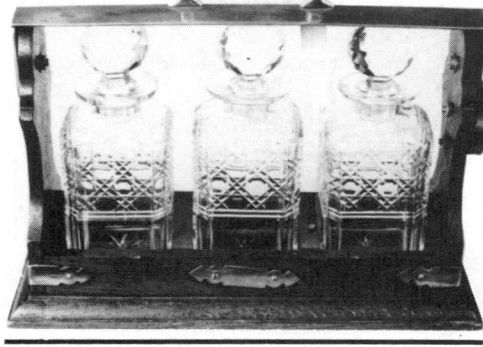

An oak tantalus with half-cut bottles, c1920.
$450-600

Bowls

A pair of English glass dishes, late 19thC.
$900-1,300

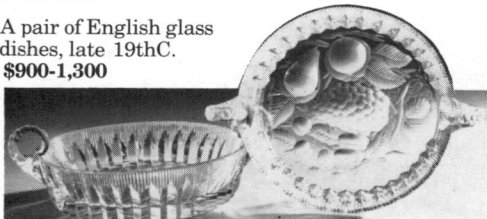

A sugar basin with diamond cut panels and fan cut rim, star cut underneath, c1820, 4½in (12cm).
$150-250

A Venetian 'revival' bowl in 'vetro a reticello', c1860-70, 4½in (12cm).
$250-350

Candelabra

A pair of ormolu and cut glass candlesticks, with pointed and undulating drip-pans, on hobnail pear-shaped stems, late 18thC, 15½in (39.5cm).
$2,500-3,500

A pair of cut glass five-light candelabra, with shaped baluster shafts and domed circular hobnail bases, the ormolu borders with entrelacs on claw feet, 34in (86.5cm).
$7,500-10,500

A pair of gilded and crystal lustre two-branch candelabra, c1830, 14½in (37cm).
$600-900

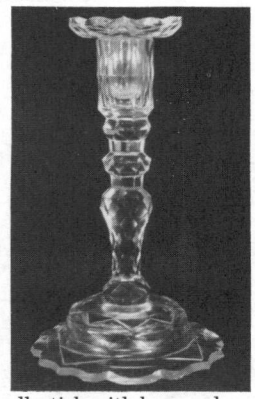

A candlestick with knopped baluster stem and domed foot, with separate sconce, diamond cut overall, c1780, 10½in (26.5cm).
$600-900

A pair of Victorian ruby glass lustre vases, with polychrome enamel decoration, each supporting 14 droppers.
$300-400

A fine pair of overlay lustre vases, cranberry and gold, c1880, 12in (30.5cm).
$1,200-1,600

A candlestick, with plain socket on a stem with single series air-twist, air-beaded knop and rib moulded folded conical foot, c1745, 7½in (19cm).
$450-600

A pair of clear glass lustre candlesticks, decorated with gilded Arabesque panels, the rims hung with cut prismatic drops, mid-19thC, 13½in (34cm).
$600-900

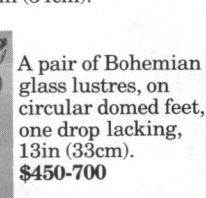

A pair of Bohemian glass lustres, on circular domed feet, one drop lacking, 13in (33cm).
$450-700

A pair of rock crystal and giltmetal pricket candlesticks, with faceted multi-baluster stems on stepped hexagonal bases, mid-19thC, 11in (28cm).
$4,000-5,500

◄ A candlestick on a plain domed foot, c1750, 8½in (21.5cm).
$750-1,000

A set of 3 plain decanters with target stoppers, c1800, 10½in (26cm).
$1,200-1,600

Chandeliers

An Empire ormolu, bronzed and cut glass chandelier of bag shape, the circlet with female masks with plumed head-dresses divided by scrolled branches with chased drip-pans and plain nozzles, the bag with alternating outstretched putti and graduated drops, with pineapple knop, with electricity, 53½in (136cm).
$15,000-21,000

A cut glass and giltmetal eight-light chandelier, with moulded drip-pans and foliate nozzles hung with swags and button drops, 34in (86cm).
$2,500-3,500

A Swedish ormolu and cut glass six-light chandelier, with pierced circular corona hung with circles of drops, the body reaching to scrolling candle-arms joined by a pierced waved frieze centering a circular blue glass plate hung with coffin drops.
$4,000-5,500

A Swedish neo-classical giltmetal and cut glass six-light chandelier, fitted for electricity, 40in (100cm).
$10,000-13,000

A pair of Irish decanters, with moulded base fluting and moulded mushroom stoppers, c1800, 9in (22.5cm).
$800-1,200

On a pair of black papier mâché coasters with gilt decoration, in original condition, c1800, 5in (13cm) diam.
$750-1,000

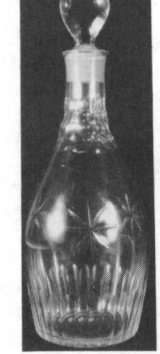

A Cork decanter, with loose radially moulded target stopper, impressed mark 'Waterloo Co. Cork', c1810, 8½in (21cm).
$600-900

Decanters

A club-shaped decanter, c1780, 9½in (23.5cm).
$300-500

A spirit decanter cut overall with prism cutting, with star cut base and cut bevelled lozenge stopper, c1810, 7½in (18.5cm).
$250-350

A decanter with club-shaped body with overall diamond cutting, c1810, 9½in (24cm).
$400-500

A pair of club-shaped spirit decanters with a band of egg-and-tulip engraving, c1780, 7½in (19cm).
$400-500

A pair of half-size Georgian decanters, with original cut target stopper, well cut triple neck ring, 9in (23cm).
$300-400

A pair of Victorian globe and shaft decanters, with facet neck and engraving, 11in (28cm).
$250-350

A pair of Edwardian deeply cut decanters, 13in (33cm).
$300-400

A Victorian decanter with cut swag and medallion decoration and target stopper, 10½in (26.5cm).
$250-350

A Victorian engraved decanter with barley-twist handle, cork stopper, silver mount, 8½in (21cm).
$300-400

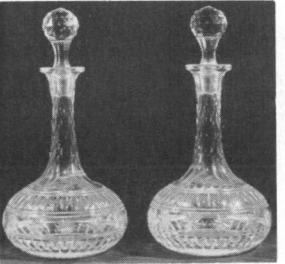

A pair of late Victorian thistle engraved Scottish decanters, 11in (28cm).
$400-500

A pair of decanters with facet cut neck, 1860-70, 12in (31cm).
$300-400

A pair of cranberry glass decanters with stoppers.
$60-100

A wine glass on plain conical foot, c1745, 7in (17cm).
$300-400

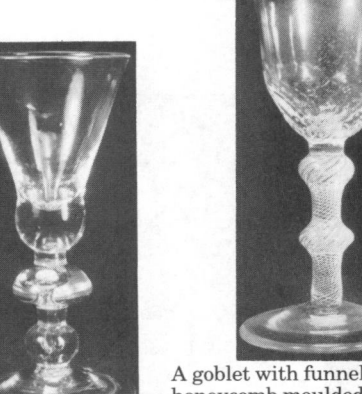

A pair of late Victorian carafes and tumblers, up-and-overs, acid edged, 8in (20.5cm).
$250-350

A goblet with funnel bowl, honeycomb moulded on lower half, on multiple spiral air-twist stem with shoulder and central knops, on plain conical foot, c1750, 6½in (16cm).
$450-700

Drinking Glasses

A heavy baluster wine glass, the slender thistle bowl on a stem with mushroom knop over a plain section and teared ball knop, with folded conical foot, c1705, 7in (17.5cm).
$2,500-3,500

A wine glass engraved with the arms of Amsterdam, the reverse with the inscription 'T. Welvaren Van Amsterdam', on a star studded pedestal stem, folded conical foot, c1750, 7in (17cm).
$1,000-1,400

An engraved Jacobite wine glass, on a stem with a multiple spiral air-twist, on plain conical foot, c1750, 6in (15.5cm).
$1,000-1,400

An ale glass, with deep round funnel bowl engraved with hops and barley, on a corkscrew mercury air-twist stem, c1750, 7½in (19.5cm).
$450-600

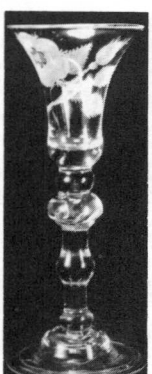

A Jacobite wine glass, the trumpet bowl engraved with rose and single bud, on a composite stem with cushion, air-beaded inverted baluster and base knops, c1750, 7in (17.5cm).
$1,200-1,600

A goblet with bucket bowl on a plain stem, with folded conical foot, c1740, 7in (19.5cm).
$250-350

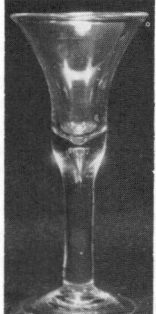

A wine glass, with trumpet bowl on a plain drawn stem with air-tear, on folded conical foot, c1745, 6½in (17cm).
$150-250

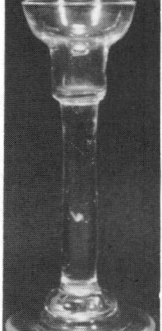

A rare cordial glass, the small bowl with pan top, on a plain stem, c1745, 6in (15.5cm).
$450-600

A plain stemmed engraved wine glass, c1745, 6in (15cm).
$300-400

A pair of Jacobite plain stemmed wine glasses, the funnel bowls engraved, the reverses with star and oak leaf, on conical feet, c1750, 6½in (16.5cm).
$750-1,000 each

Two wine glasses, the trumpet bowls on drawn stems, with air-tears on folded conical feet, c1750, 6in (15cm).
$150-250 each

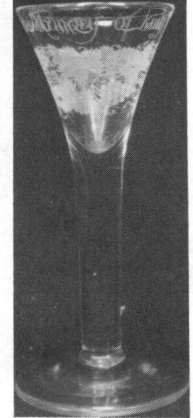

A Williamite wine glass, engraved with fruiting vine and inscription 'Glorious Memory of King William', c1750, 7in (18cm).
$1,500-2,600

An air-twist ale glass, 8½in (20.5cm).
$450-600

Three wine glasses, the trumpet shaped bowls engraved with a band of baroque scrolling, c1750, 7in (18cm).
$600-900

An English glass with shoulder knop and multi-air-twist, 18thC, 6in (15cm).
$250-350

A cordial glass, the small trumpet bowl rib moulded and engraved with a band of stylised roses, on a stem with double series 'mercury' air-twist, plain conical foot, c1740, 6½in (16cm).
$900-1,300

A baluster wine glass with bell bowl, on a stem with inverted baluster knop containing an air-tear, on plain domed foot, (18cm).
$300-500

A wine glass with waisted bowl, on a drawn stem with multiple spiral air-twist, c1745, 7in (17.5cm).
$300-400

l. A wine glass with multiple spiral air-twist stem, pan top bowl and swelling knop stem, on plain conical foot, c1745, 6in (15cm).
$300-500

r. A wine glass with multiple spiral air-twist stem, bell bowl with shoulder and centre knop stem, on plain conical foot, c1745, 6in (15cm).
$300-500

A heavy baluster goblet, supported on an inverted baluster stem enclosing tears, with folded conical foot, c1700, 8in (20cm).
$1,300-1,800

A pedestal stemmed moulded sweetmeat glass, the double ogee bowl with everted lip moulded with all-over honeycomb decoration, c1745, 6½in (16.5cm).
$750-1,000

A large master sweetmeat, on domed folded foot, c1750, 7½in (18.7cm).
$450-600

Three balustroid wine glasses:
l. The round funnel bowl on a plain stem with shoulder cushion knop, c1750, 6½in (16.5cm).
$150-250

c. The trumpet bowl on a stem with air-tear and swelling shoulder knop, plain domed foot, c1745, 7in (17.5cm).
$250-350

r. The conical bowl on a stem with air-teared bladed knop and base, ball knop, with domed folded foot, c1740, 5½in (14.5cm).
$300-500

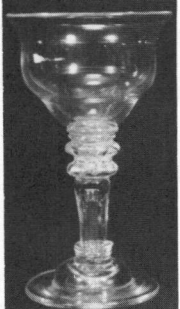

A sweetmeat, the double ogee bowl on a stem with collar, air-beaded knop and pedestal stem with base collar, plain domed foot, c1750, 6½in (16cm).
$300-400

A sweetmeat or champagne glass, with double ogee bowl, on domed folded foot, c1750, 6in (15cm).
$450-600

A wine glass with trumpet bowl on a composite stem, with multiple spiral air-twist section, and air-beaded knop, c1745, 7in (18cm).
$300-500

A heavy baluster wine glass, the conical bowl with a solid section, with mushroom and ball knops, folded conical foot, c1710, 6in (16cm).
$2,250-3,000

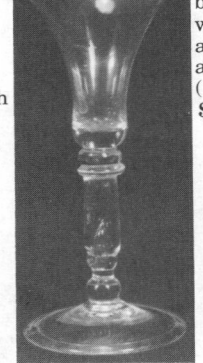

A balustroid gin glass, with trumpet bowl on a stem with cushion knop, c1750, 6½in (16cm).
$450-600

A composite stemmed wine glass, with beaded inverted baluster section, c1750, 7in (17.5cm).
$600-900

A 'Newcastle' wine glass, decorated with a band of engraved and polished baroque design, c1750, 7in (18cm).
$1,000-1,400

A baluster goblet, on a stem with wide angular knop, short plain section, base knop, folded conical foot, c1715, 6½in (16.5cm).
$1,000-1,400

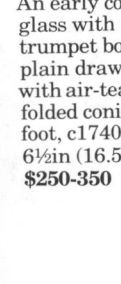

An engraved 'Newcastle' light baluster glass, c1745, 7in (17.3cm).
$600-900

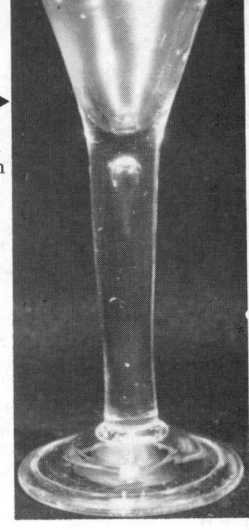

An early cordial glass with trumpet bowl, on plain drawn stem with air-tear on folded conical foot, c1740, 6½in (16.5cm).
$250-350

A champagne or sweetmeat glass, with hexagonal stem and domed foot, 18thC, 7in (18cm).
$250-350

A rare wine glass, the bowl engraved with a band of chrysanthemum and parrots, on a double series opaque twist stem, radially moulded foot, c1760, 6in (15cm).
$1,200-1,600

A heavy vine and grape shell cut wine goblet from a service, 6in (15cm).
$45-70

A set of 6 'Bristol' green rummers, 4in (10cm).
$60-100 each

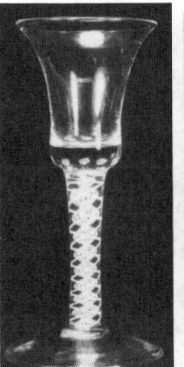

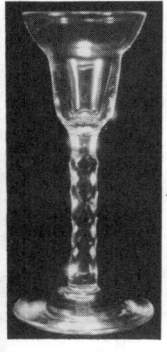

A colour twist wine glass, the stem with central opaque white spiral and outer translucent red and green spiralling tapes, c1775, 5½in (14cm).
$1,500-2,600

A Georgian panel cut rummer, c1820, 5½in (14cm).
$75-150

◀ A wine glass, with double ogee bowl on a stem with diamond facet cutting, on plain conical foot, c1770, 7in (18cm).
$250-350

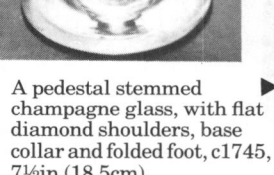

A wine glass, with bell bowl and air-beaded base, on double series opaque twist stem, c1760, 7in (17.5cm).
$250-350

A pedestal stemmed champagne glass, with flat diamond shoulders, base collar and folded foot, c1745, 7½in (18.5cm). ▶
$400-500

A wine glass with engraved ogee bowl, on a diamond cut facet stem with centre knop, on plain conical foot, c1770, 5½in (14.5cm).
$300-500

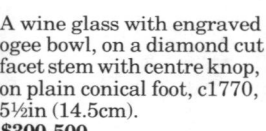

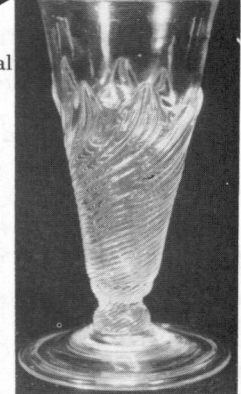

A dwarf ale glass, the conical bowl with flammiform wrythen moulding, on folded conical foot, c1740, 4½in (11cm). ▶
$150-250

◀

A plain Georgian champagne flute, 7in (18cm).
$60-100

A toasting glass, 18thC, 8in (20.5cm).
$250-350

▶

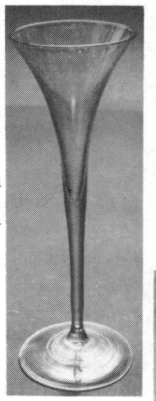

A set of Edwardian facet stem wine glasses, with engraved vine and grape, 6in (15cm).
$150-200

A goblet with honeycomb moulded ovoid bowl, on a drawn stem with hexagonal cut facets, c1770, 6½in (17cm).
$300-400

Two full and half wrythen dwarf ale glasses, 1760-80, 5 and 5½in (12.5 and 14cm).
$45-70 each

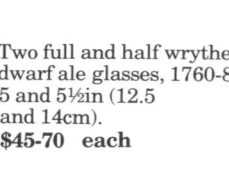

Three trumpet bowl firing glasses with heavy disc feet, c1760:
l. 4½in (11.5cm).
$75-150

c. 3½in (9.5cm).
$75-150

r. 4½in (11.5cm).
$75-150

Three dwarf ale glasses:
l. The conical bowl engraved with hops, barley, birds in flight, and initials on a plain drawn stem, c1790, 5½in (13.5cm).
$60-100

c. The wrythen moulded conical bowl with bladed knop, c1820, 5½in (14cm).
$60-100

r. The conical bowl wrythen moulded on lower half, engraved with hops and barley on top half, c1810, 4½in (12.5cm).
$45-70

l. A tumbler with acid etched crown above a rope knot, c1830, 4in (10cm).
$60-100

r. A tumbler engraved with a greyhound crest and initials 'E.T.M.' and dated '1802', c1803, 4in (10cm).
$150-200

Ovoid glasses with collars and square lemon squeezer bases:
l. An engraved rummer, c1800, 5½in (13.5cm).
$75-150

c. A pair of glasses, c1810, 3½in (9.5cm).
$75-150

r. A rummer, c1810, 5in (12.5cm).
$75-150

l. A tumbler engraved with hops and barley, c1780, 5in (12.5cm).
$150-200

r. A North Country mug with moulded fluting at base, the body engraved with floral sprays and bird in flight, c1840, 4½in (12cm).
$75-150

A set of 6 Bristol green wine glasses, c1850, 5in (12cm).
$75-150   each

A 'Sunderland Bridge' rummer, early 19thC.
$300-400

A Bohemian glass, with ruby red and green body and yellow border, c1840.
$1,000-1,400

A German betrothal goblet and cover, engraved with lovers, the reverse with mirror monograms within an elaborate crowned cartouche, inscribed with the figure '3' below, Hesse, mid-18thC, 16in (41cm).
$6,000-8,000

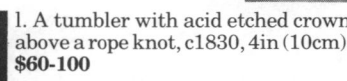

Three small stirrup glasses with flute cut conical bowls and stems, c1820, 5in (13cm).
$150-250

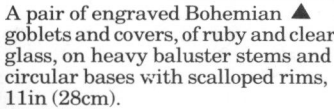

A pair of engraved Bohemian goblets and covers, of ruby and clear glass, on heavy baluster stems and circular bases with scalloped rims, 11in (28cm).
$750-1,000

A set of 6 bucket rummers with flute cut bowls, on knopped stems and plain conical feet, c1825, 5in (13cm).
$300-500

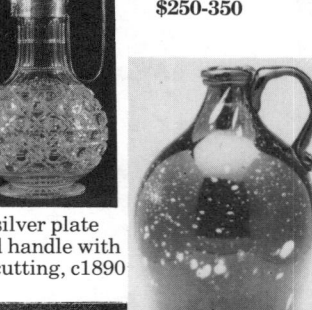

A pear shaped claret jug with star cut foot, engraved with fruiting vine, with hard metal silver plated mount, c1880, 10in (25cm).
$250-350

A Victorian Greek key cut claret jug, 11½in (29cm).
$250-350

A Victorian silver mounted glass claret jug, the hinged cover with lion finial above, Elkington & Co, Birmingham, 1878, 10½in (26cm).
$1,500-2,600

A claret jug, with silver plate mounted cover and handle with mask lip, hobnail cutting, c1890
$250-350

A large black Nailsea pitcher with splashed opaque white decoration, 10in (25.5cm).
$450-700

A late Victorian cut and engraved celery jug, 10in (25.5cm).
$100-200

A Bohemian ruby-flash faceted cream jug with solid gilt handle, gilt with fruiting vine, 5in (12.5cm) wide.
$150-250

Paperweights

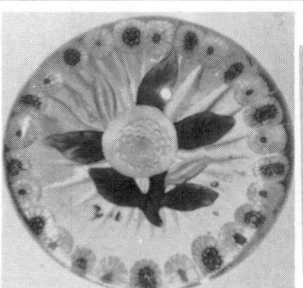

A Baccarat garlanded white pom-pom weight, the flower with a yellow stamen centre and green leaves, set within a garland of red, white and blue arrowhead and star canes, on a star cut base, 2½in (6cm) diam.
$900-1,300

An engraved claret jug with plated mounts, the handle formed as a seated grotesque terminating in a foliage scroll, enclosing a flowerhead, c1880, 10½in (27.5cm).
$300-500

A Baccarat red and white primrose weight, the flower with ribbed white petals edged in red, on a star cut base, 2in (5cm) diam.
$450-700

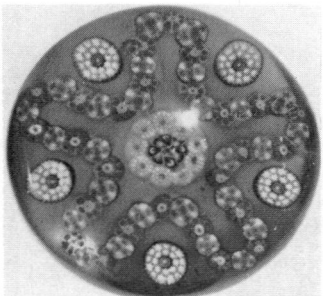

A Baccarat red ground garlanded millefiori weight, the circle of green centred white star canes enclosed by a cinquefoil garland, in shades of green, white and pink, on a translucent red ground, 3in (7cm) diam.
$1,000-1,400

A Baccarat concentric millefiori sulphide weight, the centre with portrait of Queen Victoria, enclosed by 3 circles of canes in shades of red, white, pale blue, green and pink, 3in (7.5cm) diam.
$1,000-1,400

A Baccarat close concentric millefiori mushroom weight, the coloured concentric rings of canes set within a torsade of white gauze entwined by cobalt blue threads, between mercury bands, on a star cut base, 3in (8cm) diam.
$900-1,300

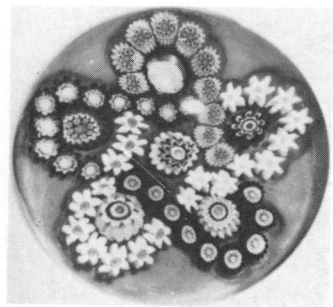

A Clichy turquoise ground patterned millefiori weight, the 2 trefoil garlands in shades of claret, pink and white, about a central green and white setup on an opaque turquoise ground, 3in (7.5cm) diam.
$1,500-2,600

A Baccarat faceted upright bouquet weight, the bouquet with a central white flower in shades of red, white and blue, set within a torsade of white gauze entwined with cobalt blue spiral thread beneath a mercury band, cut with a window, 3in (8cm) diam.
$1,300-1,800

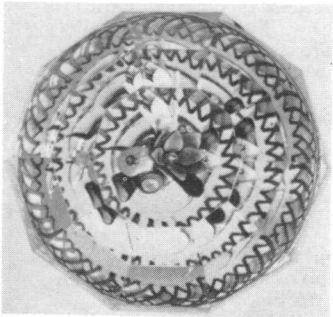

A St Louis faceted upright bouquet weight, with 3 gentian-type flowers in shades of orange, white and blue, within a torsade of white latticinio corkscrew entwined by cobalt blue threads, the fluted sides cut with graduated facets, 2½in (7cm) diam.
$1,000-1,400

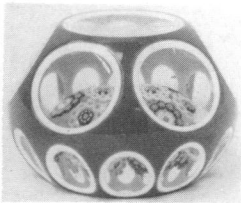

A French overlay paperweight, of 20 windows cut through blue and white opaque glass layers, encasing millefiori, 3in (7.5cm) diam.
$600-900

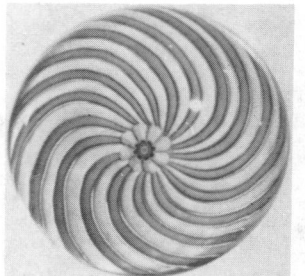

A Clichy swirl weight, with alternate pale mauve and white staves radiating from a green-centred white pastry-mould cane, 2½in (6.5cm) diam.
$1,200-1,600

A St Louis jasper ground flower weight, the flower with 2 rows of pink petals about a bright blue dot centre, surrounded by 3 serrated green leaves, set on a green and white jasper ground, 2in (5.5cm) diam.
$700-900

A Paul Ysart coloured ground garlanded bouquet weight, the flowers in shades of orange, yellow, blue, pink and white among green leaves, with a small cane at the base of the bouquet inscribed 'PY', within a garland of alternate blue and pink canes, on a translucent grey ground, 3in (7.5cm) diam.
$400-500

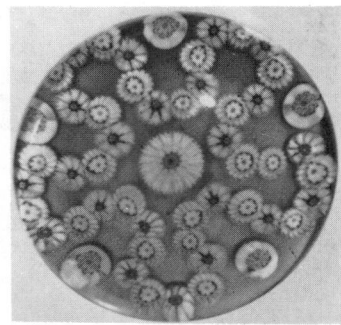

A Clichy green ground patterned millefiori weight, in shades of blue, pink and white with a large turquoise centred white star cane, with 5 large green and white canes at the periphery, set on a translucent emerald green ground, 3in (7.8cm) diam.
$750-1,000

A Clichy 'Barbers' Pole' chequer weight, with a concentric arrangement of brightly coloured canes, divided by blue and white twisted thread, on a bed of horizontal cable, 3in (7cm) diam.
$1,500-2,600

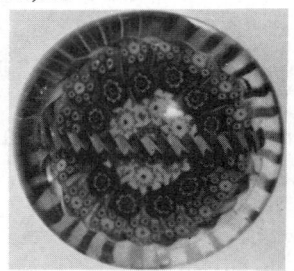

A rare Bohemian close concentric millefiori basket weight, the coloured circles of canes contained in a basket of white staves edged in pink and white twisted ribbon and with pink and white loop handle, on a star cut base, 2½in (6.5cm) diam.
$1,500-2,600

Scent Bottles

An early Victorian hand cut crystal scent bottle, 1850-60.
$150-250

A Baccarat enamelled cut glass scent bottle with giltmetal screw cover, enamelled in colours on gilt-foil with Cupid standing in a chariot, the reverse with fan cutting beneath a band of diamonds, 3½in (9.5cm) long.
$1,500-2,600

Four clear glass double ended scent bottles:
l. Cut overall, with embossed silver gilt mounts, c1870, 5in (13cm).
$100-200

lc. Flute cut with silver gilt mounts, c1870, 5in (13cm).
$100-200

rc. Facet cut opera glass type, with chased silver mounts, c1860, 5in (13cm).
$150-250

r. Facet cut opera glass type, with plain silver gilt mounts, c1860, 5½in (13cm).
$150-250

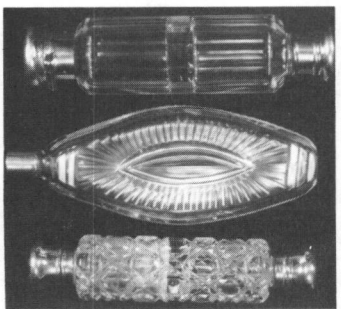

Top A double ended scent bottle with plain silver gilt mounts, c1870, 5in (12.5cm) long.
$100-200

c. An Irish cut scent bottle, with silver mount, c1800, 5½in (13.5cm).
$100-150

Bottom A double ended scent bottle, with silver gilt mounts, c1870, 5in (12.5cm).
$150-200

A Victorian ruby glass scent bottle, the unmarked silver gilt cap and cagework mounts engraved with flowers and set with turquoise beads and bosses, small chip to neck, c1860.
$300-400

A Victorian cut glass scent bottle, with embossed silver lid, London 1894, 5in (13cm).
$150-250

An Apsley Pellatt sulphide and cut glass scent bottle, inset with a portrait of a gentleman, his hair 'en queue', the sides and reverse with strawberry within hobnail cutting, chips to rim, 3½in (9.5cm).
$600-900

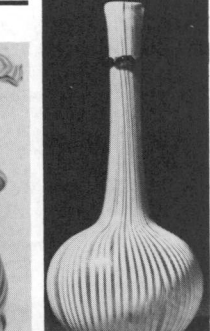

A green facet-cut scent flask, decorated by James Giles, with a frieze of garden ornaments, the short neck with everted gilt dentil rim, minute chip to rim and foot rim, 1765-70, 6in (15cm).
$1,500-2,600

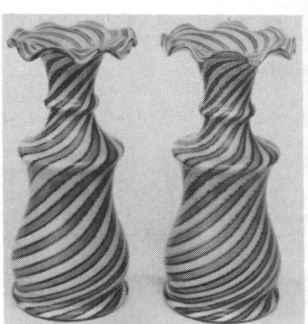

An unusual double ended scent bottle, with gold mounts with blue and white enamel, one cap in the form of a kettle drum, c1800, 5in (12.5cm).
$450-600

Vases

A pair of St Louis green and white spirally striped vases, the knopped flared necks with crenellated rims, 11in (28cm).
$900-1,300

Make the most of Miller's

Every care has been taken to ensure the accuracy of descriptions and estimated valuations. Price ranges in this book reflect what one should expect to pay for a similar example. When selling one can obviously expect a figure below. This will fluctuate according to a dealer's stock, saleability at a particular time, etc. It is always advisable to approach a reputable specialist dealer or an auction house which has specialist sales.

A 'Façon de Venise' bottle in 'vetro a fili', decorated with vertical lattimo thread and applied with a blue vermicular collar below the rim, Low Countries, 17thC, 12in (30.5cm).
$1,500-2,600

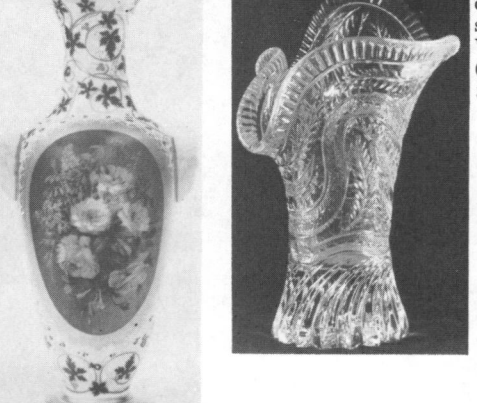

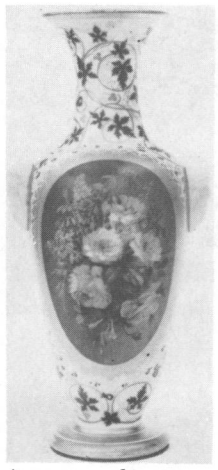

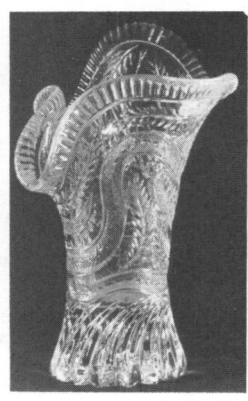

An unusual vase cut to imitate rock crystal and engraved with entwined snakes, signed 'E. Wood', Thomas Webb & Co., early 20thC, 9in (23cm).
$400-500

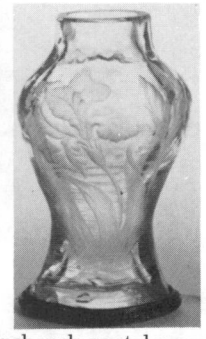

An engraved opaque white glass vase, decorated with an oval panel of summer flowers, on scrolling green and gilt foliage ground, mid-19thC, 24in (61cm).
$1,300-1,800

A pair of French rock crystal vases, engraved with flowers and foliage, the spreading bases with giltmetal borders, stamped 'E.Enot Paris', 7in (17.5cm).
$900-1,300

A Bohemian white overlay ruby glass comport, with integral cylindrical support, boldly painted with 2 bands of roses in enamel colours, on a gold decorated ground, 13½in (34cm).
$600-900

Miscellaneous

An unusual pair of oval salts, with looped, flute and prism cutting on star cut bases, c1790, 3½in (9.5cm) diam.
$100-200

A small Irish cut butter dish, stand and cover, body with looped prism cut decoration and fan cut ends, c1790, stand 7½in (18.5cm) diam.
$750-1,000

A comport, with star cut foot and mushroom finial to lid, c1830, 7½in (18.5cm).
$100-200

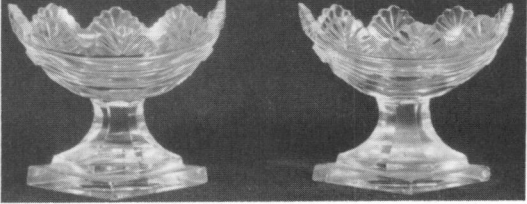

A pair of oval cut salts with prism cut bowls and fan cut rims, on diamond shaped bases, c1800, 4in (10cm) diam.
$150-250

l. A small lacemaker's lamp with plain stem and folded conical foot, c1760, 3½in (9cm).
$150-250

r. A lacemaker's lamp with drip pan, knopped stem and handle, c1800, 6in (15cm).
$300-400

A butter dish, cover and stand, with diamond and flute cutting, the cover with mushroom knop, c1825, dish 6in (15.5cm) diam.
$250-350

A pressed glass coffee jar in brown malachite vitro-porcelain by Henry Greener of Sunderland, marked, the finial in the form of a coffee bean, c1880, 6in (15cm).
$100-200

A matchstriker in brown malachite vitro-porcelain by George Davidson of Gateshead, Trade Mark, c1885, 3½in (9cm).
$75-150

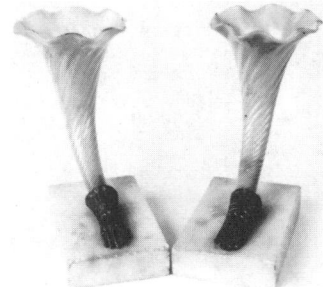

A pair of cornucopia on marble bases, unusual blue, 7in (17cm).
$450-700

A turquoise enamelled glass tazza, 19thC, 7in (18cm) diam.
$100-200

A Palais Royale ruby-stained casket with giltmetal mounts, handles and scroll feet, the cover applied with a plaque painted with ladies and gentlemen, 5in (12cm) wide.
$750-1,000

Top A potichomania rolling pin, decorated with 'The New Novel', a girl reading a book, and with figures and a verse, 12½in (32cm).
$60-100

c. A potichomania rolling pin, profusely decorated with soldiers, sailors, policemen, female figures and animals, 17in (43.5cm).
$75-150

Bottom An opaque white rolling pin, with wave pattern in blue and pink, 13in (33.5cm).
$60-100

A gadrooned oil lamp for 6 burners, mid-18thC.
$1,500-2,600

A large hexagonal inkwell with hinged lid.
$75-150

Top A pipe of opaque white glass, with a waved design in red and blue, the stem with 3 knops, 18in (46cm).
$100-150

Bottom A ruby glass pipe with a combed wave pattern in opaque white, with 3 knops in the stem, 14½in (37cm).
$75-150

A model of a ship in clear, opaque white and pink spun glass, with 3 sailors in blue and red in the rigging, a small ship and a lighthouse, 12½in (32cm), with a glass dome and base.
$300-400

Top A 'yard of ale' in ruby glass, with spherical base and funnel mouth, 36in (91cm).
$60-100

Bottom A 'coaching horn' in dark blue glass with baluster end, 40in (103cm).
$150-200

Prices

The never-ending problem of fixing prices for antiques! A price can be affected by so many factors, for example:
- *condition*
- *desirability*
- *rarity*
- *size*
- *colour*
- *provenance*
- *restoration*
- *the sale of a prestigious collection*
- *collection label*
- *appearance of a new reference book*
- *new specialist sale at major auction house*
- *mentioned on television*
- *the fact that two people present at auction are determined to have the piece*
- *where you buy it*

One also has to contend with the fact that an antique is not only a 'thing of beauty' but a commodity. The price can again be affected by:
- *supply and demand*
- *international finance – currency fluctuation*
- *fashion*
- *inflation*
- *the fact that a museum has vast sums of money to spend*

Oak & Country Furniture

TURNED TABLE LEGS
CENTURY

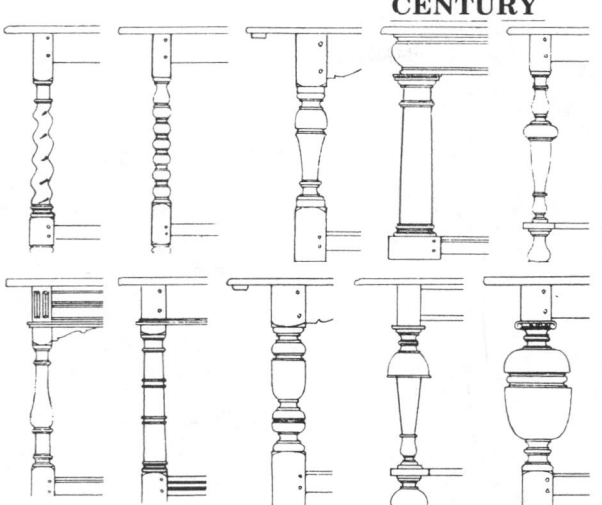

MONARCH CHRONOLOGY

Dates	Monarchs	Period
1558-1603	Elizabeth I	Elizabethan
1603-1625	James I	Jacobean
1625-1649	Charles I	Carolean
1649-1660	Commonwealth	Cromwellian
1660-1685	Charles II	Restoration
1685-1689	James II	Restoration
1689-1694	William & Mary	William & Mary
1694-1702	William III	William III
1702-1714	Anne	Queen Anne
1714-1727	George I	Early Georgian
1727-1760	George II	Georgian
1760-1812	George III	Late Georgian
1812-1820	George III	Regency
1820-1830	George IV	Late Regency
1830-1837	William IV	William IV
1837-1860	Victoria	Early Victorian
1860-1901	Victoria	Late Victorian
1901-1910	Edward VII	Edwardian

Bureaux

A Queen Anne burr-walnut bureau, inlaid with feather bandings, with a fitted interior, on later bracket feet, 35in (89cm).
$4,000-5,500

A small walnut bureau, early 18thC.
$7,500-10,500

A George I pollard oak bureau, cross and herringbone banded, with fitted interior, 37½in (95cm).
$4,000-5,500

A Queen Anne walnut bureau, with crossbanded sloping flap enclosing a re-fitted interior, later bracket feet and back, 32½in (82.5cm).
$4,000-5,500

A George I oak bureau crossbanded with walnut, with secret locking drawers and original brasses, c1725.
$5,500-7,000

A George I oak bureau, on later bracket feet, 36in (91cm).
$3,000-4,500

An early Georgian walnut and featherbanded bureau, the hinged slope enclosing a fitted interior and well, on bracket feet, 33in (84cm).
$7,000-9,000

An oak bureau, early 18thC.
$1,500-2,600

A George III oak bureau, the fall flap with mitred edges enclosing a panel with burrwood crossbanding and inlaid with a central star motif enclosing a fitted interior, inlaid with burrwood bands and on bracket feet, restored, 37in (94cm).
$1,500-2,600

An oak and mahogany crossbanded bureau, with mahogany fitted interior, 18thC, 42in (107cm).
$1,300-1,800

A walnut bureau, with fully fitted interior and secret drawers, c1730, 38½in (97cm).
$4,500-7,000

A George III oak bureau, with fall front writing slope enclosing a fitted interior, 39in (99cm).
$1,300-1,800

A George III yew and walnut veneered bureau, restored.
$1,500-2,600

Cabinets

An oak bureau, with fitted interior, on bracket feet, c1780, 36in (91cm).
$1,500-2,600

An oak bureau, with a fitted interior and well, 18thC, 34in (86cm).
$1,500-2,600

A Georgian oak cabinet on block feet, 75in (190.5cm).
$1,500-2,600

A Charles II oak cabinet with adapted dentilled top, 43in (109cm).
$2,500-3,500

An unusual walnut marquetry and oak bureau, the inlaid fall flap enclosing a fitted interior, the marquetry Dutch, 17thC, 35½in (90cm).
$3,000-4,500

A William and Mary oak escritoire, the upper section with a cushion moulded drawer, the fall enclosing an interior of drawers around a cupboard, 41½in (105cm).
$3,000-4,000

A rare Jacobean oak child's armchair, the crest rail with initials 'E.H.', the solid seat late 17thC.
$1,500-2,600

A Charles II carved oak armchair, c1685.
$3,000-4,000

A set of 5 Charles II walnut side chairs.
$2,250-3,000

A William and Mary walnut chair, c1690.
$1,000-1,400

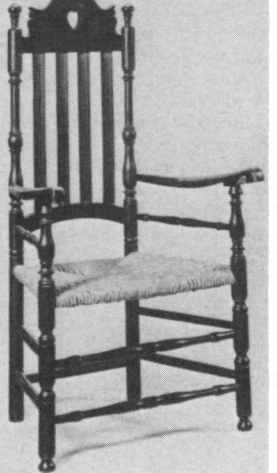

A black painted bannister back armchair, on baluster and ring turned legs, joined by turned stretchers.
$1,200-1,600

A rare Charles II mulberry armchair, c1680.
$5,500-7,000

A pair of Lancashire carved oak side chairs, c1700.
$2,250-3,500

A pair of oak wainscot armchairs, parts 17thC.
$1,200-1,600

This price reflects the enormous amount of restoration and reconstruction on these chairs.

A maple slat back child's armchair, with 3 arched slats flanked by turned stiles with lemon shaped finials, above a trapezoidal rush seat, on cylindrical legs joined by a box stretcher, feet reduced, American, 19thC, 24in (61cm) high.
$350-450

An oak chair, 17thC, 19in (48cm).
$450-700

A James II walnut open armchair, the green velvet-covered seat formerly caned, re-railed.
$2,250-3,500

A yew Windsor elbow chair, 18thC, 19in (48cm).
$1,300-1,800

A green painted sack back Windsor child's armchair, with bowed crest rail, continuing to shaped arms with turned supports over a shaped seat, stamped twice H. Cate, American, 19thC, 27in (68cm) high.
$9,000-11,000

A continuous arm Windsor armchair, with arched crest above 9 bamboo turned spindles, on bamboo turned legs joined by swelled H stretcher, repair to back, Pennsylvania, early 19thC, 35in (89cm) high.
$800-1,200

A green painted bow back side chair, with 9 tapering rods, the seat on vase and ring turned legs joined by a bulbous H stretcher, stamped twice S. Tucke, Boston, c1790, 36½in (92cm) high.
$1,500-2,000

A child's Windsor rocker, late 18thC.
$300-500

A primitive Welsh chair, c1780.
$1,000-1,400

A child's Welsh comb-back chair, c1780.
$1,300-1,800

A comb back Windsor armchair, the serpentine crest with scrolled ears above 7 spindles over a curved armrail with scrolling grips, on baluster and ring turned legs joined by a swelled H stretcher, seat once fitted as a commode, Pennsylvania, c1780, 44in (112cm) high.
$1,800-2,200

A West Country Windsor armchair, c1800.
$600-900

A set of 6 fancy painted thumb back
Windsor side chairs, each painted
grey with floral rectangular crest,
on bamboo turned legs joined by box
stretchers, American, early 19thC,
33½in (85cm) high.
$1,500-2,000

A pair of bow back Windsor side
chairs, by Ebenezer Tracy, Lisbon,
Connecticut, on bamboo turned
swelled H stretchers, c1780, 37½in
(95cm) high.
$1,700-2,000

A Shaker side chair,
marked Shaker's No.3.
Mt. Lebanon, NY,
early 20thC,
41in (104cm) high.
$400-600

A bow back Windsor side chair, with
a moulded seat on bamboo turned
legs, joined by a swelled H stretcher,
stamped Sanborn, Boston, late
18thC, 37½in (95cm) high.
$900-1,200

A set of 6 black painted Windsor
side chairs, each with a shaped crest
with gilt outline on a black ground,
above a slightly scooped seat on
bamboo turned legs, joined by a box
stretcher, the underside of the seat
stamped J R Hunt, Maker,
restorations to paint, New England,
c1820, 17in (43cm).
$3,500-4,500

A black painted bow back Windsor
side chair, by Ebenezer Tracy,
Lisbon, Ct, the upholstered seat
above vase and reel-turned legs
joined by a bulbous H stretcher, the
bottom impressed with EB. Tracy,
c1790, 39in (99cm) high.
$1,500-2,000

A set of 6 oak country dining chairs
with drop-in rush seats, 19thC.
$1,300-1,800

A Shaker slat back rocking
armchair, with turned shawl bar
over 4 arched and shaped slats, over
a rush seat, on cylindrical legs,
joined by a double box stretcher, on
rockers, stamped Shaker's
trademark No.6, Mt. Lebanon, New
York, late 19thC, 41in (104cm) high.
$1,500-1,700

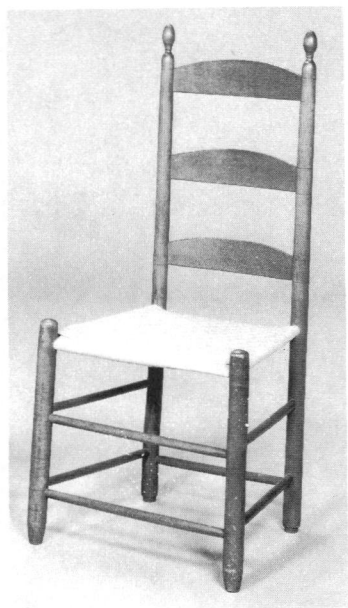

A Shaker side chair, with a taped seat, on cylindrical legs joined by a double box stretcher, marked Shaker's No.3. Mt. Lebanon, NY, early 20thC, 41in (104cm) high.
$800-1,000

A carved and turned maple rocking armchair, with straight turned crest rail above 7 turned spindles, with baluster turned arm supports above a splint seat over cylindrical legs, joined by a double box stretcher, on rockers, splits to legs, probably Enterprise Chair Manufacturing Company, Oxford New York, late 19thC, 37in (94cm) high.
$900-1,200

A Shaker maple slat back side chair, with a taped seat, on cylindrical legs joined by a double box stretcher, rear legs with original tilters, probably Enfield, Connecticut, mid-19thC, 40½in (103cm) high.
$1,500-2,500

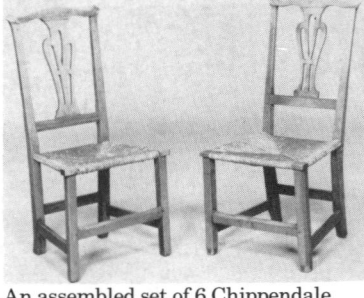

An assembled set of 6 Chippendale maple side chairs, each with shaped crest and moulded ears above a pierced vase shaped splat, feet damaged, New England, c1770, 40½in (102cm) high.
$2,000-2,300

A Shaker slat back rocking armchair, with baluster shaped arm supports, over a taped seat above cylindrical legs joined by a double box stretcher, on rockers, Mt Lebanon, New York, late 19thC, 32½in (82cm) high.
$500-800

A Shaker slat back rocking armchair, with shaped arm rests ending in mushroom carved hand holds above tapered arm supports over a padded seat, the legs joined by a double box stretcher, on rockers, retains original black paint, probably New York, early 19thC, 43in (109cm) high.
$8,500-10,000

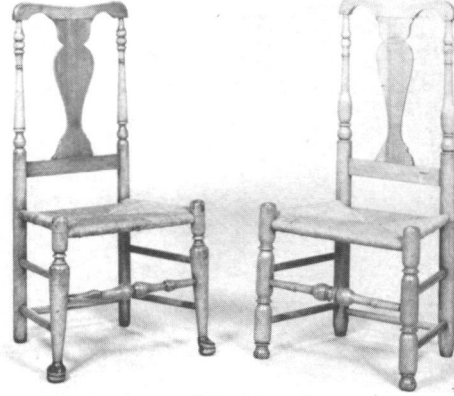

An assembled pair of 'York' maple side chairs, each with a yoke crest above a vase shaped splat, on cylindrical ring turned legs joined by box stretchers, with pad and disc feet, New England, 18thC, 41in (104cm) high.
$800-1,200

A pair of William and Mary bannister back maple side chairs, each with shaped crest rail, on baluster and block turned legs joined by a shaped double box stretcher, restoration and repairs to splats, New England, c1720, 42in (106.5cm) high.
$1,800-2,300

A rare George III child's box settle, c1800.
$2,250-3,000

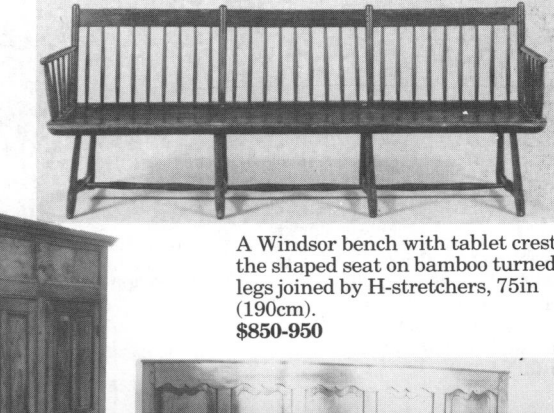

A Windsor bench with tablet crest, the shaped seat on bamboo turned legs joined by H-stretchers, 75in (190cm).
$850-950

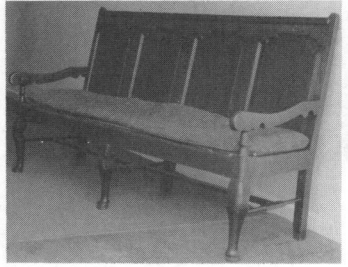

A Georgian country oak settle, on cabriole legs with pad feet.
$300-400

A free-standing figured elm bacon settle, the slightly overhanging upper part with 2 doors to a cupboard, with a drawer in the base, 18thC.
$2,250-3,500

A North Country settle in oak and fruitwood, crossbanded with walnut, early 19thC, 72in (182.5cm).
$750-1,000

Chests

A rare inlaid James I oak coffer, c1620.
$7,500-10,500

An oak coffer, with original lock plate and hinges, early 17thC.
$1,200-1,600

A small rare Charles I elm carved plank coffer, c1640.
$4,000-5,500

A fine Charles I block fronted oak mule chest, c1640.
$2,250-3,500

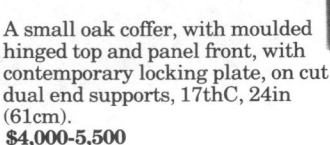

A small oak coffer, with moulded hinged top and panel front, with contemporary locking plate, on cut dual end supports, 17thC, 24in (61cm).
$4,000-5,500

A rare Charles II oak coffer with drawer, decorated with split baluster mouldings, c1675.
$4,000-5,500

A Commonwealth oak coffer, the panelled top above a vigorously carved frieze, with the date 1653, the three-panel front similarly carved, 57in (145cm).
$1,000-1,400

An oak chest with carving, mid-17thC, 36in (91cm).
$700-900

A small Charles II oak arcaded coffer, c1685.
$1,500-2,600

An oak and walnut coffer with parquetry inlay, 17thC.
$750-1,000

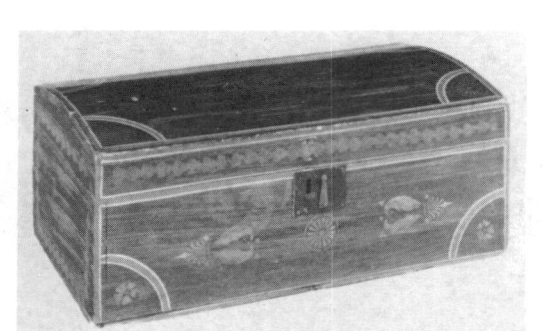

A small stencilled maple trunk, the dome top grain painted centering a gold stencilled floral decoration, American, mid-19thC, 24in (61cm).
$700-900

An oak carved panelled coffer, c1680.
$1,500-2,600

An early Georgian oak linen chest, with floral marquetry panelled front, sectionalised lid, the interior complete with candlebox and 2 small drawers, 56in (142cm).
$900-1,300

An oak panelled and planked coffer, c1680.
$1,500-2,600

A three-panelled oak coffer, c1760.
$800-1,200 ▶

A Queen Anne oak chest ▲ of drawers, veneered with figured ash and crossbanded with walnut, c1710.
$5,500-7,000

A Lake District panelled, lozenge-carved coffer, c1680.
$1,300-1,800

A Jacobean oak chest, with 4 · drawers and Stuart drop handles.
$600-900

An oak chest, the drawers with geometrically moulded panels, c1680.
$1,000-1,400

A crossbanded oak chest, early 18thC.
$1,200-1,600

A George I oak chest on original stand, c1725.
$5,500-7,000

A William and Mary walnut and oak chest, the plank top with an ogee cornice above 2 short and 3 long graduated crossbanded drawers, on later bun feet, 39½in (100cm).
$1,500-2,600

A George I oak chest of drawers, crossbanded with pearwood, c1725.
$2,500-3,500

An oak chest on stand, with geometrical applied mouldings to front, shaped stretcher to base, 17thC.
$1,000-1,400

An oak chest of drawers, 18thC, with later handles, 37in (94cm).
$750-1,000

A Norfolk style oak chest of drawers, with centre cupboard enclosing 3 smaller drawers with chamfered and reeded sides and pierced Georgian brass handles and escutcheons, the drawer faces veneered with walnut and inlaid with boxwood stringing, on bracket feet, 30in (76cm).
$2,250-3,000

An oak tallboy chest in 2 sections, the drawers crossbanded in walnut and fitted with ornate pierced brass plate handles, with dentil cornice, on bracket feet, 18thC, 46in (117cm).
$1,500-2,600

A George II oak chest on stand, with quartered columns of burr oak and original brasses, c1750.
$7,000-9,000

A small George II oak chest on stand, inlaid with yew-wood, with original brasses, possibly Welsh, c1745.
$7,500-10,500

An oak court cupboard decorated with carved foliate panels, lozenges and fluted pilasters, the lower section with a fall flap, on plinth base, 17thC and later, 57in (144.5cm).
$1,500-2,600

A Westmorland oak press cupboard, the overhanging frieze dated '1693' with incised S-scroll, enclosed by similar panel doors between projecting spirally turned columns, with cupboard below, late 17thC, 73½in (186cm).
$4,000-5,500

Cupboards

An oak food cupboard with lunette-carved frieze, early 17thC, 50in (127cm).
$5,500-7,000

A Queen Anne oak press cupboard with original carved cornice, initialled 'I.W.', dated '1712'.
$5,500-7,000

An oak court or press cupboard, the central panel sliding to reveal 3 secret drawers, 17thC, with later cornice, 58in (147cm).
$4,000-5,500

A Lancashire carved oak press cupboard, initialled 'I.F.', dated 1716.
$6,000-8,000

A dark oak court or press cupboard, repairs, 17thC, 73in (185cm).
$1,500-2,600

A William and Mary gumwood kas, in 2 sections, the upper part with 2 panelled cupboard doors enclosing a shelved interior with one small drawer, the lower section with a single long drawer panelled to resemble 2 drawers, on ball turned feet, New York, c1735, 54in (137cm).
$4,000-5,000

An oak court cupboard, deeply carved with geometric moulded doors and drawers, on stile feet.
$3,000-4,500

A George II oak press with doors enclosing shelves, above 3 short and 2 long drawers, on ogee bracket feet, 53in (134.5cm).
$2,250-3,000

A Queen Anne oak press cupboard, inlaid with date and marriage initials, dated 1704.
$6,000-8,000

A Welsh oak deudarn, the stiles forming the feet, 18thC, 53in (134.5cm).
$2,250-3,000

An oak hall cupboard, with mahogany banding, c1740.
$4,500-7,000

An oak press cupboard, with a pair of triple fielded panel cupboard doors above 2 mock and 2 short drawers, on bracket feet, the sides with fielded panels, restorations, mid-18thC, 62in (157cm).
$900-1,300

A North Wales oak press cupboard, with fielded arched panels to front, 18thC.
$1,000-1,400

An oak court cupboard, restorations, mid-18thC, 62½in (159cm).
$1,000-1,400

A rare oak estate cupboard, with 2 panelled doors enclosing a secret drawer and pigeonholes, the concave waist moulding concealing a long drawer, early 18thC, 30in (76cm).
$800-1,200

A Carmarthen oak chest, with 4 shaped door panels to top, standing on 5 drawer base with bracket feet.
$1,500-2,600

An early oak bread and cheese cupboard, with ventilation slats to upper cupboards.
$1,500-2,600

A Georgian oak housekeeper's cupboard, the top section mahogany crossbanded with raised astragal mould and shell motif, the lower section crossbanded and with black string, original feet replaced, c1800, 86in (218.5cm).
$2,250-3,000

An oak food and spice cupboard, with ventilated doors above 2 drawers and cupboards, on stile feet.
$1,500-2,600

A gumwood kas, in 3 sections, the middle section with 2 panelled cupboard doors with applied moulded ebonized reserves opening to a fitted interior with 3 shelves, the lower section with applied mid-moulding above a long drawer, with applied moulded ebonized panels, small moulding strip replaced, Long Island, New York, 18thC, 74½in (188cm).
$7,000-9,000

A rare small George III oak hanging cupboard, c1770.
$7,000-9,000 ▶

A small George III oak standing corner cupboard, c1775.
$4,000-5,500

An oak and mahogany cupboard, with ogee cornice and one shelf interior, and mahogany twist reeded columns, turned knobs, 5 panelled ends, on bracket feet, early 19thC, 50in (127cm).
$600-900

A George II pine, grained oak architectural full length corner cupboard, with beehive blocked domed top and fitted with 4 shaped shelves, the 2 lower panelled doors revealing an open space, the fluted superstructure with scrolls and applied moulding, 48in (122cm).
$3,000-4,500

An oak housekeeper's cupboard, mahogany-banded with cove cornice, 4 panel doors with shell motifs and black string arched inlay, the base with fluted quarter columns with brass capitals, on turned feet, late 18thC, 78in (198cm).
$4,000-5,500

A French provincial walnut and oak armoire, the scrolling apron centred by a flower, on squat cabriole legs and scroll feet, early 19thC, 61½in (156cm).
$2,250-3,000

A George III oak standing corner cupboard.
$300-500

A Georgian oak hanging corner cupboard, with fitted interior enclosed by 2 framed and fielded shaped top panel doors with brass H-hinges, above a shaped apron, 54in (137cm) high.
$600-900

A Georgian oak standing corner cupboard, with a pair of arched raised panel doors, above similar smaller doors, 46in (116.5cm).
$1,500-2,600

A Yorkshire oak dresser base of good colour and patination, the 3 frieze drawers above 2 central drawers, flanked on either side by panelled doors to cupboards, 18thC, 71in (180cm).
$4,000-5,500

A George I oak baluster turned dresser base in original condition, c1725.
$7,000-9,000

Dressers

An oak dresser base, 17thC, 70½in (178cm).
$4,500-7,000

A Charles II oak low dresser, with moulded elm plank top above 3 drawers with applied roundel mouldings, deep moulded frieze, on baluster turned front supports, 64½in (164cm).
$3,000-4,500

A very small George I oak dresser base with baluster turned legs, c1720.
$13,500-17,500

An oak dresser base, with 7 drawers and a central cupboard, 18thC.
$3,000-4,500

A William and Mary oak low dresser, the plank top with moulded edge above 3 geometrically panelled frieze drawers, on baluster turned and square section legs, alterations and restoration, 65in (165cm).
$3,000-4,500

An oak dresser, with 4 frieze drawers with brass swan neck handles and escutcheons, standing on cabriole supports with pad feet, 73in (185cm).
$1,500-2,600

An oak dresser with moulded rim to the plank form top, the 3 drawers with brass swan neck handles and pierced back plates, the arched fielded panel and doors enclosing a shelved interior, early 18thC, 68in (172.5cm).
$2,500-3,500

A Georgian oak dresser base, with 3 fitted frieze drawers above 2 doors and central section, all with bevelled panels, on stile feet, probably originally with rack, 56½in (143cm).
$2,500-3,500

An oak dresser base, with 3 drawers, crossbanded top and standing on cabriole legs with pad feet.
$1,500-2,600

A George II oak low dresser, with a deep moulded top above 3 drawers with cockbeading and mahogany crossbanding, brass swan neck handles and escutcheons, 75in (191cm).
$3,000-4,500

A Georgian oak dresser base, the drawers with pierced brass escutcheons and swan neck handles, with carved frieze and raised on front cabriole legs with ball and claw feet, 66in (167cm).
$600-900

A George II oak low dresser, 56in (142cm).
$1,500-2,600

An oak low dresser, with crossbanded front, some restoration, mid-18thC, 79in (200cm).
$3,000-4,500

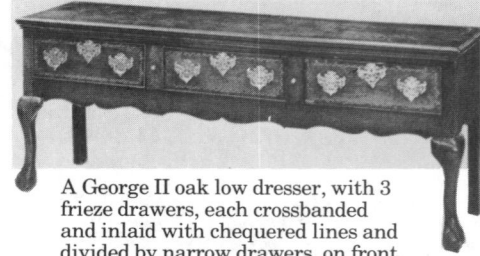

A Georgian provincial oak dresser base, with plate ledge back and 2 frieze drawers with brass handles, above a shaped apron joined by a potboard, 60in (152cm).
$800-1,200

A George II oak low dresser, with 3 frieze drawers, each crossbanded and inlaid with chequered lines and divided by narrow drawers, on front cabriole supports with ball and claw feet, 72½in (184cm).
$4,500-7,000

A George II oak dresser base.
$4,000-5,500

A George II oak dresser, with 3 spice drawers, shaped interior shelf and bracket feet, 78in (198cm).
$1,500-2,600

A George III oak dresser base, on cabriole legs, crossbanded with mahogany, c1790.
$5,500-7,000

A fine oak breakfront dresser, 18thC.
$5,500-7,000

A Welsh oak dresser, 64in (162.5cm).
$4,000-5,500

A George III oak low dresser, with 2 frieze drawers above a waved apron and 3 front turned supports, joined by a pot shelf and on later feet, possibly originally with a rack, 52in (132cm).
$1,500-2,600

A George III North Wales cupboard ▲ dresser, in original condition, c1760.
$10,000-12,000

A North Wales oak dresser, with 4 drawers and 2 cupboards, shaped fielded panels and bellied rack, 18thC.
$5,500-7,000

An oak mahogany-banded dresser with rack, on ogee feet, late 18thC, 72in (182.5cm).
$1,500-2,600

A George III Lancashire oak dresser, with an arched fielded panel door below a drawer, flanked by 6 graduated long drawers, on bracket feet, 72in (182.5cm).
$3,000-4,500

A small George III oak cupboard dresser, with spoon slots in top shelf, North Wales, c1760.
$10,000-12,000

An oak dresser, on square cabriole legs and pad feet, mid-18thC, 78in (198cm).
$6,000-8,000

An oak dresser, with pine boarded back, late 18thC, 67in (170cm).
$4,500-7,000

A George III oak potboard dresser, c1800, 63in (160cm).
$6,000-8,000

An oak dresser, with 6 drawers and cupboards.
$3,000-4,500

A late Georgian oak dresser, with a plate rack below a moulded cornice, 3 frieze drawers above a central panel flanked by 2 panelled doors, on shaped bracket feet, 64in (162.5cm).
$4,500-7,000

A Welsh oak dresser, with filled-in rack, drawers and cupboards underneath.
$3,000-4,000

An Anglesey breakfront oak dresser, with 6 drawers and 2 cupboards, c1810, 68in (172.5cm).
$4,000-5,500

An oak dresser, with 3 drawers with brass drop handles and 3 cupboards below an open plate rack, on bracket feet, 19thC, 77in (195.5cm).
$2,250-3,000

An oak dresser and rack, crossbanded with mahogany, early 19thC.
$2,250-3,500

◀

A Regency oak dresser, inlaid with geometric and radial boxwood lines in mahogany banded borders, adaptations, 83in (210.5cm).
$4,500-7,000

Stools

A tiger maple foot stool, with rectangular top above board feet, 17in (43cm).
$300-500

A rare pair of Charles I oak joint stools, c1640.
$6,000-8,000

An oak child's joint stool, dated 1643, 15½in (39cm).
$3,000-4,000

A rare oak child's joint stool, very good colour, mid-17thC, 13in (33cm).
$1,500-2,600

An oak joint stool, with moulded frieze and stretchers, 18½in (47cm).
$1,500-2,600

A carved oak joint stool, on bobbin turned legs, 17thC, 17in (44cm).
$1,000-1,400

An oak joint stool in original condition, c1660.
$1,200-1,600

An oak coffin stool, initialled 'W.C.', late 17thC, 18½in (46.5cm).
$2,250-3,000

An oak joint stool, on slightly outsplayed legs joined by moulded stretchers with bun feet, 18in (46cm).
$750-1,000

Tables

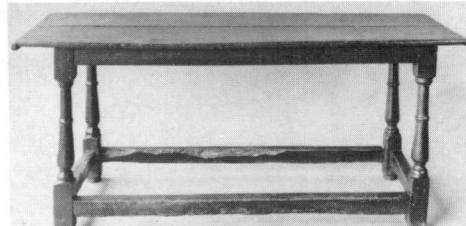

A Charles II oak side serving table, the 2 planked top raised on 4 turned baluster supports with narrow frieze, joined by square stretchers, 65½in (166cm).
$3,000-4,000

A Charles II style oak refectory table, the plank top above a foliate lunette carved frieze, on 6 massive spiral turned columns joined by floor stretcher, late 19thC, 127in (319cm).
$3,000-4,000

An oak refectory style side table with carved frieze and 6 turned legs, 17thC, 125in (317.5cm).
$25,500-36,000

An oak refectory table, with plank top above plain trestle end supports joined by a wide high stretcher, 17thC, 99½in (252cm).
$2,250-3,000

An oak refectory table, the frieze carved with foliate scrolls on one side, mid-17thC, 85½in (217cm).
$3,000-4,500

◄ An Italian walnut refectory table, with oak chamfered trestle ends, 17thC, 106in (269cm).
$6,000-9,000

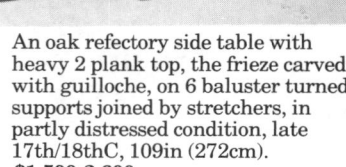

An oak refectory side table with heavy 2 plank top, the frieze carved with guilloche, on 6 baluster turned supports joined by stretchers, in partly distressed condition, late 17th/18thC, 109in (272cm).
$1,500-2,600

A Charles II oak drop-leaf gateleg table, with frieze drawer and silhouette gates, raised on turned baluster supports united with stretchers, 60in (152cm) fully extended.
$4,500-7,000

A Charles II oak gateleg table, 36in (91.5cm).
$600-900

A Charles II oak gateleg table with twin-flap and frieze drawer on spirally-turned supports and stretchers on later bun feet, some later supports, 71½in (181cm) open. ►
$6,000-9,000

An oak gateleg dining table, with 2 frieze drawers on baluster legs joined with cross stretchers, late 17thC, 63in (160cm) extended.
$2,250-3,000

An oak bobbin-turned gateleg table, c1685.
$7,500-10,500

A small Queen Anne oak trestle gateleg table, c1710.
$2,250-3,500 ►

A Charles II oak side table, c1680, 36in (91.5cm).
$600-900

A Charles II oak side table, c1680.
$4,000-5,500

A rare oak side table, c1690, 32in ►
(81cm).
$5,500-7,000

An oak side table, late 17thC, 32in (81cm).
$6,000-8,000

An oak hall table, with drawer, bobbin legs, and 4 plain stretchers, late 17thC, 33in (84cm).
$2,250-3,000

An oak side table with turned stretchers, late 17thC, 32in (81cm).
$3,000-4,500

A small oak side table, c1700, 32in (81cm).
$3,000-4,000

A Queen Anne oak side table, with moulded top and one drawer, on 4 slender cabriole supports with pad feet, 31in (79cm).
$1,000-1,400

A Queen Anne oak and pearwood side table, c1710.
$1,500-2,600

A George I burr oak lowboy, one short and 2 deep drawers with stringing in the fret-carved apron, on angular cabriole legs with scroll spandrels and pointed pad feet, 33in (84cm).
$6,000-9,000

A George I oak side table, inlaid with mahogany bands, feet replaced, 51½in (130cm).
$1,000-1,400

An oak lowboy, c1730, 33in (84cm).
$4,000-5,500

A small George I oak side table with 'H' stretcher, c1720.
$1,500-2,600

A George II oak lowboy on cabriole legs, with original brasses, c1735.
$4,000-5,500

A George II oak side table with overlapping top, the front with one long drawer and 2 small drawers in a waved apron inlaid with fruitwood lines and trailing flowers, on 4 cabriole supports, restored, 30½in (77.5cm).
$1,500-2,600

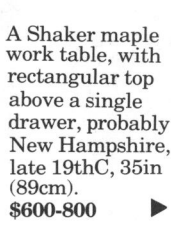

A Shaker maple work table, with rectangular top above a single drawer, probably New Hampshire, late 19thC, 35in (89cm).
$600-800 ▶

An oak dressing table or lowboy, c1760, 31in (79cm).
$3,000-4,500

An oak lowboy with shaped apron, on square legs.
$750-1,000

An oak lowboy, 18thC, 35½in (91cm).
$750-1,000

A George II oak tripod table with oak leaf carved knees and paw feet, c1745.
$1,500-2,600

A Welsh oak cricket table, 18thC.
$450-700

A George III oak dished top tripod table, c1775.
$1,000-1,400

A George III oak and elm cricket table with shelf, c1800.
$800-1,200

An oak credence table, with a semi-circular fold-over top above a deep frieze and 3 turned bulbous supports, one rear leg dividing to form the gate action support for the top, 34in (86cm).
$1,500-2,600

A Federal walnut splay leg tea table, the rectangular top with cusped corners above a plain apron, old crack to top, Valley of Virginia, c1810, 21in (53cm).
$3,000-3,500

A black painted chest, the exterior painted with gold and red birds, stars and urns, the interior lined with mid-19thC newspaper, New England, mid-19thC, 19in (48cm).
$1,500-2,000

A miniature Federal mahogany picture mirror, with a picture panel enclosing a coloured print, flanked by reeded half columns, on a moulded base, American, 19thC, 9½in (24cm).
$1,200-1,500

An early oak hanging spice cupboard, the panelled door with tulip inlay in ebony and holly, the interior with 7 drawers and 3 pigeonholes.
$600-900

Two miniature painted side chairs, l. A New York style green painted slat back chair, the central slat pierced, above a balloon rush seat, on ring turned legs, 8in (20cm) high and r. A slat back chair with yellow stencil decoration above a square rush seat on tapering cylindrical legs, 10in (25.5cm) high.
$600-700

A Shaker maple chair seat taper's work bench, the rectangular top with 2 clamps, American, 19thC, 18in (46cm).
$300-500

A miniature painted bannister back armchair, with shaped splats, flanked by baluster turned finials above ring turned stiles, restorations to the splat, one stretcher and paint, American, 19thC, 9½in (24cm) high.
$500-550

A miniature painted maple blanket chest, the black painted rectangular top with gilt decoration above a conforming case, with painted decoration on a shaped apron with flared bracket feet, American, 19thC, 6½in (16.5cm).
$1,500-2,000

A miniature Federal mahogany four-post bedstead with canopy, with a shaped headboard flanked by square tapering head posts, the footposts baluster and ring turned, American, 19thC, 15½in (39cm) high.
$300-500

Beds

An oak day bed of William and Mary style, with caned seat and russet buttoned velvet squab cushion, 72in (183cm).
$750-1,000

In the Furniture section if there is only one measurement it usually refers to the width of the piece

An Adam style mahogany inlaid four-poster bed, complete with turquoise floral drapes.
$2,500-3,500

A mahogany four-poster bed, with moulded dentilled tester, with box spring and mattress covered in pale green repp, 18thC and later, 54½in (138cm).
$10,500-14,000

A late Federal carved cherrywood four-poster bedstead, the double-panelled headboard with a shaped crest, probably New York, c1825, 53in (135cm).
$6,000-7,000

A late Federal carved birch four-poster tester bedstead, the 4 posts each reeded with double balusters above baluster turned legs, the head posts tapering octagonal, headboard restored, North Shore, Massachusetts, c1810, 54½in (138cm).
$7,000-9,000

A giltwood four-poster bed with padded headrest, on claw feet headed by acanthus scrolls, c1830, 64in (162cm).
$10,500-14,000

A William IV mahogany double bed, the panelled footrest with a coat-of-arms, the square ends with bud finials on shaped feet carved with acanthus, 73in (185cm).
$4,500-7,000

The arms are those of Pawson impaling Hargrave.

A maple lowpost bed, with baluster and ring turned head and footposts centering a shaped headboard and turned footboard, New England, mid-19thC, 49½in (124.5cm).
$650-750

A mahogany and parcel gilt day bed, upholstered in floral material, in an eagle carved frame with fluted seat rail, on claw and ball feet, 93in (236cm).
$1,200-1,600

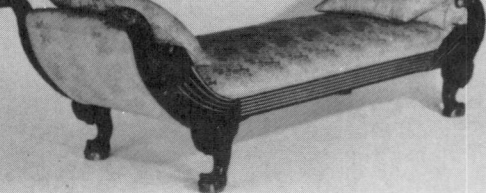

A Victorian reclining ottoman day bed, the brass hinges stamped 'Parker's Patent'.
$1,000-1,400

An Empire mahogany bed, inlaid
with brass musical trophies on an
ebony ground, 44in (111cm).
$2,250-3,000

A Portuguese rosewood bed, with
pierced open headboard, the shaped
spirally-turned uprights with
bulbous finials, the footrest with
conforming uprights, one finial
partly replaced, with box spring,
18thC, 42in (106cm).
$3,000-4,500 ▶

An Empire mahogany 'lit-en-
bateau' with chased ormolu
capitals, 48in (122cm).
$4,500-7,000

A parcel gilt and white painted day
bed, of neo-classical style, the
drop-in seat covered in a grey silk,
the open arms with winged sphinx
supports, 65in (165cm).
$4,000-5,500

A Dutch mahogany
and marquetry
cradle, 19thC,
23½in (60cm).
$2,250-3,000

A French kingwood
veneered bed,
with Sèvres style
porcelain mounted
panels, 19thC,
58in (147cm).
$4,000-5,500

Bonheur du jour

A mid-Victorian gilt metal mounted
kingwood bonheur du jour, the top
drawer inlaid 'a quatre face', the
frieze drawer with leather-lined
slide on foliate cabriole legs
reaching to conforming sabots, 28in
(71cm).
$1,500-2,600

A George III mahogany bonheur du
jour, with baize-lined folding flap
and one frieze drawer, 30in (76cm).
$4,500-7,000

A George III kingwood bonheur du
jour, with pierced brass latticework
panel, the quarter-veneered frieze
drawer on turned tapering legs,
18in (46cm).
$3,000-4,000

An Edwardian rosewood, ivory and
satinwood marquetry inlaid
bonheur du jour, with leather-lined
serpentine front surface, the inlay
depicting winged amorini,
mythological beasts and
cornucopiae, 36in (91cm).
$1,500-2,600

A Louis XV style tulipwood bonheur du jour, inlaid with foliate marquetry sprays and arabesques of various woods and applied with gilt metal mounts, engraved 'L.Grade, R. de la Paix 23. Paris', 31in (79cm).
$5,500-7,000

An Edwardian marquetry inlaid mahogany bonheur du jour, with mirror-backed shelf, flanked by a pair of glazed doors with pierced brass galleries, stamped 'Shoolbred', 42in (106.5cm).
$2,250-3,500

A Louis XV style bois satine and marquetry bonheur du jour, the hinged fall enclosing a writing surface and 3 drawers, 29½in (75cm).
$1,500-2,600

A French satinwood bonheur du jour, late 19thC. 33in (84cm).
$1,500-2,600

A Louis XVI style tulipwood bonheur du jour, with a tooled leather inset to the writing slide, the parquetry inlaid frieze with a drawer, 22in (56cm).
$2,250-3,000

A French amboyna bonheur du jour, with ormolu ornamentation, crossbanded in tulipwood with marquetry decoration, with mirror back, decorated with handpainted floral oval porcelain plaques, 60in (152cm).
$4,000-5,500

Breakfront Bookcases

A mahogany breakfront bookcase, early 19thC.
$8,000-10,500

A Georgian carved mahogany secretaire breakfront library bookcase in the Chippendale taste, with a pierced fret swan neck pediment, dentil cornice and blind fret frieze, the lower part with a fall enclosing a fitted interior, on a plinth base, 97½ by 86½in (247 by 220cm).
$13,500-17,500

A Georgian mahogany breakfront library bookcase, 101in (256cm).
$21,000-30,000

A George III mahogany breakfront bookcase, adapted, 74½in (190cm).
$13,500-15,000

An oak breakfront bookcase with open shelves, c1800.
$4,500-7,000

A George III mahogany breakfront bookcase, the base inlaid with boxwood lines, with panelled and crossbanded cupboard doors enclosing shelves, on moulded plinth, 93½ by 88in (236 by 223.5cm).
$10,000-13,000

A mahogany breakfront cabinet, the side doors each enclosing 7 cedar lined drawers with brass handles, 19thC, 89 by 79in (226 by 200.5cm).
$3,000-4,500

A Victorian walnut breakfront bookcase, with applied acanthus and floral moulded decoration, on plinth base, 112in (284.5cm).
$2,250-3,000

A George III mahogany breakfront bookcase, the geometrically glazed cupboard doors with giltwood astragals, the lower part with panelled cupboards, the central ones replaced, on plinth base, the glazing bars later, 104 by 97½in (264 by 248cm).
$9,000-12,000

A Victorian oak breakfront library bookcase, the top section with a cavetto moulded cornice, on plinth base, 88in (223.5cm).
$2,250-3,500

A mahogany breakfront library bookcase in 18thC style, with 4 astragal glazed doors enclosing adjustable bookshelves, on plinth base, 19thC, 123in (312.5cm).
$6,000-8,000

A mahogany and chequer lined breakfront bookcase, with secretaire drawer, 98in (249cm).
$4,500-7,000

A large Regency mahogany breakfront bookcase with open shelves, the base with 6 panelled cupboard doors flanked by conforming plinths, 110 by 176in (279 by 447cm).
$7,500-10,500

A mahogany breakfront library bookcase, the upper portion with a cavetto cornice above 4 glazed doors, enclosing shelves, 114 by 103in (289 by 261.5cm).
$6,000-8,000

A Victorian light oak breakfront bookcase, with applied panels to door fronts.
$750-1,000

A George III mahogany bureau bookcase, with satinwood bandings, 45½in (115cm).
$4,000-5,500

An Edwardian mahogany breakfront bookcase of Georgian design, inlaid with stringings, fitted with 9 adjustable shelves enclosed by 2 pairs of glazed doors with fine astragal mouldings, the lower part with finely figured veneers, on bracket feet, 88 by 86in (223.5 by 218.5cm).
$4,000-5,500

A small George III style satinwood bureau bookcase, with crossbanded curvilinear astragal glazed doors above a figured oval panelled fall enclosing a fitted interior, on bracket feet, 31in (78cm).
$4,500-7,000

A George III mahogany bureau, with later bookcase top, 42in (106.5cm).
$2,250-3,000

Bureau Bookcases

An oak bureau bookcase, with fully fitted interior and a well, 18thC, 77 by 33in (195 by 84cm).
$4,000-5,500

A George III mahogany bureau bookcase, inlaid with satinwood crossbanding and stringing, the fall flap enclosing a fitted interior, on bracket feet, 88½ by 42in (224 by 106.5cm).
$2,250-3,500

A George III rosewood and mahogany bureau bookcase, with later mirror glazed cupboard doors, the fall flap enclosing a fitted interior, the sides with carrying handles, on later bracket feet, 87 by 45in (221 by 114cm).
$7,500-10,500

A George III mahogany bureau ► bookcase, with moulded dentilled triangular pediment centred by a later urn, 96 by 46in (243.5 by 116.5cm).
$4,500-7,000

A George III mahogany bureau bookcase, with Gothic astragal glazed doors, the fall enclosing a fitted interior, 38½in (97cm).
$3,000-4,500

A George III mahogany bureau bookcase, with later scrolled pierced pediment and moulded cornice, the leather-lined fall flap enclosing a fitted interior, on ogee bracket feet, 100 by 49in (254 by 124.5cm).
$6,000-8,000

An elm bureau bookcase, 18thC.
$3,000-4,500

A mahogany bureau bookcase, the upper section with astragal glazed doors and dentil cornice, the bureau crossbanded in rosewood with fitted interior and the whole relieved with satinwood stringing, on ogee feet, 93 by 45in (236 by 114cm).
$4,500-7,000

An inlaid mahogany bureau bookcase with kingwood crossbanding and chevron stringing, the sloping flap inlaid with a shell, stars and quadrant fan medallions, on bracket feet, 83½ by 43½in (212 by 110cm).
$3,000-4,000

A Victorian mahogany bureau bookcase, the cylinder bureau with birch veneered fitted interior, 46in (116.5cm).
$1,500-2,600

A mahogany bureau bookcase, the fall enclosing a simple interior, on bracket feet, the bureau late 18thC with later bookcase, 46½in (117cm).
$1,300-1,800

A George III mahogany bureau bookcase, the top with an architectural pediment above glazed doors, the fall flap revealing a fitted interior, with ornate brass swan neck handles, on bracket feet, 44in (111.5cm).
$4,500-7,000

In the Furniture section if there is only one measurement it usually refers to the width of the piece

A Chippendale walnut bookcase desk in 2 sections, the upper with 2 panelled cupboard doors opening to a fitted interior with shelves, the lower section with thumb moulded slant lid opening to a fitted interior, on bracket feet, damage and restorations, Massachusetts, c1770.
$6,000-7,000

An Edwardian mahogany inlaid fall front bureau bookcase, with double astragal glazed doors, on shaped feet, 42in (106.5cm).
$900-1,300

A Chippendale mahogany desk and bookcase in 3 parts, the pediment with a swan's neck cresting with strawberry carved rosettes, the bookcase section with 2 mahogany veneered panelled doors enclosing a fitted interior, the lower section with a slant top opening to a fitted interior, old repair to pediment, probably Salem, Massachusetts, c1775, 42in (106cm).
$17,000-19,000

An Edwardian Sheraton bureau bookcase.
$2,250-3,000

Dwarf Bookcases

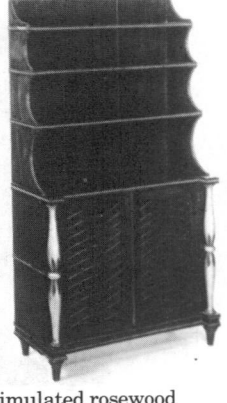

A Regency rosewood dwarf bookcase, with white marble top and Egyptian atlantes pilasters, 42in (106.5cm).
$1,500-2,600

A Regency simulated rosewood dwarf bookcase, the base with 2 wire panelled doors between gilt column angles, mounted with beaded and foliate gilt metal borders, 30in (76cm).
$4,500-7,000

A Regency mahogany open bookcase cabinet, 30in (76cm).
$3,000-4,500

A Chippendale style mahogany dwarf bookcase, on cluster column supports with wings joined with a concave platform cross stretcher, 28½in (72cm).
$1,000-1,400

An unusual George IV mahogany library bookstand, with a panelled fall flap, numbered 22, 45½in (115cm).
$1,500-2,600

A satinwood dwarf bookcase, inlaid with mahogany stylised Greek key stringing, with brass paw feet, 55½in (140cm).
$6,000-9,000

A George IV rosewood dwarf bookcase, 44in (111.5cm).
$1,500-2,600

An Edwardian mahogany revolving bookcase, 19in (48cm).
$300-400

A Victorian mahogany revolving bookcase, on a quatrefoil castered support, 24in (61cm).
$600-900

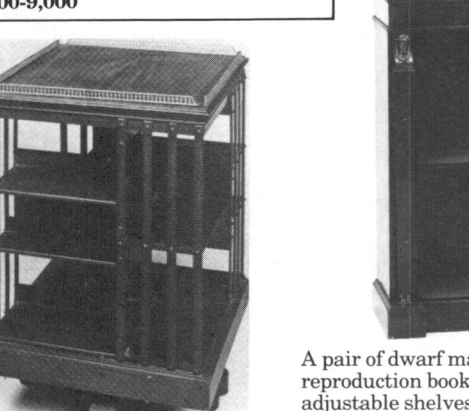

A pair of dwarf mahogany reproduction bookcases, with adjustable shelves and Empire style mounts, the tops scratched.
$400-500

A William IV rosewood dwarf breakfront bookcase.
$7,500-10,500

A Regency Boulle Revival rosewood and ormolu mounted centre bookcase, in the manner of Louis le Gaigneur, surmounted by a black marble top, the frieze veneered in tortoiseshell and inlaid in premier and contra partie brass marquetry, the reverse fitted with shelves, flanked by lotus capital stiles, the sides with silk and brass grille panels, on a plinth base, 32½in (82cm).
$10,500-15,000

Library Bookcases

A George III mahogany bookcase, the panel doors inlaid with rosewood ovals, on bracket feet, 40½in (102cm).
$4,000-5,500

A mid-Georgian mahogany bookcase, with later moulded cornice and pair of glazed doors with egg-and-dart carved astragals between possibly later volutes, 73½in (186cm).
$13,500-17,500

A George III mahogany bookcase on chest, the cornice inlaid with ebony and boxwood stringing above a pair of astragal glazed doors, the chest with crossbanded top, on narrow bracket feet, 39in (99cm).
$1,500-2,600

A George III mahogany bookcase, the base with a pair of panelled doors simulated as 2 drawers, on later bracket feet, 43½in (110cm).
$4,500-7,000

A George III carved mahogany bookcase on stand, with ribband and paterae astragal glazed doors, the stand with gadrooned apron, on scroll carved hairy paw feet, 61½in (156cm).
$4,500-7,000

A late George III mahogany bookcase, the upper section with Greek key cornice above a pair of astragal glazed doors flanked by panelled stiles, altered from a larger bookcase, 54in (137cm).
$4,000-5,500

A Georgian mahogany bookcase in two parts, the interior containing drawers and pigeonholes, 57in (144.5cm).
$4,000-5,500

A mahogany narrow bookcase, 19thC.
$1,500-2,600

An oak three-section library bookcase, with adjustable shelves, 99in (251.5cm).
$2,500-3,500

A Regency rosewood bookcase, the upper part flanked by fluted columns, the lower part with 2 glazed doors and scroll columns.
$2,250-3,000

A George IV mahogany bookcase, the whole flanked by moulded pilasters, 56in (142cm).
$3,000-4,000

A walnut bookcase enclosed by 2 glazed doors with cupboard under, on bracket feet, early 19thC.
$750-1,000

An early Victorian rosewood bookcase, with later panel backing, 36in (91.5cm).
$1,500-2,600

A Victorian rosewood library bookcase with moulded cornice, 106in (269cm).
$4,000-5,500

A Victorian walnut bookcase inlaid with ebony, 50in (127cm).
$2,250-3,000

A mahogany library bookcase, with arcaded cornice with acorn finials, 66in (167.5cm).
$2,250-3,000

A Victorian walnut and marquetry bookcase, with cavetto cornice and floral marquetry inlaid frieze, both sections with gilt metal mounts, and bandings, 53in (134cm).
$2,250-3,000

A Victorian mahogany bookcase, the lower section fitted with 3 panelled doors, the right hand door enclosing 4 drawers, 69½in (176cm).
$2,250-3,500

An Edwardian satinwood bookcase, with painted foliate decoration in the manner of Angelica Kauffman, with cresting above an arcaded cornice, 35½in (90cm).
$4,000-5,500

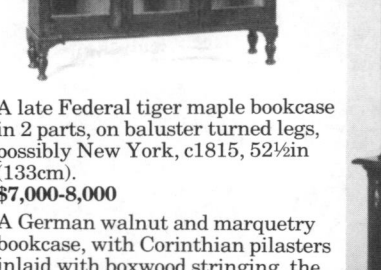

A late Federal tiger maple bookcase in 2 parts, on baluster turned legs, possibly New York, c1815, 52½in (133cm).
$7,000-8,000

A German walnut and marquetry bookcase, with Corinthian pilasters inlaid with boxwood stringing, the cupboard doors centred by marquetry cartouches and enclosing shelves, basically mid-18thC, 64½in (162.5cm).
$6,000-8,000

An Edwardian inlaid mahogany bookcase with swan neck pediment, 48in (122cm).
$2,250-3,000

Secretaire Bookcases

A George III mahogany secretaire bookcase, 44in (111.5cm).
$4,500-7,000

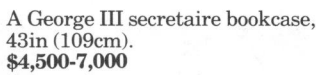

A George III secretaire bookcase, 43in (109cm).
$4,500-7,000

A George III mahogany secretaire bookcase, the lower section with a secretaire with satinwood interior, 44½in (113cm).
$4,500-7,000

A George III mahogany secretaire bookcase, 44in (111.5cm).
$4,000-5,500

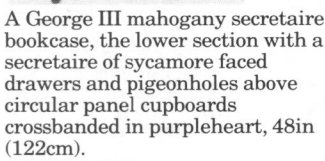

A George III mahogany secretaire bookcase, the lower section with a secretaire of sycamore faced drawers and pigeonholes above circular panel cupboards crossbanded in purpleheart, 48in (122cm).
$4,000-5,500

A George III mahogany secretaire bookcase, 43in (109cm).
$3,000-4,500

A Regency mahogany secretaire bookcase, inlaid with boxwood lines and banded in rosewood, with a deep crossbanded secretaire drawer with maple fitted interior, 45in (114cm).
$2,250-3,500

A Federal mahogany secretary in 3 sections, the lower section with hinged writing flap over a case with 3 cockbeaded and graduated long drawers, small chips, Boston, c1810, 42½in (105cm).
$7,000-9,000

A mahogany secretaire bookcase, inlaid with rosewood bands and boxwood radial lines, with a deep writing drawer, early 19thC, 43in (109cm).
$2,250-3,500

A Georgian secretaire bookcase, with brocade-lined shelves and interior, with boxwood stringing and satinwood crossbanding, on scroll legs.
$2,250-3,500

A Chippendale cherrywood secretary desk in 2 sections, the upper section with moulded swan's neck pediment, the lower section with thumb moulded slant lid opening to a fitted interior, on ogee bracket feet, 41in (104cm).
$8,500-9,500

A Regency mahogany secretaire cabinet, with shaped tablet-centred pediment and moulded corners, the base with baize-lined secretaire with burr-elm fitted interior, 48½in (123cm).
$7,500-10,500

A Regency mahogany secretaire bookcase, applied with reeded mouldings, the top drawer fitted with 8 small satinwood drawers, on reduced bracket feet, 42in (106cm).
$1,500-2,600

A mahogany secretaire bookcase, with a simulated deep writing drawer, on plinth base, early 19thC, 57in (144.5cm).
$4,000-5,500

A small Regency yew-wood and laburnum crossbanded secretaire bookcase, the fall enclosing a fitted interior, on turned feet, 37½in (95cm).
$6,000-8,000

A mahogany secretaire bookcase, early 19thC, 42in (106.5cm).
$1,500-2,600

A Victorian mahogany secretaire bookcase, the secretaire drawer with fitted interior of satin birch, 53½in (135cm).
$1,500-2,600

Buckets

A mahogany secretaire bookcase, inlaid with boxwood lines with satinwood banded borders, with a deep writing drawer, on bracket feet, 19thC, 43½in (110cm).
$4,000-5,500   *CSK*

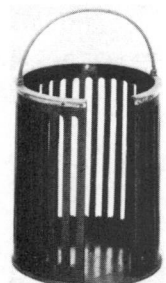

A George III mahogany plate bucket, with brass rim, 11½in (30cm) diam.
$1,500-2,600

In the Furniture section if there is only one measurement it usually refers to the width of the piece

A George III brass-bound mahogany plate bucket, with copper liner, 11½in (30cm) diam.
$1,500-2,600

An Edwardian inlaid bookcase, with writing compartment.
$750-1,000

A Scandinavian green-painted and parcel gilt secretaire bookcase, the panelled flap enclosing a fitted interior, redecorated, late 18thC, 47in (119cm).
$4,000-5,500

A George III mahogany
peat bucket.
$1,300-1,800

A pair of George III mahogany
brass-bound plate buckets, with
later tin liners, 15in (38cm) diam.
$1,500-2,600

A George III mahogany brass-bound
peat bucket, 12in (31cm) high.
$1,500-2,600

Bureaux

A pair of George III
oak and
brass-bound peat
buckets, with
pierced handles
to the sides, with
liners, 29in
(74cm) high.
$3,000-4,500

A Regency rosewood and ebonised
octagonal basket, on claw feet, 6in
(15cm) high.
$450-700

A George III mahogany bureau,
30in (76cm).
$2,500-3,500

A George III mahogany
bureau, outlined with
chequered banding,
41½in (105cm).
$1,500-2,600

An early George III
mahogany bureau,
with a crossbanded
sloping fall front
enclosing a fitted
interior,
38½in (97.5cm).
$1,300-1,800

A Federal mahogany slant front
desk, with thumb moulded slant lid
enclosing a compartmented
interior, with eagle-inlaid prospect
door, on French feet, damage,
Pennsylvania, c1800, 45in (114cm).
$8,000-12,000

A Georgian mahogany
bureau, with
fitted interior, on
bracket feet, 33in
(84cm).
$1,500-2,600

A Chippendale
maple slant front
desk, with fitted
interior, on straight
bracket feet,
New England,
c1770,
37½in (95cm).
$3,000-5,000

A Georgian mahogany fall front bureau, with Chippendale blind fretwork carving, the drawers decorated with herringbone boxwood and ebony stringing, all drawers oak lined, on ogee feet, 38in (96cm).
$4,000-5,500

A Queen Anne maple slant front desk, with a thumb moulded slant lid opening to a fitted interior, on short cabriole legs with pad and disc feet, repairs, New England, c1755, 40in (101.5cm).
$7,000-10,000

A George III mahogany cylinder bureau, with tambour shutter enclosing a fitted interior including a slide with leather-lined easel and a frieze drawer, crossbanded with rosewood on square tapering legs outlined with boxwood lines, 21in (53cm).
$7,000-9,000

A George III mahogany bureau, with hinged slope enclosing a fitted interior, 40in (101.5cm).
$2,250-3,000

A Georgian mahogany bureau, the fall flap crossbanded and inlaid with an oval shell motif, fitted interior with pigeonholes and drawers and 'book-spine' facings, 37½in (96cm).
$750-1,000

A George III mahogany and satinwood banded bureau, the broadly crossbanded fall inlaid with a shell patera enclosing a stepped fitted interior, on bracket feet, probably Irish, 38½in (97cm).
$1,500-2,600

A George III mahogany bureau-on-stand, 27in (69cm).
$3,000-4,500

A Chippendale reverse serpentine slant front desk, the slant lid enclosing a fitted interior, the moulded base with a shaped drop, on ball and claw feet, Massachusetts, c1775, 42in (106.5cm).
$7,000-8,000

A George III mahogany writing bureau, with fitted interior, on bracket feet.
$1,500-2,600

A George III mahogany bureau, with hinged slope enclosing a fitted interior, 40in (101.5cm).
$1,500-2,600

A George III inlaid mahogany
bureau, with sloping fall and fitted
interior, 32in (82cm).
$1,500-2,600

A mahogany writing bureau, with 2
short and 2 long drawers, on bracket
feet.
$1,500-2,600

A Georgian walnut veneered
writing bureau, with fitted interior,
on bracket feet.
$2,250-3,500

A George III mahogany bureau,
37in (94cm).
$1,500-2,600

A Sheraton design mahogany
bureau, crossbanded and inlaid in
satinwood and ebony with shell
corners, with fitted interior, on ogee
bracket feet, 19thC, 40in (101.5cm).
$1,500-2,600

A late Georgian mahogany bureau,
with fitted interior.
$1,300-1,800

A Georgian mahogany bureau, with
well fitted interior, on bracket feet,
39in (99cm).
$1,500-2,600

A late George III mahogany
cylinder bureau, with tambour
shutter enclosing a similarly
shuttered fitted interior, with lined
writing surface, on acanthus carved
sabre legs, 42in (106.5cm).
$2,250-3,000

A William and Mary walnut slant
front desk, the slant lid opening to a
fitted interior with 12 pigeonholes,
on ball turned feet, 35½in (91cm).
$4,000-4,500

A Chippendale cherrywood slant
front desk, the thumb moulded slant
lid opening to a fitted interior with a
prospect door, repairs, New
England, c1770, 40in (101.5cm).
$2,500-3,500

A Chippendale walnut slant front desk, opening to a fitted interior with valanced pigeonholes separated by ogee dividers, on ogee bracket feet, restorations and repairs, Rhode Islands, c1775, 40in (102cm).
$5,000-8,000

A Chippendale carved mahogany reverse serpentine slant front desk, with fitted interior centering a fan and line inlaid prospect door, on short cabriole legs with ball and claw feet, minor patches to drawer fronts, North Shore, Massachusetts, c1770, 44in (111.5cm).
$8,000-9,000

A Dutch walnut and marquetry bureau, the fall inlaid with flowers and kingfishers, enclosing a stepped fitted interior, on large claw and ball feet, 18thC, 52in (132cm).
$6,000-8,000

An Edwardian Sheraton style bureau à cylindre, veneered in satinwood with floral marquetry panels of musical instruments, ferns, swags and foliage, with fitted interior, on square tapered legs with brass casters, 42½in (107cm).
$5,500-7,000

A Chippendale mahogany slant front desk, the slant front opening to a fitted interior, on ogee bracket feet, Eastern New England, possibly Rhode Island, c1770, 38½in (97cm).
$2,500-3,500

A Dutch walnut and floral marquetry bureau de dame, 35in (89cm).
$4,500-7,000

A Dutch rosewood and marquetry bureau, with fitted interior, green baize writing surface, brass foliate escutcheons and handles, on bracket feet, 19thC, 41in (104cm).
$4,000-5,500

A Dutch marquetry bombé bureau, inlaid with birds and flowers, with fitted interior above 3 long graduated drawers.
$6,000-8,000

A Louis XV style burr walnut bureau de dame, by Gillow, the bombé fall enclosing a shaped fitted interior, the whole applied with well cast floral gilt metal mounts and mouldings, stamped 'Gillow', c1850, 33in (84cm).
$4,000-5,500

A Louis XVI ormolu-mounted mahogany bureau à cylindre, with white marble top, the shutter enclosing a fitted interior and writing slide, one drawer enclosing a 'coffre fort', 51in (129cm).
$6,000-9,000

A Chippendale mahogany reverse serpentine slant front desk, with a thumb moulded slant front opening to a fitted interior, on ogee bracket feet, repairs to lid, Massachusetts, c1775, 42in (106.5cm).
$7,000-8,000

A George III mahogany bureau, with fitted interior, on later bracket feet, 36in (91cm).
$2,500-3,500

A Dutch padouk block-fronted bureau, with fitted interior, 19thC, 36in (91cm).
$2,250-3,500

A Louis XVI style mahogany bureau à cylindre, on turned and fluted tapered legs, 51in (130cm).
$4,500-7,000

A Chippendale mahogany slant front desk, opening to a fitted interior centering a fan carved prospect door, minor repairs, probably Providence, RI, c1770, 38½in (98cm).
$10,000-12,000

Bureau Cabinets

A George II mahogany bureau cabinet, the upper part with a broken arched cornice, the crossbanded fall enclosing a fitted interior, on bracket feet, 41in (104cm).
$10,000-13,000

A William and Mary walnut cabinet-on-chest, with engraved pierced brass hinges and brass plate handles, faded golden colour, with original pierced barrel key, 43in (109cm).
$7,000-9,000

◀ A walnut crossbanded bureau cabinet, the upper part with fitted interior, enclosed by a pair of arched bevelled mirror plates, one of a later date, the lower part with a sloping crossbanded and featherstrung fall enclosing a graduated and fitted interior, parts later re-veneered and restored, late 17th/early 18thC, 49in (125cm).
$10,000-13,000

A George II walnut bureau cabinet, with plain glazed doors above candle-slides, the lower section with a crossbanded and herringbone inlaid fall enclosing fitted interior, 40in (101cm).
$7,500-10,500

A Queen Anne black japanned cabinet-on-chest, the interior fitted with various sized drawers, on a later stand with bracket feet, 26½in (67cm).
$19,500-22,500

A walnut, burr veneered and featherstrung double dome bureau cabinet, the upper part with a moulded cornice, the sloping fall with a rest and baize-lined writing surface and enclosing a fitted interior, on later bun feet, 18thC, 42in (106cm).
$6,000-9,000

A George III mahogany secretaire cabinet, with broken S-scroll pediment pierced with fretwork, with shelves, the base with a fall front writing drawer enclosing a later fitted interior, 44in (112cm).
$5,500-7,000

A walnut crossbanded and featherstrung bureau cabinet, with candle-slides, brass carrying handles to the sides, 18thC, 40in (102cm).
$27,000-30,000

A walnut crossbanded and featherstrung bureau cabinet, with fully fitted interior, enclosed by a pair of fielded panel doors, on bracket feet, 40½in (103cm).
$9,000-12,000

A Regency mahogany secretaire cabinet, with fitted secretaire drawer, with fruitwood drawer front, on splayed feet, 43in (109cm).
$4,000-5,500

A George III mahogany bureau cabinet, on high bracket feet, the two sections of different origin, 38in (96cm).
$1,500-2,600

An Italian scarlet lacquer and gilt gesso chinoiserie decorated bureau cabinet, the upper part fitted with numerous drawers, enclosed by a panel door, the bombé lower part with sloping fall enclosing a fitted graduated interior, late 18th/early 19thC, 35in (89cm).
$10,500-14,000

A pair of Italian painted and parcel gilt breakfront cabinets in the baroque style, the lower section with grotesque mask carved cupboards, the whole decorated in pinks and blues with marbelised surfaces, 88in (224cm).
$10,500-13,000

A Regency mahogany secretaire cabinet, with baize-lined secretaire drawer enclosing a fitted interior, on bracket feet, 49in (130cm).
$4,000-5,500

A Venetian decorated bureau cabinet, painted with foliate scroll panels with flowers, 51in (130cm).
$4,000-5,500

A Biedermeier mahogany secretaire à abattant, inlaid with boxwood strings, the cupboard door inlaid with chequered boxwood lines, 40in (101.5cm).
$1,500-2,600

A Louis XV marquetry secretaire à abattant, with breccia marble top and fall flap enclosing a fitted interior, 38½in (97cm).
$9,000-12,000

A Continental walnut and mahogany cabinet-on-chest, with a fitted interior of 22 small drawers, 18thC, 43in (109cm).
$2,250-3,500

A Louis XVI tulipwood and chequer inlaid secretaire à abattant, surmounted by contemporary moulded marble top and bordered with harewood and purpleheart lines, the quarter-veneered fall enclosing a fitted interior with tulipwood veneers, with later gilt metal ornament, 38in (97cm).
$2,250-3,500

A Louis XV ormolu-mounted tulipwood and mahogany secretaire à abattant, with quartered crossbanded top above a spreading frieze drawer, the leather-lined flap enclosing a fitted interior, 32in (81cm).
$5,500-7,000

A German provincial tulipwood and parquetry secretaire à abattant, with moulded chamfered white marble top, the fall flap enclosing a fitted interior, 29½in (74cm).
$2,250-3,500

Cabinets-on-stands

An Anglo-Dutch kingwood, burr yew-wood and amboyna oyster veneered bureau cabinet, veneered and crossbanded to the front and sides, the upper part of an earlier date, with fitted interior, the lower part having a sloping fall enclosing a fitted interior, on ogee bracket feet, 18thC, 47½in (120cm).
$4,500-7,000

A William and Mary walnut oyster-veneered cabinet-on-stand, inlaid and edged in boxwood, enclosing 10 crossbanded drawers, on later spiral twist legs and turned feet joined by shaped flat stretchers panelled in ebony, 44in (111.5cm).
$10,000-13,000

A small carved mahogany breakfront cabinet on later stand, in the Chippendale taste, the upper part with a swan neck pediment with a blind fret frieze, partly later, the base fitted with a frieze drawer, on blind fret square legs terminating in block feet, mid-18thC, 39½in (100cm).
$4,000-5,500

A rare pair of lacquer cabinets on later gilt ebonised cabriole stands, each with cut-out floral and bird applied exteriors, the door interiors and drawer fronts applied with coloured engravings, early 19thC, 30in (76cm).
$25,500-36,000

An early Georgian black and gold lacquer cabinet, enclosing 10 various sized drawers, decorated with rural scenes, on a George III stand, the lacquer distressed, 41in (104cm).
$3,000-4,000

A William and Mary walnut cabinet-on-stand, with fitted interior, on later spiral turned legs, 42in (106.5cm).
$4,500-7,000

A Victorian mahogany cabinet with extensive carving, the top with open shelves, the base with glazed doors, on carved cabriole legs, some damage, 93in (236cm) high.
$1,300-1,800

A Dutch burr walnut cabinet-on-stand, with fitted interior, the inner surfaces with star inlays, the stand fitted with 4 short drawers, on 5 square tapered legs and bun feet, 18thC, 70½in (179cm).
$2,250-3,000

A black japanned cabinet with fitted interior, decorated gilt Oriental style, with engraved brass hinges and escutcheons, the ebonised stand on cabriole legs with club feet, early 18thC, 41in (104cm).
$2,250-3,000

An Oriental black lacquer cabinet-on-stand, with gilt decoration, enclosing numerous drawers, 38in (96.5cm).
$4,000-5,500

An Italian scarlet and gold lacquer ▶ bureau cabinet, decorated with chinoiserie scenes, on cabriole legs and hoof feet, mid-18thC, 37in (97cm).
$4,000-5,500

A Spanish walnut vargueno on later stand, the upper part with fitted interior decorated in parcel gilt and ivory, enclosed by a fall applied with velvet and pierced gilt metal locking plates and angles, 17thC, 41in (104cm).
$4,000-5,500

A Portuguese rosewood cabinet-on- stand, the associated walnut stand with a putto and foliate carved frieze, late 17thC, 25in (64cm).
$2,500-3,500

A South German cabinet-on-stand, with oak veneer and birch panelled top, decorated with armorial marquetry, on later oak stand, 17thC, 43in (109cm).
$1,500-2,600

A Flemish ebony veneered marriage cabinet, painted with landscapes, on later stand, late 17thC, 57in (144.5cm) high.
$6,000-8,000

A Dutch Colonial teak cabinet-on-stand, with engraved and pierced decorative brass medallions and mounts, and dolphin pattern hinges, 18thC, 45in (114cm).
$1,500-2,600

An Italian ebony fall front miniature cabinet, inlaid with engraved ivory panels and arabesques, 20in (51cm).
$2,250-3,000

A walnut display cabinet-on-stand, 30in (76cm).
$4,000-5,500

In the Furniture section if there is only one measurement it usually refers to the width of the piece

A Charles II cedar table cabinet, the crossbanded top above a cushion moulded drawer and an arrangement of 14 small panel front drawers of various sizes, around a floral marquetry inlaid cupboard enclosing further small drawers and secret drawers concealed in the framing, 25in (64cm).
$3,000-4,000

A Milanese ebonised, ivory inlaid and pietra dura table cabinet on later stand, heightened in various hardstones and marble including lapis and sienna marble, the stand on polygonal tapered legs united by curved flattened stretchers, late 18thC, 30in (75cm).
$1,500-2,600

Make the most of Miller's

When a large specialist well-publicised collection comes on the market, it tends to increase prices. Immediately after this, prices can fall slightly due to the main buyers having large stocks and the market being 'flooded'. This is usually temporary and does not affect very high quality items.

A Spanish walnut vargueno with iron strapwork to the corners and front, backed by red velvet, with matching side carrying handles, decorated with gilding and with spiral carved ivory pillars and inset ivory plaques with symbols, 16thC, 37in (94cm).
$4,000-5,500

When it comes to Antique Exporting . . .
WE HAVE ALL THE ANSWERS

There are many pitfalls in the antique world awaiting the novice and experienced buyer alike. The largest doubt in the mind of the potential container buyer must be, 'How will they know what to send me and will the quality be right?' British Antique Exporters Ltd have the answers to these and other questions.

Q How many items will I get for my money?

A A typical 20-foot container will have 75 pieces of furniture and approximately 50 pieces of china-ware packed in it. We can regulate the price of the container with the quantity of small items; the higher the value of the shipment, the higher the number of small pieces. Of course the type and style of furniture, for example period Georgian, Victorian or Edwardian, also regulates the price.

Q What type of merchandise will you send me?

A We have researched all our markets very thoroughly and know the right merchandise to send to any particular country or region in that country. We also take into consideration the type of outlet eg auction, wholesale or retail. We consider the strong preferences for different woods in different areas. We personally visit all our markets several times a year to keep pace with the trends.

Q Will we get the bargains?

A In the mind of any prospective buyer is the thought that he or she will find the true bargains hidden away in the small forgotten corners of some dusty Antique Shop. It is our Company policy to pass on the benefit of any bargain buying to our client.

Q = Question
A = Answer

Q With your overheads, etc, how can you send these things to me at a competitive price?

A Our very great purchasing power enables us to buy goods at substantially less than the individual person; this means that we are able to buy, collect and pack the item for substantially less than the shop price.

Q Will everything be in good condition and will it arrive undamaged?

A We are very proud of the superb condition of all the merchadise leaving our factory. We employ the finest craftsmen to restore each piece into first class saleable condition before departure. We also pack to the highest standards thus ensuring that all items arrive safely.

Q What guarantee do I have that you will do a good job for me?

A The ultimate guarantee. We are so confident of our ability to provide the right goods at the right price that we offer a full refund, if for any reason you are not satisfied with the shipment.

Q This all sounds very satisfactory, how do we do business?

A Unlike most Companies, we do not require pre-payment for our containers. When you place your order with us, we require a deposit of £1500 and the balance is payable when the container arrives at its destination.

BRITISH ANTIQUE EXPORTERS LTD
School Close, Queen Elizabeth Avenue,
Burgess Hill, West Sussex, RH15 9RX England
Telephone BURGESS HILL (044 46) 45577
Telex 87688

Member of L.A.P.A.D.A. Guild of Master Craftsmen

Furniture

A Regency brass inlaid rosewood day bed, 76in (193cm). **$13,500-17,500**

A Biedermeier walnut cradle, 52in (132cm). **$7,500-10,500**

An Elizabethan oak tester bed, restorations, 81in (205cm). **$10,000-13,000**

A Régence beechwood duchesse en bateau. **$7,500-10,500**

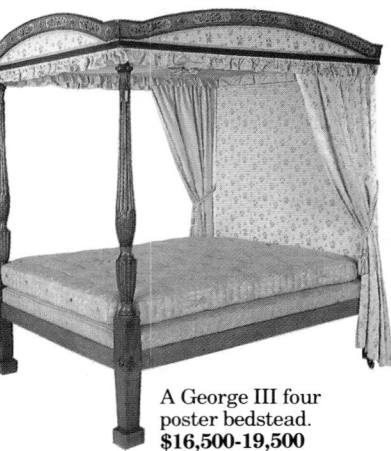

An Italian Empire four poster bed, c1825. **$30,000-34,500**

A George III four poster bedstead. **$16,500-19,500**

A George III tester bed, 74in (188cm). **$13,500-17,500**

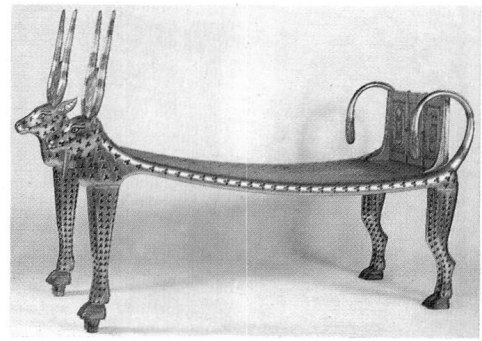

A Charles X bois clair lit en bateau, 80in (203cm). **$8,000-10,500**

A giltwood day bed in the Theban style, 79in (200cm). **$21,000-24,000**

A Continental baroque kingwood and engraved bonheur du jour, c1720, 37½in (95cm).
$36,000-39,000

A Louis XVI tulipwood and parquetry bonheur du jour, 26in (66cm).
$10,500-14,000

A painted satinwood and mahogany bonheur du jour, frieze drawer with leather-lined slide, 31½in (80cm).
$13,500-17,500

A Louis XVIII mahogany bonheur du jour, 30in.
$67,000-75,000

A Queen Anne walnut bureau bookcase, with partly fitted interior, 41½in (105.5cm).
$45,000-49,000

A Queen Anne walnut bureau bookcase, crossbanded sloping flap enclosing a fitted interior, 41in.
$28,500-34,000

A George III mahogany, satinwood, tulipwood and marquetry bonheur du jour, 28in. **$52,000-60,000**

A Queen Anne walnut bureau bookcase, with fitted interior, later bracket feet, 41½in (105.5cm).
$18,000-24,000

A George III tulipwood bonheur du jour, with leather-lined writing slide, 30in (76cm).
$6,000-9,000

A late George III mahogany breakfront library bookcase, 100in (254cm). **$19,500-24,000**

A George III mahogany bookcase, 59in (150cm). **$27,000-30,000**

A George III oak bureau bookcase, with fitted interior, 40in (102cm). **$6,000-9,000**

A George I burr walnut bureau bookcase, 41in. **$33,000-37,000**

A Regency mahogany bookcase, in the Gothic style, 29in (74cm). **$10,500-14,000**

A George III mahogany bookcase, with key pattern moulded cornice, 53in (135cm). **$31,500-34,500**

A George I walnut bureau bookcase, 39in (100cm). **$16,500-19,500**

A George III mahogany double breakfront bookcase, 124½in (316cm). **$42,000-45,000**

A Federal mahogany breakfront bookcase, Philadelphia, 1815-20, 108in. **$30,000-37,500**

A Regency ormolu mounted, parcel gilt and rosewood bookcase, marble top, 18in (46cm). **$6,000-8,000**

A Regency purpleheart pedestal bookcase, with 17thC Italian marble top, 23in (58.5cm) square. **$37,000-42,000**

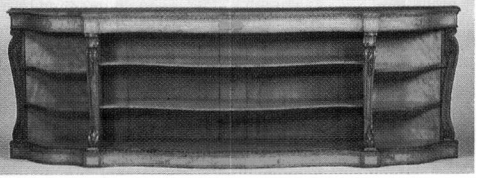

A rare Federal secretary bookcase, the lower section with writing flap, New York, 1800-10, 37in (94cm). **$30,000-36,000**

A Victorian painted and decorated pine secretary bookcase, Heywood Bros, Massachusetts, painting Edward and Thomas Hill, c1860, restorations, 49in. **$13,500-17,500**

A mid-Victorian giltmetal-mounted satinwood and walnut dwarf bookcase, the central shelves possibly later, possibly by Holland & Sons, 109in (277cm). **$6,000-9,000**

A Chippendale carved maple desk and bookcase, Rhode Island, 1750-80, 38in (96.5cm). **$27,000-30,000**

A pair of Regency rosewood bookcases, 54in (137cm). **$10,500-14,000**

A Chippendale carved mahogany blockfront desk and bookcase, signed by John Chipman, Salem, Mass, 1770-1785, 45in (114cm). **$375,000+**

A Louis XV kingwood and marquetry bureau de dame, stamped RVLC, 45in (114cm). **$16,500-19,500**

A Louis XIV ebony and floral marquetry bureau Mazarin, top inlaid with stained and engraved woods, remodelled mid-19thC, 45½in. **$30,000-36,000**

A William and Mary burr-elm bureau, 26in. **$27,000-30,000**

A Chinese export padoukwood bureau, back inscribed TH52, mid-18thC, 40in (101cm). **$19,500-22,500**

A George I walnut bureau, foot repaired, 20in (51cm). **$15,000-21,000**

A William and Mary burr walnut bureau, with later bracket feet, 38in (97cm). **$10,500-14,000**

A Louis XIV marquetry bureau Mazarin, 46in (117cm). **$21,000-24,000**

A Louis XIV ormolu mounted 'Boulle' marquetry bureau Mazarin, 48½in. **$21,000-24,000**

A George I walnut bureau, with fitted interior, 38in (97cm). **$7,500-10,500**

A German figured ash bureau, fitted compartments, early 19thC, 26in. **$6,000-9,000**

A George I walnut bureau, baize lined flap enclosing fitted interior, 29in (75cm). **$16,500-19,500**

An early Georgian walnut cabinet in 2 sections, the panelled doors enclosing numerous drawers, 108in (275cm) high. **$49,500-54,000**

A George III mahogany library cabinet, glazed cupboard doors enclosing adjustable shelves, late 18thC, 50in. **$24,000-27,000**

A Queen Anne walnut bureau cabinet, 28½in (72cm). **$13,500-17,500**

An Italian lacquer and ebonised bureau cabinet, 41in (104cm). **$21,000-24,000**

A William III figured walnut veneered bureau cabinet, the top with sliding shelves enclosed by mirror panelled doors, one mirror replaced, the bureau front with herringbone line inlay, on bracket feet, old replacements, 45in (114cm). **$13,500-17,500**

A George I oyster-veneered walnut cabinet, 45in. **$30,000-34,500**

A George III satinwood Weeks secretaire cabinet, the baize-lined fall flap enclosing fitted interior, 38½in (98cm). **$30,000-37,500**

A Queen Anne walnut bureau cabinet, with fitted interior and secret drawers, 41in. **$30,000-34,500**

A27 ANTIQUES COMPLEX

CHAUCER TRADING ESTATE
DITTONS ROAD
(A27 TRUNK ROAD).
POLEGATE, EAST SUSSEX
Tel: (03212) 7167/5301 ■ (0435) 882553 (OUT OF HOURS)

4 DEALERS OCCUPYING 26,000 SQUARE FEET OFFERING QUALITY MERCHANDISE FOR ALL MARKETS.

GRAHAM PRICE ANTIQUES LIMITED

Antique wholesalers, importers and exporters

Specialists in quality stripped pine from UK, Ireland and Europe
Country French and decorative items
Georgian, Victorian and later furniture
Container packing
– restoration workshops
– courier service

JOHN BOTTING ANTIQUES

Wholesale export specialist in Period, Victorian, Edwardian furniture and accessories.
Good call for all Overseas and UK buyers

MONARCH ANTIQUES (JOHN KING)

Specialising in quality Victorian, Edwardian and later oak mahogany and walnut furniture and accessories.
Comprehensive and varied selection of furniture changing frequently

BBC ANTIQUES (BOBBY MORLEY)

English country wood and grass seated chairs, 19th Century Pine and Oak country furniture

The most comprehensive call in Southern England
Open Mon-Fri 9am-6pm.
Weekends by appointment.
Clients met from airports or station – friendly, efficient service.
Visit us on your next buying trip.

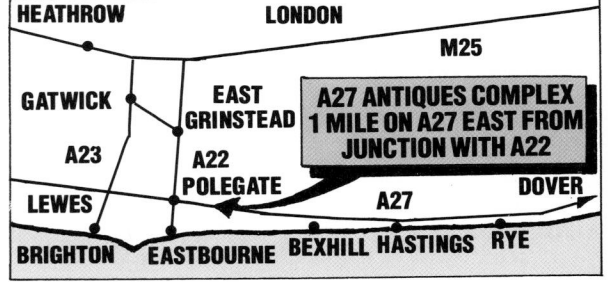

HEATHROW   LONDON   M25
GATWICK   EAST GRINSTEAD
A23   A22
POLEGATE
LEWES   A27   DOVER
BRIGHTON   EASTBOURNE   BEXHILL   HASTINGS   RYE

A27 ANTIQUES COMPLEX 1 MILE ON A27 EAST FROM JUNCTION WITH A22

A Queen Anne walnut cabinet on chest, interior with 8 drawers and pigeonholes, 26in. **$18,000-21,000**

A Dutch walnut and marquetry display cabinet, late 18thC, 60in (152cm). **$19,500-24,000**

A Chinese export black and gold lacquer bureau cabinet, mid-18thC, 42in (107cm). **$75,000-82,000**

A Louis XVI marquetry secretaire a abattant, by C Topino, with drawers, pigeonholes and coffre fort, 30in. **$82,000-97,000**

A Biedermeier mahogany secretaire a abattant, with Lancut label, 38½in (98cm). **$21,000-24,000**

A Regency mahogany chiffonier. **$30,000-34,500**

An early Victorian oak cabinet, by A W N Pugin and John Webb, 52in (132cm). **$4,500-7,000**

A Regency pollard oak cabinet, in the style of George Bullock, 61½in (156cm). **$24,000-28,500**

A mid-Victorian walnut display cabinet, A W N Pugin style, 50in. **$22,500-27,000**

A pair of mid-Victorian ormolu-mounted satinwood side cabinets, the glazed doors enclosing shelves, on bracket feet, 36in (91cm). **$7,500-10,500**

An ormolu-mounted ebonised, Japanese lacquer side cabinet, lacquer panels 17thC, 52in. **$25,000-28,000**

An Italian ebonised, tortoiseshell, giltmetal mounted cabinet on later stand, c1700, 68in. **$18,000-21,000**

A pair of late Victorian ebonised chiffoniers, 36in. **$4,000-5,500**

A pair of rosewood dwarf cabinets, 29½in (75cm). **$9,000-12,000**

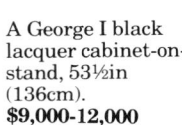

A Regency ormolu-mounted rosewood dwarf cabinet, with later marble top, 60in (152cm). **$15,000-21,000**

A George I black lacquer cabinet-on-stand, 53½in (136cm). **$9,000-12,000**

A William and Mary walnut, floral marquetry cabinet on stand, 45in. **$10,500-14,000**

A Charles II black and gold lacquer cabinet on stand, 41in. **$22,500-25,000**

A William and Mary oyster-veneered walnut and laburnum cabinet, 40in. **$7,500-10,500**

227

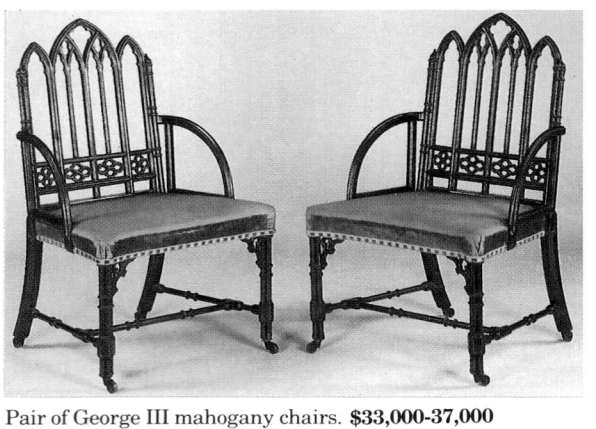

Pair of George III mahogany chairs. **$33,000-37,000**

Pair of early George III mahogany chairs, 27in (69cm). **$42,000-45,000**

A Federal mahogany chair, Massachusetts, 1790-1810. **$37,000-42,000**

George III mahogany chair. **$55,500-60,000**

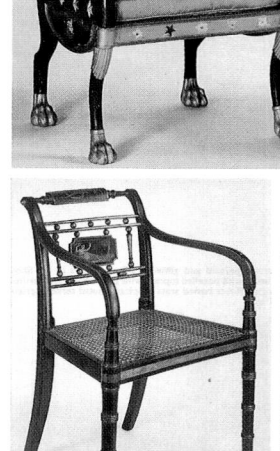

Pair of Regency bergeres. **$90,000-100,000**

Pair Rhode Island Windsor chairs. **$22,500-25,000**

Set of 4 Regency ebonised and gilt chairs. **$10,500-14,000**

A George III mahogany chair. **$13,500-17,500**

Regency 'Gothic' bergere, 19thC. **$21,000-25,000**

A set of 3 Adam carved giltwood chairs. **$8,000-10,500**

A pair of mahogany armchairs. **$4,500-7,000**

Two Dutch Colonial hardwood Burgomaster chairs, with an anthemion cresting and pierced splat.
$7,500-10,500

A pair of Chippendale carved mahogany side chairs, Philadelphia, 1765-1785.
$100,000-120,000

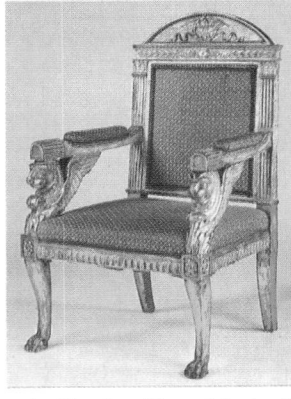

An Empire giltwood fauteuil.
$16,500-19,500

A pair of Queen Anne walnut side chairs, 21½in (51cm).
$16,500-19,500

A pair of Victorian papier mâché chairs.
$1,500-2,600

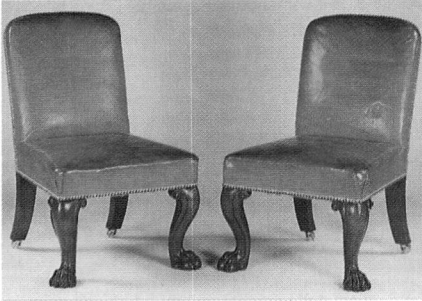

A set of 18 William IV mahogany side chairs, 23in (59cm).
$40,000-45,000

A pair of Queen Anne walnut and marquetry upholstered chairs, early 18thC.
$10,500-14,000

A set of 8 George I walnut dining chairs, 23½in (60cm).
$165,000-195,000

A pair of George II mahogany side chairs, 24½in (62cm).
$10,500-14,000

A set of 10 George III mahogany chairs. **$100,000-120,000**

A set of 6 Regency dining chairs. **$15,000-21,000**

A pair of Regency mahogany hall benches. **$90,000-100,000**

A George III mahogany serpentine chest, with moulded top and 4 graduated drawers, on bracket feet, 39in (99cm). **$13,500-17,500**

A William and Mary marquetry and oyster walnut chest, 39in (99cm). **$10,000-12,000**

A George II mahogany chest of drawers, mid-18thC, 45in (114cm). **$15,000-21,000**

A Queen Anne walnut, crossbanded bachelor's chest, 28in. **$10,500-14,000**

An early Georgian burr-walnut chest, 26in (66cm). **$24,000-27,000**

A George III mahogany chest, with 14 drawers, 25in. **$25,000-28,000**

A William and Mary oyster-veneered chest, top inlaid, 38in. **$9,000-12,000**

A George III satinwood bowfront chest, crossbanded with rosewood, 42in (107cm). **$19,500-22,500**

A George I burr-walnut chest-on-chest, 49in. **$18,000-21,000**

A George III mahogany chest of drawers. **$10,000-13,000**

An Anglo-Dutch walnut bachelor's chest, 33½in (85cm). **$10,500-14,000**

A George III mahogany serpentine commode, 50½in (128cm). **$10,500-14,000**

A George III ormolu-mounted rosewood and pollard oak commode, by Chippendale, Haig & Co, the shaped top inlaid with an oval, 49in (125cm). **$75,000-82,000**

A William and Mary kingwood chest-on-stand, the stand c1840, 49½in (126cm). **$6,000-9,000**

A Queen Anne inlaid walnut high chest of drawers, in 2 sections, Massachusetts, 1730-1740, 39in (99cm). **$45,000-49,000**

An early Louis XV kingwood and marquetry bombe commode, 51in (130cm) **$10,500-14,000**

A Chippendale maple chest-on-chest, some restorations, New England, 1760-1790, 37½in (95cm). **$25,000-28,000**

A Chippendale cherrywood chest, Conn, c1770, 42in. **$42,000-45,000**

A George III ormolu-mounted kingwood and marquetry commode, in the manner of Pierre Langlois, 39in (99cm). **$25,000-28,000**

A George III mahogany serpentine commode, with crossbanded moulded top, 49½in (126cm). **$19,500-24,000**

Butchoff Antiques

Victorian and Georgian Furniture

233 Westbourne Grove, London W11
Telephone: 01-221 8174

A Louis XV kingwood commode, Charles Cressent style, 56in. **$195,000+**

A Louis XVI tulipwood petite commode, brown and grey marble top, Lancut label, 16½in. **$6,000-9,000**

A Transitional tulipwood and kingwood petite commode, Lancut label, 16in. **$2,500-3,500**

An ormolu-mounted mahogany commode, Louis XVI style, with marble top, 76in (193cm). **$13,500-17,500**

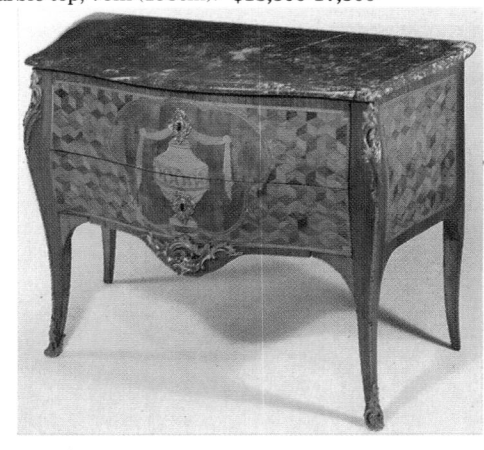

A Louis XV kingwood, bois satine and marquetry commode, stamped Macret, 50in. **$16,500-22,500**

A Louis XV tulipwood commode, 43in. **$9,000-12,000**

A Chippendale blue-painted maple chest, New England, 1810, 41in. **$6,000-9,000**

An Italian rosewood commode, with ivory, mother-of-pearl and pewter inlay, c1680, 60in. **$9,000-12,000**

PENNARD HOUSE ANTIQUES

We carry large stocks of period pine and country furniture, from England, Ireland and France.
All restorations done in our own workshops.

3/4 Piccadilly, London Road, Bath BA1 6PL Telephone: Bath (0225) 313791
Pennard House, East Pennard, Shepton Mallet, Somerset BA4 6TP
Telephone: Ditcheat (074986) 266

A George I walnut partners' desk, the moulded top inlaid with featherbanded geometric pattern, 2 frieze drawers and 9 various-sized drawers each side, 60in (152cm). **$34,000-39,000**

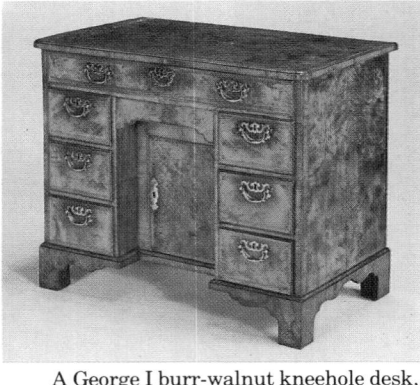

A George I burr-walnut kneehole desk, with fitted interior and dressing mirror, 36in. **$39,000-42,000**

A George II mahogany partners' desk, with leather-lined top and 9 various-sized drawers, with brass lockplates numbered 1-18, 57½in (146cm). **$22,500-25,000**

A Queen Anne walnut kneehole desk, with quartered top, 7 drawers, on restored bracket feet, 28in (71cm). **$21,000-24,000**

A William and Mary figured walnut kneehole desk, inlaid with featherbanding, on later bracket feet, 34in (86cm). **$7,500-10,500**

A George III mahogany pedestal desk, with leather-lined and gilt-tooled top, stamped SH and CP, 60in (152cm). **$22,500-25,000**

A William IV pollard oak architect's desk, with hinged easel top above adjustable shelves, early 19thC, 67in (170cm). **$21,000-24,000**

A Queen Anne burr-walnut kneehole desk, with mirror-backed baize-lined writing surface, veneered back, 37in. **$67,000-75,000**

A George III satinwood cylinder desk, with balustraded three-quarter galleried top and tambour shutter enclosing a fitted interior of pigeonholes and 2 drawers, the back with fixed tambour panel, 39½in (99.5cm). **$45,000-52,000**

A George I gilt and gesso wall mirror, with palmette cresting flanked by eagles heads, 36 by 19in (91 by 48cm). **$7,500-10,500**

A mid-Victorian black, gilt and mother-of-pearl japanned papier mâché davenport, with velvet-lined writing slope and pen drawer to the side, 27in (69cm). **$4,000-5,500**

A Regency ormolu-mounted mahogany and ebonised Carlton House desk, with leather-lined easel slide, 3 drawers with twin dolphin handles, 57in (145cm). **$100,000-120,000**

A Chippendale maple slant-front desk, attributed to Dominy, Long Island, New York, 1760-1780, minor repair to lid, 36in (90cm). **$10,500-14,000**

A George III mahogany roll-top desk, the interior with satinwood fronted drawers and pigeonholes, the pull-out writing slope with leather-inset, 42in (107cm). **$6,000-9,000**

A William III giltwood mirror, with later oval plate, 74½ by 46in (189 by 117cm). **$9,000-12,000**

A Queen Anne giltwood mirror, with shaped divided bevelled plate, 69 by 44in (175 by 112cm). **$55,500-60,000**

A pair of George I gilt-gesso pier glasses, with later plates, 87 by 33½in (221 by 85cm). **$60,000-67,500**

A George I giltwood mirror, lacking candle sconces, 60 by 29½in (152 by 75cm). **$22,500-25,000**

An early George III giltwood mirror, 38in. **$10,500-14,000**

A William and Mary black and gold lacquer mirror, 35in (89cm) wide. **$7,500-10,500**

A George II white-painted overmantel, 64 by 63in. **$10,500-14,000**

A George II giltwood mirror, with carved rococo frame, 41in (104cm) wide. **$15,000-21,000**

Early Chippendale period glass. **$10,500-14,000**

A George I burr-walnut and parcel gilt mirror, with later bevelled plate, 23in wide. **$10,500-14,000**

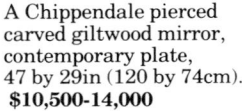

A Chippendale pierced carved giltwood mirror, contemporary plate, 47 by 29in (120 by 74cm). **$10,500-14,000**

An early George III giltwood mirror, 57 by 29in (145 by 74cm). **$10,500-14,000**

A George II giltwood overmantel, with later bevelled plate, 79 by 76½in (200 by 193cm). **$19,500-22,500**

A George II walnut and parcel gilt mirror, 52 by 27in (132 by 69cm). **$24,000-27,000**

An early George III giltwood mirror, by Thomas Chippendale. **$82,000-90,000**

A George III giltwood mirror, 42 by 31in. **$25,000-30,000**

A George III giltwood overmantel, with shaped divided plate and carved frame, adapted, 40in wide. **$15,000-21,000**

A pair of George III giltwood mirrors, 48½ by 22½in (123 by 57cm). **$30,000-34,500**

A Dieppe ivory mirror, with carved frame, 34in wide. **$10,500-14,000**

A Chippendale carved giltwood mirror, 32 by 46½in (82 by 118cm). **$9,000-12,000**

An early George III giltwood mirror, with later plate, C-scroll frame crested with a squirrel, 32in wide. **$18,000-21,000**

An early George III giltmetal automaton toilet mirror, one side magnifying, by James Cox, 11½in. **$100,000-120,000**

A Chippendale giltwood mirror, 50in (127cm) high. **$13,500-17,500**

A pair of George III giltwood mirrors by Thomas Chippendale, repairs and replacements, 29in wide. **$97,000-100,000**

239

A George III giltwood mirror, later oval plate, out-scrolled rush frame with splayed base, 39 by 26½in (99 by 67cm). **$7,500-10,500**

An Italian lead-framed mirror, early 18thC, 60½ by 28in (153 by 71cm). **$13,500-17,500**

A pair of Regency giltwood pier glasses, 98 by 52½in (249 by 133cm). **$15,000-21,000**

Chippendale mirror. **$13,500-17,500**

A Queen Anne mirror. **$6,000-9,000**

A George III satinwood and mahogany mirror, 19in wide. **$6,000-9,000**

A late 18thC mirror. **$9,000-12,000**

A Regence giltwood mirror, 26in wide. **$7,500-10,500**

A Regence giltwood mirror, 40in wide. **$9,000-12,000**

A pair of pier glasses. **$10,500-14,000**

240

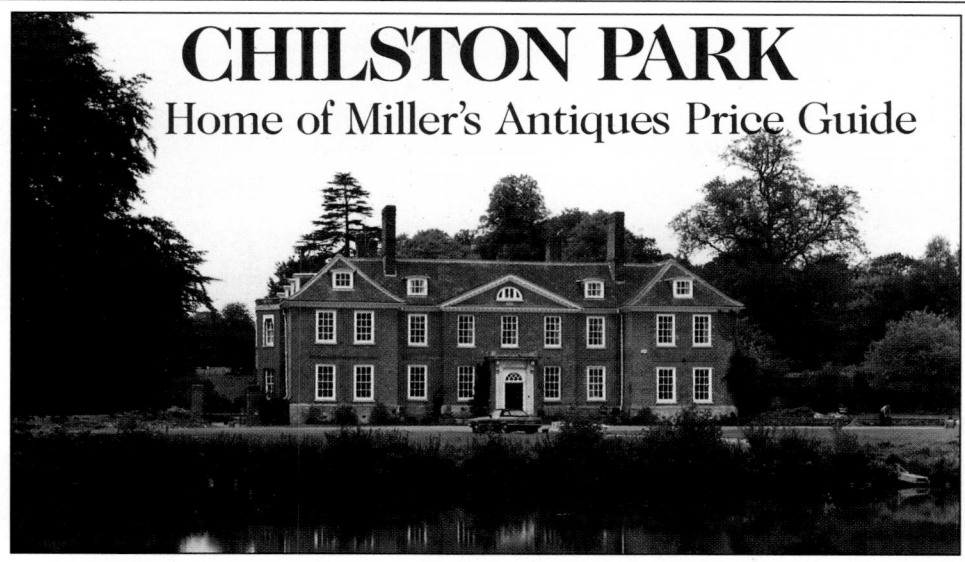

A George I walnut and beechwood settee, 64in (162cm). **$67,000-75,000**

A Regency giltwood settee in the Grecian taste, by Gillow's of London, 78in (198cm). **$120,000-135,000**

A George III cream painted and parcel gilt triple chairback settee, c1770, 57in (144cm). **$27,000-33,000**

A walnut canape, the padded back and bowed seat upholstered in petit point needlework, on fluted tapering legs, late 18thC, 76in (193cm). **$6,000-8,000**

A pair of George IV rococo revival giltwood sofas, with shaped padded backs, arms and seats with squab cushions, 124in (315cm). **$21,000-24,000**

A George III cream painted and gilded sofa, 78in (198cm). **$9,000-12,000**

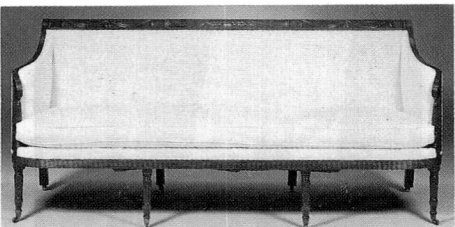

A Federal carved mahogany sofa, the shop of Duncan Phyfe, New York, 1800-20, 80in (203cm). **$51,000-57,000**

A George III mahogany sofa, with arched padded back and cushion seat, on square tapering legs, 73in (185cm). **$8,000-10,500**

A Regency Anglo-Indian mahogany sofa, 90in (228cm). **$4,000-5,500**

A Regency mahogany sideboard, inlaid with bands of brass ovals on an ebonised ground, drawers enclosing divided interiors, 88½in (224cm). **$21,000-24,000**

A George III faded mahogany sideboard, early 19thC, 64in (163cm). **$7,500-10,500**

A Regency mahogany sideboard, with brass rail centred by candle sconces and spherical top, 81½in (207cm). **$10,500-14,000**

A Regency mahogany breakfront sideboard, George Smith style, with 3 frieze drawers, 87in (221cm). **$13,500-17,500**

A pair of giltwood torchères, the tops decorated with chinoiserie lacquer, adapted, 13½in (34cm). **$10,500-14,000**

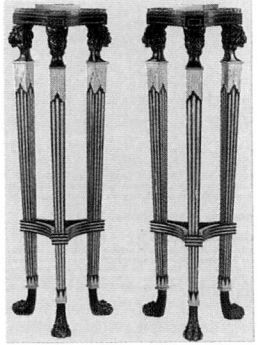

A pair of Regency parcel gilt and simulated green patinated bronze torchères, 16½in. **$75,000-90,000**

A George III mahogany stand, attributed to Thomas Chippendale, 24½in diam. **$7,500-10,500**

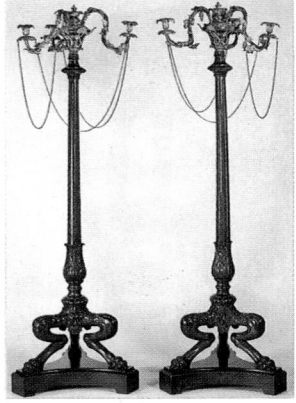

A pair of George IV ormolu and mahogany torchères, George Smith style, 68½in (174cm). **$15,000-21,000**

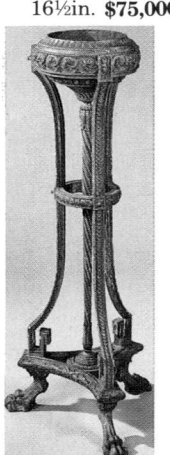

A Regency giltwood tripod Athenienne in Louis XVI taste, 38in high. **$10,500-14,000**

A mid-Victorian oak, walnut and marquetry sideboard, with mirrored centre, 132in (335cm). **$7,500-10,500**

A Regency brass inlaid rosewood breakfast table, the faded well-figured top crossbanded with rosewood and inlaid with brass lines and leaves, the base set with brass panels cut with stylised anthemia and scrolls, early 19thC, 51in (129.5cm) diam.
$13,500-17,500

A Federal inlaid mahogany corner stand, the bowed top with line inlaid front, supports and legs with ebonised reserves, New York, c1800, 23in (58.5cm).
$9,000-12,000

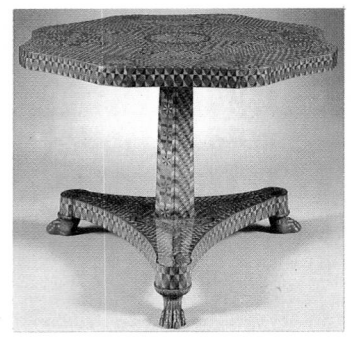

A Continental parquetry breakfast table, with lobed tilt top on hexagonal support and tripartite base on paw feet, inlaid with cube pattern and radiating stars, mid-19thC, 42½in (108cm) diam.
$4,500-7,000

A William IV rosewood architect's table, with moulded well-figured rising easel top and twin book rests, early 19thC, 45in (114cm).
$10,500-14,000

A Louis XVI tulipwood and parquetry two-tier gueridon, stamped C TOPINO JME, with adjustable ormolu galleried marble top, above an inlaid tier in stained and engraved woods, restorations, late 18thC, 29in (74cm) unextended.
$6,000-8,000

A George I burr walnut architect's table, the crossbanded easel top inlaid with chevron pattern banding, with pop-up book rest and brass candlesticks, the frieze with narrow drawer above a pull-out fitted drawer, early 18thC, 34in (86cm).
$10,500-14,000

A Louis XVI tulipwood and parquetry porcelain mounted gueridon, by Martin Carlin, date letter X for 1775.
$135,000-165,000

A Louis XVI mahogany table à la Tronchin, the adjustable top with easel and candle-slide, 34in (86cm).
$15,000-21,000

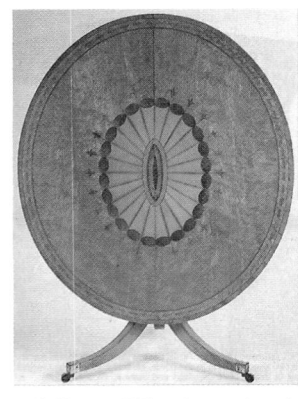

A George III satinwood and inlaid breakfast table, crossbanded in tulipwood, the top with a central radiating fan medallion, 48in (123cm).
$13,500-17,500

An oak and pollard oak centre table, with crossbanded top on entwined triple dolphin support, on concave-sided platform and bun feet, 19thC, 41in (104cm) diam. **$24,000-27,000**

A George II walnut and fruitwood card table, in the manner of Benjamin Goodison, panelled frieze and sides, concertina action, hinges stamped S. Johnson, 36½in (92.5cm). **$30,000-34,500**

A pair of Regency rosewood card tables, with boxwood stringing, the rounded swivelling baize-lined tops enclosing compartments, on twinned supports with concave sided platforms, one repaired, 36in (91.5cm). **$16,500-19,500**

A pair of Regency brass inlaid rosewood and simulated rosewood card tables, with twin-flap baize-lined rounded rectangular tops, on scrolling quadripartite base, with claw feet, 36in (91.5cm). **$7,500-10,500**

A Chippendale mahogany card table, the hinged top opening to a baize-covered surface, above a conforming apron centering a cockbeaded drawer, Pennsylvania or Maryland, some restoration, 1750-80, 35in (90cm). **$15,000-21,000**

A Queen Anne yew-wood centre table, with inset marquetry ivory centre, 27½in (70cm). **$45,000-52,000**

A Regency parcel gilt and rosewood centre table, with specimen marble top, 28in (71cm). **$22,500-25,000**

A Queen Anne laburnum-wood card table, with baize-lined top enclosing wells and candle-stands, 34in (86cm). **$16,500-19,500**

A walnut centre table, with moulded specimen marble top, 47in (119cm).
$7,500-10,500

A Dutch oyster veneered walnut and marquetry centre table, highlighted in ivory and ebony, 45½in (115cm). **$6,000-8,000**

A Portuguese ebony and kingwood centre table, the top inlaid with trelliswork and geometric bands, the frieze with clasps and grotesque beasts, 66½in (168cm).
$9,000-12,000

An English walnut specimen marble top centre table, with brass edge, c1845, 26½in (67cm) diam. **$10,500-14,000**

A parcel gilt rosewood and mahogany centre table, late 19thC, 39in (99cm).
$6,000-9,000

A Louis XIII walnut centre table, with tray top and ebonised border, on octagonal tapering legs, 21½in (54.5cm).
$4,000-5,500

A Victorian pollard oak and painted centre table, the top crossbanded with rosewood
29in (74cm). **$18,000-21,000**

A Regency faded rosewood centre table, inlaid with beechwood lines and scrolls, 44½in (112cm). **$27,000-30,000**

A pair of George I style giltwood console tables, late 19thC, 61in (155cm). **$16,500-19,500**

A George IV grained rosewood and parcel gilt console table, 42½in (106.5cm). **$15,000-21,000**

An Italian parcel gilt and black-painted console table, late 18thC, 29½in (75cm). **$4,500-7,000**

An Empire ormolu mounted mahogany console table, with later marble top, 64in. **$37,000-40,000**

An ormolu mounted tulipwood and ebony centre table, 28½in (72cm). **$6,000-9,000**

A Louis XV giltwood console table, 38½in (97cm). **$9,000-12,000**

A George IV giltwood console table, the carving mainly mid-18thC, 77½in (196cm). **$16,500-19,500**

A pair of Italian Empire parcel gilt and blue painted console tables, 42in. **$15,000-21,000**

A Chippendale mahogany drop-leaf dining table, on stop-fluted square legs, Townsend School, Newport, Rhode Island, c1770, 43in (109cm). **$27,000-30,000**

A Dutch walnut and marquetry games table, the top with 2 inlaid lifting panels, with chessboard on the reverse, partly 17thC, on later turned legs, 45in (114cm) wide. **$9,000-12,000**

A Regency rosewood drum table, the top with 4 drawers divided by hinged flaps, on turned foliate stem, 41½in (105cm) diam. **$10,500-14,000**

A Regency brass inlaid rosewood games table, with crossbanded twin-flap top, 56½in (143cm). **$4,500-7,000**

An Italian walnut and yew-wood trestle table, with crossbanded top, the fluted frieze partly filled with spindles, on twinned square feet and trestle ends, joined by a moulded stretcher and scrolling foliate feet, 90in (228cm) long. **$4,500-7,000**

A Charles II oak gateleg table, with oval double flap top and a drawer, tips of leaves renewed, 70in (177cm). **$13,500-17,500**

A late Louis XVI mahogany dining table, with ormolu bordered D-shaped ends with flaps, on ormolu-capped tapering legs, 51½in (130cm). **$9,000-12,000**

249

A late Victorian Anglo-Indian Imperial mahogany dining table, with moulded D-shaped end sections, on ring turned ribbed bulbous legs, with mother-of-pearl plaques, Shearwood & Co, Calcutta, 76in (193cm), with 8 extra leaves in mahogany case.
$10,500-14,000

A George III mahogany 4 pedestal D-end dining table, with a moulded edge, the snap tops raised on ring turned gun barrel columns and tripod inswept legs with brass cappings and casters, including 3 extra leaves, 190in (485cm) extended.
$28,500-31,500

A George III faded mahogany 2 pedestal dining table, c1800, 45in (114cm).
$13,500-17,500

A George III mahogany dining table, early 19thC, 141in (358cm), with 2 extra leaves.
$34,500-37,000

A George III faded mahogany 3 pedestal dining table, engraved Marshall Patent, No.21, Gerrard Street, Soho, 136in (345cm). **$21,000-24,000**

A Regency padoukwood and mahogany patent dining table, inscribed 'Butlers Patent', 65in (165cm). **$22,500-25,000**

An early Victorian Gothic Revival refectory table, 127in (322cm).
$37,000-40,000

An oak draw-leaf refectory table, basically early 17thC, 268in (680cm). **$10,500-14,000**

Huntington Antiques Ltd.

A Queen Anne carved and inlaid walnut dressing table, Portsmouth, New Hampshire, c1740, 36in (91.5cm). **$82,000-90,000**

A George III mahogany and marquetry spider gateleg table, in the manner of John Cobb, 35½in (90cm), open. **$25,000-28,000**

A late George III mahogany library table, with leather-lined top and 6 inlaid frieze drawers, 49in (124cm). **$15,000-21,000**

A William and Mary fruitwood gateleg table, the crossbanded top with one flap and hinged compartment, 29in (73cm). **$10,500-14,000**

A Regency mahogany library table, the leather-lined swivelling top with gilt key pattern border, 52in (132cm). **$10,500-14,000**

A late Louis XV kingwood table de nuit, stamped P.A. Veaux, J.M.E. **$4,000-5,500**

A Louis XVI kingwood, marquetry and parquetry petit table, by N A Lapie, 26in (66cm). **$7,500-10,500**

A Transitional ormolu mounted tulipwood and marquetry gueridon, 14in (35cm) diam. **$19,500-22,500**

A Louis XV/XVI Transitional tulipwood, marquetry and ormolu mounted gueridon, stamped Dusautoy, 19½in. **$7,500-10,500**

A Louis XVIII ormolu gueridon, the inset porphyry top with beaded gadrooned border, 45in (114cm) diam. **$150,000+**

An early George III harewood and satinwood veneered Pembroke writing table, the top with inlaid marquetry panels, 25in. **$40,000-45,000**

A Regency rosewood library table by Richard Goodman, made in commemoration of the explorer Captain James Cook and his ship HMS Resolution, the parquetry top of various exotic woods centred by a medallion inlaid with an urn of oak reputedly from HMS Resolution, together with ivory plaques with inscriptions, 58½in (148cm). **$90,000-100,000**

An early Victorian ebony and marquetry library table, by Edward Holmes Baldock, banded with kingwood, the frieze with flowering panels, fitted with 4 drawers, 58in. **$13,500-17,500**

A George III mahogany Pembroke table, with well-figured twin-flap top above a concave frieze drawer, 42in (107cm) extended. **$13,500-17,500**

A George III mahogany Pembroke table, with matched flame-grained mahogany top, 35in (99cm) wide, extended. **$5,500-7,000**

An early Victorian black, gilt japanned papier mâché pedestal table, Jennens and Bettridge, 20in. **$4,000-5,500**

A George IV rosewood library table, attributed to Gillows, with leather-lined top and border inlaid with cut-brass foliage, edged with ormolu gadrooning, the concave frieze with single full width drawer, 66in (168cm). **$15,000-21,000**

A George III satinwood and harewood Pembroke table, the crossbanded serpentine twin-flap top with later inlaid flowerhead oval, with 2 frieze drawers, 49½in (126cm), open. **$10,000-13,000**

A Federal inlaid mahogany Pembroke table, attributed to Michael Allison, New York, c1820, 28in (71cm) high. **$10,500-14,000**

A George I walnut lowboy, with crossbanded quartered top with re-entrant front corners, one leg spliced, 30in (76cm). **$16,500-19,500**

A George III satinwood Pembroke table, the twin-flap top crossbanded with mahogany, 39½in (100cm) open. **$13,500-17,500**

A George III harewood and marquetry Pembroke table, the hinged twin-flap easel top crossbanded and inlaid, 43in (109cm) open. **$9,000-12,000**

A George III mahogany rent table, the leather lined top with central lid and turned ebony handle, enclosing a well, 64½in (164cm). **$52,000-60,000**

A George III rent table, with gilt tooled leather crossbanded top, fitted with a well, late 18thC, 43in (109cm). **$21,000-24,000**

A painted satinwood Pembroke table, the twin-flap top crossbanded with rosewood, 36in (91cm). **$7,500-10,500**

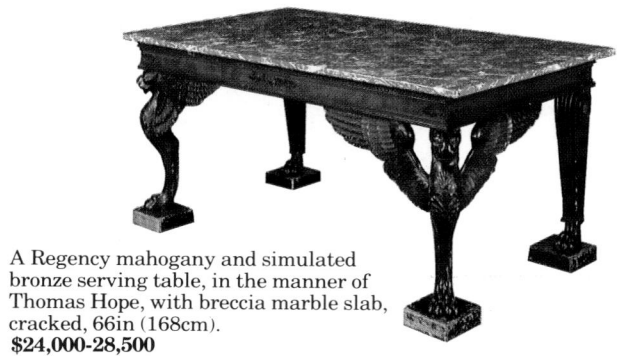

A Regency mahogany and simulated bronze serving table, in the manner of Thomas Hope, with breccia marble slab, cracked, 66in (168cm). **$24,000-28,500**

A gilt and gesso japanned side table, decorated with figures and landscapes, some restoration, early 18thC, 33in (82cm). **$15,000-21,000**

A George II walnut side table, with panelled frieze centred by a cartouche and framed by 2 well-carved putti, 69½in (176cm). **$18,000-21,000**

A George II walnut side table, with moulded grey-veined white marble top, elaborately carved, 65in (165cm). **$31,500-34,500**

A Regency ormolu-mounted mahogany breakfront serving table, the convex frieze fitted with 3 drawers edged with egg-and-dart decoration, 81in (205cm). **$15,000-21,000**

A pair of George III mahogany serpentine serving tables, with moulded tops and plain friezes, slight damage, 67in (170cm). **$19,500-22,500**

A late George III mahogany serpentine serving table, inlaid with boxwood and chevron lines, possibly Scottish, 75in (190cm). **$10,500-14,000**

A pair of George II gessoed pine side tables, with later breccia marble tops, the cabriole legs headed by masks with fruiting swags, 55in (140cm). **$45,000-52,000**

A Queen Anne walnut lowboy, the crossbanded top with re-entrant corners, 30in (76cm). **$4,500-7,000**

An important George II giltwood side table, made for St Giles's House, Dorset, with marble top, the deeply fluted frieze elaborately carved, mid-18thC, 68in (172.5cm).
$225,000+

A pair of George III satinwood and marquetry side tables, late 18thC, 44in (112cm).
$16,500-19,500

A giltwood side table, with eared verde antico marble top, 40in (101.5cm).
$13,500-17,500

A pair of George III mahogany side tables, 31in (78.5cm).
$27,000-30,000

A George III yew and marquetry side table, with inlaid frieze drawer, 22½in (57cm).
$13,500-17,500

A pair of George III satinwood side tables, the top painted with a fan lunette with medallion of a Muse, 47in (119cm). **$34,000-39,000**

A George III satinwood and giltwood side table, the top banded with rosewood and tulipwood, 57½in (145cm).
$18,000-21,000

A pine and yew side table in George II style, with crossbanded chamfered and eared top, 54in (137cm).
$6,000-8,000

A Regency rosewood, parcel gilt and painted side table, of concave sided and inverted breakfront form, 58in (147cm).
$18,000-21,000

A Regency brass-inlaid rosewood sofa table, the canted twin-flap top with ebonised border, 2 frieze drawers, 61in (153cm) open. **$13,500-17,500**

A William IV rosewood sofa table, with 2 fitted frieze drawers, stamped T. & A. Blain, Liverpool, 58in (145cm). **$6,000-9,000**

A Regency rosewood and brass mounted sofa table, with top crossbanded in satinwood, 61in (152cm). **$42,000-48,000**

A Regency rosewood sofa table, with 2 frieze drawers, 58in (145cm). **$10,000-13,000**

A Regency rosewood sofa table, with brass inlay, 2 frieze drawers, some restoration, 58in. **$15,000-21,000**

A Regency rosewood sofa table, crossbanded with satinwood, 62in (154cm) open. **$15,000-21,000**

A Regency fiddleback mahogany sofa table, crossbanded with rosewood and inlaid with lines, 61½in (154cm). **$10,500-14,000**

A Regency mahogany sofa table, inlaid with ebonised stringing, twin-flap top with reeded edge, 55½in (141cm) open. **$7,500-10,500**

A George II mahogany tripod table, the cabriole legs with scroll feet and leather casters, mid-18thC, 25in (63.5cm).
$13,500-17,500

A Regency ormolu mounted rosewood work table, with canted pierced galleried hinged top, with glazed panel and floral needle-work, enclosing a well, 16in (40.5cm).
$2,250-3,500

A mahogany tripod table, with moulded lobed top, 17in (43cm).
$4,500-7,000

A mid-Victorian black, gilt and mother-of-pearl japanned papier mâché pedestal sewing box, 15in (38cm).
$3,000-4,500

A classical mahogany work table, the hinged top enclosing a fitted interior, New York, c1820, 27in (68.5cm).
$13,500-17,500

An early Victorian black and mother-of-pearl japanned papier mâché pedestal sewing box, 32½in (82cm) high.
$2,250-3,500

A Chippendale mahogany tilt-top tea table, Massachusetts, c1780, 29in (73.5cm) high.
$30,000-37,500

A Regency rosewood and Boulle work table, the canted top banded with stylised foliage, 21½in (54cm).
$13,500-17,500

A George III plum pudding mahogany metamorphic writing table, with fitted interior and dummy drawers, 49in (123cm). **$10,500-14,000**

A George III mahogany writing table, with russet leather-lined top, 68in (173cm). **$13,500-17,500**

A German rococo kingwood and marquetry table à écrire, with crossbanded inlaid top, restored, mid-18thC, 45½in (114cm). **$13,500-17,500**

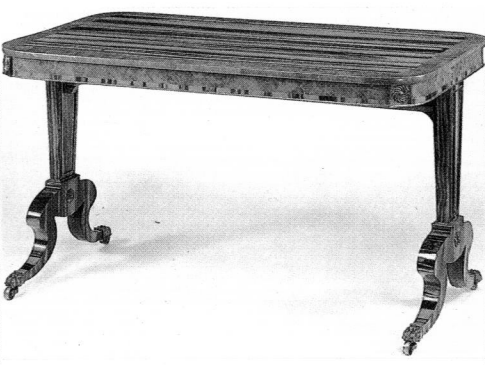

A Regency calamanderwood and pollard oak writing table, the rounded top with kingwood border, 46in (116cm). **$10,000-13,000**

A George III mahogany writing table, with orange leather-lined top, 54in (137cm). **$13,500-17,500**

A fine Regency rosewood and brass inlaid writing table, early 19thC, 45in (113cm). **$45,000-52,000**

A George III mahogany writing table, with tooled leather top above 6 drawers, c1775, 48½in (121cm). **$27,000-30,000**

A George III satinwood, mahogany and harewood writing table, c1800, 59in (148cm). **$22,500-25,000**

A Louis XVI brass mounted mahogany bureau plat, with leather-lined top and 3 panelled frieze drawers, with panelled sides and fluted tapering legs, 65in (165cm). **$27,000-30,000**

An ormolu mounted walnut and marquetry writing table of Transitional style, stamped Edwards & Roberts, possibly by H Dasson, 35½in (90cm). **$10,000-13,000**

An ormolu mounted mahogany bureau plat, after the model by G Beneman, 78in (198cm). **$13,500-17,500**

A Louis XVI sycamore and marquetry table à écrire, in the manner of Topino, stamped P. Roussel, JME, 23in (58cm). **$9,000-12,000**

A Louis XV tulip-wood and parquetry table à écrire, repairs, chateau mark CT beneath a coronet, mid-18thC. **$13,500-17,500**

A Louis XVI ormolu mounted mahogany bureau plat, late 18thC, 65in (165cm). **$13,500-17,500**

A Louis XV kingwood, tulipwood, marquetry and ormolu mounted table à écrire, stamped Migeon, 38½in (98cm). **$67,000-75,000**

An ormolu mounted scarlet Boulle bureau plat of Régence style, the moulded top inlaid with Bérainesque strapwork and figures, with scallop clasp borders and gadrooned border, 50in (127cm). **$10,500-14,000**

The John Penn Chippendale carved mahogany slab-top table, with white and grey marble top, Philadelphia, c1770, 45in. **$675,000+**

An Italian scagliola table top, inset into a mid-Georgian mahogany table, the panel, cracked, early 18thC, 48in (122cm). **$40,000-45,000**

An Italian scagliola panel, painted with putti and scrolls, 18thC, set in a red lacquer table, 50in (125cm). **$4,000-5,500**

A pair of mahogany stools, the padded seats with petit point needlework sprays. **$7,000-9,000**

A George III mahogany stool, inscribed William Flars t. Sept 1768, 38in. **$13,500-17,500**

A pair of George III carved mahogany stools. **$13,500-17,500**

A pair of George III mahogany stools, with cane-filled seats, 22in (55cm). **$7,500-10,500**

A Louis XIV giltwood folding stool, the X-frame carved with acanthus foliage and scrolls, 26in (65cm). **$10,500-14,000**

A pair of Italian Empire parcel gilt and fruitwood stools, 27½in (68.5cm). **$7,500-10,500**

261

A Regency ormolu mounted ebonised and pollard oak wine cooler, in the manner of George Bullock, the domed top centred by a lotus flower, with scrolling foliate handles, the interior with a detachable tin liner, 40½in (102cm).
$30,000-37,500

A Regency pollard elm covered wine cooler, the domed panelled top enclosing a divided, lined interior, early 19thC, 30in (76cm).
$6,000-9,000

A Regency rosewood canterbury, 20in (51cm).
$4,500-7,000

A George III satinwood canterbury, the hinged top with gallery above 3 dividers and turned supports, the frieze with 2 drawers on ring turned tapering legs.
$13,500-17,500

A George III satinwood and marquetry cellaret, the segmented top centred by a bat's-wing lunette with crossbanded border, 25in (63.5cm).
$28,500-34,000

A Regency mahogany wine cooler, the top crossbanded in rosewood, enclosing a tin-lined interior, 29in (73.5cm).   **$6,000-9,000**

A pair of Regency terrestrial and celestial globes, dated March 1816, the terrestrial globe with corrections and additions to 1829, and re-supported, 24in (61cm) diam. **$24,000-27,000**

A pair of George III terrestrial and celestial globes, by D Adams, 1809, with mid-Victorian mahogany stands, 22½in (57cm) diam.
$9,000-12,000

Two mid-Victorian black, mother-of-pearl japanned papier mâché whatnots, 26½in (67cm). **$1,500-2,600 each**

A pair of George III mahogany and brass dumb waiters, early 19thC, 44½in (111cm) high. **$27,000-30,000**

A pair of mid-Victorian ebonised and gilt japanned papier mâché polescreens, 56½in (141cm) high. **$4,500-7,000**

A George III brass bound mahogany plate bucket, later brass liner, stamped 'O', 14½in (37cm) diam. **$4,500-7,000**

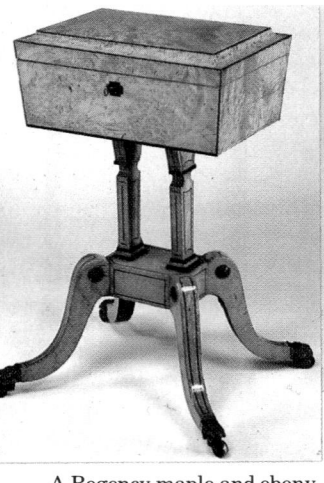

A Regency maple and ebony teapoy, top enclosing baize-lined interior, 16in (40cm). **$4,500-7,000**

A Directoire ormolu-mounted mahogany jardinière, 29in (73cm). **$13,500-17,500**

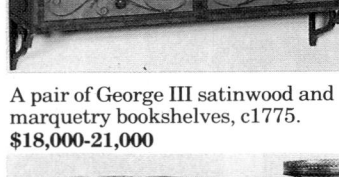

A pair of George III satinwood and marquetry bookshelves, c1775. **$18,000-21,000**

Two Regency ormolu-mounted mahogany dumb waiters, 26½in (66cm) diam.

(l.) **$10,000-13,000** r.) **$7,500-10,500**

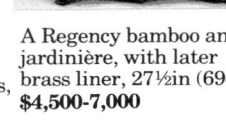

A Regency bamboo and birch jardinière, with later brass liner, 27½in (69cm). **$4,500-7,000**

A pair of Italian walnut and marquetry jardinières, late 18thC, 15in. **$10,000-13,000**

A Dutch gilt leather screen, painted with birds of paradise, ducks, cockerels and song birds amid flowering and fruiting foliage, the borders with vases of flowers and baskets of fruit, early 18thC, each leaf 84 by 22in (213 by 56cm).
$10,500-14,000

A Louis XVI giltwood four-leaf screen, with arched leaves inset with panels of floral silk brocade, the panelled frame crisply carved, the angles headed by acanthus whorls, the crestings centred by foliate clasps, each leaf 49½ by 29in (125 by 74cm).
$13,500-17,500

A Regency black and gold lacquer six-leaf screen, with scenes of a sailing boat, pavilions, animals, figures, birds, flowers and bordered by a key pattern and foliage, within an outer border of foliate scrolls, the reverse with leaves and flowers, each leaf 108 by 24in (274 by 61cm).
$10,500-14,000

A pair of Italian giltwood columns, late 17thC, 78½in (199cm) high.
$6,000-9,000

A Dutch polychrome painted leather six-leaf screen, 18thC, each leaf 84 by 22in (213 by 56cm).
$33,000-37,000

A Chinese coromandel lacquer twelve-leaf screen, 18thC, each leaf 94 by 19in (238 by 48cm).
$64,000-70,000

A Dutch painted and gilt leather six-leaf screen, with chinoiserie figures, birds and shrubs, the borders with flowers and fruits, 18thC, each leaf 96 by 22in (243 by 56cm).
$10,000-13,000

BRITISH ANTIQUE EXPORTERS LTD

WHOLESALERS, EXPORTERS PACKERS SHIPPERS

HEAD OFFICE: QUEEN ELIZABETH AVENUE, BURGESS HILL, WEST SUSSEX, RH15 9RX ENGLAND

TELEPHONE BURGESS HILL (04446) 45577

TELEX 87688 ANTIQE G

To: Auctioneers, Wholesalers and Retailers of antique furniture, porcelain and decorative items.

Dear Sirs

We offer the most comprehensive service available in the UK.

As wholesalers we sell 20ft and 40ft container-loads of antique furniture, porcelain and decorative items of the Georgian, Victorian, Edwardian and 1930's periods. Our buyers are strategically placed throughout the UK in order to take full advantage of regional pricing.

You can purchase a container from us for as little as £5,000. You could expect to pay approximately £7,000 to £10,000 for a shipment £25,000 would buy a Georgian, Queen Anne and Chippendale style container.

Containers can be tailored to your exact requirements - for example, you may deal only in office furniture and therefore only buy desks, file cabinets and related office items.

Our terms are £1,500 deposit, the balance at time of arrival of the container. If the merchandise should not be to your liking for any reason whatsoever, <u>we offer you your money back in full</u>, less one-way freight.

We have now opened a large showroom where you can purchase individual items.

If you wish to visit the UK yourself and purchase individually from your own sources, we will collect, pack and ship your merchandise with speed and efficiency. Our rates are competitive and our packing is the finest available anywhere in the world. Our courier-finder service is second to none and we have experienced couriers who are equipped with a car and the knowledge of where to find the best buys.

If your business is buying English antiques, we are your contact. We assure you of our best attention at all times.

Yours faithfully
BRITISH ANTIQUE EXPORTERS LTD

Norman Lefton
Chairman & Managing Director

A. FIELD, MSC FBOA DCLP FSMC FAAO

DIRECTORS: N. LEFTON (Chairman & Managing), P. V. LEFTON, THE RT. HON. THE VISCOUNT EXMOUTH, REGISTERED No. 893406 ENGLAND
REGISTERED OFFICE: 12/13 SHIP STREET, BRIGHTON THE CHASE MANHATTAN BANK, N.A., 410 PARK AVENUE, NEW YORK
BANKERS: NATIONAL WESTMINSTER BANK LTD 155 NORTH STREET, BRIGHTON, SUSSEX

THERE ARE A GREAT MANY

but few, if any, who are as quality conscious as Norman Lefton, Chairman and Managing Director of British Antique Exporters Ltd of Burgess Hill, Nr Brighton, Sussex.

Twenty-five years' experience of shipping goods to all parts of the globe have confirmed his original belief that the way to build clients' confidence in his services is to supply them only with goods which are in first class saleable condition. To this end, he employs a cottage industry staff of over 50, from highly skilled, antique restorers, polishers and packers.

Through their knowledgeable hands passes each piece of furniture before it leaves the BAE warehouses, ensuring that the overseas buyer will only receive the best and most saleable merchandise for their particular market. This attention to detail is obvious on a visit to the Burgess Hill showrooms where potential customers can view what must be the most varied assortment of Georgian, Victorian, Edwardian and 1930's furniture in the UK. One cannot fail to be impressed by, not only the varied range of merchandise but also the fact that each piece is in showroom condition awaiting shipment.

As one would expect, packing is considered somewhat of an art at BAE and the manager in charge of the works ensures that each piece will reach its final destination in the condition a customer would wish. BAE set a very high standard and, as a further means on improving each container load their customer/container liaison dept. invites each customer to return detailed information on the saleability of each piece in the container, thereby ensuring successful future shipments.

This feedback of information is the all important factor which guarantees the profitability of future containers. 'By this method' Mr Lefton explains, 'we have established that an average £7,500 container will the moment it is unpacked at its final destination realise in the region of £11,000 to £14,000 for our clients selling the goods on a quick wholsesale turnover basis'.

When visiting the warehouse various container loads can be seen in the course of completion. The intending buyer can then judge for himself which type of container load would best be suited to his market. In an average 20-foot container BAE put approxiamtely 75 to 150 carefully selected pieces to suit the particular destination. There are always at least 10 outstanding or unusual items in each shipment, but every piece included looks as though it has something special about it.

BAE have opened a spacious new showroom based at its 13,500 square feet headquarters in Burgess Hill. The showrooms together with the restoration and packing departments will be open to overseas buyers and all potential customers.

Based at Burgess Hill 7 miles from Brighton and on a direct rail link with London 39 miles (only 40 minutes journey) the Company is ideally situated to ship containers to all parts of the world. The showrooms, restoration and packing departments are open to overseas buyers and no visit to purchase antiques for re-sale in other countries is complete without a visit to their Burgess Hill premises where a welcome is always found.

BRITISH ANTIQUE EXPORTERS LTD
School Close, Queen Elizabeth Avenue, Burgess Hill, West Sussex, RH15 9RX England
Telephone BURGESS HILL (044 46) 45577
Telex 87688

ANTIQUE SHIPPERS IN BRITAIN

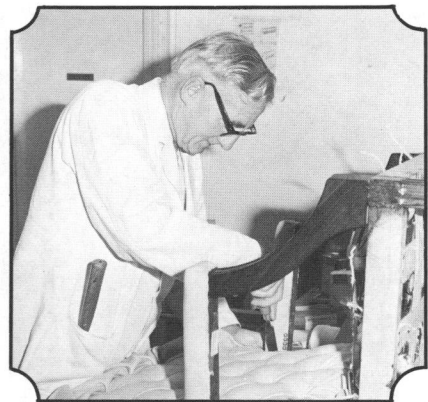
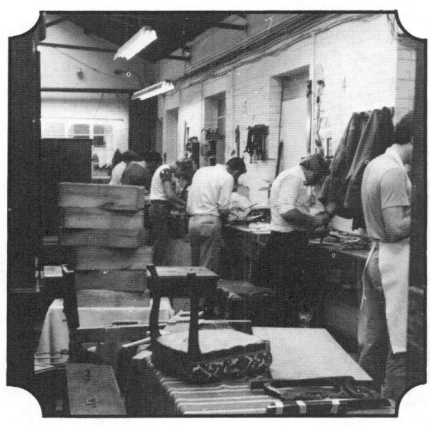

Member of L.A.P.A.D.A. Guild of Master Craftsmen

A late Victorian mahogany display cabinet with astragal glazed doors, on cabriole supports, 48in (122cm). **$1,500-2,600**

A late Victorian satinwood display cabinet, set with harewood panels, inlaid with ribbon tied husk chains and trophies, on tapering square legs with spade feet, 67 by 54in (170 by 137cm). **$1,500-2,600**

A late Victorian mahogany display cabinet, inlaid with Vitruvian scroll and foliate marquetry, on a stand with a three-quarter galleried undertier on cabriole legs with carved paw feet, 55½in (140cm). **$3,000-4,000**

A Victorian mahogany inlaid display cabinet on cabriole legs, 27in (68cm). **$750-1,000**

A mahogany serpentine-fronted display cabinet, by S. J. Waring & Sons, with kingwood and satinwood crossbanding, boxwood, ebony and parquetry lines, on tapering square legs with spade feet, early 20thC, 91 by 54in (231 by 137cm). **$4,000-5,500**

An Edwardian mahogany veneered display cabinet, inlaid with scrolls, foliates and urns, the shaped back above an oval glazed door enclosing 3 shelves, on square tapering supports with spade feet, 27in (68.5cm). **$750-1,000**

An Edwardian mahogany inlaid display cabinet, with a flame and cup finial, 74 by 42in (188 by 106.5cm). **$3,000-4,500**

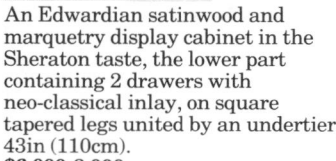

An Edwardian satinwood and marquetry display cabinet in the Sheraton taste, the lower part containing 2 drawers with neo-classical inlay, on square tapered legs united by an undertier, 43in (110cm). **$6,000-8,000**

An Edwardian marquetry inlaid mahogany serpentine fronted display cabinet, on splay feet, 39in (99cm). **$3,000-4,000**

An Edwardian inlaid mahogany display cabinet, on square tapered legs, 48in (122cm). **$1,500-2,600**

An Edwardian inlaid mahogany display cabinet.
$2,500-3,500

An Edwardian mahogany inlaid cabinet, 46in (116.5cm).
$450-600

An Edwardian inlaid mahogany display cabinet, 38in (97cm).
$2,500-3,500

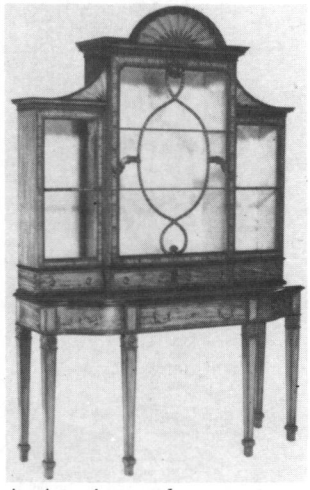

An American mahogany neo-classical style breakfront display cabinet, inlaid with satinwood fans, chequered and geometric boxwood lines, 50in (127cm).
$2,250-3,500

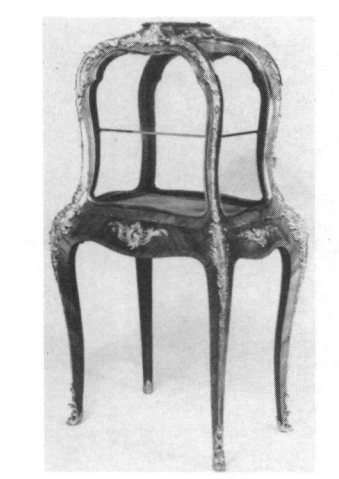

A French kingwood and ormolu mounted vitrine in the Louis XV taste, with glazed panel sides, enclosed by a door with scrolling foliate and rocaille decorated projecting angles, the mahogany veneered panel apron fitted with a drawer, on cabriole legs, headed with C-scrolls and leaves trailing to sabots, 19thC, 31in (78cm).
$5,500-7,000

A Louis XVI style mahogany vitrine, applied with ormolu mounts and decorated with painted panels, 52in (132cm).
$3,000-4,500

A scarlet Boulle and ebonised breakfront vitrine cabinet, with mirrored interiors, on an eared plinth, 64in (162.5cm).
$4,500-7,000

A Louis XV style kingwood serpentine front vitrine, with rich ormolu mounts, 5 hand-painted lower panels, signed 'W. Deluc', with velvet back, on splay feet, 84in (213cm) high.
$6,000-9,000

A Boulle vitrine, the top with a pierced foliate cast gilt metal crest, cast gilt metal banded cornice, above a plain and bevelled glazed door, the ebonised sides applied with gilt metal putti mounts, late 19thC.
$5,500-7,000

A French mahogany vitrine.
$2,500-3,500

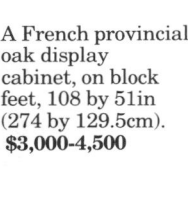

A French provincial oak display cabinet, on block feet, 108 by 51in (274 by 129.5cm).
$3,000-4,500

A Dutch floral marquetry cabinet with arched pediment, the door enclosing a shaped shelf, 18thC, 29in (73.5cm).
$450-700

A George III mahogany secretaire display cabinet, with lancet astragal glazed doors, the lower section with 4 small drawers enclosing a fitted interior, 95 by 52in (241 by 133cm).
$4,500-7,000

A Dutch marquetry display cabinet, with carved cornice, 48in (122cm).
$2,250-3,500

A French walnut D-shaped vitrine with rouge marble top and gilt brass gallery, with velvet lined interior, the door with bowed glazed panel and conforming side panels on cabriole legs, 55 by 27in (139.5 by 68.5cm).
$600-900

A small Dutch walnut display cabinet, the top with applied moulding, raised on scroll feet, 18thC, 89 by 60in (226 by 152cm).
$7,000-9,000

A Dutch oak display cabinet, 18thC, 60in (152cm).
$2,250-3,000

A small Victorian oak collectors cabinet, the front with a frieze drawer opened by a spring, with a brass plaque inset with black jasper portrait panels and a central bronze panel of Bacchantes, enclosing 15 drawers, some containing part of a fossil and shell collection, 38 by 24in (96.5 by 61cm).
$1,500-2,600

A late Victorian oak Shannon filing cabinet, with arched centre with the initials 'AHB' above a panelled frieze, 106 by 72in (269 by 182cm).
$6,000-9,000

A Victorian fruitwood collectors cabinet, 37in (94cm).
$900-1,300

A Victorian figured walnut and ebony banded secretaire/music cabinet, with fitted interior and glazed cabinet below.
$800-1,200

A Federal inlaid cherrywood corner cabinet in 2 sections, the upper section with moulded cornice above 2 glazed cupboard doors, the lower section with 2 line inlaid cupboard doors opening to a shaped shelf, probably Connecticut, early 19thC, 45½in (115cm). **$5,000-6,000**

A pair of Regency mahogany wall cabinets, with glazed fronts and sides, 12½in (31.5cm).
$2,250-3,500

An inlaid mahogany bow front drinks cabinet, with rising top and brass carrying handles, 19thC.
$450-700

A Victorian inlaid figured walnut music cabinet, with brass gallery and turned side pillars, on casters, 22in (56cm).
$600-900

A mahogany veneered dressing cabinet, with scroll shaped uprights and paw feet, the lift-up top revealing lidded toilet compartments, 19thC, 32 by 30in (81 by 76cm).
$1,300-1,800

Side Cabinets – Credenzas

A French Boulle cabinet, 19thC.
$1,500-2,600

A pair of Louis XV style mahogany display cabinets, of serpentine bombé outline and applied with gilt brass foliate mounts, 34½ by 20½in (87.5 by 51cm).
$2,250-3,000

A Victorian walnut side cabinet, with boxwood inlay and gilt metal mounts, 59in (149cm).
$1,500-2,600

A Victorian burr walnut credenza, banded in mahogany, inlaid with decorative bands and string lines, the 2 doors with porcelain plaques, gilt metal mounts, and turned feet, 73½in (185cm).
$3,000-4,000

A Victorian walnut side cabinet, inlaid with scrolling foliate motifs and applied with gilt brass mouldings, 46 by 63in (116.5 by 160cm).
$1,500-2,600

A Victorian walnut and foliate marquetry credenza applied with ormolu mounts, with ebonised panel door and 2 glazed doors between uprights headed by female mask clasps, on plinth, 75in (190.5cm).
$4,500-7,000

A red tortoiseshell and Boulle credenza, with gilt masks and mounts.
$1,500-2,600

A rosewood drawing room cabinet with inverted bow ends, inlaid with boxwood stringing and amboyna crossbanding, mid-19thC, 64in (162.5cm).
$1,500-2,600

A Victorian ebonised Boulle work cabinet, decorated with applied ormolu mounts and pietra dura panel to the single door, enclosing lined shelves, raised on turned feet, 50in (127cm).
$2,250-3,000

A Victorian walnut credenza/ display cabinet, with gilt metal mounts and porcelain plaques to door fronts.
$1,500-2,600

A burr yew and harewood credenza with marquetry, 19thC.
$4,500-7,000

A Victorian walnut veneered French design credenza/cabinet, with gilded mounts.
$1,500-2,600

A Victorian inlaid walnut credenza, with gilt metal and porcelain mounts, the frieze set with 5 Sèvres style porcelain plaques, 66in (167.5cm).
$4,000-5,500

A Boulle credenza with gilt metal mounts, 19thC.
$1,500-2,600

A Victorian ebonised and brass inlaid side cabinet, bow-ended with low gallery back, the frieze inlaid with brass banding and foliate scroll panels, on cabriole supports, 54in (137cm).
$750-1,000

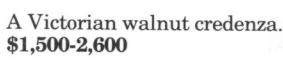

A Victorian walnut credenza.
$1,500-2,600

Side Cabinets – Chiffoniers

An Edwardian inlaid figured walnut bow fronted chiffonier, with mirror panel doors and shaped marble top, 48in (122cm).
$300-400

A Regency mahogany breakfront side cabinet, with cupboard doors enclosing 3 slides, stamped twice 'Gillows Lancaster', 76in (193cm).
$4,000-5,500

A Regency simulated rosewood chiffonier, with chased brass mounted border, original brass handles, 52in (132cm) high.
$5,500-7,000

A rosewood chiffonier, with 2 frieze drawers above 2 panelled doors, flanked by flat columns, the superstructure supported by 2 tapering columns, early 19thC.
$750-1,000

A pair of Regency ormolu-mounted rosewood side cabinets, with pierced gilt trelliswork and flowerheads, on a pleated café-au-lait silk ground, adapted, 19in (48cm).
$4,500-7,000

A pair of mahogany cabinets, crossbanded with satinwood and harewood, with satinwood and painted panels, 37½in (95cm) high.
$7,500-10,500

A Regency rosewood secretaire chiffonier, with shelf and mirror superstructure, drawer enclosing fitted interior, glazed door below, door impressed 'Wyman', 27in (69cm).
$1,000-1,400

A Regency rosewood side cabinet, the cupboard doors filled with pleated green repp, possibly formerly with a gallery, 42in (107cm).
$2,250-3,000

A late Regency rosewood breakfront dwarf cabinet, the doors filled with gilt trellis and pleated green repp, 64in (162.5cm).
$4,500-7,000

A satinwood cabinet, in late 18thC style, 19thC.
$8,000-10,500

A simulated rosewood chiffonier, early 19thC, 30in (76cm).
$400-500

A Regency mahogany chiffonier, with turned brass supports with finials, 48½in (123cm).
$1,000-1,400

A Regency rosewood chiffonier, 38in (96.5cm).
$1,200-1,600

A Regency rosewood chiffonier, with brass grille cupboards flanked by rope-twist pilasters, continuing to paw feet, 36½in (92cm).
$4,000-5,500

A Regency figured mahogany chiffonier, 37½in (95cm).
$1,500-2,600

A Regency mahogany chiffonier, the doors without original linings, 22½in (57cm).
$150-250

A mahogany ▶ chiffonier, with finely flared veneers to doors, carved decoration to back, 19thC.
$300-400

A George IV rosewood chiffonier, with a pair of upholstered brass grille doors, between pilasters with acanthus and paterae headings, 44in (111.5cm).
$1,500-2,600

A mahogany side cabinet, with 2 small drawers, on bracket feet, early 19thC, 29in (74cm).
$300-400

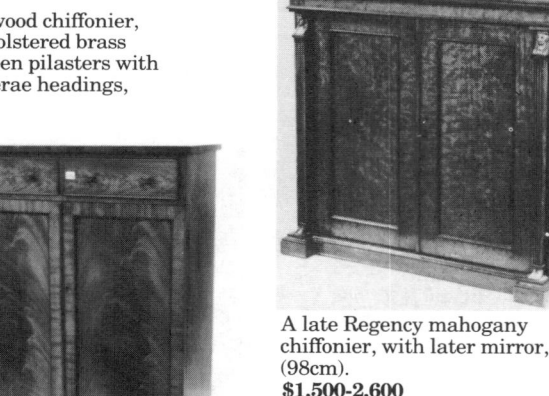

A late Regency mahogany chiffonier, with later mirror, 38½in (98cm).
$1,500-2,600

An early Victorian rosewood pier cabinet, with brass grille doors, 36in (91cm).
$1,500-2,600

A William IV rosewood chiffonier, with convex frieze drawer, 38in (96.5cm).
$1,500-2,600

STONE HALL
antiques

We have one of the largest and most varied stocks of good quality English and Continental Furniture in England. (20,000 sq. ft. furniture).

Always a large selection of Georgian, Victorian, Edwardian and Shipping Goods for the trade buyer.

We specialise in Linen Presses, Inlaid Sideboards, Chest on Chest, Desks, Writing Tables, Chest of Drawers, Chairs, Bookcases etc.

Plus small and decorative items.

All items in mint condition.
Restored in our own workshop.

1 hour drive from London
10 minutes from Stanstead Airport

Open 9 a.m. – 5.30 p.m. Monday to Friday. Weekends by appointment

STONE HALL
DOWNHALL ROAD
MATCHING GREEN
NR. HARLOW
ESSEX

Telephone: Peter, Chris or Trevor
011 44 279 731440

An early Victorian oak cabinet, fitted with a pair of Gothic panelled doors enclosing 17 drawers, 44in (111cm).
$1,000-1,400

An early Victorian rosewood chiffonier, on a plinth, stamped 'W. Stratford', 50in (127cm).
$1,000-1,400

A rosewood secretaire chiffonier of reverse breakfront form, with small drawers faced in satin birch, adjustable bookshelves beneath, 2 flanking panel doors with needlework panels enclosing shelves, mid-19thC, 86in (218.5cm).
$2,250-3,000

A Victorian walnut chiffonier, 44in (111cm).
$700-900

A pair of late Victorian ebonised and gilt etched Aesthetic side cabinets, inset with burr walnut and amboyna veneered panels, with boxwood line borders, 36in (91cm).
$1,500-2,600

An Italian walnut pedestal cabinet, 21in (53cm).
$1,500-2,600

A pair of ormolu-mounted Boulle dwarf cabinets, with well inlaid doors enclosing shelves, on scrolled triple supports, early 19thC, 41in (104cm).
$4,000-5,500

A pair of Continental walnut veneered side cabinets, with variegated marble tops, with cast brass escutcheons, on shaped bracket feet, 19thC, 30in (76cm).
$1,500-2,600

Canterburies

A Regency mahogany canterbury, with colonnaded rectangular frame and central division, on square legs, 18in (46cm).
$4,000-5,500

A Regency mahogany canterbury, with one cedar lined frieze drawer, on ring turned tapering legs, 18in (46cm).
$2,250-3,500

A mahogany music canterbury, with swept top, early 19thC, 22in (56cm).
$900-1,300

An unusual Regency rosewood canterbury, 27½in (69.5cm).
$3,000-4,000

A Regency rosewood canterbury, 20½in (52cm).
$2,250-3,500

A Victorian walnut music canterbury with 3 divisions, drawer, fretted gallery, barley twist supports and turned feet.
$750-1,000

A Regency mahogany canterbury, with the trade label 'And-w Fleming & Co., manufacturers of cabinet and upholstery furniture, undertakers and appraisers Kirkaldy', 20in (51cm).
$3,000-4,500

Kirkaldy with a K, the old spelling of Kirkcaldy, 'the lang town', Kingdom of Fife.

A mahogany music canterbury, early 19thC, 19in (48cm).
$1,200-1,600

A William IV rosewood canterbury, 21½in (54cm).
$1,200-1,600

Chairs – Open Armchairs

A George IV mahogany canterbury with 4 divisions, slatted sides with turned supports, a drawer below and on reel-turned feet, 21in (53.5cm).
$1,000-1,400

A Victorian burr walnut canterbury/whatnot, 13in (33cm).
$450-700

A pair of walnut Jacobean style high backed elbow chairs, with carved fretwork.
$600-900

A George II mahogany open armchair. $27,000-30,000

A pair of walnut open armchairs of late 17thC style, with dolphin arm supports on similar legs and front stretchers. $3,000-4,500

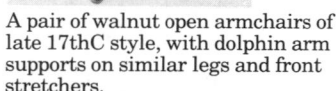

A Victorian carved oak bishop's chair, with cane seat and back. $400-500

A George III mahogany library armchair, upholstered in needlework, the back with dancing figures, later blocks, partly re-railed. $7,000-9,000

A George III mahogany open armchair, upholstered in red leather. $7,500-10,500

An early George III mahogany open armchair. $18,000-21,000

An ebonised mahogany open armchair, with high removable panel back, the scrolling arms with greyhound-mask terminals, mid-18thC. $6,000-8,000

A George III mahogany armchair of Gainsborough type, with a stuffover floral gros point needlework back and seat, on square legs terminating in brass cappings and casters. $1,500-2,600

A Georgian carved and ebonised elbow chair, in the manner of John Linnell, on reeded square tapered legs. $700-900

A pair of George III mahogany open armchairs, the seats upholstered with yellow floral damask, stamped 'BAH'. $3,000-4,500

A George III mahogany open armchair, restored. $2,250-3,500

A George III painted satinwood open armchair, decorated with flowerheads and trailing foliage.
$1,500-2,600

A mid-Georgian mahogany open armchair, with solid splat and drop-in seat, the splat possibly later.
$750-1,000

A mahogany elbow chair, 18thC, seat 23in (58.5cm).
$600-900

A George III mahogany open armchair, and another similar, both with later arms.
$1,500-2,600

A pair of George III mahogany open armchairs, attributed to Gillows, with trelliswork splats and caned-filled seats, one distressed, the frames painted with flowerheads.
$7,500-10,500

A set of 6 Queen Anne maple chairs, comprising an armchair and 5 side chairs, on block and baluster turned legs with paintbrush feet, repairs and restorations, New England, c1745, armchair 44in (111.5cm) high.
$7,000-10,000

A George III mahogany open armchair, with interlaced top rail and splat, reinforced back rail.
$2,250-3,000

Three George III mahogany elbow chairs in the Louis XV style.
$2,500-3,500

A Chippendale walnut armchair, with shaped arms ending in scrolled knuckles above shaped supports, over a trapezoidal slip seat, on shell carved cabriole legs with trifid feet, repaired, Philadelphia, c1775, 28in (70cm).
$7,000-10,000

A George III giltwood open armchair, 25½in (65cm).
$8,000-10,500

A set of 6 Federal mahogany armchairs, each with a shield back, with shaped forward scrolling arms, legs with leaf carved capitals and spade feet, repairs and restorations, Massachusetts, c1800, 37in (94cm) high.
$22,000-30,000

An Adam period giltwood frame armchair.
$3,000-4,500

A George III carved beech and gilded open armchair.
$1,500-2,600

A George III carved and later gilt elbow chair.
$750-1,000

An Edwardian satinwood open armchair of George III style, painted with roses, plumes, swags and paterae.
$1,500-2,600

A set of 6 mahogany open armchairs, the down-curved arms decorated with stiff leaves, extensive restorations, late 18thC.
$3,000-4,000

A set of 4 late George III painted beech elbow chairs.
$6,000-8,000

A pair of Sheraton ebonised and gilt decorated elbow chairs.
$4,000-5,500

A Chippendale period carved mahogany library open armchair, of Gainsborough type in the French taste, on cabriole legs with scroll feet, spandrels missing.
$6,000-8,000

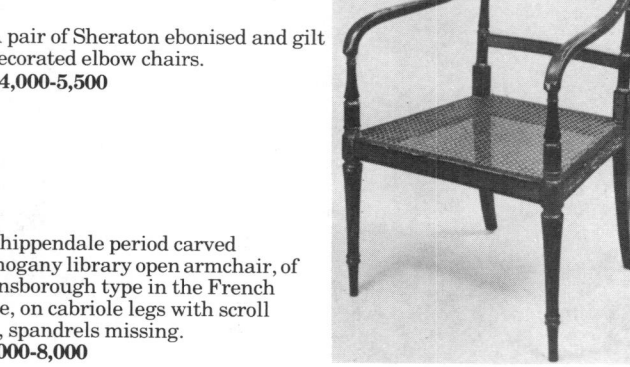

A pair of Sheraton style elbow chairs, the back panels embossed with putti.
$300-400

A pair of cream painted and giltwood elbow chairs in the Sheraton taste.
$1,500-2,600

A George III mahogany cockpen open armchair, with pierced trelliswork back and arms.
$2,250-3,000

A pair of carved hardwood fauteuils in the Louis XV style, with stuffover cartouche shaped backs and serpentine stuffover seats, the seat rails inscribed 'G.H.', late 18th/early 19thC.
$4,500-7,000

A mahogany bergère, on reeded front legs, some damage, early 19thC.
$400-500

A Regency mahogany library armchair, with cane filled back.
$1,500-2,600

A pair of Regency mahogany scroll arm carvers, with carved backs, on turned legs.
$1,300-1,800

A Regency mahogany reading chair, with deeply buttoned green leather upholstery and yoke shaped top rail, the waisted seat on turned legs.
$1,000-1,400

A set of 11 Regency simulated rosewood and gilt elbow chairs, re-decorated.
$31,000-38,000

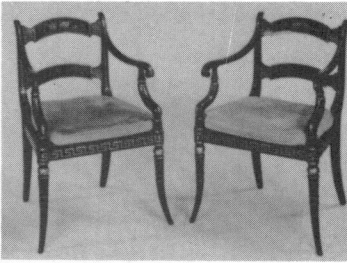

A pair of Regency simulated rosewood on beechwood armchairs, with Grecian key bands and flowersprays, and inset caned panel seats.
$8,000-10,500

A George IV mahogany armchair, with channelled scroll back, the downswept arms with a roundel on channelled legs, stamped 'W. Hodge', 22in (56cm).
$3,000-4,000

A Regency mahogany metamorphic library armchair, attributed to Morgan and Saunders, on sabre legs converting into library steps, minor restoration.
$4,500-7,000

A Regency mahogany open armchair, inlaid with ebony, and a George III mahogany open armchair with channelled solid back rail and bar splats with drop-in seat and square tapering legs, with moulded stretchers.
$1,000-1,400

A Regency mahogany armchair, the back with a shaped scroll and lobe carved top rail.
$450-600

A late Regency mahogany armchair, with caned back.
$1,500-2,600

A late Regency rosewood library armchair, on turned lappeted tapering legs, with sabre legs at the back, headed by applied scrolling foliage.
$2,250-3,000

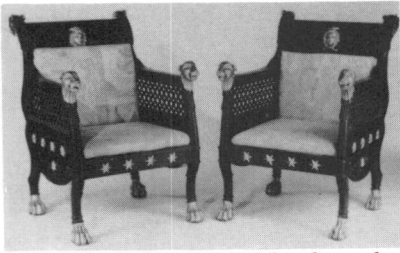

A pair of green painted and parcel gilt open armchairs, early 19thC style.
$4,000-5,500

A Chippendale walnut armchair, the skirt shell carved on acanthus carved cabriole legs with ball and claw feet, repairs, Philadelphia, c1770, 29in (73cm).
$3,000-5,000

A pair of William IV mahogany library armchairs, on lotus turned front supports and brass casters.
$1,200-1,600

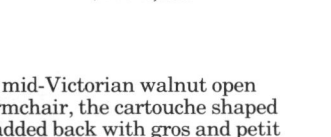

A Victorian walnut framed button back armchair, on cabriole legs.
$800-1,200

A mid-Victorian walnut open armchair, the cartouche shaped padded back with gros and petit point needlework panel.
$1,500-2,600

An unusual Victorian mahogany easy chair, with angelic busts with wing supports.
$1,200-1,600

A pair of early Victorian simulated rosewood open armchairs.
$1,000-1,400

A Victorian ebonised gentleman's armchair, inlaid with intarsia and applied with gilt metal mounts, and a lady's chair en suite.
$750-1,000

A fine Victorian carved walnut framed settee and matching armchairs.
$4,000-5,500

A mid-Victorian black, gilt and mother-of-pearl japanned papier-mâché open armchair, with split caned seat.
$1,500-2,600

A large mahogany armchair with lion mask arm rests and additional back rest, 27in (69cm).
$900-1,300

A pair of Victorian walnut spoon back easy chairs, upholstered in floral tapestry, with buttoned backs, comprising a gentleman's chair with open arms and a lady's chair without arms.
$900-1,300

A Victorian walnut framed open armchair, with carved decoration, on cabriole legs.
$800-1,200

A Victorian walnut framed spoon back chair, with carved frame, on cabriole legs.
$750-1,000

A pair of Victorian oak armchairs, the back with cabochon crestings flanked by lions, the arms with lions' mask terminals.
$750-1,000

A late Victorian mahogany drawing room suite, comprising: a settee, the shaped panelled back below a rockwork cresting with a splat pierced with foliage, 55in (139.5cm) wide, 2 open armchairs and 4 side chairs. ▶
$1,000-1,400

283

A mahogany office ▶
chair with
winged horse arm
supports and
carved baluster legs,
19thC.
$1,000-1,400

A pair of Edwardian satinwood
armchairs, the arcaded spindled rail
backs inset with ebonised lines and
fleur-de-lys motifs above
upholstered figured tapestry seats.
$1,500-2,600

A set of 6 Dutch Colonial mahogany
open armchairs.
$2,250-3,000

A pair of Edwardian carved
mahogany frame shield back elbow
chairs, with upholstered seats, on
cabriole legs.
$400-500

An Edwardian inlaid mahogany
seven-piece drawing room suite in
the Sheraton style, with carved and
pierced backs, comprising:
two-seater settee, 2 elbow chairs
and 4 single chairs.
$3,000-4,000

A pair of Dutch mahogany and
marquetry inlaid open armchairs,
with cabriole legs and claw-and-ball
feet, and a double chairback settee
en suite, 50in (127.5cm).
$4,500-7,000

A Flemish elm and beechwood open
armchair, with high rectangular
nailed back and seat covered in
floral needlework centred by a
cartouche, late 17thC.
$1,300-1,800

An Edwardian satinwood
three-piece music room
suite, inlaid
with figure panels, swags and
crossbanded decoration.
$1,300-1,800

A pair of carved giltwood fauteuils,
in the Louis XV taste.
$2,250-3,000

◀

A pair of Louis XV fauteuils by
Jean-Baptiste Sené, with later
caned cartouche shaped backs and
serpentine seats, both stamped
'I.Sene'.
$6,000-9,000

I. B. Sené, mâitre in 1769.

A pair of walnut armchairs, one
with later blocks, partly re-railed,
probably French, late 17thC.
$4,000-5,500

A set of 3 Louis XV carved walnut
fauteuils.
$4,500-7,000

A pair of French Empire mahogany
open armchairs, with bowed
cresting rails, conforming
rectangular splats, lotus-carved and
reeded downswept arms with
anthemion-carved supports, cane
seats with loose squabs, on
lotus-carved sabre legs.
$2,250-3,000

A pair of Louis XVI walnut
fauteuils, both covered in close
nailed floral needlework, the
moulded frame with twinned
flowerhead cresting and centre to
the seat rail, on fluted turned
tapering legs.
$2,500-3,500

A set of 4 Louis XV style gilt
fauteuils, with a flower carved crest,
on cabriole legs with scrolled feet.
$1,500-2,600

A Louis XVI style giltwood chair
and matching stool.
$600-900

A pair of Empire style mahogany ▶
fauteuils, with dolphin carved arms.
$1,500-2,600

An Empire ormolu-mounted
mahogany fauteuil, upholstered
with distressed silk, the partly
ribbed arm supports headed by
caryatids, on sabre legs and brass
paw feet.
$4,000-5,500

A Regence walnut fauteuil, covered
in fruiting and foliate gros point
needlework, stamped 'C.H.',
reframed.
$3,000-4,500

A pair of Empire style mahogany
open armchairs, applied with gilt
brass foliate motifs and flowerheads,
on turned legs with brass lion paw
feet.
$2,250-3,000

A French giltwood armchair, c1810.
$4,500-7,000

A pair of well carved French fauteuils, mid-19thC.
$1,500-2,600

A German giltwood fauteuil, early 18thC, later blocks.
$2,250-3,500

A set of 4 Venetian giltwood framed armchairs, with husk and scroll carved arms, on similarly carved legs, with S-scroll stretchers, some restoration, 17thC.
$4,500-7,000

An Italian green painted and parcel gilt armchair, late 18thC.
$1,000-1,400

An Italian Directoire white painted and parcel gilt elbow chair, with winged Greek helmeted masks, on tapered legs and paw feet.
$2,500-3,500

Upholstered Armchairs

A Queen Anne design mahogany tub wing armchair, on foliate cabriole legs and claw-and-ball feet, with trade label, Howard & Sons, No. 3194-423.
$1,300-1,800

An Indian silver repoussé Throne chair, in the William IV rococo taste, the upholstered cartouche shaped back with armorial device and trailing flowers in metal thread, on sabre scroll legs terminating in paw feet, 19thC.
$6,000-9,000

A Russian birch open armchair, with deep top rail and pierced splat, the downswept arms and brown pigskin covered seat on turned baluster legs, early 19thC.
$2,500-3,500

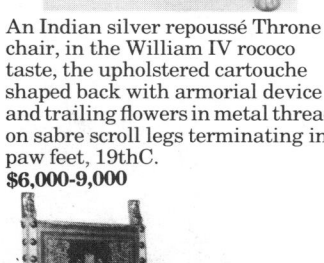

A pair of Spanish walnut open armchairs, the leather padded rectangular backs centred by coats-of-arms with foliate strapwork spandrels, the uprights with gilt finials and brass studs, with stylised claw feet, 17thC.
$4,000-5,500

A winged armchair, on carved walnut cabriole legs with shell carved knees and shaped feet, early 18thC.
$1,500-2,600

A George II style wing armchair with cushion seat, on 4 mahogany cabriole legs with shell carved knees and claw-and-ball feet.
$900-1,300

A George III mahogany framed wing back armchair, the seat on square chamfered legs joined by an H-stretcher, restorations.
$1,500-2,600

An early George III giltwood bergère, upholstered in aquamarine silk, on cabriole legs headed by shells, re-gilded.
$1,500-2,600

A walnut wing armchair, upholstered in machine cloth, on cabriole legs joined by turned and moulded stretchers with scrolled toes.
$3,000-4,500

A Federal mahogany wing chair, on moulded Marlborough legs, joined by an H-stretcher, feet slightly reduced, New York, c1800, 31in (79cm).
$2,000-4,000

A pair of late George III mahogany armchairs, upholstered in floral material, on square tapering legs with brass socket casters.
$1,500-2,600

A Regency mahogany and caned bergère, the arched bowed back continuing to arms headed by lobed and lappet-carved columns, the seat on turned tapered legs with lobed collars.
$1,500-2,600

A George III mahogany dining armchair with high curved back, covered in close nailed green leather, partly re-railed.
$2,250-3,500

An early Georgian walnut wing armchair, upholstered in floral moquette, on cabriole legs and pad feet, re-railed.
$4,000-5,500

A George III mahogany frame library tub shaped bergère, with rounded arched back and reeded splayed arm supports, on ring turned tapered legs, terminating in brass cappings and casters.
$2,250-3,000

A mahogany wing armchair, upholstered in gold fabric, on acanthus head cabriole legs and claw-and-ball feet, basically 18thC.
$4,500-7,000

A Regency mahogany library bergère, upholstered in buttoned pale green leather, on baluster turned legs.
$2,250-3,500

A Regency simulated rosewood, parcel gilt and decorated bergère library chair, with top rail and seat rail painted with foliate meander ornament 'en grisaille'.
$8,000-10,500

A William IV mahogany reclining armchair, with sliding gout stool above turned and fluted tapering supports.
$1,200-1,600

A Regency mahogany invalid's chair, upholstered in deep red velvet with footrest and ring turned legs.
$1,300-1,800

A George IV carved simulated rosewood bergère, with foliate scroll top rail and arm supports, having a beaded moulded seat rail, on scroll splayed legs and casters.
$1,500-2,600

A William IV rosewood bergère armchair, with buttoned spoon back, upholstered in stamped fabric above a lappeted show frame on crenellated turned tapering legs with patera headings.
$750-1,000

A William IV mahogany armchair with narrow spoon back, upholstered in tapestry patterned material, with a reeded lyre-shaped show frame.
$1,000-1,400

A mid-Victorian walnut tub armchair, with padded back and seat.
$1,300-1,800

A pair of William IV mahogany armchairs, with buttoned green covers and reeded legs.
$1,200-1,600

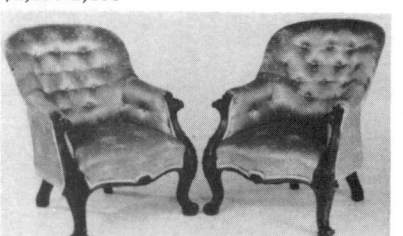

A pair of Victorian rosewood armchairs, on cabriole legs with scroll feet and carved flowerheads.
$1,500-2,600

In the Furniture section if there is only one measurement it usually refers to the width of the piece.

A mid-Victorian walnut folding armchair, with button upholstered slung seat and back in chamfered moulded frame, with grotesque mask cresting and rounded arm supports pierced with trefoils, on sabre legs.
$1,200-1,600

A Victorian easy armchair with buttoned floral upholstery, on turned legs, stamped 24916 and 5758.
$1,500-2,600

A pair of Victorian easy armchairs, with union cotton floral loose covers and ring turned tapering legs, both stamped 'Howard & Sons, numbered 1643-5007'.
$1,500-2,600

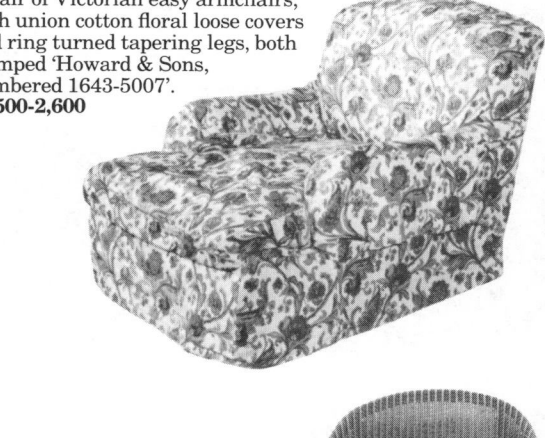

A Victorian lady's mahogany framed button back chair on carved cabriole legs.
$450-600

Six green Lloyd Loom armchairs with padded seats, and a matching circular table with plate glass top.
$450-700

A Louis XV walnut bergère, upholstered in raspberry damask, with moulded frame and cabriole legs.
$3,000-4,500

A Victorian mahogany easy chair on cabriole legs.
$450-700

A Louis XVI walnut bergère, the top rail carved with ribbon tied foliage, the channelled seat rail on shaped tapering legs.
$2,250-3,000

A Louis XV stained beechwood duchesse brisée, the moulded frame with scrolling crestings and flowerhead centres to the seat rails, on flowerhead cabriole legs.
$2,250-3,000

A pair of Louis XVI walnut bergères, the spade shaped upholstered backs with overlapping leaf carved finials, the arms with stop fluted supports continuing to turned and fluted legs.
$7,500-10,500

A Louis XVI white painted bergère, upholstered in pink striped brocade, re-decorated.
$3,000-4,500

A pair of giltwood bergères, each covered in green floral glazed cotton, the moulded frame with twinned flowerheads to the cresting and seat rail, possibly Scandinavian, c1830.
$3,000-4,500

A Louis XVI stained beechwood bergère, covered in plum velvet within a moulded frame carved with foliate finials, on paterae headed fluted tapering legs.
$2,250-3,000

Corner Chairs

A Queen Anne walnut child's commode, c1710.
$1,000-1,400

A late George II Cuban mahogany corner commode armchair, the outscrolling arms with pierced splats and turned supports.
$600-900

A George I carved red walnut corner chair, with shell pendant ornament and pointed pad feet.
$3,000-4,500

A Georgian mahogany commode.
$800-1,200

Dining Chairs

A set of 5 Queen Anne walnut chairs.
$8,000-10,500

A set of 6 Queen Anne style walnut dining chairs, including 2 armchairs.
$1,500-2,600

A mahogany corner chair, 18thC.
$600-900

Unless otherwise stated, any description which refers to 'a set' or 'a pair' includes a valuation for the entire set or the pair, even though the illustration may show only a single item.

A set of 8 George III style mahogany ladderback chairs, including a pair of armchairs, with pierced horizontal splats, late 19thC.
$4,000-5,500

A set of 8 Queen Anne design mahogany dining chairs, 2 carvers and 6 singles, the drop-in seats covered in wine brocade.
$7,500-10,500

A pair of scarlet lacquer chairs of Queen Anne design, with shaped vase splats and bowed drop-in seats, on cabriole legs and pad feet.
$2,250-3,000

A set of 14 George III mahogany ladderback dining chairs, including a pair of armchairs, some splats replaced, some partly re-railed and with later blocks.
$10,500-14,000

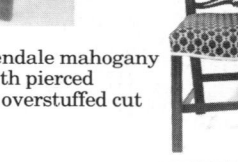

A set of 8 Chippendale mahogany dining chairs, with pierced ladderbacks and overstuffed cut velvet seats.
$10,000-12,000

A set of 8 George III mahogany dining chairs, including a pair of armchairs.
$7,000-9,000

A pair of mid-Georgian mahogany dining chairs, with later blocks, one with spliced back leg.
$3,000-4,500

A set of 8 mahogany dining chairs, in the George III manner, including 2 armchairs.
$5,500-7,000

A set of 7 mahogany dining chairs, 6 single and one carver, c1765.
$4,000-5,500

A set of 8 George III mahogany dining chairs, 6 single and 2 elbow chairs, mostly re-railed.
$5,500-8,000

A set of 8 mahogany dining chairs, including a pair of armchairs, on square tapered legs, part George III.
$2,250-3,500

A set of 4 George III mahogany dining chairs, with finely pierced vase splats.
$600-900

A set of 5 George III mahogany dining chairs, upholstered in yellow satin on square chamfered legs.
$1,300-1,800

A set of 8 George II style mahogany dining chairs, including 2 armchairs, with floral chain carved frames, the seats on acanthus carved cabriole legs with claw-and-ball feet.
$4,000-5,500

An early George III mahogany dining chair, the pierced splat carved with rockwork, the drop-in seat covered in green mercerised cotton.
$1,300-1,800

A set of 6 George III mahogany chairs.
$4,000-5,500

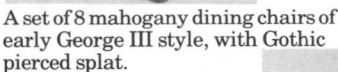

A set of 8 mahogany dining chairs of early George III style, with Gothic pierced splat.
$3,000-4,000

A set of 6 mahogany dining chairs in the Chippendale style, 19thC.
$2,250-3,500

A George III mahogany dining chair, with vase shaped splat, re-railed.
$1,000-1,400

A set of 12 Chippendale style mahogany dining chairs, with ornately carved pierced back splats, on claw-and-ball feet.
$6,000-8,000

CHAIRS

Elizabethan Chairs
oak

Charles II and William and Mary
walnut and veneers, elaborate carving

Queen Anne
cabriole legs (often carved with a shell at the knee) at first stretchers, later disappeared, hooped back and vase or fiddle-shaped splat introduced, winged armchair introduced

George I
mahogany began to be used around 1720, but not in large quantities until 1730-35, many good chairs made in walnut

'Chippendale' Chairs
noted for fine mahogany chairs, beautiful back splats, with curving uprights, usually measures 3ft 1in to 3ft 2½in from back to floor, main types, 'ribband' back, Gothic back, fret back, perforated ladder-back, rococo back

Robert Adam
oval, heart or lyre-shaped backs, legs tapered, turned or fluted, often made of beech, classical motifs, known as paterae often applied

George Hepplewhite
shield-backs, often with an enclosed central splat, often decorated with 'Prince of Wales' feathers, wheat ear, classical urn or flowers, seats usually square, legs generally straight, tapered, often with spade foot, revival of the cabriole – a very graceful example was called 'French Hepplewhite'

Sheraton
lighter, plainer, more square, much painted decoration, known for cane-work, disliked marquetry

★ in the provinces these chairs copied in cheaper more available woods – oak, birch, yew, elm, ash...

★ the ladder-backs and spindle-backs were made in large quantities by 18thC country cabinet makers

★ Thomas Hope's 'X'-back chair greatly influenced Regency cabinet makers

★ balloon-backs introduced about 1830 – very popular until early 1870's, usually made in rosewood, mahogany or walnut

★ Victorian spoon-back was a revival of the Queen Anne chair

A pair of George III carved mahogany elbow chairs, with pierced interlaced Gothic splats and outswept scroll arm supports.
$1,500-2,600

A set of 3 Chippendale carved mahogany dining chairs, on ribband-and-egg carved chamfered legs.
$1,500-2,600

A set of 8 dining chairs, with carving to backs and knees.
$2,500-3,500

A set of 8 Chippendale design mahogany dining chairs, including 2 elbow chairs.
$3,000-4,500

A pair of mid-Georgian mahogany dining chairs, with baluster splats pierced with interlaced scrolls.
$2,250-3,500

A set of 8 George II style mahogany dining chairs, including 2 armchairs, with gadrooned seat rails on acanthus carved cabriole legs, with claw-and-ball feet.
$2,250-3,500

A set of 6 mahogany dining chairs in Hepplewhite style.
$1,500-2,600

A set of 10 Chippendale style mahogany dining chairs, including 2 carvers, on cabochon headed cabriole legs with carved scroll feet.
$9,000-12,000

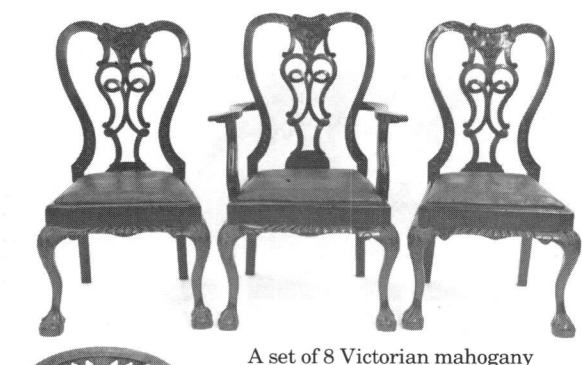

A set of 8 Victorian mahogany dining chairs in the Chippendale style.
$4,000-5,500

A set of 9 George III style mahogany dining chairs, including 2 carvers, with pierced splat applied with the Prince of Wales feathers, upholstered in floral tapestry.
$5,500-7,000

A set of 5 Georgian mahogany dining chairs, with pierced splat backs and raised on tapering square legs.
$1,300-1,800

A pair of George III mahogany dining chairs, the backs headed by a wheatsheaf and centred by a satinwood spandrel, the serpentine seats covered in close nailed floral needlework.
$1,500-2,600

A set of 8 Hepplewhite revival mahogany dining chairs, including 2 armchairs, applied with flutings, paterae and bellflower sprays.
$3,000-4,500

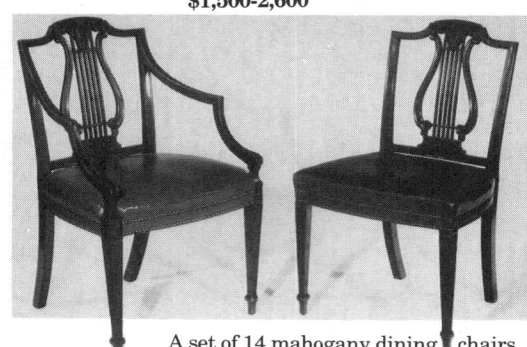

A set of 14 mahogany dining chairs of George III style, including 2 open armchairs, with Prince of Wales feathers and pierced lyre splats, the seats covered in red leatherette, on ribbed square tapering legs.
$10,000-13,000

A set of 8 Hepplewhite style dining chairs.
$900-1,300

A set of 10 George III style mahogany dining chairs, the shield backs with a pierced plume and drape carved splat.
$2,500-3,500

A set of 6 George III painted shield back chairs.
$5,500-7,000

A set of 8 Georgian mahogany
dining chairs, including 2 carvers,
with X-back supports, on turned
legs.
$6,000-9,000

A set of 6 George III carved
mahogany dining chairs in the
Sheraton taste, including an elbow
chair, with crossbanded panel splats.
$3,000-4,500

A set of 8 George III style mahogany
dining chairs, including 2
armchairs, carved with bellflowers
and drapery, with drop-in seats, on
square legs with spade feet.
$1,500-2,600

A set of 6 George III mahogany
dining chairs, with reeded abacus
rail backs.
$2,500-3,500

A set of 8 country Sheraton
mahogany dining chairs.
$1,300-1,800

A set of 6 George III mahogany
dining chairs, the shaped solid seats
with buttoned squabs covered in
yellow silk.
$4,500-7,000

A set of 8 mahogany dining chairs in
the Sheraton design, including 2
carvers, having triple pierced
moulded splats centred with inlaid
oval vignettes, late 19thC.
$3,000-4,000

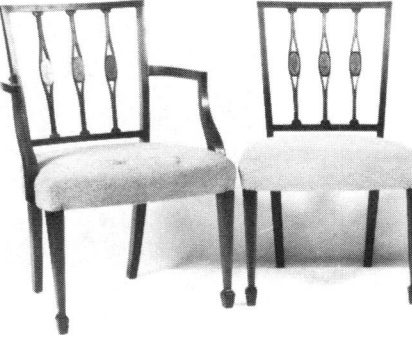

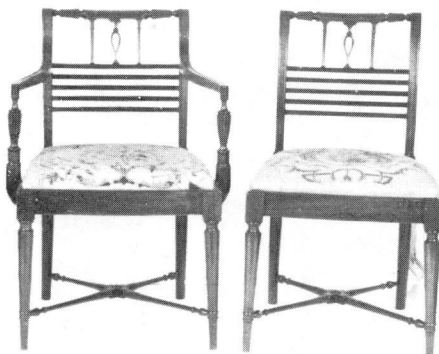

A set of 6 Georgian mahogany
dining chairs, with rope twist
cresting rails, on sabre legs.
$2,500-3,500

A set of 7 mahogany dining chairs in
the Sheraton style, including one
carver, the loose seats upholstered
in wool needlework of various
designs, early 19thC.
$4,000-5,500

A set of 8 George III carved mahogany dining chairs, including a pair of elbow chairs, with column upright reeded arm supports.
$7,500-10,500

A set of 6 mahogany dining chairs, c1790.
$10,500-14,000

A set of 6 Regency rosewood, part simulated, dining chairs.
$1,500-2,600

ENGLISH CHAIRS

★ c1630 backs of chairs were like panelled sides from a coffer
★ early 17thC chairs very square and made of oak
★ in Charles II period principal wood walnut – such chairs tend to break as walnut splits easily and is relatively soft
★ chairs have carved top rails, often with a crown, the stretcher will then be similarly carved, the legs are either turned or plain and simple spirals – sometimes called barley sugar twists; the caning in the backs is usually rectangular – any chair with oval caning is highly desirable
★ by the end of the 17thC backs were covered in needlework, the cabriole leg made its appearance, now stretchers have subtle curves
★ the beginning of the 18thC – the Queen Anne spoon back chair – with upright shaped splat, plain cabriole front legs, pad feet
★ George I – carved knees and ball-and-claw feet, solid splats were walnut or veneered, often in burr-walnut
★ William Kent – introduced heavy carved mouldings – greatly influenced by Italian baroque
★ from this time on chairs became lighter in design through the work mainly of Chippendale and Hepplewhite
★ splats now pierced, legs square or tapered
★ the square legs were also much cheaper than the cabriole legs, so they appealed to the large and growing middle class
★ many of the designs came from France
★ Hepplewhite, in particular, developed the chair with tapered legs, no stretchers and very plain splats
★ during the 19thC the taste was once again for heavier more substantial furniture

A set of 6 Regency mahogany dining chairs, including one armchair, inscribed 'Young upholsterer, 1809 Wm. Teiocks frame maker' and another chair with the initials 'WFL'.
$9,000-12,000

A set of 7 George III mahogany dining chairs in the Hepplewhite taste, including one elbow chair.
$4,000-5,500

A set of 6 Georgian mahogany dining chairs on turned legs, with upholstered seats.
$2,500-3,500

A set of 8 Regency mahogany dining chairs, including a pair of armchairs with overscrolled arms.
$6,000-8,000

A set of 10 George III mahogany dining chairs, including 2 elbow chairs.
$7,500-10,500

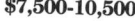

A set of 6 mahogany rail back chairs, including one elbow chair.
$3,000-4,500

A set of 8 Regency carved mahogany dining chairs, including a pair of scroll arm elbow chairs, the curved scroll top rails with reeded borders and ebony stringing, stamped 'KL', one with later top rail.
$6,000-8,000

A set of 12 Regency mahogany dining chairs, including a pair of elbow chairs, with slip-in seats on ring turned tapered legs.
$7,500-10,500

A set of 6 mahogany dining chairs, with drop-in seats, c1820.
$6,000-8,000

A set of 4 Regency mahogany dining chairs, including one armchair, c1820.
$3,000-4,500

A set of 6 mahogany dining chairs, including one carver, English, c1820.
$4,500-7,000

A set of 6 Regency mahogany ▶ dining chairs.
$3,000-4,500

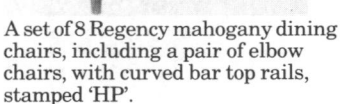

A set of 5 Regency mahogany dining chairs.
$1,000-1,400

A set of 8 Regency mahogany dining chairs, including a pair of elbow chairs, with curved bar top rails, stamped 'HP'.
$7,500-10,500

A set of 6 Regency mahogany dining chairs, and a similar pair of Regency armchairs.
$4,500-7,000

A set of 7 Regency simulated bamboo rush seated chairs, with painted decoration, raised on turned bamboo supports.
$1,200-1,600

A set of 3 Regency simulated rosewood dining chairs mounted with gilt metal.
$600-900

A set of 6 Regency mahogany dining chairs, the bar top rails carved with anthemions, on sabre legs.
$2,250-3,500

A set of 6 Regency rosewood dining chairs, with scroll cresting rails inlaid with brass foliage.
$4,500-7,000

A set of 12 Regency mahogany dining chairs, including two armchairs, with leather upholstered seats, on moulded front sabre supports.
$15,000-21,000

A set of 8 Regency mahogany dining chairs, including 2 armchairs.
$4,500-7,000

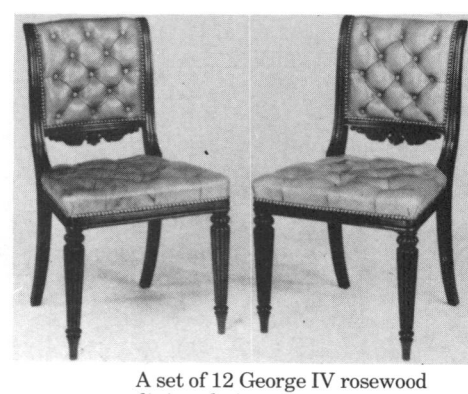

A set of 12 George IV rosewood dining chairs.
$9,000-12,000

A set of 6 late Regency mahogany chairs.
$1,500-2,600

A set of 6 mahogany framed dining chairs, including 2 elbow chairs, some woodworm to seat rails, early 19thC.
$1,500-2,600

A set of 6 George IV rosewood dining chairs.
$1,200-1,600

A set of 6 William IV mahogany
dining chairs, including 2 carvers,
with rail backs and on turned
reeded legs.
$1,500-2,600

A set of 7 William IV mahogany
dining chairs, the drop-in seats
upholstered in green cotton, on
ribbed tapering legs.
$3,000-4,500

A set of 6 mahogany dining chairs,
c1835.
$4,500-7,000

A set of 6 William IV rosewood
dining chairs.
$2,250-3,000

A set of 8 William IV mahogany
dining chairs, including a pair of
armchairs.
$4,500-7,000

A set of 9 William IV mahogany
dining chairs, with inverted
baluster reeded front supports, 3
with damage.
$1,500-2,600

A set of 7 early Victorian mahogany
dining chairs, including one elbow
chair, with turned and tapered
octagonal legs.
$1,500-2,600

A set of 12 William IV carved
mahogany dining chairs, with brass
cappings and casters.
$10,500-14,000

A set of 4 Victorian mahogany
dining chairs with carved rails,
Trafalgar seats, on turned and
carved front supports.
$750-1,000

A set of 4 Victorian ebonised dining
chairs, with gilt decoration and
fluted legs.
$600-900

A set of 8 early Victorian rosewood
dining chairs.
$3,000-4,500

A set of 6 mid-Victorian mahogany buckle back standard dining chairs.
$1,300-1,800

A set of 6 Victorian dining chairs with yoke backs, the upholstered seats raised on turned hexagonal tapering supports.
$1,000-1,400

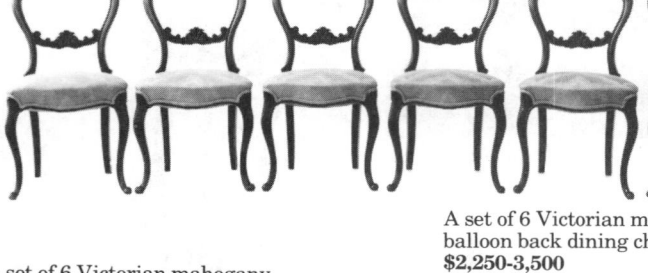

A set of 6 Victorian mahogany balloon back dining chairs.
$2,250-3,500

A set of 6 Victorian mahogany balloon back dining chairs with stuffover seats, on turned and reeded front supports.
$1,500-2,600

A set of 6 Victorian balloon back dining chairs, on moulded cabriole legs and knob feet.
$1,500-2,600

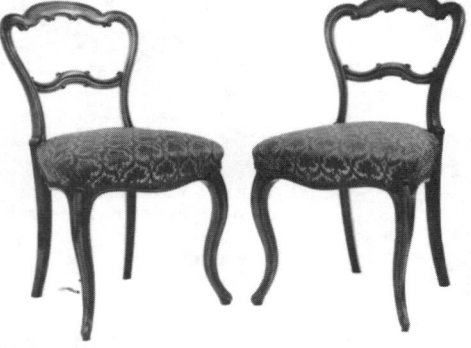

A set of 6 Victorian balloon back chairs.
$1,500-2,600

A set of 6 Victorian mahogany balloon back dining chairs.
$1,500-2,600

A set of 6 Victorian walnut framed dining chairs.
$1,500-2,600

A set of 6 Victorian rosewood dining chairs, with cabriole legs, c1840.
$2,250-3,500

CHAIRS

- ★ check seat rails are the same, with equal patination
- ★ top rail should never over-hang sides
- ★ carving should not be flat
- ★ if stretchers low, chair could have been cut down
- ★ the height from floor to seat should be 1ft 6in

A set of 6 Victorian mahogany balloon back dining chairs, on turned legs.
$1,500-2,600

A set of 8 walnut framed dining chairs.
$3,000-4,500

A set of 4 Victorian mahogany balloon back dining chairs.
$300-500

A set of 6 late Victorian walnut dining chairs, with carved frames, on turned legs.
$1,000-1,400

A set of 7 Victorian mahogany dining chairs, including a lady's and gentleman's armchairs.
$1,500-2,600

A set of 6 Victorian walnut dining chairs, including one carver, buttoned and upholstered in red leather.
$1,500-2,600

A set of 8 carved walnut chairs, c1880.
$1,300-1,800

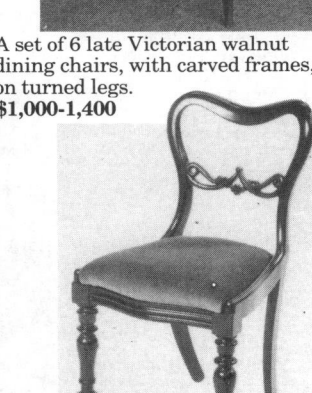

A set of 6 Victorian mahogany dining chairs.
$2,250-3,000

A set of 8 Austrian elm dining chairs, including 2 armchairs, upholstered in pale orange and white cotton, on square tapering legs, early 19thC.
$4,500-7,000

A set of 6 Victorian mahogany dining chairs, with conforming scroll carved splats, the upholstered seats on baluster legs.
$1,500-2,600

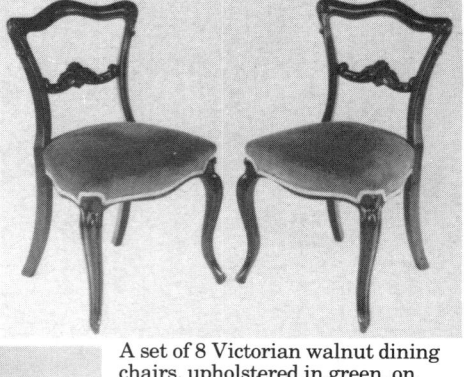

A set of 6 Victorian rosewood open back chairs, the backs with scroll carving, serpentine fronted upholstered seats, on moulded cabriole front legs.
$1,500-2,600

A set of 8 Victorian walnut dining chairs, upholstered in green, on cabriole legs and knob feet.
$2,250-3,000

A set of 6 mahogany dining chairs, in the French Empire style, the oval backs inlaid with brass lines, early 19thC.
$4,500-7,000

A set of 6 Dutch walnut and foliate marquetry dining chairs, upholstered and close-nailed in tapestry, 19thC.
$4,000-5,500

A matched set of 6 Burmese teak chairs, including a pair of armchairs, carved with deities and scrolled foliage, the seats carved as rattan work.
$600-900

A set of 4 Edwardian inlaid dining chairs, with capped feet.
$400-500

A pair of Dutch walnut veneered and marquetry balloon back dining chairs in the Queen Anne taste, with hoof feet, late 18th/early 19thC.
$900-1,300

GUIDE TO STYLES

Dates	Monarch	Period	Woods
1603-1625	James I	Jacobean	
1625-1649	Charles I	Carolean	Oak period
1649-1660	Commonwealth	Cromwellian	up to c1670
1660-1685	Charles II	Restoration	
1685-1689	James II	Restoration	
1689-1694	William and Mary	William and Mary	
1694-1702	William III	William III	Walnut period 1670-1735
1702-1714	Anne	Queen Anne	
1714-1727	George I	Early Georgian	
1727-1760	George II	Early Georgian	Early mahogany period 1735-1770
1760-1811	George III	Late Georgian	
1812-1820	George III	Regency	Late mahogany period 1770-1810
1820-1830	George IV	Regency	
1830-1837	William IV	William IV	
1837-1901	Victoria	Victorian	
1901-1910	Edward VII	Edwardian	

Hall Chairs

A pair of Georgian mahogany hall chairs, with shaped oval backs, on reeded legs.
$900-1,300

A pair of Georgian mahogany hall chairs.
$300-500

A carved walnut chair, after Daniel Manot, early 19thC, 20in (51cm).
$900-1,300

A pair of Regency mahogany hall chairs, with scallop shell backs.
$1,500-2,600

A pair of William IV mahogany hall chairs, on ring-turned ribbed tapering legs headed by scrolling capitals.
◄ **$1,500-2,600**

A pair of George IV mahogany hall chairs, with Gothic arched panelled backs, centred by a blank cartouche.
$900-1,300

A pair of oak Gothic style hall chairs, c1850.
$250-350

Side Chairs

A set of 6 James II ebonised side chairs, upholstered in green velvet, some replaced seat rails and minor restoration.
$9,000-12,000

A George I walnut veneered chair.
$4,000-5,500

A pair of Queen Anne walnut side chairs.
$10,500-14,000

A pair of Queen Anne carved walnut side chairs, each with a shaped crest centering a scallop shell above a solid vase shaped splat, flanked by S-shaped stiles over a compass seat, on cabriole legs with shell carved knees and panelled trifid feet, some damage, Philadelphia, c1740, 41in (104cm) high.
$170,000-200,000

A William and Mary painted maple side chair, with a later rush seat, on baluster turned legs, the legs joined by a turned H-stretcher, on Spanish feet, the surface painted in imitation of wood grain, Boston, c1710, 45½in (115cm) high.
$5,000-6,000

The back of one stile bears the punched initial 'T' associated with early Boston caned chairs and presumed to be a caner's mark.

A Chippendale mahogany side chair, the serpentine crest centering a carved shell flanked by moulded ears, on moulded Marlborough legs, Pennsylvania, c1775, 37in (94cm) high.
$1,000-1,500

A Queen Anne carved walnut side chair, with vase shaped splat flanked by tapering stiles, on cabriole legs with trifid feet, Pennsylvania, c1750, 40½in (103cm).
$4,000-5,000

A William and Mary painted maple side chair, on baluster turned legs centering a tripartite turned stretcher, with later black paint and green fabric upholstery, Boston area, Massachusetts, c1710, 41½in (105cm) high.
$3,000-3,500

A Chippendale carved walnut side chair, with serpentine eared crest centering a carved ruffled shell, on shell carved cabriole legs with ball and claw feet, Philadelphia, c1770, 40in (101.5cm) high.
$3,000-5,000

A Queen Anne maple side chair, on cabriole legs with pad feet joined by block and arrow turned stretchers, repairs, Newport, Rhode Island, c1760, 21½in (54cm).
$2,500-3,500

A Chippendale mahogany side chair, with over-upholstered seat, on Marlborough legs with open brackets and joined by a moulded H-stretcher, Massachusetts, c1775, 39½in (100cm) high.
$1,500-2,000

A Chippendale mahogany side chair, on cabriole legs with ball and claw feet joined by block and ring turned stretchers, Massachusetts, c1775, 22in (55cm).
$2,500-3,000

A Chippendale mahogany side chair, the pierced strapwork splat flanked by fluted stiles, on cabriole legs with acanthus carved knees and ball and claw feet, Philadelphia, c1770, 39in (99cm) high.
$10,000-12,000

A Chippendale mahogany side chair, the serpentine crest rail centering a carved fan flanked by moulded ears, with moulded square slip seat, on cabriole legs with ball and claw feet with raking talons, minor old repairs, probably Boston, c1770, 38in (96.5cm) high.
$5,000-6,000

A pair of Chippendale mahogany side chairs, the shaped crest of each with stylised leaf carving, the open Gothic style latticework splat above a trapezoidal slip seat, on leaf carved peaked knees with claw and ball feet, Salem, c1780, 37in (94cm) high.
$22,000-25,000

A set of 5 late Federal mahogany side chairs, each with a tablet crest rail veneered with a figured panel outlined by stringing, over a carved stylised foliate splat, on sabre legs, probably Philadelphia, c1800, 31in (78cm) high.
$3,000-3,500

A Chippendale carved walnut side chair, with serpentine crest rail centering a ruffled shell, over a trapezoidal slip seat within a thumb moulded frame centering a pendant shell, original upholstery, Philadelphia, c1775, 39½in (100cm).
$18,000-20,000

A set of 4 Chippendale cherrywood side chairs, with shaped crest with scrolled ears, the square legs with quarter moulding joined by an H-stretcher, minor repairs, New England, late 18thC, 37in (94cm) high.
$2,600-3,200

A Chippendale carved walnut side chair, with shell carved cabriole legs ending in trifid feet, minor repairs, Philadelphia, c1770, 23in (58cm).
$6,000-8,000

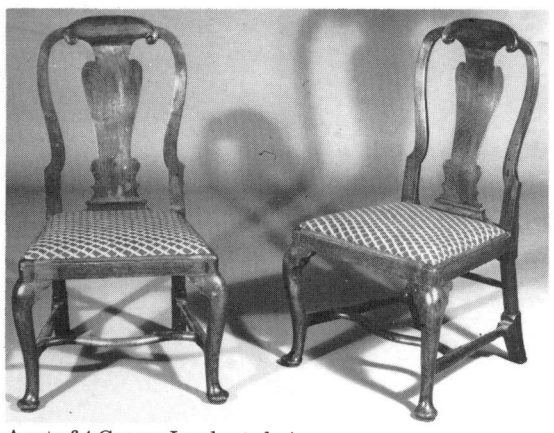

A set of 4 George I walnut chairs.
$7,500-10,500

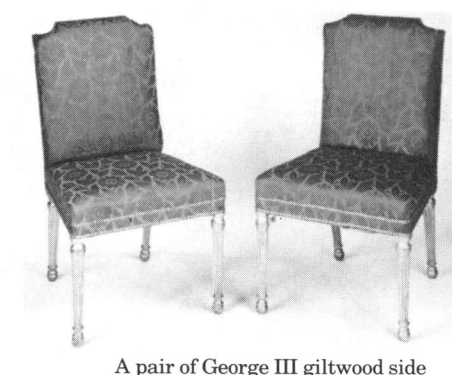

A pair of George III giltwood side chairs, upholstered in close-nailed red damask, 20in (51cm).
$2,250-3,500

A carved gilt and gesso side chair in the George I style, the vase splat with painted recess depicting the child Zeus.
$600-900

A pair of George II walnut chairs, upholstered in crimson cut velvet.
$6,000-9,000

A set of 4 George III cream painted side chairs.
$2,250-3,500

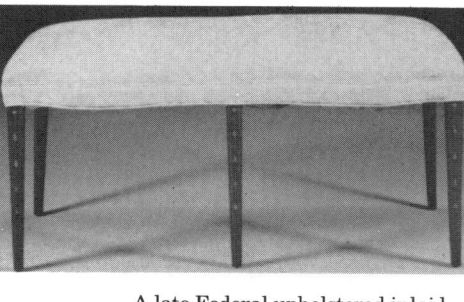

A late Federal upholstered inlaid mahogany bench, the seat with reverse serpentine front edge, on square tapering legs inlaid with bellflowers and stringing, New England, 19thC, 41½in (105cm).
$2,000-2,500

A George II mahogany side chair, on oak leaf headed cabriole legs with claw-and-ball feet.
$750-1,000

A set of 6 Regency parcel gilt and ebonised side chairs, the pierced splats centred by lion masks, with cane filled seats, 3 stamped 'BB'.
$2,500-3,500

A pair of Regency rosewood side chairs of Gillows design.
$1,500-2,600

A set of 5 Regency parcel gilt and ebonised side chairs, one with reinforced seat rails.
$2,500-3,500

A Regency correction chair in imitation bamboo, c1820.
$300-400

A Regency mahogany side chair, after a design by Thomas Hope, with buttoned scroll back, the frame with stepped roundels on reeded sabre legs.
$6,000-9,000

A set of 6 Regency ebonised, parcel gilt and painted bedroom chairs.
$2,250-3,000

A Federal carved mahogany window seat, attributed to the shop of Duncan Phyfe, New York, c1815, with double klismos-type chairback ends, on sabre legs with hairy carved shanks and paw feet, 40in (102cm).
$25,000-30,000

A green painted Bath chair, upholstered in green leatherette beneath a canopy on 3 spoked wheels, 19thC.
$1,000-1,400

Small Chests

A William and Mary oyster laburnum veneered chest, crossbanded and strung with box, raised on bun feet, 33½in (85cm).
$10,500-14,000

A Queen Anne walnut bachelor's chest, with crossbanded hinged top, 29in (74cm).
$9,000-12,000

A walnut bachelor's chest with rounded rectangular crossbanded hinged top, partly replaced bracket feet, 29in (75cm).
$8,000-10,500

A Queen Anne walnut chest, with later quarter veneered and crossbanded top, on later bracket feet, 34½in (87cm).
$1,300-1,800

A George I walnut chest with crossbanded moulded top, later back, 36in (92cm).
$3,000-4,500

A Federal inlaid mahogany and maple veneered chest of drawers, the top with outset rounded corners and lunette inlaid edge above a case with 4 line inlaid maple veneered and cockbeaded moulded drawers, top with splits, probably Boston, Massachusetts, c1800, 44in (111cm).
$6,000-7,000

A Queen Anne walnut chest, on bun feet, 43in (109cm).
$900-1,300

Originally top half of a tallboy or chest-on-stand.

A Georgian mahogany bachelor's chest, with fold-over top and brass swan neck handles, 30in (76cm).
$6,000-8,000

A George II red walnut bachelor's chest, with original brass handles, 39in (99cm).
$10,000-12,000

A George II mahogany bachelor's chest with hinged top, on later bracket feet, 28in (71cm).
$4,000-5,500

A George II mahogany chest, 32in (81cm).
$6,000-8,000

A George II mahogany bachelor's chest with baize-lined dressing slide, on later bracket feet, 31in (79cm).
$2,250-3,500

A small George II mahogany chest, 26in (66cm).
$2,250-3,500

A George II mahogany chest, 30in (76cm).
$2,250-3,500

A George II mahogany chest, 33in (84cm).
$3,000-4,500

A George III mahogany serpentine chest, 40½in (102cm).
$10,500-14,000

An early George III mahogany chest, on later ogee bracket feet, 31½in (80cm).
$2,250-3,500

An early George III mahogany chest, 33½in (85cm).
$3,000-4,000

A George III mahogany bachelor's chest, the fold-over top concealing a folding rectangular swivel mirror, various lidded compartments and a well, above one dummy drawer, 30in (76cm).
$2,250-3,500

A George III mahogany chest, with alterations and restorations, 33in (84cm).
$1,200-1,600

A Georgian mahogany chest, with brass swan neck handles, on bracket feet, 28½in (72cm).
$3,000-4,500

A George III mahogany chest, 43½in (110cm).
$2,250-3,500

A small George III mahogany chest, 31in (79cm).
$2,250-3,500

A walnut and oyster veneered chest, decorated and inlaid with boxwood lines, part 18thC, 37in (94cm).
$4,000-5,500

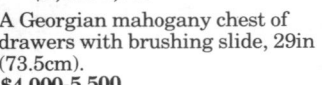

A George III satinwood bowfront chest, banded in harewood and inlaid with stringings, on French bracket feet, 42in (106.5cm).
$6,000-8,000

A Georgian mahogany chest of drawers with brushing slide, 29in (73.5cm).
$4,000-5,500

A George III burr elm chest, inlaid with geometric chequered boxwood lines, 26in (66cm).
$4,000-5,500

A Chippendale tiger maple chest of drawers, with shaped apron with fan-carved drop pendant, on straight bracket feet with traces of red paint, repairs, Massachusetts, c1770, 37in (94cm).
$3,000-3,500

A Chippendale cherrywood chest of drawers, with 4 long graduated cockbeaded drawers, the case flanked by concave quarter columns, on ogee bracket feet, repairs, Connecticut, c1775, 39in (99cm).
$4,000-4,500

A Federal walnut chest of drawers, the doors opening to 2 shelves, Mid-Atlantic States, c1800, 42in (106.5cm).
$2,500-3,000

A Federal inlaid cherrywood chest of drawers, with graduated line inlaid and incised drawers, on straight bracket inlaid feet, probably New Hampshire, c1800, 38in (97cm).
$4,000-5,000

A Federal mahogany bowfront chest of drawers, on French feet, repaired, Massachusetts, c1800, 41in (104cm).
$1,200-1,500

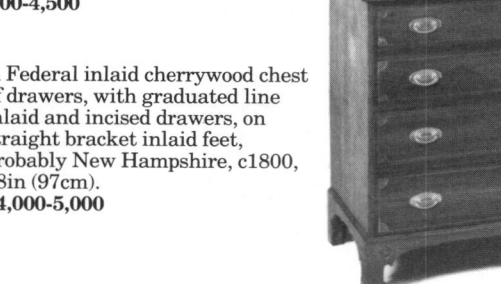

A Federal inlaid mahogany bowfront chest of drawers, the top edged with patterned stringing, with apron inlaid with a band of patterned stringing, on bracket feet, small chips, Massachusetts, c1800, 42in (106.5cm).
$2,000-3,000

A Federal inlaid mahogany bowfront chest of drawers, some inlay restored, Massachusetts, c1800, 40in (101.5cm).
$2,500-3,500

A Federal mahogany bowfront chest of drawers, Massachusetts, c1810, 37in (94cm).
$800-1,200

A Chippendale walnut chest of drawers, with fluted quarter columns over a moulded base, on ogee bracket feet, restored, Pennsylvania, c1770, 37½in (95cm).
$3,000-4,000

A Federal mahogany bowfront chest of drawers, with D-shaped top, on flared French feet, patches, Massachusetts, c1800, 39½in (100cm).
$1,000-1,200

A Federal cherrywood serpentine chest of drawers, with moulded serpentine top above a conforming case, on straight bracket feet, repairs, New England, c1800, 42in (106.5cm).
$5,000-7,000

A late Federal grain painted chest of drawers, the rectangular top with outset rounded corners, with reeded corner columns, on tapering baluster feet, with all-over grain painting in imitation of figured mahogany, Massachusetts, c1820, 41in (104cm).
$5,000-5,500

A late Federal mahogany butler's chest, with 2 short and 4 long cockbeaded drawers, the first long drawer with 2 astragal veneered panels opening to a butler's desk, minor veneer chips, probably New York, c1815, 47in (119cm).
$4,000-5,000

A Federal inlaid mahogany bowfront chest of drawers, with a banded and shaped skirt, on French feet, minor repairs, New England, c1800, 41in (104cm).
$3,000-4,000

A miniature grain painted bowfront chest of drawers, with a double stack of 5 graduated drawers, each grain painted and with ivory pulls, on straight bracket feet, American, 19thC, 12in (30.5cm) high.
$1,200-1,700

An American mahogany upright chest, the eared rectangular top with a gadrooned border and brass spindle half gallery with torch finials, the top drawer moulded with shells between fluted column uprights, that on the right forming a locking stile, on cabriole legs, 28in (71cm).
$800-1,200

A Federal mahogany veneered bowfront chest of drawers, the graduated beaded long drawers each with figured veneer, New England, 41½in (105cm).
$3,000-4,000

A Chippendale mahogany reverse serpentine chest of drawers, with 4 conforming graduated bead-moulded drawers, on ogee bracket feet, Massachusetts, c1775, 41½in (105cm).
$10,000-12,000

A pair of late Federal mahogany bowfront chest of drawers, Mid-Atlantic States, c1820, 44in (111.5cm).
$5,000-6,000

A Georgian mahogany serpentine chest, the sides inlaid with satinwood, with brass urn embossed laurel ring handles, on bracket feet, 48in (122cm).
$4,500-7,000

A Chippendale period carved mahogany serpentine chest, with moulded edge, baize-lined slide, and on claw-and-ball feet with casters, 36in (92cm).
$18,000-21,000

A Chippendale mahogany serpentine chest, containing a brushing slide and 4 graduated drawers with decorated brass bail handles, on bracket feet, 40½in (103cm).
$3,000-4,500

A George III mahogany serpentine dressing chest, with fitted top drawer.
$10,500-14,000

A George III mahogany serpentine chest, the top formerly fitted with a brushing slide, on moulded plinth base, the drawers relined, 42in (106.5cm).
$5,500-7,000

A Georgian mahogany chest with marquetry inlay, with brushing slide, 34in (86cm).
$3,000-4,500

A George III mahogany bowfront chest fitted with a brushing slide, bearing the label 'J. Weight, Cabinet Maker, Upholsterer and Undertaker, Long Acre, London', 39½in (100cm).
$1,500-2,600

Heal records a John Weight, Cabinet and Chair Maker at the Savoy Steps in the Strand in 1796.

A George III mahogany serpentine fronted chest, the top drawer fitted with a slide.
$4,500-7,000

A George III mahogany chest, 31in (79cm).
$2,500-3,500

A George III mahogany bowfront chest, 39in (99cm).
$900-1,300

A George III mahogany secretaire chest, with a secretaire drawer as 2 shallow drawers enclosing a fitted interior, 40in (101cm).
$1,000-1,400

A George III mahogany chest, with later top and later bracket feet, adapted, 47in (119cm).
$1,500-2,600

A George III mahogany bowfront chest, inlaid with boxwood stringing, 37½in (95cm).
$1,500-2,600

An unusual George III mahogany bachelor's chest, the central 8 drawers enclosed within 2 sliding boxes, on later bracket feet, possibly adapted, 39in (99cm).
$5,500-7,000

CHESTS

★ 17thC oak coffers were made in sufficient numbers to allow a reasonable supply today

★ still expect to find original wire or plate hinges; original lock and hasp; original candle box; reasonably tall feet

★ the *best* English chest of drawers of the walnut period will be veneered on to pine or other cheaper timber, the drawer linings will be oak, but the interior of the drawer front will not be; only the top surface visible when the drawer is open will have a slip of oak attached

★ an oak drawer front veneered with walnut suggests either Continental provenance or an early oak chest veneered at a later date; check that holes for handles are compatible inside and out for further evidence of this

★ feet on William and Mary chests were either formed by the stile continuing down to the floor or by large turned 'buns'. The former were often retained and used as blocks to be encased by the later more fashionable bracket feet; the 'buns' were often removed in the same cause. To ascertain this, remove the bottom drawer and a hole in each front corner will be present if bun feet were originally used

★ by the end of the 18thC, turned wood knobs were fashionable. They were at first fine and small, but soon became the flat bulbous mushrooms so popular on most bedroom and staff quarters furniture. If these are original, it is better to resist the temptation of removing them and applying reproduction brass handles

★ accept proper restoration but avoid improvements

A George III mahogany bowfront chest, 28in (71cm).
$4,000-5,500

A mahogany chest, the upper drawer with a baize-lined slide enclosing lidded compartments and an easel inlaid with satinwood fan rosettes, 40½in (102cm).
$4,500-7,000

A late Georgian mahogany bowfront chest, crossbanded and inlaid with boxwood lines, 36in (91.5cm).
$1,000-1,400

A George III mahogany serpentine chest, with chamfered corners above a writing slide, on later bracket feet, 37in (94cm).
$2,250-3,500

◀

A George III mahogany chest with moulded bowed top, on ogee bracket feet, 38in (96.5cm).
$2,250-3,500

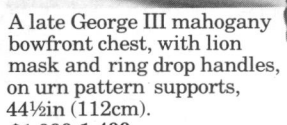

A late George III mahogany bowfront chest, with lion mask and ring drop handles, on urn pattern supports, 44½in (112cm).
$1,000-1,400

An early Victorian teakwood secretaire military chest in 2 sections, the detachable acanthus carved three-quarter gallery above a central folding writing drawer, 41in (104cm).
$2,500-3,500

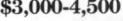

A George III mahogany campaign secretaire chest with crossbanded top, the drawers with inset ivory handles, 34in (86.5cm).
$3,000-4,500

A Regency bowfront mahogany chest, on swept bracket feet, some damage.
$1,000-1,400

A Regency mahogany chest, with waved apron, on splayed feet, 40½in (102cm).
$2,500-3,500

A George III mahogany bowfront chest, the crossbanded frieze above 2 short and 2 long drawers, on narrow bracket feet, 31½in (80cm).
$1,500-2,600

An early Victorian teakwood secretaire military chest, with writing frieze drawer and wrought metal side carrying handles, 40in (101.5cm).
$1,500-2,600

An English Colonial camphorwood and ebony chest, with lobed cabriole legs, 19thC, 32½in (82.5cm).
$2,250-3,500

A Regency mahogany chest, with satinwood inlaid frieze, 41½in (105cm).
$450-700

A Dutch walnut and foliate marquetry bombé chest, decorated with chequered boxwood lines, late 18thC, 36in (91.5cm).
$4,000-5,500

A Federal mahogany bowfront chest of drawers, with reeded pilasters, on baluster and ring turned reeded legs with ball feet, Philadelphia, c1810, 42in (106.5cm).
$1,800-2,200

A Victorian mahogany secretaire with reeded pillar corners, 52in (132cm).
$600-900

A burr maple veneered campaign secretaire chest, mid-19thC, 39in (99cm).
$2,250-3,000

An Anglo-Dutch satinwood bowfront chest, the top inlaid with a bats-wing medallion, the top drawer with a band of parquetry, late 18thC, 28in (71cm).
$6,000-9,000

A Dutch walnut and oyster veneered chest, on later cabriole legs, early 18thC, 38½in (98cm).
$1,200-1,600

An Austrian burr ash and ebonised secretaire chest, with a fitted interior and hinged lined writing slope, 19thC, 50in (127cm).
$2,500-3,500

A Chippendale cherrywood chest of drawers, some damage, probably Connecticut, c1770.
$4,500-5,000

A Dutch marquetry upright chest with coffered rectangular top, each drawer centred by 2 cornucopiae, early 19thC, 41in (104cm).
$3,000-4,500

An Italian walnut and marquetry chest, late 18thC, 24in (61cm).
$4,500-7,000

A pair of Dutch oak chests, each with a serpentine shaped moulded top above a bombé front, on shaped bracket feet, late 18thC.
$1,500-2,600

An Italian walnut and marquetry chest, inlaid with scrolling foliage, the drawers partly relined, mid-18thC, 57in (144.5cm).
$4,500-7,000

A Dutch mahogany chest inlaid with brass, 38in (96.5cm).
$2,250-3,000

Chests-on-Chests

A Chippendale walnut tall chest of drawers, with coved and dentilled cornice above a frieze of 3 thumb moulded drawers, Pennsylvania, c1770, 43in (109cm).
$4,000-6,000

A Chippendale mahogany tall chest of drawers, the drawers flanked by fluted quarter columns over a moulded base, on ogee bracket feet, drawer fronts re-veneered, minor repairs, Pennsylvania, c1750, 42in (106.5cm).
$5,000-6,000

A Georgian mahogany tallboy.
$3,000-4,500

A Georgian mahogany tallboy.
$2,250-3,500

A George III mahogany chest-on-chest of good colour, with ogee and key pattern cornice, on later turned feet, 42in (106.5cm).
$1,500-2,600

An early Georgian walnut tallboy, on later bracket feet, 67 by 41½in (170 by 105cm).
$9,000-12,000

An early Georgian walnut and oak tallboy, on bracket feet, 41½in (105cm).
$3,000-4,500

A walnut veneered chest-on-chest with 11 drawers, on bracket feet.
$1,500-2,600

A mahogany chest-on-secretaire chest, with Greek key applied cavetto moulded cornice, the base with secretaire flap fronted drawer, enclosing a fitted interior, requires restoration, 19thC, 75 by 48in (190.5 by 122cm).
$1,500-2,600

A walnut chest-on-chest, 18thC.
$2,250-3,500

A George I walnut tallboy, the bottom drawer with recessed sunburst arch, on reduced and partly replaced bracket feet, 71½ by 45½in (181 by 115cm).
$9,000-12,000

A George III mahogany tallboy, 44½in (112cm).
$2,250-3,500

A Georgian mahogany tallboy, the upper part with canted angles, fitted with a brushing slide, 48in (122cm).
$2,500-3,500

A Georgian mahogany chest-on-chest, on bracket feet, 44in (111.5cm).
$1,500-2,600

A George III mahogany chest-on-chest, the top section with cornice applied with Grecian key pattern mouldings, blind fret frieze and canted corners, 45in (114cm).
$2,250-3,000

A late George III mahogany chest-on-chest, 42in (106.5cm). ▶
$1,300-1,800

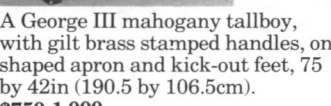

A George III mahogany tallboy, with gilt brass stamped handles, on shaped apron and kick-out feet, 75 by 42in (190.5 by 106.5cm).
$750-1,000

A George II walnut chest-on-chest, with a cavetto cornice above 8 featherbanded drawers, on bracket feet, 69 by 39½in (175 by 101cm).
$2,500-3,500

A Chippendale inlaid walnut tall chest of drawers, with a frieze of compass-drawn line inlay, the drawers with line inlay and a thumb moulding, flanked by fluted chamfered corner columns, base restored, Pennsylvania, c1770, 44½in (112cm).
$3,000-5,000

A George II walnut chest-on-stand, inlaid with rectangular herringbone lines, feet replaced, 49½ by 41in (125 by 104cm).
$2,250-3,000

A George I walnut and oak tallboy with feather line inlay, adaptations, 40in (101.5cm).
$4,500-7,000

A Chippendale maple chest-on-chest, with a cove cornice above 3 short drawers, the centre with fan carving, with a shaped skirt on straight bracket feet, probably New Hampshire, c1775, 38½in (98cm).
$14,000-16,000

A George III mahogany tallboy, the base with brushing slide, 44½in (112cm).
$4,000-5,500

A walnut crossbanded and featherbanded tallboy, parts 18thC, 40in (101.5cm).
$3,000-4,500

WALNUT

- ★ the walnut period is generally accepted as running from c1670-1740, when mahogany took over as the major wood used
- ★ walnut had many advantages: beautiful colour, suitable for veneer work, the burr and curl were particularly desirable, easy to carve
- ★ it was, however, prone to worm
- ★ cabinet makers replaced joiners as supreme craftsmen
- ★ London became furniture making centre
- ★ the first time one was able to distinguish between town and country pieces
- ★ country chests were lined in pine
- ★ Charles II reign heralded return of exiled aristocracy plus continental fashions in furniture

Plus factors with walnut:—
- ★ patination and colour
- ★ good choice of veneers
- ★ with chests – a quartered top
- ★ herringbone inlay
- ★ crossbanding
- ★ stringing
- ★ marquetry

A George III mahogany tallboy, on ogee bracket feet, 44½in (112cm).
$2,250-3,500

A walnut veneered cabinet chest inlaid with boxwood lines, the 2 panelled doors enclosing 9 drawers, recesses and cupboard, late 17thC, 41in (104cm).
$6,000-9,000

A crossbanded walnut tallboy, on bracket feet, early 18thC, with later brass drop handles, 38in (96.5cm).
$6,000-9,000

A George III mahogany tallboy, on ogee bracket feet, 44½in (112cm).

A mahogany tallboy, the 2 halves of different origin, 18thC, 59½in (151cm).
$2,250-3,500

A Dutch walnut and marquetry secretaire chest, the fall panel enclosing a hinged lined writing surface and fitted interior, on shortened block feet, late 18thC, 42in (106.5cm).
$4,000-5,500

A late George III Channel Islands mahogany tallboy, with boxwood strung frieze and canted corners, 44½in (113cm).
$1,500-2,600

A mahogany tallboy, on ogee bracket feet, 18thC, 42in (106.5cm).
$2,250-3,500

A Georgian mahogany chest-on-chest, on bracket feet, 43½in (110cm).
$1,500-2,600

A George III mahogany tallboy, fitted with brass swan neck drop handles, 43in (109cm).
$3,000-4,500

A George II walnut tallboy, on later bracket feet, 71 by 43½in (180 by 110cm).
$4,500-7,000

Chests-on-stands

A George III mahogany tallboy with key pattern cornice, 44½in (112cm).
$3,000-4,500

A figured walnut chest-on-stand, inlaid with chevron banding, with reduced stand, late 17thC, 42in (107cm).
$3,000-4,500

A William and Mary walnut and seaweed marquetry chest-on-stand, decorated with panels of stylised foliate inlay within shaded foliate borders, 38½in (98cm).
$4,000-5,500

A William and Mary oyster veneered walnut chest-on-stand, on stretchered stand with barley-twist legs and drawer in frieze, 48 by 37in (122 by 94cm).
$9,000-12,000

A William and Mary style burr walnut veneered chest-on-stand, inlaid with geometric chequered boxwood lines, 44in (111.5cm).
$2,250-3,500

A William and Mary walnut and marquetry chest-on-stand, the crossbanded rectangular top inlaid with song birds amid arabesque foliage, on later bracket feet, 38½in (97cm).
$4,500-7,000

A William and Mary honey oyster veneered chest-on-stand.
$13,500-17,500

A Queen Anne maple high chest of drawers, with moulded pediment centering 3 turned finials, the lower case with mid-moulding above a centre fan carved drawer, 38in (96.5cm).
$4,000-5,000

A Queen Anne maple and walnut chest-on-frame, in two sections, the upper case with cove moulded cornice, the lower case with applied mid-moulding above a scalloped apron centering a shaped pendant, on tapering cylindrical ring turned legs with pad and disc feet, New York State, c1750, 38in (97cm).
$9,000-12,000

A Queen Anne walnut chest-on-stand, inlaid with fruitwood compass medallions, on later spirally turned legs, waved stretchers and bun feet, 42in (106.5cm).
$3,000-4,500

A William and Mary inlaid walnut high chest of drawers, in two parts, the upper section with moulded cornice fitted with a secret drawer, each drawer with line inlay and bead moulded dividers, above a shaped apron on cabriole legs, with modified pad feet, feet restored, New England, c1740, 42½in (107cm).
$15,000-17,000

A Queen Anne walnut chest-on-stand, crossbanded and inlaid with featherbanding, on later cabriole legs and pad feet, 40½in (101.5cm).
$5,500-7,000

A Queen Anne carved maple high chest of drawers, in 2 parts, on cabriole legs with pad and disc feet, minor patches, New England, c1740, 41in (104cm).
$14,000-18,000

A George I walnut and elm chest-on-stand, inlaid with lightwood stringing, 38½in (97cm).
$4,000-5,500

A Queen Anne maple high chest of drawers, in two parts, the upper case with a cove cornice above 5 graduated and thumb moulded drawers, the lower case with the centre fan carved, New England, c1750, 39in (99cm).
$19,000-22,000

A small walnut chest-on-stand, early 18thC.
$2,250-3,500

A George I burr elm chest-on-stand, 63½ by 40in (161 by 101.5cm).
$25,000-28,000

A George II oak chest-on-stand, crossbanded in walnut, with brass cut card drop handles, on cabriole legs, 36in (91.5cm).
$3,000-4,500

An Anglo-Dutch walnut and inlaid chest-on-stand, early 18thC.
$1,300-1,800

A Chippendale walnut high chest of drawers, in two parts, the upper case drawers flanked by fluted quarter columns, the lower case over a scrolled skirt centering a carved scallop shell, flanked by fluted quarter columns, on cabriole legs with shells on the knees and claw and ball feet, Pennsylvania, c1780, 43in (109cm).
$18,000-20,000

A Queen Anne cherrywood high chest of drawers, in two sections, the upper case with 5 thumb moulded long drawers, over an applied moulding, the lower case with a shaped skirt, on cabriole legs with pad and disc feet, New England, c1750, 41in (104cm).
$12,000-15,000

Wellington Chests

A black lacquered and scarlet Boulle serpentine secretaire chest, with shaped Carrara marble top, the fall front as 3 dummy drawers enclosing a fitted interior, 19thC, 34in (86cm).
$1,300-1,800

A mahogany Wellington chest in 3 sections with side locking stiles, and carrying handles to each section.
$2,250-3,500

A Victorian walnut wellington secretaire chest, with fitted interior faced in maple wood, 24in (61cm).
$1,500-2,600

A Victorian walnut wellington chest, the drawers with turned handles, on a plinth base, 24in (61cm).
$1,300-1,800

A small mid Victorian walnut wellington chest, 27½ by 17in (70 by 43cm).
$450-700

A mahogany wellington chest of 7 drawers, 19thC.
$450-700

Coffers

A grain painted blanket chest, the moulded top lifting above a compartment with a till, above a conforming dovetailed case, later orange paint now removed, probably Mid-Atlantic States, early 19thC, 28in (71cm) high.
$700-1,000

A fine grain painted blanket chest, with moulded rectangular top lifting above an open compartment over a conforming case, decorated with a grain painted sunburst design on shaped board feet, New England, early 19thC, 40in (101.5cm).
$4,000-6,000

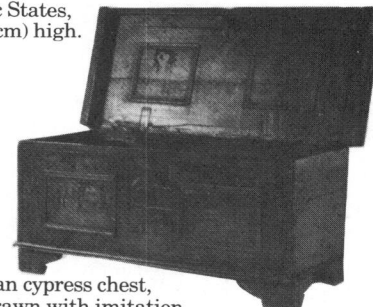

A North Italian cypress chest, incised and drawn with imitation inlay and elaborately decorated, late 16th/early 17thC, 46in (116.5cm).
$1,000-1,400

A small painted dome top trunk, the top lifting above a rectangular compartment, the interior lined with newspapers dated 1843, the top and front painted black and decorated with red, green and yellow flowers, and bearing the initials 'DOD', American, mid-19thC, 27in (68.5cm).
$2,000-3,000

An Italian walnut cassone, carved with foliage, the frieze of caryatid putti centering on a coat-of-arms, partly 17thC, 80in (203cm).
$7,500-10,500

A South German walnut chest with guilloche and fluted borders, on paw feet, late 17thC, 62in (157cm).
$750-1,000

Commodes

A Flemish gilt metal-mounted ebony casket, inlaid with engraved silvered panels and marbles with foliate studs, with partly fitted interior, 17in (43cm).
$3,000-4,500

A yellow grain painted dome top trunk, the top lifting above a green sponge decorated interior with a till, over a rectangular case above a moulded base with shaped skirt, on baluster turned feet, back feet replaced, probably New Hampshire, c1830, 42in (106.5cm).
$2,500-3,500

A Dutch oak marquetry commode elaborately inlaid, 18thC, 36in (91.5cm).
$4,000-5,500

A George III mahogany bombé commode.
$67,000-75,000

An early George III mahogany serpentine commode, with finely cast gilt metal rococo handles, 39½in (100cm).
$7,500-10,500

A pair of George III style mahogany, rosewood and satinwood demi-lune commodes, the tops inlaid with a fan patera, rosewood, tulipwood and satinwood crossbandings, 49in (124cm).
$7,500-10,500

A small Dutch marquetry commode, inlaid with shaped panels of flowers on a kingwood ground, reduced in height, 18thC, 36½in (92cm).
$4,500-7,000

A French chestnut commode, 18thC, 49½in (126cm).
$4,000-5,500

A Dutch coromandel and satinwood veneered serpentine commode, with neo-classical brass handles, 18thC, 47½in (120cm).
$4,000-5,500

A Dutch mahogany and marquetry commode, the waved top inlaid with a parrot perched amid an urn of flowers, the inlay on the sides conforming to the top, on later feet, 49in (124.5cm).
$7,500-10,500

A Louis XV style tulipwood and marquetry bombé commode, with serpentine rouge brêche marble slab, c1870, 54½in (138cm).
$5,500-7,000

A Directoire walnut and gilt metal mounted rectangular commode, surmounted by a marble top, 52in (132cm).
$3,000-4,500

A Louis XV style marquetry serpentine bombé commode, 35 by 43in (89 by 109cm).
$4,000-5,500 ▶

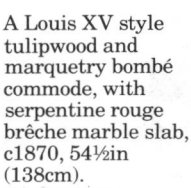

A Directoire mahogany secretaire commode with a fall front writing drawer, on toupie feet, possibly adapted, labelled 'Au Chateau de Bellevue. Rue Saint-Honoré, entre !a rue des Poulies..... Maison de la Citoyenne Poupart..... Tuart, Marchand, tient Magasin d'Ebénisterie....', the back inscribed with the inventory number LW 647, 39½in (100.5cm).
$9,000-12,000

The painted inventory number resembles the double V brand for Versailles.

A Louis XV provincial walnut commode of serpentine shape, the drawers with rococo cast brass handles and escutcheons, on short scroll supports, with defects, 35½ by 51in (90 by 129.5cm).
$4,500-7,000

A Louis XV ormolu mounted parquetry commode of serpentine form, with lozenge inlaid top and exaggerated chevon banding, 50in (127cm).
$9,000-12,000

A Louis XV marquetry and parquetry commode with later breccia marble top, the bombé body inlaid 'sans traverse' within geometric parquetry, 44½in (112cm).
$9,000-12,000

A Louis XV style serpentine bombé commode, with parquetry inlaid long drawers and similar sides, on cabriole supports, 34 by 46in (86.5 by 116.5cm).
$3,000-4,500

A Louis XV walnut and fruitwood parquetry commode, with later rocaille cast gilt metal escutcheons, on cabriole legs with later foliate cast mounts, with restorations, 33in (84cm).
$1,000-1,400

A Louis XV/XVI Transitional style rosewood and marquetry commode, on straight legs with gilt metal mounted feet, 32½in (83cm).
$1,200-1,600

A Louis XV style bois satiné and marquetry bombé commode, with brown brêche marble slab and foliate cast gilt metal handles and escutcheons, 42in (106cm).
$1,200-1,600

A Louis XVI bombé commode by Jean François Lapie, 32 by 38in (81 by 96.5cm).
$10,500-14,000

A French kingwood and foliate marquetry commode, applied with ormolu mounts, late 19thC, 75½in (191cm).
$3,000-4,000

A small South German walnut serpentine front commode, 18thC, 42in (106.5cm).
$3,000-4,000

A George III mahogany bowfront bedside commode, 21in (53.5cm).
$1,500-2,600

A fine Italian lacca povera commode, with painted marble top, the drawers decorated with overlapping scales, flowerheads and C-scrolls in blue, red and yellow on a white ground, applied with gilt shell and pendant husk corbels, c1750, 52in (132cm).
$10,500-14,000

An Italian marquetry commode, top apparently replaced, early 19thC, 43in (109cm).
$4,500-7,000

A Portuguese rosewood commode, inlaid with boxwood stringing, with rocaille carved waved apron, mid-18thC, 51in (130cm).
$6,000-9,000

A George III mahogany bedstep commode with a hinged rectangular lid and triple carpeted treads, with glazed ware liner, 19in (48cm).
$800-1,200

An Italian tulipwood, walnut, purpleheart and inlaid commode, 19thC, 38in (96cm).
$3,000-4,000

A Maltese walnut veneered serpentine commode, banded in cedar with chequer line inlay and Maltese crosses of St John, with later brass lion mask ring handles, on cabriole legs, 18thC, 65in (165cm).
$2,250-3,500

A mahogany commode with fitted interior to top.
$450-700

l. A George III mahogany commode.
$600-900

r. A George III mahogany commode.
$450-700

A George II mahogany converted box seat commode, 20in (51cm).
$750-1,000

Cupboards – Armoires

A French provincial oak armoire, the fielded panel doors divided and flanked by imbricated panels, enclosing shelves and 2 drawers, on squat cabriole legs, late 18thC, 60in (152cm).
$4,500-7,000

A Dutch walnut armoire, on claw-and-ball feet, 18thC, 72in (183cm).
$4,000-5,500

A Dutch mahogany armoire, the chamfered angles with fluted Corinthian ormolu mounted pilasters enclosing shelves and various small drawers, on fluted tapering feet, late 18thC, 74in (188cm).
$2,250-3,500

A Flemish rosewood and ebony armoire, the pair of fielded and panelled cupboard doors carved, with secret drawers behind, flanked by pilasters with grotesque mask capitals, 17thC, 91in (231cm).
$4,000-5,500

A carved Normandy marriage armoire in pitch pine, c1780, 45in (114cm).
$3,000-4,500

A walnut armoire from the Burgundy region of France, 65in (165cm).
$1,500-2,600

A South German walnut armoire, the cornice and frieze applied with cherubic masks and fruit, the spiral twist uprights with grotesque mask capitals, 88in (223.5cm).
$5,500-7,000

A German walnut armoire, with geometrically panelled doors, part 18thC, 72in (183cm).
$13,500-17,500

A Louis XV cherrywood armoire with moulded chamfered cornice, on cabriole legs, 90½ by 56in (229 by 142cm).
$7,500-10,500

A George III mahogany bedside cupboard, with an adapted commode drawer, 21in (53cm).
$1,500-2,600

Cupboards – Bedside

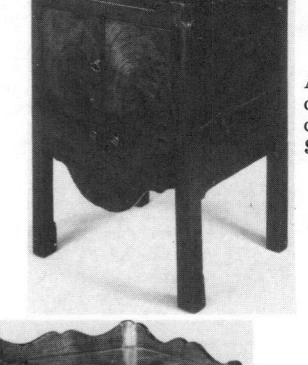

An early George III mahogany bedside cupboard with a commode drawer, 22in (56cm).
$2,250-3,500

A French kingwood veneered and porcelain mounted armoire, 19thC, 44in (111.5cm).
$6,000-9,000

A walnut veneered bedside cabinet, with inlay, 19thC, 16in (41cm).
$300-500

A Louis XV fruitwood 'table-de-nuit', with waved moulded apron and cabriole legs, restorations, 14in (35.5cm).
$1,500-2,600

A pair of mahogany bedside cupboards of Louis XVI style, with white marble tops, each with 2 drawers opening to the front and one to the side, 16½in (42cm).
$4,000-5,500

Cupboards – Corner

A George III inlaid mahogany bowfront corner cupboard, 31in (79cm).
$750-1,000

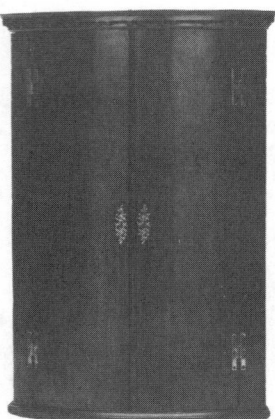

A George III style mahogany
bowfront corner cupboard, 44in
(111.5cm) high.
$750-1,000

A Regency black, red and gold
japanned hanging corner cupboard,
partly redecorated, 23in (58cm).
$1,200-1,600

A Federal walnut corner
cupboard, with shaped
pediment above a dentilled
moulding over 2 panelled
cupboard doors opening to 3
shelves above a short drawer
over 2 panelled cupboard
doors, probably Kentucky,
c1810, 50in (127cm).
$3,000-4,000

CORNER CUPBOARDS

★ these cupboards were
made right through the
18thC in various woods
including walnut and
mahogany, as well as oak

★ examples in oak are
usually 'country' versions
of the more sophisticated
pieces made in walnut or
mahogany

★ corner cupboards with
glazed doors, that are
suitable for the display of
porcelain or other objects,
are the most sought after
type. They are, however,
far more difficult to find
and are consequently
more expensive

★ bow fronted examples are
usually considered the
most desirable, especially
if they are fitted inside
with two or three small
drawers and the shelves
are shaped

★ these cupboards are
usually constructed in two
parts; 'marriages' do exist
and whilst these may be
acceptable, it should be
reflected in a lower price.
Check that the backboards
of the two parts match and
that the quality of timber
and style of construction
correspond

A fruitwood corner cupboard, 19thC.
$300-400

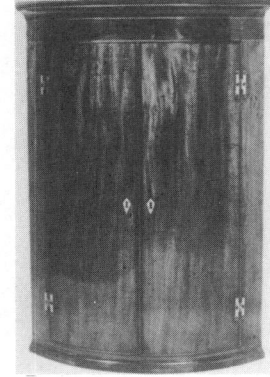

A mahogany bowfront hanging
corner cupboard, with 3 shaped
shelves and 3 spice drawers, late
18thC.
$2,250-3,000

An Edwardian mahogany corner
cupboard, with crossbanded bowed
top and cupboard doors, stamped
Howard & Sons, Berners St., 44in
(111cm).
$900-1,300

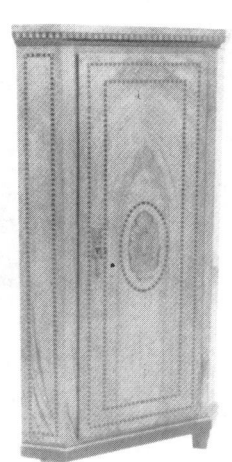

A South German kingwood and
tulipwood crossbanded encoignure
of 'arc en arbelète' outline, 18thC,
34½in (88cm).
$2,250-3,500

A Dutch inlaid walnut corner
cupboard, 19thC, 27½in (70cm).
$1,000-1,400

Cupboards – Linen Presses

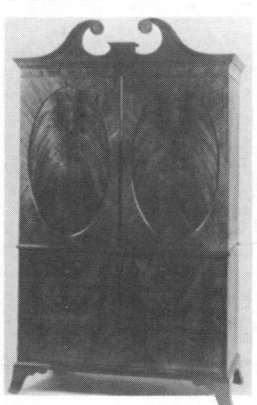

A George III mahogany linen press, the swan neck pediment carved with flowerheads, 52½in (133cm).
$6,000-9,000

A Chippendale poplar linen press, in 2 sections, the upper with moulded cornice above a patterned frieze over 2 arched panelled doors, flanked by fluted pilasters, the lower case with a moulded and gadrooned base, on straight bracket feet, New Jersey, c1770, 46in (116.5cm).
$6,000-6,500

A George III mahogany linen press with dome shaped cornice, panelled doors enclosing sliding trays, 90 by 48in (228.5 by 122cm).
$1,500-2,600

A George III mahogany clothes press, the figured doors panelled with waved moulding and foliate motifs at the angles, 50in (127cm).
$2,250-3,000

A George III mahogany secretaire press, with a deep fitted secretaire drawer as 2 dummy drawers above 3 long graduated drawers, on bracket feet, 41in (104cm).
$4,000-5,500

A George III mahogany linen press with a pair of 'plum pudding' veneered panel doors with satinwood ovals, 53in (134cm).
$1,500-2,600

A Georgian mahogany linen press, inlaid with stringing, framing bands of rosewood, 74 by 49in (188 by 124.5cm).
$4,000-5,500

A George III mahogany linen press, the fielded panelled doors enclosing slides, 49½in (126cm).
$1,300-1,800

A Regency mahogany clothes press, geometrically inlaid with boxwood strings, 51in (129.5cm).
$2,250-3,500

A mahogany linen press with fluted side flanges, late 18thC.
$1,500-2,600

A Regency mahogany linen press, 50in (127cm).
$1,300-1,800

A Regency mahogany clothes press, on later splayed and tapering feet, 88½ by 56½in (224 by 143cm).
$4,500-7,000

A George IV mahogany linen press, on bulbous turned legs, 51in (130cm).
$1,200-1,600

An oak linen press with mahogany crossbanding, mid-19thC, 49in (124.5cm).
$1,000-1,400

A large bowfront mahogany linen press, the panelled doors, with brass stile to the top, enclosing 4 linen slides, 54in (137cm).
$3,000-4,000

Cupboards – Wardrobes

A George IV gentleman's mahogany wardrobe, inlaid with satinwood bands and boxwood lines, adaptations, 51in (129.5cm).
$2,250-3,000

An Irish Sheraton style inlaid mahogany linen press, 19thC.
$600-900

A Dutch mahogany clothes press, with partly fitted interior, on fluted square tapering legs, 63in (160cm).
$4,000-5,500

A Regency mahogany breakfront wardrobe, 93 by 102in (236 by 259cm).
$7,500-10,500

An Adam style mahogany breakfront wardrobe, applied with rams head, paterae, foliate and bellflower festoons, 86in (218.5cm).
$1,500-2,600

A Victorian burr walnut double wardrobe, 72in (182.5cm).
$450-700

A late Victorian walnut breakfront wardrobe, the cornice slightly distressed, 90 by 87in (228.5 by 221in).
$1,500-2,600

Davenports

A Regency mahogany davenport, 17in (43cm).
$4,000-5,500

A Regency davenport with gilt metal pierced gallery, and a fitted interior with hinged pen drawer, the other side with dummy drawers, 20½in (52cm).
$4,000-5,500

A Victorian walnut davenport, the sliding top section with a three-quarter galleried top, stamped 'M. Wilson, Great Queen Street', 23½in (59.5cm).
$2,500-3,500

A Victorian walnut davenport with pop-up stationery compartment.
$2,250-3,000

An early Victorian figured walnut davenport, the surprise pop-up top with a pierced three-quarter gallery above a piano type slope enclosing a fitted interior, 22½in (57cm).
$3,000-4,500

A mid-Victorian burr walnut davenport, with serpentine piano lid enclosing retractable writing surface and 2 small drawers, and secret compartment to gallery, mechanism damaged, 39in (99cm) high.
$2,250-3,000

A Victorian burr elm davenport, 22in (56cm).
$2,250-3,000

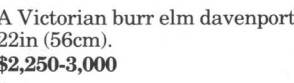

A walnut davenport, with 4 false and 4 real drawers.
$1,200-1,600

An Irish inlaid yew davenport, the hinged writing slope inlaid with trailing shamrocks enclosing a fitted interior, 19thC, 25½in (64.5cm).
$4,000-5,500

A mid-Victorian davenport of Gothic style, 30in (76cm).
$4,500-7,000

A Victorian walnut davenport, with rising stationery compartment, the piano front enclosing a fitted interior, 43½ by 23in (110 by 58cm).
$3,000-4,000

A walnut davenport with sliding top, 22½in (57cm).
$3,000-4,500

DAVENPORTS

★ the name derives from Gillow's cost book where an illustration of this piece of furniture appeared for the first time. Beside the illustration was written 'Captain Davenport – a desk'

★ first examples date from the late 1790's

★ they were extremely popular during the Regency and well into Victoria's reign

★ there are two quite distinct types of davenport – the quite severe Regency as opposed to the more generous and often highly carved Victorian

★ they are bought by a quite different market – at the moment the walnut well carved Victorian can be said to be selling much better than the earlier Regency

★ points to look out for: burr-walnut, satinwood, secret drawers or complex interior arrangement, good quality carving and cabriole legs, galleried top

★ unless stated all davenports in this section are fitted with 4 real opposed by 4 dummy drawers

A Victorian walnut satinwood inlaid davenport, 22in (56cm).
$2,250-3,500

A Victorian walnut veneered harlequin davenport, with piano front, fitted interior and pop-up back.
$2,250-3,000

A Victorian ebonised davenport with maple banding, some damage.
$600-900

A Victorian walnut davenport.
$2,250-3,500

Desks

A Victorian figured walnut davenport.
$1,200-1,600

A Victorian walnut davenport, having carved scrolled supports, 34in (86cm).
$1,500-2,600

A George I walnut kneehole desk, on later bracket feet, 33in (84cm).
$6,000-9,000

A burr ash kneehole desk, 32½in (82cm).
$4,000-5,500

A walnut kneehole desk, early 18thC.
$4,500-7,000

A George II mahogany kneehole desk with a moulded edge and re-entrant corners, containing a frieze, arched apron and 6 short drawers, about a recessed enclosed cupboard, on bracket feet, 32½in (83cm).
$3,000-4,500

A late Federal carved mahogany ladies writing desk, the top with outset corners above a conforming case with one sham drawer fitted as a writing compartment, on spiral turned tapering legs, patch to one corner, Massachusetts, c1820, 27½in (69.5cm).
$1,700-2,500

A small Georgian design mahogany kneehole desk, on ogee bracket feet, 30½in (77.5cm).
$1,000-1,400

A Federal inlaid mahogany and bird's-eye maple secretary, the 2 cupboard doors opening to a fitted interior, the lower section with hinged writing flap, minor inlay loss, Massachusetts, c1800, 40in (101.5cm).
$7,000-7,500

A George III mahogany architect's desk with double flap top, one previously inset with baize, the back with fielded panels, on later bracket feet, 54in (137cm).
$4,500-7,000

A George III mahogany kneehole desk, 40½in (102cm).
$4,000-5,500

A Chippendale mahogany kneehole desk, with original brass swan neck handles, each side with a large brass plate carrying handle, 18thC, 50in (127cm).
$3,000-4,500

KNEEHOLE DESKS

★ kneehole desk is like a pedestal but with a recessed cupboard in between the pedestals
★ it was most likely an 'upstairs' piece – hence being used as a dressing table/desk
★ they were first made c1710 in walnut
★ most then had 3 drawers across the top and 3 down each pedestal
★ this piece of furniture has suffered from demand and there are many fakes and gross alterations
★ many are made from chests of drawers (check the sides of the small drawers and if the desk has been made from a chest of drawers they will have a new side)
★ it is unusual to have a brushing slide in a kneehole desk – this *could* point to a conversion

A George III mahogany cylinder desk, the tambour shutter enclosing a fitted interior, 47½in (120cm).
$16,500-19,500

A George III mahogany partners' pedestal desk, 49in (124.5cm).
$8,000-10,500

A small George III mahogany kneehole desk, with fold-over top, 32½in (82.5cm).
$3,000-4,500

A George III mahogany pedestal desk, one bracket foot defective, 55½in (140cm).
$9,000-12,000

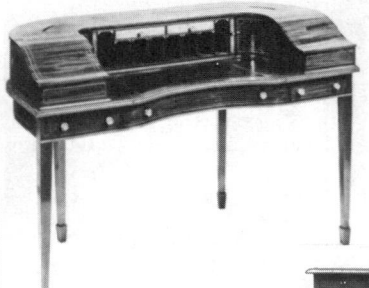

A mahogany two-pedestal desk, early 19thC, 48in (122cm).
$2,250-3,500

A George III mahogany partners' pedestal desk, the 3 frieze drawers with replacement wood knob handles, the drawers all oak lined, enclosed by outline panel doors, the sides with cast rococo shaped plate brass carrying handles, the plinth on casters, 53in (134.5cm).
$16,500-19,500

A late George III mahogany partners' desk.
$10,500-14,000

A George III style mahogany Carlton House desk, on square tapered legs with spade feet, 54in (137cm).
$4,500-7,000

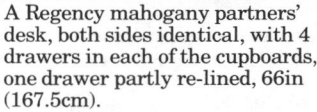

A mahogany serpentine front desk, 18th/19thC, 45in (114cm).
$7,500-10,500

A Victorian mahogany desk, the top lined with gilt tooled green leather, 42in (106.5cm).
$2,250-3,500

An early Victorian mahogany four-pedestal desk, the top lined in gilt tooled green leather, 54in (137cm).
$4,500-7,000

A Regency mahogany partners' desk, both sides identical, with 4 drawers in each of the cupboards, one drawer partly re-lined, 66in (167.5cm).
$5,500-7,000

A mahogany cylinder top pedestal desk, on plinth bases, mid-19thC.
$1,000-1,400

An early Victorian mahogany partners' desk, 60in (152cm).
$4,500-7,000

A William IV mahogany partners' pedestal desk with side flaps, the pedestals with 2 deep drawers, mahogany lined, with false fronts, 62in (157cm) closed.
$13,500-17,500

A Federal inlaid mahogany writing desk, the folding writing surface opening to reveal a frieze and 3 short drawers, above a covered writing surface opening to reveal a well, the lower case with a banded skirt, on square tapering legs, repairs to front legs at top of posts, left front leg splined at back, Eastern Massachusetts, 29in (73.5cm).
$3,500-5,000

An early Victorian desk, 60in (152cm).
$2,250-3,000

A mid-Victorian mahogany pedestal desk, the back later labelled 'Trevor Page & Co. Cabinet Makers & Upholsterers, Exchange Street, Norwich', 45in (114cm).
$2,250-3,500

A Chippendale mahogany kneehole desk, the top above a fitted long drawer over a cupboard door flanked by 3 short drawers, on ogee bracket feet, 33in (84cm).
$4,000-4,500

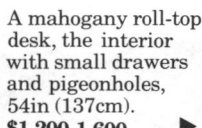

A mahogany roll-top desk, the interior with small drawers and pigeonholes, 54in (137cm).
$1,200-1,600 ▶

A mid-Victorian mahogany pedestal desk, stamped 'Holland & Sons', 60in (152cm).
$4,000-5,500

A Victorian mahogany desk with cupboards, 60in (152cm).
$1,500-2,600

A walnut roll-top desk, 54in (137cm).
$750-1,000

A Wooton's Patent desk, of walnut and burr walnut, the curved front with letterbox and matching plaque inscribed 'Manufactured by the Wooton Desk Co. Indianapolis, Ind. pat Oct 6 1874', enclosing an elaborately fitted interior, late 19thC, 39½in (100cm).
$9,000-12,000

A purple heartwood pedestal partners' desk, c1870, 60in (152cm).
$5,500-7,000

A late Victorian oak library desk, 113in (287cm).
$4,000-5,500

A Federal inlaid mahogany writing desk, the hinged lid opening to a slanted writing surface with 2 flaps concealing storage compartments, above a single long drawer flanked by panels of birch veneer outlined by patterned stringing, small veneer chips, feet pieced, Coastal Massachusetts, c1800, 30in (76cm).
$1,500-2,500

A mahogany pedestal partners' desk, the moulded top with leatherette insert, late 19thC, 72in (182.5cm).
$3,000-4,500

A Federal inlaid mahogany tambour desk, the tambour doors opening to a fitted interior, some restorations, Eastern Massachusetts, c1800, 40½in (102cm).
$3,000-3,500

A walnut partners' desk of octagonal form, with 4 frieze drawers and 4 dummy drawers, 64in (162.5cm).
$4,000-5,500

An Edwardian mahogany pedestal desk, 59½in (151cm).
$1,300-1,800

An Edwardian mahogany kneehole desk inlaid with satinwood.
$1,300-1,800

An Edwardian rosewood kneehole writing desk, inlaid with boxwood lines, trailing foliate marquetry, bellflowers and urns, 44½in (112cm).
$2,250-3,000

A Biedermeier fruitwood kneehole writing chest, with a sliding top enclosing fitted interior and foliate frieze, with slide and hinged and ratcheted slope, 43in (109cm).
$6,000-9,000

A mahogany partners' desk, with 18 drawers, c1920, 60in (152cm).
$2,500-3,500

An Edwardian satinwood kidney-shaped writing desk, inlaid with chequered boxwood lines, 60in (152cm).
$4,000-5,500

A pollard oak twin pedestal desk, with a pair of cupboards to the reverse, c1925, 61in (155cm).
$1,500-2,600

A walnut bowfront pedestal desk, c1930, 54in (137cm).
$1,200-1,600

Dressers

A rare George III mahogany breakfront Lancashire dresser, with crossbanded top and cupboard doors, 82in (208cm).
$7,500-10,500

A Louis XV style walnut serpentine fronted kneehole desk, the top with geometric handing, 44in (111.5cm).
$1,500-2,600

A George II style walnut dresser, on cabriole legs with pad feet and shell headings, 82in (208cm).
$1,500-2,600

An Anglo-Indian teakwood side buffet, late 19thC, 96in (243.5cm).
$1,500-2,600

Dumb Waiters

An unusual French Provencal dresser in cherrywood and walnut, 102in (259cm).
$4,000-5,500

A large Brittany dresser, c1880, 72in (182.5cm).
$2,500-3,500

A George III satinwood and mahogany two-tier dumb waiter, on ribbed tapering supports, 22½in (57cm).
$5,500-7,000

A mid-Georgian mahogany three-tier dumb waiter, 45in (114cm) high.
$1,300-1,800

A mahogany dumb waiter, 18thC, 43in (109cm) high.
$900-1,300

A George III mahogany two-tier dumb waiter, the tiers with drop leaves, 37½in (95cm) high.
$3,000-4,500

Lowboys

A Scottish red walnut lowboy, 18thC, 33½in (85cm).
$4,000-5,500

Globes

A terrestrial globe by Malby & Co, on mahogany stand with compass, 1847, 16in (41cm) diam.
$7,500-10,500

A Malby's terrestrial globe on a mahogany stand with turned shaft, 1848, 40½in (102cm) high.
$3,000-4,500

A Regency mahogany new terrestrial globe, the globe signed by Cruchley, the stand with silver plaque inscribed 'on this globe Lieut. Wagborn traced the overland route', 47in (119cm) high.
$9,000-12,000

An early Georgian walnut lowboy, the drawers with fruitwood stringing, back feet replaced, 30½in (77cm).
$7,000-9,000

A George II walnut lowboy, 30in (76cm).
$1,500-2,600

An early George III mahogany lowboy, 32in (81cm).
$6,000-9,000

A George II mahogany lowboy.
$4,500-7,000

Mirrors

A William and Mary silvered mirror, 60 by 20½in (152 by 52cm).
$3,000-4,500

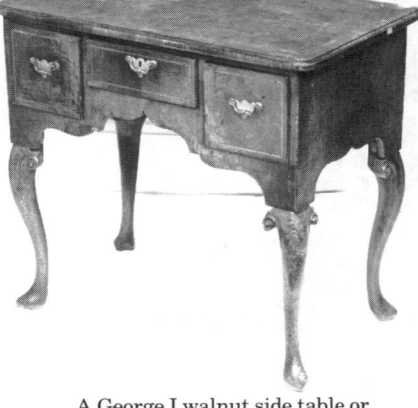

A George I walnut side table or lowboy, the crossbanded top inlaid with narrow chevron bands, legs possibly not original, top 31 by 19in (79 by 48cm).
$4,500-7,000

A Dutch walnut and foliate marquetry lowboy, 19thC, 27in (68.5cm).
$1,500-2,600

A Charles II giltwood mirror with later bevelled plate, 43 by 33in (109 by 84 cm).
$2,250-3,500

A looking glass, with walnut frame and inner carved gilt gesso border, early 18thC, 45½ by 27½in (115 by 70cm).
$7,500-10,500

A Chippendale mahogany mirror, with scrolled pediment flanked by scrolled ears above a reeded frame, repairs, American, c1775, 16½in (41cm) high.
$800-1,200

A mirror overmantel with triple bevelled plate glass panels in gilt frame, early 19thC, 52½in (133cm).
$1,200-1,600

A George II gilt gesso mirror, possibly Irish, 44 by 24in (112 by 61cm).
$2,250-3,000

An early Georgian walnut mirror with later bevelled plate, 38 by 21½in (97 by 54cm).
$2,500-3,500

A George I carved giltwood and gesso wall mirror, 38½ by 19½in (98 by 50cm).
$4,500-7,000

A pair of parcel gilt and mahogany mirrors of early Georgian style, with scrolling broken pediment crestings centred by pierced scallop and foliate clasps, 52 by 26in (132 by 66cm).
$3,000-4,500

A George II gilt and gesso wall mirror, inset with later plate, 47½ by 25in (120 by 63cm).
$6,000-8,000

A George II walnut and parcel gilt mirror.
$6,000-9,000

A Queen Anne mahogany mirror, the shaped pediment above a moulded frame, later glass, American, c1750, 16½in (41cm) high.
$400-600

An unusual neo-classical parcel gilt and cream painted mirror, partly redecorated, late 18thC, 54 by 19½in (137 by 49.5cm).
$7,500-10,500

A large giltwood wall mirror, 19thC, 100 by 60in (254 by 152cm).
$3,000-4,500

Use the Index!

Because certain items might fit easily into any of a number of categories, the quickest and surest method of locating any entry is by reference to the index at the back of the book.
This has been fully cross-referenced for absolute simplicity.

A George II giltwood mirror, the bevelled plate with tortoiseshell banded border, in a gesso moulded frame, 50 by 23½in (127 by 59cm).
$3,000-4,000

A giltwood mirror, early 19thC, 48 by 36in (122 by 91cm).
$6,000-9,000

A pair of English carved and gilded frames, 18thC, 5 by 4in (13 by 10cm).
$150-250

A Queen Anne mahogany mirror, the scrolled pediment above a moulded frame, later glass, American, c1750, 19 by 11in (48 by 28cm).
$200-400

An early George III giltwood mirror, with later shaped plate, 33½ by 21in (84 by 53cm).
$10,500-14,000

A Georgian mahogany wall mirror, with carved gilt mirror surround to the original plate, 40 by 22in (101.5 by 56cm).
$1,000-1,400

A George III giltwood mirror, 43½ by 32½in (110 by 82.5cm).
$7,500-10,500

A George III giltwood and composition girandole with 2 scrolling candle branches and fruiting boss, 43 by 18½in (109 by 47cm).
$7,500-10,500

An English carved and gilded frame, 18thC, 13 by 9½in (33 by 24cm).
$300-400

A George III giltwood mirror, ▶ 39 by 22in (99 by 56cm).
$4,500-7,000

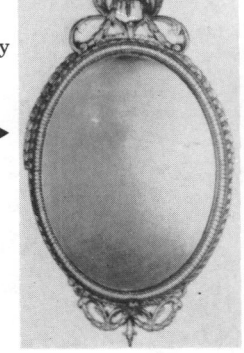

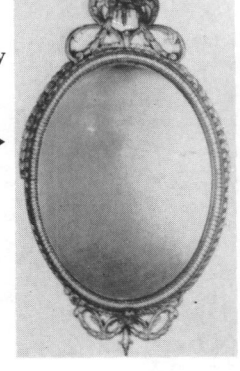

A late George III giltwood mirror, the frieze with later painted panel of a coaching scene, 32 by 15in (81.5 by 38cm).
$2,250-3,000

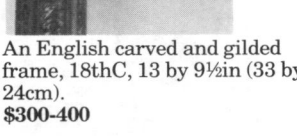

A mahogany mirror, 18thC.
$450-600

A Regency carved giltwood frame convex mirror, ▶ 44 by 33in (111.5 by 84cm).
$1,500-2,600

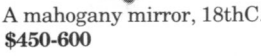

A Regency giltwood convex mirror.
$10,500-14,000

A Regency giltwood and gesso overmantel mirror, with ebonised panel applied with an outspread eagle and laurel leaf ornament, 63 by 41in (160 by 104cm).
$7,500-10,500

A Regency giltwood convex mirror with a reeded ebonised slip in a flowerhead and ball studded cavetto frame, 41 by 25in (104 by 63.5cm).
$1,500-2,600

A Regency giltwood mirror, with later rectangular plate, 35 by 28in (89 by 71cm).
$4,500-7,000

A Regency carved giltwood convex mirror, with ribband tied laurel leaf surround hung by drapery cresting from a water lily, 51½ by 31in (131 by 78cm).
$16,500-19,500

A Regency giltwood circular mirror, with later plate, 72 by 44in (182.5 by 111.5cm).
$13,500-17,500

A Regency cream painted and parcel gilt overmantel, with later rectangular plate, 57 by 57½in (144 by 146cm).
$10,500-14,000

A Regency carved giltwood and gesso convex girandole, 40½ by 23½in (103 by 59cm).
$4,500-7,000

A Regency giltwood mirror, 48 by 30in (122 by 76cm).
$1,500-2,600

An Edwardian giltwood mirror, 42 by 30in (106 by 76cm).
$1,500-2,600

A Regency giltwood mirror, 44 by 26in (111 by 66cm).
$1,300-1,800

Make the most of Miller's

Miller's is completely different each year. Each edition contains completely NEW photographs. This is not an updated publication. We never repeat the same photograph.

A Victorian giltwood overmantel,
88 by 65in (223.5 by 165cm).
$2,250-3,000

Two Continental mahogany
veneered pier glasses, early 19thC,
39½ by 15½in (100 by 38cm).
$900-1,300

A Chippendale mahogany mirror,
labelled by John Elliott Jr,
Philadelphia, 1784-1804, the
scrolled pediment flanked by shaped
ears above a shaped mirror frame,
restoration to pendant, 23in (56cm).
$3,000-5,000

A French carved oak and gilded
frame in Louis XIII manner, 17thC,
28 by 22in (71 by 56cm).
$4,500-7,000

A French carved and gilded frame,
18thC, 29 by 24in (74 by 61cm).
$750-1,000

A French gilt carved framed mirror,
c1850.
$3,000-4,500

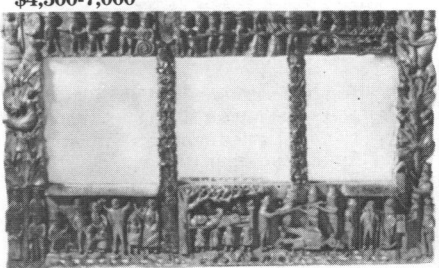

An unusual Irish carved yew and
oak three-division narrative mirror,
the frieze depicting scenes relating
to the Phoenix Park Riots, 41½in
(105cm).
$1,500-2,600

*The Phoenix Park Riots occurred in
Dublin, August 1871, and resulted
in the deaths of several Home Rule
sympathisers.*

An Italian giltwood mirror, 114 by
64in (289.5 by 162.5cm).
$1,000-1,400

A George II walnut toilet mirror, on
later bracket feet, 17in (44cm).
$750-1,000
◄

An Italian Florentine style carved
and gilded frame, 18 by 13in (46 by
33cm).
$600-900

A Venetian mirror, late 18thC.
$4,500-7,000

An early Georgian walnut toilet mirror, 17in (43cm).
$900-1,300

A George II mahogany toilet mirror, 17in (43cm).
$2,250-3,000

An Italian giltwood mirror, the frame with a central bird upon a grotesque mask, late 18thC, 86 by 57½in (218.5 by 145cm).
$12,000-15,000

A Regency mahogany cheval mirror with associated rectangular plate, on reeded downswept legs and acanthus feet, 32in (81cm).
$1,500-2,600

A Queen Anne mahogany shaving mirror, the plate with scalloped and gilded edge, flanked by square moulded supports, above a serpentine base, on conforming bracket feet, American, c1750, 17in (43cm).
$1,200-1,600

A late Federal mahogany dressing glass, the mirror tilting between 2 column-turned supports with acorn finials, the supports flanked by S-scrolls with brass mounts, on a case with a bowed front flanked by brass mounts, on turned feet, Pennsylvania, c1810, 29½in (74cm).
$800-1,200

A Regency mahogany frame cheval mirror, flanked by adjustable bronzed candle sconces, on ebonised line inlaid splay feet.
$1,500-2,600

A Chippendale mahogany mirror, with arched and scrolled pediment flanked by scrolled ears, above a mirror plate with moulded frame over a scrolled pendant, minor damage, American, c1770, 41in (104cm) high.
$3,000-4,000

A George III mahogany cheval mirror, the sliding plate flanked by brass telescopic candle sconces, on cleft feet, 25in (63.5cm).
$5,500-7,000

A George IV mahogany cheval mirror.
$1,200-1,600

A mid-Victorian satin birch cheval mirror, on scrolled feet with guilloche panels, 35in (89cm).
$800-1,200

Screens

A set of 5 chinoiserie leather panels, originally a screen, more recently a built-in cupboard, 82 by 24in (208 by 61cm) each panel.
$6,000-9,000

MIRRORS

★ until 1773, 18thC English looking glass plates were produced from blown cylinders of glass. This restricted the size and so large mirrors of the period were made up of more than one plate. In 1773, a new process enabled the production of the large single piece mirrors which became fashionable thereafter

★ 18thC carved and gilded mirror frames will be of wood covered with gesso, or occasionally of carton pierre

★ in the 19thC, cheaper and greater production was achieved by the use of plaster 'stucco' or composition 'carved' decoration built up on a wire frame. This has tended to crack and is thus detectable. Stucco work cannot be pierced with a needle. Carved wood can

★ do not have the old mirror plate re-silvered if it has deteriorated, carefully remove and store; replace it with a new specialist made plate. This particularly applies to toilet and dressing mirrors

★ store original mirror upright, never flat, using 8 batons slightly larger than the plate – 6 upright and 2 across to crate the mirror around bubble paper

---

A decorated four-fold screen, depicting 17thC scenes, late 18th/early 19thC, 114 by 79in (290 by 201cm) overall.
$9,000-12,000

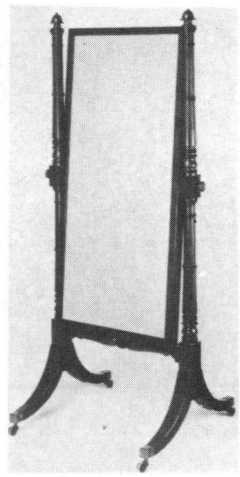

A George IV mahogany cheval glass with later plate, the splayed legs inlaid with ebonised stringing, 62in (157cm) high.
$900-1,300

A cheval mirror in the style of A W N Pugin, 34½in (87.5cm).
$4,000-5,500

A six-fold screen, 18thC, 96in (243.5cm) high.
$6,000-9,000

A painted leather four-leaf screen, 66 by 19½in (167.5 by 49cm) each leaf.
$2,250-3,500

345

A mid-Victorian four-leaf strapwork screen, 76 by 26in (193 by 66cm) each leaf.
$1,500-2,600

A Dutch painted leather four-leaf screen, with geometrically patterned border, one panel distressed, early 19thC, 72 by 21in (182.5 by 53cm) each panel.
$3,000-4,500

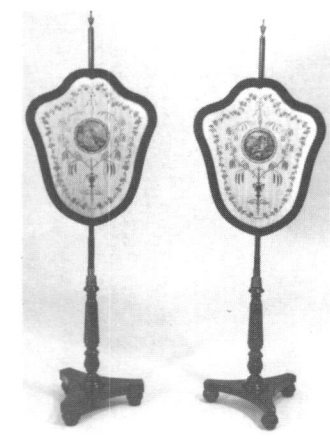

A pair of late Regency mahogany pole-screens.
$900-1,300

An early Victorian rosewood pole-screen, the adjustable glazed panel with embroidered silk and chenille vase of flowers, 61in (155cm) high.
$600-900

A George III mahogany pole-screen, with adjustable rectangular banner inset with floral tapestry, 61½in (156cm) high.
$1,300-1,800

A pair of mahogany pole-screens, painted with chinoiseries and floral borders, early 19thC, 56in (142cm) high.
$1,300-1,800

A pole-screen with needlework panel, 19thC.
$300-400

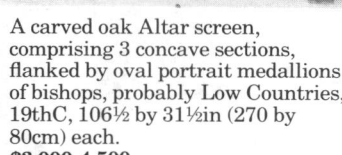

A carved oak Altar screen, comprising 3 concave sections, flanked by oval portrait medallions of bishops, probably Low Countries, 19thC, 106½ by 31½in (270 by 80cm) each.
$3,000-4,500

A mid-Victorian ebonised and gilt japanned papier mâché cheval fire-screen, with shaped panel painted with a view of Venice, signed 'Jennens & Bettridge', 26in (66cm).
$3,000-4,000

A mid-Victorian black, gilt and mother-of-pearl japanned fire-screen, with cartouche shaped stumpwork needlework panel of roses and a parrot, 52in (132cm) high.
$3,000-4,500

A mid-Victorian walnut cheval screen, in the style of A W N Pugin, with maroon velvet panel, 51 by 28½in (129.5 by 72cm).
$2,500-3,500

Settees

A mid-Georgian red walnut twin-chairback settee, the shaped arms on crook supports, 61in (155cm).
$1,500-2,600

A mid-Georgian mahogany twin-chairback settee, with cabriole legs headed by shells on pad feet, 53in (134.5cm).
$1,500-2,600

A walnut settee, 52in (132cm).
$3,000-4,000

A George III mahogany sofa, covered in pale blue striped silk, 78in (198cm).
$3,000-4,000

A George III style ▶ mahogany sofa, with block feet joined by fretwork stretchers, 19thC, 68½in (174cm).
$3,000-4,500

A George III mahogany four-chairback settee with carved and pierced shields.
$2,500-3,500

A George III carved mahogany scroll end sofa in the French taste, 84½in (215cm).
$4,500-7,000

A George III mahogany sofa, 77½in (196cm).
$2,500-3,500

An early George III mahogany frame settee.
$1,500-2,600

A late Georgian settee, on 8 mahogany supports, strengthened, 36½ by 76in (92 by 193cm).
$2,250-3,000

A Georgian settee, with original decoration, 82in (208cm).
$6,000-8,000

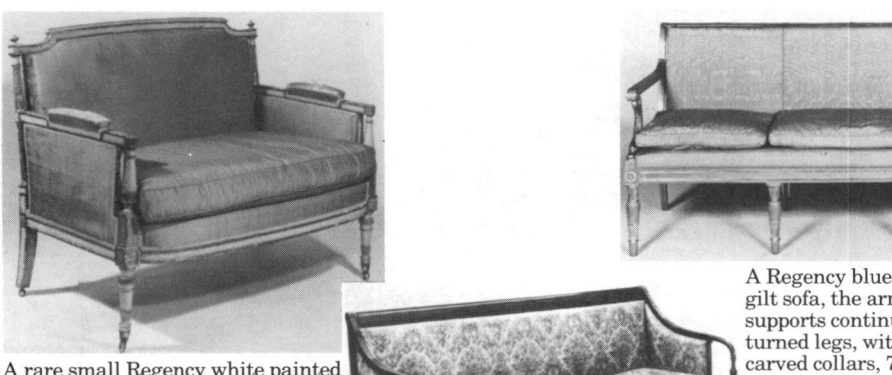

A rare small Regency white painted and parcel gilt settee in the Louis XVI taste, on ring turned tapered legs, brass cappings and casters, 43in (109cm).
$5,500-7,000

A Regency blue painted and parcel gilt sofa, the arms on dolphin supports continuing to baluster turned legs, with overlapping leaf carved collars, 70in (177cm).
$5,500-7,000

A Regency mahogany settee, with reeded curved arms and baluster supports, with cane seat and 4 front reeded tapering legs with brass casters, repairs, 35 by 72in (89 by 182.5cm).
$1,500-2,600

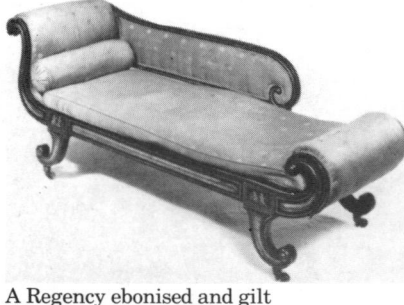

A Regency rosewood sofa mounted with brass scrolls, anthemions, masks and paterae, 96in (243.5cm).
$4,000-5,500

A Regency simulated rosewood chaise longue, painted in gold with scrolling designs, 83in (210.5cm).
$1,300-1,800

A late Regency rosewood window seat.
$750-1,000

A Regency ebonised and gilt decorated sofa or chaise longue, the fluted seat rail and scroll supports headed with panels of putto 'en grisaille'.
$7,500-10,500

A Regency beechwood chaise longue, 80in (203cm).
$1,500-2,600

A George IV brass-inlaid mahogany and rosewood chaise longue, on gilt metal scallop feet, 82in (208cm).
$1,500-2,600

A William IV mahogany window seat, 45½in (114cm).
$1,500-2,600

A mahogany five-seater settle, with rexine upholstered seat, early 19thC, 97in (246cm).
$1,000-1,400

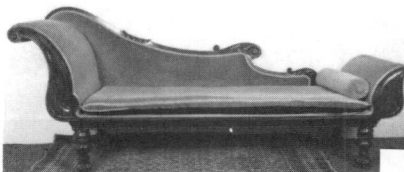

A William IV
rosewood chaise
longue, 86in (218.5cm).
$1,000-1,400

A George IV mahogany
settee, 75in
(190.5cm).
$1,500-2,600

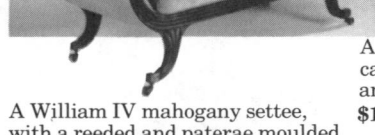

A William IV mahogany settee,
with a reeded and paterae moulded
showframe, 78in (198cm).
$2,250-3,000

A Victorian chaise longue with
carved mahogany showframe
and cabriole legs.
$1,000-1,400

A Victorian walnut framed chaise
longue.
$750-1,000

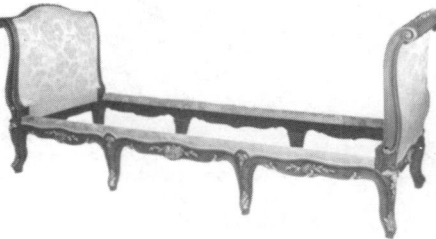

A carved and decorated 'lit de repos'
in the Louis XV taste, with base
board, mattress, bolsters and
curtains, 19thC.
$1,500-2,600

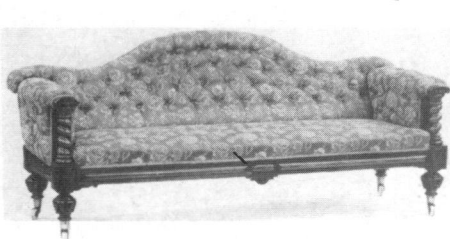

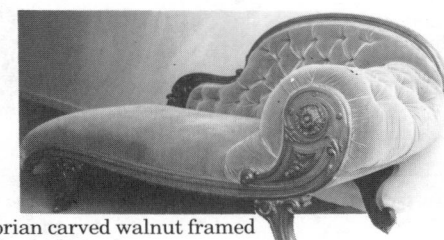

A Victorian rosewood hump-back
settee, 88in (223.5cm).
$750-1,000

A Victorian carved walnut framed
button back chaise longue.
$1,500-2,600

A mid-Victorian
centre sofa, 40in
(101.5cm).
$4,000-5,500

A mid-Victorian parcel gilt and
white painted sofa, in the manner of
A W N Pugin, upholstered in pale
green damask with deep olive fringe
and 2 associated scatter cushions,
76in (193cm).
$3,000-4,500

A Victorian button backed walnut
framed chaise longue.
$800-1,200

A Victorian double ended settee.
$750-1,000

A Victorian walnut framed settee, 88in (223.5cm).
$2,500-3,500

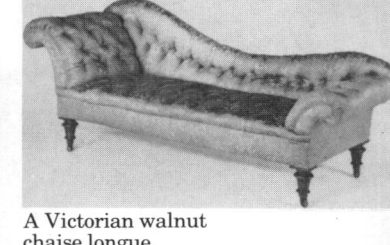

A Victorian walnut scroll framed chaise longue, deep buttoned, on cabriole legs.
$900-1,300

A Victorian walnut chaise longue, 83in (210.5cm).
$2,250-3,500

An inlaid mahogany two-seater settee, late 19thC, 49in (124.5cm).
$400-500

A late Victorian confidante, with ring turned tapering stained beech legs, one partly replaced, 48in (122cm).
$1,500-2,600

A Victorian walnut four-seater conversation seat.
$3,000-4,500

A Louis XV walnut canape, 53in (134.5cm).
$6,000-9,000

In the Furniture section if there is only one measurement it usually refers to the width of the piece.

FRENCH FURNITURE

★ France had started, during the High Renaissance of the late 16thC, to move away from the strong Italian influence
★ the reign of Louis XIV saw a period of great expansion of the industry. Colbert and Fouquet, his two senior Ministers, were great patrons of the arts. In 1662 Colbert set up the Gobelins factory to produce furniture for the Sun King; based on the classical concepts but with strong baroque adornment. Furniture was also made in the galleries of the Louvre by André Charles Boulle (or Buhl). He created two major decorative forms; inlaying on tortoiseshell ground, and use of bronze mounts, now known as ormolu
★ some great French cabinet-makers of the subsequent periods:–
    ★ Regence – Poitou and Cressant
    ★ Louis XV – Messonier (1695-1750)
        – Pineau (1684-1754)
        – Van Risenburgh

★ from 1742 the cabinet-maker's guild instructed that each piece should be stamped by the maker
★ if it was up to standard 'J.M.E.' (juré des menuisiers-ébenistes) was added after the name
★ cabinet-makers to the King and foreign cabinet-makers did not have to stamp their work
★ the main styles of this time: Louis XV – rococo, Transitional, Louis XVI – neo-classical
★ Louis XVI's main cabinet-maker was Riesener
★ Jacob and family were some of the few cabinet-makers to survive the revolution and prosper in the Directoire
★ the sons formed a partnership called Jacob Freres in 1796
★ this was changed to Jacob-Desmalter in 1803 and prospered in the Empire period
★ the 19thC saw the creation of a large number of factories and workshops
★ this culminated in the Art Nouveau styles of Gallé, Majorelle and Vallin

A Louis XVI grey and blue painted duchesse brisée, with needlework upholstery, later painted, indistinctly stamped, 77in (195.5cm).
$3,000-4,000

A Victorian conversation seat, on short giltwood and fluted legs.
$2,500-3,500

An Edwardian two-seater settee and 2 armchairs, the mahogany frame inlaid.
$750-1,000

A Scandinavian mahogany framed sofa, the waved back with a lobed fan crest, on scrolled lobed legs, 19thC, 80½in (204cm).
$1,000-1,400

A French walnut framed sofa, on foliate carved cabriole legs with scrolled feet, late 19thC, 81½in (206cm).
$1,500-2,600

An Edwardian mahogany settle in the Adam style, 78in (198cm).
$4,000-5,500

A Venetian giltwood settee in 18thC style, 19thC, 51 by 81in (129.5 by 205.5cm).
$1,500-2,600

Shelves

A pair of late Georgian mahogany hanging shelves, 26½in (67cm).
$3,000-4,000

A set of George III mahogany standing bookshelves, with carrying handles to the sides, 49½ by 20in (126 by 51cm).
$6,000-9,000

A Regency simulated rosewood hanging open bookshelf, the brass columns with X-frame supports on ball feet, 29½ by 22½in (75 by 57cm).
$3,000-4,500

A Regency mahogany open shelf, 29½ by 41in (75 by 104cm).
$800-1,200

Sideboards

A George III mahogany tulipwood crossbanded and inlaid sideboard, 60½in (153cm).
$7,500-10,500

A George III mahogany and tulipwood crossbanded bowfront sideboard of Hepplewhite design, the top and back reduced in size, originally made for an alcove, 65½in (166cm).
$3,000-4,500

A George III mahogany bowfront sideboard, 39in (99cm).
$3,000-4,500

A George III mahogany bowfront sideboard, inlaid with ebony strings with crossbanded top, on square tapering legs, 60½in (153cm).
$4,500-7,000

A George III mahogany sideboard, inlaid with ebony lines, on square tapering legs, 41in (104cm).
$1,300-1,800

A George III Scottish mahogany and inlaid sideboard, the inlay possibly later, 84in (213cm).
$8,000-10,500

A George III design serpentine fronted sideboard, by F A Matthews of Canterbury, with central single drawer with cupboard under.
$1,200-1,600

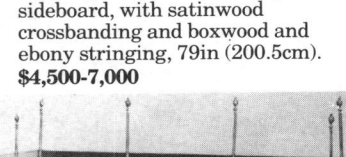

A George III mahogany serpentine sideboard, with satinwood crossbanding and boxwood and ebony stringing, 79in (200.5cm).
$4,500-7,000

A George III mahogany bowfront sideboard, inlaid with geometric boxwood lines, 56in (142cm).
$4,500-7,000

A George III mahogany veneered breakfront sideboard, with inlaid stringing and urn capped brass columns for curtains, the drawers oak lined with brass handles, 85in (216cm).
$4,500-7,000

SIDEBOARDS

★ the sideboard, as opposed to the side table, was initially designed by Robert Adam probably in the 1770's

★ most 18thC sideboards have six legs

★ although most sideboards of the 18thC had square tapering legs, some still retained turned legs, although most of these are Victorian

★ handles; started with circular plates with rings suspended from top, 1790's ovals became the vogue, in the Regency period they retained these shapes but also the 'lion's mask and ring' handle; after 1800 the central drawer often had no handles

★ all 18thC sideboards had tops made from a single piece of timber; the Victorians often made tops with two or three pieces of wood

★ again the narrower the better, especially if under 4ft; however, restorers have been known to cut down larger sideboards

★ sideboards tended to become ugly and ungainly after 1850

A Sheraton period mahogany sideboard, 53in (134.5cm).
$3,000-4,500

A George III mahogany serpentine sideboard, on canted square tapered legs with spade feet, 75in (191cm).
$4,000-5,500

A George III bowfront mahogany sideboard, 53in (134.5cm).
$4,500-7,000

A George III mahogany sideboard, the satinwood banded bowed top above a similarly banded napery drawer, flanked by 2 cellaret drawers, 54in (137cm).
$4,500-7,000

A George III bowfront mahogany and inlaid sideboard, 61in (155cm).
$4,500-7,000

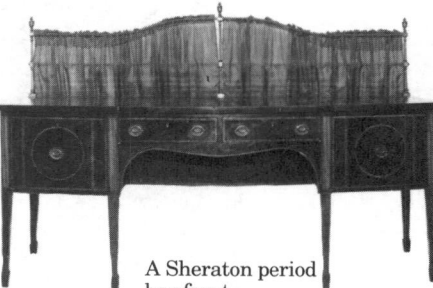

A Sheraton period bowfront mahogany sideboard, with 2 central drawers above an arched apron with tambour shutter, flanked by deep drawers, one fitted for bottles, with gilt brass handles, plates stamped with Egyptian Sphinxes, 84in (213cm).
$4,500-7,000

A Federal inlaid mahogany sideboard, with serpentine shaped top edged with light line inlay above a conforming case, on square tapering line inlaid legs with cuffs, top re-set, Middle Atlantic States, c1800, 73½in (186cm).
$5,500-6,500

A Regency mahogany bowfront sideboard, on square tapering legs with spade feet, 62in (157cm).
$1,500-2,600

A Regency mahogany breakfront sideboard, inlaid with ebonised lines, with crossbanded top, on turned tapering reeded legs and feet, 71½in (181cm).
$3,000-4,500

A Federal inlaid carved mahogany sideboard, with serpentine top above a conforming case over 2 cockbeaded cupboard doors, all with shield shaped escutcheons centering fluted pilasters, on 6 tapering ring-turned reeded legs with leaf carved capitals, minor restoration and repairs, Philadelphia, c1800.
$9,000-12,000

A Federal inlaid mahogany sideboard, the serpentine top with line inlaid edge above a conforming case, the cupboard doors each with line inlaid and quarter fans flanked by flame birch reserves, on trapezoidal tapering legs with bellflowers and cuffs, some restorations, probably New York, c1800, 63in (160cm).
$2,500-3,500

PATINATION

★ means layers of polish, dirt, dust, grease, etc., which have accumulated over the years – really the whole depth of surface of a piece of antique timber

★ the patination on different woods varies considerably but the same piece of wood will basically colour to the same extent (always allowing for bleaching by sunlight, etc.)

★ walnut furniture often had an oil varnish applied to give it a good base to take the wax polish – this has led to the lovely mellow patina which is virtually impossible to fake

★ dirt and grease from handling are important guides (especially under drawer handles, on chair arms, etc.) – these areas should have a darker colour – if they don't beware!

★ pieces which have carving or crevices, dirt will have accumulated, giving dark patches

★ colour and patination are probably the most important factors when valuing a piece of furniture

★ by repolishing a piece of furniture and removing evidence of patination, a dealer can conceal replacement or conversion

A late Georgian figured mahogany sideboard fitted with one short drawer, cupboard and cellaret, on square tapering supports with spade feet, 60in (152cm).
$1,200-1,600

A George IV mahogany sideboard, 55in (139.5cm).
$2,250-3,500

An inlaid Federal style mahogany sideboard, the D-shaped top with inlaid edge, the conforming case with drawers inlaid with flame birch panels and patterned stringing over 2 cupboard doors flanked by 2 bottle drawers, 60in (152cm).
$3,000-5,000

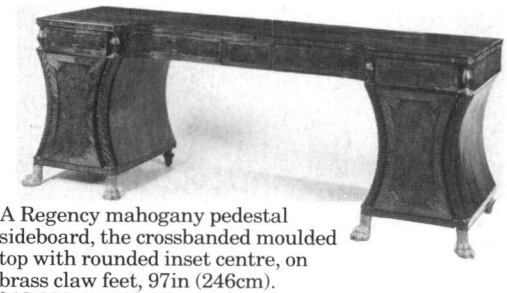

A Regency mahogany pedestal sideboard, the crossbanded moulded top with rounded inset centre, on brass claw feet, 97in (246cm).
$12,000-15,000

A mahogany sideboard, 19thC.
$1,300-1,800

A Federal inlaid mahogany sideboard, the D-shaped top above a conforming case, 2 cupboard doors flanked by 2 bottle drawers and 2 other cupboard doors, all edged with patterned stringing and hollowed line inlay, some restoration, Pennsylvania, c1800, 81½in (207cm).
$2,000-2,500

A buffet on column supports, with acanthus leaf carved mounts, early 19thC.
$3,000-4,500

A William IV mahogany pedestal sideboard with shaped gallery, 3 drawers, 2 side cupboards and cellaret, 84in (213cm).
$400-500

Stands

A George III mahogany reading stand, the adjustable top with a hinged ratcheted slope and sprung folio stay, with a candle slide to either side, 27½in (70cm).
$5,500-7,000

A Victorian lyre shaped ebonised music stand.
$250-350

A Victorian mahogany folio stand, with brass ratcheted adjustable open slatted slopes and book press on stand, 30in (76cm).
$3,000-4,500

A George IV mahogany folio stand with adjustable pierced rectangular sides, 31in (79cm).
$1,500-2,600

A set of 4 classical mahogany and giltwood pedestal urns, the vase with carved and gilt waterleaf, lotus and anthemion decoration, the mid-moulding with carved and gilt waterleaf decoration, some restorations, probably New York, c1830, 55in (140cm) high.
$40,000-60,000

An ebonised and gilded wood duet stand, by Erards, London, with folding brass candle sconces, hinged music slopes, fluted adjustable column, restored leg, 19thC, 46½in (117cm) high minimum.
$4,500-7,000

A William ► IV carved torchère, 59in (149.5cm) high.
$450-700

A pair of rosewood free standing pedestals, finely inlaid with coloured marquetry, raised on inlaid stepped bases, 19thC, 15½in (39cm).
$1,500-2,600

A Federal inlaid walnut cellaret on stand, the dovetailed and inlaid case with a hinged lid lifting above a compartment fitted with dividers for 6 bottles, 18½in (46cm).
$3,000-4,000

A pair of Victorian ebonised and gilt metal mounted pedestals, with grey and brown marble slabs and gilt metal floral mouldings, c1880, 41in (104cm) high.
$1,500-2,600

An early Victorian mahogany hall stand, 80in (203cm) high.
$800-1,200

A pair of mid-Victorian oak and ebonised coat racks, applied with brass Gothic hooks, the cross-struts joined by turned spindles, 97in (246cm).
$1,500-2,600

A Federal inlaid mahogany corner stand, the bowed top surmounted by a pierced brass gallery above a conforming apron with stringing over a medial shelf, with one inlaid drawer flanked by 2 sham drawers, probably New York, c1800, 25½in (64cm).
$3,000-4,000

Steps

A George III mahogany folding library step and table, labelled 'Meschain & Hervé Fecit No. 32, John Street, Tottenham Court Road', c1775, 32in (81cm) closed.
$6,000-9,000

Stools

A James II stool, partly re-railed, 21½in (54.5cm).
$2,250-3,500

A set of late George III mahogany library steps.
$7,500-10,500

A set of mid-Victorian oak and pine library steps, formed as a bridge with Gothic arches and square shaped finials, 26in (66cm).
$3,000-4,500

A George I red walnut stool with a slip-in seat and shaped apron, on cabriole legs united by an H-stretcher.
$6,000-9,000

A George I walnut stool, 22in (56cm).
$4,500-7,000

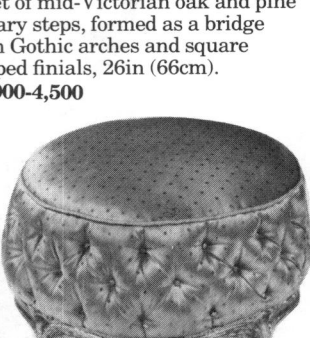

A pair of giltwood tabourets, mid-19thC, 21in (53.5cm) diam.
$4,000-5,500

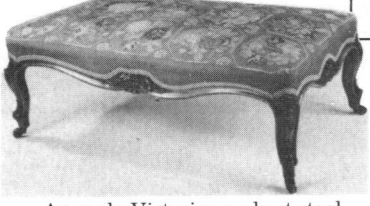

An early Victorian walnut stool, with petit point tapestry upholstered seat, 41in (104cm).
$2,500-3,500

A walnut long stool, with upholstered seat, on cabriole legs with pad feet, with foliate and rimmed C-scroll headings, 18thC, 49½in (125cm).
$4,500-7,000

A Regency mahogany X-framed stool in the manner of Thomas Hope, with slatted seat and X-frames supported with ram's mask terminals and hairy cleft feet, 30½in (77.5cm).
$9,000-12,000

STOOLS

★ until the middle of the 17thC stools were virtually the only form of seat for one person
★ many 17thC 'joint' or 'joyned' stools have been reproduced
★ look for good patination, colour and carving on oak examples. Yew-wood examples with good turning are highly desirable
★ by the end of the 17thC the chair was taking over and the oak stool became less popular, walnut stealing the show from about 1670
★ stools now tend to follow the style of chairs of the period, they also tend to be upholstered
★ many Queen Anne stools have stretchers
★ these have usually disappeared by George I
★ when mahogany was introduced from 1730-40, stools became simpler, the cabriole leg being replaced with the straight leg, often with stretchers
★ mid 18thC the 'drop-in' seat became fashionable
★ some stools made from chairs (this can increase the value of the chair 20 times
★ check for hessian under the seat – never used until 1840. Often conceals some alterations

A mid-Victorian X-framed oak stool in the style of A W N Pugin, 19½in (49cm).
$1,200-1,600

A Victorian walnut rise-and-fall music stool.
$300-400

A buttoned seat stool on a gilded base, 19thC.
$250-350

A pair of mid-Victorian oak stools in the style of A W N Pugin, 17in (43cm).
$7,000-9,000

A Dutch walnut and floral marquetry stool, 19thC.
$900-1,300

A late Victorian oak bench of Gothic style, with ring-turned back, 53½in (135cm).
$1,000-1,400

A bead and tapestry upholstered fender stool in Tunbridgeware walnut frame.
$250-350

A Napoleon III giltwood stool, designed by A M E Fournier, 29½in (75cm) diam.
$4,500-7,000

A pair of grey painted X-frame stools, of Louis XVI design, with padded cushions worked in silver thread and silk, one stamped 'Lexcellent Paris', 19thC, 24in (61cm).
$13,500-17,500

These stools were acquired by Sir Fairfax Cartwright, British Ambassador in Vienna from 1906 to 1913, and were used in the Embassy there. They are closely copied from a set of 64 supplied by Jean Hauré and made by Jean-Baptiste-Claude Sené to Marie Antoinette for her gaming rooms at the Château de Fontainebleau and the Château de Compiègne in 1786.

Etienne Lexcellent worked in Paris in the rue de Charenton from 1867 onwards, specialising in copies of 18thC furniture.

Tables – Architects

A George III mahogany architect's table.
$4,500-7,000

A Regency mahogany architect's table, with leather-lined double easel top, with hinged border and 2 drawers opening to the side, 36in (91.5cm).
$2,250-3,500

Tables – Breakfast

A Georgian rosewood snap-top breakfast table, with shaped inlaid design to border, on quadruple support with brass feet and casters, 66in (167.5cm).
$6,000-8,000

A Georgian circular mahogany snap-top breakfast table, 47in (119cm).
$2,250-3,500

A George III mahogany breakfast table, on ring turned vase shaped shaft and splayed fluted quadripartite base, 55in (139.5cm).
$3,000-4,500

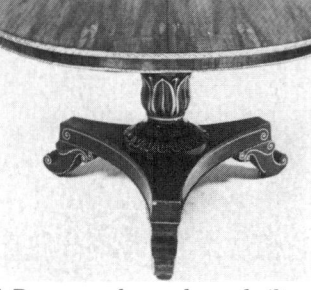

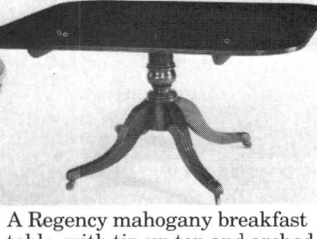

A rare Federal mahogany breakfast table, the moulded edge top above a concave apron with drawer flanked by maple veneered panels over a double baluster turned pedestal, on 4 reeded sabre legs, Massachusetts, c1800, 45in (114cm).
$3,000-4,000

A Regency calamander and gilt metal mounted breakfast table, with overlapping leaf and ribbon cast edge, on a lotus carved column decorated in green and parcel gilt, the concave triform plinth inlaid with brass stringing, column restored, 51½in (130cm) diam.
$2,250-3,500

A Regency mahogany breakfast table, with tip-up top and arched ribbed quadripartite base, 57in (144.5cm).
$4,000-5,500

A Federal inlaid mahogany breakfast table, the top with incurved ends flanked by leaves above a conforming apron edged with lunette banding and with a single drawer, on tapering reeded legs with casters, Boston, c1800, 39½in (100cm).
$6,500-7,500

A Regency mahogany and brass inlaid breakfast table, the tilt-top banded in rosewood, the reeded legs with brass caps and casters, 65½in (166cm).
$4,500-7,000

A Regency mahogany breakfast table with brass inlay.
$1,500-2,600

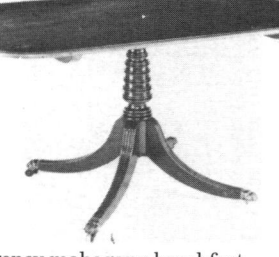

A rosewood and brass inlaid breakfast table in the Regency taste, the crossbanded snap-top with stylised foliate cut brass marquetry, 49in (124cm) diam.
$6,000-8,000

A Regency mahogany breakfast table with moulded tip-up top, 53in (134.5cm).
$1,500-2,600

A George IV mahogany breakfast table, on a quadripartite turned support, the down curved channelled legs headed by stiff leaves with brass caps and casters, 56in (142cm).
$1,200-1,600

A Regency mahogany breakfast table, with rosewood banded borders and an ebonised inlaid frieze, 47in (119cm) diam.
$4,000-5,500

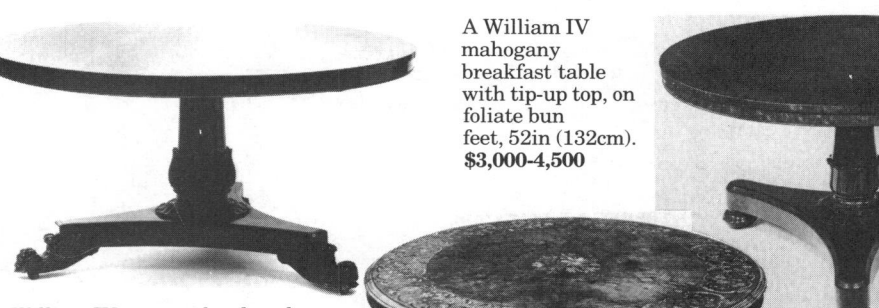

A William IV mahogany breakfast table with tip-up top, on foliate bun feet, 52in (132cm).
$3,000-4,500

A William IV rosewood pedestal breakfast table, on 3 carved feet, 53in (134.5cm) diam.
$1,500-2,600

A Victorian burr walnut and marquetry breakfast table, the top inlaid with a floral spray within a broad border of C-scrolls, 54½in (138cm) diam.
$3,000-4,500

Tables – Card

A George III mahogany card table, with baize-lined eared top, 34in (86cm).
$4,500-7,000

A Federal mahogany inlaid card table, the hinged shaped top with outset corners above a conforming apron with birch panel inlay, North Shore, Massachusetts, c1820, 36in (91cm).
$1,500-2,500

A classical carved mahogany card table, with canted corner hinged top rotating above spiral turned and ribbed urn supports over a medial shelf, on acanthus carved paw feet with castors, New York, c1820, 36in (91.5cm).
$2,000-3,000

A Federal inlaid mahogany card table, the top folding above a conforming skirt inlaid with pattern stringing centering an inlaid oval, on square tapering legs on tapering feet, Eastern Massachusetts, c1800, 35½in (90cm).
$3,500-5,500

A satinwood demi-lune card table, inlaid in the Sheraton style, with baize-lined interior, late 18thC, 38in (96.5cm).
$6,000-8,000

CARD TABLES

★ the commonest 18thC form has the fold-over top supported on one back leg hinged to wing out at 90 degrees. Better is the model with both back legs hinged, each opening to 45 degrees from the frame

★ best of all is the 'concertina' or folding frame

★ popular during the early 19thC and thereafter was the swivel top allowing use of the central column support

★ the swivel top was also used on French Revival models after 1827, particularly those decorated with Boulle marquetry

★ 19thC Boulle work, revived in 1815 in London by Le Gaigneur, was thinner than the 18thC original. Can be spotted by the brass being prone to lift and the tortoiseshell to bubble. Presence of this plus a swivel top eliminates 18thC origin. The four flap 'envelope' or bridge table was a development of the Edwardian period Sheraton Revival. The best examples are of rosewood with a degree of fine inlay. In view of comparatively recent age, condition should be excellent to command a high price

★ many plain Sheraton period card tables were inlaid during the Edwardian period. To spot, view obliquely against the light; original inlays will conform perfectly with the rest of the surface; new inlay will not, unless completely resurfaced, when shallow colour and high polish will be evident

★ all carving to English cabriole legs should stand proud of the outline of the curve; such decoration within the outline indicates recarving

A late Federal carved mahogany card table, the top with canted corners over ring-turned leaf carved baluster supports, centering a medial shelf, restorations, New York, c1820, 36in (91cm).
$1,000-1,500

A George III mahogany, tulipwood crossbanded and inlaid D-shaped card table, with baize-lined top and chequer inlaid frieze, 36in (92cm).
$3,000-4,500

Two kingwood and marquetry card tables, 19thC, a near matching pair.
$5,500-7,000

A Federal inlaid mahogany card table, the hinged circular top centering an inlaid shell, above a conforming apron with line inlaid panels, 36in (91cm).
$1,500-2,500

A Regency mahogany and satinwood banded D-shaped fold-over card table, 36in (92cm).
$2,250-3,500

A mahogany card table with swivel top, early 19thC.
$750-1,000

A late Federal carved mahogany card table, the serpentine top above a conforming skirt with carved basket of flowers and floral carved corners on punchwork ground, Salem, Massachusetts, c1810, 36in (91cm).
$3,000-4,000

A Regency mahogany card table with mahogany crossbanded fold-over swivel top, 36in (91.5cm).
$750-1,000

A pair of Regency rosewood card tables, banded with maple, each with hinged top, enclosing a well, on possibly later simulated rosewood columns and base, 36in (91.5cm).
$4,000-5,500

A Regency rosewood and brass inlaid card table, 35½in (90cm).
$1,300-1,800

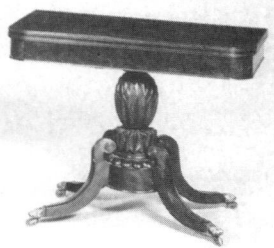

A pair of classical carved mahogany card tables, each with hinged top rotating above a conforming apron over a waterleaf carved pineapple pedestal, Boston, c1820, 34½in (86cm).
$2,500-3,500

A Federal inlaid cherrywood card table, the hinged top with inset rounded corners above a conforming apron with applied rectangular reserve, flanked by inlaid floral sprays, diamonds and pineapples, Eastern Connecticut, c1800, 36in (91cm).
$10,000-12,000

A red walnut card table, with baize-lined folding rectangular top with sunken counter wells, on cabriole legs, perhaps added, 18thC, 32in (81cm).
$2,250-3,500

A mid-Victorian black, gilt and mother-of-pearl japanned papier mâché card table, the folding top centred by a circular painting entitled 'The Friendly Meal', 36in (91.5cm).
$3,000-4,500

A Federal inlaid mahogany card table, the hinged serpentine top above a conforming apron inlaid with rectangular line-inlaid maple reserves flanked by patterned stringing and banded edges, Massachusetts, c1800, 36in (91cm).
$3,500-4,500

A Federal mahogany card table, the top with canted corners folding above a figured mahogany veneer skirt, New York, c1810, 35in (88cm).
$2,500-3,000

A Chippendale mahogany card table, with hinged top above a moulded short drawer, on cabriole legs with claw and ball feet, repairs and restorations, Philadelphia, c1780, 35in (88cm).
$8,000-9,000

A Federal inlaid mahogany circular card table, the hinged top with banded maple edge above a conforming line inlaid skirt, with oval reserves edged with maple banding, on square tapering legs inlaid with stringing, bellflowers and cuffs, minor veneer patches, Massachusetts, c1800, 36in (92cm).
$8,000-9,000

A Federal inlaid mahogany card table, the hinged top with astragal 'swept' front corners and pattern inlaid edge above a conforming apron centering an oval inlaid panel against a field of vertical bar inlays, on legs with pattern inlaid cuffs, Massachusetts, c1800, 35in (88cm).
$6,000-7,000

A pair of George IV rosewood card tables, with baize-lined tops, the spreading square shafts with panelled bases, 36in (91.5cm).
$3,000-4,000

A pair of William IV rosewood card tables, 36in (91.5cm).
$1,500-2,600

A Victorian walnut card table, with fold-over swivel top, carved with reel-and-bobbin border and circular red baize interior edged with a tooled leather band, 36in (91.5cm).
$1,500-2,600

A Federal inlaid card table, the serpentine top with outset corners folding above a conforming top, over an apron inlaid with 2 flame birch panels centering an oval birch reserve, repairs, New Hampshire, c1800, 36in (92cm).
$5,000-6,000

A William IV bird's-eye maple and yew wood banded card table, the top with beaded edge, on carved lion paw feet, 36in (91.5cm).
$750-1,000

A William IV rosewood card table with fold-over top, 36in (91.5cm).
$1,000-1,400

A pair of early Victorian rosewood card tables, the fold-over swivel tops inset with circular green velvet panels, 36in (91.5cm).
$2,250-3,000

A Federal inlaid mahogany card table, the hinged shaped top with banded edge above a conforming apron with flame birch panels, above a pattern inlaid skirt, Massachusetts, c1800, 37in (94cm).
$6,500-7,500

A Victorian walnut veneered folding card table, on birdcage base with scroll feet.
$1,300-1,800

A Victorian walnut card table with serpentine front, 39in (99cm).
$1,500-2,600

A Louis XV style rosewood and marquetry card table, the serpentine hinged quarter veneered top with floral marquetry above a bowed frieze, on gilt metal mounted cabriole legs, 32in (81cm).
$600-900

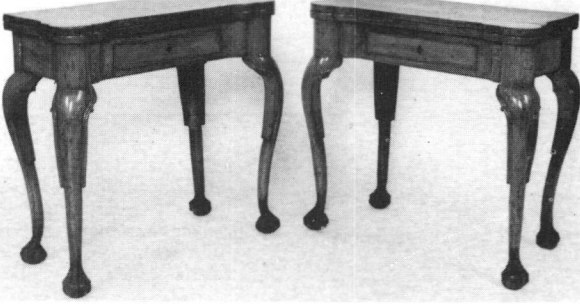

A pair of Continental card tables in polished chestnutwood, each with a fold-over top, early 18thC, 31in (79cm).
$5,500-7,000

Tables – Centre

A mid-Georgian mahogany centre table, carved with Gothic tracery, 42in (106.5cm).
$4,000-5,500

A George III sycamore centre table with waved crossbanded top, centred by an amboyna oval edged with chequered stringing, 24in (61cm).
$4,000-5,500

A Regency rosewood, satinwood, mahogany and amboyna centre table with crossbanded segmented top, 26in (66cm).
$2,250-3,500

A Regency black and gold lacquer centre table, painted with summer flowers and edged with scrolling foliage on turned spreading shaft, 28in (71cm) diam.
$1,500-2,600

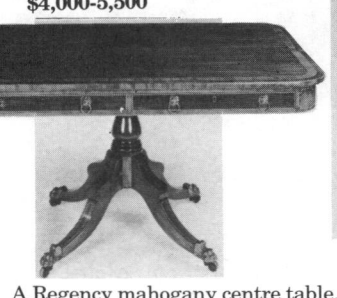

A Regency mahogany centre table, with crossbanded top and lion mask ring handles to drawers, on baluster shaft, 51in (129.5cm).
$4,500-7,000

A Regency stinkwood octagonal centre table, the top crossbanded in rosewood and inlaid with brass and ebony bands, 44in (111cm).
$6,000-8,000

A Victorian ebonised, parcel gilt and mother-of-pearl centre table, the tilt-top painted with a landscape, 37in (94cm).
$1,300-1,800

▶

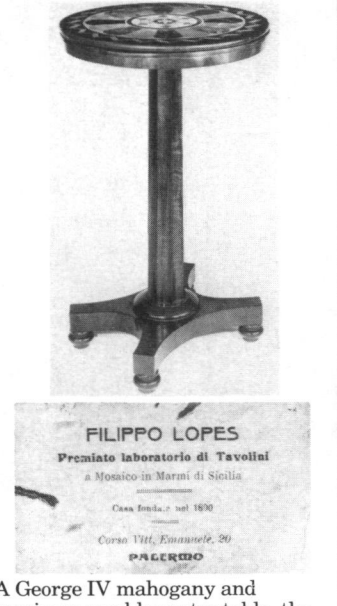

A mid-Victorian veneered burr walnut centre table, with serpentine shaped top, on carved end supports, on porcelain casters, 54in (137cm).
$1,500-2,600

A Victorian burr walnut quatrefoil shaped centre table, with crossbanding and gilded metal mounts terminating in sabots to the cabriole supports, 50in (127cm).
$1,500-2,600

A Victorian centre table.
$10,500-14,000

A George IV mahogany and specimen marble centre table, the top inlaid with grey, yellow and red marbles, the top bearing label 'Filippo Lopes, Corso Vitt. Emanuele, 20 Palermo', 19½in (49.5cm) diam.
$3,000-4,500

A late Victorian bird's-eye maple centre table, the top inlaid with a band with the emblem of the Union, with foliage gadrooned border, 65in (165cm).
$8,000-10,500

An Edwardian satinwood and marquetry centre table, the top inlaid and engraved, 30in (76cm).
$2,250-3,500

A Belgian rosewood and painted table by Jean Joseph Chapuis, early 19thC.
$9,000-12,000

An ormolu mounted mahogany centre table of Louis XVI style, the top inset with mottled breccia marble, 26in (66cm).
$1,500-2,600

Tables – Console

A Regency serpentine gilt console table, with green marble top, 44in (111.5cm).
$2,250-3,500

An Italian specimen marble low table, the top with bands of various marbles including malachite, porphyry and lapis-lazuli on gilt metal legs, 31in (79cm) diam.
$6,000-9,000

A Louis XV style inlaid walnut and kingwood centre table, with ormolu mounts, 19thC, 39in (99cm).
$1,500-2,600

A pair of painted and parcel gilt console tables of William Kent design, each with a rounded rectangular top, one marble, the other marbelised, supported by an eagle perched on a naturalistic rocky base, 36in (92cm).
$4,500-7,000

A Louis XV/XVI Transitional carved giltwood console table of bowed outline, with Languedoc marble top, 49in (125cm) high.
$4,500-7,000 ▶

A pair of mahogany console tables with D-shaped tops, on partly channelled tapering legs, headed by vases, filled with husks, 58in (147cm).
$4,500-7,000

A pair of Italian giltwood console tables in early 18thC style, with pink veined marble slab tops, 55in (140cm).
$7,500-10,500

A pair of Spanish Colonial painted console tables, each with a marbelised top and carved frieze, previously a centre table, 33in (84cm).
$2,250-3,500

Price

Prices vary from auction to auction – from dealer to dealer. The price paid in a dealer's shop will depend on:
1) *what he paid for the item*
2) *what he thinks he can get for it*
3) *the extent of his knowledge*
4) *awareness of market trends*
It is a mistake to think that you will automatically pay more in a specialist dealer's shop. He is more likely to know the 'right' price for a piece. A general dealer may undercharge but he could also overcharge.

Tables – Dining

A Georgian D-end mahogany dining table, the friezes with rosewood bands, later centre section and leaf, 104in (264cm).
$2,250-3,000

A Federal three-part dining table, the centre section rectangular with 2 drop leaves, the flanking end sections demi-lune with one drop leaf, repairs to legs, c1800, 155in (393cm).
$12,000-15,000

A Federal mahogany dining table with 4 swing legs, the top flanked by drop leaves above movable ring turned tapering reeded posts and moulded sabre legs, top restored, Boston, c1820, 62½in (158cm).
$5,000-6,000

A Regency D-end dining table, c1820.
$4,000-5,500

A William IV flame mahogany dining table, with segmented figuring veneer to the top, 48in (122cm) diam.
$1,500-2,600

A mid-Georgian mahogany gateleg dining table, with rectangular crossbanded single flap top, on club legs and pad feet, 52½in (133cm).
$3,000-4,500

A George III style mahogany three-pillar dining table, each pedestal with a blind fret carved and spirally fluted pillar on rockwork, 140in (355.5cm).
$5,500-7,000

A large George III mahogany oval twin flap dining table, 59in (150cm).
$4,500-7,000

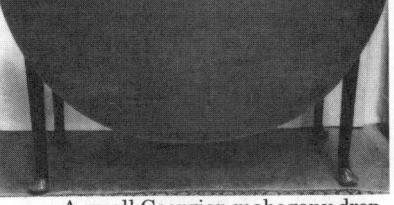

A small Georgian mahogany drop leaf six-seater dining table.
$1,200-1,600

A late George III mahogany extending dining table with concertina action, the frame stamped 'Wilkinson Patent, Moorfields'.
$4,000-5,500

A Regency mahogany dining table, c1820.
$4,000-5,500

A Regency mahogany twin pedestal dining table with D-shaped rounded ends, one being detachable, having a reeded edge, the rectangular snap top with extension runners to support the leaves, including an extra leaf, 106in (269cm) extended.
$13,500-17,500

Tables – Dressing

A Chippendale carved walnut dressing table, the top with cusped corners, the centre drawer carved with a concave shell and trailing leaf tendrils above a scalloped apron, on acanthus carved cabriole legs with ball and claw feet, Philadelphia, c1775, 36in (91.5cm).
$250,000-300,000

A French mahogany vitrine table, banded in rosewood and inlaid in foliate marquetry, 19thC, 32in (81cm).
$1,300-1,800

A Georgian mahogany folding top dressing table, with fitted interior, c1790.
$800-1,200

A George III mahogany veneered dressing table, 38in (96.5cm).
$4,000-5,500

A Queen Anne walnut dressing table, with valanced apron above cabriole legs ending in pad feet, restorations, probably Massachusetts, c1760, 34in (85cm).
$9,500-12,000

An Edwardian inlaid mahogany bijouterie table, 25in (63.5cm).
$600-900

A Federal inlaid mahogany dressing table, the top with patterned banded edge above 4 short drawers, centering a line inlaid arched opening, Massachusetts, c1810, 38in (96.5cm).
$2,500-3,000

An Edwardian inlaid mahogany bowfront dressing table.
$450-600

A Hepplewhite period mahogany dressing table, c1775.
$2,500-3,500

A Scandinavian mahogany and parquetry dressing table, the top bordered with calamander, framing 3 panels inlaid with green stained boxwood and ebonised lines, the central panel lifting to reveal a toilet mirror and well, with 3 frieze drawers and a leather-lined slide, late 18thC, 33½in (85cm).
$4,000-5,500

Tables – Dropleaf

Tables – Drum

A William IV rosewood drum table, 48in (122cm).
$2,500-3,500

A George III mahogany hunt table, 71½in (181cm).
$9,000-12,000

A Georgian mahogany drop leaf dining table, 50in (127cm) fully extended.
$1,500-2,600

An early Victorian mahogany drum table, the circular top lined in tooled brown leather above 8 frieze drawers, 53in (134.5cm).
$1,300-1,800

A Regency mahogany drum top table, the leather inset top above 4 frieze drawers, 47in (119cm).
$5,500-7,000

A mahogany ebony strung and brass mounted drum top library table, 19thC, 40in (101cm).
$4,000-5,500

Tables – Games

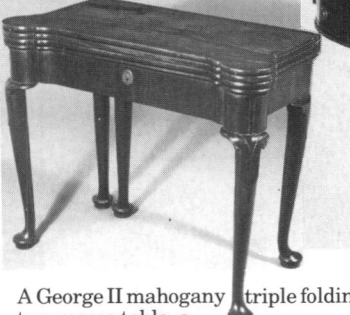

A George II mahogany triple folding top games table, a section rising to reveal a recess.
$10,500-14,000

A mahogany drum top library table, the 4 drawers stamped 'A. Blain, Liverpool', with dummy drawers, all with brass ring handles, 47in (119cm) diam.
$3,000-4,500

An early rosewood games table, the chequered top with sunken well, above real and dummy drawers.
$1,500-2,600

A Regency style rosewood games table, with tooled red leather top and fitted backgammon drawer, on centre column and quatrefoil base, late 19thC.
$4,500-7,000

A small Regency rosewood games table, inlaid with other woods, with chess set, c1830.
$450-600

An early Victorian rosewood games table, 22in (56cm) square.
$800-1,200

A mid-Victorian mahogany roulette table, by W Thornhill & Co, 144 Bond Street, London W, lacking pea, 68in (172.5cm) open.
$3,000-4,500

A Victorian walnut and parcel gilt etched pedestal games table, 33in (84cm).
$4,500-7,000

A Victorian inlaid burr walnut games table with chequer top, folding and swivelling to reveal a baize-lined interior with counter wells and cribbage score boards, above long drawer fitted for sewing and sewing bag, 30in (76cm).
$1,300-1,800

Tables – Gateleg

A Georgian mahogany gateleg dining table, 60in (152cm).
$6,000-9,000

A carved walnut gateleg table, late 19th/early 20thC, 35in (89cm).
$150-250

A George III mahogany hunt table, with double gateleg action on square tapering legs, one later, 47in (119cm) open.
$6,000-8,000

Tables – Library

A Regency maple and rosewood marquetry library table, 51in (130cm).
$10,000-13,000

A rosewood library table, crossbanded, and with brass stringing, the frieze with 2 small drawers, and with panels of brass foliate inlay and beaded borders, early 19thC, 54½in (138cm).
$13,500-17,500

A George III mahogany library table, 46in (116.5cm).
$6,000-9,000

An early Victorian mahogany library table, 49 by 47in (124.5 by 119cm).
$2,250-3,500

A William IV/early Victorian mahogany library table, the crossbanded top with mitred edge above 6 cedar-lined frieze drawers, 65in (165cm).
$1,200-1,600

A Regency mahogany library table, on twin ropetwist turned end column supports and foliate carved outswept legs, 54in (137cm).
$6,000-8,000

Tables – Loo

A burr walnut loo table, with shaped frieze on carved quadruple support, 54in (137cm). **$2,250-3,000**

A Renaissance style walnut library table, the top carved at the corners with masks, the frieze fitted with 2 drawers on 8 column supports, 50in (127cm). **$1,000-1,400**

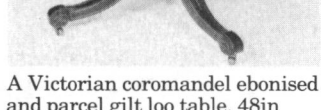

A Victorian coromandel ebonised and parcel gilt loo table, 48in (122cm). **$1,500-2,600**

A mid-Victorian walnut and inlaid loo table, manufactured by Oetzmann & Co, London, 48in (122cm). **$750-1,000**

A mahogany loo table, late 19thC. **$250-350**

Nests of Tables

A set of 4 satinwood quartetto tables, the tops with ebony stringing and crossbanded rosewood borders, from 14 to 19½in (35.5 to 49cm). **$7,500-10,500**

An Edwardian nest of 4 mahogany and inlaid tea tables. **$1,000-1,400**

A nest of 4 mid-Victorian black and mother-of-pearl japanned papier mâché quartetto tables, the tops centred by: a painting entitled 'Crossing the Tay'; a chessboard; and two with oval paintings, from 15 to 25in (38 to 63.5cm). **$3,000-4,000**

Tables – Occasional

A George III urn table, c1770. **$4,000-5,500**

A Georgian mahogany bedside table with centre drawer and undershelf, 13in (33cm). **$300-400**

An early George III mahogany night table, 22in (56cm). **$1,000-1,400**

Tables – Pedestal

An Italian pietra dura and giltwood table, 19thC, 23in (59cm) diam.
$2,500-3,500

An early Regency mahogany occasional table, 21½in (54cm).
$1,300-1,800

A Regency mahogany and brass mounted occasional table, 24in (61cm) diam.
$4,500-7,000

An early Victorian black and gilt japanned papier mâché pedestal table, painted with Italian classical lakeside landscape, 24½in (62cm).
$1,500-2,600

Tables – Pembroke

An early George III mahogany Pembroke table, with moulded serpentine twin flap top and one frieze drawer, 34in (86.5cm) open.
$2,250-3,000

A Chippendale cherrywood Pembroke table, the top with 2 leaves above an apron with a single drawer, on chamfered Marlborough legs, bottom drawer restored, Pennsylvania, c1775, 39in (99cm).
$2,000-2,500

A Federal inlaid mahogany Pembroke table, the oval top with 2 drop leaves above a bowed drawer, flanked by inlaid paterae, the legs with bellflowers, stringing and cuffs, Mid-Atlantic States, c1800, 39in (99cm).
$9,000-10,000

A George III mahogany Pembroke table, the oval twin flap top crossbanded with tulipwood, 35½in (90cm).
$3,000-4,000

A Chippendale mahogany Pembroke table, the top with 2 drop leaves above a drawer, on moulded Marlborough legs, Rhode Island, c1775, 42½in (108cm).
$1,700-2,200

A George III mahogany Pembroke table, with original brass ring handles and brass lock, on original leather covered brass roller casters, c1785, 30in (76cm).
$3,000-4,500

A George III rosewood Pembroke table, inlaid with chequered boxwood lines, 40in (101.5cm).
$1,500-2,600

A Federal inlaid mahogany Pembroke table, the oval top with 2 drop leaves above a veneered frieze and bowed drawer, with patterned stringing, Massachusetts or New Hampshire, c1810, 41in (104cm).
$2,500-3,500

PEMBROKE TABLES

★ became popular in the mid to late 18thC, possibly designed and ordered by Henry Herbert, the Earl of Pembroke (1693-1751)
★ on early examples the legs were square which are by far the most desirable
★ many 18thC Pembroke tables have chamfering on the insides of the legs
★ those with oval or serpentine tops more desirable
★ flaps should have three hinges
★ rounded flaps and marquetry again increase desirability
★ satinwood was greatly favoured, particularly with much crossbanding and inlay
★ later tables had turned legs
★ the turned and reeded legs are less popular
★ the Edwardians made many fine Pembroke tables which have been known to appear wrongly catalogued at auction

A Georgian mahogany drop leaf Pembroke table, 28in (71cm).
$700-900

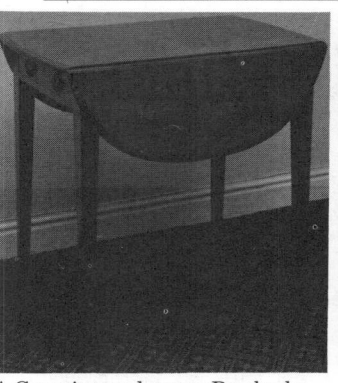

A Georgian mahogany Pembroke table, inlaid with satinwood stringing, 28in (71cm).
$700-900

A Federal mahogany table, with serpentine shaped drop leaves above an incise-beaded frieze drawer, Philadelphia, c1800, 30in (75cm).
$3,000-5,000

Tables – Pier

A George III satinwood and marquetry half-round pier table, surmounted by a grey veined white marble top, 36in (92cm).
$3,000-4,000

Make the most of Miller's

When a large, specialist, well-publicised collection comes on the market, it tends to increase prices. Immediately after this, prices can fall slightly due to the main buyers having large stocks and the market being 'flooded'. This is usually temporary and does not affect very high quality items.

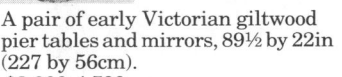

A pair of early Victorian giltwood pier tables and mirrors, 89½ by 22in (227 by 56cm).
$3,000-4,500

A small Regency mahogany Pembroke table, the top crossbanded with satinwood, on splayed quadripartite legs with claw feet, 34in (86.5cm).
$1,500-2,600

A small Regency ebonised and painted Pembroke table, 27½in (70cm) open.
$2,500-3,500

A Regency rosewood and parcel gilt pier table, with later rectangular moulded white marble top, the sides adapted, some re-mounting, 60in (152cm).
$16,500-22,500

Tables – Reading

A rare mahogany reading table,
c1765.
$7,500-10,500

Tables – Side

A George I walnut side or serving
table.
$10,500-14,000

A George II mahogany side table
with marble top, 51½in (130cm).
$15,000-21,000

Tables – Serving

A mahogany serving table,
72in (182.5cm).
$3,000-4,000

A Chippendale period carved
mahogany half round side table
surmounted by a breche violette
marble top, 51in (129cm).
$6,000-9,000

A late Federal mahogany serving
table, the serpentine top over a long
drawer above an arch, the outset
rounded corners above posts carved
with flowers against a star-punched
ground, on reeded legs, Salem,
Massachusetts, c1820, 36in
(91.5cm).
$2,500-3,500

A mahogany side table with single
drawer, c1755.
$4,000-5,500

A Chippendale style carved
mahogany side table, 32in (81.5cm).
$1,500-2,600

A small rosewood side table, with
rouge marble top and petticoat
mirror at the back, c1808, 34½in
(87cm).
$4,000-5,500

For similar patterns see Design of
Household Furniture *by George
Smith, plate 120.*

A Chippendale cherrywood side
table, the top with cusped corners
and a moulded edge, on
Marlborough legs, repairs, probably
Connecticut, c1775, 34in (85cm).
$1,000-1,500

A Chippendale style mahogany side table, 19thC.
$5,500-7,000

A late Georgian mahogany metamorphic side table, by W Wilkinson, 14 Ludgate Hill, extending scissor action with 4 leaves to a dining table, 90in (228.5cm).
$5,500-7,000

A black lacquer and gilt side table, the mottled green marble top with moulded edge, 19thC, 46in (116.5cm).
$4,000-5,500

A late George III mahogany bowfront side table, 29½in (75cm).
$1,000-1,400

A late Georgian mahogany kneehole side table, with tray top, 42in (106.5cm).
$750-1,000

A late Victorian oak side table, with 2 frieze drawers, 49in (125cm).
$1,200-1,600

Tables – Silver

A George II red walnut silver table, adaptations, 30in (76cm).
$5,500-7,000

A Régence period carved giltwood side table after designs by Nicolas Pineau, the pierced apron with a foliate scroll ornament centred by a cartouche with masks, on scroll supports, with sculptured female masks, top missing, 46½in (118cm).
$21,000-24,000

A peitra dura table, the top probably Italian in English mount, in a parcel gilt and ebonised frame, 29 by 12in (74 by 30cm).
$3,000-4,500

A George II Irish carved mahogany tray top silver or tea table, the dished top with paper scroll rim and slight re-entrant corners.
$10,500-14,000

A George III mahogany silver table, the top with Gothic arch and foliate scroll fretwork gallery above a foliate pierced frieze, 33in (84cm).
$7,500-10,500

Tables – Sofa

A George III mahogany sofa table, 57½in (145cm) open.
$5,500-7,000

A mahogany and decorated sofa table, 19thC, 60in (152cm).
$6,000-9,000

A George III mahogany sofa table with satinwood and rosewood banded top, 59½in (151cm).
$4,500-7,000

SOFA TABLES

★ an elegant feminine writing table, usually with two shallow drawers
★ genuine ones are rarer than it might appear
★ either had two vertical supports or a central pillar
★ many fine examples made in mahogany with satinwood or rosewood stringing and crossbanding
★ rosewood examples can be of exceptional quality
★ examples with stretchers tend to be later
★ lyre end supports, particularly with a brass strip, are likely to increase value
★ many sofa tables have been made from old cheval mirrors
★ if the stretcher rail is turned and has a square block in the centre – it could be from a converted cheval mirror
★ many good sofa tables have been carved with Egyptian heads in the manner of Thomas Hope
★ long drawers are undesirable but many have been cut down

A Regency rosewood and brass inlaid sofa table, the crossbanded hinged top with interlaced stringing, on lyre-shaped and dual splayed end supports, stamped 'T. Sharples, Liverpool', 65½in (166cm).
$7,500-10,500

A Regency mahogany and rosewood sofa table, with satinwood crossbanding and inlay, 69½in (176cm).
$4,500-7,000

A Regency rosewood sofa table, the twin flap top with ropetwist brass border, 58in (147cm) open.
$4,000-5,500

A Regency mahogany sofa table, crossbanded in rosewood and inlaid with satinwood stringing, 62in (157cm).
$2,500-3,500

A Regency rosewood sofa table, 36in (91.5cm).
$4,500-7,000

A Regency rosewood sofa table, 58in (147cm) open.
$7,500-10,500

A Regency mahogany sofa table, the top inlaid with a central shell motif outlined with stringing, with fan motif spandrels and edged with chequered lines, 56in (142cm) extended.
$1,500-2,600

A Regency mahogany and coromandel crossbanded sofa table, some damage, 58in (147cm).
$1,500-2,600

Tables – Sutherland

A Regency mahogany sofa table, with satinwood edge, on 4 curved feet with brass casters and mounts, 60in (152cm).
$3,000-4,000

A Victorian inlaid rosewood Sutherland table, 30in (76cm) extended.
$450-700

A George III serpentine tea table, with moulded square chamfered legs headed by pierced angled brackets, restored, 36in (91.5cm).
$3,000-4,500

Tables – Tea

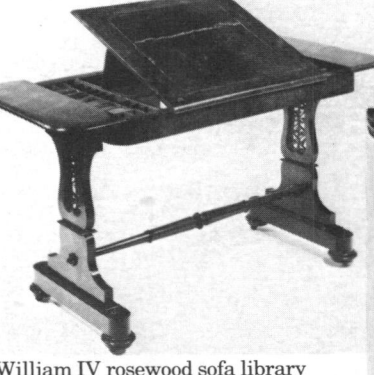

A William IV rosewood sofa library table, with hinged adjustable ratcheted centre slope inset with a panel of tooled leather, the sliding D-shaped ends concealing fitted compartments for writing and sewing, with extra leaves of a slightly later date, 51in (130cm) extended.
$1,500-2,600

A George II walnut and mahogany tea table, with later semi-circular folding top enclosing a well, one hinge stamped Cross, 30½in (77cm).
$2,250-3,000

A mahogany and burr walnut tea table, the top inlaid on both sides with a spreading fan divided by boxwood stringing, 34in (86cm).
$1,000-1,400

A sofa table veneered and decorated as satinwood, and painted with a design of flowers with ribbon borders, 60in (152cm) extended.
$1,500-2,600

An early George III mahogany tea table, 36in (91.5cm).
$5,500-7,000

A George III satinwood and banded D-shaped tea table, with painted band of flowers with ribbon ties, the apron with panels of purpleheart, 38in (96.5cm).
$6,000-9,000

Tables – Supper

A Regency mahogany supper table, the top crossbanded with stringing, fitted with a drawer each end with ebony stringing, oak lined, 41½in (105cm).
$1,200-1,600

A George III Irish carved mahogany folding top table, 46in (117cm).
$6,000-9,000

A Regency mahogany folding top tea table, the frieze with line inlay, 34in (86.5cm).
$1,500-2,600

A Chippendale mahogany tilt top tea table, the top tilting above a vase turned pedestal on cabriole legs with shod slipper feet, probably Newport, Rhode Island, c1770, 31in (78cm) diam.
$2,000-3,000

A Regency mahogany tea table, 40in (101.5cm).
$600-900

A Chippendale carved cherrywood tilt top tea table, the serpentine top with outset shaped corners tilting above a birdcage, over a tapering compressed ball pedestal, on tripod arched cabriole legs with ball and claw feet, underside of top inscribed 'E.B.W. Parsons, 145 Capitol Ave. Hartford, Conn.', repairs, c1770, 36½in (92cm) diam.
$20,000-25,000

A Regency mahogany tea table, in the manner of Gillows, Lancaster, 36in (91cm).
$1,500-2,600

A William IV rosewood tea table, 36in (92cm).
$900-1,300

Tables – Tripod

A Georgian mahogany snap top table, 35in (89cm) diam.
$300-500

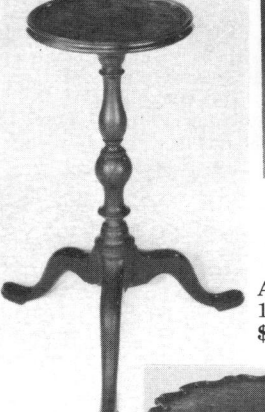

A George III carved mahogany occasional table, with later dished top with re-entrant undulating moulded edge, and birdcage action, 22in (56cm).
$1,500-2,600

A Victorian rosewood tea table with swivel top.
$1,200-1,600

A George II mahogany tripod table, 10in (25.5cm) diam.
$1,500-2,600

A George II mahogany tripod table, the circular top on a birdcage action turned column, 30in (76cm) diam.
$1,500-2,600

A mahogany tripod table with a circular galleried top, 23in (58cm) high.
$3,000-4,500

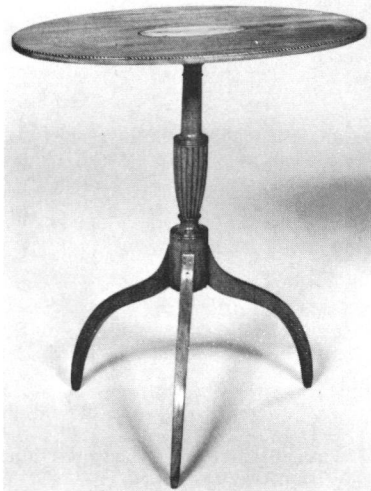

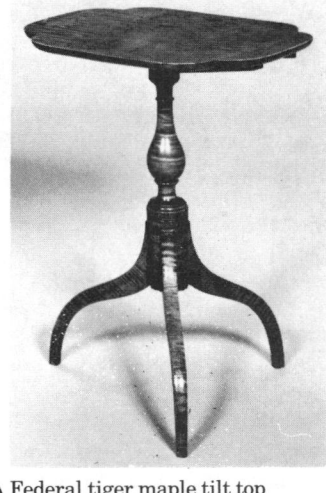

A Federal inlaid mahogany tilt top candlestand, the oval top centering an oval birch reserve, tilting above a reeded urn turned pedestal, on 3 arched square tapering legs with inlaid cuffs, minor damage, Massachusetts, c1800, 26½in (66cm).
$2,000-3,000

A maple black painted and decorated candlestand, the top with notched corners above a bulbous ring turned standard, on cabriole legs, the top painted with stylised yellow and red star motif, New England, c1775, paint early 19thC, 26in (65cm) high.
$700-800

A Federal tiger maple tilt top candlestand, with clover shaped top tilting above a baluster turned pedestal, on arched square tapering legs, New England, c1810, 20½in (51cm).
$2,000-2,500

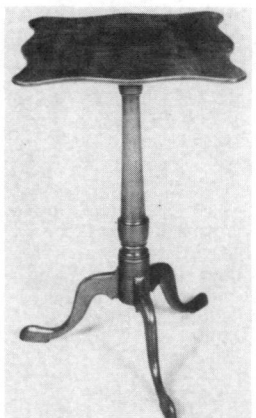

A Chippendale cherrywood tilt top stand, with serpentine outlined square top tilting above an urn turned tapering columnar pedestal, on tripod cabriole legs, Massachusetts, c1790, 28in (70cm) high.
$1,800-2,000

A Georgian mahogany tripod table.
$750-1,000

Tables – Work

A George III Scottish black and gold lacquer work table, stamped 'Bruce & Burns, Edin^R', 18½in (47cm).
$1,300-1,800

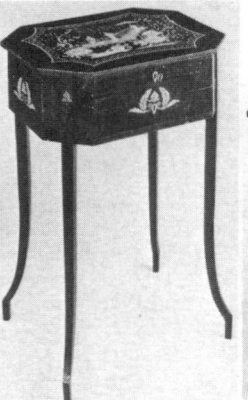

A rare mahogany octagonal top work table, c1775.
$6,000-8,000

A Regency pollard oak work table, with marbled top above a frieze drawer on a U-shaped support, with 4 down-curved legs, lacking fabric to work basket, 27in (68cm).
$2,250-3,500

A George III satinwood work table, the crossbanded octagonal top decorated at a later date, 19in (48cm).
$1,500-2,600

A Regency brass inlaid two-drawer
drop leaf work table, 20in (51cm).
$1,500-2,600

A late Federal mahogany
worktable, the top above 2
mahogany veneered drawers
flanked by panels with brass
stringing, with shaped medial shelf
on baluster and ring turned legs
with casters, New York, c1820, 23in
(58cm).
$3,500-4,500

A late Georgian mahogany work
and writing table.
$1,500-2,600

A late Regency mahogany and
ebony strung work table, 28½in
(73cm).
$1,500-2,600

A rosewood work table with drawer,
early 19thC, 17in (43cm).
$900-1,300

A George IV rosewood sewing table,
21in (53cm).
$1,300-1,800

A William IV burr elm work table,
the top with rosewood banded
borders, 33½in (85cm).
$1,500-2,600

A William IV rosewood work table,
adapted, 20in (51cm).
$3,000-4,500

A Federal walnut and maple
worktable, with tiger maple short
drawer, on reeded baluster and
turned legs on ball feet, New
England, c1820, 20in (50cm).
$1,000-1,500

A Federal mahogany worktable, the
top with outset rounded corners,
over a drawer fitted with
compartments, above a deep
drawer, flanked by reeded corner
columns, on tapering legs with ball
feet, Pennsylvania, c1810, 19in
(48cm).
$3,500-4,500

A mid-Victorian black, mother-of-pearl, japanned papier mâché sewing table, enclosing a fitted interior, 18½in (46cm).
$1,200-1,600

A Victorian burr walnut and inlaid needlework table.
$1,000-1,400 ▶

A Victorian burr walnut work table, with a pierced brass gallery, 27in (68.5cm).
$1,200-1,600

A Victorian figured walnut sewing and games table for draughts, backgammon and cribbage, 23in (58cm).
$1,300-1,800

Tables – Writing

A Regency mahogany writing table.
$1,500-2,600

A Victorian walnut work table, the hinged top inlaid with a chessboard, enclosing a fitted interior with well, 22in (56cm).
$750-1,000 ▶

A Georgian mahogany extending writing table, with fitted interior and writing surface.
$2,500-3,500

A George III mahogany and inlaid kidney-shaped writing table, 35½in (90cm).
$4,500-7,000

A George IV mahogany kidney-shaped writing table, previously with a slide, 44½in (113cm).
$2,500-3,500

A Victorian walnut and tulipwood writing table, 42in (106cm).
$1,300-1,800 ▶

An early George III mahogany writing table, the top drawer with leather-lined slide and inkwell opening to the side, the lower drawer opening to the back, 37in (94cm) open.
$2,250-3,000

An early Victorian rosewood library writing table, 64in (162.5cm).
$4,500-7,000

A mid-Victorian walnut and oak writing table, in the style of A W N Pugin, with leather-lined top above 2 frieze drawers, with carved sides, on moulded shaped trestle ends carved with oak leaves, joined by a channelled stretcher, 54in (137cm).
$4,500-7,000

An Edwardian Sheraton style kidney-shaped writing table, 30in (76cm).
$450-700

A Victorian walnut and ebonised kidney-shaped writing table, 'Gillow & Co., 6555', 45½in (115cm).
$1,300-1,800

A Louis Phillipe kingwood crossbanded and ormolu mounted table à ecrire, in the Louis XV taste, 25½in (65cm).
$3,000-4,500

A French walnut bureau plat in the Louis XV taste, c1870, 45½in (115cm).
$1,300-1,800

Teapoys

Whatnots

A William IV walnut pedestal teapoy, the interior fitted with 2 cannisters and 2 glass mixing bowls, stamped 'Gillows', 28½in (72cm) high.
$1,300-1,800

A Regency mahogany teapoy.
$600-900

An unusual George III mahogany four-tier corner étagère, early 19thC, 28in (71cm).
$7,500-10,500

An Abbotsford style heavily carved oak teapoy, with lion mask handles, the coffered lid enclosing 4 cavities for tea and 2 for bowls, late 19thC, 33½in (85cm) high.
$450-700

A Georgian mahogany four-tier whatnot, 18in (46cm).
$800-1,200

A mid-Victorian black and mother-of-pearl japanned papier mâché teapoy, with divided interior, 18in (46cm) high.
$1,300-1,800

A Regency mahogany three-tier whatnot, the rising top with easel support as a reading stand, 21in (53.5cm).
$1,500-2,600

A pair of George IV rosewood whatnots, with bead-and-reel moulded tops, ring-turned baluster uprights and ribbed bun feet, 53½in (135cm) high.
$9,000-12,000

A mid-Victorian oak étagère, in the style of A W N Pugin, 48in (122cm) high.
$2,500-3,500

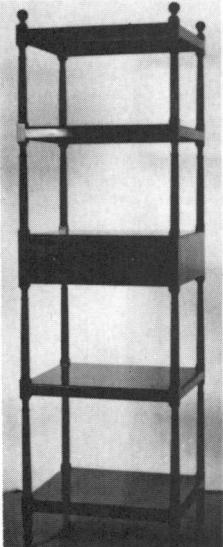

A Victorian burr walnut three-tier shaped whatnot, 37in (94cm).
$1,300-1,800

A Victorian five-tier whatnot, with barley twist supports.
$450-700

A George IV mahogany five-tier whatnot, with drawer to the centre tier, 66in (167.5cm) high.
$900-1,300

A Victorian rosewood whatnot of serpentine outline, 56in (142cm) high.
$600-900

A rosewood canterbury whatnot, 19thC.
$1,500-2,600

A French tulipwood, mahogany and ormolu mounted three-tier étagère, with a mirrored and pierced galleried detachable top, 34½in (87cm).
$3,000-4,000

A mid-Victorian black, gilt and mother-of-pearl japanned papier mâché whatnot, stamped 'Jennens & Bettridge', 51in (129.5cm) high.
$7,500-10,500

Wine Coolers

A mahogany wine cooler, late 18thC.
$6,000-9,000

An Empire carved mahogany cellaret, with coffered hinged rectangular top opening to a fitted tin-lined interior, above a trapezoidal panelled base with brass lion's head carrying handles, on carved recumbent lion supports, probably New York State, c1820, 27in (68cm).
$3,000-5,000

A George III brass bound mahogany hexagonal cellaret with carrying handles, on later base, 15in (38cm).
$2,500-3,500

A George III mahogany wine cooler, 28in (71cm).
$4,500-7,000

A George III mahogany cellaret.
$6,000-9,000

A Georgian mahogany wine cooler, with crossbanded top, inlaid with string lines, 19in (48cm).
$1,500-2,600

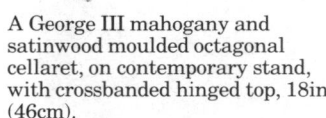

A George III mahogany and satinwood moulded octagonal cellaret, on contemporary stand, with crossbanded hinged top, 18in (46cm).
$3,000-4,000

A George III mahogany wine cooler, the tapering oval lead-lined body inlaid with lines, 24½in (62cm).
$4,500-7,000

A Georgian mahogany wine cooler, 18in (46cm) diam.
$3,000-4,500

WINE COOLERS

★ cisterns for cooling wines were noted back in the 15thC and as objects of furniture became popular after about 1730. The cellaret is basically a cooler with a lid and fitted with a lock

★ there are two main types: those made to stand on a pedestal or sideboard and those with legs or separate stands to stand on the floor

★ octagonal, hexagonal, round or oval, the commonest form is of coopered construction with a number of brass bands

★ a cooler made to stand on a pedestal will often have the lowest brass band as near to the base as possible; a cooler made to fit into a stand will have the band slightly up the body to allow a snug fit

★ it is important that all mounts are original and condition should be good, but the absence of the old lead lining is not serious. An octagonal cooler or cellaret on stand may command a slightly higher price than a hexagonal model, but both are much in demand

★ after 1800, the sarcophagus shape became popular and later Regency models were made with highly figured mahogany veneers and large carved paw feet

★ there were not many new designs after the 1850s

Miscellaneous

A miniature Chippendale walnut slant front desk, the top above a hinged moulded lid with star inlay, enclosing a fitted interior, the case with 3 drawers, on straight bracket feet, restorations, late 19thC, 7¼in (18cm) high.
$1,500-2,500

A miniature white painted tilt top tea table, with octagonal top tilting above a baluster turned standard, on cabriole legs, early 19thC, 8in (20cm) high.
$700-900

A miniature Queen Anne maple and pine slant front desk, the top above a moulded hinged lid opening to a fitted interior, on cabriole legs with pad feet, together with a carved Queen Anne cherrywood mirror, 18thC, desk 11in (28cm) high.
$3,500-4,500

A miniature George III mahogany side table, with moulded top above one long drawer above a central arch flanked by 2 short drawers, English, late 18thC, 6in (15cm).
$300-500

A miniature Chippendale style mahogany bombé chest of drawers, 13in (33cm).
$1,700-2,000

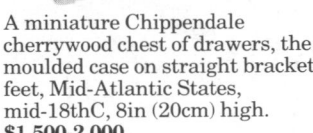

A miniature Chippendale cherrywood chest of drawers, the moulded case on straight bracket feet, Mid-Atlantic States, mid-18thC, 8in (20cm) high.
$1,500-2,000

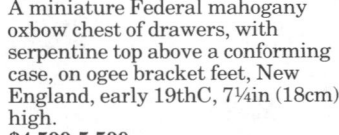

A miniature Federal mahogany oxbow chest of drawers, with serpentine top above a conforming case, on ogee bracket feet, New England, early 19thC, 7¼in (18cm) high.
$4,500-5,500

 A miniature Federal mahogany tilt top tea table, with octagonal top tilting above a baluster turned standard, on 3 arched legs ending in pad feet, early 19thC, 9in (22.5cm) high.
$1,000-1,500

A miniature Chippendale mahogany desk and bookcase in 2 parts, the upper case with a moulded cornice above 2 panelled doors, the lower case with a hinged slant lid opening to a fitted interior, above 3 drawers, on straight bracket feet, Rhode Island, c1770, 16in (40cm) high.
$2,000-3,000

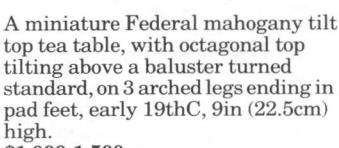

A miniature Chippendale mahogany chest-on-chest in 2 sections, on ogee bracket feet, restorations, English, late 18thC, 17in (42cm) high.
$2,000-2,500

ARCHITECTURAL ANTIQUES

One of the areas which has seen an enormous increase in interest and hence price is the rather wide term architectural antiques. It began with interior designers buying decorative items to dress rooms but is now more concerned with the actual fittings. Fireplaces, baths, WC's, door handles etc. are now in great demand. People are more concerned with creating the correct period feel and hence want to purchase suitable period fittings or good reproductions. Gone are the days of ripping out all features in the guise of modernisation. The buzz words are now 'authentically restored'.

It is still possible to find reasonably priced old fittings but one should check whether they have been reconditioned. Often the tap holes on old baths do not take modern fittings.

We have produced a book, called *Period Details* which deals with all aspects of interior period details, with special emphasis on choosing the correct fittings for the period of house and a 24 page directory of where to buy them.

A George III Carrara marble fire surround, the interior with coloured marble slips and cast iron back plates.
$10,500-14,000

A decorative arched marble fireplace, with floral carvings and cast iron grate, mid-late 19thC.
$1,200-1,600

A Regency cast iron insert, with anthemion decoration, 36 by 38in (91 by 96cm).
$450-700

A cast iron insert, with hobs and egg-and-dart pattern to arch, mid-19thC, 36 by 38in (91 by 96cm).
$450-600

A cast iron insert, with hobs and very fine casting of birds to front panels, set with blue and white Minton tiles, with a matching hearth, mid-19thC, 36in (91cm) square.
$600-900

An arched cast iron grate, with acorn motifs, mid-19thC, 38 by 36in (96 by 91cm).
$450-700

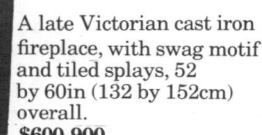

A late Victorian cast iron fireplace, with swag motif and tiled splays, 52 by 60in (132 by 152cm) overall.
$600-900

A cast iron grate and surround, early-mid-19thC.
$750-1,000

An Ashburton marble fire surround.
$750-1,000

A cast iron hob grate, mid-19thC.
$400-500

A steel club fender with curved leather seats.
$800-1,200

A decorative cast iron grate with scrollwork and scalloped backplate, 38 by 32in (96 by 81cm).
$300-500

A highly decorative cast iron grate, early-mid-19thC, 36 by 34in (91 by 86 cm).
$450-600

A Victorian cast iron and tiled grate, with Four Seasons picture tiles, 34 by 36in (86 by 91cm).
$450-700

A late Victorian cast iron grate, with tiled splays and canopy, and stripped pine surround, 50 by 63in (127 by 160cm) overall.
$600-900

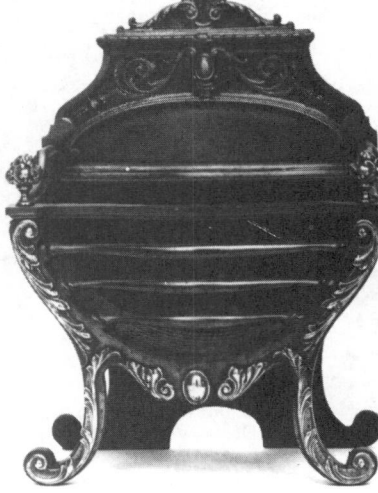

A fire grate with brass detail, 19thC.
$400-500

A mottled black, white and grey marble fire surround, c1900, later inset with fire grate and tiles, 83in (211cm) wide.
$750-1,000

A wrought iron basket grate, after a design by Sir Robert Lorimer, 32in (81cm) wide.
$600-900

See: Peter Savage, Lorimer and the Edinburgh Craft Designers, *1980. Lorimer usually used the services of local blacksmith Thomas Hadden for all his ironwork; 'he soon came to rely on Thomas Hadden for almost all his wrought iron work because Hadden was a rare bird, a working blacksmith with an imagination of his own'. Similar examples of the work of Thomas Hadden are illustrated by Christopher Hussey,* The Work of Sir Robert Lorimer, *1931, pl. 261.*

A late Victorian cast iron grate, with tiled splays and canopy, and a panelled surround also in cast iron, 52 by 66in (132 by 168cm) overall.
$750-1,000

A typical late Victorian fireplace in white marble, with a cast iron grate, having splays of tiles depicting musical instruments, 48 by 72in (122 by 183cm) overall.
$1,200-1,600

A mid-late Victorian cast iron grate, with brown and white Minton tiles depicting scenes from Shakespeare, reduced in size at some time to 36 by 32in (91 by 81cm).
$300-500

A Coalbrookdale cast iron surround with foliate panel.
$750-1,000

An Edwardian Sicilian marble fire surround.
$600-900
An Art Nouveau cast iron and tiled inset with continuous pattern, 38in (96.5cm) square.
$450-600
An Edwardian brass fender.
$250-350

A set of 4 heavy ornate cast iron garden chairs, late 19th/early 20thC.
$600-900

A set of 6 granite staddle stones, 30in (76cm) high.
$450-700

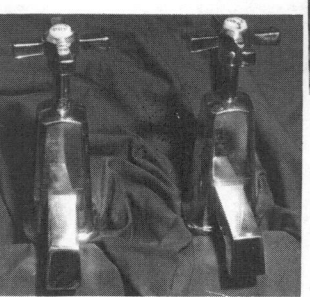

A pair of heavy brass Shanks' Deco-style bath taps, 6in (15cm) high.
$100-150

A large Georgian style brass and iron fire grate, 38in (96.5cm) wide.
$1,500-2,600

An Edwardian shield shape grate screen.
$30-50

An unusual oak window or screen with 4 leaded casements, each with a double folding shutter, all mounted with triple action hinges and sprung catches, made in decorative wrought iron, Flemish, probably 19thC, in the style of the late 16th/early 17thC, 70 by 50in (178 by 127cm).
$1,300-1,800

A wrought iron and steel basket grate, after a design by Sir Robert Lorimer, 32½in (82.5cm) wide.
$800-1,200

A cast iron grate with honey pot and thistle decoration, early 19thC, 24in (61cm).
$300-400

A cast iron bath with roll top and ball and claw feet, fitted with brass and porcelain shower mixer taps.
$450-700

An early Victorian rosewood firescreen, the glazed panel with a raised carpetwork basket of flowers, 40in (101cm) wide.
$1,000-1,400

A cast iron grate with fine floral and foliate repeat decoration, late 18thC, 34in (86cm).
$400-500

A small cast iron kitchen range, typically found in Devon where it is known as a 'Bodley' from 1850 onwards, 18 by 36in (46 by 97cm).
$250-350

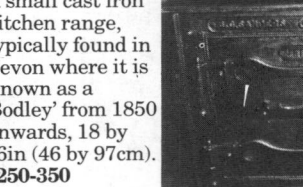

A cast iron grate with classical decoration and pierced apron, late 18thC, 36in (91cm).
$450-700

A set of six pairs of ebonised wood door handles, with decorative brass collars, 19thC.
$100-200

A heavy brass door knocker with letter slot, late 19th/early 20thC, 9in (23cm) long.
$45-70

An ornate French firescreen and matching fender, 19thC.
$1,000-1,400

A Victorian stained wood door, with painted glass panel, 89 by 30in (226 by 76cm) overall.
$1,000-1,400

An unusual oven in cast iron with brass handles, possibly late 18thC, 24 by 24in (61 by 61cm).
$300-400

A pair of heavy five panel oak double doors.
$450-600

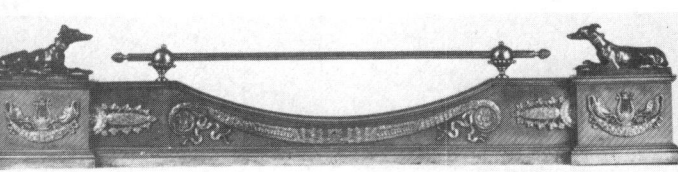

An Empire ormolu and bronze fender, the frieze with a ribbon-tied flowerhead swag with halved flowerheads and lyre and swan swags, 43½in (110cm) wide.
$4,500-7,000

A late Victorian Jacobean style oak door, showing rectangular panel design typical of the late 16th/early 17thC, 82 by 36in (208 by 91.5cm).
$300-500

A decoratively moulded WC with roses and borders of blue on a white background.
$300-400

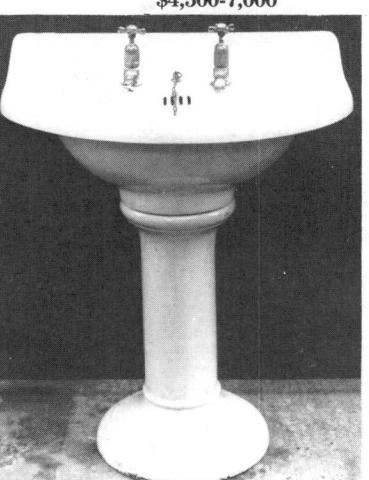

A Royal Doulton white porcelain washbasin on column pedestal with porcelain headed brass taps, 36in (91cm) high.
$300-500

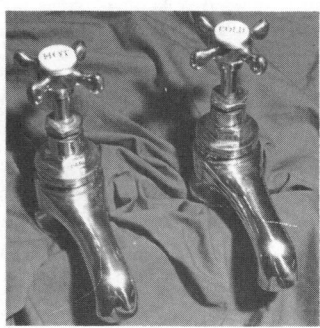

A pair of good quality brass bath taps with porcelain 'hot' and 'cold', 19thC, 6in (15cm) high.
$100-150

Note the absence of the later outer sleeve covering the body of the tap.

A cast iron roll top bath with shell shaped porcelain soap trays and concealed water inlets and outlets, with porcelain headed brass controls.
$450-600

Clocks – Longcase

An oak longcase clock by Barlow, Ashton-under-Lyne, with walnut crossbanded trunk door, the caddy top hood with free standing pillars, the 12in (30cm) brass dial signed, with date aperture and rolling moon aperture, 4-pillar rack striking movement, with anchor escapement, 18thC, 85in (216cm).
$3,000-4,500

A longcase clock by Thomas Atkinson, Ormskirk, with 8-day movement and deadbeat escapement, in original mahogany case, 94in (238cm).
$6,000-8,000

A George III mahogany longcase clock, the brass dial with subsidiary seconds dial and date aperture, inscribed Thomas Barton, Manchester, 90in (228.5cm).
$3,000-4,500

An 8-day Scottish longcase clock in a mahogany case, with rack striking movement, painted dial with seconds and date hand, signed Cameron, Kilmarnock, c1860, 90in (228.5cm).
$1,500-2,600

A mahogany longcase clock by John Benning of Windsor, 8-day movement, brass dial showing the phases of the moon, hourly striking on a bell, c1770, 99in (252cm).
$6,000-9,000

l. A mahogany longcase regulator clock, with 12in (30cm) silvered dial with seconds and hour rings, engraved 'Regulator', 'Louth', 19thC, 79in (200.5cm).
$4,000-5,500

r. A Queen Anne walnut longcase clock, with 11in (29cm) brass dial, by Wm Atkinson, London, case perhaps modified, 80in (203cm).
$2,500-3,500

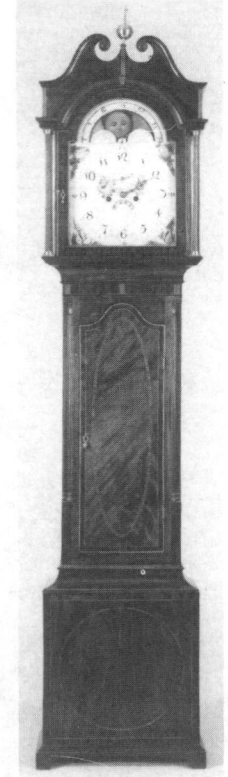

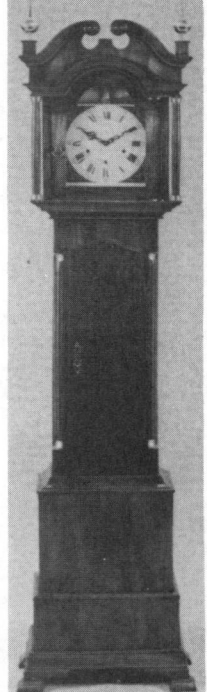

An oak longcase clock, with brass and silvered dial, date aperture and 8-day movement, maker John Barrow, London, 18thC.
$4,000-5,500

A Federal inlaid mahogany longcase clock, with painted lunar dial, the spandrels with painted shells, on straight bracket feet, dial repainted, feet restored, New Jersey, c1800, 93in (236cm).
$5,000-6,000

A Federal style mahogany grandmother clock, the painted dial with a rocking ship, 61½in (156cm).
$700-900

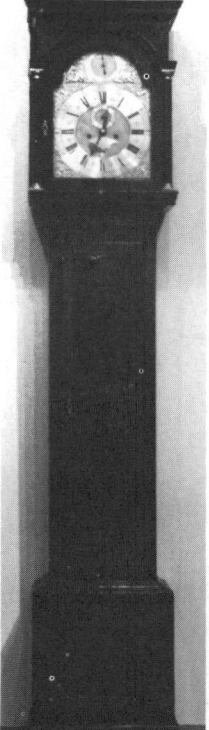

A Dutch longcase clock with 10in (25cm) silvered chapter ring inscribed Jean Baron a Utrecht, in seaweed marquetry case with brass cornice, the aperture with a bronze figure of Father Time, case probably modified, early 18thC.
$4,000-5,500

A mahogany veneered and crossbanded longcase clock, with 2-train 8-day movement striking on a bell, gilded floral and foliate spandrels, subsidiary seconds dial and calendar aperture, inscribed A. Bioletti, Wincanton, early 19thC, 88in (224cm).
$2,250-3,500

An 8-day walnut longcase clock with brass dial, silvered chapter ring, subsidiary dial for seconds, calendar aperture, figured walnut case, made by John Blake, Fulham, c1750, 90½in (230cm).
$6,000-9,000

A George III oak longcase clock, with mahogany banding and chequered stringing, the 8-day movement with brass and silvered arched dial, signed Jonathan Graham, Langholm, c1770, 87in (221cm).
$2,250-3,500

A mahogany inlaid longcase clock, with 8-day striking movement, the arched painted face with date and seconds hand, by Benjamin Cope, Franch, with key, c1786, 96in (244cm).
$2,500-3,500

An Edwardian mahogany longcase clock, the brass dial with subsidiary seconds dial and date aperture, inscribed Robert Coats, Hamilton, the case on later ogee bracket feet, 90in (228.5cm).
$2,250-3,500

A George III Lancashire mahogany longcase clock, the dial signed Saml. Collier Eccles round the moonphase, with subsidiary seconds and calendar sector, rack striking 4-pillar movement with anchor escapement, 98in (249cm).
$4,500-7,000

A highly unusual combination of painted and brass dial.

A walnut and floral marquetry month going longcase clock, the 11in (29cm) square brass dial with winged cherub's head spandrels, the silvered chapter ring signed at the VI, Phillip Corderoy, London, with subsidiary seconds, 5-ringed pillared movement with latched plates, outside countwheel strike and anchor escapement, early 18thC, 80in (202cm), the base now reduced.
$6,000-9,000

LONGCASE CLOCKS

Longcase clocks are generally ordered alphabetically by the makers name

---

A longcase clock by John Gee, Dockhead, Southwark, formerly japanned, with 12in (30cm) brass dial, 5-pillar 8-day rack striking movement, with anchor escapement, 18thC.
$1,500-2,600

An 8-day mahogany longcase clock with brass face, by Wm Blight, Plymouth.
$4,500-7,000

A George II red lacquer longcase clock, the case with gilt and black chinoiserie decoration, the movement with anchor escapement and rack strike, the brass dial with silvered chapter ring, signed Tho. Burges, Gosport, the matted centre with seconds ring and date aperture, restorations, 84in (214cm).
$3,000-4,500

A mahogany longcase clock, the 8-day movement rack striking, the 12in (30cm) broken arched painted dial with arabic numerals, subsidiary seconds and date aperture, signed J.Couzens, Langport, the arch painted with a Chinese scene, 96in (244cm).
$3,000-4,500

A walnut month going longcase clock, the 12in (30cm) brass dial with engraved wheatsheaf border, silvered chapter ring and matted centre, with strike/silent above the XII, signed on a cartouche in the arch Alexr. Giroust, Coventry Street, London, 18thC, 87in (221cm).
$4,500-7,000

A Georgian oak longcase clock with square brass dial, 8-day movement, by Mark Hawkins, Bury St Edmunds.
$1,200-1,600

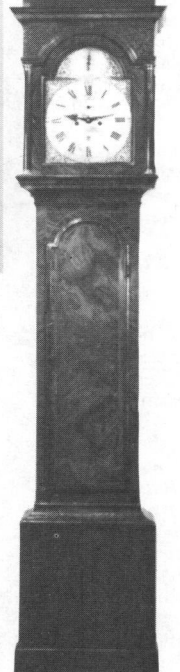

An 8-day walnut longcase clock, with brass face, by Wm Hill, Walsingham.
$7,500-10,500

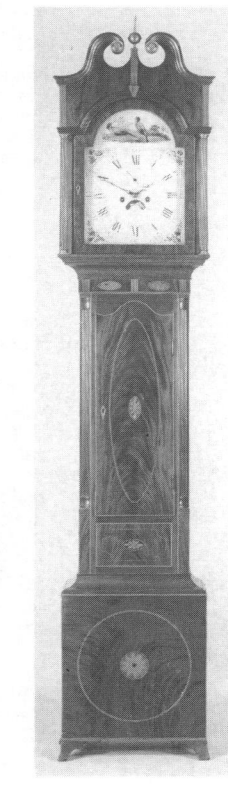

A Federal inlaid mahogany longcase clock, on French feet, the saddle board signed 'Made by Isaac Schoonmaker, April 7, 1808', Patterson, New Jersey, 96in (244cm).
$25,000-30,000

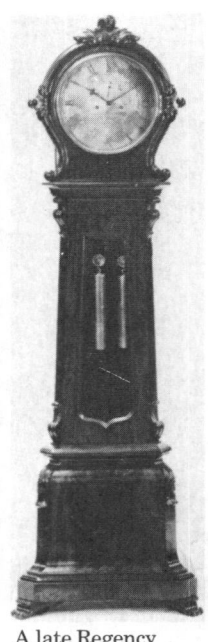

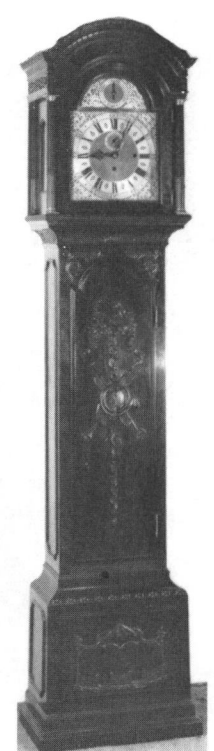

A Regency mahogany longcase clock, the brass dial with silvered chapter ring, subsidiary seconds and date dials, inscribed John Hamilton, Glasgow, 87in (221cm).
$750-1,000

A figured mahogany longcase clock, the top with fretwork panel, the hood with brass enriched columns, the silvered dial with 8-day movement, strike and silent seconds and date dials, H Hopkins, Deptford, 18thC, 94in (238cm).
$4,500-7,000

A late Stuart walnut and marquetry longcase clock, the convex moulded case with flower marquetry panel to plinth, with later caddy top, the 11½in (29cm) dial signed Peter Mallett London on the chapter ring, with 5-ringed pillar movement with inside countwheel strike and anchor escapement, 90in (229cm).
$13,500-17,500

A late Regency mahogany longcase clock, silvered dial with subsidiary seconds dial, inscribed James & Andrew Kelley, Glasgow, 81in (206cm).
$1,500-2,600

A George II longcase clock by John Hocker, Reading, with 8-day 3-train striking movement, chiming on 4 or 8 bells, in Cuban mahogany case, 92in (234cm).
$4,500-7,000

A mahogany longcase clock by Charles Haley, 18thC.
$2,250-3,500

A mahogany longcase clock, the 8-day movement rack striking and with brass cased weights, the 12in (30cm) brass dial with silvered chapter ring, urn and eagle spandrels, the engraved centre with subsidiary seconds dial and date aperture, signed on the chapter ring Wm. Hornsey, Exon, the arch with a silvered arc inscribed 'High Water at Topsham Bar', 104in (264cm).
$2,250-3,500

An oak longcase clock, with 8-day movement, painted face, by Jas Kenway, Bridport.
$1,500-2,600

An 8-day longcase clock, with brass face, blue lacquer, by Jos Herring, London.
$3,000-4,500

An 8-day longcase
clock, with brass
face, blue lacquer,
by Thos Hutley,
Coggeshall.
$6,000-8,000

A George III
Salisbury mahogany
veneered 8-day
longcase clock, the
movement striking
on a bell, the arched
brass dial engraved
with an eagle with
Tempus Fugit,
inscribed Edward
Marsh, Sarum, 92in
(234cm).
$4,000-5,500

A George III Scottish
mahogany longcase
clock, the brass dial
signed on the
silvered strike/silent
ring in the arch Jas.
Mylne Montrose,
inset seconds ring,
movement with
anchor escapement
and rack strike,
restorations, 87in
(221cm).
$3,000-4,500

A George III mahogany
longcase clock, the dial
signed Henry Jenkins
Cheapside London No.
2619 on a button in the
arch, with subsidiary
seconds and calendar
aperture, 5-pillar
movement with rack
strike and anchor
escapement, 99in
(251cm).
$6,000-9,000

A late Georgian oak
and mahogany
longcase clock, by
Wm Kirk, Stockport.
$4,000-5,500

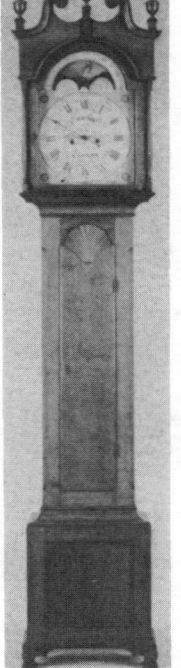

A mahogany
longcase clock of
Chippendale design,
with arched brass
face with dolphin
and scroll spandrels,
subsidiary seconds
dial and date
aperture, 8-day
movement with bell
strike, maker
Lanrie, Carlisle,
18thC, 89in (226cm).
$4,500-7,000

A mahogany
quarter-chiming
longcase clock, the
case in Chippendale
style, with silvered
dial, subsidiary
seconds and strike/
silent in the arch,
signed for Maple
& Co. London, the
3-train movement
with maintaining
power and deadbeat
escapement chiming
on 4 gongs, late
19thC, 100in
(254cm).
$4,500-7,000

A Chippendale cherrywood
longcase clock, the works by
G Bush, Pennsylvania, c1800, the
white painted dial inscribed
'G.Bush/Easton', restorations to
feet, 99½in (253cm).
$7,000-10,000

A Chippendale walnut longcase
clock, the works by Peter Stretch,
Philadelphia, c1755, face and works
of different origin, case re-carved
and other restorations, 94½in
(239cm).
$4,000-6,000

A late Georgian mahogany longcase clock, the brass dial with boss in the arch signed Robert Martin Glasgow, the movement with anchor escapement and strike on bell, 83in (211cm).
$1,200-1,600

An inlaid mahogany longcase clock, with painted dial, signed J. Milner, Sunderland, with 8-day movement, early 19thC.
$1,500-2,600

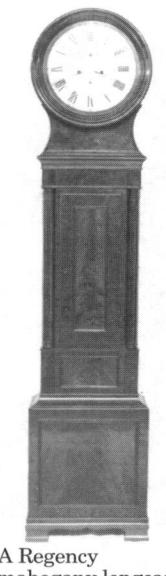

A Regency mahogany longcase clock, having circular dial, 8-day movement, by A Miller, Edinburgh, the case with balloon hood and pendulum flanked by columns, raised on ogee feet.
$1,500-2,600

A George III mahogany 8-day striking longcase clock, the movement with deadbeat escapement, striking on a bell, subsidiary seconds and date dial, inscribed Jno. Morse, Southampton, 81in (206cm).
$4,500-7,000

A 30-hour oak and mahogany longcase clock, with painted dial, Tho Pearce, Chard, 81in (205.5cm).
$1,000-1,400

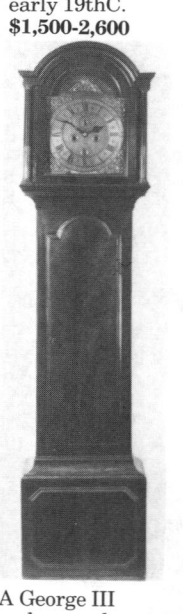

A mahogany longcase clock, by Miller, Edinburgh, with painted face, 8-day movement, subsidiary dial for seconds and calendar, replaced door lock, 84in (213cm).
$2,500-3,500

A George III mahogany longcase clock, the earlier movement with 12in (30cm) brass dial, silvered chapter ring, signed Rich Penny, London, the ringed pillared movement with inside countwheel strike and anchor escapement, the plinth missing, 82in (208cm).
$3,000-4,500

A mid-Georgian oak longcase clock, with crossbanded chequer and star inlay decoration, 8-day movement, arched brass dial, lunar and calendar date, by Thomas Ogden, Halifax.
$4,000-5,500

An oak longcase clock by William Oxley of Worksop, late 18thC.
$2,250-3,500

A George II walnut longcase clock, the dial signed Willm. Pearce Plymouth, and a button in the arch engraved Tempus Fugit, 4-pillar movement with rack strike and anchor escapement, some restoration, 98in (249cm).
$4,500-7,000

A 30-hour longcase clock, the plated movement with 10½in (26cm) brass dial, the spandrels engraved with mottos reading 'Behold this Hand', 'Observe ye motion's Tipp', 'Man's life and Time' and 'Away like these do Slipp', with later oak and mahogany case, 73½in (186cm).
$900-1,300

John Ogden, Darlington, recorded working c1730.

HINTS TO DATING LONGCASE CLOCKS

Dials

8in square	to c1669	Carolean
10in square	from c1665-1800	
11in square	from 1690-1800	
12in square	from c1700	from Queen Anne
14in square	from c1740	from early Georgian
Broken-arch dial	from c1715	from early Georgian
Round dial	from c1760	from early Georgian
Silvered dial	from c1760	from early Georgian
Painted dial	from c1770	from early Georgian
Hour hand only	to 1820	
Minute hand introduced	c1663	
Second hand	from 1675	post-Restoration
Matching hands	from c1775	George III or later

Case finish

Ebony veneer	up to c1725	Carolean to early Georgian
Walnut veneer	from c1670 to c1770	Carolean to mid-Georgian
Lacquer	from c1700 to c1790	Queen Anne to mid-Georgian
Mahogany	from 1730	from early Georgian
Softwood	from c1690	from mid-Georgian
Mahogany inlay	from c1750	from mid-Georgian
Marquetry	from c1680 to c1760	from Carolean to mid-Georgian
Oak	always	

A Georgian oak longcase clock, with enamel painted arch dial, 8-day movement, by Rider Pool.
$1,200-1,600

A longcase clock with painted face, subsidiary dial for seconds, calendar aperture, 8-day movement, oak case with reeded column to the trunk, 87in (221cm).
$4,000-5,500

A Federal inlaid mahogany longcase clock, on ogee bracket feet, restorations but original lower section, Massachusetts, c1800, 95in (241cm).
$2,500-3,000

A mahogany longcase clock, with 8-day movement, brass arch dial, bearing makers name Paul Rimbault, London, 18thC.
$6,000-8,000

A mahogany longcase clock with painted face, 8-day movement, by David Rough, Dundee, with subsidiary dial for seconds and calendar, the case inlaid with burr elm and boxwood stringing, c1820, 86in (219cm).
$5,500-7,000

A Chippendale walnut longcase clock, with an arched glazed door opening to an engraved brass and copper dial with a circular medallion with a gilt sun, dial originally silvered, finials restored, dial signed by Thomas Crow, Wilmington, Delaware, c1770, 89in (226cm).
$6,000-9,000

A mahogany longcase clock, with 12in (30cm) painted dial, signed Simmons Coleman St., and with strike/silent above the XII, the 5-pillared movement with maintaining power and deadbeat escapement, 19thC, 79in (201cm).
$3,000-4,500

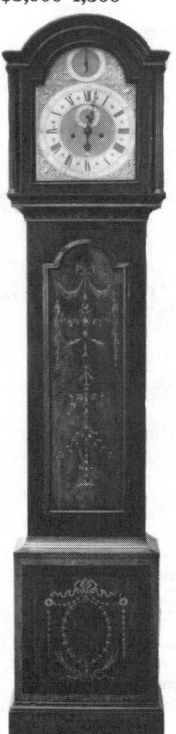

An Edwardian inlaid mahogany longcase clock, with 8-day movement, brass dial and silvered chapter ring inscribed Jabez Stock, Whitechapel, London, the case crossbanded with satinwood and decorated with ribbons, swags and harebells, 86in (219cm).
$2,250-3,000

A mahogany striking longcase clock, with 8-day movement, 3 original brass eagle and ball finials, with key, by John Smith, Chester, c1790, 93in (236cm).
$2,250-3,500

A North Country, Cheshire, 8-day grandfather clock, with burr walnut/pollard oak case with feathered fruitwood crossbanding, with engraved circular silver boss with eagle, Tempus Fugit, striking movement with countwheel, with key, maker Gabriel Smith, c1735, 20in (50cm) wide.
$13,500-17,500

A Georgian mahogany longcase clock, with 3-train movement and anchor escapement, quarter chiming on 8 bells, the brass dial with silvered chapter and Whittington/Cambridge tune selection ring in the arch, silvered plaque in the later centre, signed Wm. Webster, Exchange Alley, London, some alterations, 91in (231cm).
$2,250-3,500

A George II black and gold lacquer striking longcase clock, with 8-day movement, brass and silvered dial, subsidiary seconds hand and date aperture, cast brass urn scroll corner spandrels, the arch with a plate inscribed Wm. Stapleton, London, flanked by dolphin spandrels, c1730, 96in (244cm).
$10,500-14,000

A walnut longcase clock, by Marm'd Storr, 18thC.
$4,000-5,500

A longcase clock by Stephenson, Congleton, with 8-day chiming movement, brass and ormolu decorated dial, 85in (216cm).
$5,500-7,000

A mahogany longcase clock, with subsidiary seconds dial and date aperture, 8-day strike, maker Stockell & Stuart, Newcastle, 1779 engraved on a circular plate, 88in (224cm).
$1,500-2,600

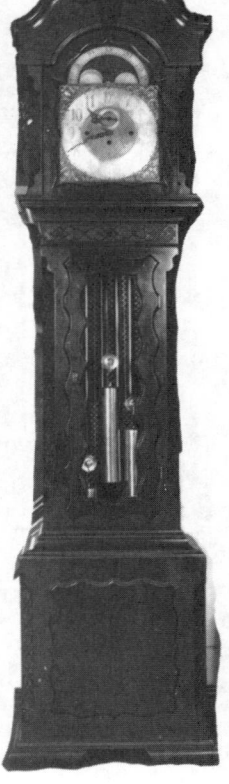

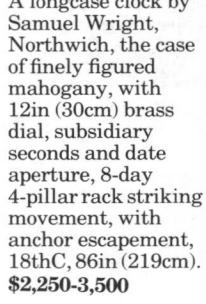

A George III mahogany longcase clock, the 12in (30cm) brass dial with brass chapter ring, subsidiary seconds, signed Rich Winch, Hackney, strike/silent in the arch, the 5-pillared movement with anchor escapement, 97in (246cm).
$3,000-4,500

A mahogany and marquetry longcase clock, with glazed face and later chapter ring with seconds hand, strike/silent, Westminster/Whittington chimes, the top with painted lunar calendar, 101in (256.5cm).
$5,500-7,000

An Edwardian mahogany longcase clock, with 12in (30cm) brass dial, substantial 8-day 3-train quarter striking movement constructed to regulator standards, with deadbeat escapement, maintaining power, striking on 5 gongs, with 2 strike/silent alternatives, triple brass cased weights and brass faced pendulum, 100in (250cm).
$6,000-9,000

A longcase clock by Samuel Wright, Northwich, the case of finely figured mahogany, with 12in (30cm) brass dial, subsidiary seconds and date aperture, 8-day 4-pillar rack striking movement, with anchor escapement, 18thC, 86in (219cm).
$2,250-3,500

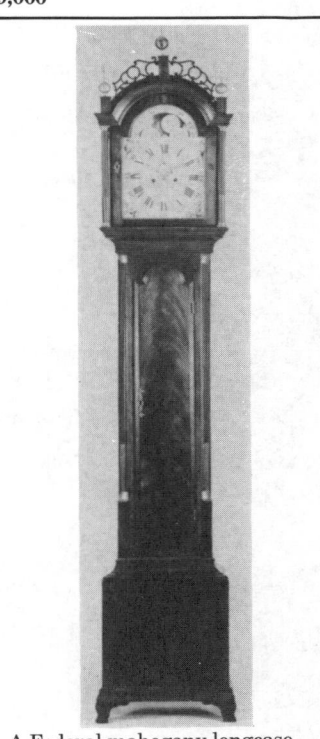

A miniature Continental painted longcase clock, with coffered hood above applied cove moulding over an arched glazed door on an inlaid waisted case, flanked by patterned inlay on a bombé base, with French feet, late 18th/early 19thC, 17in (42.5cm) high.
$600-700

An American pine longcase clock, with painted wood dial, Lancaster County, PA, 91in (231cm).
$1,000-1,500

A Federal mahogany longcase clock, dial signed Aaron Willard, the case Massachusetts, c1800, bearing label of Aaron Willard, Roxbury, dial repainted, other restorations, 103in (262cm).
$10,000-12,000

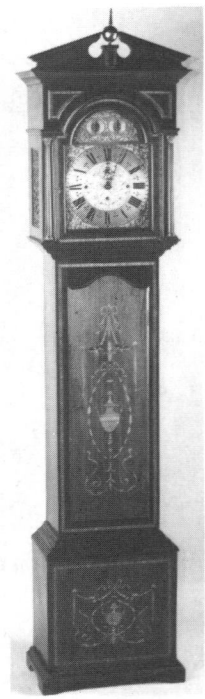

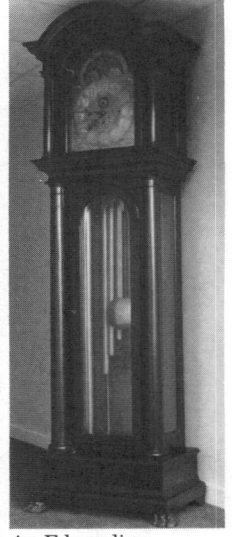

A Scottish mahogany longcase clock, with 8-day movement, painted dial, by Winter Lang & Co Glasgow, c1840, 92in (234cm).
$2,500-3,500

An Edwardian longcase clock in marquetry inlaid mahogany case, with 8-day movement, the arched brass dial with silvered chapter and playing 2 musical airs.
$4,000-5,500

A Continental mahogany longcase clock, the 11in (29cm) brass dial with subsidiary seconds and date aperture, with a monogrammed cartouche in the arch, the 5-pillared movement with anchor escapement, 18thC, 103in (262cm).
$2,250-3,500

An Edwardian 9-tube 3-train chiming longcase clock, with brass filigree arched lunar dial and pillared case.
$4,000-5,500

A Dutch walnut longcase clock, with 8-day movement, moon in the arch, subsidiary dial for seconds, calendar aperture and alarm, Dutch striking, c1740, 93in (236cm).
$9,000-12,000

An Edwardian inlaid mahogany musical longcase clock, the brass face with silvered chapter ring showing moon phases, subsidiary seconds and month dials, 8-day quarter striking movement with Westminster chimes on 5 gongs, the movement by Winterhalder & Hofmeir, Nestad, Baden, Germany, 94in (238cm).
$5,500-7,000

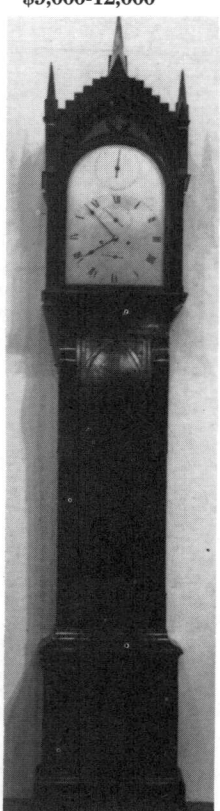

A late George III mahogany longcase clock.
$1,500-2,600

An Edwardian oak longcase clock with glass panel door, 8-day chiming movement on 8 bells and 5 gongs, with brass dial.
$3,000-4,500

A black lacquer longcase clock by Thorogood, London, with silvered dial, strike/silent in the arch, in original lacquered pine case, with original finials, c1780, 97in (246cm).
$3,000-4,000

An 8-day mahogany longcase clock, with subsidiary dial for calendar and seconds, original glass fret and wood rod pendulum, by I Thwaites, London, 1802, 98in (250cm).
$10,500-14,000

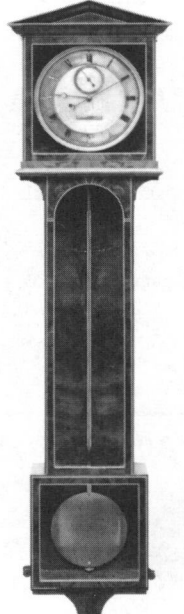

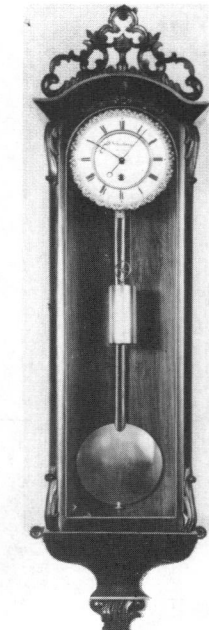

A dwarf 2-weight Vienna regulator, in walnut, with pull repeat, c1840, 35in (89cm).
$1,500-2,600

An 8-day 2-train Vienna wall regulator, striking the hours and half-hours on a gong, in walnut case, c1885, 53in (135cm).
$1,000-1,400

A single weight Vienna regulator wall clock, by Gustav Becker, German, c1875, 48in (122cm).
$750-1,000

A 2-weight Vienna regulator wall clock, with ivory dial and gong strike, German, c1890, 48in (122cm).
$800-1,200

A month going lantern clock of the Biedermeier period, with metal dial with engine-turned bezel and centre, steel shafted pendulum, signed Carl Zuchy in Prague, 43in (109cm).
$18,000-24,000

A small Biedermeier regulator, in rosewood case with stringing, by W Schönberger in Wien, 2-piece dial with piecrust bezel and wood rod pendulum, 32in (81cm).
$5,500-7,000

A single weight Vienna regulator wall clock, in ebonised case, German, c1880, 52in (132cm).
$600-900

Clocks – Bracket

A Regency mahogany striking bracket clock, with painted dial signed Collett Chelsea, the movement with anchor escapement, strike on bell, signed and border engraved backplate, 15½in (39cm).
$1,500-2,600

A small mahogany bracket clock, inlaid with brass, with single fusee and 8-day movement, by Ashley & Sons, Clerkenwell, c1860, 11in (29cm).
$700-900

A Charles II ebonised timepiece alarm, with pull quarter repeat, by William Cattell, London, the fusee movement (now wire lines) with knife edge verge escapement, pull wind alarm and pump action quarter repeat, the backplate tulip engraved and signed William Cattell Londini Fecit, some restoration, 13½in (34cm).
$6,000-9,000

A 2-weight Vienna regulator wall clock, striking on a gong, German, c1880.
$800-1,200

A 2-weight Vienna regulator wall clock in a walnut case, rack striking, German, c1880, 50in (127cm).
$800-1,200

HINTS TO DATING BRACKET CLOCKS

Dials

Square dial	to c1770	pre-George III
Broken arch dial	from c1720	George I or later
Round/painted/silvered	from c1760	George III or later

Case finish

Ebony veneer	from c1660 to c1850	Carolean to mid-Victorian
Walnut	from c1670 to c1870	Carolean to Victorian
Marquetry	from c1680 to c1740	Carolean to early Georgian
Rosewood	from c1790	from mid-Georgian
Lacquered	from c1700 to c1760	Queen Anne to early Georgian
Mahogany	from c1730	from early Georgian

A rare Eureka electric striking clock, signed Eureka Clock Co. Ltd. London Pat.No.14614-1906 No.196 above the regulation 'star' with timing screws, striking on a gong, ivorine annular chapter ring, on wood base for the battery, not now present, 11in (28cm) overall.
$3,000-4,500

A George III period mahogany bracket clock, with brass handle, the 8-day striking movement chiming on 8 bells, with pull repeat, inscribed John Drury, London, 21½in (54cm) high including handle.
$3,000-4,500

A Georgian bracket clock in ebonised case, with 8-day fusee movement, verge escapement and brass arch dial, by Felix Barnet, Westminster.
$2,250-3,500

A Georgian mahogany bracket clock, with 8-day striking movement and silvered arch dial, by Harris, London.
$1,300-1,800

A Regency bracket clock, by James McCabe, Royal Exchange, London, with double fusee movement.
$2,250-3,500

A mahogany cased bracket clock, by Frodsham, Gracechurch Street, London, with engraved backplate and 8-day strike, with pull cord hour repeat, 19thC, 18in (46cm).
$1,500-2,600

A Regency mahogany bracket clock by Vincent, Bath, with double fusee movement.
$1,500-2,600

A George II mahogany striking bracket clock, by Ellicott, London, with brass handle, engraved silvered dial with strike/silent lever top left and signed in the bottom corners, the twin fusee movement (now wire lines) with signed rococo-engraved backplate and now converted to anchor escapement, 16in (41cm).
$4,000-5,500

A Regency brass inlaid chiming bracket clock, by Frodsham, Gracechurch St, London, the painted dial with chime/silent aperture, 8-day striking movement with 9 bells and signed again by the maker on the backplate, 20in (51cm).
$1,500-2,600

A Queen Anne ebonised timepiece bracket clock, signed Fromanteel London, with brass handle, the dial with false pendulum aperture, silvered chapter ring, fusee movement (now wire line), with latches to the dial feet and 5-ringed pillars, pull quarter repeat and rebuilt verge escapement, restorations, 14in (36cm).
$3,000-4,500

A 'silent verge' mahogany bracket clock, with 5-pillar repeating movement, signed Thomas Harrison, Liverpool, the re-silvered dial with pierced blued steel hands and signed Thos. & Finney Harrison, Liverpool, 18in (46cm).
$1,500-2,600

A George II mahogany striking bracket clock, with brass handle, the dial signed William Gough London on a silvered sector plaque, with false pendulum and calendar apertures, silvered chapter ring, scroll spandrels and strike/silent ring in the arch, twin fusee movement, now converted to anchor escapement, 18½in (47cm).
$4,000-5,500

An ebonised quarter repeating bracket timepiece, the movement now with anchor escapement, signed on a silvered plaque Ben.Huntsman, Doncaster, 19½in (49cm).
$1,500-2,600

A mahogany and brass inlaid bracket clock, with enamelled dial signed James McCabe, London, 2088, the twin fusee movement with anchor escapement, shaped plates and engraved border, signed in a cartouche, 19thC, 15½in (40cm).
$1,500-2,600

An early George III ebonised striking bracket clock, engraved silvered dial signed Sam. Toulmin Strand London, with false pendulum and calendar apertures, twin fusee movement (now wire lines), pull quarter repeat, now converted to anchor escapement, some alterations, 18½in (47cm).
$1,500-2,600

A mid-Georgian ebonised striking bracket clock, the dial signed Stepn. Rimbault London, with strike/silent in the arch, twin fusee movement (now wire lines), with rebuilt verge escapement and pull quarter repeat, possibly associated case, 19½in (49.5cm).
$3,000-4,000

A rosewood bracket clock by Thos Richards of London, with lion ring handles and thistle mount, 19thC.
$700-900

A Regency mahogany bracket clock, with 8-day double fusee movement, bearing makers name John Rigby, London.
$900-1,300

A bracket clock by Nicolls, London, in polished fruitwood case, with single fusee movement, brass frets, signed on the backplate, c1820, 15½in (39cm).
$1,500-2,600

A small mahogany bracket clock, by F Job, London, the case with brass inlay, striking on a bell, repeater, c1820, with later pendulum, 10in (25cm).
$4,000-5,500

An ebonised repeating bracket clock, with automata, by Robert Henderson, 18thC.
$5,500-7,000

A George II ebonised striking bracket clock with brass handle, the dial signed Thos. Shipman London on a silvered arc, with false pendulum and calendar apertures, the twin fusee movement with verge escapement, trip repeat and engraved backplate, 21in (53cm).
$3,000-4,500

A bracket clock in rosewood case, with double fusee movement and anchor escapement, by Stanley of 41 Princes St, Leicester Square, c1870, 14in (36cm).
$1,500-2,600

An Edwardian chiming bracket clock, with mahogany case, chime/silent, slow and fast regulator, 12in (30cm).
$250-350

An Austrian giltwood petite sonnerie bracket clock, with 3-train repeating movement, anchor escapement, silk suspension and striking on 2 bells, with gilt brass dial engraved overall with scrolls, silvered chapter ring, alarm setting disc, pierced blued steel hands and signed Conrad Vogt, 26½in (67cm).
$1,500-2,600

A George III ebonised miniature striking bracket clock, with gilt metal mouldings, signed Williams 168 Shoreditch, on Arabic enamel chapter disc, with strike/silent disc in the arch, twin chain fusee movement with anchor escapement and lightly engraved backplate with monogram J.W., 14½in (37cm).
$5,500-7,000

An ebony veneered quarter repeating bracket clock, the 2-train fusee movement with verge escapement, signed Jos. Windmills, London, restored, 18in (46cm).
$7,500-10,500

A French ormolu mounted Boulle bracket clock in Louis XV style, with striking movement.
$1,200-1,600

An Austrian ebonised quarter striking bracket clock, the dial with false pendulum, brass chapter ring and Schlagt/Nicht Schlagt ring in the arch, triple going barrel movement with hour bell and quarter bell, verge escapement and engraved backplate, 18thC, 12in (30cm).
$2,500-3,500

A Continental tortoiseshell bracket timepiece, the 6½in (16cm) dial with false pendulum, silvered chapter ring, the tapered narrow movement with fusee and verge escapement, some alterations, c1700, 16in (41cm).
$2,500-3,500

Clocks – Carriage

A French gilt brass carriage clock, the lever movement with grande sonnerie striking on 2 gongs, with the Drocourt trademark on the backplate numbered 13871, the enamel dial signed for J.F. Bautte, Geneve, 19thC, 7in (17cm).
$4,000-5,500

A French carriage clock, by Brevetee, with grande sonnerie striking 8-day movement, with alarm, in gilded case, c1880, 9in (23cm).
$2,500-3,500

A gilt metal striking carriage clock for the Chinese market, with strike/repeat and alarm on bell, enamel dial with sweep centre seconds, early style gorge case, stamp of Japy Frères, 6in (15cm).
$1,000-1,400

A French brass carriage clock, the 2-train movement with anchor escapement, gong striking, repeating at will, and stamped L.F. in a shield, 7in (18.5cm).
$750-1,000

The initials L.F. are those of Louis Fernier of Besançon and Paris.

A French gilt brass carriage clock, the lever movement striking on a gong, with push repeat, bearing the Drocourt trademark and signed for Klaftenberger, Paris, 12762, in a numbered one-piece case, 19thC, 6½in (17cm).
$750-1,000

A French brass carriage clock, the lever movement striking on a bell and signed on the backplate for Ollivant & Botsford, Paris & Manchester, in one-piece case, 19thC, 6½in (17cm).
$750-1,000

A gilt metal striking oval carriage clock, with uncut bimetallic balance to silvered lever platform, strike/repeat on gong, enamel dial, 5½in (14cm).
$1,000-1,400

A brass cased quarter striking carriage clock, the movement with lever platform, strike/grande sonnerie repeat and alarm on gongs, the backplate signed L. Leroy & Cie, with alarm setting disc, the silvered dial with signature at base, with leather travelling case, 6in (15cm).
$1,500-2,600

A French brass carriage clock, the movement with later lever escapement, gong striking and stamped R. & Co. Paris, 6in (16cm).
$450-700

An English striking carriage clock, the movement with lever platform, free sprung overcoiled blued spring, split bimetallic balance, fusee and chain, strike on gong, the mottled plates signed Chas. Frodsham 115 New Bond St W.No.2188, 9in (23cm).
$9,000-12,000

A brass calendar and moon phase carriage timepiece, the movement with later lever escapement, stamped H.B. and numbered 260, the white enamel dial with inner ring for days of the week and subsidiary dials for month and date, 6in (16cm).
$2,250-3,000

A gilt metal cased carriage clock, the movement with backplate and gilt metal dial inscribed James McCabe, Cornhill, London, 19thC, 7in (17cm).
$4,000-5,500

A brass carriage clock, the movement with later lever escapement, gong striking and repeating at will, together with outer carrying case, 7in (18cm).
$900-1,300

A gilt metal grande sonnerie oval carriage clock, with uncut bimetallic balance to lever platform, alarm and strike/repeat on 2 gongs, 6in (16cm).
$4,000-5,500

The handle has an unusual peg to one side to prevent it from depressing the repeat button when swung forward.

A small French brass carriage timepiece, the lever movement with enamel dial signed Le Roy & Fils, 4in (9.5cm).
$750-1,000

A silver plated striking carriage clock, with split compensated balance to gilt lever platform, strike/repeat on gong, in rococo revival case, 6in (16cm).
$1,000-1,400

A brass grande sonnerie carriage clock, with split compensated balance to lever platform, 6in (15cm).
$1,000-1,400

A gilt metal striking carriage clock with centre seconds, for the Chinese market, with strike on bell, slight corner chips and cracks to dial, 6in (15cm).
$1,200-1,600

A gilt brass quarter striking carriage clock, with cut bimetallic balance to lever platform, strike/repeat and alarm on 2 gongs, 6in (15cm).
$900-1,300

A brass carriage clock, with French movement and alarm.
$450-600

A gilt metal striking carriage clock, with uncut bimetallic balance to lever platform, strike/repeat on gong, 6½in (17cm).
$750-1,000

A French gilt brass carriage clock, the lever movement striking on a gong, with push repeat, numbered 597, 19thC, 6in (15cm), with travelling case.
$600-900

A small silver carriage clock on bun feet, engraved with initials and the date 1917, marks indistinct, probably Birmingham 1912, 3½in (9cm).
$600-900

A French carriage clock, with original lever escapement and case, 8-day repeater alarm movement.
$700-900

A French petite sonnerie carriage clock, the case applied with emblematic figures to the sides, the door with winding hole shutter, numbered 3695, late 19thC, 6in (15cm).
$3,000-4,500

A French carriage clock in gilded brass case, with 8-day movement, hourly and half-hourly striking on a gong, 5in (13cm).
$600-900

A French brass carriage clock with lever movement, striking on a gong with alarm and push repeat, the enamel alarm set on the backplate and numbered 1803, 19thC, 7½in (19cm).
$1,500-2,600

Clocks – Mantel

An unusual French carriage clock, mid-19thC.
$750-1,000

A miniature French carriage clock, with porcelain painted enamel dial, 8-day movement, c1890, 3in (8cm).
$900-1,300

An Empire ormolu mantel clock, the dial signed F. B. Adams, London, 17in (43cm).
$1,500-2,600

A Louis XVI ormolu mounted marble mantel clock, the enamel dial signed Hartingue a Paris, 21in (53cm) wide.
$6,000-8,000

Claude François Hartingue active c1773.

A Victorian rosewood 4-glass mantel clock, the dial signed Ashdown Finchlake, timepiece fusee movement with anchor escapement and pendulum securing nut, 10in (25.5cm).
$900-1,300

A George III gilt metal, alabaster and white marble mantel clock, the engraved backplate signed J. Burrows, Goodge Street, London, 19in (48cm).
$750-1,000

A porcelain mounted ormolu mantel clock, with porcelain dial decorated with enamel, the backplate signed Ducasse Claveau & Co., Paris, 19½in (49cm).
$3,000-4,500

A French ormolu and champlevé enamel mantel clock, the gilt dial signed for Howell & James, 19thC, 17in (43cm).
$1,000-1,400

An ormolu and crystal mantel clock, the glazed enamelled dial signed Cristalleries de Baccarat, 17in (43cm).
$2,500-3,500

An electric mantel timepiece, the movement with circular enamel dial signed Dollond, London, with mirrored back, 17½in (44cm).
$1,000-1,400

A French ormolu and porcelain mantel clock, the enamel dial signed Grohe A Paris, the signed movement with silk suspension, 19thC, 11in (28cm).
$800-1,200

An early Victorian mantel clock, with 3½in (9cm) silvered dial signed Horatio Finer, Holborn, London, the 8-day movement with chain fusee going train and stopwork and anchor escapement, with pendulum, 10in (25.5cm).
$800-1,200

A French bronze mantel clock, movement by Lenoir, Paris, c1850, 20in (50cm).
$2,250-3,000

A Louis XVI ormolu mantel clock, the dial signed Imbert L'aine a Paris, the striking movement similarly signed, the case with Cupid holding an oval medallion of Henry IV, 18½in (47cm).
$4,000-5,500

Jean Gabriel Imbert, maître 1772-1789.

A French oval 4-glass and brass mantel clock, the movement with Brocot type suspension, mercurial pendulum and bearing the trade stamp of S. Marti, 11½in (28cm).
$600-900

A Federal mahogany shelf clock, the hinged door opening to a kidney-shaped white painted dial with gilt spandrels, above a box base on flared French feet, lacking pediment, Massachusetts, c1800, 31in (77cm).
$8,000-9,000

A French gilt brass mantel clock, the enamel dial with visible escapement, signed Le Roy & Fils, the movement with twin glass mercury pendulum, 19thC, 14in (35.5cm).
$800-1,200

An Empire ormolu mantel clock with enamel dial, signed Le Roy Hr du Roi a Paris, 14½in (36.5cm).
$1,200-1,600

A silvered bronze and ormolu mantel clock, the dial with backplate signed Le Roy a Paris, now set on a mahogany 2-tune musical base with bowed ends, mid-19thC, 26½in (65cm).
$1,500-2,600

An Empire ormolu mantel clock, with steel dial signed Le Roy & fils Hrs du roi, surmounted by a classical warrior grasping a parchment and with a helmet, 25in (63.5cm).
$1,500-2,600

A mid-Victorian burr walnut mantel clock of Gothic style, the dial signed Reid & Sons, Newcastle-on-Tyne, with strike/silent and chimes, 24in (61cm).
$2,250-3,000

A late Victorian walnut cased
mantel clock with gilt metal mounts.
$750-1,000

A bronze and gilt bronze mantel
clock, by Webster, Cornhill, London,
with 8-day movement and anchor
escapement, 19thC, 12in (30.5cm).
$3,000-4,500

A Victorian 3-dial, lunar,
barometer, mantel clock with 8-day
striking movement and exposed
escapement.
$600-900

A mahogany cased mantel clock,
inlaid with boxwood, with 8-day
movement and French cylinder
escapement, c1910, 7in (19cm).
$250-350

A French white marble and ormolu
mantel clock, the movement with
Brocot type suspension, stamped
Rollin a Paris, and bearing the trade
stamp of Vincenti, 14in (35.5cm).
$900-1,300

A large repeating mantel clock in
ebonised case, with 8-day brass
movement striking hours and
quarters on 9 bells, with ornate
engraved backplate, 19thC, 30in
(76cm).
$2,250-3,500

An Edwardian inlaid mahogany
mantel clock, with 8-day striking
and chiming movement, the brass
face applied with foliate scroll
decoration and silvered dial, the
case with boxwood stringing inlay,
13in (33cm).
$300-500

A William IV mahogany 4-glass
mantel clock, by W J Thomas, New
Road, London, with twin fusee
5-pillar 8-day movement with back
mounted bell, 12½in (31.5cm).
$1,000-1,400

A mid-Victorian slate and marble
mantel clock, the dial flanked by 2
earlier thermometers, signed Paris
1838, with a lunar calendar and a
barometer beneath, on plinth base,
18in (46cm).
$1,500-2,600

A French brass and champlevé
enamel 4-glass clock, the 2-train
spring driven drum movement
striking on a gong, with mercury
compensated pendulum, late 19thC,
11in (28cm).
$1,000-1,400

A French ormolu and champlevé
enamel mantel clock, with circular
gilt chapter ring, 19thC, 9½in
(24cm).
$450-600

A French gilt brass and champlevé
enamel 4-glass mantel clock, 19thC,
10in (25cm).
$750-1,000

A brass and porcelain 8-day striking
mantel clock, under a glass dome.
$450-700

An Empire ormolu mantel clock, the
dial and movement contained in a
chariot with Minerva and
charioteer, 17in (43cm).
$3,000-4,500

A French gilt bronze mantel clock,
raised on brass ball feet, 15in (38cm).
$250-350

A gilt metal mantel clock, with
French 8-day striking movement,
early 19thC.
$750-1,000

A French striking mantel clock in
ormolu mounted case.
$150-250

A French brass and marble mantel
clock, with a figure of a Crusader,
with silk suspension, 8-day
movement, hourly and half-hourly
striking on the bell, 19in (48cm).
$750-1,000

A Black Forest quarter striking
clock, with blue floral enamel dial,
c1865, 21in (53cm).
$250-350

A mantel clock on marble base, the
clock face surmounted by bronzed
lovers.
$750-1,000

Clocks – Lantern

A rare lantern clock, with automata in the arch, with fruitwood pencil case and cow tail verge escapement, c1680, 79in (200cm).
$15,000-21,000

A Japanese brass lantern clock, the posted frame 30-hour iron movement with double foliot verge escapement, countwheel European strike and alarm on bell above, the dial with fixed black enamel chapter ring and single pierced hand on the central alarm disc, 11½in (28cm) excluding later wood stand.
$2,500-3,500

A brass lantern clock, with pendulum verge escapement, signed Stephen Tracy London on a button in the arch, 15in (38cm).
$1,500-2,600

Clocks – Skeleton

A skeleton clock with double fusee movement, striking on a gong, by B Russell, Norwich, c1870, 13in (33cm).
$1,300-1,800

A Victorian brass epicyclic skeleton clock with chain fusee movement and deadbeat escapement, the black slate base with plaque signed W. Wigston, Derby, No.51, W. Strutt Esq., Inv, 10in (25.5cm).
$5,500-7,000

A quarter chiming skeleton clock, the movement with anchor escapement, fusee and chain, chiming on 8 graduated bells, 21in (53.5cm).
$4,000-5,500

A brass steeple skeleton clock, with 8-day movement and passing hour strike, under a glass dome, 19thC.
$300-400

A brass skeleton clock, the 2-train fusee movement with anchor escapement, striking one on the half-hour on a bell, and the hours on a coiled steel gong, the later glazed mahogany case with drawer in the base, 29in (74cm).
$1,500-2,600

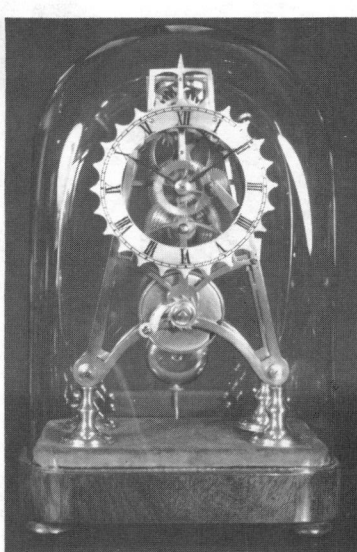

A single fusee skeleton clock on walnut base with glass dome, 12in (30.5cm).
$750-1,000

Clocks – Wall

An American walnut and floral marquetry drop dial wall clock, with circular white painted dial, 26½in (66cm) high.
$250-350

HINTS TO DATING WALL CLOCKS

Dials

Square	to c1755	George II or later
Broken arch	from c1720 to c1805	early to late Georgian
Painted/round	from c1740	George II or later
Silvered	from c1760	George III or later

Case finish

Ebony veneer	from c1690	to William and Mary
Marquetry	from c1680 to c1695	from Carolean to William and Mary
Mahogany	from c1740	from early Georgian
Oak	always	

A double fusee drop dial wall clock inlaid with brass, by Jas Fairey, Weymouth.
$750-1,000

A circular wall timepiece in mahogany case, with fusee movement, the white painted dial inscribed City Clock Co, 8 Cullum St, City, mid-19thC, 12½in (31.5cm) diam.
$300-400

A single fusee drop dial wall clock by Fox, Bournemouth.
$400-500

A Georgian mahogany wall timepiece, the 19in (48cm) diam painted wood dial signed Field, Bath, the 8-day 4-wheel movement with anchor escapement, restored, 43in (109cm).
$1,200-1,600

A giltwood ship's wall clock, the single going barrel movement with anchor escapement, 19thC, 30in (76cm).
$1,500-2,600

An Austrian Biedermeier mahogany quarter striking wall clock, with marquetry patera inlay, the enamel dial with crescent moon hands, 3-train movement, slightly distressed, striking on gongs, 41½in (105cm).
$3,000-4,000

An American walnut and marquetry drop dial wall clock, the circular white painted dial inscribed 'G.W. Harvey, 9 Market St. Wellington', 29in (72.5cm) high.
$100-200

A carved and gilded wall clock by Jacob Holmgren, Stockholm, early 19thC.
$1,500-2,600

A Georgian giltwood wall dial clock, the 14in (35.5cm) enamel painted dial signed Geo. Yonge, London, with regulation arc below XII, the timepiece fusee movement with tapered plates and anchor escapement with rise-and-fall regulation, 24in (61cm) diam.
$2,500-3,500

A drop dial wall clock in a mahogany case, with fusee movement, c1870.
$450-600

An 8-day single fusee drop dial nightwatchman's wall clock, by Tilley, Dorchester.
$300-400

An 8-day fusee wall clock, in a mahogany case, the circular cream painted dial inscribed Ganthony, 83 Cheapside, London.
$1,000-1,400

An Act of Parliament clock by Matthew Hill, Devonshire St.
$2,500-3,500

A drop dial wall clock in shaped case, with floral and mother-of-pearl inlaid panels, 19thC.
$400-500

A German wall clock in a walnut case, striking on a gong, with enamel dial, c1900, 26in (66cm).
$400-500

An American drop dial wall clock, the walnut case inlaid with Sorrento ware banding and floral marquetry decoration, the 8-day 2-train movement striking on a bell, late 19thC, 32in (80cm) high.
$100-150

Clocks – Garnitures

A French ormolu and porcelain clock garniture, the clock case surmounted by a twin-handled urn, applied with rams' heads, the enamel dial signed Lenoir a Paris, 20½in (52cm), with a matching pair of 3-branch candelabra, 19½in (48cm), 19thC.
$4,000-5,500

A French garniture de cheminée, comprising a Louis XVI style gilt brass mantel clock with white marble urn surmount, the 8-day movement half-hour striking on a bell, impressed and numbered Vincent, 2806, on the backplate, 12in (30.5cm), and a pair of matching 2-branch candelabra, 10½in (26cm), late 19thC.
$750-1,000

A French white marble and ormolu mounted lyre clock, the decorated enamel dial surrounded by the pendulum ring, 19thC, 16in (40.5cm).
$1,500-2,600

A French clock garniture for the Chinese market, the gilt dial with annular chapter ring 'oriental' Arabic numerals, the 8-day movement by Ad Mougin, in turquoise blue porcelain case, 14in (35.5cm), with 2-branch candelabra, 15½in (39cm).
$1,000-1,400

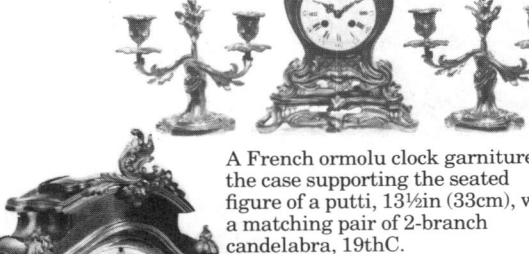

A French ormolu clock garniture, the case supporting the seated figure of a putti, 13½in (33cm), with a matching pair of 2-branch candelabra, 19thC.
$1,500-2,600

A French gilt brass composite clock garniture, comprising a mantel clock, with French movement striking on a gong, 16in (41cm), and a pair of 2-handled vases.
$750-1,000

A French clock garniture comprising mantel clock with 8-day chiming movement, the Sèvres porcelain dial painted with figures, the ormolu mounted turquoise porcelain case with urn and pineapple finials, on gilt wood base and ebonised stand, under glass dome, 19½in (49.5cm) overall, with 2 urns, the covers with pineapple finials and reversible candleholders, 9½in (23cm), 19thC.
$1,000-1,400

A French gilt metal and simulated malachite clock garniture.
$4,000-5,500

Clocks – Table

A French clock garniture, the clock with enamelled dial, 8-day movement striking on a bell, with lyre shaped bleu-de-roi porcelain frame with gilt metal mounts, 20in (51cm), with candelabra, 17in (43cm).
$2,250-3,500

A French ormolu and porcelain mounted 3-piece clock garniture.
$450-700

A spring driven vertical table clock, 18thC.
$9,000-12,000

A rare early English alarm table clock, the movement signed Eduardus, East Londini, possibly original barrel and fusee, but later going train, spring balance and regulation disc, lacking countwheel and striking hammer for the underslung bell, lacking one foot, 4in (10cm) diam of dial.
$10,500-14,000

A gilt brass table clock, the front with later chapter ring decorated with a female portrait, the back with countwheel indicating dial, and a male portrait, the sides showing a man in armour and his lady, the posted iron movement with steel fusees and wheels, converted to verge bob pendulum escapement and originally with alarm, now missing, 17thC, 6½in (17cm).
$5,500-7,000

Clocks – Miscellaneous

A Federal mahogany giltwood and églomisé banjo clock, with gilt lemon finial, the gilt and églomisé panel depicting 2 ships with flag and inscribed 'Hull', restoration to églomisé, Massachusetts, c1820, 40in (101.5cm) high.
$1,500-2,500

A rosewood table clock by Charles Frodsham, 19thC.
$15,000-21,000

Make the most of Miller's

Unless otherwise stated, any description which refers to 'a set' or 'a pair' includes a valuation for the entire set or the pair, even though the illustration may show only a single item.

A French 4-glass clock, striking on a gong, with mercury pendulum, c1900, 14in (35.5cm).
$900-1,300

A French striking ormolu cartel clock, by De Hemant, Paris.
$1,200-1,600

An ormolu strut clock, in the manner of Thomas Cole, the movement with lever escapement, with folding stand, silvered dial signed Hunt & Roskell, London, 5½in (14cm), with leather travelling case.
$1,500-2,600

A miniature lantern wall clock by Hemmings of Bicester, short duration and alarm, c1720, 9in (23cm).
$4,000-5,500

A German iron chamber clock of Gothic pattern, with posted frame for the 3 back-to-back trains, with verge and foliot escapement, countwheels for the quarter and hour strike on 2 bells, probably 17thC, 30in (76cm).
$6,000-9,000

A miniature wall clock, with painted dial, 30-hour movement, hourly strike on the bell, c1860, 8½in (21.5cm).
$250-350

An unusual Japanese rack clock, the circular gilt dial with pierced steel pointer and adjustable register, the movement with verge escapement and spring driven countwheel strike, powered by its own weight descending a vertical rack, the rack and stand missing, 19thC, 4in (10cm) diam.
$1,000-1,400

A miniature brass dial wall clock, 30-hour movement, c1860, 5in (13cm).
$450-600

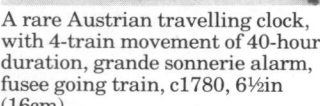

A rare Austrian travelling clock, with 4-train movement of 40-hour duration, grande sonnerie alarm, fusee going train, c1780, 6½in (16cm).
$3,000-4,000

A miniature Black Forest porcelain dial wall clock, 30-hour movement, c1860, 5in (13cm).
$450-600

A German oak novelty clock, with simulated fountain, c1890, 18in (46cm).
$450-700

A Germanic iron chamber clock, the posted frame 30-hour movement with fabricated wheels, anchor escapement and countwheel strike, lacking pendulum, 22in (56cm).
$5,500-7,000

A miniature skeleton clock, with calendar and alarm, c1850, 9in (23cm).
$1,000-1,400

A French clock in the Egyptian taste, with mirror base, c1900, 12½in (31cm).
$250-350

A brass Congreve rolling ball clock, the chain fusee train with 6-armed wheels within gabled pierced plates with annular silvered chapter ring to the front, on marble base, 16in (41cm) high overall.
$2,250-3,500

An ornamental miniature grandfather clock, with decorative enamel panelled front, 11in (29cm).
$150-250

An unusual Irish inlaid mahogany clock and pier table, the clock with 8-day striking movement, the whole inlaid with cherubs, foliate scrolls and mythological beasts, 88in (223cm).
$5,500-7,000

Watches

An 18ct gold hunter cased quarter split second watch by Huguonin Berthoud, 19thC.
$1,500-2,600

A platinum keyless lever dress watch by Cartier, the steel bar movement jewelled to the centre and signed Cartier Paris, with silvered dial, 4.5cm.
$2,250-3,500

A gilt metal and leather covered verge watch, the movement with square baluster pillars and pierced winged cock, inscribed Quare, London, 2567, with gilt champlevé dial, 6cm diam.
$750-1,000

An early gilt metal puritan oval verge watch, the movement signed Charles Whitwel, with 3-wheel train, fusee and chain, symmetrically pierced cock with stud and pin, steel ratchet and click, engraved border, simple dial with single hand, solid ring pendant, restorations, early 17thC, with boxwood outer case, crank key with later handle, 7.6cm over pendant.
$10,500-14,000

A gold pair cased pocket watch, the fusee movement with verge escapement, and with dust cover inscribed John Walker Newcastle-upon-Tyne 736, the inner gold case pierced and engraved, 18thC.
$800-1,200

An Austrian silver verge clockwatch with quarter repeat, signed Andre Hochenadel, Wienn Fecit 615 on the bridge cock movement with chain fusee for the going, resting barrel for the strike and pull wind quarter repeat, in fitted chamois and galloon lined tooled leather case, 12.3cm.
$7,500-10,500

A red enamel watch with pearl surround and diamond centre, c1880.
$1,200-1,600

Wristwatches

A Swiss 18ct gold watch and bracelet by Gubelin, c1950.
$1,500-2,600

A Swiss gold cased quarter repeating musical watch, the frosted and gilt movement with cylinder escapement, musical train playing on the hour or at will, quarter repeating on gongs, white enamel dial with gold serpentine hands, case engine-turned with reeded band, early 19thC, 5.8cm.
$5,500-7,000

A Swiss gilt metal and enamel verge watch, wound through Arabic enamel dial, case with paste-set bezels, the reverse enamelled with a mother and child, 5.4cm.
$750-1,000

A gentleman's bracelet watch by Cartier, the 'tank' model, with off-white dial, the case bearing factory numbers, on heavy flexible gold brickwork strap with 'D' fastener, 2.2cm wide.
$10,000-13,000

A gentleman's gold automatic bracelet watch by Cartier, the 'tank' model, with white dial, in gold case with sapphire winding crown, leather strap.
$1,500-2,600

A gentleman's yellow gold bracelet watch by Cartier, with white dial, the case signed Delano, with fawn leather strap and Piaget 'D' bracelet.
$1,500-2,600

A gentleman's gold calendar wristwatch, nickel plated 15 jewel movement, the silvered dial signed Movado, with raised Arabic chapters, concentric calendar ring and apertures.
$700-900

A white gold 'retro' buckle-shaped watch by Cartier, on Jaeger Le Coultre's patent, signed on the silvered dial, in white gold case with looped lugs and leather strap, 1.6cm diam.
$900-1,300

An 18ct Swiss automatic wristwatch by Patek Philippe, c1960.
$3,000-4,000

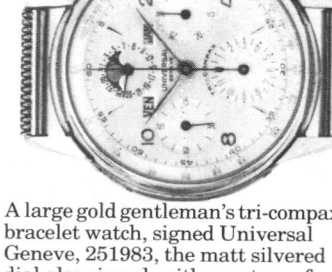

A large gold gentleman's tri-compax bracelet watch, signed Universal Geneve, 251983, the matt silvered dial also signed, with apertures for week-day and month, subsidiary date ring, fly back sweep centre seconds with 30-minute recording at 3 o'clock, 12 hour recording ring at 6 o'clock and continuous seconds at 9 o'clock, outer tachometric scale, gold chapters and hands, case plain, 18ct with factory marks, 3.7cm diam, on heavy 18ct gold woven mesh bracelet.
$4,000-5,500

A gold gentleman's bracelet watch with chronograph, by Vacheron & Constantin, Geneve, 437415, the matt silvered dial also signed with gold chapter bars, fly back sweep centre seconds hand, with outer tachometric scale, subsidiary minute recording ring at 3 o'clock and continuous seconds at 9 o'clock, in original polished gold case with factory marks and numbers, 3.6cm diam.
$6,000-9,000

A gentleman's gold chronograph bracelet watch by Rolex, signed on the nickel finished and jewelled movement, the silvered dial with gold chapter bars, outer tachometric scales, continuous seconds at 9 o'clock and minute recording at 3 o'clock, with fly back sweep centre seconds, case plain 18ct with factory marks and numbered 50691/3484, 3.2cm wide.
$5,500-7,000

A 9ct gold Swiss Rolex oyster watch, c1930.
$1,500-2,600

Barometers
Stick

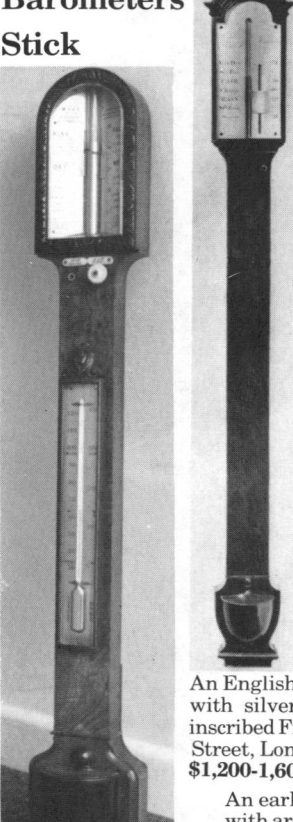

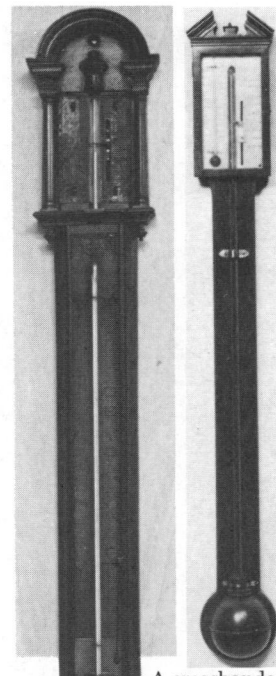

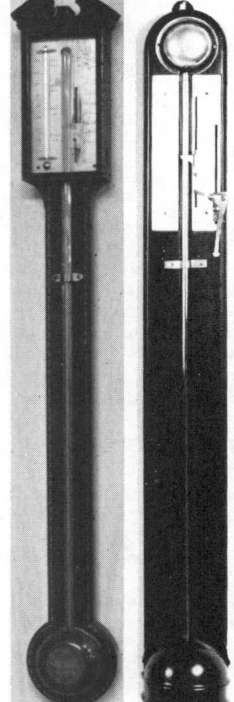

A Georgian mahogany stick barometer, with silvered and engraved dial bearing makers name, Joseph Tory & Co., London.
$1,000-1,400

An English barometer, with silvered dial, inscribed Fraser, Bond Street, London, c1800.
$1,200-1,600

An early walnut stick barometer with architectural top, with silvered and engraved dial plates, John Patrick, Old Bailey, London.
$5,500-7,000

A crossbanded mahogany stick barometer, the silvered scale signed Sharp, Faversham, 19thC, 38in (97cm).
$450-700

A Georgian mahogany stick barometer, the silvered brass plate signed J. Search, London, fitted with brass cantilever fine adjustment, the case with moulded edge, domed cistern cover, brass cap and rounded top, 38in (96.5cm).
$3,000-4,500

A stick barometer with thermometer in figured walnut, with silvered dial plates, by W Cox, Devonport, Plymouth, 19thC.
$800-1,200

Wheel

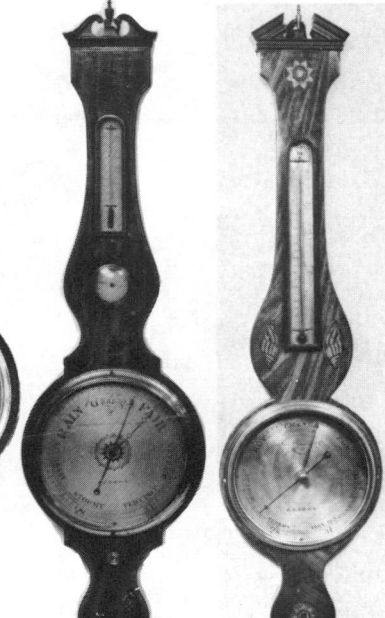

Miller's price ranges

The price ranges reflect what one should expect to pay for an item in similar condition to that illustrated. If you're selling you may be offered 30% less. Dealers have to make a profit too! However if the market has moved upwards, or your piece is a particularly good example – you could be offered more.

An inlaid mahogany wheel barometer, the dial signed P. Donegan & Co., Fecit, London, with inset spirit thermometer, 38½in (97.5cm).
$450-600

A rosewood wheel barometer, with 5in (12.5cm) silvered dial, the level signed J. Cetta, Stroudwater, bowfront thermometer and hygrometer, inlaid with mother-of-pearl, late 19thC, 37in (94.5cm).
$1,300-1,800

A mahogany wheel ▶ barometer with 10in (25.5cm) silvered dial signed Lione & Somalvico, 14 Brook Strt. Holbn. London, 19thC, 44in (111.5cm).
$800-1,200

A Sheraton mahogany shell wheel barometer, the silver dial signed Lione, Somalvico & Co., No.125 Holbn Hill, London, the case inlaid with boxwood and ebony stringing, mounted with Fahrenheit scale thermometer, restored, c1805, 39½in (100cm).
$450-700

Chronometers

An 18ct gold pocket chronometer, with Earnshaw type spring detent escapement, freesprung compensated balance, helical spring and diamond endstone, signed Barraud & Lund, Cornhill, London, $\frac{2}{847}$, 5.2cm diam.
$7,500-10,500

A silver gilt deck chronometer, with Earnshaw type spring detent escapement, freesprung compensated balance and helical spring, signed Widenham, London, No.1149, the case marked London 1829, 6.2cm diam, with original box, early 19thC.
$4,000-5,500

A banjo barometer with silvered and engraved dial, the case decorated with inlaid mother-of-pearl.
$300-400

A 2-day marine chronometer, No.7715, by Kelvin & James White Ltd, Glasgow, with auxiliary compensation, in brass case, gimballed in mahogany carrying case, 7in (18cm) square, bezel 5in (12.5cm) diam.
$1,500-2,600

A satinwood wheel barometer, the silvered dial signed D. Ortelly & Co. Bath, mounted with Fahrenheit scale thermometer and hygrometer, c1800, 39in (99cm).
$750-1,000

Miscellaneous

A brass thermobarograph, the drum rotating by clockwork, the base with 2 inset ink bottles of green and blue ink, the whole contained in a bevel glazed oak case, with circular aperture for equalising internal and external temperatures, the outset moulded base with drawer in the frieze containing spare charts, 14in (36cm).
$450-600

A mahogany cased sympiesometer signed Stebbing, Southampton, the tube flanked by thermometer in a moulded case, tube broken, 23½in (59cm).
$750-1,000

A rare Francis Watkins mahogany angle tube 'Perpetual Regulation of Time' barometer, with brass 28in (71cm) to 31in (78.5cm) scale, magnified 6½ times, 19½in (49cm) long, signed F. Watkins, London, brass Fahrenheit scale thermometer, and printed paper calendar and tables for 1753 to 1852, the case with boxwood and ebony stringing, hygrometer and gadrooned cistern cover, lacks one cistern cover and finials, c1760, 38½in (98cm) high.
$13,500-17,500

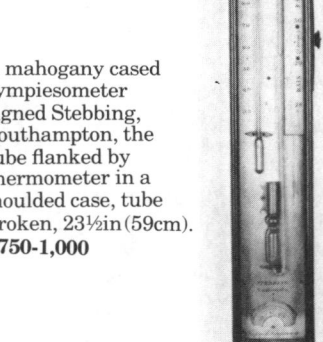

A lacquered and anodised brass barograph with dial, retailed by Harrods Ltd, with instructions, 14½in (37cm) wide.
$600-900

A combined oval brass framed timepiece and barometer, centred by a thermometer scale, raised on an onyx base, 6½in (16cm).
$300-400

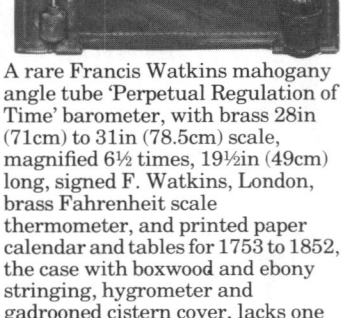

Scientific Instruments

Dials

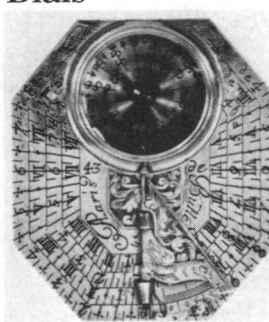

A brass sundial signed W & S Jones, 30 Holborn, London, calculated for latitude 52° 9′ 30″, Pentlow Rectory, the centre with engraved star to the cardinal points and with a plain gnomon, 10in (25.5cm) diam.
$400-500

A lacquered and silvered brass universal equinoctial dial, 2½in (6cm) diam, the silvered compass box with blued needle, the hinged equinoctial ring signed Bleuler, London, with spring-loaded gnomon and folding latitude arc, in case, late 18thC, 3in (7.5cm) wide.
$600-900

A French silver Butterfield dial, signed Butterfield A Paris, the base engraved with the names and latitudes of 27 continental cities and towns, the upper surface inset with a compass with blued steel needle, in case, 18thC, 2½in (6cm) long.
$1,200-1,600

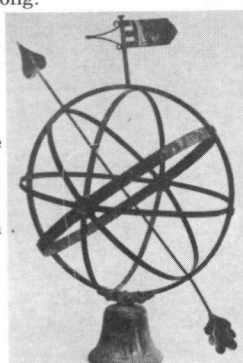

A garden sundial, the gnomon in the form of an arrow, the lower ring set within the equatorial ring, surmounted by a weather vane and fixed to a bell mounting, 19thC, 18in (46cm).
$600-900

A bronze heliochronometer by Pilkington & Gibbs Ltd, Preston & London, with sights, calendar and hour rings, on a turned stand, 9in (23cm) diam.
$450-700

A gilt brass universal equinoctial dial, signed J.N. Hölderich, Augsburg, inset with a compass, engraved with the signature and the latitudes of 6 European cities, the silvered hour ring with spring-loaded gnomon, with hinged latitude arc in a leather case, 18thC, 3in (8cm) square.
$600-900

Globes

A 'Cary's pocket globe, agreeable to the latest Discoveries, pubd by J & W Cary, Strand, London, April. 1791', the continents coloured, in case, the interior applied with 'A Table of Latitudes & Longitudes of Places not given on this Globe', and a small map of 'The World as Known in Caesar's time agreeable to D'Auville', late 18thC, 3in (7.5cm).
$3,000-4,000

A silvered brass equinoctial compass dial, unsigned, the horizontal plate engraved with the latitude of 6 continental capitals, mounted with a latitude arc, hour ring and spring loaded pin gnomon, in mahogany case, 19thC, 4in (10cm) wide.
$300-500

A terrestrial globe by S S Edkins
Son in Law, 12in (30.5cm) globe.
$1,000-1,400

A Malby's terrestrial globe on
original mahogany stand, dated
January 1st 1851.
$4,000-5,500

A star globe signed 'The Hudson
Star Globe, H. Hughes & Son Ltd.,
London, 1920, Serial No. 4093', with
4 altitude pointer stowed in lid,
contained in wooden case, 10½in
(27cm) square.
$450-700

A 12in (31.5cm) terrestrial globe by
G Thomas 44, Rue N.D. de Champs,
Paris, the coloured paper gores
printed with the continents,
currents, tracks of famous
navigators and explorers and other
relevant information, mounted on a
cast iron stand, late 19thC.
$450-700

Surveying

A brass mounted sextant, in
mahogany case.
$400-500

Telescopes

A brass 2⅝in (7cm) four-draw
telescope with leather covered outer
tube signed Dollond, London, the
eye piece incorporating shades, with
a dust cap and brass tripod, 19thC.
$450-600

A surveyor's brass level, the
telescope with rack and pinion
focusing, the compass with silvered
dial signed Troughton & Simms,
London, in the original mahogany
case, 19thC, 25in (63cm) wide, with
a tripod.
$600-900

A lacquered brass 3in (7.5cm)
refracting telescope, signed Wray,
London, with 39½in (100cm) long
body tube, mounted on a horizontal
plate with 3-screw adjustment and
bubble level, a folding mahogany
tripod with 2 Newtonian eye pieces
and 3 supplementary eyepieces in 2
fitted pine cases, 19thC.
$2,250-3,500

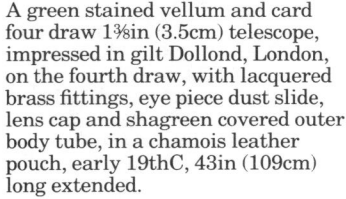

A green stained vellum and card
four draw 1⅜in (3.5cm) telescope,
impressed in gilt Dollond, London,
on the fourth draw, with lacquered
brass fittings, eye piece dust slide,
lens cap and shagreen covered outer
body tube, in a chamois leather
pouch, early 19thC, 43in (109cm)
long extended.
$3,000-4,000

A black enamelled brass plane table
alidade sighting telescope, by
W Ottway & Co Ltd, Ealing, folding
to fit in a plush lined leather case,
16in (40cm) wide, and 2 surveyor's
chains.
$400-500

Microscopes

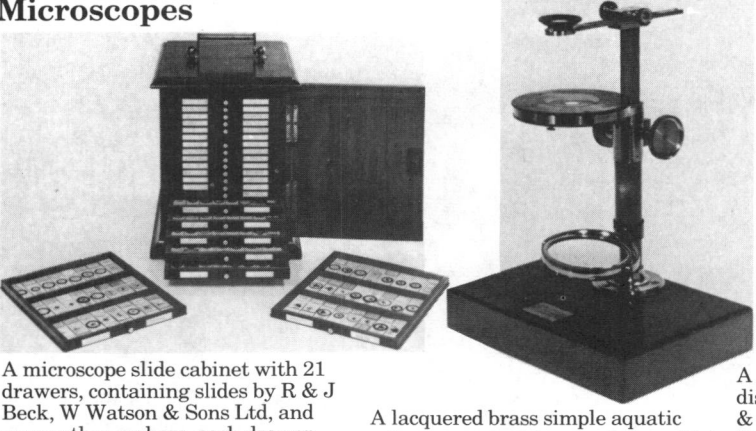

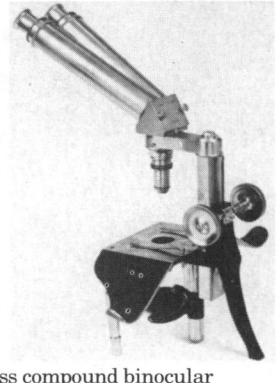

A microscope slide cabinet with 21 drawers, containing slides by R & J Beck, W Watson & Sons Ltd, and many other makers, each drawer labelled, the collection 90% complete, late 19thC, the cabinet 14in (35.5cm) high.
$1,000-1,400

A lacquered brass simple aquatic microscope on mahogany base, with inset plate R & J Beck, 31 Cornhill, London, the limb with swivel mirror, rack and pinion focusing and rack and pinion aquatic movement, with 6 objectives, 2 watch glasses and 4 lenses, in mahogany case, 8in (20cm) wide.
$400-500

A brass compound binocular dissecting microscope by J Swift & Son, London, No.13802 HY, 13in (33cm) high, in lowered position.
$300-400

A lacquered brass simple microscope, with sliding stage, live box and 3 objectives in leather covered card case, 19thC, 3½in (8.5cm) high.
$250-350

A fruitwood and decorated paper card Nuremburg monocular microscope fitted with an eyepiece dust cap, objective and mirror, the body tube and circular base, the underside impressed with the mark M, united by 3 slender turned supports, 19thC, 12in (30cm) high.
$1,300-1,800

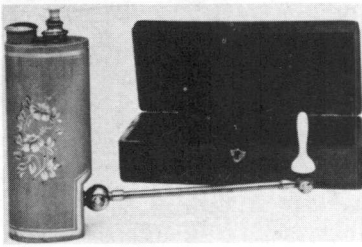

A brass screw barrel simple microscope, with sprung stage and stained ivory eyepiece, contained in fishskin covered etui, 4in (10cm) long, with associated accessories, late 18thC.
$750-1,000

A lacquered brass Martin-type drum microscope, unsigned, with sliding draw tube focusing and swivel mirror, with accessories in a fitted mahogany case, 19thC, 10½in (26.5cm) wide.
$300-400

Medical Instruments

An enema or douche, the container painted and decorated and outlined with gold, the hinged brass arm with ivory nozzle, and the pump with ivory knob, contained in a mahogany case with blue velvet lining, 19thC, 10½in (27cm).
$400-500

A silver plated ear trumpet, profusely engraved and signed F.C. Rein & Son, Patentees, inventors & makers, 108 Strand, London, the bell mouth inset with pierced scrollwork, 19thC, 3in (7.5cm) long.
$250-350

A brass bound mahogany domestic medicine chest, 19thC, 10in (26cm) wide.
$1,000-1,400

A Varney's electric life invigorator, c1900.
$100-150

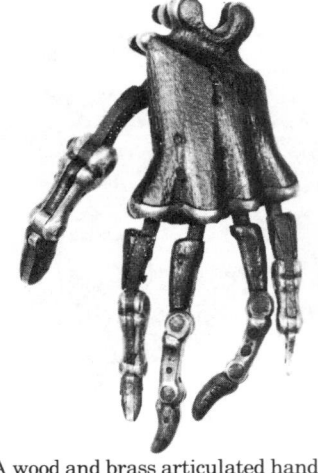

A wood and brass articulated hand, 19thC, 7in (17.5cm) long.
$250-350

An induction coil with adjustable contact breaker points, brass terminals and rheostat mounted on a mahogany base, mid-19thC, 8½in (21.5cm).
$300-400

An unusual laryngoscope by Edward Messter, Berlin, late 19thC, 10in (26cm).
$400-500

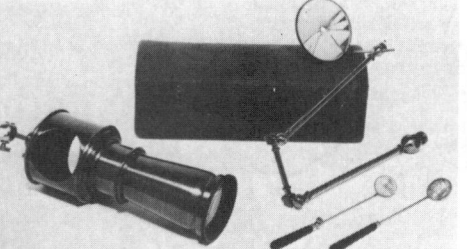

A coloured plaster instructional torso, on a wood base, 33in (84cm) high.
$150-250

A fully fitted mahogany domestic medicine chest, the rear poison compartments with 5 bottles, 19thC, 12in (30.5cm) wide.
$1,300-1,800

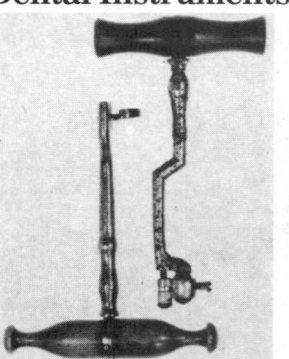

A brass bound mahogany instrument case, by Down Bros, the upper tray containing a variety of ivory handled instruments by Down, Weiss Arnold and Wood, the lower tray containing accessories in compartments, 3 missing, the case 12in (30.5cm).
$750-1,000

Dental Instruments

A French experimental transmitting and hearing machine by A Zund Burguet, with electrophonic adjustment dials for transmission and receiving with 2 ammeters and rheostats, 38½in (98cm) high, with the companion instruction book.
$100-200

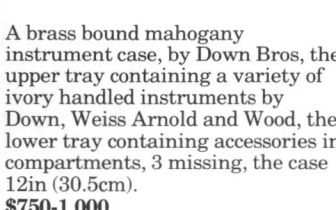

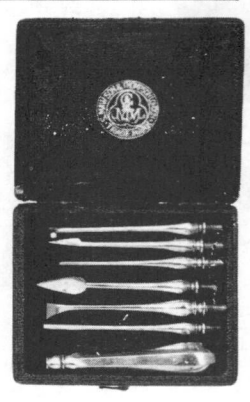

An ivory cane top phrenology head, signed Levesley, 19thC, 3½in (8.5cm).
$1,500-2,600

A burnished iron tooth key with cranked shaft and ebony handle, and another tooth key with fruitwood handle, early 19thC.
$250-350

A pocket dental scaling set by Maw Son & Thompson, the 6 instruments with baluster turned shanks and universal handle, in case, 19thC, 3in (7.5cm).
$400-500

Miscellaneous

A rare coin balance, by V Anscheutz and J Schlaff, the silver plated scale signed Anfcheutz & Co No. 1940, arranged to fold into the shaped case, the lid with label of instructions, 18thC, 6in (15cm) long.
$900-1,300

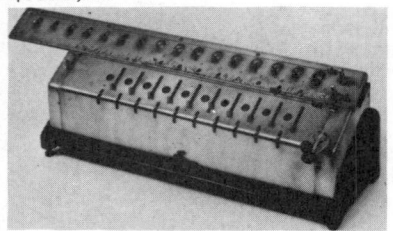

A German brass cased mechanical calculator by Ludwig Spitz & Co, the mechanism bearing the numbers 15538 and 02242, complete with crank handle on a black enamelled base lined in gilt, 18in (45.5cm).
$750-1,000

Cameras

A lacquered brass Cagniard-Latour siren, 12in (31cm) high, with associated foot operated bellows by Fletcher Russell & Co, Warrington.
$300-400

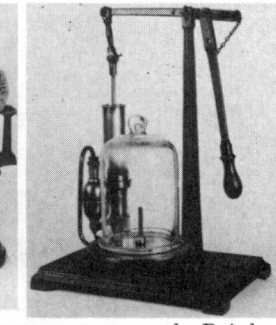

A brass vacuum pump by Baird & Tatlock, with copper expansion chamber, iron stand and base, 17in (43cm).
$300-400

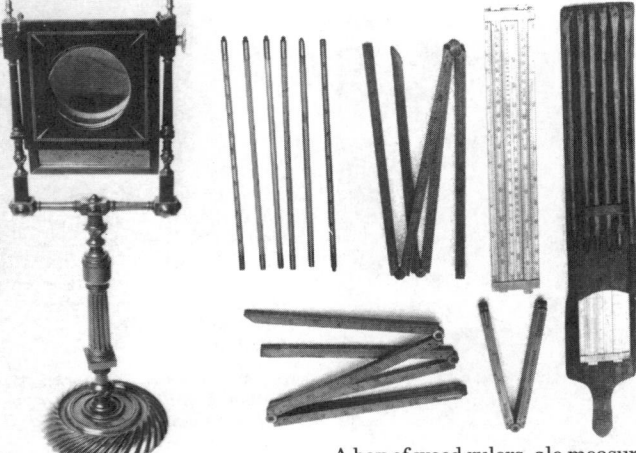

A zograscope, on turned walnut stand, c1820, 27½in (69.5cm) high.
$600-900

A box of wood rulers, ale measure and ivory slide rule.
$450-700

A set of 6 Geissler's tubes of various shapes including spiral, twist and snake, some with pale green glass sections in a cardboard case, 9in (23cm).
$300-400

An Adams tropical Minex 4 by 5in (10 by 12.5cm) reflex camera, having brass bound teak body with Ross Xpres f4.5 7¼in (18cm) lens in Adams patent shift front, lacks focusing screen, with a non-matching Adams lens board and film pack back, and 2 various d.d.s.
$3,000-4,500

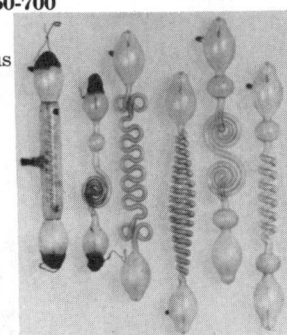

An Ansco photo vanity 'detective' camera, with box camera concealed in fitted mirror-lined vanity case.
$1,000-1,400

A wet plate sliding box camera with rising front, with a C Barr lens No. 3489, with iris diaphragm and rack and pinion barrel focusing, 6½ by 6½in (16.5 by 16.5cm).
$900-1,300

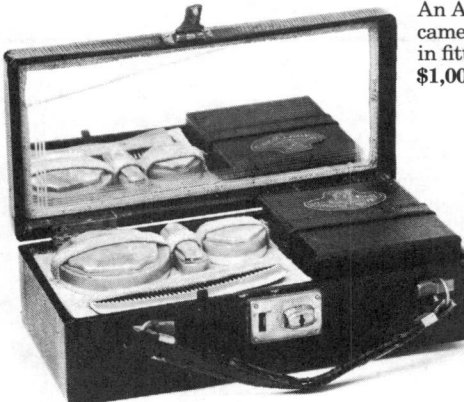

A Plasmat Roland 120 camera, with Compur shutter.
$800-1,200

A Bell & Howell Foton spring motor driven rangefinder camera, with Cooke Amotal f2 2in (5cm) lens.
$450-600

A mahogany Biokam combined cinematograph/still camera, by Alfred Darling, Brighton, with Voigtlander Euryscop f7.7 38mm lens.
$750-1,000

A Kodak super six-20 automatic exposure, roll film camera, with Kodak Anastigmat Special f3.5 100mm lens, c1940.
$900-1,300

A Kruegener's Patent book camera, No.1510, made in Germany for Marion & Co, The Sole Agents, 22A-23 Soho Square, London W, No.1419, in embossed black morocco finish with eleven 1½ by 1½in (3.5 by 3.5cm) plate holders.
$2,500-3,500

A rare derivative of the more commonly found German and French versions, manufactured c1888-1892.

An H J Redding's Patent 'Luzo' mahogany and brass roll film camera, by J Robinson & Sons, London, in original leather case, c1890.
$600-900

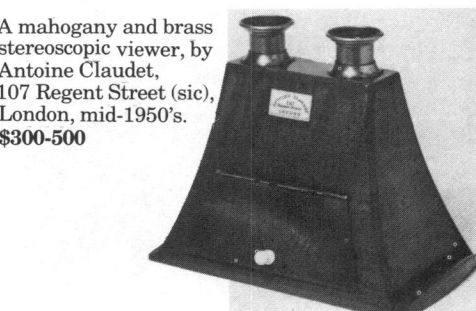

An Edwardian portrait camera, on unusual cast iron adjustable stand.
$300-400

A George III mahogany 'Camera Obscura', inlaid with stringings and rosewood crossbandings, with rectangular removable cover, enclosing the collapsible instrument with reflecting mirror and well, 42½ by 23in (107 by 58.5cm).
$4,000-5,500

Viewers

A mahogany and brass stereoscopic viewer, by Antoine Claudet, 107 Regent Street (sic), London, mid-1950's.
$300-500

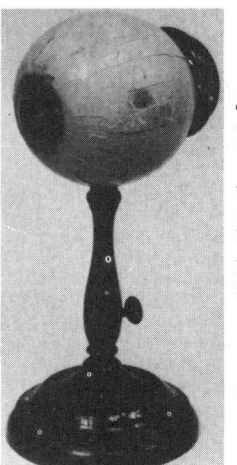

A rare camera obscura, in the form of a human eye, unsigned, with frosted glass and other lenses, the body paint in white over blue, defective, raised on a turned ebonised stand, 19thC, 8½in (21.5cm) high.
$1,500-2,600

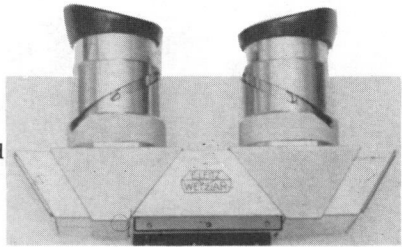

A Leitz Leica stereo Betrachtungsapparat (stereo viewer), code VOTRA in nickel and chrome finish, in presentation case.
$300-500

A Polyorama Panoptique day-night tissue diapositive viewer, in green paper-covered wood casing, with sliding focusing, matching paper bellows and 6 day-night diapositive plates, 7½ by 9½in (19 by 24cm), in wood box.
$600-900

A rare pair of Carl Zeiss 'Marine-Glas in Revolver' twin x5 and x10 power rotating 'turret' prismatic binoculars, 5½in (14cm) long.
$300-500

A kaleidoscope, with red painted card tube and eyepiece, brass rotating wheel, stamped C. G. Bush & Co., Patent Reissued Nov 11, 1873, on turned mahogany stand with collapsible four-foot stand, 19thC, 13½in (35cm) high overall.
$900-1,300

Art Nouveau Carpets

Four lengths of Morris & Co woven wool fabric, with green, pink and pale blue design, on a darker blue ground, 164 by 123in (416 by 312cm) and smaller.
$1,200-1,600

Four lengths of Morris & Co Wilton woollen stair runner, with a running pattern of dark pink, ochre and green on a dark green ground, 155 by 27in (395 by 69cm), 79 by 27in (201 by 69cm), 148 by 27in (378 by 69cm).
$1,500-2,600

Ceramics

A Poole Pottery vase by K Hickisson, the oviform body painted in polychrome, with impressed and painted marks, 13in (33cm).
$400-500

A Royal Lancastrian lustre vase, 8½in (21.5cm).
$300-500

A pair of stoneware slender oviform vases, decorated by Hannah Barlow, with various animals on a buff ground within bands of leaves and jewelled borders, one repaired, impressed marks, Doulton Lambeth and 1879, 12½in (32cm).
$750-1,000

A large earthenware vase, the tan ground decorated with blue fish, olive frogs and blue and scarlet berried black trees outlined in gilt, inscribed Rookwood Pottery, 1881, 16in (40.5cm) diam.
$1,200-1,500

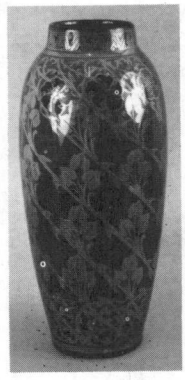

A rare Burmantoft pottery jardinière and stand, with figurative decoration of bulldogs in shades of vibrant blues, greens and yellows, 35½in (89cm).
$1,200-1,600

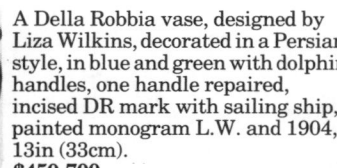

A Della Robbia vase, designed by Liza Wilkins, decorated in a Persian style, in blue and green with dolphin handles, one handle repaired, incised DR mark with sailing ship, painted monogram L.W. and 1904, 13in (33cm).
$450-700

A ceramic baluster vase with bronze mounts, painted in natural colours by S Pascault, on revolving foot, signed on side 'J. Pascault', 22½in (56.5cm).
$1,000-1,400

Two Royal Lancastrian lustre vases, one decorated with fish in blue, silver and red, 6in (15cm).
$250-350 each

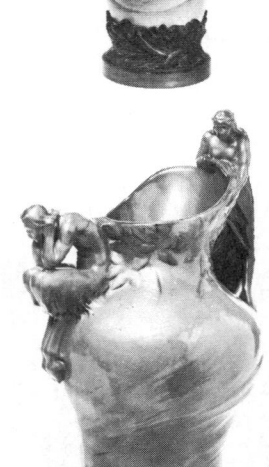

A gilt metal mounted pottery vase, the mounts each centred with a woman's head, impressed B.G. Imperial about a crown.
$150-250

A ceramic vase, decorated with a large brown, black and white moth against a light blue dripping background, the lower part painted in dark brown, embellished with gilt, signed EG Déposé on the base, 5½in (14cm).
$1,200-1,600

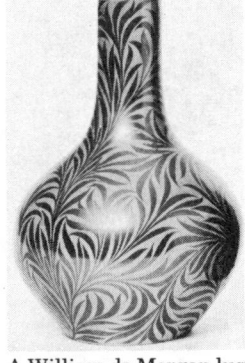

A large Zsolnay figural vase, modelled in high relief with a satyr sitting with his elbows on his knees and a maiden behind him, covered overall in a deep flambé red lustre glaze, impressed spires mark and Zsolnay Pecs in a circle, No. 6129, 23, 18in (45cm).
$1,200-1,600

A Linthorpe earthenware vase, moulded on each side with grotesque fish faces among algae, covered in an olive green and brown glaze, moulded vase mark and impressed 457, 7in (18cm).
$750-1,000

A William de Morgan lustre vase, painted in red lustre with branches of willow leaves against a pink ground, unmarked, 8in (21cm).
$300-400

A pair of metal mounted flambé stoneware vases, designed by Otto Eckmann, covered in a streaked ox-blood and olive green glaze, with pierced metal collar and handles extending to metal foot, each stamped with OE monogram, 20½in (52.5cm).
$3,000-4,000

A Poole Pottery earthenware vase, painted by Anne Hatchard, the grey white glaze painted in green, puce, lavender and blue, incised marks 212x, underglaze blue monograms AH NT, 11in (28cm).
$450-600

A Linthorpe earthenware jug designed by Dr Christopher Dresser, covered in a streaked lustrous olive brown and turquoise glaze, impressed Linthorpe with Chr Dresser facsimile signature, 7½in (19.5cm).
$300-500

A Carltonware limited edition punch bowl, moulded in relief with a frieze of Henry VIII and his wives and children, glazed in bright colours and heightened with gilding, with full inscription on base, numbered 50 of an edition of 250, 8in (21cm).
$600-900

An earthenware vase, with a dark brown ground, impressed Louwelsa Weller K and painted K Kappes, 16in (40.5cm).
$700-1,000

A ceramic câche pot by Max Laueger, the celadon ground decorated with green branches and black fruit, hairline crack, impressed with firm's mark on the base, 8in (21cm).
$450-600

A William de Morgan deep bowl, decorated by Fred Passenger in copper, blue and silver lustre, the exterior in golden and ruby lustre with scroll motif, painted marks W. de Morgan Fulham FP, 16½in (41.5cm) wide.
$7,000-9,000

A Scottie Wilson ceramic plate, painted in colours, signed on the plate 'Scottie', 14in (35.5cm), mounted, framed and glazed.
$300-400

A 'tube line' decorated plant trough, Austrian, 4 by 11in (10 by 28cm).
$150-250

A Carltonware plaque painted in gilt, orange, blue, green and white, printed mark, design No.7898, 3787, 15½in (39cm).
$300-400

A large earthenware vase, by Rookwood, decorated by Matthew A Daly, with yellow magnolias amongst olive and brown leaves and branches in a 'standard' glaze, impressed with firm's mark and 463BS and inscribed M.A.D. L., 1889, 19in (48cm).
$2,600-3,000

A Bing & Grondahl porcelain model of a monkey, factory marks and signed beneath glaze 'Dahl Jensen 1902', 'R' on tortoise, 13in (32.5cm).
$400-500

A Goldscheider pottery bust, impressed factory mark, 14½in (37cm).
$600-900

An earthenware plaque, 'Green Pastures', by Rookwood, decorated by Lenore Asbury, in a 'vellum' glaze, painted LA, and impressed with firm's marks and V, 1917, 5 by 8in (12.5 by 20cm), in original frame with firm's paper label.
$1,000-1,300

A pair of Rockwood stoneware bookends, light brown glaze, impressed mark Rookwood Pottery XXI 2503, 7in (18cm).
$300-400

A Royal Dux centrepiece, painted in typical muted enamel colours and gold, firing crack, 16½in (42cm).
$450-600

A Goldscheider pottery figure designed by E Tell, cold painted in a cream, green and brown finish, incised 'E. Tell' and Goldscheider Wien pictorial mark, 2357/584/19, 25½in (65cm).
$800-1,200

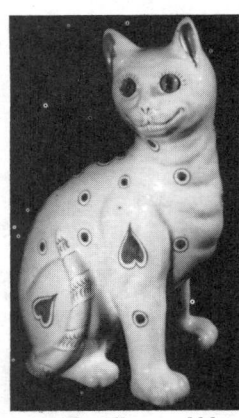

A Gallé cat with yellow and blue hearts.
$1,500-2,600

An earthenware plaque, 'January', by Rookwood, decorated by Sara Sax, in a 'vellum' glaze, painted SAX and impressed with firm's marks, 1920, 6 by 8in (15 by 20.5cm), in original frame with firm's paper label.
$1,400-1,700

Clocks

A Longwy ceramic tile panel, the 30 glazed tiles with a cockatoo perched on a pomegranate branch, in turquoise, yellow, red, green and white, inscribed Longwy, in oak frame, 48½ by 41½in (123 by 106cm).
$1,500-2,600

A Foley Intarsio pottery timepiece, inscribed 'The Days May Come the days may go', printed factory marks, Rd. 379152, 3455, 10½in (26.5cm).
$600-900

A Favrile glass and bronze mantel clock in the 'pine needle' pattern, impressed Tiffany Studios New York 879, clock face painted Tiffany & Co., 10in (25cm).
$2,500-3,500

A Goldscheider pottery timepiece by Simon, inscribed 'AMICITIA-VINCIT HORAS' with circular copper dial, signed 'Simon', and with impressed and applied factory marks 'Wein', 15½in (40cm).
$600-900

A Liberty pewter clock, 7in (18cm).
$1,000-1,400

A Foley Intarsio earthenware clock, with painted underglaze polychrome decoration, the top entitled 'Prithee Whats O'clock', printed marks, No.3116 Rd No.337999, 13in (33.5cm).
$750-1,000

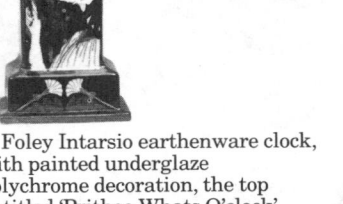

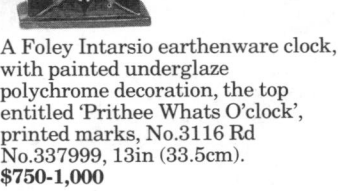

A Liberty pewter clock, 4½in (11.5cm) diam.
$400-500

Furniture

A satinwood inlaid stand and a pair of chairs.
$450-600

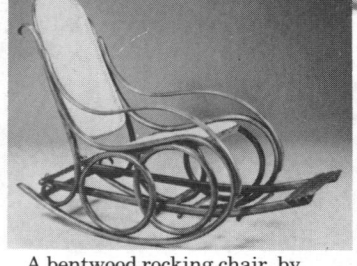

A bentwood rocking chair, by Thonet, c1904.
$1,000-1,400

A French oak dining chair, designed by Charles Plumet and Anthony Selmersheim.
$600-900

A Bugatti corner chair, the sides slung with circular beaten copper and kid drums, inlaid with pewter and ivory, 28in (71cm) high.
$1,500-2,600

A Wylie and Lochhead oak chair, the design attributed to E A Taylor.
$600-900

> In the Furniture section if there is only one measurement it usually refers to the width of the piece

An English mahogany and marquetry settle, the top and frieze inlaid with various fruitwoods, c1890, 73in (185cm).
$1,500-2,600

A mahogany armchair, 48in (122cm) high.
$450-700

An American Arts and Crafts oak upright chair, with a W-shaped top rail and openwork centre, the sides inlaid in ebony with lozenges, with paper label 'Made by United States Speciality Company – Makers of Welbilt Furniture, number 907A'.
$300-600

An oak chalet desk and chair, by Onandago Shops, of L & J G Stickley, the desk with narrow slats on either side resting on shoe feet, unsigned, model No.395, the chair with rise on crest rail and vertical slats, leather seat, unsigned, model No.788, c1905.
$1,500-2,000

An oak and leather highback spindle chair, by Gustav Stickley, c1905.
$4,500-5,500

An oak settle, by Gustav Stickley, the posts at the back and arms with chamfered tops, red decal 'Stickley' outlined, model No.161, c1901, 50in (127cm).
$1,500-2,000

An oak and leather high back spindle chair, by Gustav Stickley, with original soft leather seat, unsigned, paper label under seat, model No.384, c1905, 46in (116.5cm).
$4,000-5,000

An oak trestle table by Gustav Stickley, the top with dark brown replaced leather and original tacks, with red decal 'Stickley' outlined, model No.401, c1902, 48in (122cm).
$1,600-2,000

An oak and leather footstool, by Gustav Stickley, the red decal with logo outlined, model No.729, but similar to the later model No.301, c1902, 20in (51cm).
$1,200-1,500

An oak magazine stand, designed by Harvey Ellis, executed by Gustav Stickley, the top with overhang and curving apron above 3 shelves, red decal, model No.72, c1909, 21½in (54cm).
$1,200-1,500

A mahogany dresser and mirror, by Stickley Bros, Grand Rapids, Michigan, the sloping sides with heart cut-outs, c1908, 45½in (115cm).
$500-800

An oak table, by Gustav Stickley, with cross stretchers joined by a pyramidal 'button', unsigned, c1903, 40in (101.5cm) diam.
$900-1,200

An oak dining table, by L & J G Stickley, the square top splined and supported on a square non-dividing pedestal with six 12in (30.5cm) leaves, in their original storage crate with L & J G Stickley Handcraft paper shipping label attached, with red decal, c1910, 124in (315cm) extended.
$3,000-4,000

An Emile Gallé fruitwood and marquetry table a deux plateaux, inlaid signature E. Gallé, 20½in (52.5cm).
$1,000-1,400

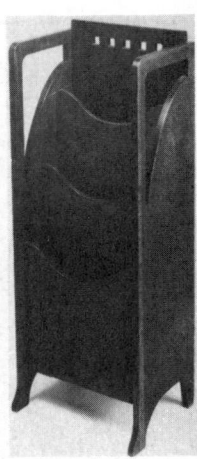

An oak bent arm Morris chair, with original finish and leather cushions, 'The Work of L & J G Stickley' white decal, model No.410, c1915.
$5,500-6,500

An oak sideboard, by L & J G Stickley, the doors with copper strap hangers, the top with plate rail, unsigned, model No. 735, c1912, 56in (142cm).
$1,900-2,200

A Scottish oak newspaper rack, 14in (36cm).
$900-1,300

An oak settle, by Gustav Stickley, with red decal, model No.225, c1910, 78½in (199cm).
$6,000-7,000

A mahogany and inlaid dressing table, with marquetry 'landscape' panels in various woods including yew, sycamore, satinbirch and partridgewood, 48in (122cm).
$900-1,300

A tip table, by L & J G Stickley, with tilt-top mechanism, the top supported by a pedestal base, unsigned, model No.588, c1912, 28in (71cm) square.
$800-1,000

An oak gong stand, by Gustav Stickley, unsigned, model No.812, lacking Chinese gong and striker, 31in (79cm).
$1,600-2,000

l. An English umbrella stand, inlaid with several woods.
$300-400

r. An oak umbrella stand with chequered inlay.
$150-250

An Arts and Crafts oak firescreen, with a panel of Morris & Co fabric woven with 'The Tulip and Rose' in blue, grey and beige wools, 22in (55.5cm) high.
$400-500

An Arts and Crafts mahogany four-fold silk embroidered screen, 60in (152cm) high.
$1,500-2,600

A Gallé cameo glass, 23½in (60cm).
$4,500-7,000

Glass

A Gallé enamelled bowl, the clear green glass with orchids and etched foliage, engraved 'Gallé' signature incorporating mushroom, 11½in (29cm) wide.
$2,250-3,000

A Gallé cameo vase, with riverside landscape decoration, in brown and ochre on a peach ground, 3½in (9cm).
$1,000-1,400

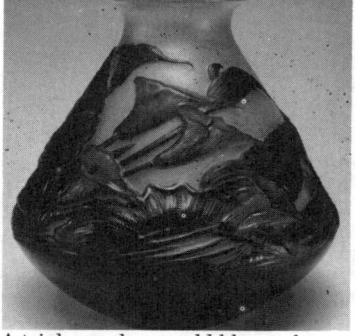

A triple overlay mould-blown glass vase by Emile Gallé, of flared baluster form, the translucent yellow ground overlaid in red, chestnut and burgundy etched with large flowering cala lilies, with cameo signature 'Gallé', 14½in (36.5cm) high.
$28,500-34,000

GALLÉ, Emile (1846-1904)

If not the father, certainly one of the foremost figures of the French Art Nouveau movement, Emile Gallé was the founder of the Nancy school. After a liberal education, he began his working life as apprentice to his father, a studio glassmaker. The development of his unique Art Nouveau style is considered to have dated from about 1884, and within six years he was running a factory supplying large quantities of studio glass to, among others, the Parisian shop of Sebastian Bing, the international entrepreneur. The shop was called l'Art Nouveau. Gallé was widely imitated by other glass workers, but few, if any, could match his technical skill or artistic feeling. In 1880 he began to produce Art Nouveau furniture of extremely high quality, often embellishing his products with inlays – notably mother-of-pearl – and characteristically delicate marquetry designs. Following his death in 1904, articles produced by his factories continued to be signed 'Gallé', but all were marked with a star from that time onward.

A cameo double overlay glass perfume bottle, by Emile Gallé, in frosted white glass overlaid with sapphire blue and puce, with cameo signature, the matching stopper etched with a dragonfly, 4in (10cm).
$1,500-2,600

A double overlay etched glass vase by Emile Gallé, the transparent ground overlaid in pink and green etched with umbelliferous plants, with intaglio signature 'Gallé', 7½in (19cm) wide.
$1,500-2,600

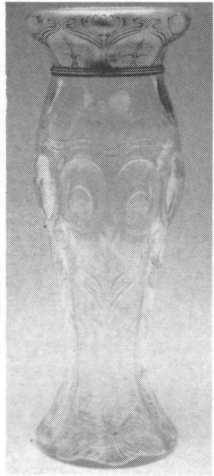

A silver mounted cut glass vase, by Tiffany & Co, New York, with a flaring silver rim engraved with waterlilies and lily pads, the glass cut with waterlily blossoms, marked, 1907, 11in (28cm).
$1,400-1,700

A Gallé cameo vase, the slim body overlaid in brown and green and carved with trees in a lakeland setting against a frosted pink tinged ground, signed, 8in (20.5cm).
$900-1,300

A tall Gallé cameo glass vase, the greyish body with evidence of slight vertical ribbing overlaid with ruby glass acid-etched with waterlily blooms, tendrils and leaves, fire-polished, etched on leaf with vertical signature 'Gallé', 22½in (57cm), applied with brass rim to base.
$1,000-1,400

An etched and double overlay glass vase, the light amber ground overlaid in green and brown, etched 'Gallé', 5in (12.5cm).
$1,000-1,400

A triple overlay etched glass vase by Emile Gallé, with cameo signature 'Gallé', 14in (35.5cm).
$3,000-4,500

A glass vase by Emile Gallé, the green streaked translucent yellow ground etched, enamelled and gilded on the obverse with a medallion, inscribed Cristallerie Emile Gallé a Nancy, 7in (17cm).
$9,000-12,000

A Gallé vase, the pale amber coloured glass with gold foil inclusions overlaid with white and blue, engraved 'Gallé' on the base, 7½in (18.5cm).
$4,000-5,500

A plum triple overlay mould-blown glass vase, by Emile Gallé, the translucent yellow ground overlaid with sapphire, purple and chestnut brown, cameo signature, 15½in (39cm).
$6,000-8,000

A Gallé cameo glass vase, with mountainscape in blue and brown overlaid on amber, with a trefoil shaped rim, signed in cameo 'Gallé' 8½in (21.5cm).
$2,250-3,000

A Gallé flask-shaped scent bottle, enamelled with stylised flowers, branches and dragonflies in yellow and green against green tinted glass, enamelled signature 'E. Gallé Nancy depose', rim chip, 5in (12.5cm).
$750-1,000

An enamelled glass jug with stopper by Gallé, enamelled signature on the bottom, 'E. Gallé a Nancy', chips on handle and rim, 8in (20cm).
$750-1,000

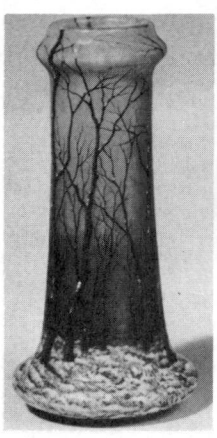

A Daum cameo and engraved martele flattened globular glass vase, the hammered amethyst and blue opalescent ground overlaid with cornflowers, inscribed 'Daum Nancy' with Cross of Lorraine, 5½in (13.5cm).
$3,000-4,000

A Daum vase, with cameo cut and enamel painted wintry landscape on acid-treated matt pale amber ground, enamelled signature 'Daum Nancy' with Cross of Lorraine, 10in (25cm).
$1,500-2,600

DAUM BROTHERS, Auguste (1853-1909), Antonin (1864-1930)

Makers of decorative domestic glassware, the Daum Brothers turned to art glass production following the Paris Exhibition in 1889. Since they worked in Nancy, it is not unnatural that they should have been greatly influenced by Gallé – with whom they are invariably unfavourably compared. Inevitable as such comparison is, it is unfortunate, because their work is highly competent and frequently displays a high standard of artistic merit.

A Daum cameo vase, with dark amethyst coloured glass cut back to an acid-treated ground shading from frosted to purple, engraved 'Daum Nancy' with Cross of Lorraine, 18in (46cm).
$3,000-4,000

A small cameo glass dish, signed, 3½in (9cm) diam.
$75-150

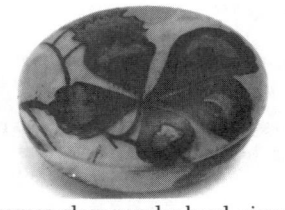

A cameo glass powder bowl, signed 'Leune', decorated with leaves in orange, yellow and purple, 4in (10cm) diam.
$150-250

An 8-piece gold Favrile glass cordial/sherry service, by Tiffany Studios, the decanter inscribed L.C. Tiffany-Favrile, 5 liqueurs inscribed L.C.T. Favrile, one L.C.T. Favrile Favrile, one unsigned, 9½in (24cm) height of decanter.
$2,250-3,000

A French glass vase, within a silver coloured metal mount, embossed and chased with chyrsanthemum and leaves, stamped with poinçon and maker's mark 'JM' in lozenge, 9½in (24.5cm).
$700-900

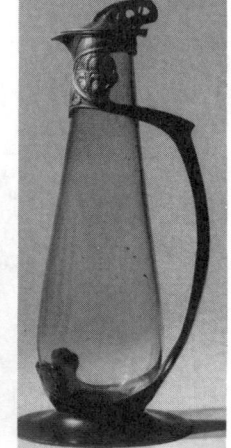

A Liberty & Co Tudric pewter mounted claret jug, the bottle green glass body cast with pierced pewter neck mount and hinged cover, the handle stamped 4, Tudric 0634 Rd 427856, 15in (38cm).
$450-700

A bronze mounted glass vase, the heavy clear glass etched and enamelled in the Japanese taste, signed 'Escalier de Cristal Paris', 9in (23.5cm).
$1,500-2,600

l. A cameo silver mounted scent bottle overlaid in white, with clear inner stopper, minor chips to body, the silver mount London 1884, 10in (25.5cm).
$450-600

r. A cameo silver mounted scent bottle overlaid in white, on a red ground, minor chips to body, c1885, 10½in (26.5cm).
$450-600

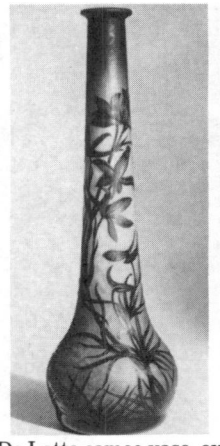

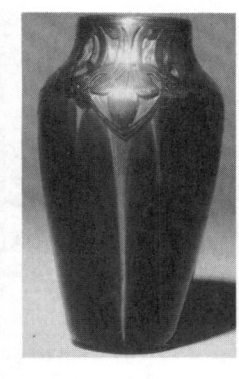

A Loetz white metal mounted baluster vase, the metallic orange glass with pulled loop metallic green and white decoration, 7½in (19cm).
$1,000-1,400

A De Latte cameo vase, overlaid in deep amber coloured glass with sprays of orchid against a mottled amber and russet ground, signature 'De Latte Nancy', 19½in (50cm).
$800-1,200

An etched and overlay glass vase by Charles Schneider, the milky white and pink mottled glass overlaid in shades of claret and orange, etched 'Le Verre français' on the base, 14in (36cm).
$900-1,300

l. A Loetz orange glass vase, designed by Michael Powolny, decorated with a brown band around the rim and vertical brown stripes, 11in (28cm).
$250-350

r. A Loetz orange glass vase, designed by Michael Powolny, decorated with brown stripes, 5½in (13.5cm).
$150-250

A cameo vase, 'Chestnuts' by Le Gras, 20in (51cm).
$3,000-4,000

An enamelled glass plate, by Gabriel Argy-Rousseau, decorated with orange and white fish and silvered waves, signed, 8in (20.5cm) diam.
$1,500-2,600

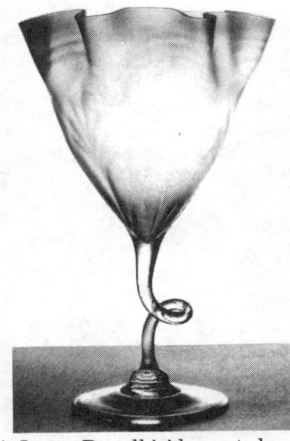

A James Powell decanter, 12½in (32cm).
$250-350

A James Powell iridescent clear glass vase, 11in (28cm).
$750-1,000

A Hukin and Heath silver mounted claret jug, with ebony handle, designed by Christopher Dresser, stamped JWH, JTH and with London hallmarks for 1880, 9in (22.5cm).
$1,500-2,600

An iridescent liquor glass by A de Caranza, the mustard ground decorated with red and gilt iridescent flowers, signed 'Duc A. de Caranza' on the base, 6in (15.5cm).
$900-1,300

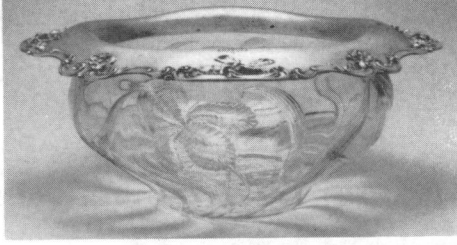

A silver mounted cut glass punch bowl, by Gorham Manufacturing Company, Providence, c1900, 17in (43cm) diam.
$3,500-4,500

An oil and vinegar cruet set, early 20thC.
$60-100

Jewellery

A Murrle Bennett gold wirework oval brooch, with opal matrix and 4 seed pearls, stamped MB monogram and 15ct on the pin, c1900, 3cm wide.
$400-500

l. A stained glass panel in the style of Morris & Co, 36in (91.5cm) high.
$1,000-1,400

r. 'Spring', a stained glass panel in the style of Morris & Co, 36in (91.5cm) high.
$300-400

A German plique-à-jour brooch, the design ascribed to Otto Prutscher, with shaded green translucent enamels, with an opal cabochon, flanked by small opals and an opal drop, maker's mark of Heinrich Levinger of Pforzheim, 'deposé' and '900', 3.3cm wide.
$450-600

A turquoise necklace by Murrle Bennett.
$750-1,000

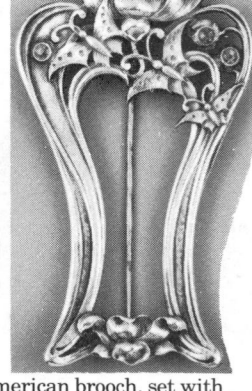

An American brooch, set with amethysts and butterflies in flight, with Gorham maker's marks and 'Sterling', 9.5cm long.
$250-350

A gold plique-à-jour brooch.
$1,500-2,600

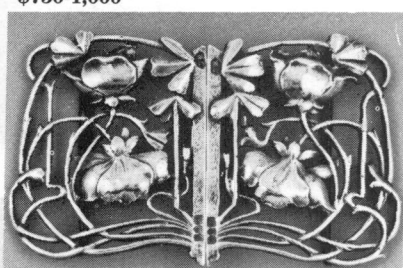

An unusual plique-à-jour brooch, formed as a locust, in shaded green translucent enamels, set with pastes, stamped with maker's mark and '900', probably Austrian, 10.6cm long.
$750-1,000

A Liberty & Co silver buckle, designed by Oliver Baker, set with 4 lapis lazuli cabochons, marked 'L & Co.,' and Birmingham marks for 1900, 4in (10cm) wide.
$300-400

A William Comyns silver buckle, marked 'W.C.' for London 1900, 9cm wide.
$150-250

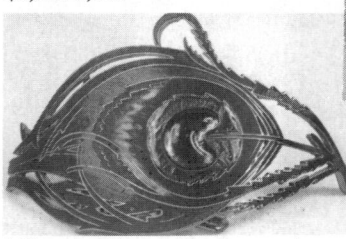

A French gilt metal and enamel peacock feather buckle, the 'eye' set with blue paste, c1900.
$300-400

A silver and carnelian brooch by Georg Jensen.
$2,250-3,500

A gold and tortoiseshell comb.
$400-500

A German horn comb, surmounted by panels of green plique-à-jour enamels set with marcasites and a faceted green stone, marked '900' and 'deposé', 8.5cm wide.
$150-250

A gold, opal and plique-à-jour pendant, the wings of pale brown and turquoise plique-à-jour enamels and a pearl drop, stamped 'Jules', 9cm wide.
$700-900

A gold and tortoiseshell comb, 4in (10cm).
$400-500

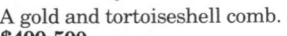

An unusual George Hunt necklace and pendant in ivory and enamels, on an elaborate chain with initials 'M' and 'R' and foliate panels, stamped 'GH' in shield, length of pendant 5cm.
$1,000-1,400

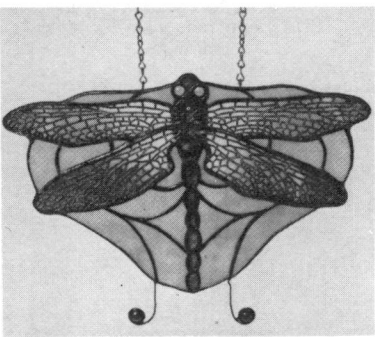

A Tiffany Studios stained glass dragonfly pendant, with shaded pink and white wings with bronze veining, a green body and red eyes against a honey-coloured ground.
$900-1,300

Lamps

A Tiffany style lamp on bronze base, modelled as lilies and reeds.
$4,000-5,500

A painted ivory and silver pendant, possibly Austrian, the frame enclosing an ivory plaque, with silvermarks, 4.7cm.
$400-500

A leaded glass and bronze table lamp, by Tiffany Studios, the shade with yellow and apricot daffodils amongst blue stems and green leaves on a light mauve ground, impressed 'Tiffany Studios New York', 22in (56cm).
$10,500-14,000

A pair of Favrile glass and gilt bronze 'bamboo' candle lamps, by Tiffany Studios, the shades in transparent yellow glass with a gold iridescence, shades inscribed 'L.C.T.', bases impressed 'Tiffany Studios New York 1205', 15in (38cm).
$3,000-4,500

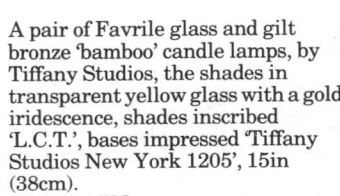

A German silvered pewter and nautilus shell desk lamp, supported on cast stem of a reclining nymph among bulrushes, stamped marks, 11½in (30cm).
$4,500-7,000

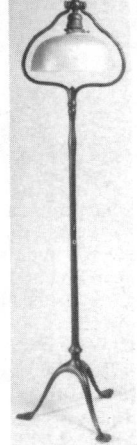

An unusual Bohemian cut glass table lamp, the pale amber body overlaid with rich ruby glass, 21in (53.5cm), on separate marble base.
$1,200-1,600

A Favrile glass and bronze floor lamp, by Tiffany Studios, the shade of white-cased yellow glass with a heavy gold iridescence, inscribed 'L.C.T. Favrile', with minor chips to top rim, the base impressed 'Tiffany Studios New York 5209 423', 54½in (138cm).
$4,000-5,500

A rare glass and copper clad iron table lamp, by Gustav Stickley, the domical shade suspending 16 square amber glass plates, stamped with firm's logo, model No.755, c1912, 38in (96cm) high.
$7,000-8,000

A table lamp, the base and shade inset with pebbles in red, blue and opalescent glass, on oval wooden base, 19½in (49cm).
$900-1,300

A metal figure lamp, signed by the artist, 23in (58.5cm).
$900-1,300

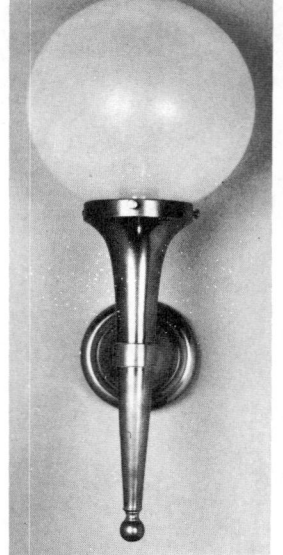

Two brass and glass wall sconces, designed by Frank Lloyd Wright, executed by Will Lau for the B Harley Bradley House, Kankakee, Illinois, the spherical opalescent glass globe on trumpet turned brass supports extended on bell form wall mounts, one sconce corroded and missing glass globe, c1900, 18in (45.5cm).
$600-900

Martin Bros

A Martin Brothers stoneware bird, the detachable head modelled with the eyes humorously looking up, the head signed 'R.W. Martin Brothers, London & Southall, 2nd April 1902', and the base inscribed the same, 9½in (24cm).
$9,000-12,000

A Noke Martin Brothers style grotesque bird tobacco jar and cover, signed, 10½in (26.5cm).
$750-1,000

A Martin Brothers stoneware model of a bird, with incised plumage picked out in muted browns, whites and blue, the head and base signed 'Martin Brothers, London & Southall', the head only dated '9-1898', 14½in (36cm).
$6,000-9,000

A Martin Brothers grotesque bird, covered in blue and olive green glaze, the head incised 'R. W. Martin & Bros. Southall 193 1915', 7½in (18.5cm).
$3,000-4,500

A Martin Brothers stoneware vase, incised 'R. W. Martin & Bro. London & Southall, dated '3-1892', 8½in (21cm).
$6,000-8,000

MARTINWARE

★ in 1873 Robert Wallace Martin set up a studio in Fulham
★ Southall studio pottery founded in 1877 by the four Martin Brothers
★ many designs derived from traditional English pottery jars and jugs but also influenced by Italian majolica, Gothic gargoyles and many other European and Far East sources
★ the chief sculptor, Wallace Martin's main speciality was the grotesque birds known as Wally birds
★ often done as caricatures of famous people
★ the more unusual the bird the higher the price
★ record price was £47,300 paid in May 1985 at Sotheby's for an 1893 owl which was 27in (68.5cm) high
★ production from the factory was not large and demand being strong prices seem set to increase

A Martin Brothers stoneware double face jug, in buff coloured glaze, inscribed on base 'R. W. Martin Brothers, London & Southall, 2.2.1903', 7in (18cm).
$1,500-2,600

A Martin Brothers stoneware spirit flask, the tan glazed body moulded with a grinning face, with silver mounted stopper, inscribed on base 'R. W. Martin Brothers, London and Southall, 11.1901', 9½in (24cm).
$1,300-1,800

A Martin Brothers stoneware jug, with mottled blue ground, incised on base 'Martin Brothers, London & Southall June 1897', 10½in (26cm).
$1,300-1,800

A Martinware stoneware vase, decorated with incised fish and watersnakes among seaweed, in mottled brown glaze, incised 'R. W. Martin London & Southall 3.1891', 7in (18cm).
$750-1,000

A Martinware stoneware jug, with incised decoration of an underwater scene with grotesque fish in shades of brown, green and blue on a cream coloured ground, inscribed 'Martin Bros. London & Southall, 1888', 9in (23cm).
$400-500

The tremendous increase in value of grotesque birds has not yet been reflected in an increase in the small incised vases.

A Martin Brothers stoneware bottle vase, incised with 2 grotesque frogs painted in shades of green and brown against a light honey-coloured ground, incised 'Martin Bros. London & Southall 4.1913', 5in (12.5cm).
$750-1,000

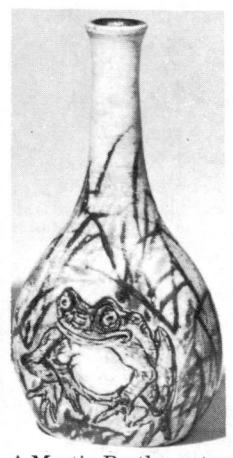

A Martin Brothers stoneware bottle vase, incised with 2 frogs among grasses painted in shades of green, brown and white, incised 'Martin Bros. London & Southall 4.1913', 4in (10cm).
$750-1,000

A rare Martin Brothers stoneware sundial, the base glazed in various shades of brown, green, blue and yellow, below brass sundial, incised 'R. W. Martin & Brothers, London & Southall 4-1888', 33in (84cm).
$4,500-7,000

A Martinware stoneware vase, painted with orchids in shades of ochre and pale lilac on a brown ground, inscribed 'Martin Bros. London & Southall 3.1898', 13in (33cm).
$750-1,000

Metal

A Liberty & Co Tudric pewter box and cover, designed by Archibald Knox, the stylised flowers with blue enamel centres, 'Made in England Tudric 0194 3 E', 4½in (12cm).
$450-600

A bronze figure of a pierrot by L Alliott, 13½in (34cm).
$1,500-2,600

A bronze group of a man and a poodle, inscribed 'D. de Chemellier', 23½in (59cm).
$1,200-1,600

A bronze figure cast from a model by Marius Vallet, on marble base, signed 'Mars Vallet', 'Siot-Decauville Fondeur Paris', 12in (30cm).
$4,000-5,500

A Lorenzl bronze figure of a dancer, signed, on an onyx base, 9in (23cm).
$600-900

A silvered bronze group, 'Carthage', cast after a model by Théodore Rivière, signed in full on the front, marks for 'Susse Freres Editeurs Paris', 22in (56cm).
$4,000-5,500

A WMF silver pewter table mirror, stamped marks 'W.M.F. 70g', 13½in (35cm).
$1,500-2,600

A silver, copper, bronze and oak chafing dish, set in a silver bordered copper dish supported on 3 scrolled silver and copper legs, each surmounted by a bronze standing rabbit, impressed 'Copper and Silver', c1910, 11in (28cm).
$800-1,000

A bronze bust, 'La Sibylle', cast from a model by E Villanis, signed in the bronze 'E. Villanis' and with Société des Bronzes de Paris foundry mark, 28½in (72cm).
$4,000-5,500

A pewter mirror, 18in (45.5cm).
$450-700

A silver photograph frame, decorated with blue and green enamel, 5 by 5½in (12.5 by 14cm).
$450-700

A French gilded metal mirror, signed 'A. Rety', 16in (40.5cm).
$450-700

A three-piece demi-tasse service and a circular tray, by Tiffany and Company, New York, c1920, coffee pot 7in (18cm) high, 60oz gross.
$2,800-3,200

A six-piece tea and coffee service and tray, by Porter Blanchard, Pacioma, California, comprising a hot water kettle on stand with a burner, a coffee pot, a teapot, a cream pitcher, a covered sugar bowl, a waste bowl and a tray, with ivory finials and insulating rings, each inscribed on base, marked, c1915, kettle 14in (35.5cm) high, 212oz 10dwt gross.
$5,000-6,000

A five-piece tea and coffee service, by Tiffany & Company, New York, comprising a teapot, coffee pot, kettle on stand, covered sugar bowl, a cream pitcher, with ivory insulating rings, each marked, 1907-47, coffee pot 9in (23cm), 125oz gross.
$2,500-3,000

A punch bowl, tray and 12 cups, by Whiting Manufacturing Company, Bridgeport, Connecticut, each with an applied scrolling border, each marked, 1913, 16in (40.5cm) diam, 210oz 10dwt.
$4,000-5,000

A pair of martele dishes, by Gorham Manufacturing Company, Providence, with a stylized monogram 'MS', each marked, c1900, 7in (18cm) diam, 14oz 10dwt.
$1,800-2,200

A part dinner service, by Tiffany and Company, New York, comprising 3 graduated oval trays, a two-handled bread tray, 8 dessert bowls on stands, 2 covered entrée dishes with removable handles, and a sauceboat on stand, each with a monogram, marked, c1920, tray 21½in (54cm) wide, 488oz 10dwt.
$10,000-12,000

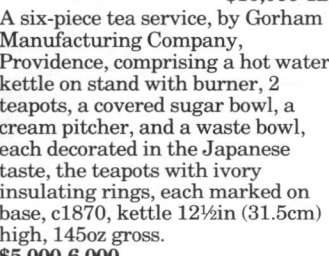

A six-piece tea service, by Gorham Manufacturing Company, Providence, comprising a hot water kettle on stand with burner, 2 teapots, a covered sugar bowl, a cream pitcher, and a waste bowl, each decorated in the Japanese taste, the teapots with ivory insulating rings, each marked on base, c1870, kettle 12½in (31.5cm) high, 145oz gross.
$5,000-6,000

A six-piece tea and coffee service with a plated tray, by the Mulholland Brothers, Evanston, Illinois, comprising a coffee pot, a teapot, a kettle on stand, a covered sugar bowl, a cream pitcher, and a waste bowl, marked on base with initial 'M' within an anvil shaped cartouche, with inscription 'Hand Wrought Sterling', the tray marked 'S.H.M. & Co.', the tray, waste bowl and kettle each engraved with inscription 'Margaret Lombard Wingfield, Clarksdale, Miss. Dec. 25, 1918', coffee pot 9in (23cm), 170oz gross.
$4,000-5,000

A six-piece tea and coffee service, by Bigelow, Kennard and Company, Boston, comprising a kettle on stand, a coffee pot, a teapot, a covered sugar bowl, a cream pitcher, and a waste bowl, the handles with ivory insulating rings, each engraved with a coat of arms, the bases engraved 'RLM to JMM, June 6, 1901' and 'GWM June 19, 1912', each marked, kettle 12in (30.5cm) high, 168oz gross.
$4,000-5,000

A pitcher, by Gorham Manufacturing Company, Providence, three sides with applied copper and silver maple leaves, in the Japanese taste, with an engraved name on the base and date 1905, marked, 1897, 9in (23cm) high, 31oz gross.
$2,000-3,000

A set of 12 plates, by Gorham Manufacturing Company, Providence, the brim with relief swags and cartouches, marked, 1907, 10in (25.5cm) diam, 204oz.
$4,500-5,500

An ivory and silver cigar holder, by Tiffany & Company, New York, the holder a section of ivory tusk with a bevelled glass bottom, mounted in a hammer faceted silver base, marked, 1881, 6½in (16.5cm).
$5,500-6,500

A New York Yacht Club trophy flagon, by Whiting Manufacturing Company, the handle in the form of a stylized dolphin, the front with inscription 'N.Y.Y.C. Squadron Runs 1892', 10in (25.5cm) high, 35oz 10dwt.
$800-1,200

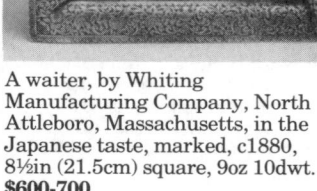

A waiter, by Whiting Manufacturing Company, North Attleboro, Massachusetts, in the Japanese taste, marked, c1880, 8½in (21.5cm) square, 9oz 10dwt.
$600-700

A copper lamp, by Gorham Manufacturing Company, Providence, in the form of a globular teapot, the body etched with a sparrow on one side and a flowering plant on the other, one side with cast applied silver butterfly and frog, marked, 1882, 2½in (6.5cm) high.
$300-500

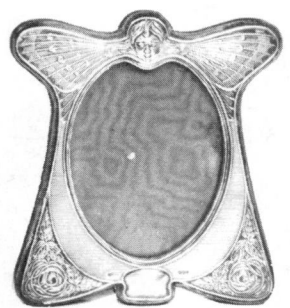

A photograph frame, maker's initial probably G.W. & Sons, London 1905, 8in (20.5cm).
$700-900

A pewter picture frame, 7in (18cm) diam.
$250-350

A William Hutton & Sons Arts and Crafts silver picture frame, enamelled in green and dark blue, stamped with maker's mark and London hallmarks for 1903, and number 404509, 8in (20cm).
$2,250-3,500

A pair of WMF silver coloured metal candlesticks, 11in (28cm).
$450-700

A chrysanthemum pattern flatware service, comprising 164 pieces, by Tiffany & Company, New York, marked, monograms removed and added later, c1885, 206oz 10dwt excluding knives.
$12,000-15,000

A Liberty pewter ice bucket of Archibald Knox design, 7in (18cm).
$150-250

An Unger Brother silver bowl, stamped maker's monogram, Sterling 925 Fine, 0850, 6in (15.5cm) diam, 3oz.
$150-250

A Scottish silver bowl, designed by D Carleton Smythe and produced through the Glasgow School of Art, set with a crystal cabochon, 3 now missing, bearing Glasgow hallmarks for 1905, 19in (48.5cm) diam.
$750-1,000

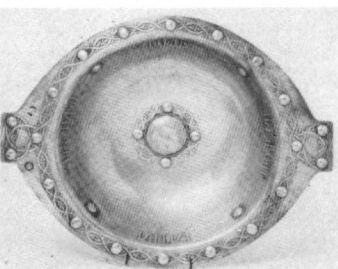

A tray, by Howard & Company, New York, with an applied relief grapevine border, centering engraved foliate initials 'NBD', marked, c1900, 18in (46cm) diam, 78oz 10dwt.
$1,500-2,000

A pair of James Dixon & Sons silver candlesticks, stamped maker's marks and Sheffield hallmarks for 1904, 8½in (22cm).
$1,300-1,800

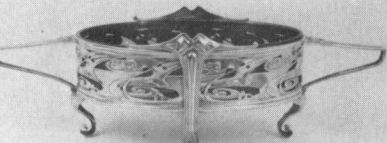

A Connell two-handled bowl, designed by Kate Harris, with bottle green glass liner, stamped maker's mark and London hallmarks for 1904, 'Connell 83 Cheapside Rd, 352424', 15½in (39cm) diam, 22oz 15dwt.
$1,500-2,600

A Hukin and Heath silver sugar bowl, designed by Dr Christopher Dresser, stamped maker's marks J.W.H., J.T.H., London hallmarks for 1883, 5½in (13.5cm), 5oz 2dwt.
$300-400

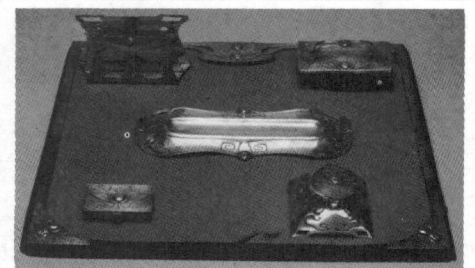

A six-piece silver desk set, by
George W Schiebler & Company,
New York, with an Egyptian
inspired repoussé design featuring
scarabs, each impressed with firm's
mark and 'Sterling 283D', c1925,
the blotter frame 23in (58cm) long.
$1,800-2,500

An American ivy-chased jug by
Tiffany & Co, later inscribed 'Corrie
Cup won by "Burnswark", nos. by
David Bell Irving, Esq. 1886', c1870,
9in (23cm), 27.5oz.
$4,000-5,500

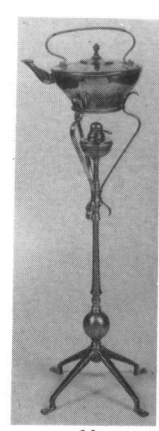

A W A S Benson copper and brass
kettle on stand, with copper burner,
stamped 'Benson', 34in (86cm).
$400-500

A Hukin and Heath silver
condiment set, designed by
Dr Christopher Dresser, stamped
maker's marks and London
hallmarks for 1881, 5½in (14cm).
$2,250-3,000

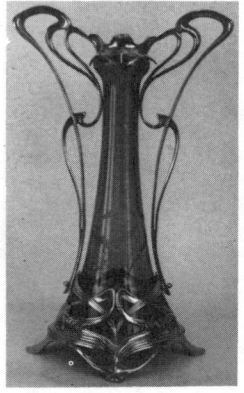

A pair of large WMF pewter
mounted green glass vases, 19in
(48cm).
$1,500-2,600

A white metal hors d'oeuvres dish,
14½in (36.5cm) wide.
$700-900

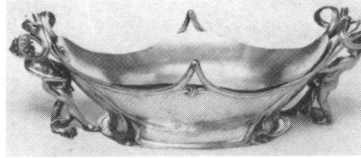

A silver coloured metal centrepiece,
with an alpaca liner, unmarked,
possibly Austrian or German,
22½in (57.5cm) wide.
$3,000-4,000

A Hukin and Heath electroplated
picnic teapot, designed by
Dr Christopher Dresser, stamped
maker's 'H & H, 2109 Designed by
Dr. C. Dresser' with registration
lozenge for 18th October 1879, 3½in
(9cm).
$250-350

A large French white metal vase
with 2 scantily clad females draping
the body, with various marks,
signed and dated '1902', Marcelle
Devuit foundry seal, 26½in (66cm).
$1,500-2,600

A mythologique pattern flatware
service, by Gorham Manufacturing
Company, Providence, comprising
271 pieces, c1900, 265oz excluding
knives.
$7,000-8,000

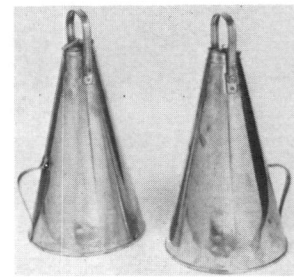

A pair of copper and brass vacuum
flasks, attributed to W A S Benson,
with pewter liners, brass strap
hinges, wooden lids and brass
carrying handles, 19in (48cm).
$600-900

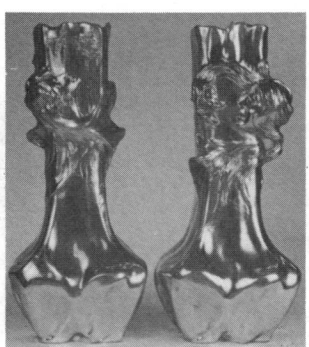

A pair of silvered pewter vases, each cast 'Flora' with copper liners, 16½in (41.5cm).
$1,500-2,600

A bronze metal inkwell, 9in (23cm) wide.
$300-400

A silver dressing table set, decorated with ladies heads, c1900.
$450-700

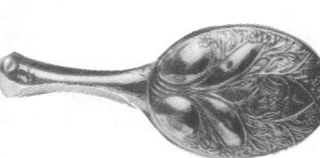

A Guild of Handicraft silver hand mirror, stamped marks 'G of H Ltd' and London hallmarks for 1905.
$450-600

An unusual French lacquered copper and brass pill-making machine, the rotating copper bucket operated via a gear mechanism and driving wheel, 19in (48cm) high.
$450-700

A gold, turquoise and diamond lady's mesh evening purse, stamped with '9ct', import marks for London 1905, 4in (10.5cm) wide.
$750-1,000

A pair of bronze firedogs, 24in (61cm) high.
$250-350

An English Arts and Crafts brass and copper gas fire, c1880, 37 by 16½in (94 by 42cm).
$300-400

Moorcroft

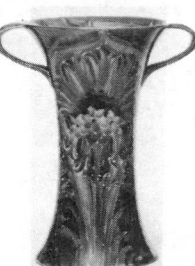

A Moorcroft Macinytre brown cornflower vase, decorated in maroon, blue and butterscotch against a green ground, signed 'W. Moorcroft', printed Macintyre mark and 'Made for Brown & Co. Wigan', 8in (20cm).
$450-700

A Moorcroft Macintyre vase, c1892, 9½in (24.5cm).
$150-250

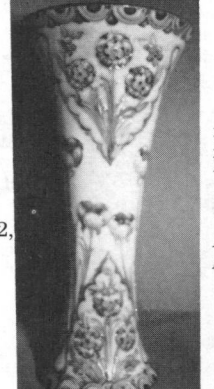

A silver coloured metal trophy by Ernest Sichel, apparently not hallmarked, engraved signature, 12½in (31.5cm).
$1,300-1,800

Ernest Sichel 1862-1941 worked in Bradford.

A Florian style bulbous vase with daffodil motif, signed 'W. Moorcroft des', c1900, 6in (15.5cm).
$450-700

A pair of Moorcroft vases, painted in the pomegranate pattern in shades of pink, green and purple on an inky blue ground, impressed marks, signed in green, 15in (38cm).
$750-1,000

A giant nib silver inkwell, Birmingham 1894, 8in (20.5cm).
$600-900

A Moorcroft vase, in the Dawn pattern, painted in blue against a pale sky between borders of white, yellow and blue, impressed marks, 3½in (8.5cm).
$100-150

A Moorcroft pottery vase, decorated in the Claremont pattern with toadstools in shades of red, yellow, green and blue on a blue to green streaked ground, printed marks, signed in green, 6in (15.5cm).
$900-1,300

A trumpet shaped vase with grape and pomegranate decoration, backstamp, Moorcroft Burslem, c1914, 10½in (26.5cm).
$300-400

A Moorcroft pottery flambé vase and cover, decorated with irises in shades of yellow and green on a dark red flambé ground, impressed marks, signed in blue, 11in (28cm).
$750-1,000

A Moorcroft pottery vase, decorated in the Hazeldene pattern in shades of yellow, green and blue, painted signature, c1915, 6in (15.5cm).
$750-1,000

MACINTYRE/ MOORCROFT

★ first Art Pottery produced in 1897. Early wares marked Macintyre and/or W Moorcroft des
★ William Moorcroft established his own works in 1913
★ 1913-21 wares impressed MOORCROFT BURSLEM with painted W.Moorcroft signature
★ after 1916 impressed ENGLAND
★ 1921-1930 impressed MADE IN ENGLAND
★ 1930-1949 paper label, BY APPOINTMENT, POTTER TO H.M. THE QUEEN used
★ 1949-1973 label states BY APPOINTMENT TO THE LATE QUEEN MARY
★ rivals copied patterns and colours

A pair of Macintyre plates, attributed to William Moorcroft, decorated in white slip trailing with blue irises and green leaves against an off-white ground, printed Macintyre marks, Rd. no. 211991, 8in (20cm) diam.
$150-200

A Moorcroft Spanish pattern pot pourri with pierced cover, decorated with large blue and green bloom s on green scrolling stems, reserved against a pale green ground, signed 'W. Moorcroft 12/1911', impressed '189 W', 4in (10cm).
$300-400

A Moorcroft Macintyre pottery jar, painted in the 18thC pattern with swags, roses and forget-me-not in shades of yellow, green, pink and blue on a cream coloured ground, printed mark, signed in blue, 4in (9.5cm).
$450-600

A Moorcroft Florian ware twin-handled vase, decorated in white, yellow, blue and pale green, reserved against a shaded blue ground, signed 'W. Moorcroft des', printed Florian Macintyre mark, 8in (20cm).
$600-900

A four-piece pewter mounted tea service, painted in red, purple and green on a blue ground, impressed 'Moorcroft, Made in England' and signature.
$750-1,000

A Moorcroft wheat ear motif vase, with green and purple tones on an off-white ground, blue signature, 13½in (34.5cm).
$750-1,000

A Moorcroft Tudor rose pattern vase, decorated in white tube-lining, glazed in green, blue and heightened with red and reserved against a turquoise ground, signed 'W. Moorcroft des', printed 'Made for Liberty & Co., Rd. no. 431157', 10in (25.5cm).
$400-500

Posters

'Etienne Driau': 'Mdlle Gaby Deslys', drypoint etching, signed in full bottom right, No.45, image area 25 by 15½in (64 by 40cm), framed and glazed.
$450-600

Maurice Denis: 'La Dépêche – Grand Format', a chromolithographic poster, signed en block 'M. Denis', printed 'Edw. Ancourt & Cie, 83 Frd St. Denis Paris', framed and glazed, 57½ by 39½in (145.5 by 100cm).
$150-200

Horace Warner: 'Who's a Pretty Boy Then?', a watercolour on grey paper, 43½ by 21½in (108.5 by 54cm), framed and glazed.
$250-350

This picture has been re-backed but bears the old label signed Horace Warner 1920.

Mucha: 'Printemps', a panel decoratif, chromolithograph on silk, signed en bloc 'Mucha 1900', 28½ by 12½in (72.5 by 31.5cm), framed and glazed.
$150-250

Miscellaneous

An Arts and Crafts hand woven wool rug in the style of Charles Voysey, woven in coral red, brick red, green and blue, worn, 102 by 34½in (259 by 87.5cm).
$600-900

A set of 5 miniature rectangular paintings, after Hans Mackart, painted in water colour on ivory, 6½ by 1½in (17 by 4.5cm).
$1,200-1,600

A photograph frame with brass trim and painted design, 10 by 13in (25.5 by 33cm).
$100-200

A leather bound vellum plaque painted with the Madonna and Child, signed 'H. Granville, Fell' and dated 06, the leather surround tooled in gold by Cedric Chivers, Bath, 19½ by 14in (49.5 by 35.5cm), in fitted leather case.
$1,000-1,400

A naturalistically coloured stone carving of a chimpanzee, 21in (53.5cm).
$600-900

Doulton

A Doulton Lambeth stoneware salad bowl, in buff, chocolate and deep blue, with silver rim mount, Sheffield 1878, marked with monogram of Florence E. Barlow, and a pair of matching silver servers with stoneware handles.
$250-350

A Doulton Lambeth stoneware box and cover, modelled in the form of a leather hat box, covered in a\brown saltglaze, faint r.m., 5in (12.5cm).
$250-350

A Doulton Lambeth stoneware biscuit barrel by Florence Barlow and Lucy Barlow, glazed in greens, brown and blues, having metal collar, handle and cover, incised F.E.B. no. 9.7., L.A.B. 456, r.m., 1883, 8in (20cm).
$750-1,000

A Doulton Lambeth jug, by Arthur B Barlow, glazed in shades of blue and brown, artist's monogram, No.777, ?'SG' assistant mark, o.m. dated 1873, 6½in (17cm).
$250-350

DOULTON WARES
Doulton marks – abbreviations

o.u.m.	– oval updated mark
o.m.	– oval mark, dated
c.m.	– circular mark
r.m.	– rosette mark
r.m. & e.	– rosette mark and England
d.l.e.	– Doulton Lambeth England
d.s.l.	– Doulton Silicon Lambeth
d.s.p.	– Doulton & Slaters Patent
c.m.l. & c.	– circle mark, lion & crown
c.m. & l.	– circle mark and lion
r.d.e.	– Royal Doulton England
s.c.m.	– slip-cast mark
i.c.f.m.	– impressed circular faience mark
r.d.f.	– Royal Doulton Flambé
b.r.m. & c.	– Burslem rosette mark & crown

A Doulton Lambeth stoneware jug, decorated by Hannah Barlow, Florence Barlow and Mark V Marshall, glazed in greens, brown and beige, incised H.B.B., monogram No.214, F.E.B. No.341, M.U.M. No.3., r.m. & e., 9½in (24.5cm).
$1,000-1,400

A tapering mug decorated by Hannah Barlow, impressed Doulton Lambeth, incised H.B.B., 209, dated 1874, 4in (10cm).
$450-600

A Doulton stoneware jug, decorated by Hannah Barlow and probably Lucy Barlow, inscribed and printed marks, dated 1884, 9½in (23.5cm).
$400-500

A Doulton stoneware jardinière, in blues, browns and grey, incised 'H. Doulton Lambeth', 7½in (19cm).
$750-1,000

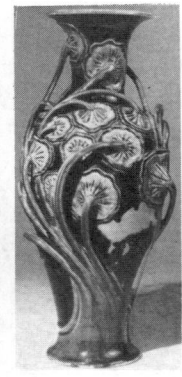

A Doulton stoneware vase, designed by Frank Butler, modelled in relief, with blue, brown and green glaze, impressed Royal Doulton mark and incised artist's monogram FAB, 18½in (47.5cm).
$1,300-1,800

A Doulton Lambeth stoneware baluster vase, by Florence E Barlow and Frank A Butler, in rich blues, browns and greens, the neck rim carved as a row of scrolls, r.m. & e., F.E.B. and F.A.B. monograms, numbered 345 and 385 respectively and RHM monogram as assistant, 21in (53cm).
$1,300-1,800

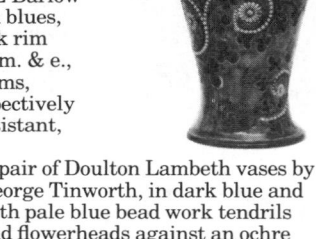

A Doulton Lambeth faience tile panel, printed c.m. on reverse of each tile, indistinct painted monogram on one, R to bottom tile, 24.5 by 8½in (61.5 by 20.5cm).
$400-500

A pair of Doulton Lambeth vases by George Tinworth, in dark blue and with pale blue bead work tendrils and flowerheads against an ochre coloured ground, d.l.e., both with incised monogram to body, 11in (28cm).
$400-500

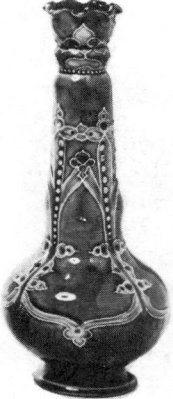

A Doulton Lambeth Silicon ware vase, by Edith D Lupton and Ada Dennis, in white, brown and blue, top reduced, ED.L artist's monogram, numbered 378, AD monogram, numbered 16, dated 1885, 8in (20.5cm).
$400-500

A Doulton Lambeth stoneware vase by Mark V Marshall, glazed in mottled brown, blue and cream, r.m. artist's monogram, No.3 and assistant's mark, 10in (25cm).
$450-600

A Doulton Lambeth vase by Emily Stormer, glazed in blues, greens, white and brown, artist's monogram, numbered 825 and EM for Emma Martin, c.m. dated 1877, 9½in (24.5cm).
$300-400

Royal Doulton Figures

'In The Stocks', 1st version, HN14/4, designer L Harradine, introduced 1931, withdrawn by 1938, 5in (13cm).
$1,500-2,600

'The Beggar', HN526, designer L Harradine, introduced 1921, withdrawn by 1949, 6½in (16.5cm).
$300-400

'Butterfly', HN719, designer L Harradine, introduced 1925, withdrawn by 1938, 6½in (16.5cm).
$900-1,300

'London Cry, Turnips and Carrots', HN752, designer L Harradine, introduced 1925, withdrawn 1938, 7in (17cm).
$750-1,000

'A Jester', HN45, signed C. J. Noke, introduced 1915, withdrawn by 1938, 10in (25.5cm).
$1,500-2,600

'Pierrette', HN644, 1st version, designer L Harradine, introduced 1924, withdrawn 1938, 7in (18cm).
$750-1,000

'Pierrette', no number, should be HN644, pilot decoration, designer L Harradine, introduced 1924, withdrawn by 1938, 7in (18cm).
$150-250

'The Modern Piper', HN756, designer L Harradine, introduced 1925, withdrawn by 1938, 8½in (21.5cm).
$1,500-2,600

'Guy Fawkes', HN98, designer C J Noke, introduced 1918, withdrawn by 1949, 10½in (26.5cm).
$900-1,300

'An Orange Vendor', HN72, designer C J Noke, introduced 1917, withdrawn 1938, 6in (16cm).
$600-900

'Henry Irving as Cardinal Wolsey', HN344, designer C J Noke, introduced 1919, withdrawn 1949, hair cracks in base, 13in (34cm).
$2,250-3,000

'Geisha', no number, should be HN376, designer H Tittensor, dated February 1927, 11in (27cm).
$2,250-3,500

'Harlequinade Masked', no number, should be HN768, designer L Harradine, introduced 1925, withdrawn by 1938, 6½in (16.5cm).
$1,000-1,400

'Judge and Jury', HN1264, designer J G Hughes, introduced 1927, withdrawn 1938, 6in (15cm).
$4,000-5,500

'Negligée', HN1219, designer L Harradine, introduced 1927, withdrawn 1938, 5in (12.5cm).
$1,000-1,400

'Siesta', HN1305, designer
L Harradine, produced February
1931, 5in (12cm).
$1,500-2,600

'Lady Jester' 2nd version, HN1284,
designer L Harradine, introduced
1928, withdrawn 1938, 4in (10cm).
$1,500-2,600

'Tulips', HN1334, introduced 1929,
withdrawn 1938, 9½in (23cm).
$450-700

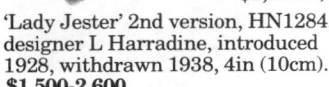

'Folly', HN1335, designer
L Harradine, introduced 1929,
withdrawn by 1938, 9in (23cm).
$1,000-1,400

'Sweet Lavender', HN1373,
designer L Harradine, introduced
1930, withdrawn by 1949, 9in
(23cm).
$450-600

'The Courtier', HN1338, designer
L Harradine, introduced 1929,
withdrawn 1938, 4½in (11.5cm).
$2,250-3,000

'Doreen', HN1389, designer
L Harradine, introduced 1930,
withdrawn 1938, 5in (13cm).
$400-500

'Iona', HN1346, designer
L Harradine, introduced 1929,
withdrawn 1938, 7½in (19cm).
$1,500-2,600

'Tildy', HN1576, designer
L Harradine, introduced 1933,
withdrawn by 1938, 5½in (14cm).
$450-700

'Phyllis', HN1420, designed by
L Harradine, introduced 1930,
withdrawn by 1949, slight chips to
flower, 9in (23cm).
$150-250

'Calumet', HN1428, designer
C J Noke, introduced 1930,
withdrawn 1949, 6in (15cm).
$900-1,300

'Teresa', HN1683, designer
L Harradine, introduced 1935,
withdrawn 1938, hair cracks in
base, 6in (15cm).
$450-700

'Dreamland', wrongly numbered
HN1471, should be HN1473,
designer L Harradine, introduced
1931, withdrawn 1938, 4½in
(11.5cm).
$1,500-2,600

'Molly Malone', HN1455, designer
L Harradine, introduced 1931,
withdrawn 1938, slight hair crack to
base, 7in (18cm).
$1,500-2,600

'Court Shoemaker', HN1755,
designer L Harradine, introduced
1936, withdrawn 1949, hair cracks
in base, 7in (17cm).
$700-900

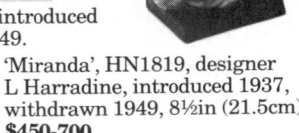

'The Squire', HN1814, introduced 1937, withdrawn by 1949.
$300-400

'Henry VIII', 2nd version, HN1792, No. 39 of a limited edition of 200, designer C J Noke, introduced 1933, withdrawn by 1939, hair crack in base, 11½in (29cm).
$3,000-4,500

'Miranda', HN1819, designer L Harradine, introduced 1937, withdrawn 1949, 8½in (21.5cm).
$450-700

'Mariquita', HN1837, designer L Harradine, introduced 1938, withdrawn 1949, 8in (20cm).
$1,500-2,600

'The Young Miss Nightingale', HN2010, designer Margaret Davies, introduced 1948, withdrawn 1953, 9in (23cm).
$450-700

'Pearly Boy', 2nd version, HN2035, designer L Harradine, introduced 1949, withdrawn 1959, 5½in (13.5cm).
$250-350

'The Corinthian', no number, should be HN1973, designer H Fenton, introduced 1941, withdrawn 1949, 8in (20cm).
$1,500-2,600

'Granny's Heritage', HN1873, 7in (18cm).
$300-500

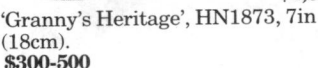

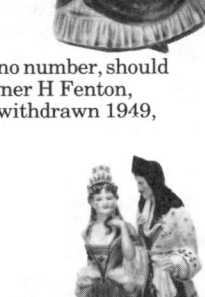

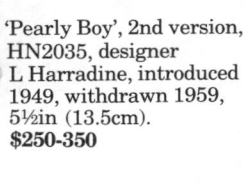

'Promenade', HN2076, designer Margaret Davies, introduced 1951, withdrawn 1953, 8in (20cm).
$1,200-1,600

'Sleepyhead', HN2114, designer Margaret Davies, introduced 1953, withdrawn 1955, 5in (12.5cm).
$900-1,300

'St George', HN2067, designer Stanley Thorogood, ARCA, introduced 1950, withdrawn 1976, 16in (40.5cm).
$1,200-1,600

'Pearly Girl', 2nd version, HN2036, designer L Harradine, introduced 1949, withdrawn 1959, 5½in (14cm).
$150-250

'Lady in blue ballgown', no number, a pilot figure, slightly defective, 9in (23cm).
$1,500-2,600

'The Tailor', HN2174, designer M Nicoll, introduced 1956, withdrawn 1959, 4in (10cm).
$700-900

'Jolly Sailor', HN2172, designer M Nicoll, introduced 1956, withdrawn 1965, 6½in (16.5cm).
$400-500

'St George and the Dragon', 3rd version, HN2856, designer W K Harper, introduced 1978, 16½in (42cm).
$1,000-1,400

'The Perfect Pair', 7in (18cm).
$600-900

A rare pilot figure believed entitled 'The Logsman', not produced, Block No. 1767, 6in (15cm).
$2,250-3,000

Four Royal Doulton character jugs:
l. 'Parson Brown'.
$100-200

lc. 'White-haired Clown'.
$750-1,000

rc. 'Toby Philpot'.
$100-200

r. 'Vicar of Bray'.
$150-250

A Royal Doulton flambé Buddha, signed Noke, 8in (21.5cm).
$750-1,000

l. 'Ard of 'Earing, designer D Biggs, D6588, registered numbers 913137, 45356, 9681, 811/63, 7½in (19cm).
$800-1,200

c. 'The Clown', brown haired version, designer H Fenton, registered number 810520, 6in (15cm).
$1,500-2,600

r. 'Old King Cole', designer H Fenton, 6in (15cm).
$150-250

'Lord Nelson', D6336, designer M Henk, introduced 1952, withdrawn in 1969, 7in (18cm).
$150-250

A Royal Doulton 'Jester' wall mask.
$300-400

A Royal Doulton Lonsdale leaf and floral decorated toilet jug and basin.
$60-100

l. A Royal Doulton flambé model of a leaping salmon, 12in (30.5cm).
$300-400

r. A Royal Doulton flambé model of a seated fox, 9in, (23cm).
$250-350

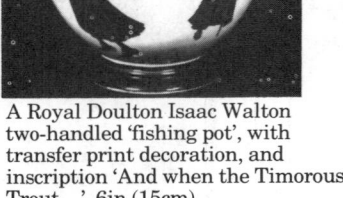

A Royal Doulton Isaac Walton two-handled 'fishing pot', with transfer print decoration, and inscription 'And when the Timorous Trout ...', 6in (15cm).
$150-200

A Royal Doulton Kingsware 'golfing' jug, decorated with embossed golfing figures in period costume, printed factory mark, c1935, 9in (23cm).
$400-500

'The Gondolier', D6589, printed Royal Doulton England marks, 8in (20cm).
$450-700

Make the most of Miller's.

We do not repeat photographs in Miller's. However, the same item may appear in a subsequent year's edition if our consultants feel it is of interest to collectors and dealers

A rare Lalique car mascot, 'Longchamps', in clear and satin finished glass, moulded signature R. Lalique, France, 5in (13cm).
$13,500-17,500

A Lalique car mascot, 'Archer', in clear and satin finished glass, etched R. Lalique France, 4½in (12cm).
$2,250-3,000

RENÉ LALIQUE

The work of René Lalique spans both the Art Nouveau and Art Deco periods. He began his career as a designer of jewellery and was an innovator among goldsmiths in the 1890s, being more concerned with the craftsmanship and decorative elements of the work than its intrinsic value. His pieces of this time are recognised as the finest examples of Art Nouveau jewellery.

By the 1900 Paris Exposition – 'the triumph of Art Nouveau' – the movement was actually on the wane. This, combined with the fact that he had more commissions than he could cope with and that numerous imitations of his work were appearing, made him turn elsewhere for inspiration. He found it in glass and exhibited some pieces at the Salon in 1902. In the same year he designed a new studio and set up a workshop where his most notable cire-perdue and glass panels were produced.

He was introduced to commercial glass production around 1907 when François Coty asked him to design labels for perfume bottles. In fact, Lalique designed the bottles as well. These were manufactured by Legras et Cie, until he opened his own small glassworks at Combs in 1909 to cope with the demands of this and other work. After the First World War he opened a larger glassworks which was responsible for the bulk of his output.

Just as Lalique had triumphed at the 1900 Paris Exposition with his Art Nouveau jewellery, so he dominated the 1925 Exposition, establishing himself as the leading exponent of mass-produced glassware. His designs by now were in the Art Deco style but the earlier Art Nouveau influence was still apparent in some of the decorative elements.

He was very much concerned with the commercial mass-production of his designs and it is as much as a pioneer of mass-produced art glass that he should be remembered as for his earlier imaginative jewellery.

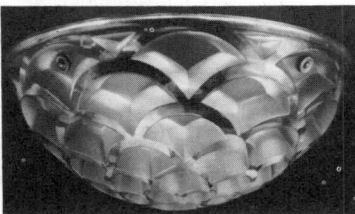

A Lalique plafonnier, in clear and satin finished glass, acid stamped signature R. Lalique, France, 14½in (37cm) diam.
$1,500-2,600

A pair of Lalique opalescent glass plafonniers, each bowl with acid signature R. Lalique France, 16½in (41cm) diam.
$1,500-2,600

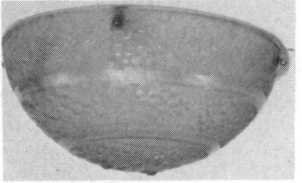

A Lalique amber plafonnier, 'Saint Vincent', moulded signature R. Lalique, inscribed France, 13½in (34.5cm) wide.
$1,000-1,400

A Lalique plafonnier, the yellow frosted glass moulded with peaches and leaves, moulded R. Lalique, France, 15in (38cm) wide.
$1,500-2,600

A Lalique car mascot, 'Perche', in clear and satin finished glass, engraved Lalique France, 3½in (9.5cm).
$1,500-2,600

A Lalique St Christopher car mascot.
$1,300-1,800

Make the most of Miller's

When a large specialist well-publicised collection comes on the market, it tends to increase prices. Immediately after this, prices can fall slightly due to the main buyers having large stocks and the market being 'flooded'. This is usually temporary and does not affect very high quality items.

A Lalique opalescent globular vase, 'Formose', moulded signature R. Lalique, 6½in (17cm).
$750-1,000

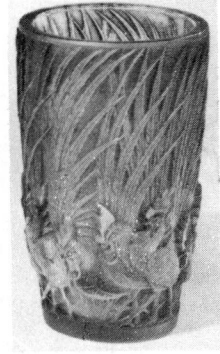

A Lalique blue opalescent glass vase, 'Soucis', in clear and satin finished glass, acid stamped signature R. Lalique, 6½in (17cm).
$900-1,300

A Lalique glass vase, 'Coqs et Plumes', heightened with blue staining, signed R Lalique, France, 6in (15.5cm).
$750-1,000

A Lalique vase, 'Gui', the clear satin finished glass with turquoise staining, engraved signature Lalique, rim slightly ground, 7in (17cm).
$300-400

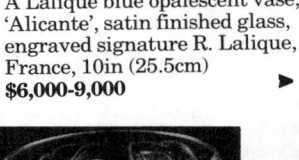

A Lalique blue opalescent vase, 'Alicante', satin finished glass, engraved signature R. Lalique, France, 10in (25.5cm)
$6,000-9,000 ▶

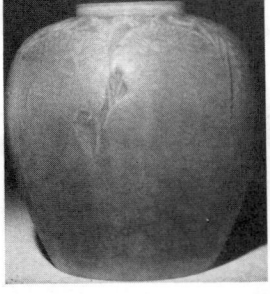

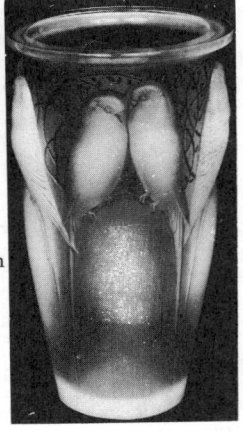

A Lalique frosted glass vase, 'Carmargue', acid stamped R. Lalique, France, 11in (28.5cm).
$5,500-7,000

A Lalique blue opalescent cylindrical vase, 'Ceylon', stencil engraved R. Lalique, France, 9½in (24.5cm).
$2,250-3,000 ▶

A Lalique blue opalescent cylindrical vase, 'Danaides', in clear and blue satin finished glass, engraved R. Lalique, France, No. 972, 7in (18cm).
$1,500-2,600

A Lalique opalescent vase, 'Six Figurines et Masques', moulded and etched R. Lalique, France, with lamp fitting, 10in (25cm).
$4,000-5,500

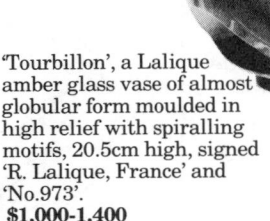

An Orrefors vase, wheel-engraved in neo-classical style with naked maidens posed on pedestals, etched signature Orrefors 1930 S Gate 238 EW, 17.5cm high.
$1,500-2,600

A Lalique baluster vase, the satin finished glass with blue staining, moulded signature R. Lalique, 9½in (23.5cm).
$750-1,000

'Tourbillon', a Lalique amber glass vase of almost globular form moulded in high relief with spiralling motifs, 20.5cm high, signed 'R. Lalique, France' and 'No.973'.
$1,000-1,400

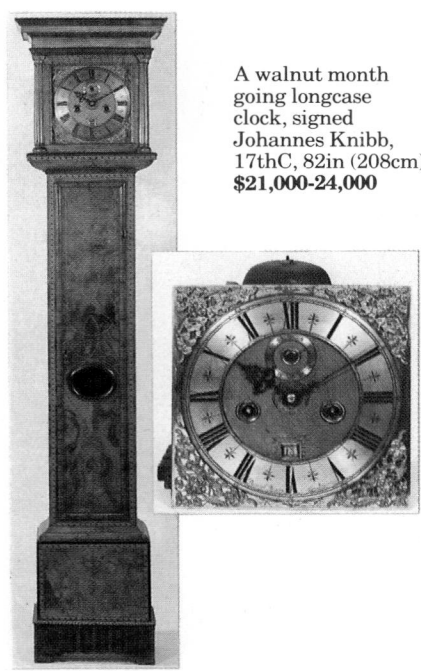

A walnut month going longcase clock, signed Johannes Knibb, 17thC, 82in (208cm). **$21,000-24,000**

A walnut longcase clock, with 10in (25cm) brass dial, the silvered chapter ring signed Daniel Quare, London, restorations to hood, late 17thC, later plinth, 80in (203cm). **$18,000-21,000**

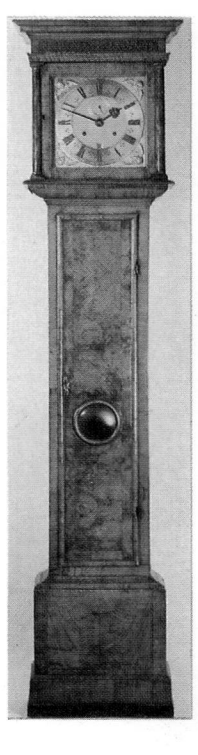

A Charles II walnut month going longcase clock, signed Thomas Tompion, Londini Fecit, alterations, 76in (193cm). **$75,000-90,000**

A walnut quarter chiming longcase clock, signed Claude Du Chesne, restored, early 18thC, 97in. **$15,000-21,000**

A Federal inlaid mahogany longcase clock, dial signed Caleb Wheaton, Providence, restoration, c1785, 90in (228.5cm). **$15,000-21,000**

l. A Federal longcase clock by Wm Cummens, Massachusetts, c1800. **$15,000-21,000**

r. A cherrywood longcase clock by T Harland, Connecticut, c1775. **$13,500-17,500**

A Chippendale mahogany longcase clock, signed by Thomas Wagstaffe, London, the case Philadelphia, c1770, 88in (223cm). **$19,500-24,000**

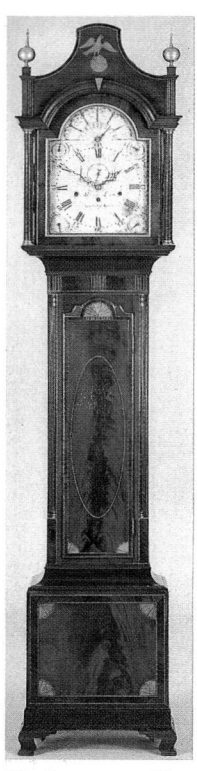

The Longstreet Family Federal inlaid mahogany longcase clock, dial signed Aaron Lane, Elizabethtown, N. Jersey, c1790, 94in (238cm). **$42,000-48,000**

An ebony veneered bracket clock, Daniel Quare, London, early 18thC, 17in (43cm). **$21,000-24,000**

A Restauration equation longcase regulator, of 6 months' duration, signed Lepaute, restoration, 83in (210cm). **$22,500-25,000**

A Louis XV ormolu mounted corne verte bracket clock, the glazed dial and back-plate signed Pierre Leroy a Paris, the bracket stamped St. Germain Jme, 37in (94cm). **$13,500-17,500**

A Louis XIV ormolu mounted Boulle marquetry religieuse, stamped, early 18thC, 22in (56cm). **$10,500-14,000**

A Louis XV ormolu bracket clock, attributed to Charles Cressent, signed Viger. **$10,500-14,000**

A mid-Georgian scarlet japanned quarter striking, musical and automaton bracket clock, in the style of Giles Grendey, 37in (94cm). **$90,000-100,000**

A Louis XV ormolu mounted Boulle marquetry bracket clock, late 18thC, 52in (132cm). **$6,000-9,000**

South Bar Antiques

DIGBETH STREET, STOW-ON-THE-WOLD,
GLOUCESTERSHIRE

Telephone: Stow-on-the-Wold 30236

*We have a large and varied selection of Clocks
(approx 50 Longcases together with Bracket,Wall
and French Clocks) and Barometers.
JEWELLERY especially a number of Cameos.
Paintings and collectables.
Pollard and Burr Furniture a speciality.*

A Regency gilt bronze automaton mantel clock, signed Hy Borrell, London, 19in (48cm). **$10,500-14,000**

A Charles X ormolu and ebony portico mantel clock, the cast dial signed Delaunoy Eleve de Breguet, 26in (66cm). **$13,500-17,500**

An Oriental gold, enamel and gem set monstrance clock, early 19thC, wood base and glazed cover, 11½in (28cm). **$10,500-14,000**

A Meissen mantel clock, by George Fritzsche, restoration and firing cracks, c1727. **$24,000-27,000**

An Empire ormolu mantel clock, with later ebonised base and glass dome, 12½in (32cm). **$9,000-12,000**

A Louis XV ormolu mounted tôle and porcelain mantel clock, signed Musson A Paris, 14in (35.5cm). **$6,000-9,000**

An ormolu mounted Samson Imari clock and candelabra, with giltwood plinths, clock 21in (53cm). **$6,000-9,000**

460

l. A porcelain panel carriage clock.
$3,000-4,500
c. A porcelain panel carriage clock, signed
Drocourt, No.8849, 6½in high. **$4,000-5,500**
r. A carriage clock with alarm, 7½in. **$4,000-5,500**

A Sicilian coral mantel clock, early
19thC, 21in (54cm). **$3,000-4,500**

A Louis XVI ormolu urn clock,
the revolving dial with
enamel numerals, the case
signed Courieult à Paris,
16½in. **$15,000-21,000**

An Empire ormolu and bronze mantel
clock, enamel dial signed L.J.
Laquesse et Fils à Paris, 16in.
$4,000-5,500

A Louis XV ormolu cartel clock,
42½in (108cm). **$13,500-17,500**

A George III satinwood mantel
clock, signed Weeks.
$6,000-9,000

A skeleton clock with calendar, signed
Julien Beliard, late 18thC.
$21,000-24,000

A mahogany mantel clock, dial signed
Breguet, 11in high. **$7,500-10,500**

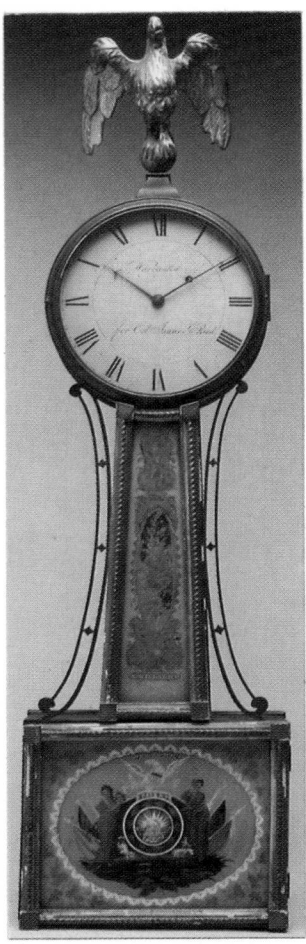

A gold and enamel verge watch, the movement signed Perigal London 482, with champlevé enamelled protective case and a gilt metal enamelled chatelaine, 4.5cm diam. **$7,500-10,500**

A Federal mahogany veneer lighthouse clock, by Simon Willard, Roxbury, Mass, with original dome and winding key, c1825, 27½in (69.5cm) high. **$112,000-127,000**

The Colonel Isaac Gardiner Reed presentation banjo clock, by Aaron Willard, Jr, Boston, c1815, 30in (76cm) high. **$127,000-150,000**

A gold cased gentleman's bracelet watch, by Patek Philippe, Geneve, 867914, signed, 3.5cm, leather strap. **$60,000-75,000**

A gentleman's bracelet watch, by Patek Philippe & Co Geneve, No.861245, 3.4cm. **$75,000-90,000**

A gold Grande Sonnerie keyless lever clock watch, A Lange & Söhne, c1910, 5.5cm. **$67,000-75,000**

A gold cased gentleman's perpetual calendar bracelet watch, signed Patek Philippe & Co., No.868331, 3.9cm. **$180,000+**

An American novelty clock, by Ansonia Clock Co, with a child on a swing, painted 4th December 1886, 15½in (38cm). **$750-1,000**

A George III mahogany perpetual calendar and elbow barometer, c1763. **\$10,500-14,000**

A Sheraton period wheel barometer, by J B Roncheti. **\$7,500-10,500**

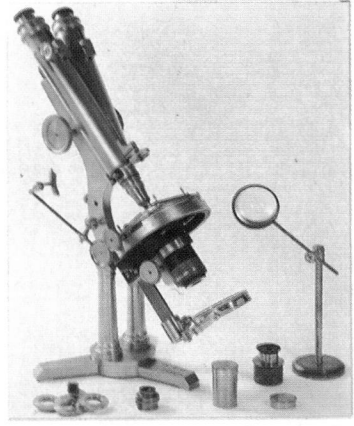

A lacquered brass compound monocular microscope, signed R & J Beck, 31 Cornhill, London, No.6164, incomplete, with original mahogany case, 20in (51cm). **\$1,500-2,600**

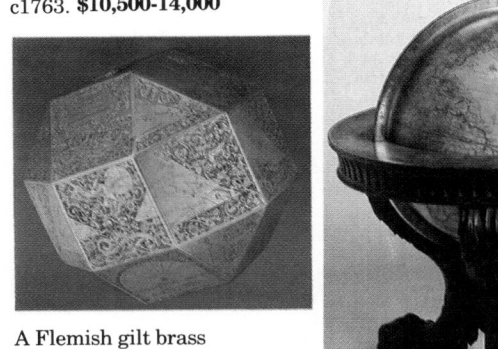

A Flemish gilt brass polyhedral sundial, by Michael Coignet, incomplete, c1590, 6in (15cm). **\$36,000-39,000**

A pair of celestial and terrestrial library globes, the terrestrial globe signed, the celestial globe unsigned, on mahogany stands, late 18thC, 12in (30cm) diam. **\$6,000-9,000**

A lacquered brass compound binocular microscope, by Ross London, Ross No.1. Stand No.5321, with accessories in original mahogany carrying case, late 19thC, 21in (53cm) high. **\$4,500-7,000**

A brass cruciform sundial, possibly Augsburg, secured by pin latches, enclosing a storage area, mid-17thC, with later suspension loop, 8in (20cm). **\$7,000-9,000**

A white wisteria leaded glass and bronze table lamp, the shade impressed 1073, the bronze tree-form base impressed Tiffany Studios New York 27770, 26½in (67cm) high. **$52,000-60,000**

A nasturtium leaded glass and bronze table lamp, the shallow domed shade impressed Tiffany Studios New York, the base similarly impressed, 8620, 24in (61cm) high. **$16,000-21,000**

A daffodil leaded glass and bronze table lamp, the shade unsigned, the twisted vine base impressed Tiffany Studios New York 443, 25½in (64cm) high. **$13,500-17,500**

An Oriental poppy leaded glass and bronze floor lamp, the shade impressed Tiffany Studios New York 1597, the base No.376, similarly impressed, 79in (200.5cm) to top of pig-tail finial. **$90,000-100,000**

A rosebush leaded glass and gilt bronze table lamp, the shade impressed Tiffany Studios New York 1915, the base No.367, 30in unextended. **$60,000-75,000**

A leaded glass and earthenware table lamp, the shade impressed Tiffany Studios, N York, base Grueby Pottery Boston USA, 21in high. **$7,500-10,500**

A Gallé bronzed mounted 'veilleuse', with 3 dragon-flies forming the stand, carved signature of Gallé, 7in (18cm) high. **$10,000-13,000**

l. A plum mould-blown triple overlay glass vase, by Emile Gallé, 13in (33cm) high. **$10,500-14,000**

r. An apple mould-blown triple overlay glass vase, by Emile Gallé, 11½in high. **$15,000-21,000**

A Gallé vase modelled as a Fu Dog, clear glass with blue and gilt enamelling, engraved with a grasshopper enriched with gilding, engraved EG incorporating the cross of Lorraine, c1875, 6in (15cm) high. **$22,500-25,000**

A Gallé blowout vase, with moulded decoration of clematis flowers, moulded Gallé signature, 10in (25.5cm) high. **$6,000-9,000**

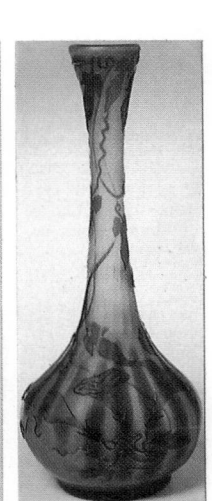

A Gallé cameo glass vase, overlaid with amethyst tone acid-etched flowers and leaves, signed in cameo form 'Gallé', 16in (40.5cm). **$4,500-7,000**

Two tall Gallé cameo baluster vases, with carved Gallé signatures, 23in (59cm) high, l. **$7,500-10,500** r. **$10,500-14,000**

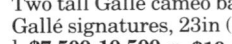

An Art Nouveau leaded stained glass panel, signed Jacques Gruber, dated 04, 101in (256cm) high. **$15,000-21,000**

465

A glass vase overlaid with a design of spring flowers, signed Gallé, c1900, 9in (23cm) diam. **$3,000-4,500**

A poppy triple overlay cameo glass vase, by Emile Gallé, with cameo signature, 24in (61cm) high. **$13,500-17,500**

A glass vase, Les Sept Princesses, by Emile Gallé, inscribed Exposit. 1900, 9in. **$27,000-30,000**

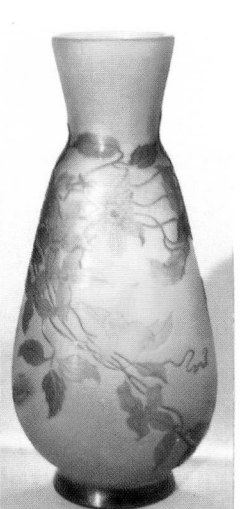

A glass vase, with a design of clematis, signed Gallé, 13in. **$3,000-4,000**

A vase overlaid on amber with a design of chrysanthemums, signed Gallé, 12½in (32cm) high. **$4,500-7,000**

A glass vase with a design of anemones, signed Gallé, c1900, 8in (20cm) high. **$4,000-5,500**

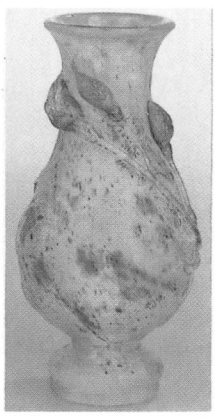

A Gallé overlay glass vase, 'Roses de France', engraved Gallé, 7½in. **$82,000-97,000**

A vase overlaid on apricot with a design of nasturtiums, signed Gallé, 9in (23cm). **$4,000-5,500**

An etched and double overlay glass vase, signed Gallé, 8in (20cm) high. **$19,500-22,500**

466

A glass vase overlaid on amber with a design of lilies and lotus rising from a pond, signed Gallé, c1900, 8½in (22cm). **$2,250-3,500**

An elephant mould-blown double overlay glass vase, incised signature Emile Gallé, 15in (38cm) high. **$30,000-34,500**

A glass vase overlaid with a design of clematis, signed Gallé, c1900, 12½in (31cm). **$2,500-3,500**

A fine glass vase, engraved with silver designs of scrolling flowers and foliage, inscribed Loetz, Austria, 9in (22.5cm). **$3,000-4,000**

A glass vase with red overlaid on amber with flowering creeper, signed Gallé, c1900, 9in (23cm) diam. **$2,500-3,500**

An internally decorated and wheel-carved cameo glass vase, signed Daum, Nancy, 8½in (21cm). **$45,000-49,000**

A wheel-carved and enamelled cameo glass vase, Daum, Nancy, c1900, 5in. **$3,000-4,500**

An internally decorated glass vase, Daum, Nancy, 14in. **$90,000-100,000**

A wheel-carved cameo glass vase, Daum, Nancy, 10in. **$20,000-22,000**

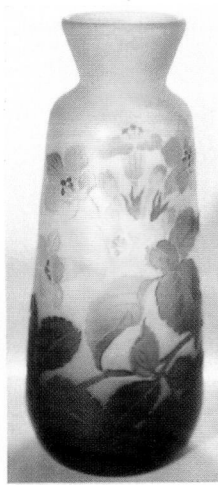

A glass vase with spring flowers, signed Gallé, c1900, 14in. **$3,000-4,000**

A glass vase with spring flowers, signed Gallé, c1900, 8in. **$1,500-2,600**

A marquetry cabinet, inlaid with flowers and butterflies, the upper section with a mirror, by Louis Majorelle, 39½in (100cm) wide. **$18,000-22,500**

A marquetry cabinet, 'Aux Grenouilles', with carved frog feet, inlaid panels with dragonflies and mushrooms, marquetry Gallé signature, 26in. **$19,500-24,000**

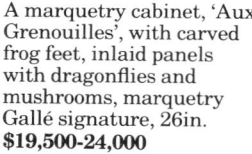

A pair of oak twin beds, designer Frank Lloyd Wright, probably by Niedecken-Walbridge Co for Ray Evans House, Chicago, Illinois, c1909, 47in (119cm) wide. **$7,500-10,500**

A carved and marquetry vitrine, branded L. Majorelle Nancy, 31in (78cm). **$10,500-14,000**

An upholstered mahogany 3-piece salon suite, carved with ferns and 2 snails, by Louis Majorelle, settee 54½in. **$6,000-9,000**

Two rare inlaid oak armchairs, designer Harvey Ellis, by Gustav Stickley, c1904, 47in high. l. **$13,500-17,500** r. **$13,500-17,500**

A marquetry umbrella stand, with original tin liner, marquetry Gallé signature, 21in (53cm). **$25,000-28,000**

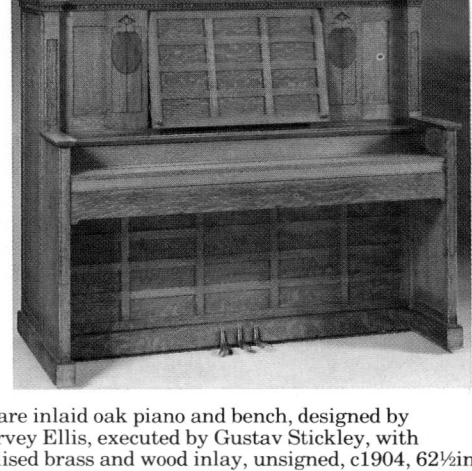

A rare inlaid oak piano and bench, designed by
Harvey Ellis, executed by Gustav Stickley, with
stylised brass and wood inlay, unsigned, c1904, 62½in
(158cm) wide. **$15,000-21,000**

A walnut fishing tackle cabinet, by Ernest Gimson,
with barber's pole inlay, the brass mounts by
Alfred Bucknell, the bottom drawer inlaid with
fruitwoods, dated 1913, 79in (197cm).
$22,500-25,000

A rare oak and leather hexagonal table,
by Gustav Stickley, with original
finish, leather and tacks, part
of craftsmans paper label, model No.
624, c1910, 48in (122cm).
$15,000-21,000

A walnut bureau cabinet-on-
stand, by Ernest Gimson,
with fitted interior, the
frieze drawer with barber's
pole inlay, on black painted
stand, c1906, 39in (99cm).
$18,000-21,000

A walnut bookcase, by Sidney
Barnsley, with 2 glazed
doors edged with rosewood,
above 2 panelled doors with
rosewood handles, 42in
(106cm). **$13,500-17,500**

Two oak high spindle back chairs, designed by
Frank Lloyd Wright, probably executed by
Neidecken-Wallbridge Co, for Ray Evans
House, Chicago, Illinois, c1908, 45in
(114cm) high. **$30,000-37,500 each**

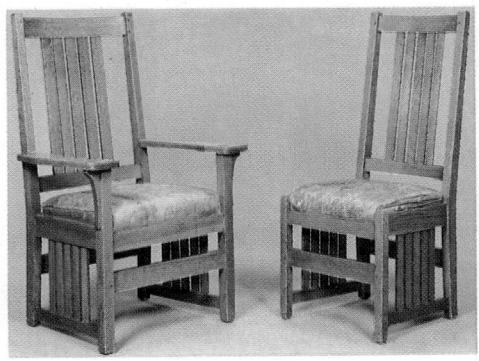

A set of 7 high back dining chairs, by
L & J G Stickley, including one carver,
with original finish and original leather
drop-in seats, model nos. 814 and 812,
c1910, 45½in (115cm) high.
$15,000-21,000

An Omar Ramsden silver punch bowl with everted rim, with inscription and stamped marks Omar Ramsden me fecit, London hallmarks for 1931, 9in (23cm) wide, 65oz 14dwt. **$7,500-10,500**

A Ramsden and Carr silver tea caddy and spoon, 1931, 4in (10cm), 13oz 7dwt gross. **$3,000-4,000**

A silver, amber and chrysolite cloak brooch, designed by Georg Jensen, c1905, executed by Georg Jensen Silversmithy, impressed G1830S I, 2oz gross. **$10,500-14,000**

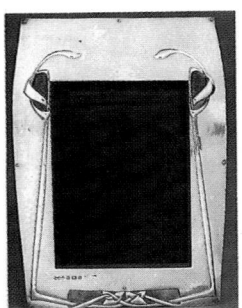

A Liberty silver and enamel picture frame, designed by Archibald Knox, with Celtic stylised turquoise and green enamelling, 2 pins set with tiny turquoise cabochons, stamped L. & Co Cymric, Birmingham hallmarks for 1904, 8½in (21cm). **$6,000-9,000**

A 6-piece tea service and tray, each with stylised monogram 'PEM', by Gorham Manufacturing Co Providence, tray 31in, 374oz gross. **$18,000-22,500**

A centrepiece with lightly hammered oval bowl on pierced stem with foliage and trendrils, stamped Georg Jensen 925.S 306, with Master C F Heise assay mark, c1928, 15in (38cm) diam, 58oz 5dwt. **$6,000-9,000**

A pair of candelabra, each with 5 cup-shaped candle nozzles and circular drip pans, stamped marks Georg Jensen 383A, 10½ (27cm). **$34,000-39,000**

A silver centrepiece, the hammered bowl with peaked and scrolled corners with clusters of grapes, engraved Joseph Ambrose and Elizabeth Genevieve Braun June 9th 1926, impressed Georg Jensen Sterling 380 Denmark GI 925S, 16in diam, 102oz. **$18,000-21,000**

A silver and ivory tea service, with hammered bodies raised on 4 short feet, impressed mark of Gorham and Martele 9584 WDL, samovar with stand 13in (33cm) high, 218oz gross.
$16,500-19,500

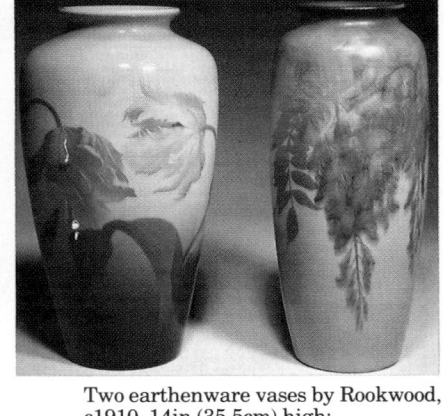

Two earthenware vases by Rookwood, c1910, 14in (35.5cm) high:

l. by Carl Schmidt. **$4,500-7,000**

r. by Edward Diers. **$1,000-1,400**

A Guild of Handicrafts mustard pot, 3½in, 4oz 11dwt, a box and cover, 8in, 16oz 15dwt, designed by C R Ashbee, stamped G of H Ltd, c1900, and a mustard pot by C R Ashbee, stamped CRA, c1900, 3in high.
l. **$1,500-2,600** c. **$7,500-10,500** r. **$1,500-2,600**

A 3-piece enamelled demi-tasse service, by Tiffany & Co New York, bearing touchmark of Pan-American Exposition in Buffalo, 1901, marked on base, coffee pot 9in, 37oz 10dwt gross.
$25,000-28,000

A Liberty & Co silver bowl with matching spoon, designer Archibald Knox, stamped L & Co, Cymric and Birmingham 1899, 4in, 21oz. **$6,000-9,000**

An earthenware vase, by Rookwood, 1900, by Carl Schmidt, impressed firm's painter mark, 8½in (21.5cm). **$7,500-10,500**

A Doulton Lambeth faience tile panel, 'Sleeping Beauty – The Fairies at the Christening', painter Margaret E Thompson, signed, 41 by 55in, in modern wooden frame. **$6,000-9,000**

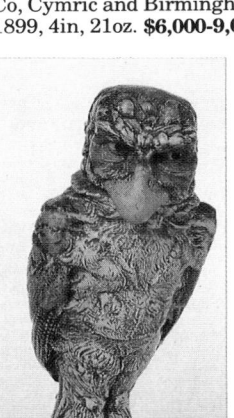

A Martin Brothers stoneware model of a grotesque bird, with removable head, signed on neck, rim and base R.W. Martin & Bros, dated 12-1900, 15in (38cm) high.
$9,000-12,000

A silver sugar bowl and teapot, by Tiffany & Co, New York, 1877-1891, with green stone finial and applied with insects, 3in and 5in high, 13oz and 15oz gross. l. **$10,500-14,000** r. **$18,000-21,000**

471

An agate, gold and enamel plate, by E Tourrette and Georges Fouquet, the enamel signed E. Tourrette. **$18,000-22,500**

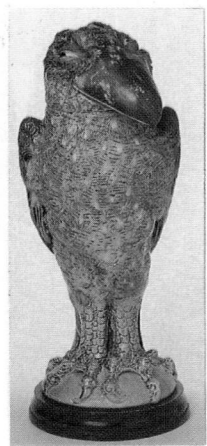

A Martin Bros stoneware grotesque bird, signed, dated 11-1899, 16½in high. **$13,500-17,500**

An Arts and Crafts pendant and chain, the design attributed to Edgar Simpson. **$4,500-7,000**

A gold, plique-à-jour enamel, diamond and pearl pendant, by G Fouquet. **$100,000-120,000**

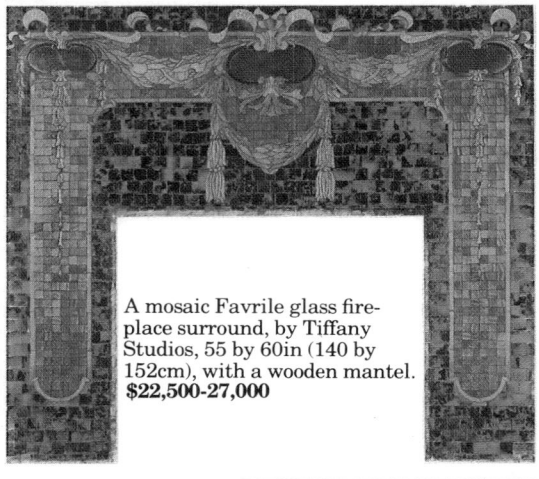

A mosaic Favrile glass fireplace surround, by Tiffany Studios, 55 by 60in (140 by 152cm), with a wooden mantel. **$22,500-27,000**

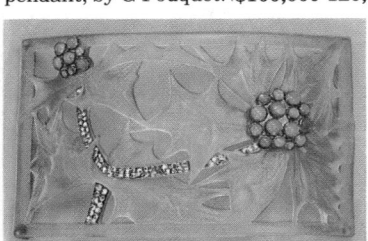

A blond horn, opal, diamond plaque of a collier de chien by Lucien Gaillard. **$13,500-17,500**

A French gold, plique-à-jour enamel, diamond, emerald and tourmaline mounted pendant. **$7,500-10,500**

A mosaic Favrile glass fireplace surround, by Tiffany Studios, 72 by 89in (183 by 226cm). **$15,000-21,000**

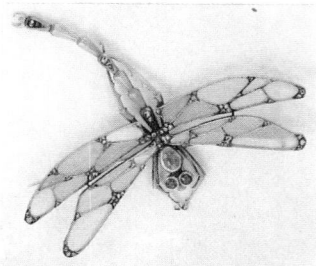

A gold, opal, ruby, emerald and diamond dragonfly brooch, by Georges Fouquet. **$30,000-37,500**

472

'Job', by Alphonse Mucha, lithograph in colours on paper, creased, signed, 20 by 15½in (51 by 39cm), framed.
$9,000-12,000

A gold, enamel, diamond and opal plaque of a collier de chien by René Lalique.
$75,000-90,000

A gold, plique-à-jour and enamel pendant watch, engraved Lalique, the dial marked Leroy Paris.
$52,000-60,000

A gold, pearl and enamel choker, by René Lalique, in fitted case.
$52,000-60,000

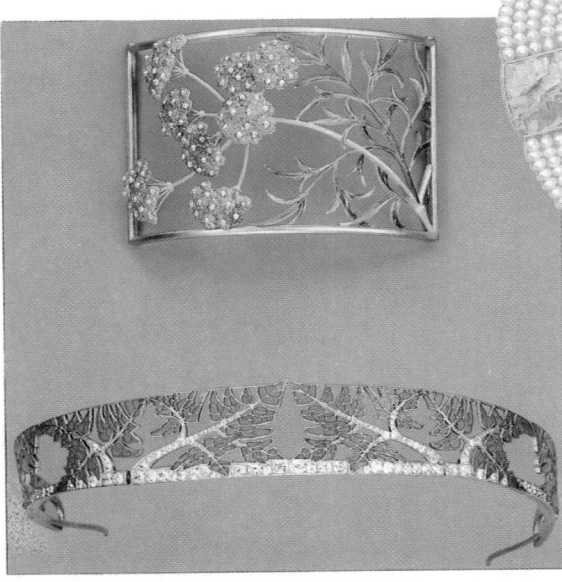

A gold, plique-à-jour, enamel and diamond plaque of a collier de chien, by Paul and Henri Vever, No.1256. **$25,000-30,000**

A gold, plique-à-jour and diamond hair ornament.
$18,000-22,500

An English bronze statuette of Peter Pan, from a model by Sir George Frampton, pipes loose, monogrammed and dated GF 1915, and inscribed P.P. within a circle, 19in (48cm).
$16,000-21,000

A bronze and ivory figure, 'Danseuse de Thebes', inscribed Cl. J.R. Colinet, 10in (25.5cm).
$15,000-21,000

Bronze and ivory figures: l. 'Mandolin Player', signed F. Preiss in marble, 23½in (59cm).
$33,000-37,000 r. 'Flute Player', from a model by F Preiss, 19in (48.5cm).
$30,000-34,500

A bronze and ivory figure, 'Towards the Unknown', signed Cl. J. R. Colinet, 18½in (47.5cm).
$7,500-10,500

A cold painted, damascened and silvered bronze and ivory group of a cabaret act, 'Two Girls', inscribed 'Laurent Hely' and 'Bronze', French, early 20thC, 21in (53cm) high.
$18,000-22,500

A cold painted, gilt bronze and white marble group of a snake charmer, 'Dance of Carthage', inscribed Cl.J.R. Colinet, Belgian, early 20thC, 22in (56cm).
$15,000-21,000

A bronze and ivory figure, 'Girl Dancer', the bronze base decorated with 3 masks above a 12-sided striated marble base, signed in the bronze O. Hoffmann, and with foundry mark, 14in (35.5cm).
$22,500-25,000

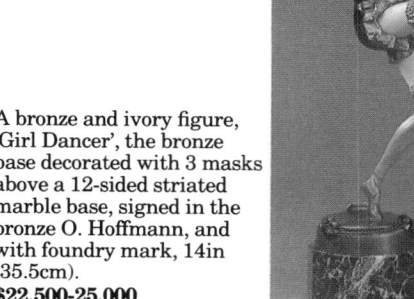

F Preiss bronze and ivory figures: 'Sonny Boy', restored, 8½in (21cm). **$4,500-7,000** r. 'Con Brio', 14½in (37cm). **$18,000-21,000** c. A Japanese lady by C Jaeger, 10½in (27cm). **$4,000-5,500**

A copper urn, designed by Frank Lloyd Wright, by James A Miller, c1903, 18in (45.5cm) high. **$87,000-93,000**

A polished bronze head of a woman, 'Divinité' Solaire', from a model by Gustave Miklos, French, 20thC, 25½in (64.5cm). **$42,000-51,000**

A painted bronze and ivory figure, stamped with PK monogram, and signed on base F. Preiss. **$13,500-17,500**

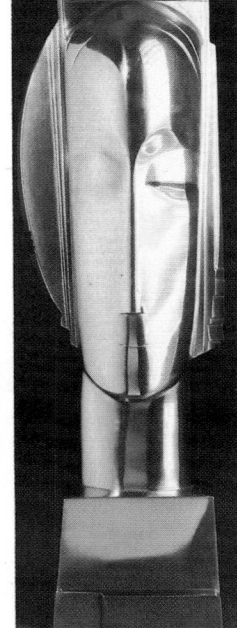

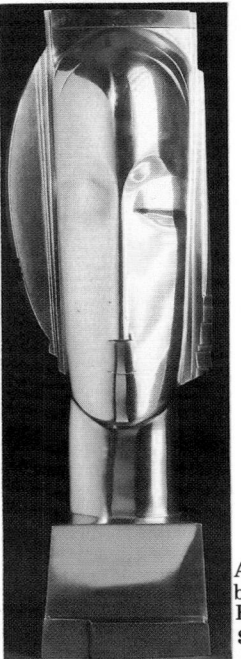

A bronze and ivory figure, 'Bayadère', by D H Chiparus, 20½in (52.5cm) high. **$18,000-21,000**

A bronze group, from a model by Jean Lambert-Rucki, French, 20thC, 23in (58cm). **$13,500-17,500**

A painted bronze and ivory figural lamp, signed 'Chiparus', and stamped on metal LN Paris JL, and Made in France, 14½in (37cm). **$15,000-21,000**

A bronze group of an amorous dancing couple, from a model by Bruno Zack, Austrian, early 20thC, 10in (25.5cm). **$6,000-9,000**

A bronze card holder, 'Chat mâitre d'hotel', by Diego Giacometti, impressed Diego, 11½in (29cm). **$37,000-42,000**

A selection of Clarice Cliff pottery, Newport and Wilkinson Ltd from **$600-1,800 each**

A platter, from a limited edition of 50, painted signature Dessin J Lurçat Sant Vincens DN 11/50, 21in (53cm) wide.
$1,300-1,800

A lacquered vase, inscribed Jean Dunand 4694, 13½in (34cm).
$9,000-12,000

A clear and frosted glass vase, engraved R. Lalique, 11½in (28cm).
$6,000-9,000

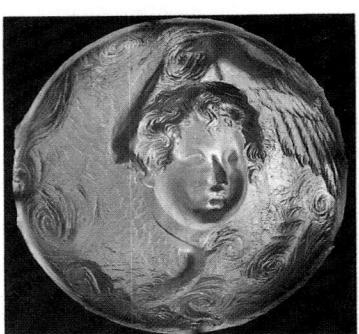

A rare Lalique 'Cire Perdue' hanging lampshade, engraved 'R. Lalique', numbered 384-22, for 1922, contemporary chromed hooks for suspension, 12½in (31cm) diam.
$9,000-12,000

A frosted amber glass vase, 'Serpent', by René Lalique, 10in (25cm).
$10,500-14,000

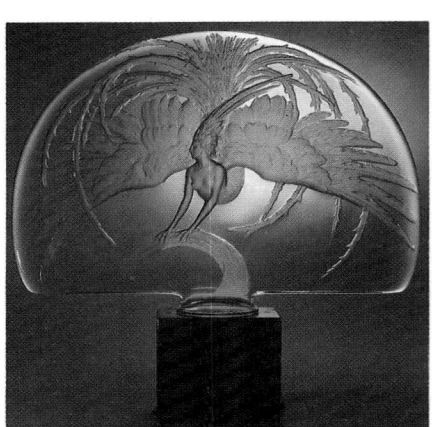

A Lalique liminaire, 'Oiseau de Feu', in clear and satin glass, moulded signature R. Lalique, fitted for electricity, 17in (43cm) high.
$15,000-21,000

Richard Garbe figures: l. Royal Doulton 'The Macaw'.
$2,500-3,500 c. terracotta maiden, 1952.
$1,200-1,600 r. bronze figure, 1933. **$4,000-5,500**

A J Dixon & Sons plated teapot, by
Christopher Dresser.
$60,000-67,500

A 'blossom pattern' coffee set, designed
by Georg Jensen, marked and numbered,
coffee pot 8in (20cm).
$4,000-5,500

A terracotta figure, by
Paul Scheurich, impressed
Karlsruhe mark and incised
Scheurich, 21in (54cm).
$6,000-9,000

A Royal Doulton vase, by
Mark V Marshall, c1910,
20in (51cm). **$10,500-14,000**

A silver tea service, by Cube Teapots Ltd,
each piece impressed trademarks, with
Birmingham hallmarks, 1925, teapot 4in (10cm),
27oz gross. **$4,000-5,500**

A Wiener Werkstätte pottery
figure by Gudrun Baudish,
9½in (24cm). **$1,500-2,600**

A pair of silver and ivory candelabra, by Tetard,
impressed with firm's mark and French poinçons,
c1930, 9in (23cm), 273oz gross. **$10,500-14,000**

A Mappin and Webb silver table service, 'Rosalind', designed by Eric Clements, comprising 114 pieces, stamped maker's marks and London hallmarks for 1963, 153oz 8dwt. **$10,000-13,000**

A calendar table clock with adjustable day and date, marked Cartier, stand stamped Cartier 2324 Paris, 11 by 7cm. **$6,000-8,000**

A lapis lazuli and jade table clock, face gilded Swiss, c1925, 10in (25cm). **$6,000-9,000**

A black lacquered metal, mother-of-pearl and glass table clock, inscribed Cartier No.1074 Made in France, 5in (12.5cm) high, with original battery movement and fitted case. **$6,000-9,000**

A cloisonné box, brass inlaid with a geometric design, incised Jean Goulden CVIII 30 and stamped J, 5in (12cm) wide. **$4,000-5,500**

A bronze and glass dining table, by Diego Giacometti, the glass top with 4 frogs for attachment above a gilt leaf band, signed Diego, 60in (152cm) diam. **$120,000-135,000**

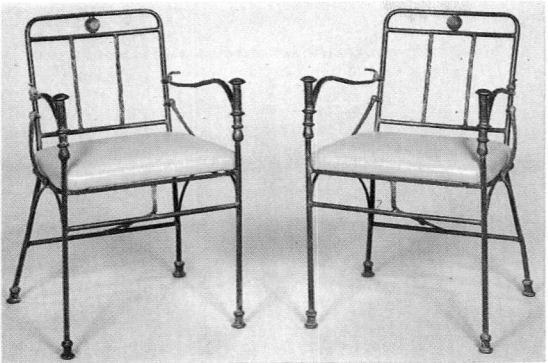

Two bronze armchairs, by Diego Giacometti, the arms formed by the front leg rising to a button top, 32in (81cm) high. **$21,000-24,000 each**

A pair of beechwood open armchairs, designer J Hoffman, branded J & J Kohn, Wein, Austria. **$6,000-8,000**

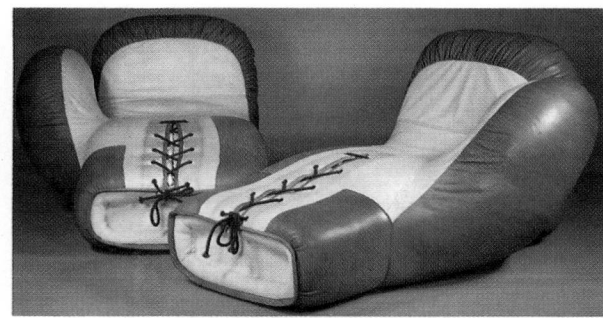

A pair of De Sede chaise longues, in the form of 2 boxing gloves, the fingers forming the back and the thumb the armrest, upholstered in hide, 70in (178cm) long. **$10,500-14,000**

A set of 6 Asprey dining chairs and two armchairs. **$37,000-42,000**
An Asprey glass and chromed metal dining table, inlaid with Lalique panels. **$150,000+**

An Apielli & Varesio chair designed by Carlo Mollino, c1945. **$7,500-10,500**

The Gerrit Rietveld '1918 Red/Blue chair', by G A v d Groenekan, in beech and plywood. **$4,000-5,500**

A Fontana Arte plate glass and chromium plated table, c1935, 67in (169cm). **$4,500-7,000**

A wrought iron and mahogany table, by Pierre Chareau, 19½in (49cm). **$13,500-17,500**

A bentwood salon suite, designed by Josef Hoffmann, by J J Kohn, c1905, settee 47½in (120cm). **$9,000-12,000**

An Art Deco cocktail bar trolley, the top with 2 inset clear and satin glass panels each inscribed R. Lalique, France, with illuminated fitted bar interior, 34in (88cm) wide.
$13,500-17,500

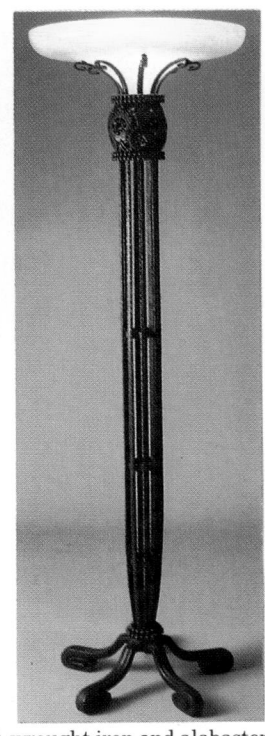

A wrought iron and alabaster floor lamp, 'Orient', by Edgar Brandt, c1925, 72in (182.5cm).
$40,000-45,000

A moulded glass, bronze mounted vitrine, on wood stand, by René Lalique, c1910, 25in (63.5cm) high.
$48,000-52,500

A George III three-piece table garniture, by Wm Pitts and Joseph Preedy, London, 1799, 21in (53cm), 143oz. **$9,000-12,000**

A bronze floor lamp, by Diego and Alberto Giacometti, cast with a woman's head, unsigned, 63in (160cm), on green marble base.
$30,000-36,000

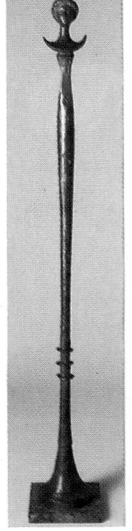

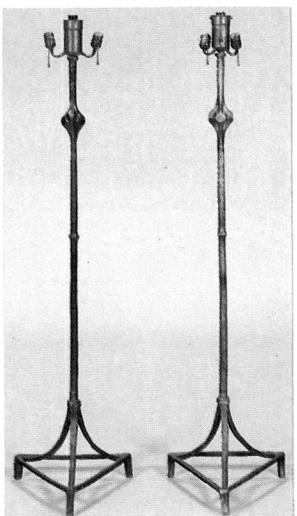

A pair of bronze floor lamps, by Diego Giacometti, one with green patina, the other gilt patina, 58in (147cm). **$34,000-39,000**

A George III epergne, by William Holmes, the centre engraved with the Hobhouse coat of arms, each basket engraved with a crest, 1771.
$10,500-14,000

A George II Irish bread basket, by George Hill, Dublin, engraved with a coat-of-arms within a rococo cartouche, c1760, 15in (38cm) wide, 72oz.
$25,000-30,000

A Lalique green tinted vase, 'Palissy', engraved signature R. Lalique, France, 6in (16cm).
$300-500

A Lalique clock, 'Inseparables', moulded signature R. Lalique, 4½in (11cm).
$1,500-2,600

A Lalique table lamp, the clear satin finished glass with amber staining, etched and engraved signature R. Lalique, 10½in (27.5cm).
$4,000-5,500

Glass

A Sabino blue opalescent glass vase, engraved Sabino, Paris, foot ground, 11½in (29cm).
$450-700

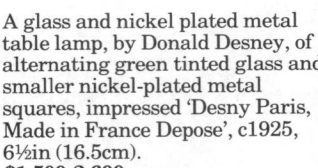

A Cenedese vase, with primitive trailed decoration, in deep amethyst coloured glass, 13½in (34cm).
$1,500-2,600

A glass and nickel plated metal table lamp, by Donald Desney, of alternating green tinted glass and smaller nickel-plated metal squares, impressed 'Desny Paris, Made in France Depose', c1925, 6½in (16.5cm).
$1,500-2,600

A chrome and glass table lamp, 15in (38cm).
$75-150

A Lalique hand mirror, 'Deux Chèvres', in original fitted case, for 'Il Rue Royale Paris', 6½in (16cm).
$1,500-2,600

A pair of chromium plated metal photograph frames, 17in (43cm).
$2,250-3,000

An amethyst glass table lamp base, moulded 'A. Hunibelle', 'Modele Dep de R Cogneville, Made in France', 11in (28cm).
$300-400

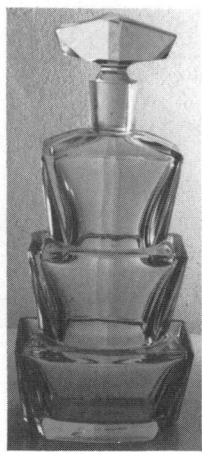

A French geometric enamel and glass decanter, with black and red decoration, 12in (30.5cm).
$300-500

Two black and white glass perfume bottles, c1930:
l. **$150-200**

r. **$150-250**

Ceramics

A Wedgwood lustre charger, by Alfred and Louise Powell, decorated with an armorial crest, stylised gilt foliage and a gilt Latin motto with blue, grey and gilt border, on a cream ground, impressed Wedgwood and with painted artist's monogram, 12½in (31.5cm) wide.
$450-600

A scent bottle in original case, 7cm.
$60-100

A French glass and enamel decanter and set of 6 glasses, decanter 9in (23cm), glasses 3in (7.5cm).
$450-700

l. A Wedgwood polar bear.
$100-150

c. A Goldscheider figure of girl with dog.
$100-150

r. A Goldscheider wall mask.
$450-700

A free standing Goldscheider head, 10in (25cm).
$450-600

A wall mask attributed to Goldscheider, orange and green on a flesh coloured ground, 11in (27cm).
$250-350

An earthenware vase by Wheatley Pottery Company, with 3 L-shaped legs, the body moulded with large leaves and small buds in a matt tan glaze, unsigned, minor flakes, 12in (32cm).
$500-600

A Shelley pottery tea service, with a design after Mabel Lucie Atwell.
$450-700

A Shelley 'Vogue' shape Sunray pattern part teaset, comprising: milk jug, sugar bowl, 6 cups and saucers, 6 plates and a cake plate, in green, orange, beige and yellow against a white ground, printed factory mark, Rd. 756533.
$400-500

An earthenware vase by Fulper, the body with a tan streaked blue flambé glaze, raised on 4 partially glazed feet, unsigned, c1915, 16in (40cm).
$500-600

An earthenware vase, with 2 angular handles in a matt green glaze, impressed 'Teco', 7in (17cm).
$400-500

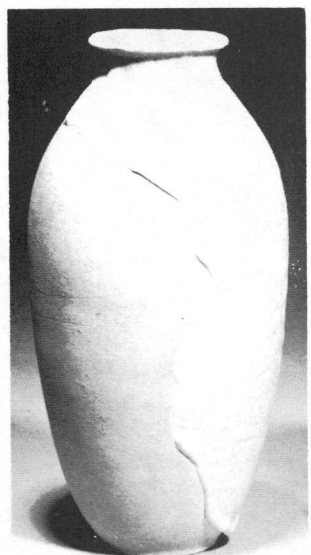

An earthenware vase, with a thick crazed white partial glaze, impressed 'Grueby Pottery Boston U.S.A.', 10in (25cm).
$700-900

An earthenware vase, moulded with broad leaves in shades of green, impressed 'Chicago Crucible Co. Chicago, Ill.', minor chips, c1925, 5½in (14cm).
$450-500

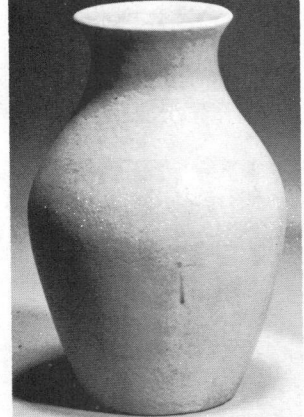

An earthenware vase in a matt mauve glaze, impressed 'Grueby Faience Co. Boston U.S.A.', 7in (18cm).
$300-350

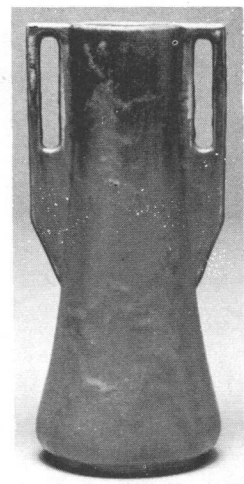

An earthenware vase in a rippled raspberry matt glaze covered with a green flambé glaze at the neck, inscribed 'Fulper', 11in (29cm).
$250-300

An earthenware vase by Grueby, executed by Ruth Erickson, the spherical body modelled with broad leaves in a matt cucumber glaze, impressed 'Grueby Pottery Boston', inscribed 'RE', and with the firm's paper label, 7in (18cm).
$700-800

A square earthenware vase, with 4 broad handles at the shoulder, in a matt green glaze, impressed twice 'Teco', 9in (23cm).
$700-900

An earthenware vase with a cobalt and lavender blue flambé glaze over a matt blue glaze, impressed 'Fulper', 10in (25cm).
$700-900

An earthenware vase by Volkmar, with an inscribed Greek key design around the neck, in a pale olive glaze with tan patches, inscribed 'V', 6in (15cm).
$140-180

A baluster earthenware vase, with twin ear-shaped handles, in a black flambé glaze with grey crystalline highlights, inscribed 'Fulper', 13in (33cm).
$450-500

A baluster earthenware vase by Grueby, in a blue-speckled light blue glaze, impressed with firm's mark, 3in (8cm).
$300-400

A Goldscheider pottery double face wall plaque, the 2 females in profile with green and orange hair and orange lips, printed marks, 12in (30.5cm).
$600-900

A Goldscheider pottery negro wall mask, impressed 'Frederich Goldscheider Wien 1613 96 21', 10½in (26.5cm).
$300-400

A Volkstedt porcelain figure, signed by 'Busse', 10in (25cm) wide.
$450-600

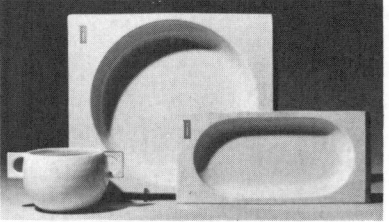

A 55-piece Jean Luce dinner service.
$750-1,000

A Crown Devon porcelain bridge set, with black and gilt geometric decoration comprising: 4 coffee cups and saucers, 2 ashtrays and a card box, printed marks Crown Devon Fieldings Made in England 2714, in original box.
$300-400

A St Ives stoneware vase by Janet Leach, partially covered with a running iron-brown glaze over a thin green glaze revealing the textured red body beneath, impressed 'St. Ives' seal, 11½in (29cm).
$250-350

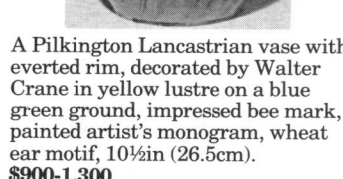

A Pilkington Lancastrian vase with everted rim, decorated by Walter Crane in yellow lustre on a blue green ground, impressed bee mark, painted artist's monogram, wheat ear motif, 10½in (26.5cm).
$900-1,300

A Belgian Modewest vase, marked Ceramique Brussels, c1930.
$150-250

A French vase, painted in the manner of René Buthaud, in black, dark green and brown against an oatmeal ground, indistinctly marked on base, 13in (33cm).
$400-500

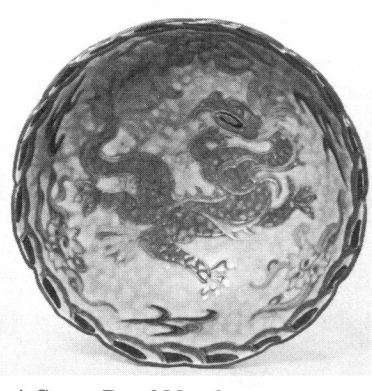

A Crown Ducal Manchu pattern bowl, designed by Charlotte Rhead, coloured in green, blue, orange and with gilding against a green ground, printed factory marks, signed 'C. Rhead', 10in (25.5cm) diam.
$150-250

A Webb & Co earthenware wall plaque, buff coloured against a grey blue background, impressed mark 'Webb & Co., Leeds-Faience', artist's signature 'E. H. Hammond' and 'Leeds art pottery', 14½in (36.5cm).
$300-400

Jazzy Art Deco

*Specialists in good quality
British art deco furniture*

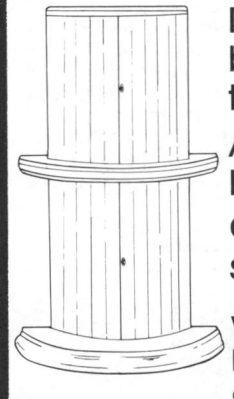

Dining room, lounge and
bedroom suites, cocktail cabinets,
tables and desks.

Also modernist, mirrored and
lacquered furniture.

Carpets, rugs, peach mirrors,
standard lamps and light fittings.

We also stock a selection of glass,
bronzes, ceramics by Clarice Cliff etc.,
and many interesting pieces of the
period.

Enquiries, call or write to:

Jazzy Art Deco Furniture Centre
67 Camden Road, Camden Town
London NW1, England
Telephone: 01-267 3342

Telephone: 011 44 1 267 3342

*We are open Tuesday-Sunday 10.00-6.00 and on
Monday's by appointment*

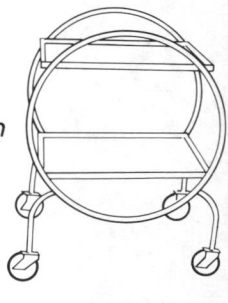

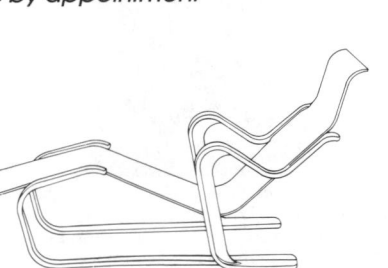

A Clarice Cliff Bizarre vase, 10in (25.5cm).
$900-1,300

A Clarice Cliff Bizarre Patina ware vase, Newport Pottery, 10in (25.5cm).
$300-400

A Clarice Cliff Bizarre Inspiration pattern jug, Newport Pottery, painted mark on base, hairline crack to handle, 10in (25.5cm).
$150-250

A Clarice Cliff Fantasque lotus shape vase, painted with large orange, green and blue sunburst enclosed by brown and white bubbles, the borders of orange, green, blue and purple banding, printed facsimile signature, Wilkinson, 9½in (24.5cm).
$600-900

CLARICE CLIFF

★ marked wares produced between 1925 and 1963
★ it would be very unusual to find unmarked examples
★ marks are nearly always black though gilt was occasionally used
★ a variety of markings are found but usually include: hand painted Bizarre by Clarice Cliff, the name of the pattern, the maker; either Newport Pottery or Wilkinson Ltd
★ pre-1935 wares in unusual shapes or rare patterns are particularly collectable

A Clarice Cliff vase in the Honey Glaze pattern, 8in (20.5cm).
$150-250

Ceramic Figures

A Clarice Cliff Inspiration charger, 'The Knight Errant', depicting a knight, reserved against a green turquoise ground, printed factory marks and facsimile signature, 18in (45.5cm).
$1,500-2,600

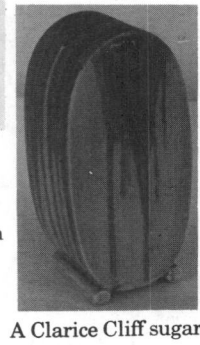

A Clarice Cliff sugar sifter, 5in (14cm).
$60-100

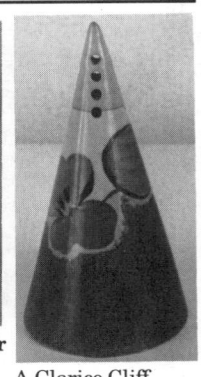

A Clarice Cliff Nasturtium pattern cone sugar sifter, 5½in (14cm).
$100-200

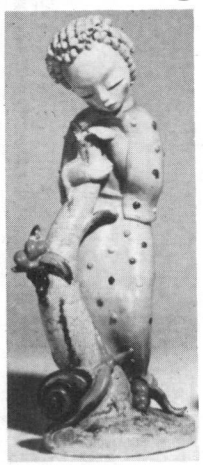

A Goldscheider figure in terracotta with polychrome glaze, printed marks Goldscheider Wien, Made in Austria, 12½in (31cm).
$250-350

A Goldscheider pottery group after a model by Lorenzl, painted in mottled shades of pink, green and brown, printed and impressed marks, 17in (43cm).
$1,000-1,400

A Clarice Cliff jardinière in Delecia pattern, 6½in (16cm) high.
$300-400

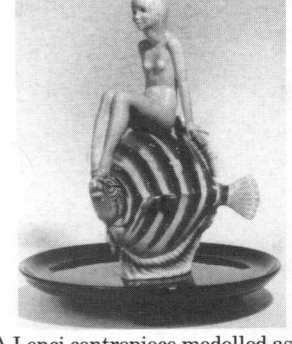

A Lenci centrepiece modelled as a young naked girl, inscribed 'Lenci Made in Italy Torino', 18in (46cm).
$1,500-2,600

A Goldscheider pottery figure of a dancing girl designed by Lorenzl, base impressed 'Lorenzl', printed marks, 16in (40.5cm).
$1,200-1,600

A Goldscheider figure of semi-naked negro girl, on Corinthian column pedestal, 55in (139.5cm).
$1,500-2,600

A Goldscheider figure from a model by Lorenzl, printed marks, column inscribed 'Lorenzl', 13in (33cm), and 9 other figures.
$300-400

A Royal Dux figure of Gandhi, c1930, 12in (30.5cm).
$300-500

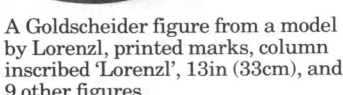

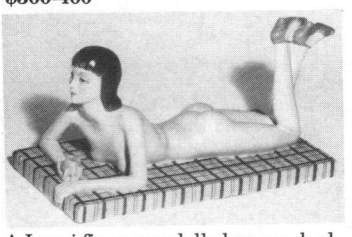

A Lenci figure modelled as a naked girl, with brown hair and wearing orange shoes reclining on a tartan blanket, black painted marks 'Lenci, Made in Italy' and printed paper label, 12in (30.5cm) wide.
$1,500-2,600

A Berlin white porcelain figure of a nymph with deer, designed by Gerhard Schliepstein, inscribed 'G. Schliepstein', underglaze blue sceptre mark and impressed 'MZ 12050', 8in (20.5cm).
$600-900

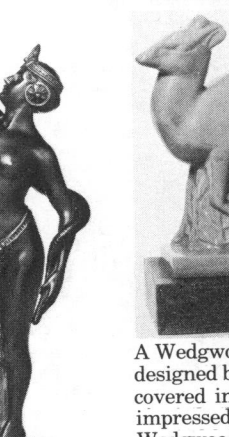

A Wedgwood animal figure, designed by John Skeaping, covered in a celadon glaze, impressed 'J. Skeaping, Wedgwood', 9in (23cm).
$250-350

An Italian china 'Galle' figure of a kneeling semi-dressed female figure, 1950s, 18in (45.5cm).
$900-1,300

A bronze figure by Fesler Felix, signed 'Fesler Felix', 14½in (37cm)
$450-600

A porcelain Katshutte figure, marked, 20½in (52cm).
$750-1,000

A Wiener Keramik polychrome figure by Gudrun Baudisch, some damage, impressed WW monogram and artist's monogram GB, 7½in (19.5cm).
$1,300-1,800

A rare Austrian miniature golfing figure, c1910.
$250-350

A green painted metal figural lamp, inscribed on the metal 'Guerbe', 19½in (50cm).
$1,300-1,800

A bronze figure cast from a model by Jaeger, signed 'Jaeger', stamped Vrais-Bronze Depose K foundry marks, 26in (66cm).
$1,200-1,600

A bronze group cast from a model by C Kauba, dark gilt patina, on marble base, signed in the bronze 'C. Kauba', 5½in (14cm).
$600-900

A bronze figure, 'Dancer with Thyrsus', cast from a model by Pierre Le Faguays, cold-painted in grey on stepped marble base, slight restoration, inscribed 'Le Faguays', 10½in (27cm).
$1,500-2,600

A bronze figure cast from a model by Ferdinand Liebermann, in various cold coloured patinas, including gilt, dark gold and red, signed in the bronze 'F. Liebermann', 15½in (40cm).
$1,500-2,600

A bronze figure of a hunter cast from a model by Pierre Le Faguays, bronze inscribed 'P. Le Faguays', 14in (35.5cm), and another similar bronze cast from a model by Le Faguays.
$1,300-1,800

A bronze figure, 'A Torch Dancer', cast after a model by Ferdinand Preiss, with dull golden bronze patina, on black and green marble pyramid base, signed on the base 'F. Preiss', 13½in (34.5cm).
$3,000-4,500

A silvered bronze figure, 'A huntress', cast from a model by G None, signed in the bronze 'G. None Gorini Fres Ed teors, Paris', 13½in (34cm).
$2,250-3,000

A bronze figure, 'The Racing Driver', cast from a model by Saalmann, inscribed 'Saalmann', stamped 'Echte Bronze', 11½in (28.5cm).
$3,000-4,000

A bronze figure, 'Bear Hug', cast after a model by F Rieder, bronze inscribed 'F. Rieder', 12in (30.5cm).
$2,250-3,000

A bronze figure, 'Con Brio', cast after a model by Ferdinand Preiss, with dull golden bronze patina, on black and green marble pyramid base, signed on the base 'F. Preiss', 13½in (34cm).
$3,000-4,500

A bronze figure, 'Girl Skipping', cast from a model by Bruno Zack, signed in the bronze 'Zack', 14½in (37cm).
$1,500-2,600

A bronze group, signed in the bronze 'JB', 25½in (65cm).
$3,000-4,500

A seated bronze study of Lucifer, 20thC, 8in (20cm).
$600-900

An Italian bronze head of a young boy, cast from a model by Vincenzo Gemito, stamped 'Gemito' and with the Fonderia Gemito seal, early 20thC, 11in (28cm).
$1,500-2,600

A bronze figure, 'The Kicking Dancer', cast from a model by Bruno Zack, on green onyx base, bronze inscribed 'B. Zack', 12½in (31.7cm).
$1,200-1,600

A large cold painted bronze figure of a young woman, by Bruno Zack, on a grey veined black marble plinth, signed, 36½in (93cm).
$16,500-19,500

A bronze figure of a panther, cast from a model by M Prost, dark patina, inscribed 'M. Prost' and Susse Fres Editrs. Paris, 7½in (18.5cm).
$1,500-2,600

A French bronze figure, 'A Seated Monkey', cast from a model by Edouard Marcel Sandoz, formed as a finial, inscribed 'Ed M Sandoz', early 20thC, 4½in (11.5cm).
$1,300-1,800

A gilt bronze figure of a girl with a dog, 12in (30cm).
$3,000-4,000

A green and gilt patinated bronze figure of a female archer, unsigned, 15in (38cm).
$750-1,000

Bronze and Ivory Figures

A Preiss bronze and ivory figure of 'Vanity', 8½in (21.5cm).
$3,000-4,500

A bronze and ivory figure of a goblin, cast and carved from a model by Ferdinand Preiss, bronze inscribed 'F. Preiss', 3½in (9cm) overall.
$900-1,300

A gilt bronze and ivory figure, 'Old Style Dancer', cast and carved from a model by Demêtre Chiparus, cold-painted in dark olive green on brown, black and green marble base, inscribed 'Chiparus', 16in (40.3cm).
$10,500-14,000

A cold-painted bronze and ivory figure of an exotic dancer, 'Dourga', cast and carved from a model by Demêtre Chiparus, French, signed 'Chiparus', early 20thC, 25in (63cm).
$10,500-14,000

A cold-painted, gilt bronze and ivory figure of an exotic dancer, cast and carved from a model by Demêtre Chiparus, French, including white alabaster base, signed 'D. Chiparus', early 20thC, 14in (35cm).
$6,000-9,000

A bronze figure, 'A Lioness', cast after a model by Demêtre Chiparus, signed in the marble 'D. Chiparus', 22½in (57.5cm) wide.
$1,500-2,600

A bronze and ivory figure of a girl, cast and carved from a model by Ferdinand Preiss, unsigned, 6½in (15.5cm).
$1,500-2,600

This model is known as 'The Necklace'; in this case the necklace she should be holding is missing.

A painted bronze and ivory figural lamp, 'Oriental Waiter', cast and carved from a model by Ferdinand Preiss, signed on base 'F. Preiss', 19in (48cm).
$3,000-4,500

A bronze figure of a reclining greyhound, cast from a model by Danniel Bartelletti, base inscribed 'Bartelletti', 20in (51cm).
$300-400

PREISS, JOHANN PHILIPP FERDINAND

Perhaps the best known of those sculptors who chose bronze and ivory as their medium, Preiss, a German, worked in Berlin. Comparison of his figures with many of those made by the Paris-based artists highlights the then German ideal of the master race. Instead of the sensuousness and sometimes frank eroticism of the French school, many of the Preiss figures display a fresh air healthiness of spirit as they earnestly pursue their sporting activities. The sheer numbers of Preiss figures in circulation preclude his having made each one individually. It is generally accepted that he designed all the figures himself, employing a number of sculptors to work, almost on a production line basis on their various component parts, which he would then assemble.

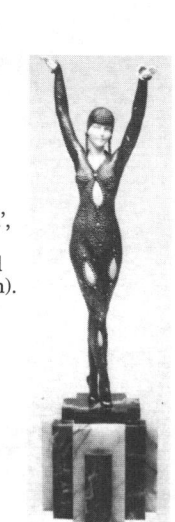

An unusual painted bronze and ivory figural lamp, unmarked but possibly by F. Preiss, 23in (58cm).
$2,500-3,500

A bronze and ivory figure, 'Madame Chrysanthemum', cast and carved from a model by A Jorel, cold-painted in brown with gilt decoration on marble base, inscribed 'A. Jorel', 16in (41cm).
$3,000-4,500

A gilt bronze and ivory figure, 'Exotic Dancer', cast and carved from a model by A Gory, on green marble base, inscribed in bronze 'Gory', one finger missing, 15in (38cm).
$3,000-4,500

A parcel gilt bronze and ivory group, 'Morning Walk', cast and carved after a model by A Becquerel, cold-painted in red on marble base, base restored, inscribed 'Becquerel', 10½in (27cm).
$2,250-3,500

A gilt metal and ivory figure, 'Girl in trouser suit', cast and carved from a model by Lorenzl, cold-painted in green and red on green onyx base, 8½in (21cm).
$1,000-1,400

A coloured bronze and ivory figure, 'The Hindu Dancer', by C J R Colinet, No. 203, damages, 14in (35.5cm).
$2,500-3,500

A Bouraine bronze and ivory figure, on a marble base, 12½in (32cm).
$1,500-2,600

A cold-painted bronze and carved ivory dancing girl figure, signed 'Lorenzl', restoration, 15in (38cm).
$1,200-1,600

A bronze figure by Prof Poertzle, 13in (33cm).
$3,000-4,500

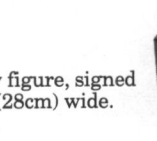

A pair of ivory figures, 'Greek Maidens', 7in (18cm).
$1,200-1,600

A bronze and ivory figure, signed 'P. Philippe', 11in (28cm) wide.
$4,000-5,500

Furniture

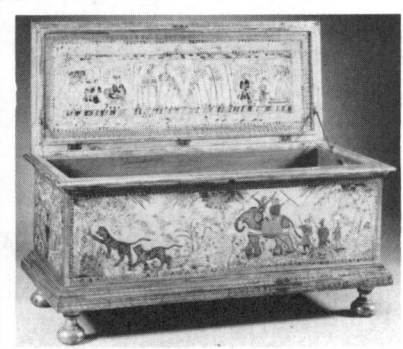

A polychrome and giltwood blanket chest, by Max Kuehne, painted and incised to depict Indian or Persian scenes in polychrome, silver and giltwood, c1930, 44½in (113cm).
$4,000-6,000

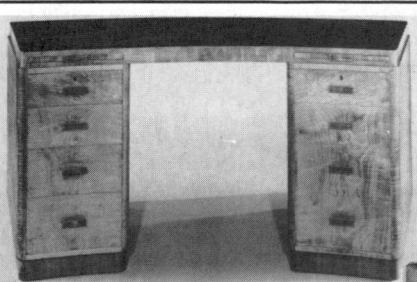

A sycamore kneehole desk, with 2 slide pulls, 7 drawers and one false drawer, inset with a circular printed ivory label, 'Tottenham Court Road, HEAL'S, London W.1.', 28in (71cm) high.
$1,500-2,600

An upholstered aluminium tub armchair, by Warren MacArthur, with 4 aluminium supports joined by a curved stretcher at mid-point, paper label, c1930, 33½in (85cm).
$1,800-2,000

A bird's-eye maplewood dining suite, comprising: table, serving table, sideboard, 10 chairs upholstered in green leather, 1930s, 120in (305cm).
$5,500-7,000

A white painted side chair by Edmund Moiret, with triple bar stretcher, c1907.
$2,250-3,500

Edmund Moiret 1883-1967 was born in Budapest and became a leading member of the Hungarian Secession Movement. He began his studies at the Academy of Art in Budapest but went on to study in Vienna and Brussels. He was awarded a major prize at the Budapest Winter Salon in 1910 and decided to settle in Hungary where he taught sculpture from 1911 at the Budapest Technische Hochschule. He later lived and worked in Vienna. In 1985 a commemorative exhibition was held at the Österreichisches Museum für Angewandte Kunst.

A set of 4 walnut side chairs.
$900-1,300

A Heal's oak writing desk, designed by Ambrose Heal, with fall flaps at each end and enclosing 6 file trays, inlaid with printed ivory label 'Heal and Son Ltd London N.W', 60in (152cm).
$5,500-7,000

An aluminium and glass centre table, in the style of Donald Deskey, with 2 U-shaped supports joined by a stretcher and surmounted by a black glass top, c1930, 60in (153cm).
$2,500-3,000

A set of 8 dining chairs.
$1,500-2,600

A Peter Waals walnut dressing table, 46in (116cm).
$900-1,300

An occasional table, veneered and inlaid with ebony, boxwood, satinwood and oysterwood, 25in (63.5cm) high.
$900-1,300

A Rowley walnut and rosewood dining room suite, printed labels 'Modern Decoration ROWLEY 140-2 Church St., W.8', comprising: an extending dining table, 72in (184cm) fully extended, 6 dining chairs, a side table, 36in (91cm) and a sideboard , 79½in (202cm).
$1,300-1,800

A nest of 3 Bakelite tables.
$150-250

A painted hall mirror, in the style of Robert Mallet-Stevens, 46½in (118cm).
$1,300-1,800

Jewellery

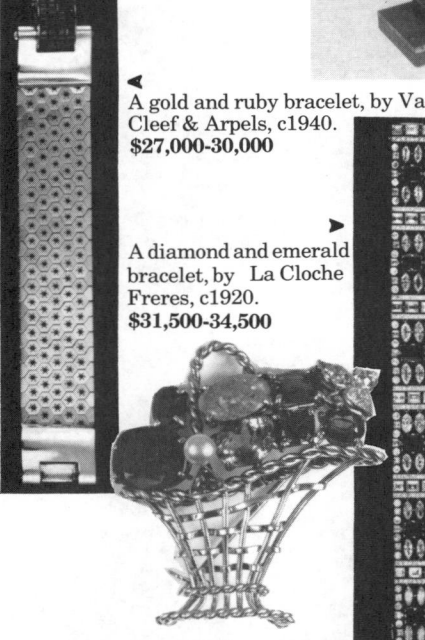

◄ A gold and ruby bracelet, by Van Cleef & Arpels, c1940.
$27,000-30,000

► A diamond and emerald bracelet, by La Cloche Freres, c1920.
$31,500-34,500

A basket brooch, set with various precious and semi-precious stones.
$300-500

A pair of pendant earrings.
$9,000-12,000

A diamond and black onyx bow brooch, 3 small onyx stones missing.
$1,500-2,600

A silver and onyx necklace and bracelet, by Antonio Pineda, necklace impressed '925 TAXCO'.
$1,300-1,800

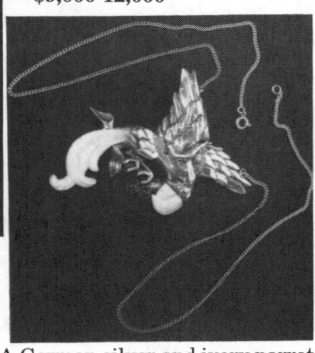

A German silver and ivory parrot necklace.
$450-700

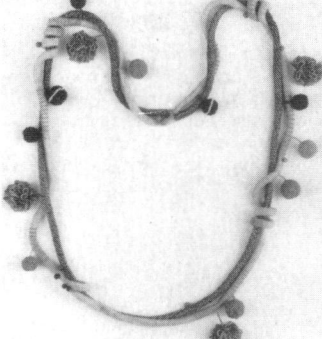

A beadwork necklace, the 2 entwined silver and yellow strands with blue, orange and pink beadwork balls and 4 lime green and steel blue looped balls, c1920.
$1,000-1,400

cf Werner J Schweiger, Wiener Werkstätte Kunst und Handwerk, 1903-1932, Vienna, 1982, p 231.

A green Bakelite leaf necklace, c1925.
$75-150
A chrome mesh necklace, c1925.
$75-150

A German necklace, set with 2 coral cabochons, suspended from 2 geometric bars on chain, stamped 'Germany-Sterling' and 'E' in lozenge, 7cm.
$300-400

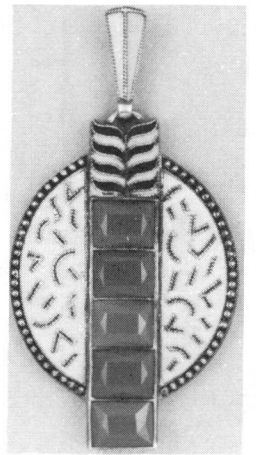

A diamond cocktail ring on platinum shank.
$800-1,200

A solitaire diamond ring, the fan shaped shoulders each set with 3 baguette diamonds, on platinum shank, 1.4ct solitaire.
$1,500-2,600

A lady's 9ct hallmarked white gold diamond set cocktail watch, with 2 baguette and 30 brilliant cut diamonds, 20thC, in Morocco fitted case.
$800-1,200

A German enamelled pendant, in the manner of Theodor Fahrner, marked 'A. Sch.' and '935', 7cm long.
$600-900

Metal

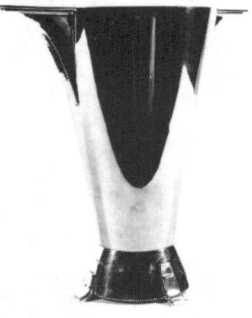

A Georg Jensen 75-piece 'Pyramid' pattern table service, designed by Harold Nielsen, stamped marks, 1926, 132oz 6dwt gross.
$10,000-13,000

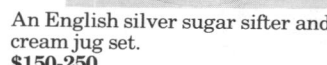

An English silver sugar sifter and cream jug set.
$150-250

A vase, Chester 1933, 8in (20.5cm), 18oz.
$300-400

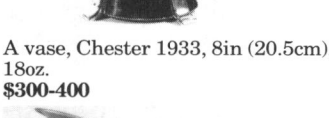

A small pitcher, designed by Johan Rohde, stamped marks 'JR Georg Jensen GJ 295 S 432A', c1928, 9in (23cm), 17oz.
$1,500-2,600

Johan Rohde first designed his famous pitcher in 1920; it was then considered to be too advanced to put into general production and did not appear until 1925. There is a slight variation on this design; a number of pitchers have a part ebony handle.

A pair of metal bookends, each formed as a standing mother bear, flanked by twin cubs, on self-shaped triangular base, gold and brown patina, impressed 'Frankart Inc. Pat. Appld. For', 7in (17cm) high.
$60-80

A pair of gilt bronze, onyx and marble table lamp bases, in the manner of Süe et Mare, 19½in (50.5cm).
$600-900

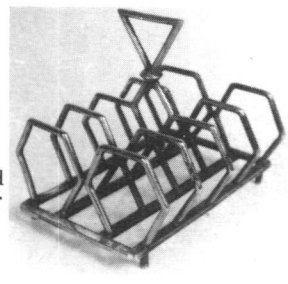

An Adie Brothers Modernist electroplated tea set, designed by Harold Stabler, stamped maker's marks 'EPNS Al' facsimile signature Stabler, 3½in (8cm) height of teapot.
$750-1,000

A James Dixon & Sons electroplated toast rack, designed by Christopher Dresser, facsimile signature and numbered '68S', 4in (10cm).
$1,500-2,600

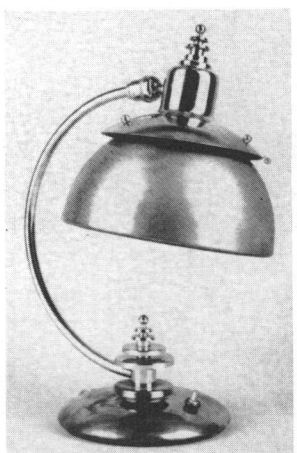

A chrome and copper desk lamp, with decorative stepped circular finials at each end, American, unmarked, c1930, 14in (35cm) high.
$600-700

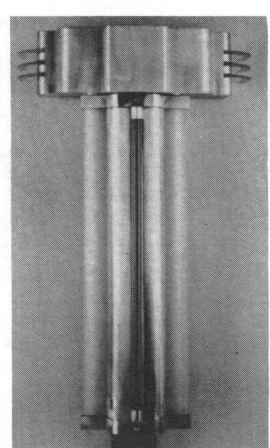

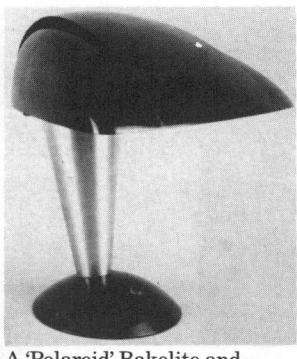

A 'Polaroid' Bakelite and aluminium desk lamp, by Walter Dorwin Teague, with paper label, 13in (33cm) high.
$900-1,200

A copper and glass wall sconce, the copper framework of stylized skyscraper form, with frosted glass wings, projecting from top sides, frosted glass panels at front centering translucent glass rod, American, unmarked, c1935, 34½in (87cm) high.
$900-1,200

A four-piece silver plated metal and ebony tea service, consisting of a semi-circular teapot, a covered cream pitcher and covered sugar bowl, fitted in a circular handled tray, designed by Jean G Theobald, patented October 9, 1928, each impressed 'Wilcox S.P. Co. International S. Co. 7036', tray 7½in (18cm) diam.
$6,500-7,500

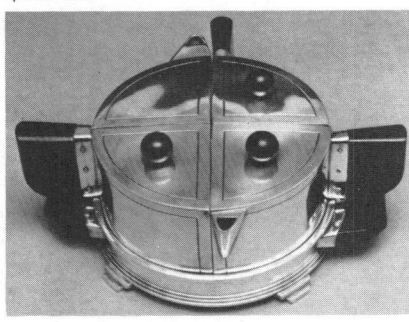

A chromed metal and Bakelite lamp, with domed shaped up-lighter, the base circular with 4 cylindrical supports, designed by Donald Deskey for Radio City Music Hall, c1932, 67½in (172cm) high.
$3,000-4,000

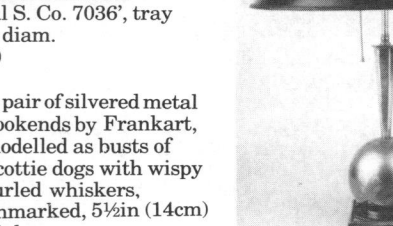

A pair of silvered metal bookends by Frankart, modelled as busts of Scottie dogs with wispy curled whiskers, unmarked, 5½in (14cm) high.
$120-150

A silvered metal lamp base, the spherical body sitting on a silver and black square platform with 4 ball feet, American, unmarked, c1935, 27in (68cm) high.
$700-900

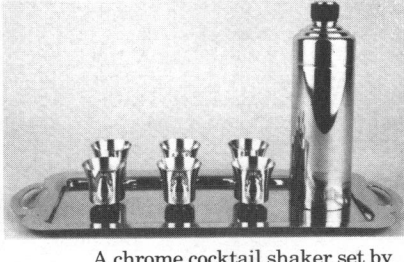

A chrome cocktail shaker set by Chase, comprising: a cylindrical shaker, 6 matching cocktail cups, each on purple Bakelite foot, on a curved rectangular two-handled tray, unmarked.
$200-300

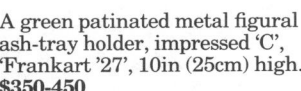

A silver compote raised on a hammered domed foot, impressed 'Sterling Peer Smed 1933', 7in (17cm) high, 14.5oz.
$800-1,000

A green patinated metal figural ash-tray holder, impressed 'C', 'Frankart '27', 10in (25cm) high.
$350-450

A wrought iron and glass chandelier, with yellow and blue mottled glass bell-shaped shades, 30½in (77.5cm).
$300-500

A Dunhill architect's lighter, silvered metal formed as a 12in (30.5cm) box ruler, surmounted by a lighter with wheel and flint mechanism, stamped Dunhill.
$1,000-1,400

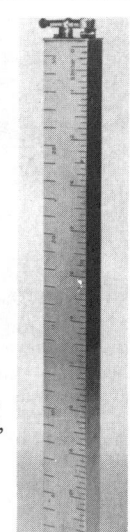

A group of chrome and Bakelite items by Chase, comprising 38 pieces, all pieces stamped 'Chase', the coffee urn by Manning-Bowman & Co, rectangular tray unmarked, the largest item 13½in (34cm) high.
$600-800

A pair of fine and important wrought iron gates, designed by Eliel Saarinen for the Cranbrook Academy of Art's Museum, the interior with stepped skyscraper device surmounted by a foliate motif, c1928, 36in (91cm) wide.
$5,000-7,000

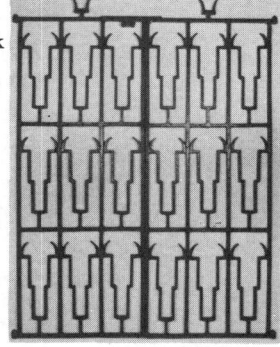

Miscellaneous

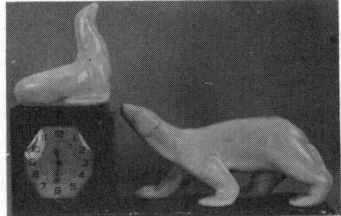

A French marble effect clock with polar bears, 17in (43cm) wide.
$300-400

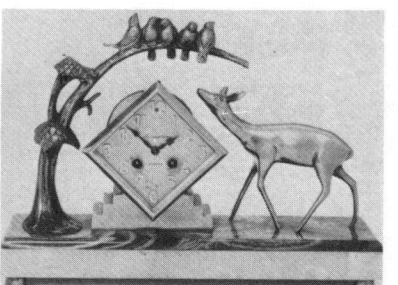

A clock garniture, the clock signed 'Sellier & Tondu, Lisieux', 16in (40cm) wide, and a matching pair of side tazze, 9in (23cm).
$300-400

A Louis Vuitton cabin trunk, covered in brown hide, secured by brass pins and mounted with brass lockplate and hinged, fitted with amber coloured interior and 4 laminated beechwood coat hangers, 45in (114cm) wide.
$1,500-2,600

A bronze, ivory and onyx timepiece, cased in green onyx and flanked by bronze seals balancing ivory balls on their noses, the clock made by Phillips & Macdonald, London, 12in (30.5cm).
$400-500

An Alfred Dunhill marble mantel clock, the face in mottled turquoise, white and black enamel, the number 12 forming release button for sprung hinged top enclosing fitted gilt metal cigarette case, 9in (23cm).
$1,000-1,400

A suede handbag in soft brown, with Bakelite handle, 9 by 8in (23 by 20.5cm).
$100-200

These have to be of excellent quality and condition to make good money.

A gilt embossed leather wallet, designed by Josef Hoffmann, the black leather embossed with radiating linear crescents, embossed mark Wiener Werkstätte, 5½in (14.5cm).
$900-1,300

A marbelised Bakelite radio by Addison, cathedral shape in black and green marbelised ground, the fabric covered speaker with amber Bakelite grillwork, marked, 9in (23cm) high.
$900-1,000

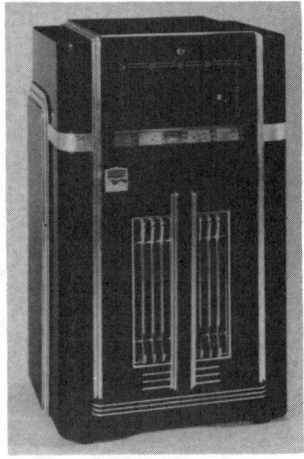

An amber Bakelite radio by Emerson, with cream and black horizontal grillwork at left, having black Bakelite handle, marked, 9in (23cm) high.
$500-600

A black lacquer and silver leaf juke-box, 'Symphonola', by J P Seeburg Corp, Chicago, the rectangular case with glazed frame having phonograph with 12 selections, over chrome grillwork and selector knob, serial no. S.7461, c1930.
$3,000-4,000

A white marble head of a woman, American School, signed 'Lonzar', 20thC, 9in (23cm), on wood cube.
$600-900

A glass, nickel-plated metal and wood radio, designed by Walter Dorwin Teague, in a peach mirrored glass body, intersected by 3 nickel-plated bands, raised on a black painted wood base, face printed 'Spartan Jackson, Michigan Made in U.S.A.', 15in (38cm) high.
$1,200-1,500

A tufted wool carpet, designed by Marion Dorn, woven signature 'Dorn', 87 by 49in (221 by 125cm).
$2,500-3,500

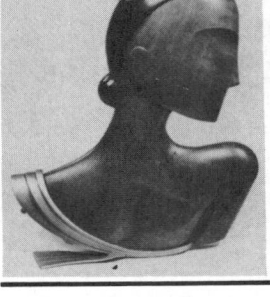

A Hagenauer carved wood and metal bust of a woman, stamped monogram, Hagenauer Wien, 12½in (31.5cm).
$1,500-2,600

A wool carpet fragment, designed by Ruth Reeves for Donald Deskey for Radio City Music Hall, depicting abstract guitars and banjos in alternating rectangular repeats in shades on salmon, grey, cinnamon and tan, pieced, c1932, 24½ by 38in (62 by 96cm).
$350-450

Post-War Design

A brushed steel and chromium plated table, the design attributed to Ringo Starr, 48in (121cm) wide.
$400-500

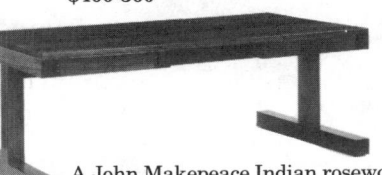

A teak serving table, designed by Terence Conran, 30in (76cm).
$100-200

A John Makepeace Indian rosewood library table, 1966, 72in (183cm).
$4,000-5,500

A Minton hexagonal garden seat, marked No. '1364', 18in (45.5cm) high.
$600-900

A diamond back upholstered wire armchair, by Harry Bertoia for Knoll Associates, upholstered in beige hopsacking, supported on chrome frame, with original tag from Knoll, 28in (70cm).
$300-500

A wicker patio chair, designed by Terence Conran.
$150-250

A pair of laminated beechwood armchairs, designed by Gerald Summers for 'The Makers of Simple Furniture'.
$13,500-17,500

A Brianco self-assembly mahogany and metal rod bench, 60in (152cm).
$100-150

A set of 6 Fornasetti porcelain plates, 'Mongolfiere', transfer printed in black and white with yellow, red, blue, green and brown enamels, each depicting various ballooning events, each printed 'Mongolfiere Fornasetti Milano, Made in Italy 1955', 10in (25.5cm) diam.
$1,000-1,400

A pair of Barcelona chairs, designed by Mies van der Rohe.
$1,200-1,600

A solid rosewood table lamp, c1950, 18in (45.5cm).
$3,000-4,500

A Stilnova painted metal lamp by Gaetano Scolari, with light fitment inside, Italian, c1959, 26½in (67cm).
$250-350

An unusual bronze model of a fox modelled in highly stylised fashion with the creature sitting upright on its haunches with its ears erect, on square black marble base, 35cm high, stamped on reverse 'Seiden-Stücker'.
$450-700

There is a cutting from a magazine on the base of this piece showing Friedrich Seidenstücker, a Berlin Press Photographer, and is dated in pen 1962. It is possible that this piece is a presentation trophy

'Saint John the Baptist', a glass panel by John Hutton, acid-etched and engraved with standing figure of Saint John, engraved signature John Hutton, in mahogany frame, 127.5 x 43.4cm including frame.
$600-900

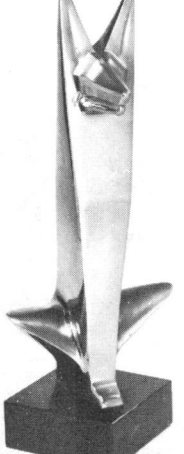

A laminated wood drinks trolley designed by Alvar Aalto, executed by Finmar Ltd, the two tiers with two laminated wood supports dipping and rounded to accommodate two white wheels, 23in high.
$1,000-1,400

A 1950's desk and chair by Silvio Cavatorta, the desk with curved top, with lower tier fitted with two units of double drawings, the chair upholstered in red leather, the desk 66in wide, the chair 30in high, metal label.
$1,000-1,400

A cherrywood dining room suite, by
George Nakashima, comprising: a
trestle table on sled feet, and 2
spindle-back benches, on tapered
legs, c1960, table 60in (153cm) long.
$4,000-5,000

A wire and steel desk chair by
Charles Eames, the scoop back
composed of white plastic covered
wire grid, set on black and chrome
steel pedestal flaring to 4 legs with
wheels, 32in (81cm) high.
$500-700

A rear-view mirror chrome and
lucite vanity chair, the revolving
cushioned stool upholstered in black
ground fabric with beige and white
jungle print, c1940, 51½in
(130.5cm) high.
$300-400

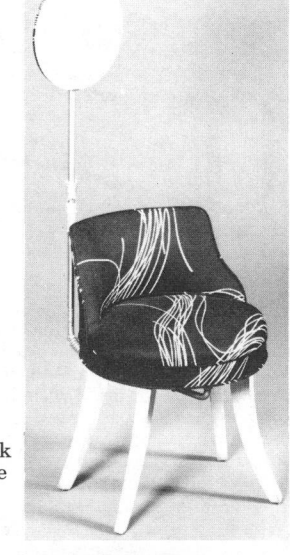

A black Formica and chrome
'surf-board' coffee table, by Charles
Eames, 89in (226cm) long.
$2,000-3,000

A pair of caned walnut and black
steel armchairs by George Nelson
for Herman Miller, seat upholstered
in purple, orange and green striped
fabric, unmarked, 33in (84cm) high.
$300-400

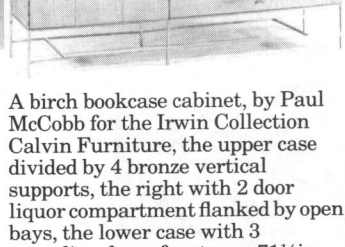

A clear and frosted glass and black
lacquered dining table, by
Modernage, unmarked, c1950, 32in
(82cm) high.
$1,400-1,600

A birch bookcase cabinet, by Paul
McCobb for the Irwin Collection
Calvin Furniture, the upper case
divided by 4 bronze vertical
supports, the right with 2 door
liquor compartment flanked by open
bays, the lower case with 3
accordion doors for stereo, 71½in
(182cm) long.
$700-900

A rosewood and chrome dresser by
George Nelson for Herman Miller,
the drawers with plastic waisted
knobs, marked with metal tag,
numbered model 385, 30in (75cm).
$1,200-1,400

A cork and walnut coffee table by
Paul Frankl, the rectangular cork
top having curved ends, on 4 short
wooden legs, unmarked, 70in
(177cm) long.
$800-1,200

A blonde mahogany kneehole desk
by George Nelson, on 4 cylindrical
chrome legs, the drawers with
curved chrome handles, 60in
(153cm) long.
$800-1,200

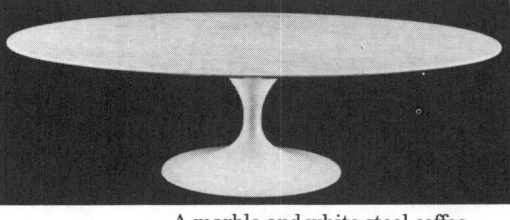

A marble and white steel coffee table by Eero Saarinen, 36in (91cm) long.
$1,700-2,000

A walnut, rosewood and leather roll-top desk, designed by Edward J Wormley for Dunbar, the top with 2 tambour sections fitted with double compartmentment leather letter trays, flanking a flat central section, supported on a trestle shaped base, c1959, 75in (190cm) wide.
$2,800-3,500

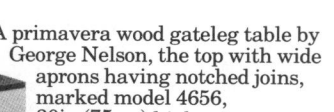

A primavera wood gateleg table by George Nelson, the top with wide aprons having notched joins, marked model 4656, 30in (75cm) high.
$1,200-1,500

A rosewood and Formica miniature chest, by George Nelson for Herman Miller, with white enamelled metal waisted knobs, metal tag, stamped 224, 30in (75cm) long.
$900-1,200

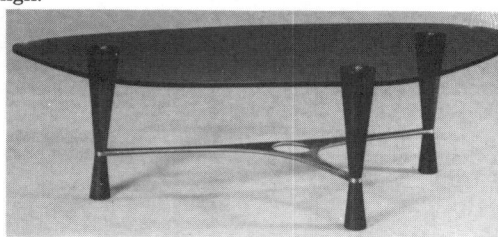

A walnut, bronze and glass coffee table, by Edward J Wormley for Dunbar, 16½in (41cm) high.
$700-900

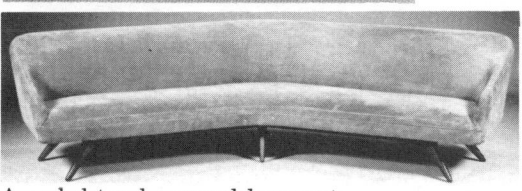

An upholstered rosewood davenport by Vladmir Kagan for Kagan-Dreyfuss Inc, L-shaped, on tapered rosewood legs, stamped, 1959, 107in (272cm) long.
$800-1,200

A Bentwood magazine rack attributed to Herman Miller, unmarked, 16in (40cm) high.
$300-400

A rosewood, walnut and white lacquered miniature chest, by George Nelson for Herman Miller, Zeeland, Michigan, the drawers with porcelain knobs, marked with paper label, 20in (52cm) wide.
$1,800-2,000

An upholstered armchair by Paul Lazlo for Herman Miller Furniture Company, re-upholstered in brown and beige striped fabric, unmarked, model L.689, 27in (69cm).
$500-600

A primavera wood sideboard by George Nelson for Herman Miller, on 4 short legs, the drawers with round wood knobs, 29½in (74cm) high.
$550-650

A glass, iron, wood and leather dining room suite, by Edward Durrell Stone for the Fulbright Foundation Collection, the glass over blonde mahogany top on 2 'V' shaped wrought iron pedestals with circular cutouts, the brown leather seats on wrought iron legs, c1945, chair 29in (73cm) high.
$9,000-12,000

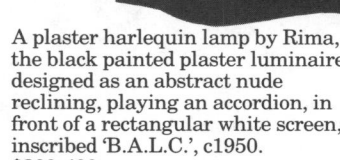

A plaster harlequin lamp by Rima, the black painted plaster luminaire designed as an abstract nude reclining, playing an accordion, in front of a rectangular white screen, inscribed 'B.A.L.C.', c1950.
$300-400

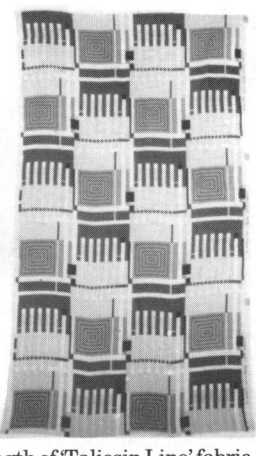

A length of 'Taliesin Line' fabric, the beige linen printed in a geometric design in shades of brown, printed 3 times 'The Taliesin Line of Frank Lloyd Wright', executed by F Schumacher and Company, 1955, 83 by 47in (210 by 119cm).
$2,500-3,500

An engraved glass bowl, 'Mariners', designed by Sidney Waugh, inscribed 'Steuben 1937', 15½in (39cm) diam with stand.
$4,500-5,500

A wooden wall clock by George Nelson for the Howard Miller Clock Company, the clock with white face from which radiate 12 spokes ending in wood knobs, black metal hour hand with triangular point, minute hand with ovoid, paper label, 13in (33cm) diam.
$350-450

A Decorastone sculpturama by Rima, in rough terracotta finish, mounted on wooden rectangular plaque, paper label, 28 by 34in (70 by 85cm).
$700-800

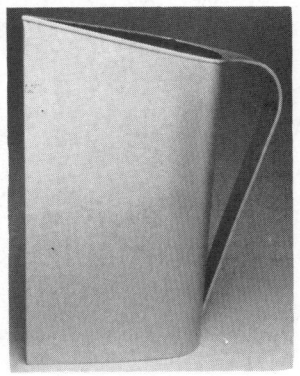

A nickel-plated metal pitcher, 'Normandie', designed by Peter Muller-Munk, executed by Benedict Manufacturing Company, impressed 'revere ROME N.Y.', 12in (30cm) high.
$2,500-3,500

A Chronopak walnut and brass desk clock, by George Nelson for the Howard Miller Clock Company, 7in (17cm).
$200-250

A suite of 3 gilt bronze figural plaques, depicting a clipper ship, a train against city-scape and a family group amongst trees, c1940, 15 by 28in (38 by 70cm).
$600-800

Did you know
MILLER'S Antiques Price Guide builds up year by year to form the most comprehensive photo-reference system available.

A glass vase, engraved with a partially clad man holding the reins of a muscular horse, inscribed 'G. de Chirico Steuben 1939', 12in (30cm) high.
$6,500-7,500

Silver Baskets

A George III swing-handled cake basket, with 4 applied oval medallions, the handle with 2 applied small plaques and with central oval cartouche engraved with a monogram, Andrew Fogelberg, London 1778, the handle repaired, 14in (35.5cm) wide, 37.75oz.
$2,500-3,500

A George III Scottish sugar bowl, crested, by John Leslie, Aberdeen, c1785, 9.5cm, 10.5oz.
$800-1,200

A large boat-shaped bread basket, by Paul Storr, 1810, 17in (42.5cm) wide, 54oz.
$10,500-14,000

A George III sugar basket, by Charles Hougham, 1790, 3in (8cm) high, 4oz.
$450-700

A George IV cake basket, the centre engraved with a crest and motto, Battie, Howard & Hawksworth, Sheffield 1829, 13in (33cm) 36oz.
$900-1,300

A George III swing-handled cake basket, by Robert Hennell, 1794, 15½in (40cm) wide, 27oz.
$4,000-5,500

A George III sugar basket, George Brasier, London 1799, 6in (15.5cm) wide, 7oz 15dwt.
$600-900

A George IV cake basket, the centre embossed, Silenus riding an ass with fauns and satyrs, IET, J E Terry & Co, London 1829, maker's mark, 12½in (32cm) diam, 40oz.
$1,000-1,400

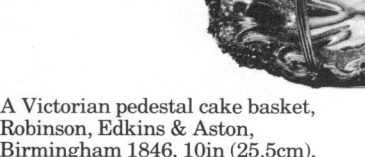

A Victorian pedestal cake basket, Robinson, Edkins & Aston, Birmingham 1846, 10in (25.5cm), 17oz.
$600-900

A Victorian silver gilt sweetmeat basket, in the George II style, engraved with a crest, by E, E, J, and W Barnard, London 1843, marked on base and handle, 6in (16cm) wide, 6oz.
$1,500-2,600

A pair of silver pierced baskets, maker W C London, 13oz.
$450-700

A silver basket, London 1883.
$3,000-4,000

A set of 3 Victorian baskets, with gilded interiors, by Stephen Smith, London c1883, 156oz, in fitted oak case.
$10,500-14,000

A foliate pierced boat-shaped cake basket, James Dixon & Sons, Sheffield 1919, 9in (23cm), 17.5oz.
$600-900 ▶

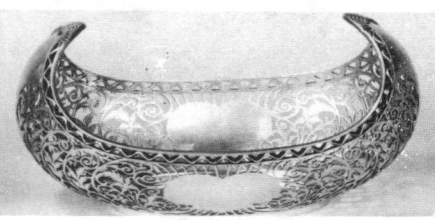

A silver swing-handled basket.
$750-1,000

Beakers

A pair of beakers, by John Taylor & Horace Hinsdale, one engraved with script initials 'EBN', the other with 'HMM', each marked bruises, New York, c1820, 3½in (9cm), 9oz.
$800-900

A beaker, by Hudson & Dorflinger, with a moulded and beaded rim and footrim, marked on base, Louisville, Kentucky, c1855, 4in (10cm), 4oz.
$500-600

A pair of beakers, by Curtis H Clark and Maltby Pelletreau, the front engraved with a castle crest above script initials 'JCB', marked on base 'C & P', New York, c1820, 4in (10cm), 9oz.
$1,500-2,000

A Commonwealth beaker, pricked with initials and date CSL 1678, maker's mark TS in monogram, Norwich, c1665, 5in (12cm) high, 6oz 11dwt.
$7,500-10,500

A Provincial beaker, the underbase punched with spiked rose mark, the letters SV(?) and also possible TG., c1675, 4in (10cm) high, 3oz.
$1,500-2,600

A Charles II beaker, pricked beneath the flared lip with initials WC DC and dated 1685, maker's mark TC with a fish above, 1684, 4in (10cm) high, 5oz 6dwt.
$3,000-4,500

A German parcel gilt beaker, by Gerdt Eimbke (Eimeke) III, Brunswick, c1690, 5in (13cm) high, 8oz.
$3,000-4,500

A German parcel gilt beaker, probably by Abraham Bartmann, Lüneburg, c1690, and a cover with ball finial by Matthaus Schmidt, Augsburg, c1680, 7.5oz.
$1,500-2,600

A William and Mary plain beaker, pricked with initials 'AL.IM', by James Daniel, Norwich, 1689, 3½in (9cm) high, 3oz 3dwt.
$4,000-5,500

A Scandinavian beaker, engraved with script initials around rim 'THS MMD', maker's mark only FM conjoined in a shaped punch, stamped twice, probably Norwegian, late 17th/early 18thC, 3½in (9.5cm) high, 4.25oz.
$750-1,000

Bowls

A James II silver twin-handled porringer, with pinpointed 'Ann Petter 1689', maker YT, London 1689, 3½in (9cm) diam, 5.5oz.
$5,500-7,000

A Queen Anne punch bowl, 1706, 10in (25.5cm) diam, 36oz.
$6,000-8,000

A Victorian covered bowl with blue glass liner, by C T and G Fox, London 1854, fully marked, 6½in (16.5cm) diam, 20oz.
$3,000-4,500

A Latvian tapering cylindrical beaker and cover, engraved with 3 coats-of-arms, below a partly fluted ball finial, later engraved with names and date, by Christoffer Dey, Riga, c1740, 10½in (26.5cm) high, 23oz.
$3,000-4,000

A George II sugar bowl and cover, by Edward Vincent, London 1735, cover unmarked, 4½in (11cm) diam, 9oz 10dwt.
$2,250-3,500

A George III punch bowl, engraved with coat-of-arms, crest and motto, by Paul Storr, London 1805, 11½in (29cm) diam, 75oz.
$19,500-24,000

Two pairs of George III interlocking beakers, each pair engraved with a coronet, crest and motto, by C Aldridge and H Green, 1778, barrels 5in (13.5cm) high, 16oz 18dwt.
$4,000-5,500

A covered beaker, Augsburg 1745.
$1,500-2,600

A pair of George III plain goblets, the undersides engraved with initials, by John Wakelin and William Taylor, 1779, 6in (15cm) high, 15oz.
$3,000-4,000

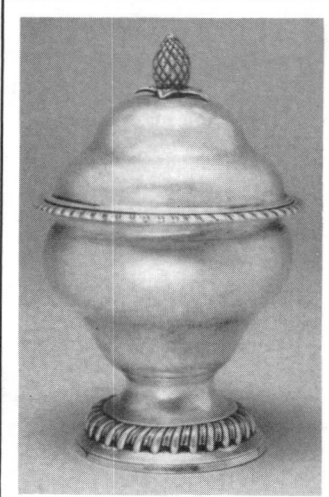

A covered sugar bowl, by Edmund Milne, with a domed pyriform cover with a cast pineapple finial, mark struck twice on base, Philadelphia, c1785, 7in (18cm) high, 11oz.
$4,000-5,000

A centrepiece bowl, by Simeon Coley, the front engraved 'TS' in foliate script, marked on base, New York, c1768, 9in (23cm) diam, 21oz 10dwt.
$30,000-35,000

A late Victorian rose bowl, Goldsmiths & Silversmiths Co Ltd, London 1900, 10½in (26.5cm), 32.25oz.
$1,000-1,400

A Victorian punch bowl in William III style, Walker & Hall, Sheffield 1898.
$1,300-1,800

An 18thC style spiral fluted punch bowl, with applied cherubs' mask, D & J Wellby, London 1919, 12in (30.5cm), 56.25oz, and ebonised wood plinth.
$1,500-2,600

A late Victorian spiral fluted rose bowl, James Dixon & Sons, Sheffield 1893, 9in (23cm), 22.75oz.
$600-900

A silver fruit bowl, Sheffield 1947, 15in (38cm), 42oz 10dwt.
$1,200-1,600

Boxes

A Charles II oval silver gilt tobacco box, with detachable cover, maker's mark WH only, struck twice on the base, the cover once, c1675, 4in (10cm) long, 5oz 10dwt.
$1,500-2,600

A commemorative box, the base decorated in relief with a portrait of King George II, the detachable cover decorated with a portrait of King George III, unmarked, 18thC, 2in (5cm).
$400-500

A Continental silver gilt snuff box, probably German, possibly late 18thC, 3in (7.5cm).
$450-600

An unusual German parcel gilt box, by Joachim Albert Finck(e), Hamburg, c1720, 4in (10cm) wide, 6oz 13dwt.
$7,000-9,000

A Dutch plain shaped octagonal casket, by J Logerat, The Hague, 1728, 5in (13cm) wide, 14oz 16dwt.
$9,000-12,000

A George II cartouche shaped silver snuff box, repoussé and chased with Venus, Cupid and a dolphin, the gilt interior inscribed R.H.S.B. in memory of H.S.B., August 4th, 1875' by Francis Harache, c1732-58, 7cm wide.
$750-1,000

A George II silver gilt toilet box, the hinged cover inset with a velvet covered pin cushion, by Aymé Videau, 1755, the cover unmarked, 7in (17cm), 36oz.
$5,500-7,000

A Louis XV cartouche shaped silver gilt snuff box, with later mirror inside the lid, slight wear to base, with the décharge of Julien Berthe, 1750-56, and the countermark of Eloy Brichard, 1756-62, Paris, 3in (8cm) wide.
$1,500-2,600

An Austrian snuff box inset with miniature, maker's mark HV, Vienna 1861, the miniature c1775, 7.5cm.
$1,200-1,600

A George III oval silver gilt seal box, by Peter, Ann and William Bateman, 1802.
$600-900

A Continental cartouche shaped snuff box, with gilt interior, maker's mark F.H., c1780, 2½in (6.5cm), 2.1oz.
$750-1,000

An oval snuff box, with bright engraved decoration, Paris, c1810, 3½in (9cm) wide.
$450-600

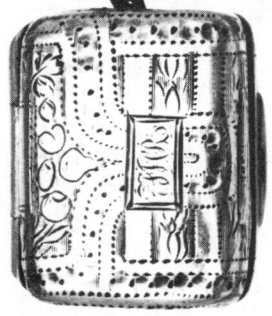

l. A silver box, Paris c1781, 7cm, 2oz.
$1,000-1,400

r. A Victorian silver table snuff box, by Charles Rawlins and William Summers, London 1849, 5½oz.
$750-1,000

A William IV presentation snuff box with bombé sides, with presentation inscription dated 1836, by Nathaniel Mills, Birmingham 1833, 3in (7.5cm) wide.
$300-400

A George III vinaigrette, in the form of a purse, the gilt interior with a pierced grille, by Lawrence and Co, Birmingham 1817, the grille with standard mark, 2.3cm.
$100-200

A George IV snuff box, the cover engraved with the Nassau Balloon rising over Norwich, by Thomas Shaw, Birmingham 1824, 3in (8cm) wide.
$750-1,000

A George IV silver gilt table snuff box, with double hinged cover, the inner cover engraved twice with an inscription, by Thomas Edwards, 1820, 4in (9cm) wide, 9oz 4dwt.
$1,300-1,800

A William IV table snuff box, the cover applied with trophies of arms, Garter star and regimental colours of the 12th East Suffolk Regiment, the interior engraved with presentation inscription, the front with applied gold rectangular plaque, engraved with crest and motto, by Charles Reily and George Storer, 1835, 4in (10cm) wide, 10oz 12dwt.
$1,200-1,600

A George III silver gilt snuff box, makers Phipps & Robinson, London 1813 (6 by 4cm).
$300-400

A George IV vinaigrette, by Lawrence and Co, Birmingham 1827, the grille with standard mark, 2cm.
$150-250

A William IV vinaigrette, the cover chased in relief with Kenilworth Castle, by Nathaniel Mills, Birmingham 1836.
$600-900

A William IV vinaigrette, by William Simpson, Birmingham 1836, the grille with maker's and standard marks, 2.6cm.
$250-350

An early Victorian vinaigrette, the cover chased in relief with a view of Windsor Castle, by Francis Clarke, Birmingham, 1838.
$450-700

A Victorian snuff box, the cover inscribed 'Coronation 1841 The Derby Winner', by Francis Clarke, Birmingham 1841, 3½in (8.5cm) wide.
$450-700

A Victorian vinaigrette, decorated in relief with a view of Windsor Castle, by John Tongue, Birmingham 1844.
$450-600

An early Victorian Scottish table snuff box, the interior of the cover engraved with a presentation inscription, by James Nasmyth, Edinburgh 1838, 4in (10cm).
$300-400

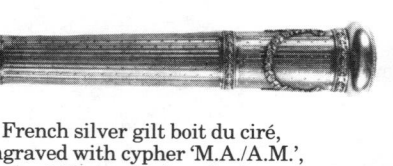

A French silver gilt boit du ciré, engraved with cypher 'M.A./A.M.', Paris, .950 standard, maker's mark S & E over an encircled star in a lozenge, 19thC, 6in (15cm).
$300-400

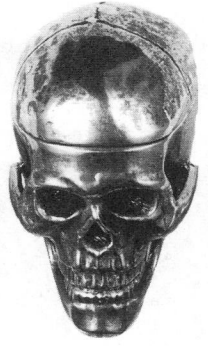

A small silver snuff box, modelled as a skull with articulated jaw, the hinged head with snuff compartment, 19thC, 4.2cm long.
$900-1,300

A Swiss silver gilt and enamel singing bird box, the top painted with a landscape, by Charles Bruguier, 19thC, with hinged key compartment, key and original fitted case, 4in (10cm) wide.
$5,500-7,000

A French silver gilt snuff box, c1860, 4½in (11cm) wide.
$450-600

A French combined vesta case and tinder box, inscribed in cover 'J.V. 1st Jany. 1870', c1870.
$300-400

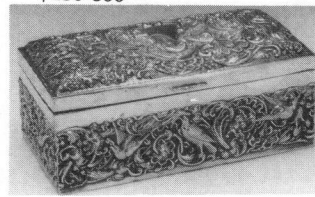

A Victorian table cigarette box, William Comyns, London 1894, 9in (23cm) long.
$750-1,000

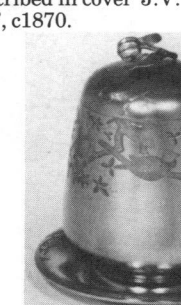

A silver gilt box, by Martin Hall and Company, Sheffield 1876, 8in (20.5cm) high, 26oz.
$1,500-2,600

A Victorian sentry box vesta case, enamelled on the front with a guardsman of the Grenadier Guards, by Sampson Mordan, 1886.
$900-1,300

A late Victorian silver mounted tortoiseshell stamp box, the cover with 2 Victorian stamps behind glass, Birmingham 1893.
$250-350

A late Victorian oblong card case, CC, Birmingham 1894, 4in (10cm).
$300-400

A late Victorian tortoiseshell and silver gilt oval trinket box, on shell and foliate feet, GF, London 1899, 4½in (12cm).
$700-900

An Edwardian card case, die-stamped with maidens' heads in the Art Nouveau taste, Crisford and Norris, Birmingham 1902, 3½in (9cm).
$300-400

A silver casket, by Alwyn Carr, London 1927, for the British Waterworks Association.
$3,000-4,500

An Austrian silver-mounted rock crystal casket, the hinged cover surmounted by a clock, the dial enamelled with a French coat-of-arms between winged griffons, damage, late 19thC, with key, 9in (23cm) high.
$6,000-8,000

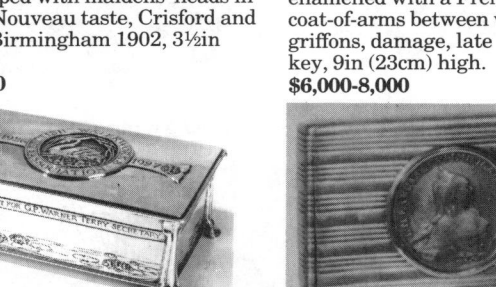

A silver box, probably French, with gilt interior, 7cm.
$300-400

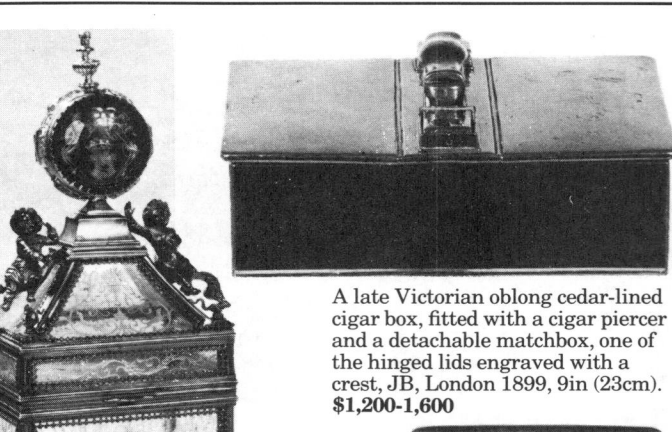

A late Victorian oblong cedar-lined cigar box, fitted with a cigar piercer and a detachable matchbox, one of the hinged lids engraved with a crest, JB, London 1899, 9in (23cm).
$1,200-1,600

An Edwardian card case, in the style of Angelica Kaufmann, HM, Birmingham 1904, 4in (10cm).
$150-250

A Fabergé gilt lined ribbed cigarette box, the lid inset with a medallion depicting Catherine the Great, with sapphire thumbpiece, August Fredrik Hollming, some damage, 3½in (9cm).
$800-1,200

A cedar-lined cigar box, the cover with applied plaques with polychrome enamelled nautical signal flags, 8½in (21.5cm).
$450-600

A pair of early 18thC style two-light candelabra, 10in (25.5cm), 56oz.
$1,300-1,800

Candelabra

A Victorian seven-light candelabrum centrepiece, by Joseph and John Angell, London 1845, 31½in (80cm) high, 215oz.
$6,000-9,000

A pair of George III three-light candelabra, engraved with coat-of-arms and crest, by John Green & Co, Sheffield 1800, 20½in (52cm) high, weight of branches 58oz.
$9,000-12,000

A pair of George III three-light candelabra, engraved on bases with coat-of-arms and on wax pans and detachable nozzles with crest, by John Scofield, London 1795, fully marked, 2 nozzles unmarked, 17in (43cm) high overall, 119oz.
$30,000-34,500

A pair of George III three-light candelabra, with detachable nozzles, by Matthew Boulton & Co, Birmingham 1809 and 1810, 19in (48cm) high, weight of branches 62oz, the candlesticks engraved with scratchweights 13:15 and 13:13.
$10,000-13,000

A Victorian seven-light candelabrum, engraved with presentation inscription, by Robert Garrard, 1854, 31in (78.5cm) high, 288oz.
$9,000-12,000

A Russian Hanukah lamp, assaymaster OC, possibly Minsk, struck with the name L. Zammer and town mark, a crescent between mullets, 1879, 21in (54cm) high, weight of branches 30oz.
$4,000-5,500

A pair of Victorian candlesticks and a matching four-light candelabrum, the central light with detachable flame extinguisher, by Walker & Hall, Sheffield 1894, 23in (58.5cm) and 11in (28cm) high, weight of branches 62oz.
$6,000-9,000

A pair of four-light candelabra, by Hawksworth, Eyre and Co Ltd, Sheffield 1917, the branches 1892, 15in (38.5cm) high, weight of branches 72oz.
$4,000-5,500

Candlesticks

A pair of George II plain candlesticks, engraved with a crest, by John Cafe, 1742, 8in (20.5cm) high, 33oz.
$4,000-5,500

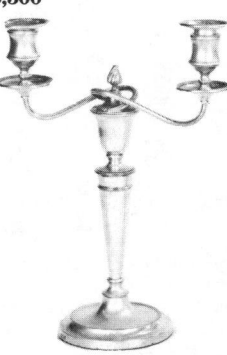

A pair of reeded two-light candelabra, 12in (30.5cm).
$750-1,000

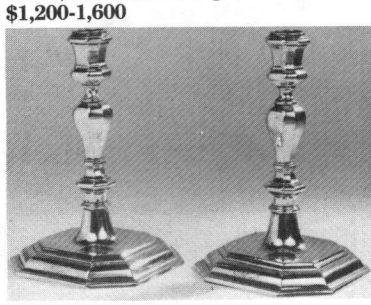

A pair of silver gilt candlesticks, probably German, unmarked, c1700, 5½in (13cm) high, 8.5oz.
$1,200-1,600

A pair of German candlesticks, Allenstein, maker's mark I.C. over S, c1750, 7in (18cm) high.
$4,000-5,500

A pair of George II candlesticks, by J Cafe, London 1754, 40oz.
$2,500-3,500

A pair of German table candlesticks, engraved with a coronet and two coats-of-arms, by Christian Lieberkühn II, Berlin, c1735, 8in (20.5cm) high, 31oz.
$12,000-15,000

A pair of George II silver
candlesticks, by John Cafe, marked
on bases, spool sconces (l) and
nozzles, 1756, 10in (25.5cm),
43.25oz.
$7,000-9,000

A set of 4 George II Scottish
Corinthian column candlesticks,
crested, by Robert Gordon,
Edinburgh, c1758, 13in (33cm)
high, 111.5oz.
$9,000-12,000

A pair of French cast candlesticks,
maker's mark $^{PI}_M$ with crown above,
untraced, possibly Lille, c1760,
8½in (21cm), 27.5oz.
$5,500-7,000

A pair of German candlesticks, by
Johann Erhard Wegelin, Augsburg,
c1768, 10in (25.5cm), 21oz.
$3,000-4,500

A pair of George III Corinthian
candlesticks, by Ebenezer Coker,
1762, 13½in (35cm), loaded.
$3,000-4,500

A pair of George III cast
candlesticks, by Ebenezer Coker,
1768, 10in (25.5cm), 34oz.
$2,250-3,500

A pair of George III candlesticks by
Ebenezer Coker, marked, one nozzle
odd and pierced, 1772, 9½in (24cm)
high, 36oz.
$3,000-4,000

A set of 4 cast candlesticks,
unmarked, c1770, the nozzles by
R Garrard, 1845, 11½in (29cm),
149.75oz.
$7,500-10,500

A pair of George III candlesticks, by
William Holmes, 1780, 11½in
(29cm), 43oz.
$5,500-7,000

A pair of George III silver table
candlesticks, by John Scofield, 1780,
12in (30cm), 36oz.
$4,000-5,500

A set of 4 George III fluted
candlesticks, maker's mark of
Daniel Smith and Robert Sharp
overstriking another, Sheffield
1783, 11in (28cm).
$9,000-12,000

A pair of German candlesticks, by
Johann Balthasar Heggenauer,
Augsburg, c1784, 9½in (23.5cm),
28oz.
$1,500-2,600

A George III chamber candlestick,
by Thomas Robins, London 1798,
5½in (14cm) diam, 8oz, also the
conical snuffer without hallmark.
$450-700

A set of 4 George III faceted tapering baluster candlesticks, crested, by John Green & Co, Sheffield 1801, 12in (30cm), loaded.
$7,500-10,500

A George III taperstick, by John Emes, London 1805, fully marked, 3in (8cm) diam, 2oz 10dwt.
$900-1,300

A pair of George IV candlesticks, John and Thomas Settle, Sheffield 1820, 9½in (24cm).
$750-1,000

A pair of George III part fluted oval candlesticks, each later chased with flowers and scrolling foliage and with a later presentation inscription, Sheffield 1805, 7in (18cm).
$1,000-1,400

A pair of George III candlesticks, each engraved with an armorial and motto, Tate and Co, Sheffield 1810, 12in (30.5cm).
$1,500-2,600

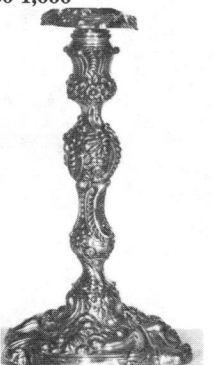

A pair of Regency baluster candlesticks, Kirkby, Waterhouse & Co, Sheffield 1818, 11in (28cm).
$1,000-1,400

A George IV taperstick by Nathaniel Mills, Birmingham 1829, marked on handle and nozzle, 3½in (9cm) wide, 1oz.
$600-900

A pair of Victorian beaded candlesticks, JKB Sheffield, 1881, 5in (12.5cm).
$600-900

A pair of late Victorian Corinthian column candlesticks, Sheffield 1897, 9in (23cm).
$600-900

A pair of Victorian candlesticks in the Adam style, by Hawksworth, Eyre & Co, Sheffield 1897, 12in (30.5cm).
$1,000-1,400

A pair of candlesticks, each with a circular removable bobêche above a vasiform candlecup, the base engraved in script 'Laura Jay from Mrs. Banyer 1841', unmarked, c1841, 8in (20cm), 19oz.
$1,200-1,500

A pair of pillar candlesticks in Georgian style, with detachable nozzles, London 1899, 11½in (29cm), loaded.
$750-1,000

A pair of baluster candlesticks, 10in (26cm).
$750-1,000

A pair of silver candlesticks, Sheffield 1920, 13½in (34cm), loaded.
$1,200-1,600

Casters

Three George I pear-shaped casters, engraved with a coat-of-arms in a foliage cartouche, by Samuel Welder, 1716 and 1717, 6in (15.5cm) and 7in (18cm), 18oz 5dwt.
$5,500-7,000

A caster, marked 'DC', marked on base, possibly American, 18thC, 4in (10cm), 3oz.
$300-500

A caster, by Zachariah Brigden, the domed pierced cover with pinecone finial, the side engraved 'MN' in script, marked 'Z+B' on base, Boston, c1775, 5in (12.5cm), 3oz.
$2,500-3,500

A caster, by Benjamin Burt, the domed cover pierced and engraved, with a bell shaped finial, marked on body, Boston, c1760, 5in (12.5cm), 3oz.
$1,500-2,000

A caster, by John Edwards, on a moulded circular foot, marked on body, Boston, c1745, 5½in (14cm), 3oz.
$3,500-4,500

A caster, by Samuel Minott, engraved on base 'SLH', marked with 'M' in script on base, small repair to cover, Boston, c1760, 5in (12cm), 2oz.
$2,500-3,500

Centrepieces

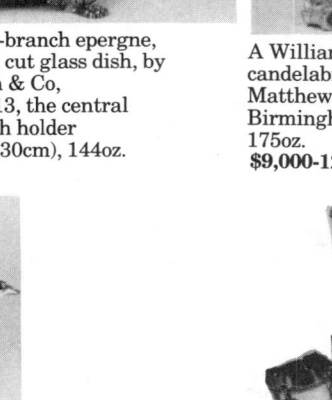

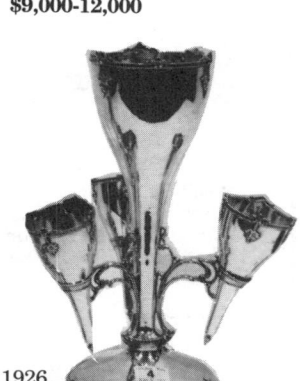

A George III openwork epergne, with 4 detachable scroll branches, each terminating in a detachable shaped sweetmeat dish, by Francis Butty and Nicholas Dumee, 1769, four branches missing, 19in (48cm), 117oz.
$10,000-13,000

A George III four-branch epergne, each branch with cut glass dish, by Matthew Boulton & Co, Birmingham, 1813, the central basket and branch holder unmarked, 12in (30cm), 144oz.
$7,500-10,500

A William IV four-branch candelabrum centrepiece, by Matthew Boulton & Plate Co, Birmingham 1832, 18in (45cm), 175oz.
$9,000-12,000

Coffee Pots

A William III coffee pot, with later baluster finial, engraved with a coat-of-arms, by John Martin Stockar, 1701, repairs, 9in (22.5cm), 17oz 12dwt gross.
$3,000-4,500

A silver epergne, London 1926, 13½in (34cm), 33.5oz.
$750-1,000

A Queen Anne coffee pot, engraved with a cypher within baroque cartouche, by William Gibson, 1704, 9in (23cm), 20oz gross.
$3,000-4,500

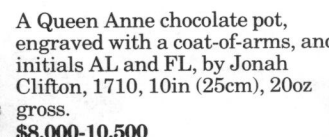

A Queen Anne chocolate pot, engraved with a coat-of-arms, and initials AL and FL, by Jonah Clifton, 1710, 10in (25cm), 20oz gross.
$8,000-10,500

A Queen Anne coffee pot, pricked with initials MS, by John Rand, 1707, 9½in (24cm), 18oz 18dwt.
$5,500-7,000

A George I coffee pot, engraved with a coat-of-arms within baroque cartouche, by Richard Bayley, 1714, 9½in (24cm), 24oz gross.
$6,000-9,000

A Queen Anne coffee pot, engraved with the coat-of-arms of Symonds impaling Croft, by Richard Raine, 1712, 10in (25cm), 24oz gross.
$6,000-9,000

A Queen Anne coffee pot, engraved with a coat-of-arms within baroque cartouche, by Anthony Nelme, 1713, 9in (23cm), 20oz gross.
$4,000-5,500

A George I coffee pot, engraved with a coat-of-arms, by John Edwards II, 1726, 9in (23cm), 25oz gross.
$4,000-5,500

A George II coffee pot, engraved with 2 crests, London 1748, 9in (23cm), 19.5oz gross.
$1,500-2,600

A George II coffee pot, by Whipham & Wright, 1757, 31oz.
$1,500-2,600

A George II coffee pot, engraved with a coat-of-arms, by Isaac Cookson, Newcastle 1737, with later silver handle, 10in (25.5cm), 30oz gross.
$2,250-3,500

A William IV melon-fluted coffee pot, by Joseph and John Angell, London 1833, 8½in (21.5cm), 23.75oz.
$900-1,300

An early George III baluster coffee pot, engraved with crests and motto, by William Cripps, 1760, the cover unmarked, 10½in (26cm), 25oz gross.
$1,500-2,600

An early George III coffee pot, by Alexander Johnston, London 1762, 11in (28cm), 29oz gross.
$2,250-3,000

A George III coffee pot, engraved with a monogram, Thomas Whipham and Charles Wright, London 1767, 11in (28cm), 31.25oz gross.
$3,000-4,500

A George III argyle, engraved with a crest, by Hester Bateman, 1775, 7in (18cm), 10oz.
$4,000-5,500

A George III coffee pot, by Robert Peat, Newcastle 1778, 11in (28cm), 30oz gross.
$3,000-4,500

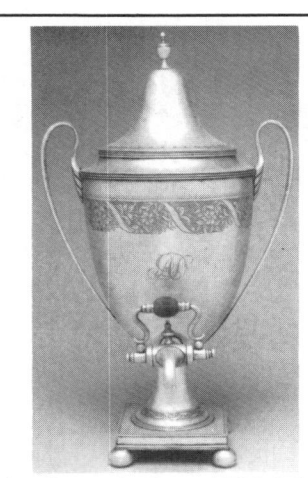

A coffee urn, by Samuel Kirk & Son, with a spigot with a wood handle, the base fitted to hold a burner, the shoulder engraved with a bright cut band of flowers above script initials 'AD', without burner, marked on base, Baltimore, c1850, 56oz 10dwt.
$3,500-4,500

Cups

A cup, by Thomas Coverly, the front engraved 'MG to EE' in script, marked on base, Newport, Rhode Island, c1750, 2½in (6cm), 2oz.
$3,000-3,500

A George II Provincial tumbler cup, engraved with a coaster, with a label floating from the mast inscribed 'Success to Trade and Navigation', by Richard Richardson (II), Chester 1752, the engraving possibly 20-40 years later, 5.9cm diam, in fitted leather case.
$2,250-3,000

A George III two-handled cup and cover, engraved with a coat-of-arms and crest, by Paul Storr, 1792, 17in (43cm), 55oz.
$6,000-8,000

A German silver gilt Kiddush cup, inscribed with a Hebrew inscription, maker's mark an incuse H, Augsburg, c1764, 5in (13cm), 3.75oz.
$5,500-7,000

A George III silver gilt two-handled cup and cover, by Philip Rundell, 1818, the cover 1819, maker's mark probably that of William Burwash, 13in (33cm), 94oz.
$4,000-5,500

A teacup and saucer, by Gorham Manufacturing Company, the cup engraved 'Hiram Powers' and the saucer engraved 'Your Pupil, 1872', marked, Providence, saucer 5½in (14cm) diam, 7oz 10dwt.
$1,000-1,500

A racing trophy cup, the lower part of the foot electroplated, bearing French export marks, c1870, 15in (38cm), 115oz weighable silver.
$4,000-5,500

Cutlery

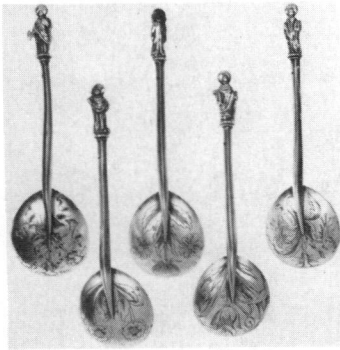

A set of 5 Swiss Apostle spoons, the finials representing St Andrew, St Phillip, St Matthias, St Simon Zelotes, and another possibly St Matthew, maker's mark, Baden in Aargau, 17thC.
$3,000-4,500

An Edwardian hammered goblet, the stem chased and applied with 4 masks representing Comedy and Tragedy joined by bows, the bowl with contemporary presentation inscription, Ramsden & Carr, London 1901, 4in (10cm).
$300-400

A Victorian Vine pattern dessert service, comprising 71 pieces, by George Adams, 1860, 139oz.
$6,000-9,000

A George IV King's shape pattern flatware service, crested, comprising 120 pieces, by Charles Eley, 1825, also 2 sauce ladles, 1825, one condiment ladle, 1825, 2 salt spoons, 1832, by William Chawner, 245.75oz.
$8,000-10,500

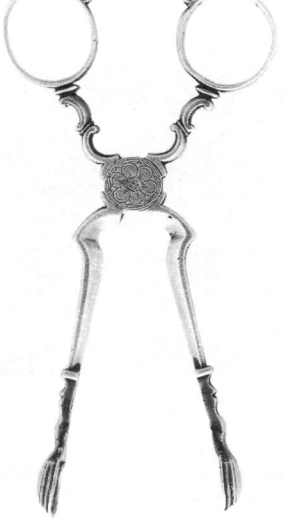

A pair of sugar tongs, by Philip Syng, Jr, the circular hinge engraved on both sides with a flower, the grips engraved 'SW', marked on inside of one tip with 'PS' in a rectangular, probably Belden touch 'a', Philadelphia, c1770, 6in (15cm), 10dwt.
$3,500-4,000

A pair of Georgian silver sugar tongs, by Charles Hougham, London, dated 1791.
$75-150

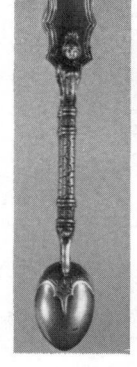

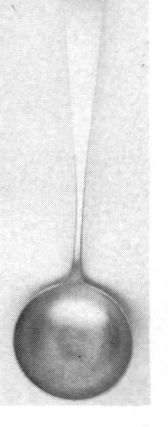

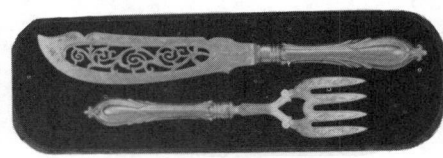

A Victorian fish slice and fork, each engraved with a crest, JG, Birmingham 1858, in a fitted case.
$250-350

A soup ladle, by Saunders Pitman, the handle coffin ended, with a round bowl, the handle engraved 'WR' in script, marked, Providence, c1800, 14½in (36.5cm) long, 6oz 10dwt.
$400-600

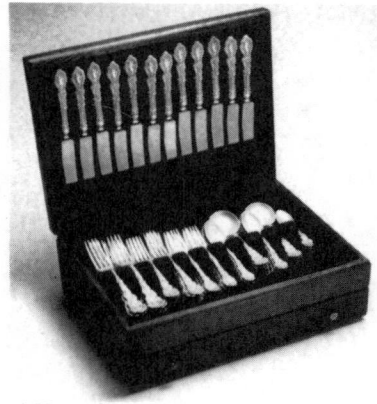

A Versailles pattern flatware service, by Gorham Manufacturing Company, comprising 126 pieces, marked, Providence, after 1888, 118oz 10dwt excluding knives.
$3,500-4,500

An assembled King's pattern flatware service, by R & W Wilson, comprising 91 pieces, Philadelphia, c1830, 175oz excluding knives.
$3,000-4,000

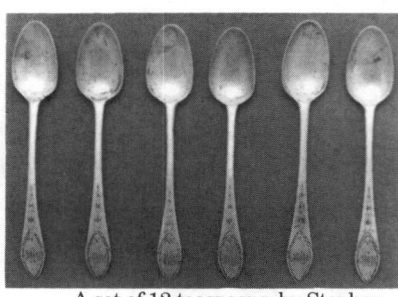

A set of 12 teaspoons, by Stephen Emery, engraved with bright cut decoration enclosing script initials 'WMW', the oval bowl with a scroll drop, each marked, Boston, c1780, 6in (15cm), 4oz 10dwt.
$1,200-1,800

A set of 5 parcel gilt servers, by Whiting Manufacturing Company, retailed by N Harding & Co, Boston, comprising 2 large spoons, a flat server, a smaller spoon, a pierced ladle, the gilt bowls each with a matt finish, in varying shapes, the large flat server with engraved decoration, each marked, North Attleboro, Massachusetts, c1870, 8 to 10½in (20.5 to 26.5cm) long, 9oz 10dwt, in original silk lined fitted box with retailer's label.
$2,000-3,000

An English King's pattern flatware service, by Tiffany & Company, comprising 157 pieces, marked, New York, c1885, 239oz 10dwt excluding knives.
$10,000-12,000

A rare set of 3 basting spoons, by Baldwin Gardiner, each with a fiddle thread handle engraved with a coat of arms, marked on back of handle, Philadelphia or New York, early 19thC, 13½in (34cm) long, 22oz.
$1,500-2,000

A pair of tablespoons, by John Edwards, each with a wavy end handle, the back of handle engraved 'MC', with added engraving '1713, AT, ARPB and MWP', each marked on back of handle, Boston, early 18thC, 7in (17.5cm), 1oz 10dwt.
$3,500-4,500

A pair of tongs, engraved on the exterior in foliate script 'JMC', engraved on the interior in script 'From George Washington to Col. John M. Clarke,', marked 'IE', marked twice on one arm, late 18thC, 5½in (13.5cm), 1oz.
$700-1,000

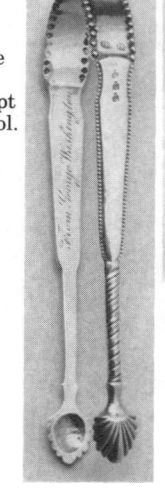

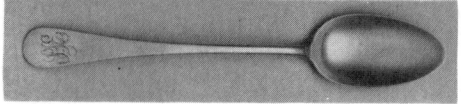

A teaspoon, by Paul Revere II, engraved with script initials 'SSE', marked on the back of handle with Belden touch 'a', Boston, c1790, 6in (15cm), 1oz.
$1,000-1,500

A flatware service, by Albert Coles & Company, comprising 122 pieces, New York, c1860, 313oz weighable silver.
$7,000-8,000

An 8-place King's pattern silver cutlery set, comprising 48 pieces, London, c1825-46, 117oz.
$2,250-3,500

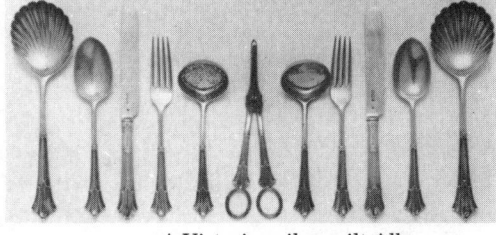

A Victorian silver gilt Albany pattern dessert service, comprising 41 pieces, by Francis Higgins, 1897, 59oz excluding knives, in brass-bound wood case.
$5,500-7,000

A fruiting vine design service, comprising 68 pieces, c1914, with a pair of pierced and engraved fish servers with bone handles, 1906, 22oz weighable silver.
$1,500-2,600

An oak canteen of silver crested lobe-ended tableware, Sheffield 1918, 148.5oz.
$2,250-3,500

A Victorian double struck beaded Old English table service, comprising 48 pieces, engraved with a crest, by George Adams, London 1873, 117oz.
$3,000-4,500

Spoons – Caddy

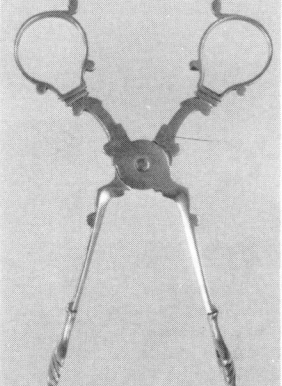

A pair of Chinese sugar tongs, 1900
$60-100

A pair of silver sugar nips, 1885.
$100-200

A George III caddy spoon, with prick dot engraved cartouche within wreath, by Joseph Taylor, Birmingham 1798.
$150-250

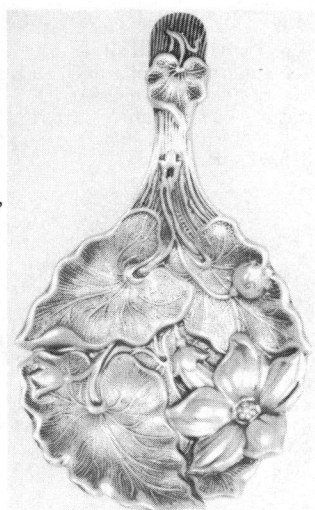

A George III caddy spoon, with fiddle stem, by J Taylor, Birmingham 1813.
$250-350

A George III caddy spoon, by Elizabeth Morley, 1809.
$400-500

A Victorian caddy spoon, the coiled tendril and vine leaf handle concealing the hallmarks, c1850.
$150-200

A Victorian caddy spoon, stamped with ivy leaves and flowers, by Alexander Hunt, Sheffield, 1850.
$400-500

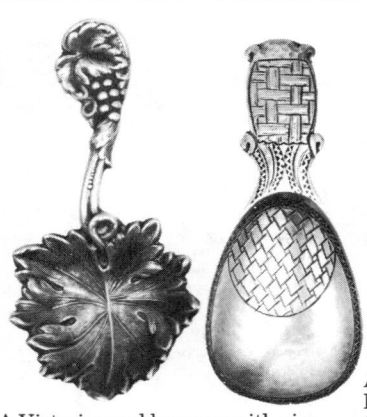

A Victorian shovel bowl caddy spoon, the handle terminating in an ancient Egyptian male head, by Hilliard & Thomason, Birmingham 1883.
$150-250

A late Victorian caddy spoon, by George Unite, Birmingham 1899.
$250-350

A caddy spoon by Liberty & Co, Birmingham 1936.
$250-350

A Victorian caddy spoon with vine leaf bowl, by Elizabeth Eaton, 1852.
$150-250

Dishes

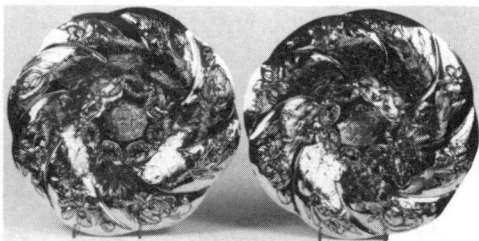

A Charles I two-handled sweetmeat dish, maker's mark IP, a bell between, 1634, later engraved, 8½in (21.5cm), 5oz 10dwt.
$5,500-7,000

A pair of silver gilt dishes, engraved with a coat-of-arms in a baroque cartouche, maker's mark only WH between rosettes and pellets, c1700, 15in (38cm), 65oz.
$6,000-9,000

A set of 4 George II dishes, each engraved with a coat-of-arms within drapery mantling, by Frederick Kandler, 1752, 10in (24cm), 76oz.
$16,000-21,000

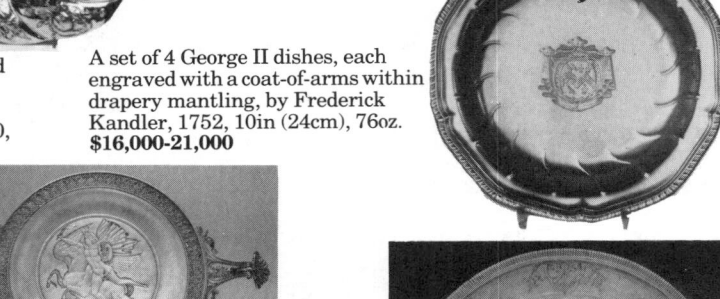

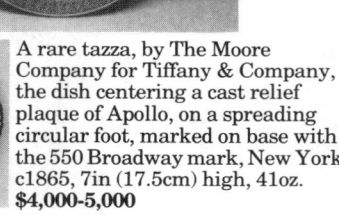

A rare tazza, by The Moore Company for Tiffany & Company, the dish centering a cast relief plaque of Apollo, on a spreading circular foot, marked on base with the 550 Broadway mark, New York, c1865, 7in (17.5cm) high, 41oz.
$4,000-5,000

A pair of George III silver gilt vegetable dishes, engraved with a coat-of-arms, the reverse with initials, by Benjamin Smith, 1807, 12in (29cm) wide, 66oz.
$16,500-19,500

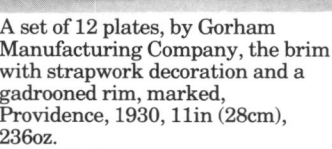

A set of 12 plates, by Gorham Manufacturing Company, the brim with strapwork decoration and a gadrooned rim, marked, Providence, 1930, 11in (28cm), 236oz.
$6,000-7,000

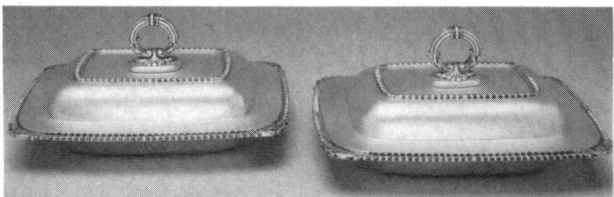

A pair of covered vegetable dishes, by Tiffany & Company, the lids with removable ring handles, marked, New York, c1950, 5in (12.5cm) high, 92oz 10dwt.
$3,000-4,000

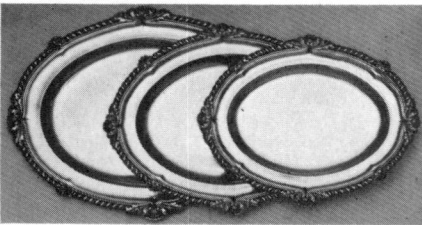

A set of 3 George IV meat dishes, by Paul Storr, 1825, 18½in (47cm) to 14in (35.5cm) wide, 155oz.
$18,000-21,000

Inkstands

A George II oblong inkstand, with a central bell with taperstick socket handle, by Edward Wakelin, 1751, unmarked, 13½in (34cm) wide, 59oz.
$10,500-14,000

An English silver penner, the octagonal stem with threaded sections, one concealing a nib and one forming the cover to the vase-shaped ink bottle, the foot with indecipherable maker's initials, early 18thC, in original fishskin case with nailhead decoration, some damage, 5in (12cm) long.
$1,000-1,400

A Victorian inkstand, part gilt, by Charles Thomas & George Fox, 1852, 9½in (24cm) diam overall, 27oz.
$1,500-2,600

A Continental inkstand, marks for Augsburg, 19thC German, import marks for 1912, 7½in (18cm), 39.5oz.
$2,500-3,500

Jugs

A George I covered milk jug, crested, maker's mark unclear, 1719, 5½in (13.5cm) high, 6.5oz.
$3,000-4,500

A Victorian four-handled tyg with gilt interior, by Robert Garrard, London 1870, 5½in (14cm) high, 22oz 10dwt.
$750-1,000

A Victorian silver beer jug with mask spout, maker AGP, 1859, 10in (25.5cm), 50.5oz.
$1,500-2,600

A cream pitcher, by Albert Coles, retailed by L H Wing, Macon, Georgia, the side engraved with a cartouche centering an inscription 'Georgia State Agricultural Soc. To Ida Feuchtwanger Best Performance on Piano. Macon, Nov 23 1869', marked by maker and retailer on base, New York, 6in (15cm) high, 6oz.
$400-500

A rare pitcher and a set of 6 beakers, by Joseph Foster, the pitcher with a hinged domed lid with a ball finial, the front engraved 'SBW' in script, marked, bruised, the beakers engraved on base with script initial 'W', each marked, Boston, c1820, pitcher 10in (25.5cm) high, 64oz 10dwt.
$9,000-10,000

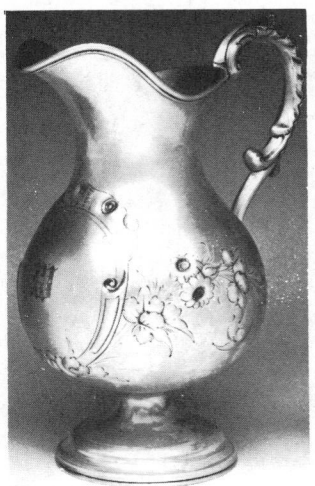

A pitcher, by Adolf Himmel, retailed by Hyde and Goodrich, repoussé and chased with flowers centering a cartouche with initial 'W', marked by maker and retailer on base, New Orleans, c1860, 11in (28cm), 25oz.
$1,500-2,000

A sauceboat, a cream pitcher, and a bowl, by Samuel Kirk and Son, the sauceboat with a figural thumbpiece, the bowl with repoussé flowers, each marked, Baltimore, 19thC, sauceboat 7in (18cm) high, 21oz 10dwt.
$1,000-1,500

A pitcher, the shoulder with a cast applied grapevine border, marked on base with unidentified eagle touchmark, c1830, 12in (30.5cm) high, 35oz.
$1,500-2,000

A pitcher, by Gorham Manufacturing Company, in the Japanese taste, with a handle in the form of a tree trunk, with leafy branches joined to the rim and sides, marked, Providence, 1885, 9in (23cm), 40oz 10dwt.
$7,000-8,000

A cream pitcher, by Zachariah Brigden, with a flaring cylindrical foot with a gadrooned moulding, the front engraved 'EH', marked 'Z+B' on base, Boston, c1775, 5in (12.5cm), 3oz.
$2,500-3,500

A small pitcher, by Charters, Cann & Dunn, the scroll handle cast in the form of a leafy branch, with a pendant blossom, and 9 oval reserves, one engraved 'MFC', marked on bottom with maker's and retailer's marks, New York, c1850, 8½in (21cm), 12oz.
$300-500

A pitcher, by Jones, Ball & Poor, the surface repoussé and chased with a vine against a punched ground, with a reserve engraved 'H.C. to C.H.M. 1852', marked, bruises, Boston, 11in (28cm), 29oz.
$1,200-1,600

A cream pitcher, by Henry J Pepper, the rim with a gadrooned border, one side engraved with script initials 'JRB', marked on base, Wilmington, Delaware, c1820, 6in (15cm), 7oz.
$600-800

A cream pitcher, by Philip Syng, Jr, the handle engraved 'SW', marked on base twice with 'PS' in script, Belden touch 'c', Philadelphia, c1760, 4in (10cm) high, 3oz.
$7,000-8,000

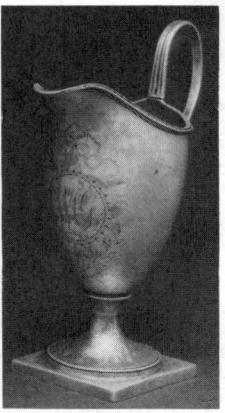

A cream pitcher, with a moulded strap handle, the front engraved with a bright cut shield enclosing script initials 'WCG', marked on base with 'ID' in conforming reserve, c1800, 7in (18cm), 5oz.
$1,000-1,500

A covered sugar bowl and cream pitcher, by Curry & Preston, each on a stepped circular foot with beaded borders, the sugar bowl cover with an acorn finial, marked, monograms removed, bruises, Philadelphia, c1830, sugar bowl 8in (20.5cm) high, 33oz 10dwt.
$800-900

Mugs

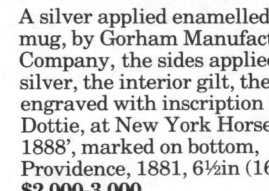

A George II mug, initialled A.C. on base, maker's mark worn, London 1727, 4½in (11cm), 11.8oz.
$600-900

A small mug, by Thaddeus Keeler, the body engraved in script 'SCJ', marked on base, minor repairs to handle joins and seam, bruises, New York, c1810, 2oz.
$500-600

A silver applied enamelled copper mug, by Gorham Manufacturing Company, the sides applied with silver, the interior gilt, the bottom engraved with inscription 'Won by Dottie, at New York Horse Show, 1888', marked on bottom, Providence, 1881, 6½in (16.5cm).
$2,000-3,000

A George IV gilt lined fluted christening mug, George Burrows and Richard Pearce, London 1829, 4in (10cm), 5.25oz.
$300-400

Salts

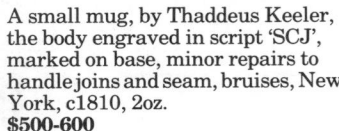

A set of 4 oval salts, by Lewis Fueter, on pedestal bases with silver gilt rims and interiors, New York, c1785, 13.75oz.
$2,000-2,500

A set of 4 George III silver gilt salt cellar stands, fitted with cut glass liners, by Robert and Samuel Hennell, 1805, 5in (13cm) wide, 28oz.
$5,500-7,000

A pair of salts, by Bigelow Bros and Kennard, the handles in the form of satyrs' masks with ring handles, marked, Boston, c1860, 3in (7.5cm) high, 7oz.
$400-500

Salvers

A pair of Dutch salts, 18thC.
$250-350

A William and Mary salver, on central spreading foot, by George Manjoy, 1694, 7cm diam, 15dwt.
$1,000-1,400

A rare small salver, by Jacob Hurd, with cusped corners and a moulded rim, on 4 scroll feet, engraved 'WLH' on base, marked near rim with Belden touch 'c', Boston, c1745, 6in (15cm) square, 5oz.
$10,000-13,000

A George II salver, on 3 scroll and lion's paw feet, by Isaac Cookson, Newcastle, 1748, 13in (33cm), 46oz.
$1,500-2,600

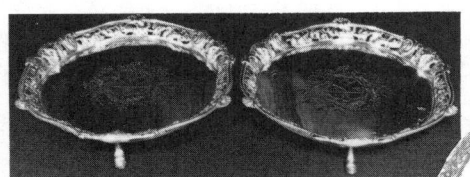

A pair of George II silver salvers, with contemporary raised cast border, each on 3 serpent head feet, by Thomas Hemming, London 1753, 8½in (21.5cm), 16oz each.
$3,000-4,000

A George II salver, on 4 eagle's wing and claw feet, by Jabez Daniell, London 1755, 26in (66cm), 202oz.
$6,000-9,000

A George III salver, on 4 vine feet, by William Cripps, 1762, 24in (61cm).
$9,000-12,000

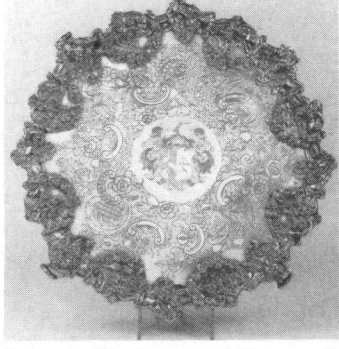

A George IV salver on 4 foliate scroll feet, applied with masks of Bacchus, by William Pitts, 1822, 22½in (57cm), 202oz.
$9,000-12,000

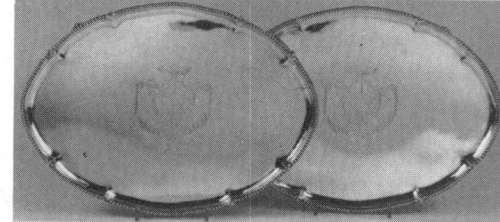

A pair of George III salvers, each on 4 shell and scroll feet, by Thomas Hannam and John Crouch, 1776, 16in (40.5cm) wide, 80oz.
$4,500-7,000

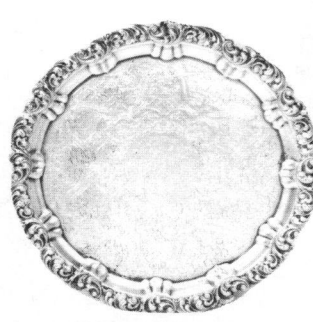

A pair of George IV salvers on foliate and shell feet, with central presentation inscriptions, S C Younge & Co, Sheffield 1825, 10½in (26.5cm), 42oz.
$900-1,300

A pair of George III bead-edged salvers, the borders applied with 6 medallions in the manner of James Tassir, the surface crested, each on 3 bracket supports, by George Crouch and Thomas Hannam, 1780, 8in (20.5cm), 30oz.
$3,000-4,500

The crest is that of George Scholloy who was Lord Mayor of London 1812/13.

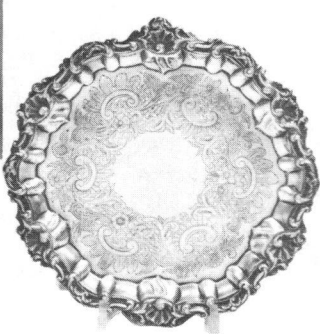

A William IV salver on scroll feet, by Richard William Atkins and William Nathaniel Somersall, London 1833, 8in (20cm), 12oz.
$450-600

A Victorian chased silver salver, in George II style, on 3 shaped feet, London 1883, 18in (45.5cm), 79oz.
$2,250-3,500

A late Victorian salver in the 18thC taste, on shell and scroll feet, the ground engraved with a crest and motto within rococo floral cartouche, Walker & Hall, Sheffield 1898, 8½in (21.5cm).
$250-350

An Edwardian salver on rococo pierced scroll feet, Walker and Hall, Sheffield 1909, 11in (28cm), 19.25oz.
$400-500

A salver, with Chippendale style border, on 4 shell feet, engraved in the centre, Chester 1927, 7½in (19cm), 12oz approx.
$150-250

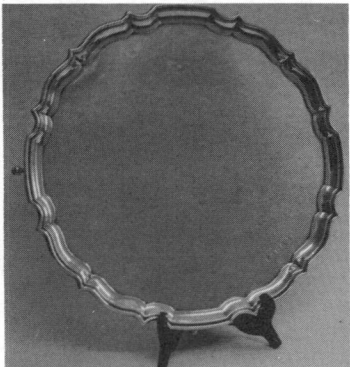

A silver salver, with Chippendale style border, on 4 tab feet, Birmingham 1935, 14in (35.5cm), 37oz.
$450-600

A German silver ornamental charger, the central panel depicting embattled Teutonic knights, 19thC, 27in (68.5cm), .8125 standard, 47oz 10dwt.
$1,300-1,800

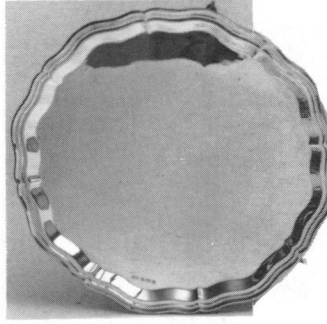

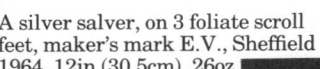

A silver salver, on 3 foliate scroll feet, maker's mark E.V., Sheffield 1964, 12in (30.5cm), 26oz.
$300-400

Sauceboats

A George I brandy saucepan, by Benjamin Brancker, Liverpool c1720, the base engraved with initials MH, marked twice STER over LING and twice with maker's mark EB a 'liver' bird above, 5in (12.5cm) wide overall, 2oz gross.
$1,500-2,600

A pair of sauceboats on hoof feet, by Viners, 7in (18cm), 17.5oz.
$300-400

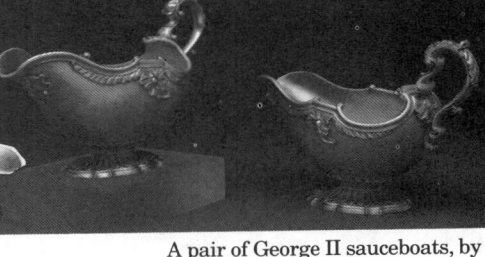

A pair of George II sauceboats, by Ayme Videau, London 1744, 9in (23cm) wide, 43oz 10dwt.
$30,000-34,500

A pair of George III sauceboats, by Ebenezer Coker, 1771, 9in (23cm) wide, 38.5oz.
$3,000-4,000

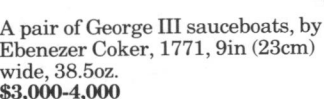

A pair of George II Irish sauceboats, on 4 lion's mask and paw feet, by John Hamilton, Dublin, c1745, 33oz.
$4,000-5,500

A pair of George II sauceboats, on 3
fluted scroll feet, by Edward
Wakelin, 1749, 9in (23cm) wide,
38oz.
$4,000-5,500

A pair of George III two-handled
double-lipped sauceboats, engraved
with a crest, by Thomas Heming,
1761, 38oz.
$6,000-9,000

A Victorian sauceboat, on 3 shell
pattern feet, London 1898, 8in
(20.5cm) wide, 10oz.
$250-350

A Victorian cylindrical scent bottle,
by Sampson Mordan, 1882, with
interior glass stopper.
$150-200

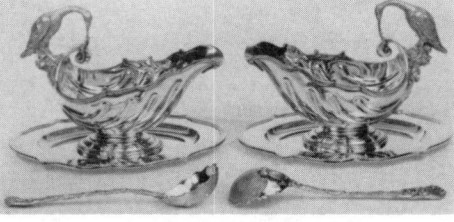

A pair of silver gilt sauceboats and
stands, in the style of David
Willaume II, 1965, with a pair of
silver gilt sauce ladles in the style of
Paul de Lamerie, 1966, 66oz.
$3,000-4,000

Scent Bottles

A Victorian silver cylindrical scent
bottle, by Sampson Mordan, 1884.
$100-200

A Victorian silver gilt cylindrical
perfume bottle, with glass liner and
stopper, S Mordan & Co London
1884, 2in (5cm) high, in fitted case.
$450-600

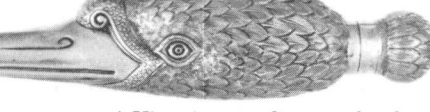

A Victorian novelty scent bottle
formed as a swan's head, maker's
mark indistinct, Birmingham 1884,
6in (15cm).
$800-1,200

A late Victorian tapering scent
flask, embossed with rococo scrolls,
flowers and a serpent motif,
engraved with a name, H and A,
Birmingham 1886, 9½in (24cm).
$400-500

Services

A George III composite four-piece
tea and coffee service.
$2,250-3,500

A George IV three-piece tea service,
by Rebecca Emes and Edward
Barnard, London 1820, 45.9oz.
$1,000-1,400

A three-piece tea set, by George
Hayter, London 1824.
$1,300-1,800

A Victorian four-piece coffee and tea
service, with basketweave bodies,
by Robert Hennell, 1859, sugar bowl
1857, 79.5oz.
$4,000-5,500

A George IV tea service, by John
and Thomas Settle, Sheffield 1824,
and a similar coffee pot, by William
Eaton, 1824, each engraved with an
inscription dated 1826, coffee pot
8in (20.5cm) high, 82oz gross.
$3,000-4,000

A William IV four-piece rococo style
tea service, London 1836, 92oz.
$4,000-5,500

A six-piece tea and coffee service, by
Samuel Kirk & Sons, each
elaborately repoussé and chased
with landscape scenes, the handles
with ram's head grip, the domed
covers with a cast grape finial, each
base with an engraved inscription
and dated 1911, each marked, the
kettle now without burner,
Baltimore, c1911, kettle 14½in
(36.5cm) high, 209oz gross.
$8,500-9,000

A three-piece tea service, by
Fletcher & Gardiner, the teapot
with an acorn finial and S-scroll
handle and ivory insulating rings
and a mask grip, and a scrolled
spout with an applied mask, the
sugar bowl with a similar cover and
2 cast mask handles, the cream
pitcher with a scrolling handle with
a bird's head grip, each marked,
Philadelphia, c1820, teapot 9in
(23cm), 87oz gross.
$7,000-8,000

A Victorian silver four-piece tea and
coffee service by Robert Harper,
London 1866, coffee pot 11in (28cm)
high, 71oz 13dwt.
$2,250-3,500

A Victorian beaded three-piece tea
service, by Stephen Smith, London
1868, teapot 5½in (14cm) high, 45oz.
$1,500-2,600

A tea and coffee service, by Geradus
Boyce, comprising: teapot, coffee
pot, sugar basin and cover, cream
jug and slop basin, the covers with
foliage finials, New York, c1825,
coffee pot 12in (30.5cm), 157oz gross.
$800-1,200

A four-piece tea and
coffee service, by Gorham
Manufacturing Company,
engraved on the side with
a stylized monogram,
marked, Providence,
1888, coffee pot 8in
(20cm) high, 67oz gross.
$1,200-1,800

A three-piece tea service, by Tiffany
& Co, comprising: a teapot, a
covered sugar bowl and a cream
pitcher, each with mid-bands of
die-rolled decoration, each engraved
with foliate initials 'GC', marked on
base, New York, c1865, teapot 9in
(23cm) high, 71oz gross.
$1,800-2,200

A three-piece part tea service, by
R & W Wilson, comprising: a coffee
pot, a teapot and a waste bowl, each
with die-rolled grapevine borders at
the shoulder, on a spreading
circular foot with a die-rolled leaf
border, marked, some bruises,
Philadelphia, c1835, pots 12in
(30cm) high, 113oz 10dwt gross.
$1,500-2,000

A three-piece tea service and a
kettle on stand, by Tiffany &
Company, the tea service
comprising: a teapot, a covered
creamer and a covered sugar bowl,
each marked, New York, tea service
c1850, kettle c1880, the kettle (14in
(35.5cm) high, 154oz gross.
$3,500-4,000

A six-piece tea and coffee service, by
R & W Wilson, comprising: a coffee
pot, 2 teapots, a cream pitcher and 2
covered sugar bowls, the covers with
acorn finials, the spouts each with
an eagle's head terminal, each
marked, Philadelphia, c1825, coffee
pot 11½in (29cm) high, 202oz gross.
$4,000-6,000

A three-piece tea service, by John
Targee, with a die rolled band of oak
leaves at the shoulder, engraved
'MAB', the handles scrolled, the
teapot handle with wooden
insulating rings, each marked, New
York, c1810, teapot 9in (23cm) high,
61oz gross.
$2,500-3,500

A four-piece tea service, by John B
Jones Co, comprising: a teapot, a
covered sugar bowl, a cream pitcher
and a waste bowl, each with applied
relief foliate decoration on the body,
on a circular base on 4 cast
winged-paw feet, each marked on
base, Boston, c1838, teapot 9in
(23cm) high, 84oz 10dwt gross.
$1,500-2,000

A six-piece tea and
coffee service with tray,
by Gorham
Manufacturing
Company, the handles
wooden, marked,
Providence, c1930,
kettle 14in (35.5cm)
high, 299oz gross.
$8,000-9,000

A Victorian tea set, initialled B
& GB, 1876, 57oz.
$1,200-1,600

A Victorian four-piece finely chased
tea service, maker Garrard's,
London 1879, 55oz.
$1,200-1,600

A Victorian four-piece tea and coffee
service, the coffee pot with fluted
bone finial, Sheffield 1879, coffee pot
8½in (21.5cm) high, 61oz gross.
$3,000-4,000

A Victorian three-piece tea service,
James Dixon & Sons, Sheffield
1891, teapot, 6½in (16.5cm) high,
26oz.
$450-700

A Victorian silver tea service, by
George Fox, London 1887, in
original cases.
$3,000-4,000

A Victorian silver tea service, the
teapot Birmingham 1899, sugar
basin and cream jug 1898, 30oz.
$400-500

A six-piece silver tea service, by
Atkin Bros, Sheffield 1905-07,
110oz.
$3,000-4,000

A five-piece tea and coffee service in
the neo-classical taste, burner
missing to kettle, 1902-3, 137oz
gross.
$5,500-7,000

A four-piece tea set in the rococo
style, Sheffield 1912, 104oz.
$1,500-2,600

An Edwardian seven-piece dessert
suite, gilt lined, by Mappin & Webb,
Sheffield 1902 and 1908, largest
17in (43cm) wide, 151oz.
$10,500-14,000

A three-piece tea service, by Colin and J W Forbes, comprising: teapot, two-handled sugar bowl, and creamer, the teapot with C-scroll wooden handle, the teapot and creamer with dolphin finial, the creamer and sugar bowl with stylized eagle's head handles, repair to foot of sugar bowl and teapot, New York, c1815, teapot 8in (20.5cm) high, 51oz 10dwt gross.
$1,200-1,800

A tea service on pedestal feet, Chester 1924, 24oz.
$300-400

A tea and coffee service in the Queen Anne style, by Sebastian Garrard, 1920, tea kettle 13in (33cm) high, 158oz gross.
$4,000-5,500

A three-piece tea service, maker 'G. Limited', Sheffield 1933, 35oz gross.
$700-900

A five-piece chased tea service and tray, Birmingham 1960, hot water jug 10in (25.5cm) high, 139oz gross.
$2,250-3,000

A five-piece tea service, Birmingham 1935, tray 21½in (54.5cm) wide, 109oz.
$1,300-1,800

Tankards

A four-piece tea service, hot water jug 8in (20.5cm) high, 41oz.
$1,000-1,400

A Charles II tankard, maker's mark lA in dotted oval, 1677, 7½in (19cm) high, 32oz.
$4,500-7,000

A Charles II tankard, maker's mark IC with a mullet below, 1679, 7½in (19cm), 41oz.
$10,000-13,000

A William III tankard and cover, the handle engraved with initials, by Thomas Brydon, 1695, 6½in (16.5cm), 24oz.
$7,500-10,500

A tankard by John Brevoort, with a flat domed cover with a crenellated lip, an S-scroll handle with a rat tail and an oval disc terminal, the cover engraved with a cypher 'WL', the base engraved with the weight, mark struck twice on either side of the handle, several old repairs to cover, New York, c1740, 7in (19cm), 26oz 10dwt.
$3,000-5,000

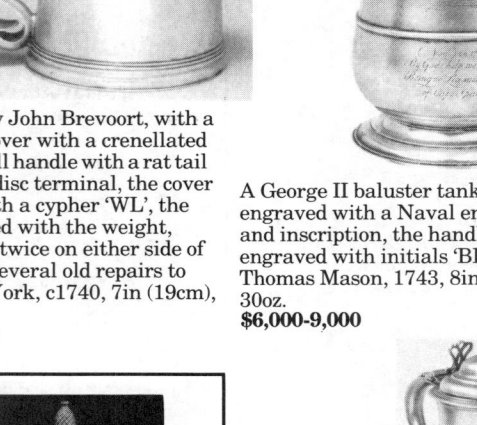

A George II baluster tankard, engraved with a Naval engagement and inscription, the handle engraved with initials 'BEH', by Thomas Mason, 1743, 8in (20.5cm), 30oz.
$6,000-9,000

A George II Provincial mug, by Langlands & Goodrick, Newcastle, 1756, 3½in (9cm) high, 7.25oz.
$600-900

A George III quart tankard, Thomas Whipham and Charles Wright, London 1764, 8in (20.5cm), 25.75oz.
$1,500-2,600

A George III tankard, engraved with coat-of-arms, by Robert Sharp, 1791, 7in (17.5cm), 30oz.
$5,500-7,000

A tankard by William Hollingshead, with a pineapple finial and a pierced strapwork thumbpiece, the double scroll handle with a moulded drop and a shield shaped moulded terminal, marked 'WH' in script on either side of handle, spout removed, Philadelphia, c1770, 10½in (26cm) high.
$3,500-5,500

A George III tankard, by Soloman Hougham, London 1804, with later chased decoration, 9in (23cm), 33.3oz.
$1,200-1,600

Tea Caddies

A pair of George II tea caddies and matching sugar box, by Samuel Taylor, 1753, 6in (15cm), 29oz.
$4,000-5,500

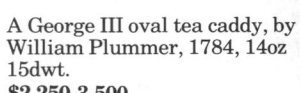

A George III oval tea caddy, by William Plummer, 1784, 14oz 15dwt.
$2,250-3,500

A pair of George II tea caddies and matching sugar box, by Robert Albin Cox, 1756, 4½in (11cm), 32oz.
$5,500-7,000

Tea Kettles

A George III tea urn, by Edward Fernell, London 1786, 20½in (52cm), 105oz, complete with plated inner frame and heating bar.
$2,250-3,500

A Victorian tea kettle, stand and lamp, with partly covered wicker swing handle, by D and C Hands, 1856, 15½in (39cm) high, 72oz.
$2,500-3,500

An Edward VII silver kettle, 1906.
$700-900

A tea kettle on stand, retailed by Starr & Marcus, the kettle with a band of ornament in the Renaissance taste, burner missing, stand marked, New York, c1910, 14½in (36.5cm) high, 53oz 10dwt.
$1,200-1,500

A Victorian tea kettle in the mid 18thC taste, fitted with an electroplated burner, WWW, London 1861, 11in (28cm), 32.25oz gross excluding burner.
$750-1,000

A George III tea caddy, by Henry Chawner, 1791, 13oz 8dwt.
$3,000-4,000

A George III tea urn, by Samuel Hennell and James Taylor, 1814, 14in (35.5cm) high, 143oz.
$5,500-7,000

A kettle on stand, by Grosjean & Woodward for Tiffany & Company, with a bail handle with ivory insulating rings, on 4 scrolling feet enclosing a burner, marked, damage to hinge of bail handle, New York, c1860, 12in (30.5cm), 30oz.
$1,000-1,500

Teapots

A Dutch teapot, maker's mark indistinct, Amsterdam 1722, 5in (12.5cm) high, 9oz 10dwt gross.
$5,500-7,000

An Edwardian silver tea kettle and stand by Goldsmiths and Silversmiths Company Ltd, London 1905, 13½in (34cm) high, 49oz 8dwt.
$1,000-1,400

A teapot, with a pineapple finial and a wooden C-scroll handle, the base engraved 'George Partridge' in script, marked 'Revere', 6in (15cm) high, 15oz 10dwt gross.
$1,500-2,000

A teapot by Bailey & Company, with a domed cover with an urn finial, the entire surface decorated with repoussé and chased flowers and leaves, with beaded borders and a Greek key border at the shoulder, marked on base, Philadelphia, c1850, 11in (28cm), 37oz gross.
$1,100-1,500

A George III cape pattern biggin and stand, by Paul Storr, 1811, 56.5oz.
$7,000-9,000

A Victorian tapering teapot, John Tapley, London 1849, 6½in (16.5cm), 21oz.
$450-600

A William IV teapot, by E E J and W Barnard, 11in (29.5cm) wide, 24.5oz.
$450-700

A Victorian oval drum teapot in 18thC style, by Hands & Son, London 1858, 19½oz gross.
$400-500

A late Victorian teapot, WG and JL, London 1897, 6in (15cm), 22oz gross.
$400-500

Trays

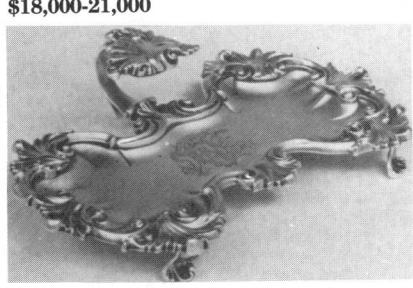

A set of 2 waiters and a mug and cover, one waiter and mug with a detachable 19thC plaque, maker's mark only perhaps AM for Arthur Mainwaring, c1690, and one waiter by Thomas Farren, maker's mark only, c1720, the waiters 7½in (19cm) diam, the mug 4½in (11cm) high, 39oz.
$18,000-21,000

A Victorian oval teapot, by Barnard Bros, London 1898, 25.25oz.
$300-400

A George III Irish tray, Thomas Jones, Dublin, 1793, 22in (56cm) wide, 77oz.
$6,000-9,000

A George II snuffers tray, by Alexander Johnston, 1750, 8in (20cm) wide, 13oz.
$1,000-1,400

A George III waiter, Robert Makepeace and Robert Carter, London 1777, 6in (12.5cm) diam, 7.9oz.
$600-900

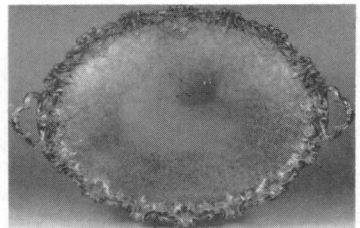

A Victorian two-handled tray, by
Robert Garrard, stamped
'R. & S. Garrard, Panton St.,
London', 1855, 33½in (85cm) wide,
214oz.
$13,500-17,500

A silver cherub pin tray, c1911.
$450-600

A silver tea tray, by Walker & Hall,
Sheffield 1911, 24in (61cm) wide,
118oz.
$2,250-3,000

A Victorian gallery tray, by Martin
Hall and Co Ltd, Sheffield 1877,
19½in (49cm) wide, 84oz.
$5,500-7,000

Tureens

A George II soup tureen and cover,
crested and inscribed, by Edward
Wakelin, 1754, 15½in (40cm) wide.
95oz.
$7,500-10,500

A set of 4 George III tureens and
covers, by Andrew Fogelberg and
Stephen Gilbert, 1782, 10in
(25.5cm) wide, 92.5oz.
$10,000-13,000

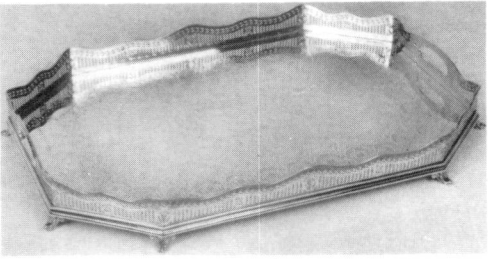

A gallery tray, by West and Son,
1913, 24in (61cm) wide, 163oz.
$6,000-8,000

A covered soup tureen, by Bailey &
Kitchen, the lid with an acanthus
ring handle, the bowl with 2 leafy
handles, on 4 lion's paw feet, the
sides engraved with later script
monograms, marked on bottom,
Philadelphia, c1840, 15½in (39cm)
high, 127oz.
$3,500-4,000

A George III Scottish soup
tureen, cover and liner,
maker's mark JN, the cover
and finial apparently
unmarked, the liner plated,
Edinburgh 1818,
16in (40cm), 132oz.
$8,000-10,500

A pair of George III entreé dishes, by
Robert Sharp, 1800, the handles
unmarked, 12in (30.5cm) wide,
115oz.
$6,000-9,000

Wine Antiques

A George III wine label, incised 'Old Hock', by John Humphris, c1765.
$150-250

A George III Provincial wine label, incised 'Claret', by Richard Richardson (II), Chester, c1770.
$150-250

A pair of George III wine labels, incised 'Shrub' and 'Lisbon', by Hester Bateman, c1790.
$150-250

A pair of George III wine labels, by Phipps & Robinson, c1795.
$150-250

A George III wine label, by John Whittingham, 1812.
$250-350

A set of 3 George III Provincial wine labels, incised 'Rum', 'Brandy' and 'Hollands', by John Watson, Sheffield 1814.
$150-250

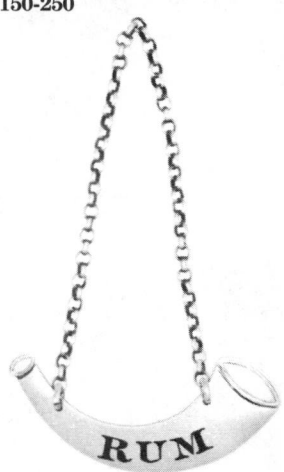

A George III hunting horn wine label, incised and filled 'Rum', by Thomas Wallis (II), 1804.
$450-600

A George III large cast wine label, by Paul Storr, 1816, 8.4cm wide.
$1,000-1,400

A wine label, possibly Irish, unmarked, c1820, possibly an unrecorded design.
$450-600

A set of 4 Regency wine labels, by T & J Phipps, London 1817.
$450-700

A William IV wine label, by Rawlings & Summers, 1834.
$75-150

A William IV wine label, by Paul Storr, 1835, 4cm wide.
$1,300-1,800

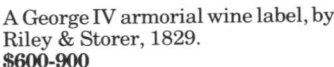

A William IV cast large single vine leaf wine label, by Benjamin Smith (II), 1834.
$250-350

A George IV armorial wine label, by Riley & Storer, 1829.
$600-900

533

A set of 4 William IV cast vine leaf wine labels, Riley & Storer, 1835.
$1,200-1,600

A Victorian wine label, by Rawlings & Summers, 1837.
$250-350

A Victorian cast wine label, incised 'Red Constantia', by Rawlings & Summers, 1843.
$600-900

An engraved silver wine jug, by Barnard Bros, London 1863.
$1,500-2,600

A ewer by Thomas Fletcher, the inside of foot engraved with inscription 'From E. Carmick to Minerva Cenas. 1838', marked on base, bruises, Philadelphia, c1838, 13in (33cm) high, 39oz.
$1,500-2,000

A late Victorian mounted glass claret jug, by Alexander Crichton, 1882, 10½in (27cm).
$4,000-5,500

A Victorian beaded vase shaped claret jug, with presentation inscription, Martin Hall & Co, London 1872, 12½in (31.5cm), 28oz.
$1,200-1,600

A Victorian Cellini pattern vase shaped claret jug, by J H Savory, London 1891, the base with Goldsmith's Alliance Ltd, trade mark, 11in (28cm), 24oz.
$900-1,300

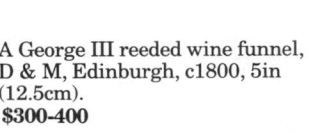

A George III reeded wine funnel, D & M, Edinburgh, c1800, 5in (12.5cm).
$300-400

A George III silver wine funnel, by Rebecca Emes and Edward Barnard, London 1816, 5in (12.5cm), 2.75oz.
$450-700

A pair of George III circular coasters, London 1779, 5in (12.5cm) diam.
$1,000-1,400

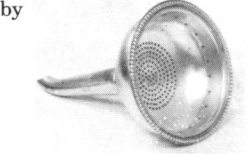

A George III beaded wine funnel, Hester Bateman, London 1777, 5in (12.5cm).
$1,000-1,400

A pair of William IV decanter stands, by Howard, Battie and Hawkesworth, Sheffield 1832, 10oz.
$1,500-2,600

A George III silver gilt covered wine cooler, by Benjamin Smith, London 1807, 15½in (39cm), 103oz.
$5,500-7,000

A silver bottle cork, the base incised around the side 'Sauterne', unmarked, c1830.
$750-1,000

A ewer by William Forbes for Ball, Black and Co, with a branch handle terminating in a grape vine, on a spreading circular foot with a pierced grapevine border, marked on base, monogram erased, New York, c1851, 16½in (41.5cm) high, 46oz.
$1,000-1,500

Miscellaneous

A late Victorian silver mounted easel mirror, by William Comyns, London 1900, 8 by 7in (20.5 by 18cm).
$450-600

A silver mounted desk blotter, by William Comyns, London 1915, 12 by 9in (30.5 by 23cm).
$450-600

A milk pot by Tobias Stoutenburgh, with a moulded mid-band, on 3 scroll legs with pad feet, cover now missing, New York, c1735, 5in (12.5cm) high, 7oz 10dwt.
$4,500-5,500

A silver mounted desk blotter, maker's mark HM, Birmingham 1901, 11 by 8in (28 by 20.5cm).
$400-500

A Victorian silver blotter with mauve velvet background, London 1885.
$450-700

A Georgian silver egg set, 1795.
$600-900

A vase by Shreve, Stanwood &
Company, with 2 cast mask handles
attached to beaded strapwork,
marked on base, Boston, c1865, 13in
(33cm) high, 24oz.
$800-900

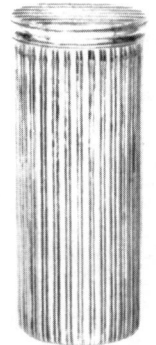

A George IV nutmeg grater,
by Charles Rawlings, 1824,
3in (7.5cm).
$300-400

A George III mustard pot, with blue
glass liner, by Edward Aldridge,
1771, 2.5oz.
$450-600

A large French jardinière, maker's
mark 'T. Freres', late 19thC, on
marbled plinth, 18in (45.5cm) high
overall, 312oz.
$16,000-21,000

A pair of historical shoe buckles,
with engraved borders of rosettes
and incised lines, with a steel
fastener, unmarked, c1770, 2½in
(6cm) long.
$9,500-11,000

A Victorian novelty propelling
pencil, modelled as a champagne
bottle, by Sampson Mordan, c1880.
$250-350

A George V silver gilt epergne
stand, London 1911, 6½in (16.5cm)
high, 30oz.
$450-600

A pair of Victorian fox mask stirrup
cups, John S Hunt, London 1846,
5½in (13.5cm), 26.2oz.
$6,000-8,000

A sugar urn, the front engraved
with script initials 'AMH', the foot
marked 'J. Shoemaker',
Philadelphia, c1800, 10in (25.5cm)
high, 11oz 10dwt.
$1,500-2,500

A two-compartment caviar
container, the cover with central
detachable caster, by Omar
Ramsden and Alwyn Carr, 10in
(25.5cm) high, 27.75oz excluding
glass liner.
$2,250-3,500

An Irish dish or 'potato' ring of
capstan form, JE monogram,
Dublin 1910, 7½in (19.5cm) diam at
base, 9oz.
$450-700

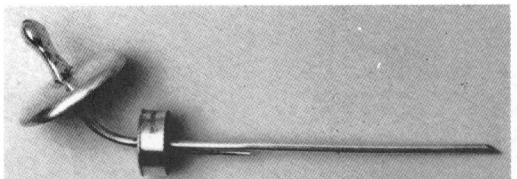

A baby feeder, the circular nipple attached to a straw fitting into a circular bottle cap, marked on cap 'E. Lownes', Philadelphia, c1820, 7in (18cm), 1oz.
$1,800-2,200

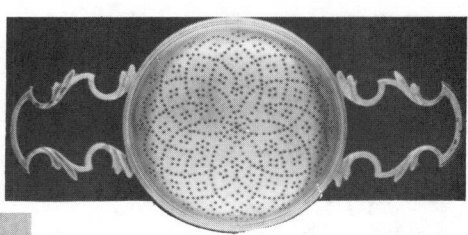

A George III orange strainer, by Adam Graham, c1765, 8in (20cm).
$450-600

An egg cruet stand, supporting 2 pepper casters and suspending 6 footed egg cups, over a spreading circular foot, the stand applied with 2 medallion profile masks, the casters and cups engraved with the initial 'G', the stand bearing a scratchmark 'T. Kirkpatrick N.Y', c1865, 9½in (24cm), 24oz 10dwt.
$800-1,200

A sugar urn by Joseph Jr and Nathaniel Richardson, the side engraved with foliate script initials 'HL', engraved on bottom 'IL to HL', marked 4 times on bottom, Philadelphia, c1790, 8½in (21.5cm) high, 12oz 10dwt.
$1,600-2,000

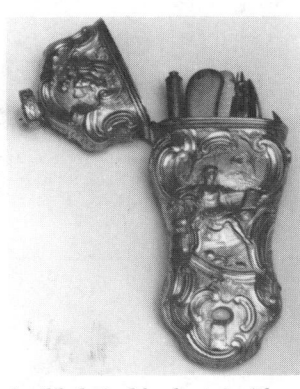

A gilded pinchbeck etui with fittings, 18thC, 4in (10cm).
$450-700

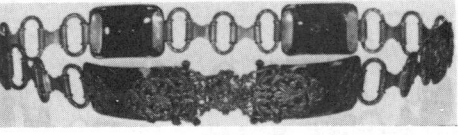

An Edwardian silver and tortoiseshell panelled linked belt, London 1905, 35in (89cm) overall.
$400-500

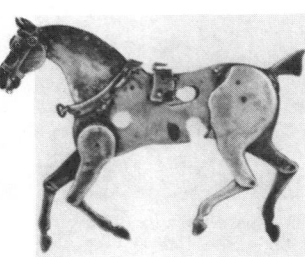

A Combmartin silver buckle of Exeter castle, c1847.
$150-200

An unusual and fully articulated model of a horse, possibly for use as an artist's model, unmarked.
$300-400

A George III silver Pontefract race ticket.
$300-500

Toys and Miniature Pieces

A Victorian Britannia standard toy sugar dredger of early 18thC style, by Horace Woodward & Co, 1869, 2in (5cm).
$150-250

A miniature model of a folding plate bellows camera, on tripod, 3½in (8.5cm).
$400-500

A silver mounted cut glass inkwell, with tilting silver stopwatch to hinged lid.
$150-250

Silver Plate Candlesticks

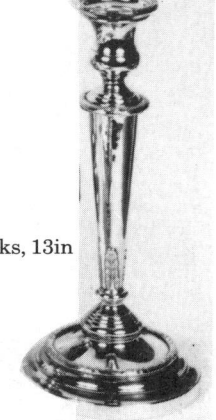

A pair of plated candlesticks, 13in (33cm).
$150-250

A five-light candelabrum, Sheffield 1916, and two pairs of candlesticks, Sheffield 1917.
$1,500-2,600

A pair of George III Sheffield plate candlesticks of neo-classical design, 11in (28cm).
$700-900

A pair of silver plated candlesticks, with lift-out nozzles, 15½in (39cm) high.
$3,000-4,500 ▶

Services

A three-piece tea set, applied with 2 reeded girdles, c1790.
$750-1,000

A George III four-piece tea and coffee service.
$2,250-3,000

A Victorian Britannia metal four-piece tea and coffee service, on tab feet.
$250-350

A Victorian four-piece tea service, comprising: teapot, Sheffield 1897, hot water jug 1898, with ebonised wood handles, sugar basin and milk jug 1896.
$750-1,000

A Victorian four-piece tea and coffee set, cased.
$450-700

An electroplated four-piece tea and coffee service, Goldsmiths and Silversmiths Company.
$450-600

A Victorian five-piece tea and coffee service, engraved with oval panels and bright cut decoration, with scroll handles.
$750-1,000

Tureens

A four-piece silver plated tea service.
\$300-400

A Victorian plated soup tureen and
cover, 11½in (28cm) wide.
\$250-350

A plated entrée dish and cover.
\$300-400

A soup tureen and cover, Elkington
& Co, late 19thC, 16in (40.5cm)
wide.
\$250-350

A pair of silver plated entrée dishes
with lids, cast borders and
decoration.
\$250-350

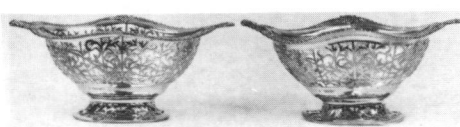

A pair of electro-plated warming
dishes, bases, liners and covers,
10½in (26.5cm) diam.
\$450-700

Miscellaneous

A pair of Victorian silver dessert
baskets.
\$1,200-1,600

A plated biscuit box, with lion mask
ring handles.
\$150-200

A Victorian biscuit box, bearing a
Victorian registration mark, c1870,
8½in (21cm) wide.
\$450-600

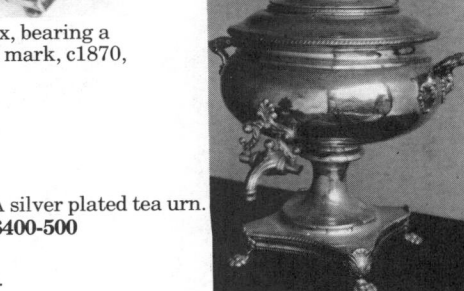

A silver plated tea urn.
\$400-500

A Victorian plated tea urn, by
James Dixon & Son, 17in (43cm).
\$150-250

An early Victorian silver plated samovar.
$450-600

A silver plated tankard on copper, by N Smith & Co.
$150-250

A three-branch plated epergne, 17in (43cm) high, with fitted box.
$1,000-1,400

An electro-plated and cut glass butter turnover dish, decorated in the Adam style, Martin Hall & Co, 5½in (14cm) high.
$450-600

A pair of Sheffield plate silver salvers, 18thC.
$450-600

A Georgian goblet, London 1769, 6in (15.5cm).
$300-400

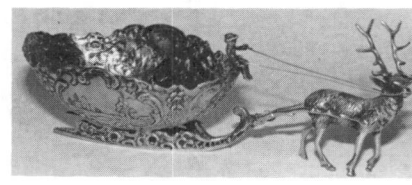

A Victorian fruit dish with faceted ruby glass liner.
$450-700

A Continental sweetmeat dish.
$250-350

A French silver plated table jardinière, with brass liner, 19thC.
$400-500

An EPNS cockerel pepper pot, 6½in (16.5cm).
$300-400

A fish serving tray, with draining well, 24in (61cm) wide.
$400-500

A Victorian Aesthetic Movement electro-plated card case, c1870.
$75-150

A toastrack, in the form of the Man in the Moon, the handle as a cast owl, c1900, 6½in (17cm) wide.
$400-500

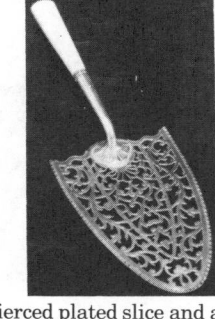

A pierced plated slice and a pair of silver sugar tongs.
$75-150

A pair of George III wine coolers, with detachable collars and liners, by Matthew Boulton & Plate Co, c1825, 9½in (24cm) high, with fitted case.
$6,000-8,000

A drum taperstick or bougie box, c1785, 6cm high.
$450-700

A Victorian plated pen and ink stand with a pair of glass inkwells, 9½in (24cm) wide.
$100-200

A serving trolley with silver plated dish cover.
$3,000-4,000

A Victorian electro-plated coffee pot, 12in (30.5cm).
$250-350

A Continental chess-set with gilt and silver-plated finish, the kings and queens in 16thC dress with jesters as bishops, mounted warrior knights and rooks as military trophies, the pawns as footsoldiers, the bases gilt or silvered (one pawn to silvered side missing), 19thC, probably French, height of kings 4in (10cm), height of pawns 3in (7.5cm).
$3,000-4,500

Make the most of Miller's

Every care has been taken to ensure the accuracy of descriptions and estimated valuations. Where an attribution is made within inverted commas (e.g. 'Chippendale') or is followed by the word 'style' (e.g. early Georgian style) it is intended to convey that, in the opinion of the publishers, the piece concerned is a later – though probably still antique – reproduction of the style so designated. Unless otherwise stated, any description which refers to 'a set', or 'a pair' includes a valuation for the entire set or the pair, even though the illustration may show only a single item.

A Victorian unusual plated spoon warmer, in the form of a Ship's Buoy, the conical-shaped body on a simulated rock base, with chain attachment, approximately 21cm long, with Victorian registration mark, circa 1870.
$250-350

Gold

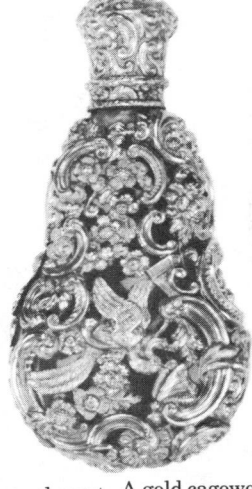

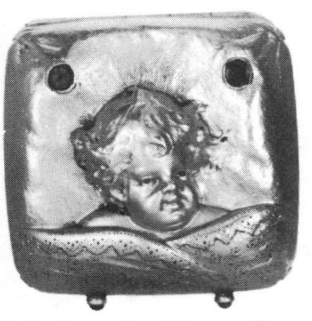

A Continental gold box, with a sapphire set either side of a cherub's head, and 2 cabochon set sapphire thumbpieces, probably Russian, but bearing an Austrian import mark for 1891-1901.
$750-1,000

A small engraved gold vinaigrette, small repair to handle, 19thC.
$1,200-1,600

A George III gold and enamel scent bottle, slight damage, c1770, 3in (8cm) high.
$3,000-4,500

A gold cagework scent bottle with glass stopper, probably 19thC, in fitted case inlaid 'Janisset 108 Rue Richelieu, Paris'.
$1,500-2,600

A gold presentation medal, the obverse engraved with a bust of George Washington surrounded by the motto 'Peter Patriae Scientlaegue Lireralis.', the reverse with a foliate border surrounding the motto 'Palmam Qui Meruit Ferat', enclosing the inscription 'Presented to Levi S. Burridge MD by Washington University of Baltimore March 1851', c1851, 1½in (3.5cm) diam, in original fitted and silk lined case.
$1,500-2,000

A 9ct gold presentation box by Omar Ramsden, dated '1879-1929' the underside inscribed 'Omar Ramsden me fecit', hallmarked London 1929, 3 by 2in (7.5 by 5cm), 2.7oz.
$1,500-2,600

A pair of French gold folding pincenez, late 19thC.
$700-900

Tortoiseshell

A tortoiseshell double inkstand, inlaid with floral mother-of-pearl design.
$1,200-1,600

A Continental tortoiseshell box, inlaid in gold, probably French, c1780.
$600-900

A late Georgian tortoiseshell tea caddy, 7½in (19cm) wide.
$750-1,000

A late Victorian tortoiseshell photograph frame, the corners with applied silver leaf and scroll mounts, Birmingham 1892, 9 by 7in (23 by 18cm).
$700-900

Metal
Brass

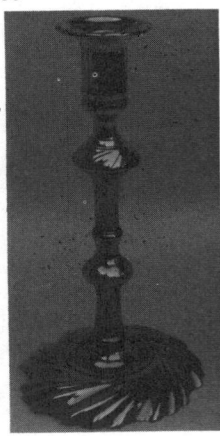

An English brass candlestick, c1760, 8in (20cm).
$150-250

An English brass candlestick, c1760, 10in (25cm) high.
$250-350

A brass 'Brighton Bun' travelling chamber candlestick, 4in (10cm) diam.
$450-600

A Spanish brass candlestick, c1700, 5½in (14cm).
$450-600

A pair of brass table candlesticks with baluster stems, on square stepped bases, 18thC, 11in (28cm).
$150-250

A Continental candleholder, the body of brass and foliate cut steel, 18thC, 8½in (21.5cm).
$450-600

A pair of Flemish brass candlesticks, with later glass storm shades, 27½in (68.5cm).
$7,000-9,000

A brass lantern, c1900, 12in (30.5cm) high.
$45-70

A brass and copper lamp, c1900, 13½in (34cm).
$45-70

A pair of brass and iron knife blade andirons, on arched legs with disc feet, c1800, 22in (55cm) high.
$900-1,200

A set of 4 brass wall oil lamps, with glass chimneys and brass adjustable shades, fitted for electricity, 12½in (31.5cm).
$300-400

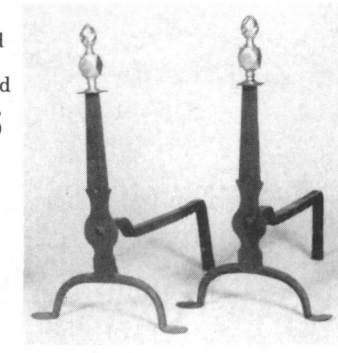

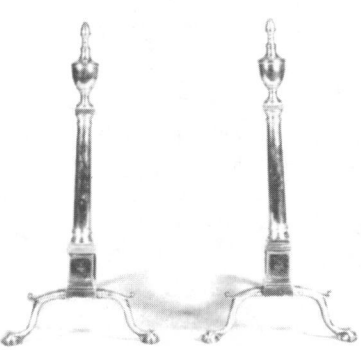

A pair of miniature Federal brass andirons, on shaped spurred legs with ball feet, early 19thC, 8in (20cm) high.
$1,200-1,500

A brass hall lamp, fitted for electricity, 27in (68.5cm).
$150-250

A pair of Federal brass andirons, engraved with a memorial scene, on spurred cabriole legs ending in ball and claw feet, Philadelphia, c1800, 29in (72cm) high.
$4,000-5,000

A brass planter with gadroon embossed decoration, and lion mask handle, 13in (33cm) wide.
$300-500

A brass and copper plant pot by W A S Benson, 10in (25.5cm).
$300-400

A late Victorian brass helmet coal scuttle, the top embossed with stylised flowers, 19in (48cm) high, and another similar with a shovel, the handle slightly distressed, 18½in (47cm) high.
$1,500-2,600

A pair of Dutch brass jardinières, with embossed stylised coats-of-arms and foliage, 25in (63cm).
$4,000-5,500

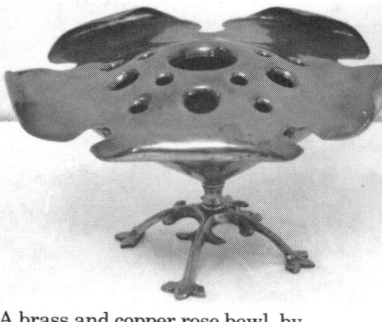

A brass and copper rose bowl, by W A S Benson, 11in (28cm) diam.
$300-500

A Continental brass fire insert, with 2 pierced decorated doors, 19thC.
$400-500

A Regency brass and steel D-shaped fender, 56in (142cm) wide.
$450-700

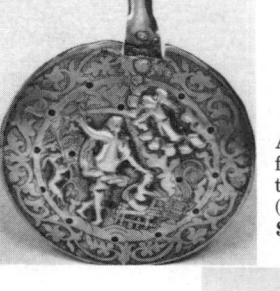

A brass warming pan with turned fruitwood handle, the cover c1700, the bowl and handle later, 44in (111.5cm) long.
$150-250

A brass and red leather upholstered fender, damaged, late 19thC, 60in (152cm).
$700-900

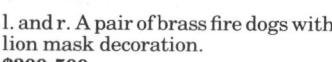

c. A Victorian polished steel coal scuttle with a lifting flap and shovel, with Gothic brass hinges.
$150-250

l. and r. A pair of brass fire dogs with lion mask decoration.
$300-500

A brass Dutch style chandelier, 19in (48cm).
$450-700

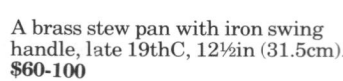

A brass stew pan with iron swing handle, late 19thC, 12½in (31.5cm).
$60-100

A Regency brass ornamental urn, 13½in (34cm) high.
$600-900

A Benham & Froud brass kettle, 9½in (24cm) high.
$450-600

A set of 7 brass standard bell weights by Bate, London, engraved 'Babergh Hundred Suffolk' and dated '1824', each stamped with numerous proof marks and lbs.
$2,500-3,500

A pair of English brass ember tongs, c1730, 8in (20cm) long.
$75-150

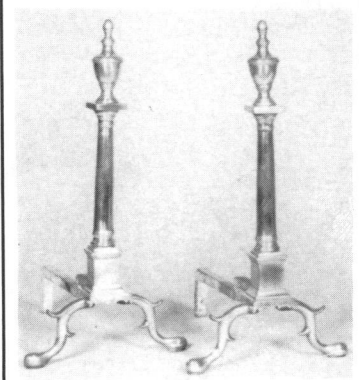

A pair of brass andirons, with an urn turned finial, on spurred arched legs with slipper feet, late 18thC, 25½in (64.5cm) high.
$4,000-4,500

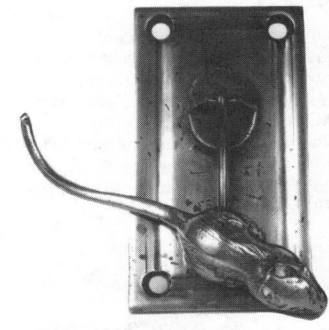

A brass bell pull, with mouse pull, 4½in (11.5cm) long.
$15-30

A brass and iron door stop, c1860, 10in (25.5cm) high.
$100-150

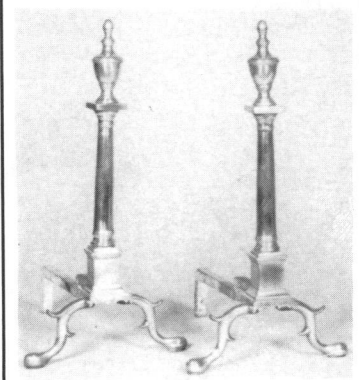

A heavy brass footman, mid-19thC, 21in (53cm) wide.
$400-500

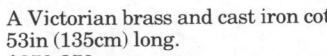

A brass face spit engine, c1750.
$1,500-2,600

A Victorian brass and cast iron cot, 53in (135cm) long.
$250-350

Bronze

An English bronze bust of G F Watts, 1817-1904, cast from a model by Sir Alfred Gilbert, signed and dated on the back, 'A. Gilbert A.R.A. Sc.1888', on an integrally cast moulded socle, collar slightly damaged, 6½in (16.5cm).
$1,500-2,600

A French bronze bust of Autumn, cast from a model by Jean Baptiste Carpeaux, signed 'J Bte Carpeaux', on wood pedestal, late 19th/early 20thC, 42½in (108cm) high.
$2,500-3,500

A hollow cast and cold-painted bronze bust of a Moor, by Wilhelm Christian Andreas Giesecke, 1854-1917, signed, 22in (56cm) high.
$3,000-4,000

A large bronze and gilt bronze clock garniture set.
$6,000-6,500

An English bronze bust of The Viscount Northcliffe, cast from a model by Courtnay Pollack, inscribed on the back 'Courtenay Pollack' and 'The Viscount Northcliffe with affectionate esteem from the staff of Carmelite House 1920', 20thC, 20½in (52cm) high.
$700-900

A pair of recumbent bronze ducks, 14 and 13in (35.5 and 33cm).
$750-1,000

A bronze hunting group, 'Gone Away', the base incised 'Elkington', 20in (51cm) high.
$6,000-9,000

A French bronze group of 'The Accolade', after Pierre-Jules Mêne, the base inscribed 'P.J. Mêne', 17 by 27in (43.5 by 69cm).
$6,000-8,000

A French bronze model of a prancing stallion, cast from a model by Christophe Fratin, the base signed 'Fratin', 19thC, 10½in (26cm) high.
$2,500-3,500

A French bronze model of a Senegalese lion with an antelope, cast from a model by Paul-Edouard Delabrierre, with greenish patina, 19thC, 18 by 31½in (46 by 80cm).
$5,500-7,000

A French bronze model of a walking stag, cast from a model by Isidore Bonheur, the base signed 'Isidore Bonheur' and with foundry marks, late 19thC, 11 by 12in (28 by 30cm).
$1,300-1,800

A bronze figure of Molière, stamped 'Molière' and bearing the sculptor's name 'Melingue', 19thC, 18in (46cm) high.
$900-1,300

A bronze patinated figure of a man holding a wreath, 19thC, 24in (61cm) high.
$300-400

A bronze figure of Sagittarius by
E M Geyger, H Gladenbeck u Sohn,
Berlin, 13in (33cm) high.
$150-250

A pair of French bronze ewers, after
Clodion, 19thC, 21½in (54cm) high.
$1,000-1,400

A French bronze statuette of a
huntsman with a pointer, cast from
a model by Pierre Jules Mêne, the
hound branded 'S', signed and dated
'P.J. Mêne, 1879', with golden
patina, rubbed, late 19thC, 19in
(47cm) high.
$4,000-5,500

A bronze group of nude female with
bust of Bacchus by Carrier.
$1,500-2,000

A French bronze statuette of a
youth, cast from a model by Albert
Ernest Carrier de Belleuse, the base
signed 'A. Carrier', waxed,
weathered patina, 19thC, 41in
(104cm) high.
$3,000-4,500

A bronze and parcel gilt Warwick
vase, with a liner, 19thC, 9in (23cm)
high, raised on a marble base.
$300-400

A pair of bronze urns, with raised
frieze, on marble plinth bases, 15in
(37.5cm) high.
$450-700

A Regency gilt bronze fender, 32½in
(81.5cm), slightly reduced.
$750-1,000

A bronze casket by Moignez, the
cover set with a pair of birds feeding
their fledglings, the sides with
strapwork panels set with birds,
signed, 10½in (27cm) wide.
$1,000-1,400

A pair of French gilt bronze chenets,
31in (77.5cm) high, and associated
rectangular pierced iron basket
grate, 36in (91cm) long, 19thC.
$1,300-1,800

A pair of bronze candelabra.
$1,000-1,400

An early Victorian bronze inkstand, one glass liner cracked, 17in (43cm) wide.
$450-700

A pair of gilt bronze candlesticks in the Dutch taste, 10½in (26cm) high.
$250-350

A bronze figural candlestick, conceived in the manner of Alfred Gilbert, inscribed indistinctly on the base, 11½in (29cm) high.
$300-400

A bronze of St John the Baptist, after Paul DuBois.
$2,500-3,000

A pair of bronze candlesticks, with Assyrian atlantes, early 19thC, 12½in (31cm) high.
$750-1,000

A pair of French bronze statuettes of seated Bacchic putti, on reddish marble half-columns, 19thC, 15½in (39cm) high.
$2,250-3,000

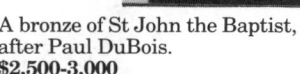
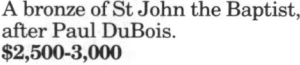

A pair of French bronze torchères of Cupid and Psyche, on naturalistic bases cast with tree-stumps, 19thC, 38in (94cm) high.
$7,000-9,000

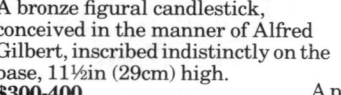

A bronze and gilt three-branch candelabrum in the form of a winged maiden.
$600-900

A pair of gilt bronze twin-light wall applique, 20½in (51cm) high.
$1,300-1,800

Copper

A pair of copper hall lanterns, with inset amber glass panels, 17in (43cm) high.
$750-1,000

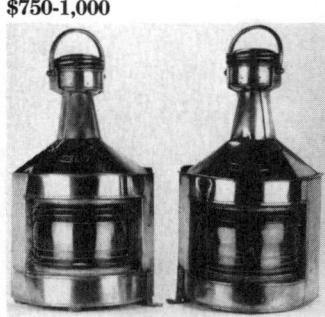

A pair of copper and brass navigation lamps, by Alder Son & Gyde Ltd, 29½in (74cm) high.
$600-900

A pair of bronzed silhouettes by Frederick Frith, in rosewood frames, both signed and dated 1844, 10½ by 8½in (26 by 21cm).
$600-900

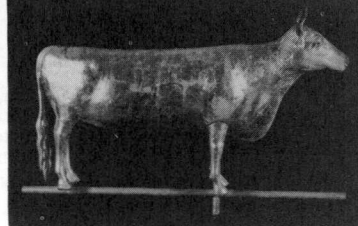

A hollow gilt copper and cast iron weathervane in the form of a bull, some re-gilding, American, c1885, 40in (101.5cm) long overall.
$3,500-4,000

A pair of copper ships' lamps, 'Bow
Port' and 'Bow Starboard'.
$250-350

A copper preserving pan, with iron
handles, 19thC, 17in (43cm) diam.
$150-200

A George III bronzed copper tea urn,
in the Chippendale style, late
18thC, 22in (56cm) high.
$600-900

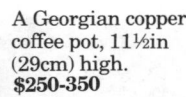

A Georgian copper
coffee pot, 11½in
(29cm) high.
$250-350

A copper hot water urn,
early 19thC, 18in
(45cm) high.
$150-250

An enamelled copper globular tea
urn with brass mounts, with silver
plaque dated London 1799 and
maker's initials 'T.H.', 12½in (33cm)
high.
$750-1,000

A moulded copper 'North Wind'
weathervane, with a stand for
display, 56½in (144cm) long.
$19,000-22,000

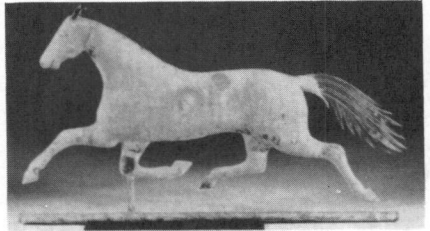

A copper weathervane in the form of
a running horse, with hollow head
and body with pressed and cut tail,
probably A L Jewel & Co, Waltham,
Massachusetts, late 19thC, 35in
(90cm) long.
$1,000-1,500

Ormolu

A copper coal helmet with matching
shovel, early 19thC, 17½in (44cm)
high.
$700-900

A pair of French ormolu seven-light
candelabra, signed 'Henry Dasson
et Cit 1891', fitted for electricity,
27½in (69.5cm).
$2,250-3,000

A charcoal burner in copper, on cast
iron stand, with two-section
chimney, 72in (182cm) high overall.
$750-1,000

A pair of Regency ormolu candlesticks, 13in (33cm).
$1,200-1,600

An ormolu lamp base, 16in (41cm) high.
$400-500

A six-branch ormolu hanging electrolier, possibly French, 67in (170cm) high overall.
$1,300-1,800

An ormolu and bronze fender of Louis XV style, 52in (132cm) wide.
$1,300-1,800

A French oval ormolu casket, the lid applied with a blue glass portrait relief of a maiden on opaline glass ground, engraved 'Maisons Boissier', 19thC, 6½in (17cm) diam.
$900-1,300

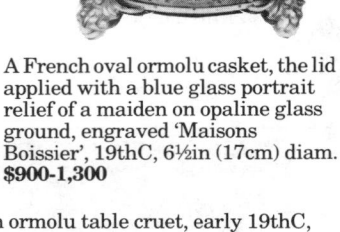

An ormolu table cruet, early 19thC, 19in (48cm) high.
$1,500-2,600

A pair of ormolu chenets of Louis XVI design, 15in (38cm) high.
$5,500-7,000

A pair of ormolu jardinières of Louis XVI design, with square blue glass liners, the ormolu struck with the C couronné poinçon, 6in (15cm).
$4,000-5,500

Iron

A pair of cast iron garden urns, on terracotta pedestals, mid-19thC, 52in (130cm) high overall.
$2,250-3,000

A French encrier in ormolu and bronze, signed 'Ferville-Suan', 19thC, 15in (38cm) wide.
$1,200-1,600

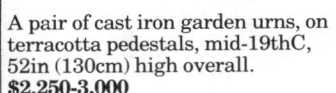

A cast iron horse weathervane, retaining old ochre paint, now on a stand, American, 19thC, 35in (88cm) wide.
$17,000-19,000

A pair of Victorian cast iron garden benches, 50in (128cm) wide.
$1,500-2,600

A sheet iron weather cock, 18thC.
$450-700

A pair of late Victorian cast iron beacon andirons, with brass acorn finials, 31in (79cm) high.
$1,300-1,800

A cast iron stick stand, 22½in (57cm) high.
$2,250-3,000

A pair of cast iron andirons, each modelled as a dolphin, impressed on back 'Pat App For', 'B & H/9512', probably New York, c1830, 14in (35cm) high.
$300-400

An iron fire back, 17thC, 24in (61cm) wide, with 2 andirons of the period with twist turned supports, knops and fleur-de-lys finials, and a large rectangular iron fire basket, 21in (53cm) wide.
$750-1,000

A Victorian cast iron figure of a classical maiden, 65in (165cm).
$1,500-2,600

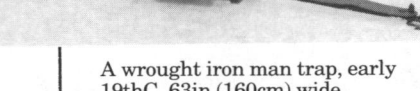

A wrought iron man trap, early 19thC, 63in (160cm) wide.
$400-500

Man traps were first used around 1780 as shocking deterrents to poachers. However, in 1820 a bill was passed through Parliament banning the use of these cruel traps – contemporary evidence proved that most victims of these savage iron jaws turned out to be the wives, children or pet dogs of country house and estate workers. After the ban of 1820 anyone caught using these traps would face a long prison sentence, and officers were appointed to travel the country to ensure landowners abided by the new laws.

Pewter

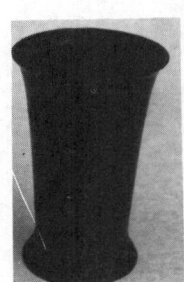

A decorative iron game hook.
$75-150

A Dutch pewter beaker, c1760, 7in (18cm).
$100-150

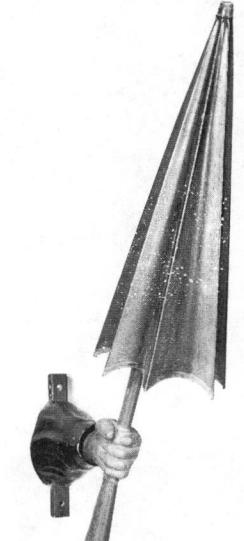

A painted iron trade sign, polychrome, with sleeved hand grasping a partly-furled umbrella, American, 19thC, 40in (101cm) high.
$2,500-3,000

A basin with a single reed brim, marked on the interior with an unidentified eagle touch, American, c1810, 8in (20cm) diam.
$200-250

A beaker by Boardman & Hart, with moulded mid-band, on moulded flaring base, marked with Laughlin touches 437a and 439, New York, c1840, 4in (10cm) high.
$350-450

A basin by Blakeslee Barnes, marked in interior with Laughlin touch 556, damage and repair to bowl, Philadelphia, c1815, 8in (20cm) diam.
$100-200

A rare small plate by Johann Christoph Heyne, marked with initial and Jacobs touch #169 on reverse, Lancaster, PA, c1770, 7in (17cm) diam.
$6,000-7,000

A basin by Samuel Hamlin, marked on the interior with Laughlin touch 330a, Providence, Rhode Island, c1785, 8in (20cm) diam.
$300-400

A beaker by Timothy Boardman Company, with single incised mid-band, on circular footrim, New York, c1825, 4in (10cm) high.
$300-400

A beaker by Timothy Boardman Company, engraved with initials, marked 'X' with Laughlin touch 432, New York, c1825, 3in (8cm) high.
$250-300

A basin with single reed brim, marked on base with 'Love' touch, Laughlin 868, dent to rim, Philadelphia, c1775, 8in (20cm) diam.
$400-500

A beaker, by Boardman & Hart, on single bead moulded base, pitting, New York, c1840, initials 'PTH' scratched on surface at a later date, 3in (7.5cm) high.
$100-150

A beaker, by Timothy Boardman & Company, marked with Laughlin touch 425, minor bruises, New York, c1825, 3in (7.5cm) high.
$200-250

A rare basin by Thomas Danforth Jr, Richmond, with a single reed brim, marked on the interior with 2 eagle touches and the 'Richmond Warranted' touch, Virginia, c1810, 12in (30cm) diam.
$2,500-3,500

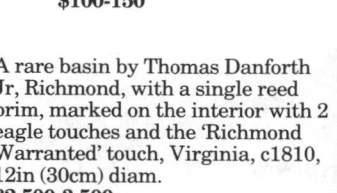

A teapot, probably by Israel Trask, with a square wood finial, one side engraved in script 'SB' marked with initial 'T' within a square punch, similar to Jacobs touch 261, repairs to handle joins and spout join, minor bruises and slight pitting, Beverly, Massachusetts, c1820, 6½in (16.5cm) high.
$200-250

A beaker, by Rufus Dunham, with everted rim, and 4 incised bands, marked with Montgomery touch p221, minor pitting, Westbrook, Me, c1850, 3½in (8.5cm) high.
$100-150

A coffee pot, by Israel Trask, with a lobed finial and 2 raised mid-bands, on a flaring circular base, marked with Jacobs touch 262, Beverly, Massachusetts, c1830, 11½in (29cm) high.
$400-500

A teapot, by Luther or Thomas D Boardman, marked 'Warranted', some dents, Connecticut, c1840, 7in (18cm) high.
$800-1,200

A lighthouse coffee pot, by Israel Trask, the body with 2 bands of reeding and engraved with a shield within a cartouche, marked, body indented at spout join, Beverly, Massachusetts, c1840, 12in (30.5cm) high.
$600-650

A lighthouse coffee pot, by George Richardson, with scrolling handle, and an S-scroll spout, marked, Cranston, c1840, 10½in (26cm).
$400-500

A teapot, by George Richardson, with a disc finial, on a flaring circular footrim, marked on base with Laughlin touch 310, bruises, Boston, c1820, 6in (15cm) high.
$300-500

A lighthouse coffee pot, by William Calder, the domed lid with a conical finial, marked on inside with Laughlin touch 350, Providence, Rhode Island, c1840, 12in (30.5cm) high.
$250-300

A teapot, on 4 ball feet, each side with a bright cut engraved shield, unmarked, dent to spout, c1800, 7½in (19cm).
$650-750

A teapot, by Roswell Gleason, on a flaring circular footrim, marked on base with Jacobs touch 147, minor pitting, Dorchester, Massachusetts, c1835, 7½in (19cm) high.
$200-300

A flagon, attributed to Henry Will, with a curved spout, and a double scrolled handle, the body with a mid-moulding, on a flaring moulded footrim, unmarked, Albany, c1780, 12in (30cm) high.
$17,000-20,000

A flagon, by William J Ellsworth, the scroll handle with a spatulate terminal, on a moulded footrim, marked on the interior and near handle, marks worn, bruise to side, New York, c1780, 9½in (24cm) high.
$4,000-6,000

A flagon, by Boardman & Company, with a double scrolled handle and bud finial, marked with Montgomery touch p217, New York, c1825, 11in (28cm).
$800-1,000

A flagon, by Boardman & Company, with a 3-tiered finial and scrolled thumbpiece, the body with a moulded mid-band, on a flaring moulded base, marked on bottom with Laughlin touch 431, New York, c1830, 12in (30.5cm) high.
$1,500-2,000

A flagon, by Boardman & Company, the domed lid with a triple tiered finial and a scrolling thumbpiece, on a flaring moulded circular foot, marked with Montgomery touch p217, New York, c1825, 12½in (31.5cm).
$2,500-3,000

A flagon, by Boardman & Company, the body with a moulded mid-rib on a flaring moulded base, marked 'XX' and Laughlin touch 431, New York, c1825, 12½in (31.5cm) high.
$3,000-4,000

A pair of fluid lamps, each with a brass double wick holder, with strap handles, foot marked 'J.B. & H.H. Graves, Middletown, Connecticut', c1850, 9in (23cm) high.
$900-1,000

A flagon, by Boardman & Company, with a narrow moulded mid-band, and a curved spout, marked 'X' and a Laughlin touch 431, New York, c1825, 8in (20cm) high.
$2,000-2,500

A fluid lamp, by Ephraim Capen and George Molineux, with a partial 'brass' double ink holder above a cylindrical font, on baluster stem, marked with Montgomery touch p218, bruising and repairs, New York, c1850, 7½in (19cm) high.
$100-150

A pair of fluid lamps, each with brass double wick holder above a cylindrical font, one slightly bruised, mid-19thC, 6½in (16.5cm) high.
$150-200

Three fluid lamps, by James H Putnam and Smith & Company, with trumpet stems and domed circular bases, 2 marked with Montgomery touch p226, the other marked 'Smith & Company', one lamp with attached snuffers, Malden, MA, c1840, 6½ to 7½in (16.5 to 19cm) high.
$450-500

A flask, with incised concentric rings, the cap cylindrical and threaded, late 18th/early 19thC, 5in (12.5cm) high.
$250-300

A mug, by Frederick Bassett, with moulded mid-band at shoulder, the scroll handle with bud terminal, marked on inside with Montgomery touch p216, repairs to handle joins and rim, some pitting, New York and Hartford, c1780, 4½in (11.5cm) high.
$1,000-1,500

A flask, by James Weekes, with a threaded cap, the lower half fitting into a cup, marked with Laughlin touch, New York, c1830, 7in (18cm).
$500-600

A ship's hanging lamp, by Yale & Curtis, the acorn font with 2 covered wick holders suspended over a stepped circular base with a ring handle, New York, c1860, 8in (20.5cm) high.
$600-650

A mug, by Henry Will, marked on inside with Laughlin touch 491, mark pitted, bruising, New York and Albany, New York, c1770, 6in (15cm) high.
$2,000-3,000

A quart mug, by Joseph Danforth, marked near handle join with Laughlin touch 374, and on inside with Laughlin touch, surface abrasion, Middletown, Connecticut, c1785, 6in (15cm) high.
$2,000-2,500

A mug, by Robert Bonynge, the S-scroll handle with a shell grip and a boot heel terminal, marked on inside with Laughlin touch 292, Boston, c1760, 5in (12.5cm) high.
$6,000-6,500

A mug, by J B Woodbury, with 3 incised mid-bands, on beaded base with scroll handle, repair to base, probably Beverly, Massachusetts, c1830, 3in (7.5cm) high, with 2 cups, with scroll handles, unmarked, minor pitting, Philadelphia, Pennsylvania, c1835, 2½ to 3in (6 to 7.5cm) high.
$250-300

A quart mug, by Thomas D and Sherman Boardman, marked on base with Laughlin touch 428, Hartford, c1820, 6in (15cm) high.
$700-900

A mug, with a scroll handle with a bud terminal, marked, probably Hartford, Connecticut, late 18th/early 19thC, 6in (15cm) high.
$650-800

A mug, by Boardman and Hart, with double scroll handle, minor repairs to base and handle base, slight bruise to body, New York, c1830, 4½in (11.5cm) high.
$500-600

A mug, by Samuel Hamlin, marked near handle with Laughlin touch 330a, Providence, c1780, 4½in (10cm) high.
$1,000-1,500

A pitcher, by George Richardson, marked with Jacobs touch 237, minor surface abrasion, Cranston, Rhode Island, c1830, 7in (18cm) high.
$300-400

A mug, by Thomas D and Sherman Boardman, engraved on either side of handle 'B5' and 'B6', marked with Laughlin touch 428, Hartford, Connecticut, c1820, 6in (15.5cm).
$600-900

A footed pitcher, by Hiram Yale & Company, with barrel shaped finial, on a turned and domed foot, marked, Wallingford, Connecticut, c1825, 13½in (34cm) high.
$500-600

A covered pitcher, by Thomas D and Sherman Boardman, with a stepped and domed cover, a disc finial, marked on base with Laughlin touch 435, few scratches to cover, Hartford, c1840, 10in (25.5cm) high.
$400-600

A pitcher, by Daniel Curtiss, on a moulded circular footrim, marked with Laughlin touch 523, Albany, c1830, 8in (20cm) high.
$800-900

A mug, by Timothy Boardman & Company, marked with Laughlin touch 432, minor pitting, New York, c1825, 4½in (11.5cm) high.
$500-600

A pitcher, by Rufus Dunham, the body with a raised mid-band, on a flaring circular footrim, marked 'R. Dunham' incuse, Westbrook, Maine, c1850, 6½in (16cm) high.
$400-500

A porringer, by Samuel Danforth, with everted brim, the Old English handle marked with Laughlin touch 399, Hartford, Ct, c1800, 5in (12.5cm) diam.
$1,200-1,500

A porringer, by William Calder, the flowered handle marked with Laughlin touch 350, some bruising, Providence, RI, c1830, 5in (12.5cm) diam.
$700-800

A porringer, by Samuel Hamlin, the flowered handle marked with Laughlin touch 337, Providence, RI, c1780, 6in (15cm) diam.
$550-650

A porringer, by Thomas D & Sherman Boardman, the crown handle marked with Laughlin touch 428, Hartford, Ct, c1820, 5in (12.5cm) diam.
$450-550

A porringer, by Thomas Melville, with Rhode Island tab handle, marked 'T.M' on handle bracket, as in Laughlin touch 847, small scratches and dents, Newport, RI, c1795, 5in (12.5cm) diam.
$2,200-2,500

A porringer, with Pennsylvania tab handle, unmarked, some pitting and bruising, late 18thC, 5½in (13cm) diam.
$100-200

A tankard, on a moulded circular foot, marked on interior 'J.S', probably English, late 19thC, 8in (20cm) high.
$500-600

A tankard, by Parks Boyd, with beaded lip, the S-scroll handle with a bud terminal, marked with Laughlin touch 546, spout probably added, lid punctured, Philadelphia, c1800, 7½in (19cm) high.
$2,000-3,000

A tankard, by Thomas D & Sherman Boardman, with a domed lid and a scrolling thumbpiece, the sides with a mid-band, marked with Laughlin touch 428, Hartford, Connecticut, c1820, 8in (20cm) high.
$5,000-6,000

A humidor, with an acorn finial, the sides with moulded bands centering an engraved cipher 'ES', opening to a flat circular inner lid, unmarked, c1800, 7in (17cm) high.
$250-300

A pair of candlesticks, with a flaring rim on baluster turned stem over a conical foot, unmarked, minor bruises, mid-19thC, 10in (25.5cm), with a modern pair of candlesticks marked 'Flagg & Homan', 7in (18cm) high.
$300-400

A tankard, possibly by Parks Boyd, on a beaded and moulded footrim, the front engraved with foliate script initials 'C.C' within a foliate cartouche, unmarked, bruises, slight tear to lid, Philadelphia, Pennsylvania, c1800, 7½in (19cm) high.
$4,000-5,000

A tankard, by Frederick Bassett, the lid with a crenellated lip and a scrolling thumbpiece, marked on interior with Laughlin touch 458, small bruises, New York, c1780, 7in (18cm) high.
$9,000-10,000

An English pewter wavy edge plate with armorial, c1760, 9½in (24cm) diam.
$100-200

A set of chalices, with moulded mid-bands, on moulded circular feet, repairs, dents, pitting and tears, mid-19thC, 8in (20.5cm) high.
$550-650

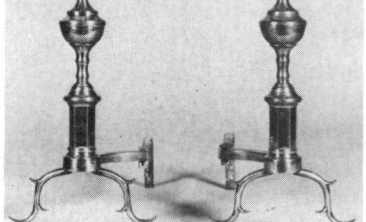

A pair of Federal bell metal andirons, on spurred arched legs and ball feet, probably New York, c1810, 25in (63.5cm) high.
$800-1,200

Make the most of Miller's

Miller's is completely different each year. Each edition contains completely NEW photographs. This is not an updated publication. We never repeat the same photograph.

l. A pewter quart measure, 17thC, 8in (20.5cm).
$750-1,000

c. A pear-shaped pewter loving cup, c1760.
$700-900

r. A pewter quart measure, 17thC, 9in (23cm) high.
$700-900

An English pewter loving cup, c1820, 5½in (14cm).
$60-100

An English pewter spice container, c1770, 4in (10cm) high.
$60-100

l. and r. A pair of pewter peppers, c1830, 4in (10cm) high.
$45-70

c. A pair of pewter taper sticks, 4½in (11cm) high.
$60-100

A pewter mustard pot, c1830, 3½in (9cm) high.
$30-50

An English coffee pot and teapot, c1940.
$1,500-2,600

An English triple reeded pewter charger, c1700, 18in (46cm) diam.
$300-500

A whale oil lamp with trumpet base, rim intact, ring handle, possibly North German or Polish, 18thC, 9in (23cm) high.
$450-600

A pair of candlesticks, possibly Dutch, 16thC, 5in (12.5cm) high.
$300-400

A pewter chamber pot, stamped with crown and other marks.
$150-250

Locks & Keys

An English huge wrought iron padlock, c1660, 9in (23cm) high.
$300-400

Two brass padlocks:
l. 2in (5cm).
$15-30

r. 1½in (4cm).
$15-25

Lead

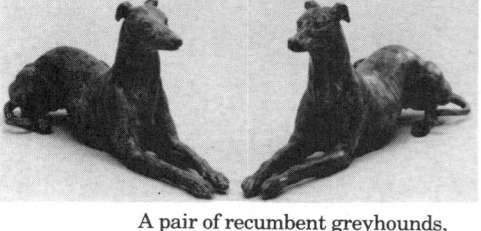

A pair of recumbent greyhounds, bases dated 1909, 71in (180cm) long.
$1,500-2,600

A lead figure of a dancing girl.
$750-1,000

A lead figure of a seated putto on a stone ball, 19thC, 28in (71cm) high.
$600-900

A pair of lead jardinières, 18thC, 32½in (82.5cm).
$13,500-17,500

Firemarks

East Kent and Canterbury Economic Fire Assurance, 1824-28 (821/65A) (E).
$450-600

A very rare mark.

A lead vase on a square plinth, 17in (43cm) high.
$250-350

A lead fountain, 25in (63.5cm) high.
$600-900

Middlesex Fire Insurance, 1874-1877, enamelled iron (956/111A) (G).
$700-900

A very rare mark.

London Assurance, copper, original paint, unissued (603/6Hi) (M).
$450-700

FIREMARKS

The first number in brackets refers to Footprints of Assurance, by Alwin E Bulau, New York, 1953. The second number refers to British Firemark, 1680-1879, by Brian Wright, published by Woodhead-Faulkner, Cambridge 1982. The letter refers to condition:

M – Mint
E – Excellent
G – Good
F – Fair

Scottish, Commercial Fire and Life Insurance, copper (948/106A) (E).
$400-500

A rare mark.

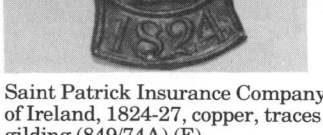

Saint Patrick Insurance Company of Ireland, 1824-27, copper, traces of gilding (849/74A) (E).
$450-600

Sun Fire Office, lead, original paint, unissued (532/3B) (E).
$250-350

Two bell metal travelling chalices, c1766, 3½ and 3in (9 and 7.5cm).
$75-150 each

A pair of large gilt metal ten-branch candelabra, on square marble plinths, 48in (122cm).
$1,000-1,400

A mid-Victorian black and gilt japanned tôle purdonium, with shovel, 12½in (31.5cm).
$750-1,000

Ivory/Shell

A fine ivory bas relief bust length portrait of a gentleman in early 18thC costume, attributed to David Le Marchand, initialled on reverse D.L.M.F., probably for David Le Marchand Fecit, 6in (14cm) high.
$52,000-60,000

David Le Marchand was born in Dieppe, worked extensively in London, specialising in ivory portraits in bas-relief. Examples of his work are in most major public collections and whilst the identity of the subject is uncertain, it bears a close resemblance to 2 studies of Sir Isaac Newton, exhibited at the Victoria and Albert Museum.

A carved ivory group of Cupid and Psyche, 19thC, 7in (17.5cm) high.
$1,300-1,800

A large ivory classical figure, 'The Bather Surprised', modelled by Sir Thomas Brock in 1902, 24in (60cm) high.
$750-1,000

A French or German ivory group of a Mediaeval woodsman and a Court jester, wooden stand, minor breaks and losses, 8in (20cm) high.
$8,000-10,500

An ivory figure of a young Victorian lady, 19thC, 5½in (14cm), on marble socle.
$250-350

A large silver gilt mounted ivory tankard, carved with the Wise and Foolish Virgins, slight damage and restoration to ivory, 17thC, the mount by Adolf Zethelius, Stockholm, 1816, 8in (20cm) high.
$21,000-25,000

A French carved ivory tankard, in the Baroque style, 19thC, 10in (26cm) high.
$5,500-7,000

A Continental ivory covered jar, probably German, 19thC, 9in (22.5cm).
$1,300-1,800

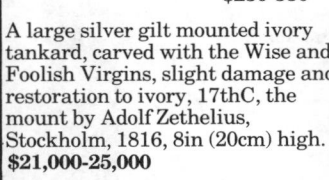

A German ivory tankard and lid, of centaurs abducting the wives of the Lapiths, shaft of club missing from hand of centaur on lid, 19thC, 13½in (34cm) high.
$5,500-7,000

A pair of plaques, probably German, each raised with a wood and ivory figure of a pedlar, 19thC, 12½in (31cm) high.
$1,200-1,600

A German ivory tankard of a battle, the handle and base of silver, stamped underneath, 19thC, 12in (30cm) high.
$4,000-5,500

An Anglo-Indian ivory veneered table, late 18thC.
$10,500-14,000

An oval seascape minutely carved in ivory, signed by Stephany and Dresch, c1790, some damage, in shaped carved giltwood frame, the seascape 3½in (9cm) high.
$3,000-4,500

A pair of shell pictures, 9½in (24cm) wide.
$300-400

A pair of ivory plaques, one showing the Battle of Milvean Bridge, the other the Battle of Arbella, after Charles Lebrun, probably Dieppe, c1840, 5 by 20in (12.5 by 50cm).
$6,000-9,000

An Anglo-Indian ivory model of a charabanc, 9in (23cm) wide.
$3,000-4,000

An ivory and steel table seal with 6 hardstone intaglios of classical busts, 3in (8cm) long.
$1,000-1,400

A French ivory panel, formerly the front panel of a casket, carved with legends of Aristotle, Alexander, Pyramus and Thisbe, 14thC, 4 by 9½in (10 by 24cm).
$40,000-45,000

A carved ivory walking cane handle of Maori influence, the silver collar with London hallmark for 1894, 6in (15cm).
$450-600

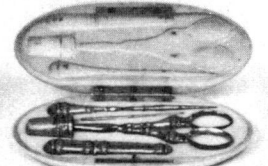

A French ivory necessaire, the fitted interior with silver gilt implements, 19thC, 5in (12.5cm).
$450-600

A pair of antique Naga ivory cuffs, Assam, India.
$750-1,000

An ivory inlaid frame.
$250-350

A Spanish ebonised, ivory and tortoiseshell cabinet, with a painted panel of the Virgin Mary in the style of Valdes Leal, late 17thC, 32½in (83cm) wide.
$5,500-7,000

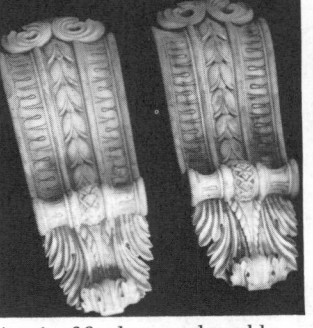

A fine German ivory hour-glass stand, 17th/18thC, 10½in (26cm) high.
$1,300-1,800

A Victorian still life of shells, on a simulated circular marble base, beneath a glass dome, 14½in (36cm) high overall.
$300-400

Marble

An Indian white marble bench, 49in (129.5cm) wide.
$2,250-3,000

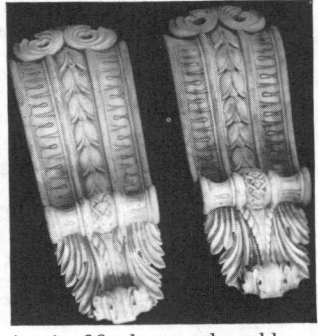

A pair of finely carved marble corbels, 30in (76cm) high.
$1,000-1,400

A white marble bust, 19thC, 9½in (24cm).
$250-350

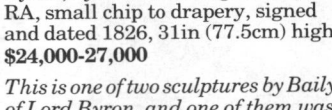

A sculptured bust of George, Lord Byron, by Edward Hodges Baily, RA, small chip to drapery, signed and dated 1826, 31in (77.5cm) high.
$24,000-27,000

This is one of two sculptures by Baily of Lord Byron, and one of them was exhibited at the Royal Academy 1826, number 1066.
The other bust is now at Harrow School.
E H Baily was the sculptor of the figure of Nelson surmounting the column in Trafalgar Square.

A marble bust of a girl, inscribed 'Poesie Prof. Garella', with a laurel garland of gilt metal, 10in (25cm) high.
$750-1,000

An Anglo-Indian marble portrait relief of Madame Josephine de Bagshawe, 1856-1942, by Baron Maurizio Marochetti, wood frame, 23 by 15in (57 by 38cm).
$800-1,200

An Italian white marble bust of a Roman matron, entitled 'Paulina', early 19thC, 34½in (86cm).
$3,000-4,500

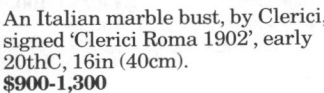

An Italian coloured marble bust of Beatrice, by F Vichi, shoulders pitted, late 19thC, 18in (45cm) high.
$3,000-4,500

An Italian marble bust, by Clerici, signed 'Clerici Roma 1902', early 20thC, 16in (40cm).
$900-1,300

An English marble group of 2 lions fighting, weathered, both tails missing, 18thC, 15 by 20in (37.5 by 50cm).
$5,500-7,000

An inlaid marble table top, with malachite and lapis lazuli heightened with mother-of-pearl, possibly Jaipur, 21in (53.5cm).
$3,000-4,000

An Italian pietra-dura rectangular plaque, 9½ by 6½in (24 by 16cm), in gilt brass mount and wood frame.
$1,000-1,400

A Carrara marble lifesize figure of Pandora, 3 fingers broken, plinth signed and dated 'C.B. Ives Fecit Romae.1858', on a scagliola mottled purple pedestal, American, 67in (170cm) high, the pedestal 36in (90cm) high.
$37,000-40,000

Chauncey Bradley Ives (1810-1894) left America for Florence in 1844 and in 1851 he moved to Rome. He first modelled Pandora in 1851 (1854 according to Craven, loc. cit.) and then remodelled it in 1863, changing the shape of the box and the tilt of her head. The present statue conforms to the earlier version. The model proved so popular that nineteen replicas, life- and half-size, were produced up until 1891.

A pair of gilt metal mounted Siena marble solid urns, 16½in (42cm) high.
$1,500-2,600

A Victorian marble figure, on octagonal plinth, 31in (77.5cm) high, on later mahogany stand.
$2,250-3,000

A black marble centre table, the octagonal top inlaid with specimen marbles and semi-precious stones, 19thC, 22½in (56cm).
$2,250-3,000

Terracotta/Stone

A French terracotta bust of a man, on marble socle, some repairs, late 18thC, 20in (51cm) high.
$3,000-4,500

A French terracotta bust of a Bacchante, cast from a model by Jean-Baptiste Clesinger, minor chips and repairs, late 19thC, 22in (55.5cm) high.
$1,000-1,400

A pair of Continental terracotta genre figures, some restoration, 19thC, 36in (91cm).
$3,000-4,500

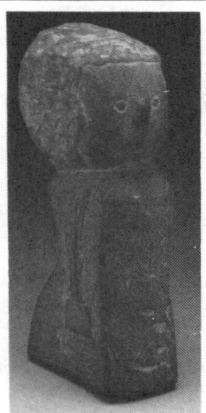

A carved limestone figure of 'Little Lady with Handbags', by William Edmondson, Nashville, Tennessee, c1935, 13in (33cm) high.
$4,500-6,500

A pair of painted and marbelised metal and terracotta ornaments, 30in (76cm) high.
$2,250-3,000

A pair of terracotta urns and stands, c1860.
$1,300-1,800

A grotesque terracotta wall bracket, 21in (53cm) high.
$600-900

An alabaster figure of Hercules, 12½in (32cm) high.
$150-250

A pair of glazed terracotta lions, c1860, 108in (274cm).
$18,000-22,500

A stone Buddha's head from a statue in Jaipur, India, c1300, 18 by 10in (46 by 25.5cm).
$600-900

A carved limestone ornament of a crouching mythical beast, 17th/18thC, 31½in (80cm).
$2,500-3,500

A pair of composition stone urns, 25in (63cm) high.
$1,000-1,400

A pair of Italian composition urns, c1880, 48in (122cm) high.
$4,000-5,500

Woodcarvings

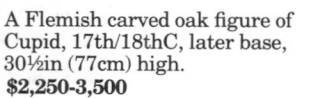

A pair of Franconian carved angels, some restoration to hands, early 16thC, 22in (56cm) high.
$9,000-12,000

A Flemish carved oak figure of Cupid, 17th/18thC, later base, 30½in (77cm) high.
$2,250-3,500

A carved stone font, c1860, 54in (137cm) high.
$1,200-1,600

A German baroque carved figure of the Virgin, restored, 17th/18thC, 57in (145cm).
$1,500-2,600

A carved and stained maple figure of an eagle, inset with glass eyes, repairs to neck, wing tip and tail, probably 19thC, 34½in (87.5cm) high.
$8,500-9,500

A carved and painted wooden ship weathervane, painted red and black with traces of original gilding, now on modern stand, 19thC, 42in (106.5cm) wide.
$700-900

A Chinese export wooden plaque, with 3 carved outer borders, the central one foliate carved and interspersed with Chinese figural vignettes, centering a gilded eagle surmounting a polychrome shield and 3 American flags, the background embellished with 13 gilded stars and a banner inscribed, 'E. Pluribus Unum', early 19thC, 12½ by 15½in (31.5 by 39cm).
$1,800-2,000

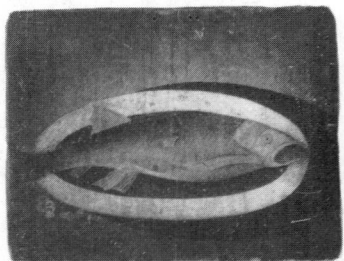

A painted and decorated wooden game board, with painted red and black chequerboard design, the reverse with a vividly painted fish on a platter in shades of blue and brown, 19thC, 14in (35.5cm) high.
$4,000-4,500

A carved and gilded wood eagle plaque, with spread wings above a shield, and holding a blue painted banner inscribed 'Live and Let Live', old repairs to wings, mid-19thC, 23in (58.5cm) high.
$4,500-5,500

Miscellaneous

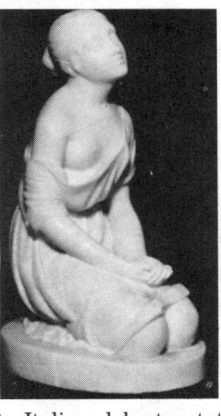

A gilt and wooden trade sign in the form of a fish, early 20thC, 57in (145cm) wide.
$4,500-5,500

A plaster bust of George II.
$1,000-1,400

An Italian alabaster statue, after Bartolini, 19thC, 8½in (21.5cm) high.
$300-400

A large blue-john vase, restored, 12½in (31cm) high.
$3,000-4,000

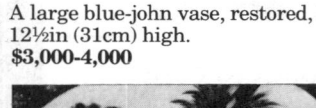

A blue-john vase of classical shape, 10in (25cm) high.
$1,500-2,600

A pair of unusual mother-of-pearl inlaid pictures, with simulated tortoiseshell frames, 23in (58cm) wide.
$1,300-1,800

A pair of George II rococo plaster brackets, attributed to John Cheere, minor damages, 20½in (52cm) high.
$9,000-12,000

John Cheere, 1709-1787. An identical pair of gilded plaster brackets from Felbrigg Hall, Norfolk, were exhibited in 'Rococo, Art and Design in Hogarth's England', Victoria and Albert Museum, 16 May-30 September 1984, Catalogue S55. These were part of the furnishings of the Cabinet Room at Felbrigg and were probably intended to support bronzed plaster busts, also supplied by Cheere. The catalogue notes the close similarity of this design to the work of Cressent and Caffieri in France in the 1730s and 1740s.

A pair of granite columns, inscribed 'A relic of old London Bridge', 15in (38cm) high.
$1,300-1,800

Old London Bridge was demolished finally in 1831, to be replaced by a new bridge designed by John Rennie.

Antiquities Pottery

An Attic red figure column krater, by the Harrow painter, 500-480 BC, 15in (38cm) high.
$15,000-21,000

An Apulian bell krater, related in style to the Eton-Nika painter, repaired, 380 BC, 14in (35.5cm).
$7,500-10,500

A stemmed Attic Kylix, c520 BC.
$1,200-1,600

An Apulian red figure pelike, late 4th Century BC, 6½in (16cm).
$300-400

An Apulian hydria, associated with the Gioia del Colle Painter and the Painter of Copenhagen 4223, repaired, 4th Century BC, 27in (68.5cm) high.
$13,500-17,500

A large Cypriot white painted ware amphora, decorated in black, c1050-950 BC, 12in (30cm).
$150-250

A Cypriot bichrome pottery oenochoe, decorated in orange and brown, base chipped, 8th-7th Century BC, 14in (35.5cm) high.
$1,000-1,400

A collection of Roman pottery vessels, c3rd Century AD.
$300-400

A gesso painted Cartonnage fragment, in orange, yellow, black and green on a white ground with a line of hieroglyphs beneath, late Dynastic Period, 11 by 8½in (28 by 21cm).
$450-600

An Egyptian gesso painted Cartonnage fragment, late Dynastic Period, 15 by 7½in (38 by 19cm).
$600-900

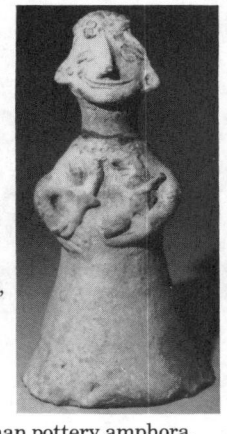

A gesso painted Cartonnage fragment, in green, yellow, orange, black and white, Late Dynastic Period, 15 by 8½in (38 by 22cm). **$600-900**

A near Eastern pottery female idol, of hollow stylised form, holding suckling twins to her breast, early 1st Millennium BC, 10in (25.5cm) high. **$3,000-4,500**

An Egyptian gesso painted wood figure, painted red with details in black, Late Period, 17in (43cm) high. **$800-1,200**

A large Roman pottery amphora, c1st Century AD, 41in (104cm) high excluding cast iron stand. **$600-900**

Metalware

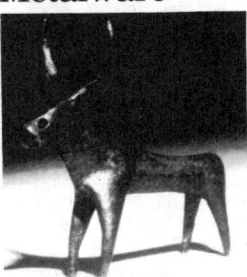

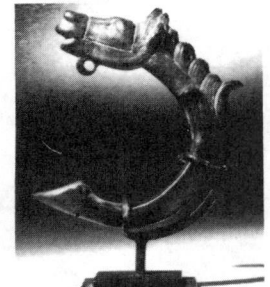

Seven Frankish bronze and niello buckle elements, c7th Century AD, 3in (8cm) long. **$1,500-2,600**

Three Iberian bronze figures of standing females, 5th-3rd Century BC, approx 3in (8cm) high. **$1,500-2,600**

A Luristan bronze bull, 9th-8th Century BC, 2½in (6cm) high. **$1,500-2,600**

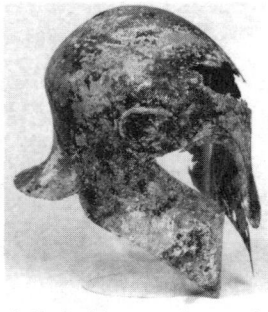

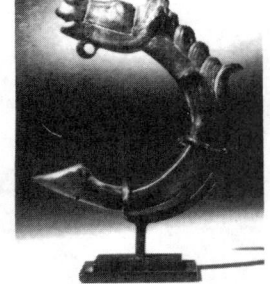

A bronze lamp handle in the form of a horse's head, Roman 1st-2nd Century AD, 3in (7.5cm) high, mounted. **$750-1,000**

A Corinthian type beaten bronze helmet, fragmentary, c6th Century BC, 10in (25cm) high. **$7,500-10,500**

A Roman bronze candelabrum and lamp, 2nd-3rd Century AD, 10in (25cm) high. **$600-900**

Marble

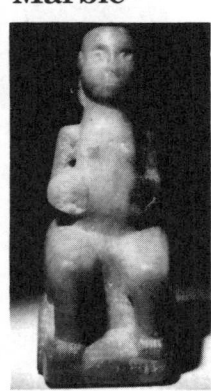

A pair of gold beaten over bronze hair rings, and 3 fragments from a similar, 8th-7th Century. **$1,000-1,400**

An Etruscan gold bulla in the form of a satyr's head, crushed, 6th-5th Century BC, 2in (5.5cm) high. **$3,000-4,500**

A South Arabian alabaster figure of a seated female idol, 1st-2nd Century AD, 8½in (21.5cm) high. **$1,300-1,800**

Miscellaneous

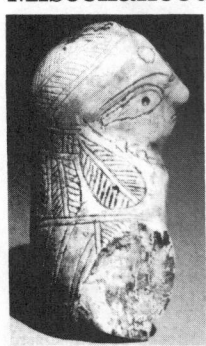

An Elamite white alabaster palette fragment, from Iran, Late Iron Age, 950-440 BC, 2½in (6cm) high.
$1,500-2,600

A marble stele of a rider and horse approaching a shrine, East Roman, 8½in (21.5cm).
$800-1,200

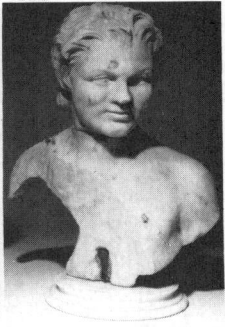

A Roman marble bust of a Satyr, neck and crown repaired, nose restored, bust fragmentary, 2nd Century AD, 16½in (41.5cm).
$10,500-14,000

A translucent green glass amphoriskos, 5in (12.5cm) high, and a chalice, 3in (7.5cm) high, both c4th Century AD.
$900-1,300

A 'Victory' beaker, mould blown, translucent amber yellow, a central band reading: 'Λ[ΑΒ]Ε ΤΗΝ ΝΕΙΚΗΝ 'Take the Victory', from Syria or Italy, repaired, with parts of one side and base restored, 1st Century AD, 2½in (6.5cm).
$2,250-3,000

A green glazed composition amulet of Tueris, 5th-4th Century BC, 2in (5cm) high.
$800-1,200

A translucent amethyst glass bowl, traces of applied white trail decoration below an everted rim, with iridescence.
$1,000-1,400

An Egyptian wood building clamp, Seti I, 19th Dynasty, 1318-1304 BC, 10½ by 4½in (26 by 12cm).
$750-1,000

A green hardstone heart scarab, 2in (5.5cm) long, Dynasty XVIII, a greyish Egyptian 'blue' scarab, 2in (5cm) long, and a turquoise glazed composition scarab, 1½in (4cm) long, Late Period.
$1,300-1,800

A gesso painted wooden sarcophagus fragment, painted in yellow and red, Later New Kingdom, 12in (30.5cm).
$900-1,300

An Egyptian gesso painted wood Anthropoid mask, coloured yellow with details in black, Late Ptolemaic Period, 9½in (24cm) high.
$450-700

A linen and gesso painted gilt mask, Late Period, 10in (26cm) high.
$800-1,200

Three South Italian terracotta figures 3rd-2nd Century BC, 5½ to 9in (14 to 23cm) high.

l. **$400-500**

c. **$450-600**

r. **$450-700**

A head of a girl with grapes in her hair, Roman, Eastern Mediterranean, 2nd Century AD.
$1,200-1,600

Rugs & Carpets

An Afshar rug, with stepped red, blue and ivory floral medallions, 63 by 47in (160 by 119cm).
$400-500

A Belouchi rug, 67 by 45in (170 by 114cm).
$450-700

A Bakhtiari carpet, with red ground, the main border with a light blue ground, with a panel bearing inscription and signature, some damage, 152 by 94in (386 by 238cm).
$4,000-5,500

A Belouchi rug, the midnight blue field with totem of 8 medallions, 49 by 105in (124.5 by 266.5cm).
$450-700

A Bidjah rug, the red field with indigo radiating medallion within powder blue spandrels, 82 by 42in (208 by 108cm).
$1,500-2,600

A Caucasian rug, the brick red field with central octagonal medallion on a blue field within a multiple border, 84 by 53in (213 by 134.5cm).
$1,300-1,800

A Bidjov rug, with indigo field, enclosed by a main ivory border of Chi-Chi influence, 72 by 50in (182 by 127cm).
$1,500-2,600

A Chi-Chi rug, with indigo field, 65 by 42in (165 by 105cm).
$1,500-2,600

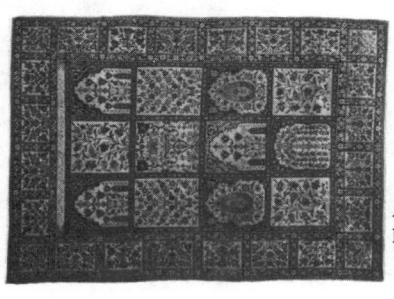

An Indian cotton durrie, the beige field within a wine and floral border, 82 by 50in (208 by 127cm).
$800-1,200

A silk Fereghan prayer rug, with ivory field and burgundy indented and cusped mihrab with floral sprays, in a light blue palmette and vine border, 79 by 53in (200 by 135cm).
$7,500-10,500

A Kashan rug, with an inscription panel at one end, 77 by 57in (195 by 145cm).
$4,000-7,000

A Fachralo Kazak rug, the bottle green field with a column of ivory and tomato red panels and stepped lozenges, in an ivory hooked lozenge border, areas of slight wear, repair and stains, 92 by 53in (233.5 by 134.5cm).
$4,000-5,500

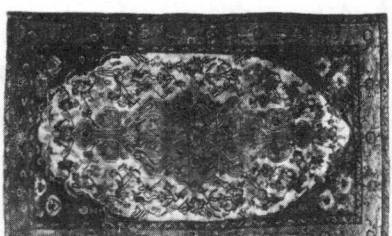

A silk Kashan rug, the ivory field with powder blue pendant medallion, purple spandrels and stylised foliate stems, 82 by 50in (207 by 128cm).
$7,500-10,500

A Kashan silk rug, in tones of magenta, ivory, green and cinnamon, 84 by 48in (213 by 122cm).
$4,000-5,500

A Fereghan Sarouk rug, the ivory field with shaded blood red palmette vine border between blue flowering vine stripes, a short Kelim strip at each end, one Kelim slightly damaged, 75 by 51in (190.5 by 129.5cm).
$7,500-10,500

A red ground bordered Kashgai rug, 79 by 46in (200 by 116.5cm).
$3,000-4,500

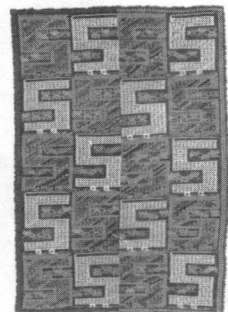

A Kirman carpet, the field with 18 ivory panels and lobed medallions in crimson and powder blue, 168 by 105in (445 by 266cm).
$3,000-4,500

A part cotton Sileh, the shaded red field with 4 columns of indigo and ivory dragon-like motifs, woven in 2 parts, old repairs, 112 by 74in (283 by 188cm).
$5,500-7,000

A Shirvan rug, the indigo field with a string of multi-coloured Lesghi medallions, in an ivory border between dark brown and ivory minor stylised floral stripes, minor repairs, 123 by 49in (312 by 124cm).
$4,000-5,500

A Lesghi rug, the sable field with 3 traditional medallions, 60 by 39in (152 by 99cm).
$2,250-3,000

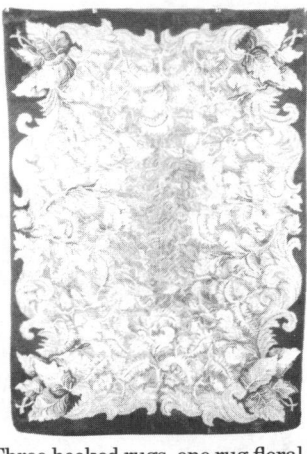

Three hooked rugs, one rug floral in hues of pink, yellow and blue, the second in a patchwork design comprising striped squares interspersed with floral squares surrounded by a brown border, the third in a wavy geometric design in greens and browns, late 19thC, the first 80 by 41½in (203 by 105cm), the second 51½ by 43in (130 by 109cm), the third 61 by 33in (155 by 84cm).
$900-1,200

A Shirvan rug, with royal blue field and an ivory crab rosette border, a short Kelim strip at each end, 95 by 57in (241 by 145cm).
$5,500-6,000

Textiles
Costumes

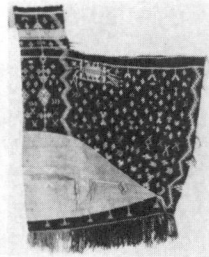

A Chinese embroidered shawl, mid-19thC.
$300-400

A Moroccan Western Atlas cloak of black wool, embroidered in red, orange, blue and white wools.
$400-500

A reversible silk shawl, the deep border worked mainly in red and blue, the reverse having a deep pink centre panel, c1880, 71in (180cm) square, fringed.
$700-900

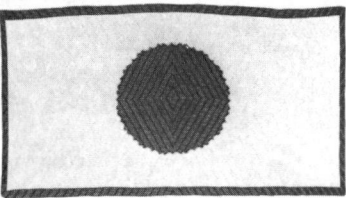

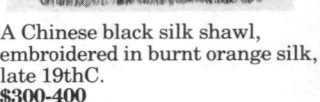

A Mexican Saltillo, woven in blue, black and sand on a cream wool ground, 53 by 96in (136 by 244cm).
$4,000-5,500

A Chinese black silk shawl, embroidered in burnt orange silk, late 19thC.
$300-400

A French shawl, c1860, 133 by 65in (340 by 164cm).
$400-500

A Paisley shawl, in mainly green, blue, crimson and orange with cones, sprays of leaves and tendrils, c1860, 133 by 65in (340 to 164cm), with original box labelled 'Nicholls & Plincke, St. Petersbourg, Magasin Anglais'.
$750-1,000

A Japanese kimono in aqua silk, embroidered with coiled thread mainly in grey and cream, with matching sash, late 19thC.
$400-500

A Chinese robe of yellow silk, embroidered in blue and ivory silks and gold thread, 19thC.
$1,300-1,800

Reputed to have belonged to the artist Frederick Whiting, 1874-1962, War correspondent and artist for The Graphic in China 1900-1.

A Chinese Taoist priest's robe of silk and gold thread k'o-ssu, mid-18thC, later lined, altered.
$15,000-21,000

A Chinese robe of eau-de-nil silk, worked in coloured silks and gold thread, having black silk border, lined.
$250-350

A muslin dress, embroidered with sprigs and garlands of flowers in mauve and white, probably embroidered in India for the European market, c1810.
$2,250-3,500

A Japanese silk embroidered kimono, 19thC.
$400-500

A Chinese dragon robe, in metallic thread and polychrome silks on an azure silk ground, 19thC.
$600-900

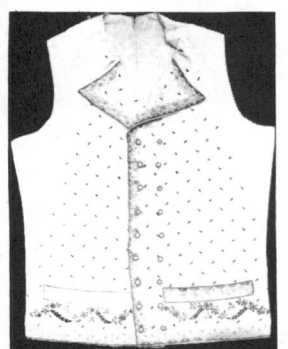

A gentleman's waistcoat of ivory silk, c1790.
$250-350

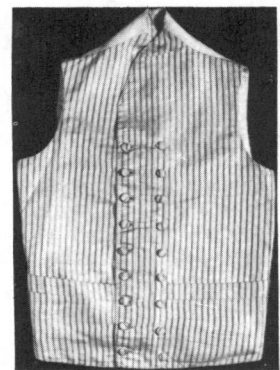

A gentleman's double-breasted waistcoat of yellow silk brocade, c1790.
$150-250

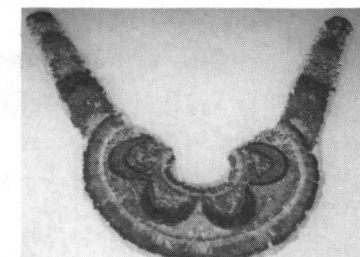

A feathered cape, c1830.
$1,000-1,400

A pelerine of aubergine coloured satin, embroidered with flowers, c1830.
$60-100

The Silver Spring Parasol, made by Week's Royal Mechanical Museum, Tichborne Street, Piccadilly, with green silk mount edged with white silk fringe and telescopic silver handle, maker's mark G.C., 1810, in red morocco case, 8in (20cm).
$250-350

A top hat of grey beaver, with narrow ribbon of cream ribbed silk, c1830, 5½in (14cm) high.
$450-600

A feathered cape, c1820.
$600-900

A pair of very high heeled shoes of ivory figured silk, worn, c1770.
$600-900

A pair of ladies' high heeled shoes of bottle green morocco, c1780.
$1,500-2,600

A pair of children's shoes of cord quilted green silk, c1740.
$2,250-3,500

A pair of young men's needlework carpet slippers of Albert pattern, c1860.
$450-700

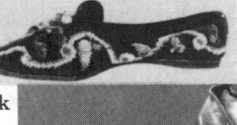

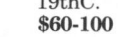
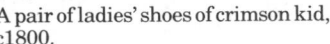

A pair of miniature clogs, late 19thC.
$60-100

A pair of ladies' shoes of crimson kid, c1800.
$750-1,000

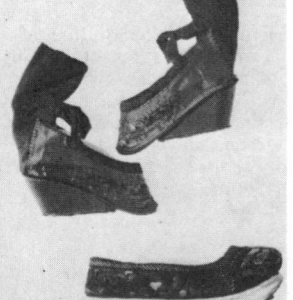

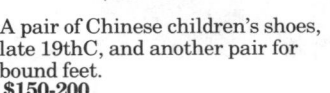

A baby bonnet of ivory silk, mid-18thC.
$700-900

A pair of Chinese children's shoes, late 19thC, and another pair for bound feet.
$150-200

A gentleman's nightcap of linen, in pink and green silks and gold and silver thread, English, early 17thC.
$4,000-5,500

Embroidery

A Stuart needlework picture, embroidered in various stitches, 13 by 18in (33 by 45cm), in ebonised and tortoiseshell frame.
$1,300-1,800

An ivory silk purse, embroidered in mainly blue, green and yellow silks, c1660.
$2,250-3,500

A silk embroidered picture, early 19thC, 24 by 18in (60 by 45cm), in walnut frame.
$150-250

A pieced and appliquéd quilted coverlet, worked in the feathered star pattern with 72 alternating blocks of white and blue pin dot fabric, American, mid-19thC, 88in (223.5cm) square.
$700-900

A rare silk-on-silk needlework picture, worked with polychrome silk threads in embroidery stitches on a natural silk moiré ground, in original black painted cavetto frame with gilt mouldings and the original gilt sand textured mat, signed on back panel 'Mary Flower her work done in the year 1764', Philadelphia, 25 by 21½in (63.5 by 54cm).
$70,000-90,000

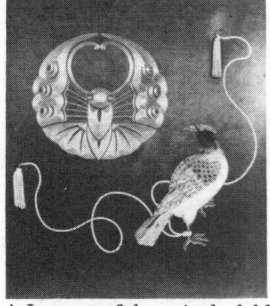

A pieced and appliquéd quilt top, predominantly red, green and yellow, with a meandering floral and vine surround, in red and green, all on a white ground, probably Pennsylvania, mid-19thC, 88in (223.5cm) square.
$2,500-3,000

A Japanese fukusa in dark blue silk, 19thC, 29 by 23in (75 by 60cm), framed and glazed.
$600-900

A pair of Turkish sash ends, late 17th/early 18thC, joined, 30 by 20in (76 by 51cm).
$1,500-2,600

For similar piece see Turkish Embroidery by Pauline Johnstone, page 38, plate 14.

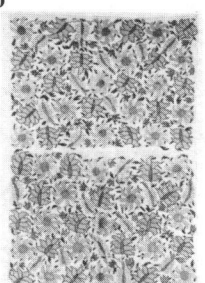

A pieced and appliquéd quilted coverlet, worked in a Rose of Sharon variation pattern, with 9 wreath blocks within a tulip and meandering vine border, all worked in red, green and yellow in a white ground, American, mid-19thC, 94in (238cm) square.
$1,500-2,000

An Italian silk velvet with silk appliqué banner, with raised silver embroidery, 17thC, 24 by 48in (60 by 121cm).
$1,000-1,400

A Japanese coverlet of chocolate brown silk, embroidered in brown, mauve, orange and ivory silks, worked in satin stitch, with matching pillow shams, 90 by 68in (230 by 174cm).
$750-1,000

An undyed linen coverlet, embroidered in coloured wools with crewel work, 88 by 83in (226 by 212cm).
$450-600

A Chinese coverlet of yellow silk, embroidered in satin stitch with pink, blue, green and ivory silks, late 19thC, 102 by 84in (260 by 214cm), fringed and lined.
$1,300-1,800

A Balkan patchwork coverlet, with Greek and Turkish muslin and linen embroideries, mainly 17th and 19thC pieces, 96 by 76in (244 by 194cm), lined.
$1,000-1,400

A Chinese silk picture, late 19thC, 20½ by 16in (52 by 41cm), in a hardwood frame and glazed.
$450-700

A Japanese wall hanging, worked in gold and brown and grey coiled thread, having brocade border, 19thC, 77 by 56in (196 by 142cm), printed cotton lined.
$1,300-1,800

Lace

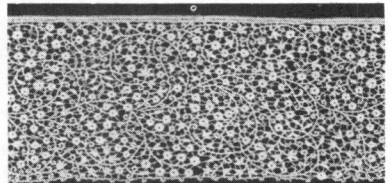

A flounce of Venetian bobbin lace, c1690, 7½ by 160in (19 by 408cm).
$900-1,300

A border of linen cutwork and embroidery, early 17thC, 5½ by 95in (14 by 240cm), joined.
$300-400

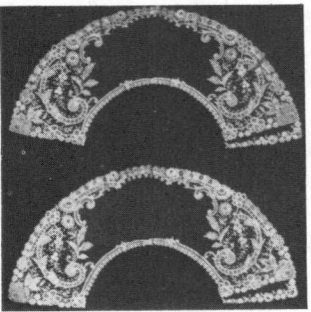

A pair of fan leaves of Brussels bobbin and needlepoint laces, 19thC, 6in (15cm) long.
$300-400

A deep flounce of point de France, late 17thC, 25½ by 137in (65 by 348cm).
$3,000-4,500

A pair of cravat ends of Brussels bobbin lace, with the monogram of the Sun King, Louis XIV, the whole with a multitude of fillings, c1710, 12½ by 16in (31 by 40cm) each.
$4,000-5,500

Probably worked to commemorate the Treaty of Utrecht, 1713.

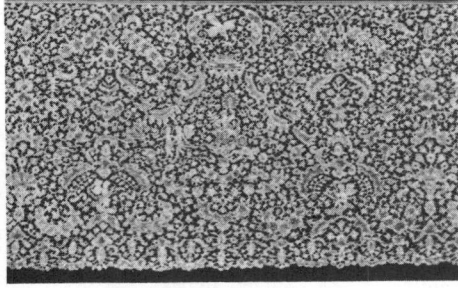

An English needlepoint flounce, c1700, 8½ by 98in (21 by 249cm), divided and mounted.
$4,000-5,500

A Flemish bobbin lace flounce, c1690, 11½ by 144in (29 by 368cm).
$2,250-3,500

Samplers

A spot motif sampler with coloured silks and metal threads, c1650, 15 by 13in (38 by 33cm).
$1,500-2,600

A sampler by Elizabeth Lewling dated 1775, worked in coloured silks, damage, 15 by 10in (38 by 25.5cm).
$300-500

A needlework sampler, 'Jane Doughtys work 1777', the linen ground embroidered in ivory, green, brown and pink silks, 24½ by 20½in (62.5 by 52.5cm), framed and glazed.
$2,250-3,500

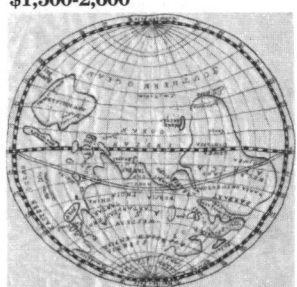

A pair of small map samplers of the World, worked in black and coloured silks against an ivory silk ground, 18thC, 8in (20.5cm) across, framed and glazed.
$1,000-1,400

A needlework sampler, with the inscription 'Maria S. Furrer's work wrot in the 12 year of her age in E. Brown's Wesleyan Seminary', dated 1829, framed, 16 by 17½in (40.5 by 44cm).
$6,000-7,000

An embroidered map sampler of England and Wales, inscribed and dated 'B. Cosier, Novr: 1800', 16½ by 14½in (42 by 36cm), gilt framed and glazed.
$250-350

A needlework sampler, worked predominantly in pink, rose red and green woollen threads on natural cotton ground, with the initials 'MD' on top and the inscription 'Jane Bell House Oswego Americ', surrounded by a floral border, slight tears and minor staining, New York, late 18thC, framed, 13in (33cm) square.
$1,500-2,000

A needlework sampler by 'Elizabeth Campling aged 12 years', the linen ground embroidered in green, brown and ivory silks, early 19thC, 12½ by 13½in (31.5 by 34.5cm), framed and glazed.
$400-500

A sampler by Mary Cooper, dated 1803, worked in shades of brown and cream silks, 17 by 20in (43 by 51cm), framed and glazed.
$800-1,200

A sampler by 'Elizabeth Wilkinson, finished in the 11th year of her age, 1812', 21 by 16in (53 by 41cm), framed and glazed.
$450-700

A needlework sampler by 'S. Parker aged 14 yrs 1817', embroidered in cross, eye and other stitches with coloured silks, 14½ by 12½in (37 by 32cm), framed and glazed.
$1,000-1,400

A needlework picture, with the inscription 'Mary Fentun her sampler and age 9 years 1789', browning, 21 by 16½in (53 by 41.5cm).
$3,000-4,000

A Flemish tapestry woven in wools and silk, restored, late 17thC, 100 by 142in (254 by 360cm).
$5,500-7,000

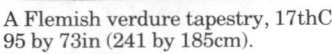

A Flemish verdure tapestry, 17thC, 95 by 73in (241 by 185cm).
$5,500-7,000

A Spanish armorial tapestry, woven in greens, blues, yellow and orange wool, in a later scrolling foliate border with paterae corners, 17thC, 133 by 118in (338 by 301cm).
$6,000-8,000

An Aubusson tapestry cushion, mid-19thC, 23½in (59cm) wide.
$1,200-1,600

A set of 6 Aubusson tapestry panels, woven in shades of rose pink, green and other colours, 19thC, 103 by 38in (261.5 by 96.5cm) each panel, framed.
$6,000-9,000

A pair of Aubusson tapestry pelmets woven in greens, blues and reds, mid-19thC, 88in (223.5cm) wide.
$4,000-5,500

A painted cloth wall hanging, after Audran at the Gobelins, depicting the departure for the hunt, with the arms of Philippe de Bourbon-Parme, 18thC, 54 by 120in (137 by 304cm).
$4,000-5,500

The design of this wall hanging is adapted from several of the panels from the series Les Chasses de Louis XV, woven by the Workshop of Audran at the Gobelins after paintings by Jean-Baptiste Oudry. The tapestries were ordered by Philippe de Bourbon-Parme in 1743 and are now in the Pitti Palace in Florence.

Miscellaneous

A crewel work picture dated 1707, darned, 18 by 12in (46 by 30.5cm).
$300-500

A patchwork quilt, worked in brightly coloured squares of printed cotton, c1840, 110 by 91in (280 by 232cm), lined.
$600-900

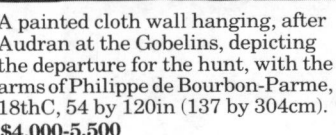

A patchwork quilt, c1840, 105 by 93in (266 by 236cm).
$400-500

A furbelow of ivory silk painted in pink, yellow, purple and green, 8½ by 112in (22 by 285cm) with 3 others all matching, of various sizes.
$450-600

'Acanthus', a pair of printed velvet curtains in blood red and caramel brown, designed by William Morris, inscribed Morris & Company 440 Oxford Street, c1880, 19 by 45in (48 by 114cm).
$1,500-2,600

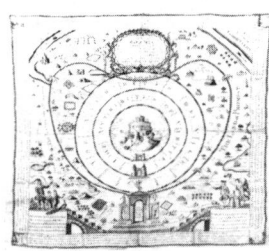

A linen kerchief, printed in madder, early 18thC, 26½ by 31in (67 by 78cm).
$600-900

A small wool ship picture, c1850, 8 by 6in (20 by 15cm).
$400-500

A sailor made wool work picture, 23 by 30in (58 by 76cm), framed.
$1,000-1,400

A Victorian beadwork pelmet, 9 by 76in (23 by 193cm).
$450-600

A pair of epimanikia of crimson silk, depicting the Annunciation, late 16thC.
$750-1,000

A flattened moose foot, North American, possibly Iroquois.
$3,000-4,000

A linen handkerchief, printed in rose madder, with 'Almanack for the Year of our Lord 1798', published by William Hanson & Son, 1798, 21 by 24in (53 by 61cm).
$700-900

A Mandarin civil rank badge in woven silks, Kossu, depicting a goose, 4th Rank, c1850.
$400-500

An ivory silk handkerchief, commemorating 'The Glorious Reform in Parliament', printed in blue, inscribed, designed by Rob Cruikshank a friend to Reform, c1832, 31 by 34in (79 by 87cm).
$150-200

A pair of Aubusson hangings woven in shades of pink, red and green, on a creamy sand ground with pale eau-de-nil border, 19thC, 120 by 49in (304 by 124cm).
$4,000-5,500

Fans

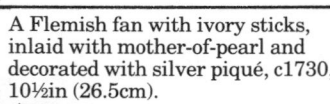

A Flemish fan with ivory sticks, inlaid with mother-of-pearl and decorated with silver piqué, c1730, 10½in (26.5cm).
$600-900

A Flemish fan, the carved ivory sticks decorated with silver piqué and mother-of-pearl clouté, early 18thC, 10½in (27cm).
$150-250

An English fan commemorating the death of Frederick, Prince of Wales, in 1751, 11in (28cm), in a box.
$1,200-1,600

A French fan, painted with bright colours, the ivory sticks pierced, c1680, 10in (25cm).
$9,000-12,000

An ivory brisé fan, carved and pierced with roundels, swags and neo-classical motifs, c1810, 7in (17cm).
$250-350

A Chinese fan with carved, pierced ivory sticks, c1850, 11in (28cm), in original black and gold lacquer box with interior fitted glass lid.
$800-1,200

A fan with carved, pierced, silvered and gilt mother-of-pearl sticks, late 19thC, 10½in (27cm).
$400-500

A fan with silvered and gilt mother-of-pearl sticks, c1880, 14in (35cm).
$600-900

A Chinese ivory brisé fan, c1830, 7½in (18.5cm), in a box.
$300-500

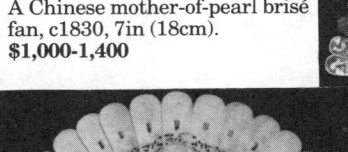

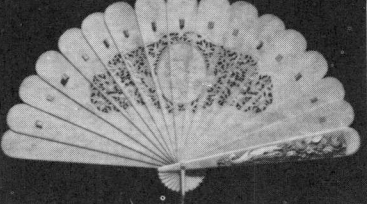

A Chinese mother-of-pearl brisé fan, c1830, 7in (18cm).
$1,000-1,400

A Chinese cabriolet fan with painted lacquer sticks, decorated with ivory and silk appliqué, c1840, 9in (22cm), in original box.
$400-500

An ivory brisé fan, the centre carved and pierced, c1860, 9in (22.5cm).
$450-600

Dolls – Wooden

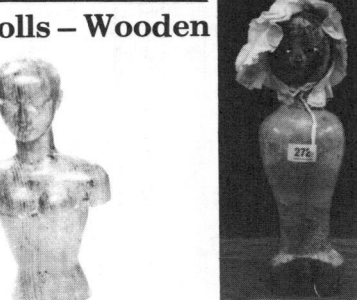

A carved wood doll, legs and arms missing, late 17thC.
$100-150

A carved wooden stump doll, the hair carved in a plait, early 17thC, 11in (28cm).
$1,500-2,600

Dolls – Wax

A North American carved pine wood doll torso, with holes in the head for wig, 19thC, 7in (18cm).
$300-500

Dolls – Bisque

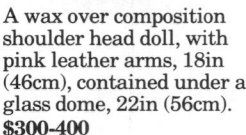

A wax over composition shoulder head doll, with pink leather arms, 18in (46cm), contained under a glass dome, 22in (56cm).
$300-400

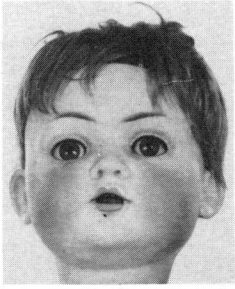

A Pierotti poured wax shoulder head doll, with inset fair mohair wig, cloth body and wax lower limbs, 21in (53cm).
$750-1,000

A wax doll with several silk and other costumes, early 20thC.
$750-1,000

A bisque headed character baby doll, with blue sleeping eyes, short wig and baby's body, marked BP in a heart for Bahr and Proschild 678 9, 18½in (47cm).
$450-600

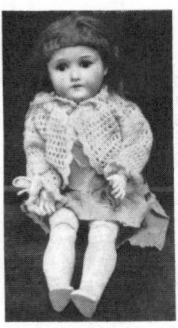

A German bisque headed doll, 17½in (44cm).
$250-350

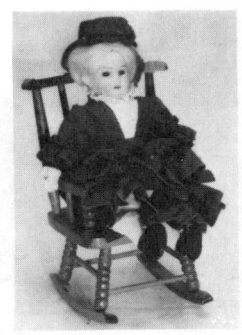

A small doll with bisque head, sitting in rocking chair.
$100-200

A bisque headed bébé, with fixed wrist jointed composition body, dressed in blue, impressed SteA.1., 16in (40cm).
$3,000-4,500

A bisque headed character boy doll, with composition baby's body, neck chipped, marked 166-13, the head 6½in (16cm).
$1,000-1,400

Bru

Gebruder Heubach

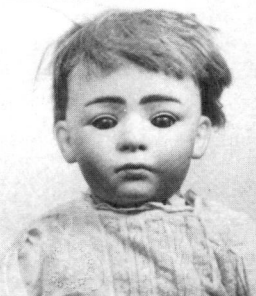

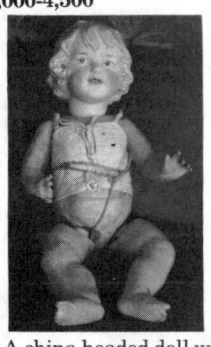

A china headed doll with composition body, marked 7 79 Heubach 58 Germany.
$150-250

A Bru teteur bisque doll, impressed BRU Jne.8, with jointed wood and composition body, stringing loose and flaking on hands, French, c1875, 19in (48cm), together with cotton and lace pillow and cover.
$6,000-9,000

A Gebruder Heubach bisque headed character boy doll, with composition toddler body dressed in whitework, marked with sunburst 12 7246, 24in (61cm).
$3,000-4,500

A bisque headed googlie eyed doll, the round blue eyes flirting by means of a wire at the back of the neck, marked with the Heubach square mark 1 and stamped in green 06, 10in (25cm).
$1,500-2,600

A Heubach coloured boy character doll's head, with open and shut eyes and closed mouth, 6in (15cm).
$750-1,000

Jumeau

A Jumeau bisque doll, with jointed composition body with blue stamp on buttocks, Jumeau Medaille d'Or Paris, legs and arms painted, stamped in red Déposé Tete Jumeau Bte. S.G.D.G.6, red check marks, French, c1880, some damage, 15in (38cm).
$2,250-3,500

A bisque headed bébé, neck chipped, mark 7 and stamped in blue on the body Bébé Jumeau Déposé, 15in (38cm).
$2,250-3,000

A bisque headed bébé, impressed 6, body stamped in blue JUMEAU Medaille D'or Paris, 15in (38cm).
$1,500-2,600

A Jumeau bisque headed doll with cork pate, replacement wig and jointed composition body, marked 12 and the body stamped Bébé Jumeau Bte S.G.D.G. Déposé, hairline to left temple, 28in (70cm).
$1,300-1,800

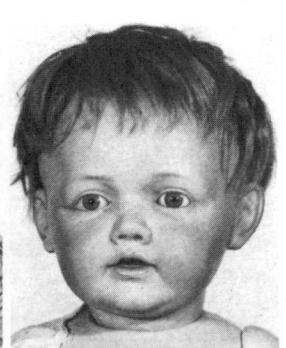

J D Kestner

A bisque headed character baby doll, marked M16. 237.J.D.K.jr. 1914. C in a circle Hilda Ges gesch N. 1070, 19½in (49cm).
$5,500-7,000

A pair of all bisque dolls house dolls, jointed at the shoulder and hip, with moulded black bows to their brown shoes, marked 1503 and 1603 on the legs, by Kestner, c1910, 5in (12cm).
$250-350

Armand Marseille

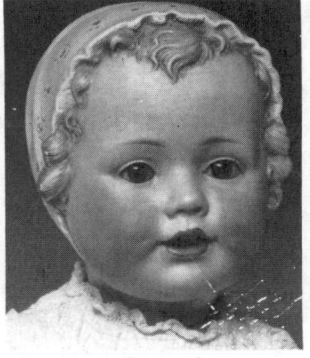

A very rare bisque bonnet headed baby doll, with brown sleeping eyes and moulded blonde curls showing under her blue and white baby's cap with indented lacework, the baby's body wearing a nightgown, marked JDK 12, 15in (38cm).
$10,500-14,000

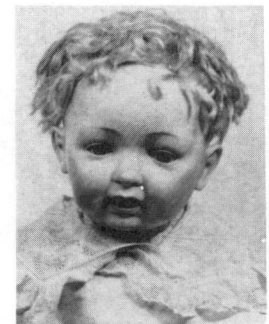

A Kestner bisque headed character doll, marked G20 211 JDK20, 26½in (66cm).
$1,500-2,600

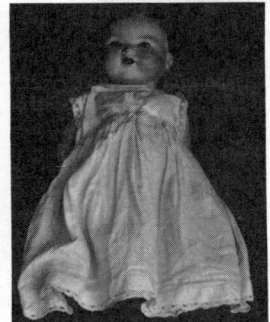

A bisque headed character doll, with brown sleeping eyes and composition jointed toddler body, marked JDK239G11, 15in (38cm).
$1,000-1,400

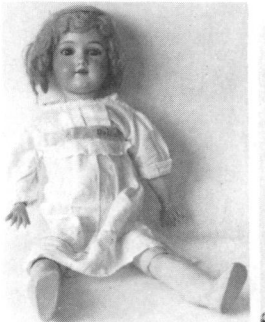

An Armand Marseille bisque headed 'Dollie', with wood and composition ball-jointed body, in original white muslin dress with blue 'Dollie' sash, impressed Made in Germany, Armand Marseille 390 A8M, 24in (61cm).
$300-400

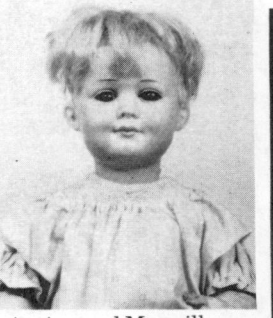

An Armand Marseille bisque headed character doll, marked 550 A 2 M DRGM, 12in (31cm).
$1,300-1,800

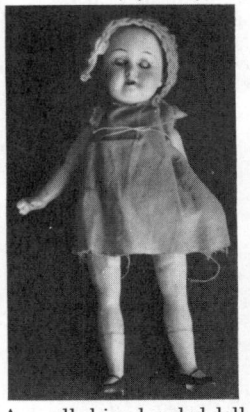

A small china headed doll, Armand Marseille, Germany, 390 A12/OX N.
$100-200

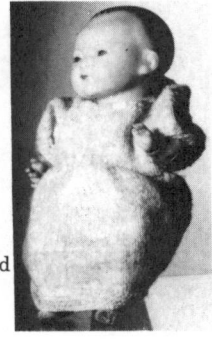

A china headed doll, with composition body, AM Germany, 351/8K.
$250-350

A china headed doll with composition body, Armand Marseille, Germany, 995, A.10.M.
$250-350

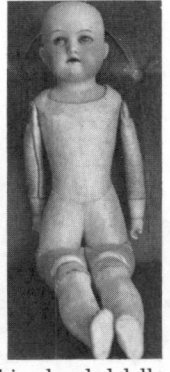

A china headed doll with leather body, Armand Marseille, 370 AM 2/OX-DEP.
$150-250

An Armand Marseille bisque headed Floradora doll, with 4 moulded teeth, ball-jointed composition body and limbs, in lilac crochet dress, impressed Made in Germany, Floradora, A2/OM, early 20thC, 14in (35cm).
$250-350

An Armand Marseille bisque headed Oriental character baby doll, with composition limbs, stamped A.Star M. Germany 3K, 11in (28cm).
$750-1,000

Schmidt

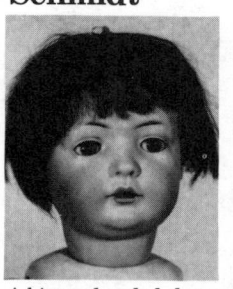

A bisque headed character doll with jointed composition body, marked BSW in a heart 2097-7 by Bruno Schmidt, c1911, 28½in (71cm).
$1,000-1,400

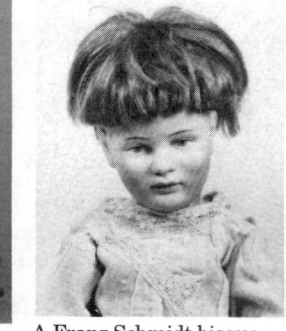

A French bébé doll by Franz Schmidt, with composition body, 9in (23cm).
$250-350

A Franz Schmidt bisque headed character doll, the ball-jointed composition body dressed in white cotton dress, marked Deponiert FS & Co, 1268/30 Germany, 12in (30cm).
$2,250-3,500

A Franz Schmidt bisque headed doll, with open and closed mouth and simulated tongue, imressed F.S. & Co, 1272-32Z, c1912, 12½in (31cm).
$450-700

Schoenau & Hoffmeister

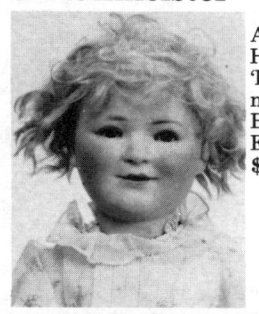

A Schoenau and Hoffmeister bisque headed 'Princess Elizabeth' doll, marked Porzellanfabrik Burggrub Princess Elizabeth 5, 20½in (51cm).
$1,500-2,600

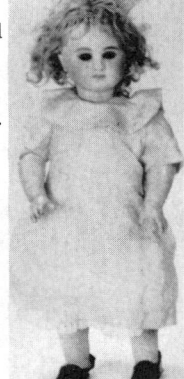

A bisque headed bébé with closed mouth, the fixed wrist composition jointed body dressed in pink with underclothes, shoes and socks, marked on the head 8 and with the Schmidt of Paris shield mark on bottom, 19in (48cm).
$4,000-5,500

SFBJ

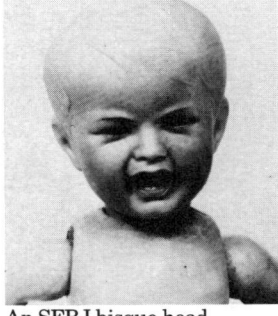

An SFBJ bisque head character doll, 233, with blue glass eyes, open and closed mouth and composition toddler body, flock hair removed, small blemish to right temple, slight damage to body, 12in (31cm).
$1,300-1,800

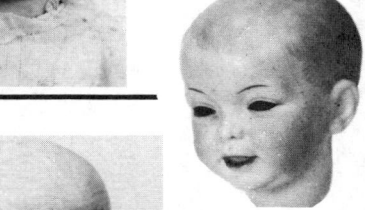

A bisque character dolls head, modelled as a boy with open and closed mouth and painted hair, marked S.F.B.J. 226, Paris 8, 5in (12.5cm).
$1,200-1,600

A bisque headed character baby, with a quantity of other items including bedding, shoes, a parasol, a box of washing items and 23 changes of clothes, marked F.S. and Co, 1272/352, Deponiert, 14½in (36cm).
$1,500-2,600

Simon & Halbig/ Kammer & Reinhardt

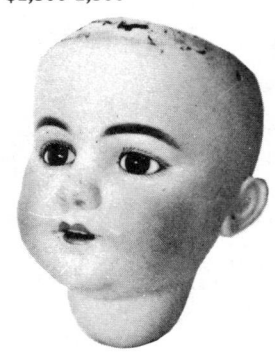

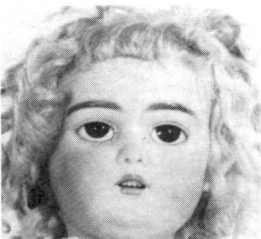

A bisque headed child doll, the jointed composition body dressed in white, marked S H 1079, 10 DEP, 21½in (54cm).
$600-900

A bisque dolls head, with fixed blue paperweight eyes, pierced ears and heavy brows, marked S & H DEP94917.50, 8in (20cm).
$1,000-1,400

A bisque headed doll with moving blue glass eyes, stamped Simon & Halbig 1079 DEP Germany, 18in (45cm).
$600-900

A doll's brass and iron bedstead with hair mattress and pillows, late 19thC, 16in (40cm) long.
$450-700

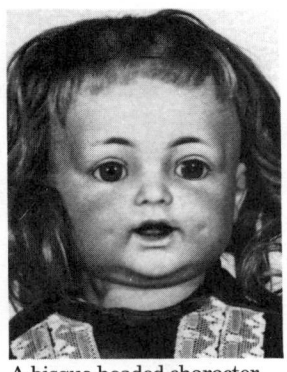

A bisque headed character child doll with dimpled cheeks, and jointed toddler body, marked K*R, Simon & Halbig 122 42, 18½in (46cm), and a composition doll.
$1,300-1,800

Jules Steiner

A bisque headed bébé, with composition jointed body with later arms, wearing nightgown, marked SteA.2 and written in red Steiner A.S.G.D.G. Paris Bourgoin jeun, 18in (45cm), and a doll's wig of blonde hair made with 3 pigtails in original box.
$3,000-4,000

Miscellaneous

An Arthur Askey fabric character doll with painted composition head, by Deans Rag Book Co Ltd, 13in (32cm).
$250-350

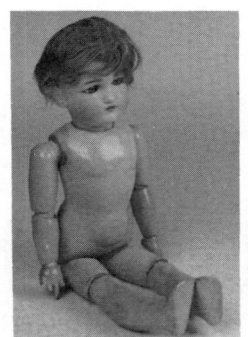

A bisque headed clockwork Bebe Premier Pas, with carton body and kid upper legs, original bronze shoes and pink outfit, by Jules Nicholas Steiner, fine hairline on left cheek, c1890, 17½in (44cm).
$1,500-2,600

A painted cloth character doll, wearing original black velvet shorts and cap with cream rayon shirt and carrying a terrier under his right arm, his hands stitched in his pockets, with Deans Rag Book Co Ltd button on left leg, c1926, 18in (45cm).
$300-400

A bisque headed character boy doll with closed mouth, blue sleeping eyes and jointed composition body, marked 1488 Simon and Halbig 4, 12½in (31cm).
$3,000-4,000

A Simon & Halbig bisque headed doll, with composition ball-jointed body, impressed 1349 Jutta s 7 h, 24in (61cm).
$450-700

A French Steiner bisque headed doll with blonde sheepskin wig, jointed composition body wearing socks, brown buckled leather shoes and ribboned straw bonnet, incised in red C O, 14½in (36cm).
$2,250-3,500

A papier mâché mask faced doll, with turquoise blue eyes, black painted short curls and remains of braid entwined plaits, the cloth and wood body in original Central European costume, c1860, 15½in (39cm).
$300-500

An English pedlar doll by C & H White of Milton, Portsmouth, the kid leather head with black pin-head eyes and painted features, the base with printed label, early 19thC, 10in (25cm).
$800-1,200

A yellow bisque headed character doll modelled as an Oriental, with black wool wig over the painted black hair, with yellow composition body, marked AM 353/4/OK, 7½in (19cm).
$800-1,200

A painted felt portrait doll wearing original clothes, modelled as Princess Elizabeth, marked with the Chad Valley label on left foot, c1938, 18in (45cm).
$450-700

Automata

An automaton doll in the form of a Turk, with painted papier mâché shoulder head, body enclosing the clockwork mechanism, 11½in (29cm), with key.
$450-600

A pair of 'Juba Dancers', hand-carved and stained wood with clockwork mechanism, USA, c1880, 10in (25cm).
$600-900

A 'Charlie Chaplin' felt covered and painted clockwork tinplate toy, probably by Schuco, c1933, 7in (17cm).
$600-900

A Lambert doll automaton guitar player, with Simon & Halbig No.6 bisque head and forearms, on plinth containing two-air musical and automaton movements, 23in (58cm).
$4,000-5,500

Dolls Houses

A painted wooden room-setting containing an Art Nouveau style set of furniture, 5 bisque and china headed dolls, the room 35in (88cm) wide, German, c1890.
$1,500-2,600

A late Victorian oak dolls house, on an oak stand with frieze drawer, 51in (128cm) wide.
$1,500-2,600

An 11 piece set of dolls house furniture, upholstered in pink silk, sofa 9in (23cm) long.
$600-900

A toy hardware market stall painted green, with wares, 15in (38cm) wide.
$2,250-3,000

A toy grocery shop painted cream and gold with labelled drawers, and label reading Art C. Niessner Wien 1913, 22in (55cm) wide.
$900-1,300

A white and blue painted toy delicatessen, 22in (55cm) wide.
$1,000-1,400

A dolls house Walterhausen 'Duncan Phyfe' secretaire, one foot missing, 6in (15cm), and a chest of 4 drawers, 3in (8cm), both transfer-printed with gilt decoration.
$600-900

A set of metal dining chairs, painted to simulate woodwork, 4in (10cm) high, and a marble topped table with metal base, 3in (7cm) high.
$1,300-1,800

A dolls house Walterhausen 'Duncan Phyfe' tapestry frame, on a fully fitted workbox, 2½in (6cm), and a drop-leaf sofa table, 5in (12.5cm) extended, one foot missing, both transfer-printed with gilt decoration.
$750-1,000

Teddy Bears

A Steiff teddy bear.
$1,500-2,600

An early black plush teddy bear, with black button eyes, some stuffing missing, 20in (50cm).
$1,500-2,600

A dark brown plush-covered teddy bear with black button eyes, with silver button on side marked GBN for Gebruder Bing Nuremburg, c1906, 20in (50cm).
$1,200-1,600

A worn plush covered teddy bear, the head moving from side to side by turning the tail, 8½in (21cm) long.
$100-200

An early blond plush teddy bear, probably by Steiff, some stuffing missing, 27in (68cm).
$1,500-2,600

A worn pink plush-covered bear on wooden wheeled stand, 15in (38cm) long.
$100-200

A large plush-covered push-along bear, on metal wheeled stand, lacks growl pull, 31in (78cm) long.
$450-600

An Edwardian teddy bear with moving limbs.
$100-200

Lead soldiers

Britains set no.31, 1st Dragoons, the Royals, dated 1.11.1902, early printer's type box label, in original box, 1908.
$1,200-1,600

Britains set no.39, Royal Horse Artillery gun team, first version, 1898.
$1,000-1,400

Britains set no.82, Colours and Pioneers of the Scots Guards, rare box-pack version with oval bases, early illustrated label, 1906.
$450-700

Britains set no.71, Turkish Cavalry, early printer's type label 'The Ertoghrul Regiment', 1910.
$450-600

Elastolin, 2 SS, peak caps, and one similar, SA, 1937.
$150-250

Britains set no.2052, Anti-Aircraft display, original box, 1958.
$900-1,300

Britains set no.144A, Royal
Field Artillery, Service
Dress, some damage, 1926.
$450-600

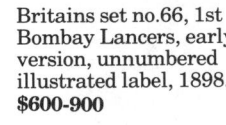

Britains set no.75, Scots
Guards, with piper and
officer, early illustrated
label, 1899.
$400-500

Lineol 70mm scale 9/37, SS
men marching, with similar
Elastolin 30/12, 1937.
$150-250

Britains set no.66, 1st
Bombay Lancers, early
version, unnumbered
illustrated label, 1898.
$600-900

Elastolin, 2 officers, Lineol
officer holding map and
binoculars, 1937.
$250-350

Elastolin 70mm scale, SA
bandsmen, a Schellenbaum
bearer and fifer by another
maker, 1937.
$250-350

Britains set no.128, 12th
Lancers, with slung lances,
dated 12.2.1903, early
printer's type label, 1905.
$400-500

A carded set of apparently
Japanese Infantry, but
carrying Union Jack, 35mm
scale, made in Japan, 1935.
$45-70

A group of 40mm semi-flats,
World War I, mostly
RAMC, 1916.
$250-350

Heyde, 80mm scale
mounted figure of George V,
original box, 1930.
$300-400

Money Banks

A metal money box.
$100-200

A repainted cast iron money
box of Paddy seated with a
pig, 'Shamrock Bank', U.S.
Pat.Aug.8, 1882, by J & E
Stevens, lacks coin trap, 8in
(20cm).
$250-350

A mechanical cast iron
money box, 'Creedmore
Bank', by J & E Stevens,
USA, c1880.
$250-350

A ceramic money bank in
the form of Donald Duck's
head, marked Walt Disney
Productions, London, 6½in
(16cm).
$75-150

A rare mechanical cast iron
money box, 'Football Bank',
damaged,.c1890, 10½in
(26cm).
$900-1,300

Tinplate

A Bing Model T Ford, clockwork, number plate 19872, German, c1927, 6½in (16cm).
$700-900

A Distler 1952 Packard tinplate tourer, clockwork mechanism, W Germany, c1955, 10in (25cm).
$450-600

A Lehmann 'Tut-Tut', box poor.
$1,300-1,800

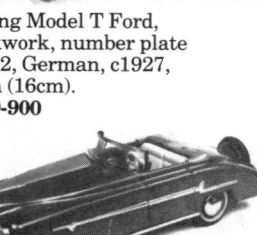

A Lehmann tinplate taxi in lemon yellow and black, no.755 c/w, Pats. Dec.1913, U.S.A. Jan.1927, late 1920, 7in (18cm).
$600-900

A fine lithographed tinplate garage, with 2 clockwork cars, Bing, c1925, in original box.
$450-600

A 'Captain Campbell's Bluebird' model of Bluebird III land speed record car, clockwork mechanism, by Gunthermann, c1931, worn, 20in (50cm).
$750-1,000

A tinplate clockwork open tourer with driver, one door missing, by Gunthermann.
$1,500-2,600

A Meccano constructor car no.1.
$450-600

A P2 Alpha Romeo repainted tinplate racing car, clockwork mechanism, by CTG France, c1926, 21in (53cm).
$1,300-1,800

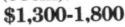

An original P2 by CIJ.
$1,300-1,800

A coloured lithographed tinplate racing car, clockwork mechanism, defective, yellow with gold lining, probably by Gunthermann, c1907, 6in (15cm).
$600-900

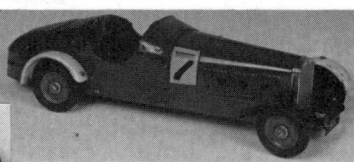

A Marklin tinplate clockwork constructor racing car, 1935, in red.
$450-600

A Tipp clockwork charabanc, reg.no. TC900, 10½in (26cm).
$1,200-1,600

A Tipp tinplate clockwork Faux Cabriolet, in beige and maroon, late 1930s, 21in (53cm).
$1,500-2,600

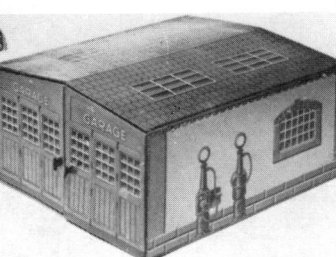

A Tipp printed tinplate garage, 10in (25cm) wide.
$150-200

A clockwork 'Kingsbury Firetruck', extending ladders, USA, c1930, 31½in (79cm).
$450-700

A spring-action tinplate delivery lorry with driver, 8in (20cm).
$100-200

A Bing clockwork tinplate battleship, entitled Möve (Seagull), pieces missing, 20½in (51cm).
$1,500-2,600

A Fleischmann tinplate clockwork liner, no.67, 20½in (51cm).
$1,300-1,800

A Bing clockwork three-funnelled liner, lacking lifeboat, 13in (33cm).
$900-1,300

A Carette carpet toy tinplate sailboat, flywheel mechanism, German, c1905, 12in (30cm).
$300-500

A rare live steam, spirit fired tinplate battleship, HMS Barfleur, by Marklin, minor damage, flags missing, c1924, 35in (88cm) long, in original box.
$30,000-37,500

A tin tank with chain tracks and clockwork motor, British, c1916, 8in (20cm) long.
$75-150

A clockwork printed and painted tinplate beetle, EPL no.431, by Lehmann, c1906, damaged, 4in (10cm).
$300-400

A German painted tinplate clockwork fish, Bassett-Lowke by Bing, 'The Plunging Pike', 14in (35cm).
$450-600

A Carette clockwork tinplate 'Man of War' gunboat, German, c1905, 10in (25cm).
$1,500-2,600

A clockwork painted tinplate fish, by Bing, c1910, 9in (22cm).
$400-500

A scarce painted tinplate cat chasing a mouse, 'Nina', EPL no.790, by Lehmann, c1907, 11in (28cm).
$1,500-2,600

A Lehmann tinplate 'Zikra', c1915.
$250-350

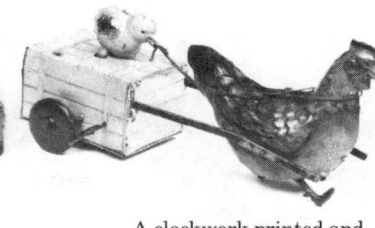

A clockwork printed and painted tinplate chicken, possibly French, one leg broken, c1910, 8in (20cm).
$150-250

A Lehmann clockwork tinplate 'Wild West Bucking Bronco', no.625.
$400-500

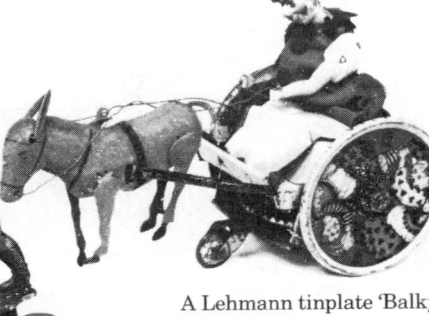

A Lehmann tinplate 'Balky Mule', c1912.
$250-350

A clockwork printed and painted tinplate beetle, EPL no.43, by Lehmann, legs missing, c1906, 4in (10cm).
$100-200

A spring-action tinplate 'Paddy and the Pig', possibly by Gebr Einfalt, 8in (19cm).
$450-700

A French clockwork nodding tiger, moving lower jaw, 19thC, 24in (60cm).
$600-900

A spring-action 'Paddy and the Pig', 5in (12cm).
$450-600

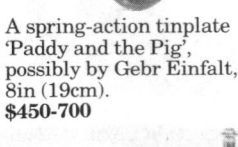

A painted cast iron horse-drawn sulky, USA, c1920, and painted wooden model of a two-horse trap.
$150-250

A tinplate brewing plant driven by a separate stationary spirit-fired engine, by Bing.
$4,000-5,500

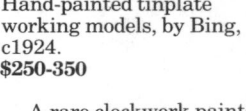

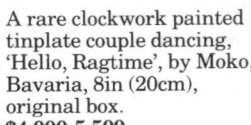

Hand-painted tinplate working models, by Bing, c1924.
$250-350

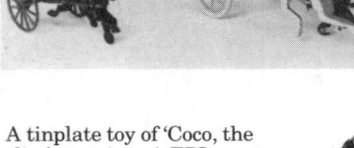

A tinplate toy of 'Coco, the climbing nigger', EPL no.185, by Lehmann, c1920, 16½in (41cm).
$700-900

A rare clockwork painted tinplate couple dancing, 'Hello, Ragtime', by Moko, Bavaria, 8in (20cm), original box.
$4,000-5,500

A lithographed tinplate clockwork 'Mickey Mouse Organ Grinder', with musical mechanisms, by Distler, some damage, c1930, 6in (15cm).
$1,000-1,400

A repainted blue Austin 'Pathfinder Special' racing car, British, lacks bumper, c1950, 63in (160cm).
$1,300-1,800

An Austin roadster pedal car, British, c1955, 64in (162.5cm).
$1,200-1,600

An Austin A40 pedal car.
$1,200-1,600

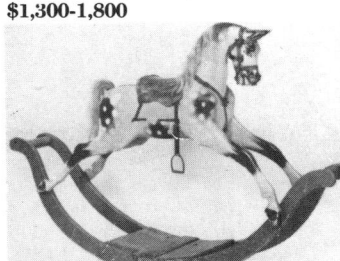

A Victorian rocking horse, 44in (111.5cm) high.
$1,500-2,600

A rocking horse, early 19thC, 48in (122cm).
$2,250-3,000

A Triang child's pedal racing car, windshield and steering wheel not original, 2 wheel hubs missing, 51in (129.5cm).
$750-1,000

A painted wood rocking horse, British, slightly overpainted, one handle missing, late 19thC, 40in (101.5cm).
$1,000-1,400

A carved and painted wood horse pull toy, painted in black, orange and silver, mounted on wooden base with wheels, wheels restored, 19thC, 11in (28cm) high.
$500-600

A carved wooden rocking horse, 19thC, 52in (132cm) high.
$1,500-2,600

A Victorian cast iron child's chain driven tricycle, 33in (84cm) long.
$900-1,300

A tin rocking horse, c1950, 35in (90cm) high.
$60-100

A rocking horse, c1930, 37in (94cm) long.
$150-200

A painted tinplate dolls pram, 6in (15cm) wide, another with blue hood and bedding, a metal folding push chair, and a bisque doll.
$450-700

A Victorian dolls pram, 39in (100cm) long.
$75-150

A Victorian pony skin covered horse on wooden base, with iron wheels, 6in (15cm) high.
$250-350

A German Noah's Ark, restored and repainted, c1870, 20½in (52cm) long.
$600-900

A painted wood Noah's Ark with 163 animals, probably made in Erzegebirge, Germany, c1870, 17in (43cm) long.
$1,500-2,600

A German carved and stained wood Noah's Ark with animals, some damage, c1880, 26in (66cm) long.
$900-1,300

A set of assorted farmyard animals.
$450-600

An Elastolin farm with animals.
$150-250

Assorted Britains Home Farm items, in original boxes.
$600-900

A Britains miniature garden.
$600-900

Ten Heyde farm workers, c1935, some damage, 4.5cm.
$150-200

A Taylor and Barrett and Timpo zoo.
$300-400

An Elastolin zoo, German, c1936.
$450-700

A painted carved wood stage coach, and 3 other coaches, by Erzegebirge, slight damage, c1920.
$75-150

A live steam spirit fired 4¾in (12cm) gauge brass model of the 2–2–2 locomotive and tender 'Express', by Steven's Model Dockyard, c1850, 30in (76cm) long.
$4,000-5,500

A 3¾in (9cm) gauge spirit fired brass model of the Great Northern Railway Stirling 2–4–0 locomotive and tender No.152, built by H J Wood, 35 Oxford St, London, late 19thC, 35in (90cm) long.
$2,250-3,000

A 3½in (8.5cm) gauge model of the Great Western Railway County class 4–6–0 locomotive and tender No.1022, 'County of Northampton', 47in (119cm) long.
$2,500-3,500

A 3½in (8.5cm) gauge model of the British Railways Class 7 4–6–2 locomotive and tender No.70013, 'Oliver Cromwell', by H C Luckhurst, Oxhey, 52½in (133cm) long.
$4,000-5,500

A 3½in (8.5cm) gauge model of the Southern Railway 0–4–2 side tank locomotive No.2036, built to the designs of Juliet by M Darlow, 1972, 21in (53cm).
$750-1,000

A 3¼in (8cm) gauge brass and steel spirit fired model 4–2–0 locomotive and tender, by H J Wood, London, late 19thC, 21½in (54cm).
$1,000-1,400

A gauge 1 London and North Western Railway twin bogie 1st/3rd class passenger coach, No.1322, by Carette for Bassett-Lowke, damage.
$300-400

A Bing candle lit signal box, No.60/630, boxed, and station indicator, and other pieces.
$75-150

A Hornby 3-rail boxed electric set, French factory Le Basque.
$250-350

A gauge 0 clockwork model of the GWR 4–4–0 locomotive and tender No.3433, 'George V', by Bing for Bassett-Lowke, with instructions.
$600-900

A Hornby gauge 0 'Cornish Riviera' electric trainset.
$1,200-1,600

A gauge 1 clockwork model of the LNWR 4–4–0 locomotive and tender No.266, 'George V', with original paintwork, by Bing for Bassett-Lowke, damage.
$750-1,000

A Bing gauge 1 four-wheeled baggage car, damage.
$250-350

A Bing spirit-fired 4–4–0 LNWR locomotive and tender No.1902, 1st/3rd bogie coach, mail van, and a quantity of rails.
$600-900

A Hornby gauge 0 electric model of the LNER E3/20 4–4–2 locomotive and tender No.4472, 'Flying Scotsman', with original paintwork.
$400-500

A Hornby gauge 0 clockwork model of the LMS No.2 special 4–4–2 'compound' locomotive and tender No.1185, in original boxes, pre-war.
$750-1,000

A Marklin clockwork 0–4–0 'Power Car'.
$600-900

A Hornby Pullman twin bogie coach, and 'Palethorpes' sausage van, c1939.
$300-400

A Marklin gauge 0 electric trainset, c1932.
$1,500-2,600

A Falk horizontal 'over type' stationary steam engine, c1912, 5½in (14cm) wide.
$400-500

A German tinplate model railway automaton locomotive and carriage on track, some damage, boxed, 14½in (36.5cm) long.
$100-200

An early Japanese tinplate Penny type train set.
$75-150

A Bowman live steam 0–4–0 locomotive model 300, boxed, 8½in (21.5cm) long, and a Meccano electric motor E06.
$75-150

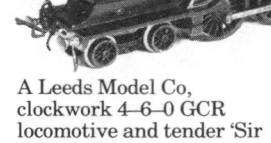

A Leeds Model Co, clockwork 4–6–0 GCR locomotive and tender 'Sir Sam Fay'.
$700-900

A Carette clockwork 4–4–0 L&NWR locomotive and tender No.513 'Precursor'.
$450-700

A carved and painted model of the paddle steamer 'City of Key West', with brown and white painted solid hull, inscribed 'City of Key West', re-rigged, American, 20thC, in wooden and glass case, 38in (96.5cm) long.
$1,200-1,500

A carved and painted model of the 'William Tapscot', with green and black painted solid hull, late 19thC, in a glass and mahogany case, 38in (96.5cm) long.
$1,500-2,000

A carved and painted model of the ocean liner 'Franconia', executed for the Cunard Lines, the white and red painted hull with portholes, in wooden and plexi-glass case, 49in (124.5cm) long.
$1,000-1,500

A carved and painted model of ocean liner 'Liberte', executed for the Companie Generale Transatlantique, the black painted hull with portholes, the deck with 27 ship's boats, funnels, 2 masts and 2 smokestacks, c1950, in wooden and plexi-glass case, 54in (137cm) long.
$6,000-7,000

A painted wooden and metal model of the 'Normandie', executed for the Companie Generale Transatlantique, with 2 plaques inscribed 'Normandie', 3 smokestacks and swimming pool, c1935, in wooden and glass case, 62½in (158cm) long.
$6,000-7,000

A carved and painted model of the schooner 'Dove', the plank on frame hull with copper sheathing, American, 20thC, in a glass and wooden case, 27in (68.5cm) long.
$700-900

A carved and painted model of the 'Royal Ark', by J R Whittemore, with white and brown painted solid hull, the beakhead with carved griffin figurehead, on a moulded wooden base, 43in (109cm) long.
$2,000-3,500

A carved and painted model of the 'Flying Cloud', by George K Meyer, with black and brown painted solid hull, the beakhead with carved figurehead, c1936, on a moulded walnut base, 37in (94cm) long.
$3,000-4,000

A carved and painted model of the runabout 'Javelin', the blue painted hull with single brass screw, white topsides, American, 20thC, in a glass and wooden case, 30in (76cm) long.
$600-800

An English barleycorn pattern ivory set, 19thC, king 5in (12.5cm).
$1,500-2,600

A Cantonese ivory chess set, probably 19thC, lances missing, king 8in (20cm).
$1,500-2,600

A leather boxed game of bézique, in gold trimmed leather case with ivory markers, 9in (23cm) wide.
$300-400

An Indian carved ivory chess set, king 7in (17cm), and a sandalwood and ivory inlaid chess and combined backgammon board.
$1,500-2,600

A rare game of 'Les Moulins', depicting an alpine stream running through a series of wheels.
$900-1,300

A game of quoits, depicting clergymen, huntsmen and naval officers, Bavarian, c1900.
$300-400

A mahogany shove ha'penny board with brass inlays, with hinged brass strips, 24in (61cm) long.
$100-200

A miniature billiard table, 20in (51cm) wide.
$1,000-1,400

A crib board made from a World War I rifle butt, standing on 3 bullet legs, silver plate trim, c1914, 12½in (30.5cm).
$150-250

Musical Instruments

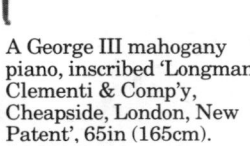
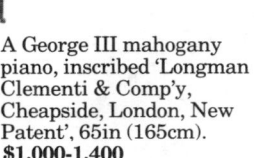

A George III mahogany piano, inscribed 'Longman Clementi & Comp'y, Cheapside, London, New Patent', 65in (165cm).
$1,000-1,400

A Steinway & Sons rosewood cased upright overstrung piano, No.157437.
$2,250-3,500

An English spinet, inscribed 'Baker Harris Londini Fecit 1766', in a mahogany case, 74in (188cm) wide, on contemporary Virginia walnut stand.
$24,000-27,000

A W Menzel secessionist piano, in a mahogany case, c1900, 49in (124cm) high.
$1,300-1,800

A game of Soccatelle, 24in (61cm) long.
$15-30

A C Bechstein concert grand pianoforte.
$2,500-3,500

A Bechstein boudoir grand piano, in ebonised case, No.79950, 72in (182.5cm).
$2,500-3,500

An Aeolian 58-note Orchestrelle, Model V No.7077, pressure type with 16 musical stops, 75in (190.5cm) wide, with stool.
$3,000-4,000

A French ten air penny-in-the-slot barrel-piano, by Simoens Lopez Rovbaix.
$2,250-3,000

A Reform Orgel disc-operated player reed organ by I P Nyström, Karlstad, lacks correct discs.
$600-900

A German portable barrel organ automaton, with retail label on mother-of-pearl engraved 'Dominick Bancalari, Proprietor, J. Hicks, Maker, Pentonville, London', mid-19thC, the plinth 26in (66cm) high.
$13,500-17,500

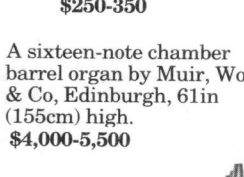

An Ariston organette, 15in (38cm) square, with cut card discs.
$250-350

A sixteen-note chamber barrel organ by Muir, Wood & Co, Edinburgh, 61in (155cm) high.
$4,000-5,500

An English violin, branded 'T. Jacques Holder', length of back 14in (35.5cm).
$2,500-3,500

An English violin, labelled 'Alfred Vincent, Maker 1923, 40 Gt. Pulteney St. Soho', with two-piece back, length of back 14in (35.5cm).
$4,000-5,500

An English violin, labelled 'Caressi, George Wulme-Hudson, fecit London 1926', length of back 14in (35.5cm).
$5,500-7,000

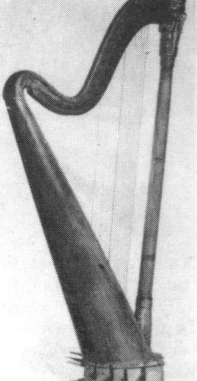

A French violin by Louis Guersan, labelled 'Ludovicus Guersan Prope Comoediam, Gallicam Lutetiae Anno 1787', with one piece back, length of back 14in (35.5cm).
$4,000-5,500

An Italian violin, attributed to Gaetano Sgarabotto, length of back 14in (35.5cm).
$4,000-5,500

A violin by Wolff Bros, with 2 bows.
$2,250-3,000

A concert size forty-three string harp with neo-classical decoration and fitted 7 brass pedals, by Muir Wood & Co Ed.
$750-1,000

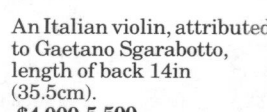
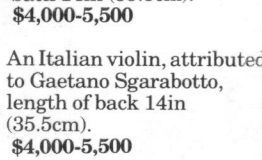

A French silver mounted violoncello bow, possibly Adam School, 73gm.
$1,500-2,600

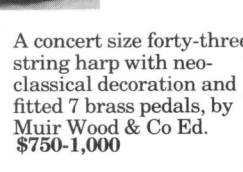
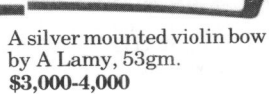

A silver mounted violin bow by A Lamy, 53gm.
$3,000-4,000

Musical Boxes

A three-bell musical box, playing 10 airs, 30in (76cm) high, the cylinder 6in (13cm).
$3,000-4,000

A 13⅝in (35cm) coin-slot wall hanging symphonion, with sublime harmony combs, 37½in (95cm) high, with 22 discs.
$3,000-4,000

A German polyphon musical box, model No.44, No.120224, imported by J H Ebblewhite, late 19thC, 19in (48cm) wide, and 62 discs.
$4,000-5,500

A 15⅝in (39.5cm) upright coin-in-slot polyphon, with 29 discs and disc bin stand, 73½in (186cm) high.
$5,500-7,000

A 24⅝in (62.5cm) upright coin-in-slot polyphon, lacking gallery, on disc bin stand with 33 discs, 75in (190.5cm) high.
$10,500-14,000

A 12in (30.5cm) symphonion disc musical box, with 100 metal discs.
$700-900

An Improved Celestina 20-note organette, with 3 rolls.
$1,200-1,600

A drum and bells-in-sight musical box, playing 12 airs, slight wear, 11in (28cm) cylinder, with key.
$1,500-2,600

A Swiss bells-in-sight cylinder musical box playing 8 airs on 3 bells, late 19thC, 6in (15cm) cylinder.
$450-700

A German symphonion, with two 4½in (11.5cm) combs, to play 10½in (26.5cm) diam discs, with key and winding handle and 25 discs.
$1,000-1,400

A concerto sublime harmony musical box, by F Conchon, Geneva, playing 12 airs, 16in (41cm) cylinder.
$4,000-5,500

A 'jeu des flutes' musical box, playing 6 airs accompanied by 17-key organ, 13in (33cm) cylinder.
$2,500-3,500

A Swiss musical box playing 6 airs, marked with initials JB to comb case, damage, 19thC, 28in (71cm) wide.
$4,000-5,500

Phonographs

An Edison phonograph, and collection of records.
$250-350

An Edison Gem phonograph in oak case.
$150-250

An Edison standard phonograph, 12½in (31.5cm) long, with cylinder records.
$300-400

A Thomas Edison phonograph, No.H203683, with a quantity of discs, early 20thC.
$300-400

An Edison standard phonograph, Model A No.S9665, with 10 brown wax blank cylinders, and an Edison Bell New Model reproducer.
$400-500

An Edison home phonograph, Model A No.H73313, the horn 30in (76cm) long.
$700-900

An Edison Model A home phonograph, with 5 cylinder records, 1901.
$450-600

A Columbia type BF 'Peerless' graphophone with 6in (15cm) mandrel, in oak case.
$600-900

Gramophones

A Gramophone Company double-spring Monarch horn gramophone with worm-drive motor, Exhibition soundbox.
$800-1,200

A Victor Gramophone by Gramophone & Typewriter Ltd, c1905, with 8in (20.5cm) turntable.
$750-1,000

A G & T single-spring Monarch gramophone, with later black Morning Glory horn, rusted, c1904, 24in (61cm) diam.
$600-900

A mahogany open pedestal gramophone with Apollo motor, Gramophone Co back bracket, 40½in (102cm) turntable height.
$400-500

An Apollo horn gramophone in mahogany case, soundbox replaced.
$1,300-1,800

A Pathéphone No.6 with oak case and brass flower horn, lacks reproducer, 17in (43cm) diam.
$700-900

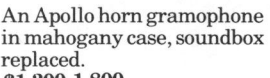

A French mahogany writing box, stamped twice Chapuis, early 19thC, 22in (56cm) wide.
$4,000-5,500

A rosewood sarcophagus shaped workbox, strung with boxwood and ebony, 12in (30.5cm) wide.
$250-350

A Regency rosewood workbox, 9in (23cm) wide.
$300-400

A Bohemian dated double overlay gilt metal mounted casket for the Persian market, c1848, 6in (15cm) wide.
$4,000-5,500

A rare painted bird's-eye maple box, the top decorated with a scene of a New England village and harbour, decorated on all 4 sides with painted flowers and fruit, the back signed, 'B. Freeman', above a verse, the interior divided into 2 compartments, on brass ball feet, Massachusetts, c1820, 9in (23cm) wide.
$5,500-6,500

A Viennese ebonised and enamel mounted table casket, with fitted interior, 13in (33cm) high.
$2,250-3,000

A silver mounted Batavian ivory and teak casket, with fitted interior, probably early 18thC, 18½in (47cm).
$5,500-7,000

A Batavian ivory and teak casket, the lid with contemporary coat-of-arms of the Duke of Newcastle, with fitted interior, probably mid-18thC, 19½in (49cm).
$7,500-10,500

An Ottoman marquetry wood casket, 18thC.
$1,200-1,600

A French carved walnut casket in the manner of Bagard of Nancy, late 17thC, 15½in (39cm).
$1,500-2,600

A brass mounted kingwood 'coffre fort', enclosing a fitted interior, late 17thC, 11½in (29cm) wide.
$1,200-1,600

A Regency penwork table cabinet, with fitted interior, 8in (20cm) wide.
$900-1,300

A Victorian walnut lap box with lift top and fall front, enclosing coromandel and satinwood interior, 14in (35.5cm) wide.
$750-1,000

An English oak salt box with brass hinge, c1790, 9in (23cm) high.
$150-200

A Victorian vanity box with silver and gilt fittings, dated 1878, 13in (33cm) wide.
$1,500-2,600

A French walnut brass mounted coach strongbox, 17thC, 11in (28cm).
$1,000-1,400

A Louis Vuitton travelling trunk, with rising top and fitted tray.
$750-1,000

A Swiss carved pine box in the form of a brown bear, late 19thC, 9½in (24cm) high.
$300-400

Enamel Miscellaneous

A Continental enamel snuff box, 18thC, 2½in (6cm) wide.
$2,250-3,000

A Continental enamel casket, probably German, c1750, 5in (12cm).
$1,500-2,600

An enamel cigarette box.
$5,500-7,000

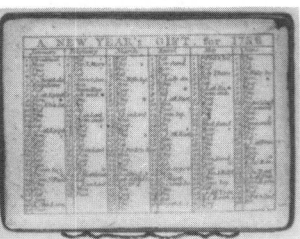

A George III enamel calendar snuff box, in the style of Anthony Tregent, dates for 1758, London, some damage, 3in (7.5cm) wide.
$1,300-1,800

An enamel and gilt metal mounted sweetmeat dish, 5in (12.5cm) diam.
$300-500

A Staffordshire enamel bird bonbonnière, probably Bilston, damaged, c1770, 3in (7.5cm) wide.
$2,500-3,500

A Viennese enamel coffee pot, by Christoph and Johann von Junger, c1770, 13½in (34cm).
$2,250-3,500

A German enamelled roundel with metal mount, Bohemia, 1692, 5½in (14.5cm) diam.
$1,000-1,400

A blue enamel easel photograph frame, by Hukin & Heath, Birmingham 1909, 5½in (14cm).
$400-500

A Limoges enamel plaque of Archbishop Fenelon, monogrammed IL, inscribed on the reverse 'Laudin Emailleur à Limoges IL 1694', in wooden frame, 4in (10.5cm).
$450-700

A South Staffordshire enamel bodkin case, with gilt metal mounts, c1770, 4½in (11.5cm).
$450-700

An enamelled nef, probably Viennese, 5in (12.5cm).
$800-1,200

Electrical
Radios

An early Marconi radio receiver, complete with headphones.
$450-600

An Addison and a Fada wireless, USA, c1935.
$1,000-1,400 each

A Gamage's Polaris Mediwaver single valve receiver.
$1,500-2,600

An early crystal receiver by Marconi's Wireless Telegraph Co Ltd, 12in (30.5cm).
$2,250-3,000

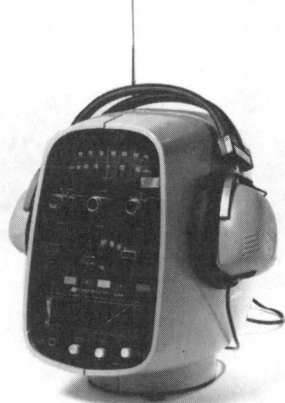

A Planetron radio and 8 track stereo, c1960.
$250-350

Miscellaneous

l. An early telephone with hand operated magnets, on black and gilt cast iron stand.
$150-200

r. An Ericson Telephones Ltd, telephone on stand, with gilt decoration.
$150-250

Typewriters

An American Hammond Number 1 typewriter.
$200-250

A typewriter by North's Typewriter Mfg Co Ltd, London, lacks one type bar.
$3,000-4,000

Transport

A 1934 MG Midget PA sports car.
$16,000-21,000

A 1951 Bentley-Mallalieu 2-door tourer.
$22,500-25,000

A 1926 Vauxhaull 14/40 4-door saloon, coachwork by Mulliner.
$10,500-14,000

A 1954 MG TF Midget 2-seater tourer in green.
$13,500-17,500

A 1933 Austin Seven 2-door saloon.
$5,500-7,000

An Alvis 12/70 touring car, 13.22hp, originally registered in 1939, for restoration.
$5,500-7,000

A 1938 Talbot-London 10 tourer, for restoration.
$1,000-1,400

A 1924/5 Indian Scout V-twin solo motorcycle.
$3,000-4,500

A 1909 Premier V-twin 499cc solo motorcycle.
$5,500-7,000

A 1961 Austin hearse.
$750-1,000

A 1922 Ariel sports 3½hp solo motorcylce.
$3,000-4,500

A 1925 model P Triumph 494cc motorcycle.
$2,250-3,000

An Ordinary bicycle, repaired, 54in (137cm) wheel.
$1,500-2,600

An Ordinary bicycle, lacking spoon brake, c1880, 51½in (130cm) wheel.
$1,500-2,600

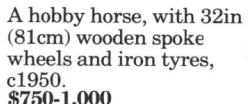

A hobby horse, with 32in (81cm) wooden spoke wheels and iron tyres, c1950.
$750-1,000

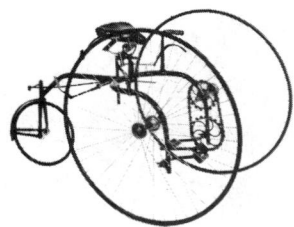

A Starley and Sutton Meteor rear steering tricycle, wheels respoked, c1882, rear wheel 18in (45.5cm).
$5,500-7,000

A 1928 Dennis 250/300 gallon turbine motor fire engine and ladder carrier, headlamps missing.
$6,000-8,000

A 1958 Bedford long chassis fire engine with Magirus hoist turntable and ladder, twin search lights and siren.
$3,000-4,500

A 1935 Morris 8cwt Post Office van.
$1,300-1,800

A baby pram in early caravan style.
$250-350

A hop picker's baby carriage, 46in (116.5cm) long.
$750-1,000

A baby carriage with maker's name plate attached, A. Mitchell, 21 Marine Drive, Margate, 31in (78cm) high.
$600-900

An Edwardian showman's caravan, by Walker Smith Jnr, Clapham Junction, London, chassis signed, with fitted interior, 144in (365cm).
$5,500-7,000

An A T Speedometer Co Ltd, Bentley 6½ or 8 litre speedometer, and an Elliot Bros Bentley rev counter.
$450-600

A motor racing trophy, Continental hallmarks, 8in (20cm) high.
$450-600

A silver cup and lid presented to the winner of a 15 mile road race 1891-1899, The Oldbury Cycling Club Championship cup, hallmarked Birmingham, 19½in (50cm) high.
$600-900

A Polkey brass fork fitting oil motorcar headlamp, c1900, 15½in (40cm) high.
$450-600

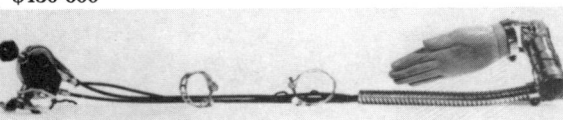

A chromium plated automatic traffic warner, inscribed Birglow Auto Signal, 42in (106.5cm) long.
$250-350

A silver trophy, presented by B Muratti Sons & Co Ltd, to the Ulster Centre of the Motor Cycle Union of Ireland, Sheffield, 1904, 34in (86cm) high.
$21,000-24,000

An unnamed Scottish pirn,
Perth, 18thC.
$150-250

An early Victorian
unnamed brass reel with
sliding handle lock, 2in
(5cm) diam.
$60-100

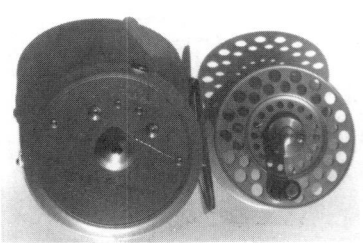

A Hardy featherweight fly
reel, 3in (7.5cm).
$45-70

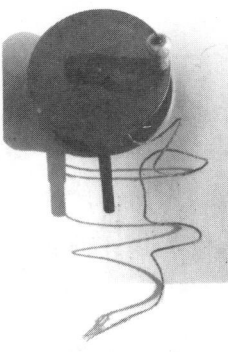

A Victorian unnamed spike
reel, with brass crank
handle, 3in (7.5cm) and
linen mixed with horsehair
line.
$75-150

An aluminium Fraser-
Killian NEO Caster level
wind reel, by Remploy,
c1955, 3in (7.5cm).
$25-35

A collection of fishing reels:

l. Blued brass, 3in (7.5cm)
diam.
$30-50

c. Wood and brass, 4½in
(11.5cm) diam.
$45-70

r. Wood and brass, 3½in
(8cm) diam.
$30-50

An American fixed spool
reel, Holliday 30, c1960.
$15-30

A level wind multiplying
bait casting reel, ABU of
Sweden, c1964.
$25-35

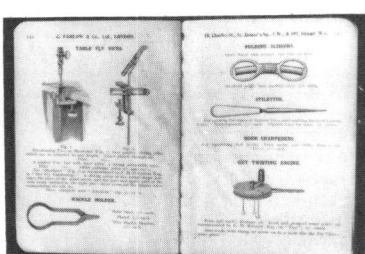

A Farlow catalogue,
slightly damaged, c1909.
$30-50

A Turnbull's of Edinburgh
fishing tackle catalogue,
1928.
$25-35

A box of 'Killer' Nature flies
by Thomas Murdoch of
Redditch, c1938.
$25-35

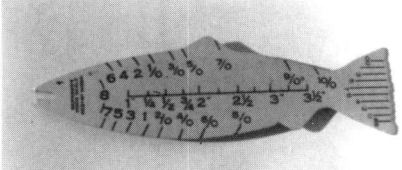

A Bernard's of London
xylonite fish-shaped device
for measuring the size of
salmon and trout flies.
$15-30

A Cummins of Bishop
Auckland boxed silver quill
minnow.
$15-30

A Hardy brass rod butt
spear.
$15-30

A Royal Doulton stoneware loving cup, the lip mounted in silver, chips and restoration, 6½in (17cm).
$450-600

A miniature portrait, signed A Howard, the case containing locks of hair and the reverse inscribed 'E.E. Leatham 1890', damage, 7cm, with fitted case.
$300-400

A Copeland blue ground pottery jug, with moulded rugby football scenes, 7½in (19.5cm).
$250-350

A cast iron W G Grace pub table, repainted.
$600-900

Twelve enamelled metal Robertson's 'golliwog' batsmen lapel badges for Surrey.
$250-350

A decorative cast iron umbrella stand, inscribed 'Footballer', 33½in (85cm).
$450-600

A large bronze figure of a footballer, 'The Left Winger', signed and dated WAL. LAW 1929, 24½in (62cm).
$2,250-3,500

A 9ct gold and coloured enamel Derby County Football League Division II Champions medal for 1911-12, inscribed to E. Scattergood.
$600-900

A George III Pontefract race ticket, dated 1803.
$300-500

A late Victorian silver and gold brooch, 2in (5cm).
$400-500

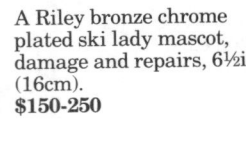

A Riley bronze chrome plated ski lady mascot, damage and repairs, 6½in (16cm).
$150-250

A collection of 3 painted decoy ducks, 13 to 14in (33 to 35.5cm) long.
$150-250

Golfing

An electroplated desk stand, by Walker & Hall, Sheffield, c1890.
$400-500

A Royal Doulton pottery
jug, 9in (23cm).
$400-500

A Copeland Spode jug, the
dark blue ground decorated
in white relief with golfers,
6in (15cm).
$600-900

A papier mâché figure of the
'Dunlop Man', 16in
(40.5cm).
$400-500

A papier mâché figure of the
'Penfold Man', repaired,
21in (53.5cm).
$250-350

A silver medal, inscribed
'Thistle Golf Club', and on
the reverse 'Winter Prize
Medal, played for over Leith
Links on 7th December,
1822, and won by Geo.
Logan Esq., W.S., Mark
Sprot, Esq., of Garnkirk,
Captain', 4cm wide.
$1,500-2,600

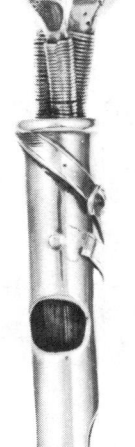

A silver cigar cutter in the
form of a golf bag containing
3 clubs, 3in (7.5cm).
$750-1,000

A feather golf ball,
unnamed, c1840.
$1,500-2,600

An Osmond's Patent caddy
automaton, a mashie golf
club and 2 golf balls, c1893.
$400-500

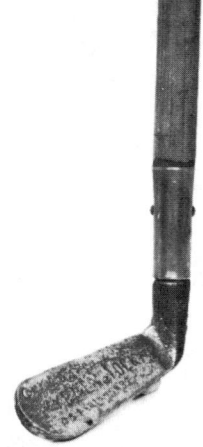

A Patent golf club with
bamboo shaft, the head
stamped C. Cooper,
Hyhenstock, Reg. Patent
15892, c1925.
$60-100

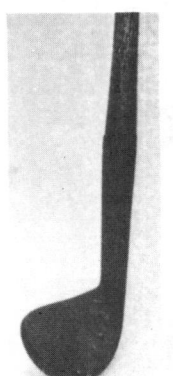

A smooth faced track iron,
the shaft stamped
Hutchison and M.B., c1860.
$450-600

Crafts

An earthenware rhyme
tankard, by Michael
Cardew, covered in a
mustard yellow slip, carved
with inscription, impressed
MC and St Ives seal.
$300-500

An unusual Abuja
stoneware casserole and
cover, by Michael Cardew,
c1960, 12½in (31.5cm).
$1,300-1,800

An oak framed dinner gong,
the base with an
electroplated plaque
inscribed 'The Captains
Prize 1892, County Down
Golf Club'.
$1,200-1,600

A pottery bowl, by Gertrud and Otto Natzler, in a heavy bittersweet orange glaze, painted Natzler, 3½in (8.5cm) diam.
$1,000-1,500

A pottery bowl, by Gertrud and Otto Natzler, in thick sea green glaze, painted by Natzler, 5in (13cm) diam.
$1,500-2,000

A pottery luminaire, by Ka-Kwong Hui, with chalice form body in black having 2 rows of blue hanging beads, with orange side handles and yellow broken pediment enclosing red light bulb, unsigned, c1980, 22in (56cm) high.
$2,500-3,000

A pottery set, comprising 77 pieces, in mustard coloured glaze, most pieces impressed Russel Wright MFG. by Steubenville, the largest 11in (28cm) high.
$450-550

A pottery bowl, by Gertrud and Otto Natzler, in deep blue crystalline glaze with swirls of paler glaze, painted Natzler, 6in (16.5cm) diam.
$3,000-3,500

An earthenware vase, by Maija Grotell, in an irregular ochre brown glaze with a dark brown rim inscribed Mg CA, 5in (12.5cm) diam.
$1,000-1,200

A stoneware jar, by Charles Vyse, covered in a greyish green glaze inlaid in white clay, incised CV 1928, 6½in (17cm).
$300-400

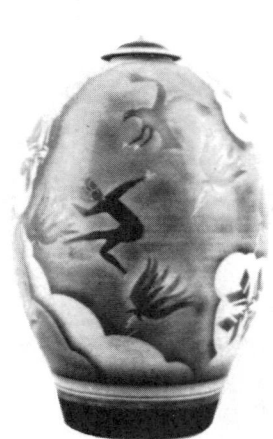

Miller's is a price Guide not a price List

The price ranges given reflect the average price a purchaser should pay for similar items. Condition, rarity of design or pattern, size, colour, pedigree, restoration and many other factors must be taken into account when assessing values.

A pottery covered jar, by J Davis, the pink/grey ground decorated with figure in landscape being pursued by a bird, marked S, 15½in (39cm) high.
$400-600

A pottery sculpture, by Ka-Kwong Hui, the blue hourglass body with twin yellow arched handles and cornice of 3 red rings flanked by blue vertical appendages, unsigned, c1980, 23in (58cm) high.
$3,000-3,500

An earthenware motto tankard, by Michael Cardew, with inscription, impressed MC and St Ives.
$300-400

An earthenware cider flagon, by Michael Cardew, c1970, 15½in (39cm).
$1,500-2,600

A laminated porcelain bowl, by Marian Gaunce, in light blue, purple and black bands, with white rim, 4in (10cm).
$450-600

A stoneware vase by Seth Cardew, covered with olive green and olive brown glaze, impressed SC and Wenford Bridge seals, c1984, 24in (61cm).
$450-600

A Raku roughly potted jar and cover, by Keiko Hasegawa, 8in (20cm).
$600-900

A stoneware jug, by Bernard Leach, covered in a mottled brown and olive green glaze, impressed BL and St Ives seal, 11½in (29cm).
$750-1,000

A stoneware oviform vase, by David Leach, covered in a rich tenmoku glaze with russet brown scrolls, impressed DL seal, 17½in (44.5cm).
$300-500

A porcelain bottle vase, by Lucie Rie, covered in a thick matt manganese glaze thinning in places to reveal white body, impressed LR seal, c1957, 8in (20cm).
$1,200-1,600

A stoneware teapot and cover, by Lucie Rie, covered in a matt manganese glaze, with cane handle, impressed LR seal, c1955, 6in (15cm).
$750-1,000

A stoneware bottle, by the Mashiko School, decorated in wax resist through an iron brown glaze with brushwork on a buff ground, 8½in (21.5cm).
$100-150

Tribal Art

A Solomon Islands wood bowl, the rim with a band of shell inlays of serrated triangles, the handle at each end carved as a frigate bird, 17½in (44cm).
$450-600

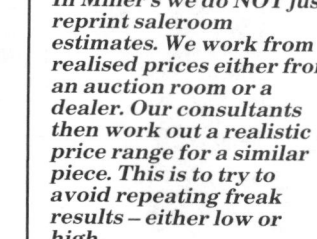

A Maori wood feather box, with a mask at each end, the lid ornamented with a reclining Tiki figure, 12½in (32cm) long.
$1,000-1,400

Four George III entrée dishes and covers, by Paul Storr, 1814, one dish repaired, plated stands by Matthew Boulton, 11in, 281oz. **$33,000-37,000**

A George III tureen and stand, the tureen with engraved coat of arms and presentation inscription on the reverse, by Robert Sharp, 1802, 18in (45cm) wide, 172oz. **$10,500-14,000**

A William IV centrepiece, with presentation inscription and coat of arms, by Benjamin Smith, 1836, 25in high, 421oz. **$10,500-14,000**

A George III Irish epergne, engraved with a coat of arms and motto, by Thomas Jones, Dublin, 1789, 17½in (44.5cm) high, 180oz. **$33,000-37,000**

l. A rare can, by John Coney, Boston, c1700, repaired, 4in high, 6oz. **$21,000-24,000**

r. A rare spout cup, by Edward Winslow, Boston, c1710, repaired, 3in high, 4oz. **$21,000-24,000**

A Charles II tankard, maker's mark only, c1670, 8in (20cm) high, 37oz. **$9,000-12,000**

A George III tureen and cover, the raised cover with beaded border and serpent and foliage handle, engraved twice with crest and motto, by Paul Storr, 1807, 13in (176oz). **$33,000-37,000**

A magnificent George II epergne, by Paul de Lamerie, c1738, the feet with maker's mark of John S Hunt, c1846, 14in (36cm) high overall, central dish 14in (35cm) wide, 301oz. **$1,275,000+**

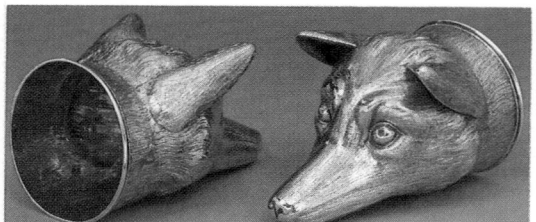

A pair of George III fox mask stirrup cups, each with realistically chased fur, engraved with the crest of Dutton, by Peter and Anne Bateman, 1805, 5in (13cm) wide, 16oz 11dwt. **$16,500-19,500**

A teapot on moulded circular foot, one side later engraved with initials 'HHD', base engraved 'IEL', by Peter Van Dyck, New York, c1730, 8in (20cm) high, 25oz. **$97,000-127,000**

A fine sauceboat, on 3 scroll legs with fluted shell feet, by John Coburn, Boston, c1750, slight damage, marked 'I. Coburn' on base, 8½in (21.5cm) wide, 14oz. **$19,500-22,500**

A set of 2 George II tea caddies and matching sugar box, by Aymé Videau, 1749, contained in later George III satinwood and tulipwood box, sugar box 4½in (11cm) high, 48oz. **$13,500-17,500**

A fine engraved snuff box, marked on inside of base, by Bartholomew Schaats, New York, c1720, 3in (7cm) long, 2oz. **$18,000-21,000**

A George II inverted pear-shaped tea kettle, stand and lamp, engraved with a coat of arms within scroll cartouche, by William Cripps, 1749, the stand unmarked, 16in (40cm) high overall, 92oz. **$13,500-17,500**

A set of 4 George III table candlesticks, by Thomas Hannam and John Crouch, 1766, 11in (28cm) high, 96oz. **$10,500-14,000**

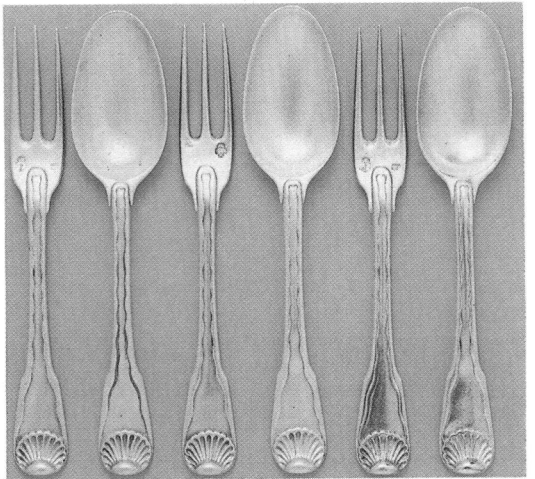

Twelve George II fiddle and shell pattern
dessert forks and 6 matching spoons, by
Paul de Lamerie, c1740, most maker's marks
overstruck with that of James Shruder, 27oz.
$22,500-25,000

A George II coffee pot, the body finely
chased, engraved with a coat of arms
within a scroll cartouche, by Samuel
Courtauld, 1753, 10½in (26.5cm) high,
40oz. **$37,000-40,000**

A George II shaped circular salver,
on 3 foliage and scroll feet, with
shell and scroll border, engraved
with a coat of arms and motto,
within rococo cartouche, by John
Swift, 1751, 23in (58cm), 136oz.
$9,000-12,000

A set of 4 George III candlesticks, with fluted
stems and detachable nozzles, by John Scofield,
1788, 12in (30cm) high, 72oz. **$15,000-21,000**

Two English silvered bronze groups of jockeys
on horseback, cast from models by John Willis
Good, signed and dated 1875.

l. 10½in (27cm) high. **$4,500-7,000**

r. 13in (32.5cm) high. **$4,000-5,500**

A fine dressing glass, the bevelled mirror plate
set into a conforming frame chased with scrolls
and flowers in the rococo taste, the mirror frame
tilting between spiral-twisted supports, engraved
inscription 'M.L. Vanderbilt 1887' on the reverse,
by Howard & Co New York, 1884, 30in (76cm) wide.
$18,000-21,000

A teapot, by William Will, Philadelphia, 1764-98, with later carved wood handle, minor repair to hinge, marked on inside with Laughlin touches 538 and 539, crowned X and name touch, 6in (15cm). **$25,000-28,000**

A set of 4 Louis XVI ormolu mounted mottled marble vases, c1780, 23in (58cm) high. **$40,000-45,000**

A George II silver gilt dressing table mirror, the frame engraved with a coat-of-arms, by Edward Feline, 1750, 24in (61cm), 62oz. **$27,000-30,000**

A Louis XV gold snuff box, chased in 3 colour gold, by Jean Baptiste Carnay, Paris, c1765, 3½in (8.5cm). **$10,500-14,000**

A pair of George III ormolu bronze and white marble cassolettes, 10in (25cm). **$6,000-9,000**

A pair of late Louis XVI ormolu mounted covered urns, possibly Russian, 17½in (44cm). **$10,500-14,000**

A gold and enamel box, by Pierre Francois Delafons, c1840, 3in (8cm). **$18,000-21,000**

A garniture of 3 ormolu mounted Kangxi black-glazed vases, the ormolu Regency, 22½ and 18½in high. **$75,000-90,000**

A pair of Louis XV style ormolu mounted Chinese porcelain vase candelabra, porcelain early Qianlong, mounts c1830, restored. **$33,000-37,000**

An ormolu mounted gros bleu Sèvres candelabrum, on stepped square base, 34½in (88cm) high. **$10,500-14,000**

Two ormolu mounted porphyry pot pourri vases,

l. 11½in (29.5cm) high. **$13,500-17,500**

r. 13in (33cm) high. **$9,000-12,000**

A pair of Louis XV ormolu mounted Chinese porcelain vases, porcelain Qianlong, 10½in. **$13,500-17,500**

A pair of Empire style malachite and ormolu obelisks, late 19thC, 34in (88cm) high. **$6,000-9,000**

A Louis XV ormolu mounted porphyry cache-pot, mid-18thC, 11½in (29cm) high. **$13,500-17,500**

A Regency ormolu and ebonised inkstand, with 2 cut glass wells flanking a taperstick with snuffer, two pen trays and foliate gadrooned border, the sides mounted with lion mask ring handles, claw feet, 13½in (34cm).
$10,500-14,000

An ormolu mounted malachite jewel casket, lined in blue silk, 19thC, 10in (25.5cm).
$10,500-14,000

A pair of Empire ormolu and patinated bronze candelabra, early 19thC, 36½in (92.5cm).
$15,000-21,000

A pair of Empire ormolu candelabra, with classical female figure stems, the scrolled branches with foliate drip pans, on cylindrical bases cast with ozier-work and square plinths, 35½in (90cm).
$10,500-14,000

A pair of Louis XVI ormolu mounted Chinese porcelain ornaments, the porcelain Kangxi, 8in (20cm).
$45,000-49,000

A pair of Louis XVI ormolu and bronze candelabra, on white fluted marble plinths, and square bases, 19in (48cm). **$7,500-10,500**

A set of 4 Empire ormolu wall lights, each with backplate cast with anthemia and central rosette, early 19thC, 21in (53cm). **$15,000-21,000**

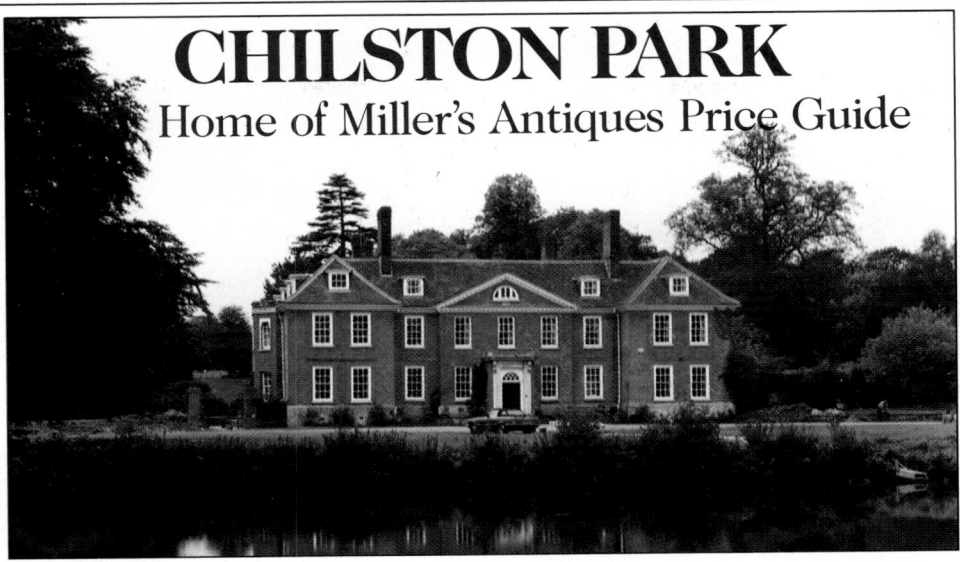

A pair of Louis XVI ormolu and bronze candelabra, 19in (48cm). **$10,500-14,000**

A pair of Regency ormolu wine coolers, after a design by J J Boileau, inscribed, alterations, c1895, 11½in (29cm). **$60,000-64,500**

A pair of Empire ormolu wall lights, the backplates with Apollo masks, fitted for electricity, 5½in (14cm) wide. **$1,300-1,800**

A Louis Philippe ormolu mounted marble and biscuit de Sèvres surtout de table. **$22,500-25,000**

A pair of Louis XVI ormolu wall lights, fitted for electricity, late 18thC, 22in (56cm) high. **$19,500-24,000**

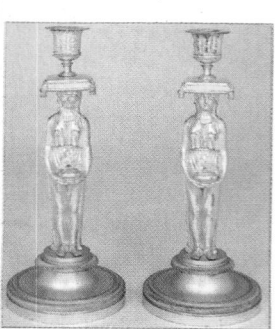

A pair of ormolu candlesticks, Thomas Hope style, 11in (28cm). **$4,500-7,000**

A pair of Louis XVI wall lights. **$13,500-17,500**

A pair of George III ormolu candelabra, Vulliamy style, engraved with coats-of-arms, 24in (61cm). **$10,500-14,000**

A pair of Regency ormolu wall lights, Thomas Hope style, 18in (46cm) high. **$19,500-24,000**

A pair of ormolu chenets, each with a bearded merman blowing a conch, on pierced scrolling foliate rockwork base, 16½in (42cm). **$18,000-21,000**

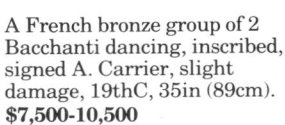

A French bronze group of 2 Bacchanti dancing, inscribed, signed A. Carrier, slight damage, 19thC, 35in (89cm). **$7,500-10,500**

An Empire ormolu and patinated bronze 20-light chandelier, fitted for electricity, early 19thC, 41in (104cm) wide. **$15,000-21,000**

An Italian bronze figure of a man on a rearing horse, he separately cast, the rough cast left unfinished, 16thC. **$13,500-17,500**

A French bronze model of a stag, signed Isidore Bonheur and dated 1893, stamped Peyrol, and inscribed Boudet 43 B^D Des Capucines, 32½in (82cm) wide. **$13,500-17,500**

A neo-classical ormolu and ruby glass 6-light chandelier, Swedish or Russian, 26in (66cm) high. **$13,500-17,500**

A pair of Régence patinated bronze and ormolu chenets, of Venus and Vulcan, early 18thC, 15in (38cm). **$10,500-14,000**

A brass 6-branch chandelier, with
gadrooned multi-baluster shaft and
scrolled branches, fitted for
electricity, 17thC, 20in (51cm).
$6,000-8,000

A French bronze group, from model by Jean-Jacques, signed
J. Pradier, c1850, 33in (84cm). **$9,000-12,000**

A French bronze statuette of
Phryne, from a model by
P E D Campagne, patina
slightly rubbed, late 19thC,
34in (85cm).
$9,000-12,000

A French bronze
statuette of
Apollo standing
on a dragon, with
Boulle base, 19thC,
32½in (82cm).
$4,500-7,000

A French statue of
Diana the Huntress,
by Marius-Jean-
Antonin Mercié,
base signed Mercié,
inscribed Epreuve
Unique, and stamped
Siot. Fonduer, Paris,
late 19th/early 20thC,
44in (111cm).
$15,000-21,000

A French bronze statuette of Diana,
signed Denécheau, patina rubbed,
plinth chipped, late 19thC, 23½in
(60cm). **$7,500-10,500**

A French bronze statue of
the Neapolitan fisherboy,
signed J.B. Carpeaux, c1900.
$10,500-14,000

A French ivory and gilt bronze
statuette of Fame, signed E. Barrias,
inscribed and stamped Susse Freres
seal, c1900. **$13,500-17,500**

An English copper electrotype bust of Eliza Macloghlin, cast by Albert Toft, from a model by Sir Alfred Gilbert, the back signed, dated and inscribed Eliza Macloghlin/ 1906i/Alfred Gilbert Bruges/ Eheu Fugaces!, marble plinth, early 20thC, 16in (40.5cm).
$18,000-22,500

A pair of mid-Victorian brass andirons, in the style of A W N Pugin, 38in (96.5cm) high.
$18,000-22,500

A rare ordos metal figure of a walking horse, some repair, 4th-3rd Century BC, 10in (25cm) long. **$7,500-10,500**

An early bronze tripod pouring vessel, some repair, six Dynasties, 8in (20cm) high.
$33,000-37,000

A fine archaic bronze gui, Transitional Shang/ Zhou Dynasty, 11th-10th Century BC, 10½in (26cm) wide. **$10,500-14,000**

An English brass doorway, the double doors attached by hinges on steel poles to the ajouré surround, with glass panes, late 19thC, 94in (238cm) high. **$25,000-28,000**

An early bronze deep tripod food bowl and cover, Warring States, damage, six-character dedicatory inscription, 9½in (24cm) diam.
$45,000-52,000

619

A gilt bronze figure of the Buddha Vairocana, Liao Dynasty, 6½in (17cm). **$16,500-19,500**

A Northern Wei gilt bronze figure of a Boddhisattva, inscribed and dated for AD 512, 7in (17.5cm). **$52,000-60,000**

A gilt bronze mirror, the face and rim not gilt, and with malachite encrustation, Han Dynasty, 3½in (9cm). **$19,500-22,500**

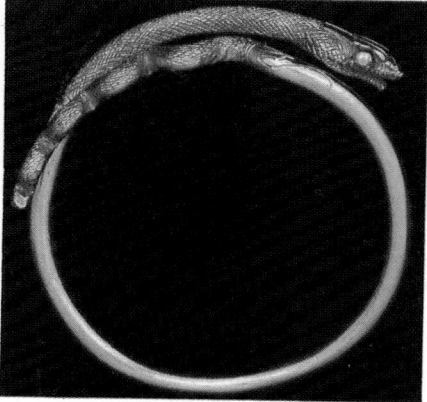

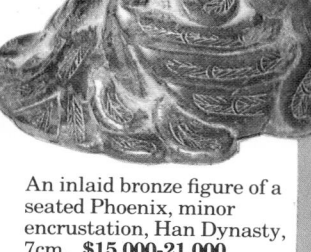

An inlaid bronze figure of a seated Phoenix, minor encrustation, Han Dynasty, 7cm. **$15,000-21,000**

An Egyptian solid gold snake bracelet, Romano-Egyptian, 150g. **$27,000-30,000**

A gilt bronze figure of Avalokitesvara, some surface rubbing, 6th-7th Century AD, 12cm. **$6,000-9,000**

An English marble group of a King Charles Spaniel watching a cat, by Joseph Gott, signed and dated on the edge of the base J. Gott. Rome. 1826., on a separate, matching marble plinth, slightly weathered and chipped around edges, early 19thC, 26in (66cm). **$4,500-7,000**

An American marble bust of Diana, by Hiram Powers, signed on the back, repairs and minor abrasions, mid-19thC, 29½in (75.5cm). **$15,000-21,000**

A pair of marble allegorical statues of day and night, chipped, 19thC. **$27,000-36,000**

A marble figure of Minerva, by Rombout Verhulst, the base incised R. Verhulst Fec Anno, c1650, 8in (20cm). **$9,000 - 15,000**

An American marble bust of Psyche, by Hiram Powers, truncated below her breasts with a foliate and beaded moulding, signed underneath the back of the moulding H. Powers. Sculp, mid-19thC, 19in (48.5cm). **$13,500-17,500**

An English marble statue of Sabrina, by Holme Cardwell, the base signed Holme Cardwell Fecit Roma 1856, on marble plinth, 40in (101cm). **$22,500-25,000**

A rare French marble group of Venus with Cupid asleep in her lap, the base signed A. Carrier-Belleuse, damage, 19thC, 22in (56cm). **$25,000-28,000**

An Indian white marble throne bench, the arched back and scrolled sides pierced with lattice work and geometric designs, 19thC, possibly Jaipur, 67½in (171cm). **$9,000-12,000**

A stone figure of 'Prometheus Bound' in the manner of Cibber, soft sandy stone, some weathering, English, late 17thC, 69in (175cm). **$18,000-21,000**

A Carrara marble figure of a girl, the base signed Heinrich Imhof Fec Roma 1844, damage, 63½in (161cm). **$21,000-24,000**

An early limestone head of a youthful Buddha, c570, 9in (23cm). **$52,000-60,000**

A pair of Italian parcel gilt and polychrome torchères, on plinth bases inscribed 'rancesco de marco vietro', lacking wings, 17thC, 48in (122cm). **$10,500-14,000**

A marble statuette of a jester, probably Yorick, by Sarah Bernhardt, signed and dated 1877, damage, 17in (43.5cm). **$34,000-39,000**

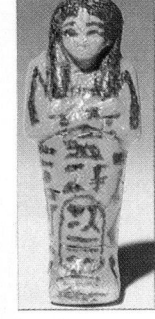

A glazed composition royal shabti of Queen Henutowy, Dynasty XXI, from the Deir el Bahri cache, 12cm. **$2,250-3,500**

A pair of Italian marble busts of maidens representing Spring and Autumn, signed A. Bottinelli Roma, inscribed, damaged, 19thC, the largest 30½in (77.5cm). **$10,500-14,000**

A large blue-john bowl, with well marked body, on hardwood stand, 14in (35.5cm) diam.
$6,000-9,000

An Apulian loutrophoros, by the School of Varrese Painter, repaired, 4th Century BC, 37in (94cm).
$30,000-37,500

A blue-john cup, with deep circular bowl, ring turned shaft and stepped base, 10in (26.5cm) high.
$7,500-10,500

A Mesopotamian steatopygous female idol, the eyes inlaid with shell, one missing, 3½in (9cm), and an alabaster elipsoid jar, 1½in (4cm), 6th Millennium BC.
$10,500-14,000

A blue and white glazed composition pectoral, in the form of a shrine, repaired, early Dynasty XIX, 4 by 3½in (10 by 8.5cm).
$18,000-21,000

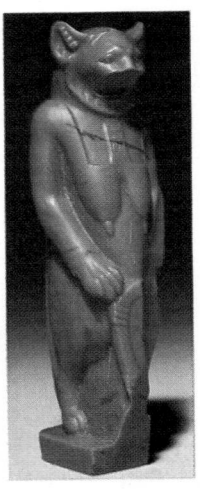

An Egyptian red granite head of a king, wearing nemes headdress, restored, 4th-3rd Century BC, 14½in (36.5cm).
$30,000-37,500

A red jasper syncretistic statuette of Tueris, 6th-4th Century BC, 7.5cm.
$22,500-27,000

A polychromed terracotta figure of a matron, Tang Dynasty, 14½in (36.5cm).
$42,000-51,000

l. and r. A pair of George III ormolu and blue-john brûle-parfums, by Matthew Boulton, 10in (25cm) high. **$10,500-14,000** and c. A Regency blue-john tazza, 7in (18cm) diam. **$6,000-8,000**

An archaic jade disc, bi, the rim with a slightly recessed flange possibly to take a metal rim, minor surface degradation, late Eastern Zhou Dynasty/Warring States, 9.5cm diam, fitted box. **$40,000-45,000**

Silver mounted blue-john solid urns, l. & r. 10in (25cm). **$3,000-4,000** lc. & rc. 13in (33cm). **$7,500-10,500** and c. 11in (28cm). **$1,500-2,600**

A pair of George III ormolu and blue-john candle vases, attributed to Matthew Boulton, 9in (23cm). **$13,500-17,500**

A Viennese ivory and enamel casket, the pediment centred by a watch movement clock, the concave-sided spreading frieze inlaid with jewelled appliqués, 19thC, 15½in (39cm) high. **$4,500-7,000**

A Dieppe troubadour style ivory tabernacle with paintings, on wooden carcase, damage, 19thC, 40 by 32½in. **$10,500-14,000**

George III ormolu and blue-john vases by Matthew Boulton, 12in (30.5cm). **$13,500-17,500**

A Russian neo-classical carved ivory dressing glass, late 18thC, 26in (66cm) high. **$15,000-21,000**

A mid-Victorian black japanned papier mâché tray, with raised rolled gallery centred by a bouquet of roses, camellias and fuchsias, in a mother-of-pearl heightened bowl, surrounded by fruiting vines and exotic flowers, 24½ by 30½in (62 by 77cm). **$4,000-5,500**

An early Victorian bronzed japanned papier mâché tray, with a shepherdess and lamb with a young man and his dog, the gallery painted with entrelac foliage, 15 by 19½in (38 by 50cm). **$2,250-3,000**

An early Victorian black, gilt and mother-of-pearl japanned papier mâché tray, stamped Jennens & Bettridge, Makers to the Queen, beneath a crown, 25½ by 32½in (64.5 by 82cm). **$3,000-4,000**

A mid-Victorian black, gilt and mother-of-pearl japanned papier mâché tray with gallery, stamped with mark of William Whiteley, and 6th March 1875. **$4,000-5,500**

A mid-Victorian black and gilt japanned papier mâché tray, the centre with a picture of the 'Queen's favourites' after Landseer, 27½ by 34½in (70 by 87cm). **$7,500-10,500**

A George III giltwood and papier mâché frame, by Thomas Chippendale, with a collage of Chinese wallpaper, damaged, 36½ by 47½in (92 by 120cm). **$13,500-17,500**

l. A Fereghan rug, very minor repairs, 76 by 58in
(193 by 147cm). **$9,000-12,000**

r. A Beshir carpet, damage and repair, 136 by 69in
(344 by 175cm). **$9,000-12,000**

l. An Aydin kilim, in 2 parts, joined, small
repairs, 194 by 73in (492 by 185cm).
$6,000-9,000

r. A Konya part cotton kilim, in 2 parts, joined,
repaired, 151 by 70in (385 by 178cm).
$3,000-4,000

An Agra carpet, 177 by 141in (450 by 360cm).
$7,500-10,500

An Agra carpet, 131 by 130in (335 by 330cm).
$15,000-21,000

A Tadouk style medallion Ushak rug,
144 by 105 in (365 by 268cm).
$9,000-12,000

A Kuba rug, with a kilim
strip at each end, 90 by
47in (228 by 119cm).
$7,500-10,500

A silk and metal thread
Koum Kapu prayer rug,
signed Zare Agha, 63 by
40in (160 by 102cm).
$37,000-45,000

A Louis Philippe Aubusson carpet, with a central spray of flowers within a foliate cartouche, 181 by 300in (460 by 769cm). **$13,500-17,500**

A Chondzoresk Karabagh rug, worn, part border missing, 77 by 63in (196 by 160cm). **$1,000-1,400**

An Afshar triclinium carpet, repairs, 199 by 120in (505 by 304cm). **$6,000-9,000**

An Aubusson carpet, restored, 19thC, 114 by 154in. **$4,500-7,000**

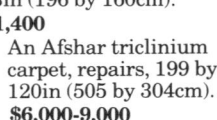

A Qum garden rug, 86 by 56in (218 by 142cm). **$1,500-2,600**

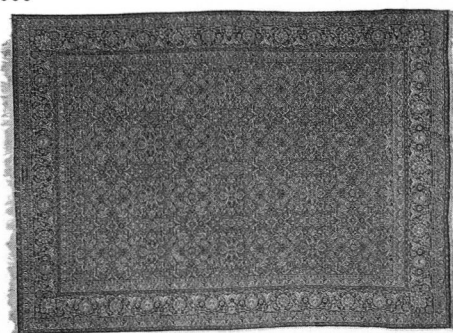

A Kashan carpet, with inscription panel dated in Arabic 1300 and signed Safarzadeh Kashani, 168 by 125in (428 by 320cm). **$10,000-13,000**

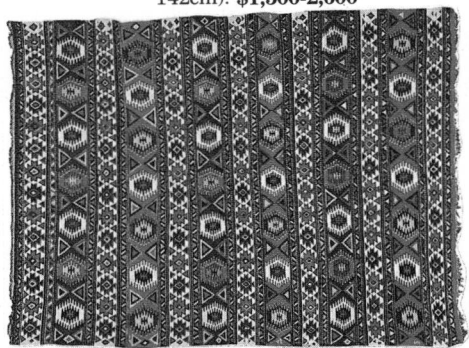

A Verneh, small tears, field backed, 78in (198cm) square. **$13,500-17,500**

A Caucasian kilim, 110 by 81in (279 by 206cm). **$4,500-7,000**

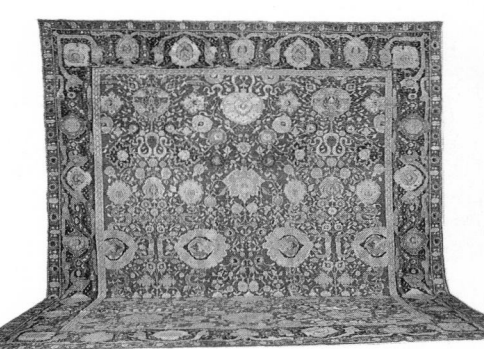

A Tabriz carpet, with indigo border between blue and ivory flowering stripes, 196 by 148in (497 by 375cm). **$9,000-12,000**

An Indo-Isfahan carpet, slight wear and small old repairs, 186 by 166in (471 by 422cm). **$7,500-10,500**

A pair of Venetian painted plaster Blackamoor figures, on waisted pedestals with acanthus foliage, 70in (177.5cm) high. **$16,500-19,500**

An overstrung grand piano-forte, seven and a quarter octaves, by Th Steinway, No.10625, with a painted satinwood case, c1864, 65in (165cm) wide. **$15,000-21,000**

A cut glass 5-light chandelier, fitted for electricity, c1830, 54in (137cm) high. **$4,500-7,000**

A Biedermeier fruitwood upright piano, enamel plaque inscribed Leopold Sauer, Instrumentmeche: in Prag, with ebonised music rests, 102in (259cm). **$6,000-9,000**

A cut glass chandelier, fitted for electricity, minor damage, late 19thC, 106in (269cm). **$60,000-75,000**

A pair of Viennese enamel, jewelled and silver gilt mounted vases, minor repair to enamel, c1880, 22in (56cm), fitted cases. **$67,000-75,000**

A Continental neo-classical ormolu, cut and amber glass 8-light chandelier, Russian or Swedish, restorations, late 18th/early 19thC, 46in (117cm) high. **$13,500-17,500**

An Empire amboyna work box, a wedding gift to the Archduchess Marie-Clémentine of Austria in 1816, 15in (38cm) wide. **$25,000-30,000**

A Regency pianoforte, by John Broadwood & Sons, 5½ octaves, 42in (106.5cm) wide. **$9,000-12,000**

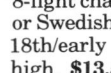

A Brussels tapestry, in brightly coloured wools and silks, with the figure of Flora by a fountain with cherubs, the borders inscribed 'Florae Sacrum', restored, early 18thC, 121in (307cm) square. **$18,000-22,500**

A Brussels tapestry, woven to a design by Teniers, signed F.V.D. Borcht, with Brussels town mark in frame borders, mid-18thC, 122in. **$13,500-17,500**

A Brussels genre tapestry, depicting 4 children playing with a dog, late 17th/early 18thC, 133 by 110in (340 by 280cm). **$9,000-12,000**

A Flemish verdure mythological tapestry, depicting Diana hunting a stag, restorations, mid-late 17thC, 137in high. **$13,500-17,500**

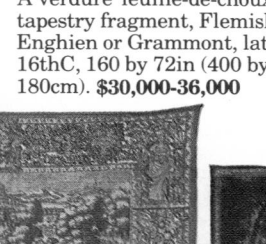

A verdure 'feuille-de-choux' tapestry fragment, Flemish, Enghien or Grammont, late 16thC, 160 by 72in (400 by 180cm). **$30,000-36,000**

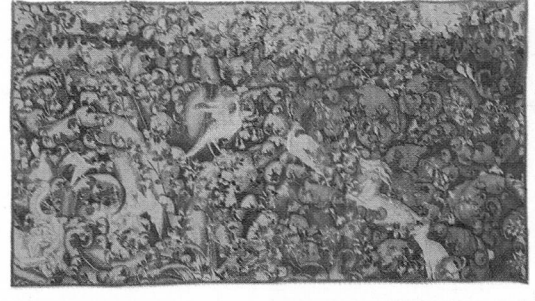

A Brussels tapestry woven in silks and wools, the border with Brussels town mark and initials CM, cut and shut with restorations, late 16thC, 132 by 130in (335 by 330cm). **$10,500-14,000**

A Brussels tapestry, woven to a design by Teniers, depicting the Kermesse, within picture frame borders, the panel folded over and reduced, mid-18thC, 128 by 222in (325 by 564cm). **$33,000-37,000**

A Noh costume, Karaori, decorated with chrysanthemum, wisteria and other flowers, late Edo period. **$24,000-27,000**

A silk kosode, embroidered with a wave pattern at the bottom and Hagoromo above, 19thC. **$4,000-5,500**

A Noh costume, Karaori, with design of ho-o and gosho-guruma, carriage for noblemen, among flowers, richly embroidered, late Edo period. **$18,000-21,000**

A Noh costume, Karaori, richly decorated in various colours on gold twill weave ground, with numerous ho-o birds among flowers, late Edo period. **$30,000-34,500**

A silk furisode, for winter wear, with gold embroidered sparrows in flight above a snow covered bamboo, with red silk and flower patterned yusoku lining, 19thC. **$3,000-4,500**

A silk kosode, embroidered with tree peonies and other plants, with a gold embroidered tatewaku patterned ground, and orange silk lining, 19thC. **$22,500-25,000**

A kosode, richly embroidered with gold, purple and green with small rafts and sprays of flowers among golden waves, 19thC. **$4,500-7,000**

A pair of Aubusson cushions, woven in silks and wools with a reaper in a coat drinking and a boy huntsman, with tasselled fringes, mid-19thC, 15½in (39cm). **$3,000-4,500**

A pair of ivory vases, late 19thC. **$4,000-5,500**
Two ivory vases, late 19thC. **$3,000-4,500**

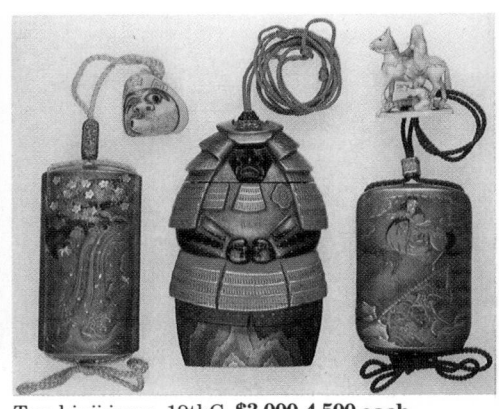

Two kinji inros, 19thC. **$3,000-4,500 each**
A yoroigata inro, late 19thC. **$9,000-12,000**

A stoneware vase, by Elizabeth Fritsch,
9in (23cm). **$6,000-8,000**

A pair of cloisonné enamel figures of Buddhistic
lions, minor damage, late Qing Dynasty, 19½in
(50cm). **$10,000-13,000**

A cloisonné enamel jar and
shallow domed cover with
knob finial, late 19thC,
23½in (59.5cm) high.
$7,500-10,500

A Momoyama period black lacquer domed chest,
decorated in hiramakie and takamakie and inlaid
with shell, old wear and damage, c1600, 20½in
(50cm) wide. **$4,000-5,500**

A Momoyama period black lacquer coffer and
hinged domed cover, engraved kanagu, old wear
and damage, c1590, 31½in (80cm) wide.
$7,500-10,500

A hand enamelled open tourer with clock work mechanism, German, c1910, 8in long. **$7,500-10,500**

A doll magician automaton, with bisque head marked Deposé Jumeau, 24in (61cm) high. **$6,000-8,000**

Part of Britains Largest Set, British Camel Corps troopers, also featured bottom right.

Britains, The Cavalry of the British Army, No.129, approx 70 pieces, c1930. **$6,000-9,000**

The Largest Set Ever Made by Britains, No.131, of approx 251 pieces, some damage. **$15,000-21,000**

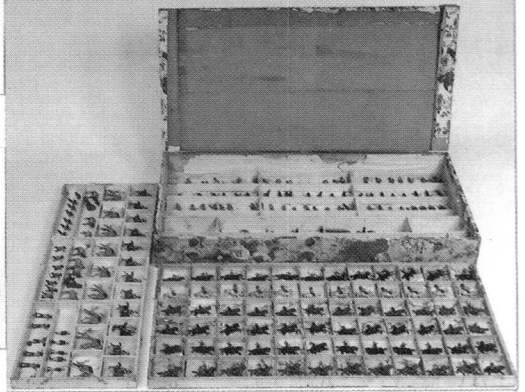

A 5in gauge model of the GWR Armstrong Class 4–4–0 locomotive and tender No.14, 'Charles Saunders', by P J Rich. **$16,500-19,500**

A 7¼in gauge model of the GWR Armstrong Class 4–4–0 locomotive and tender No.8. 'Gooch', by T Childs, Churchill. **$10,500-14,000**

A 5in gauge model of the GWR River Class 2–4–0 locomotive and tender No.69, 'Avon' by R W Gale, Newport. **$10,500-14,000**

A Baule wood male figure, 19in (48cm).
$300-400

A hermaphrodite Dogon spirit figure, 45in (114cm).
$1,200-1,600

A Maori wood figure, 15in (38cm).
$2,250-3,500

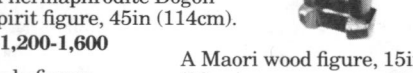

A Maori wood footrest for a digging stick, teka, 8in (20cm) wide.
$5,500-7,000

A Senufo wood rhythm pounder carved as a standing female figure, 44in (112cm) including bronzed plinth.
$400-500

Two Sinhalese masks.
$60-100

A Trobriand Islands wood staff, the finial in the form of 2 addorsed seated figures sharing a domed cap, 40in (101cm).
$250-350

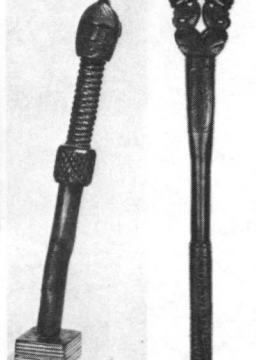

A New Guinea lime spatula, 15in (38cm).
$600-900

An African wood staff, the finial carved as a human head, 17½in (44cm), and a wood snake.
$75-150

A Trobriand Islands canoe prow, with coloured blue sections, 53in (136cm).
$300-400

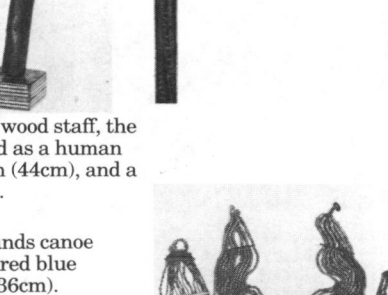

Two Naga necklaces, one with red and orange beads, the other with orange beads, and brass bells.
$300-400

A Haida Argillite spoon, carved in the style of a Welsh love spoon.
$600-900

Ephemera
Pop Ephemera

DECCA
GROUP
ADVANCE TEST RECORDING

A cardboard presentation folder, damaged, containing the first 4 45 rpm records produced by Apple Records Ltd, 13½ by 9in (34 by 23cm).
$450-600

A demonstration record by The Beatles, 'From Me To You/Thank You Girl', 45 rpm Parlophone R5015, the date 11.4.63 inscribed in biro, together with 'The Beatles Get Back', a book of colour plates by Ethan A Russell, with text by Jonathan Cott and David Dalton.
$300-400

A rare acetate by The Beatles 'Hello Little Girl/Like Dreamers' Do', 45 rpm, on 'Decca Group Advance Test Recording' label, 1962, and a letter of authenticity from Geoff Milne, Decca label manager 1952-80.
$6,000-9,000

Four polychrome Richard Avedon psychedelic posters of The Beatles produced for the Daily Express, c1967, and one black and white photograph.
$450-600

A Beatles tour magazine signed on front cover, 1964.
$300-400

633

A Beatles tin advertising tray, c1963, 13in (33cm).
$45-70

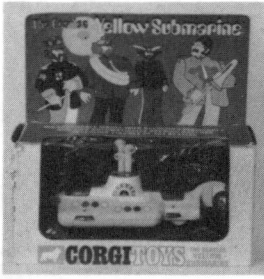

A Corgi model of 'Yellow Submarine', with opening hatches revealing figures of the Beatles, in original box, 1967, 5in (12.5cm).
$250-350

An Aria PE-180 electric semi-acoustic guitar, with Bill Haley's 'play list' fastened with Sellotape to the base, together with case, not original.
$24,000-28,500

A signed page from Film Weekly, Leslie Howard, 1932.
$60-100

The Beatles, 'Help', Parlophone, 33⅓ rpm mono, signed on cover by each, 1965, with accompanying letter of authenticity.
$1,500-2,600

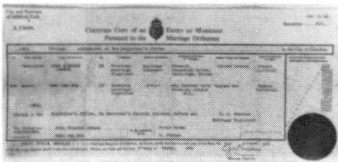

A copy of the Marriage Certificate of John Winston Lennon and Yoko Ono Cox on 20th March, 1969.
$5,500-7,000

The Beatles leaving an aircraft at Heathrow Airport, signed, slight creasing, 8 by 10in (20.5 by 25.5cm).
$600-900

Magazines

The Austin Magazine, original artwork, December 1937, signed, watercolour, unframed, 21½ by 17in (54 by 43cm).
$250-350

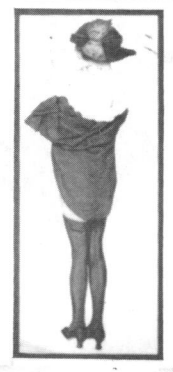

An illustration for the Beatles song 'In My Life', by Peter le Vasseur, signed and dated 1969, 8½in (21.5cm) square, framed.
$1,000-1,400

A self portrait with Yoko Ono in black felt tip pen, on Amsterdam Hilton paper, autographed by John and Yoko, 1969, 7½ by 10½in (19 by 25.5cm), mounted.
$2,250-3,000

A limited edition resin bronze GRP bust of Jimi Hendrix, by John Somerville, c1985.
$600-900

A portfolio of magazine pages, Raphael Kirchner.
$100-150

The original artwork for book sleeve of St Trinian's Story to be published by Perpetua, in gouache and ink, with some work by Searle.
$250-350

An advertising brochure for Triumph motorcycles, c1934, 12 by 8in (30.5 by 20cm).
$45-70

634

Cigarette Cards

Allen & Ginter, 'Racing Colours of the World', a complete set of 50.
$300-400

Churchman's Beauties 'CERF' 1899, a complete set of 12.
$400-500

Clarke's Cricket Terms, 1900, a complete set of 14.
$400-500

Clarke's Cycling Terms 1900, a complete set of 12.
$250-350

Clarke's Football Terms 1900, a complete set of 12.
$250-350

Clark's Golf Terms 1900, a complete set of 12.
$400-500

Edwards, Ringer & Bigg's Beauties, 'CERF' 1905, a complete set of 12.
$400-500

Edwards, Ringer & Bigg's Beauties, 'CERF', a complete set of 12.
$300-400

W & F Faulkner, 'Sporting Terms', a set of 12, 'Cricket Terms', 9/12 and 2 duplicates.
$400-500

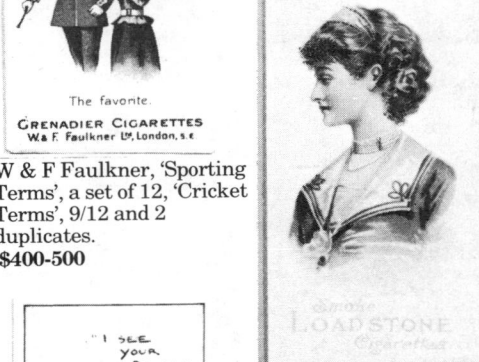

Franklyn Davey's Beauties, 'CERF' 1905, a complete set of 12.
$600-900

Cope's British Warriors 1912, a complete set of 50, loose.
$75-150

Allen & Ginter's Parasol Drill 1888, a complete set of 50, loose.
$450-600

Player's Everyday Phrases by Tom Browne, 24/25.
$150-200

Wills's Vanity Fair 1902, a complete set of 50.
$75-150

A three-dimensional Shell
advert, c1920, 4 by 6in (10
by 15cm).
$45-70

Cunard Europe America
Berengaria.
$750-1,000

A circus and balloon advert,
c1880, 22 by 6in (56 by
15cm).
$60-100

Chas Pears, SR 'There's
Nothing Equal to the
Southern sea after all', quad
royal, 1935.
$450-600

The Glasgow Herald £650
Golf Tournament at
Gleneagles Open to the
World's Players, May 1920,
letterpress, by
McCorquodale, 40 by 30in
(102 by 76cm).
$60-100

Hudson's Soap for the
People, In Packets, 20 by
27½in (51 by 70cm).
$60-100

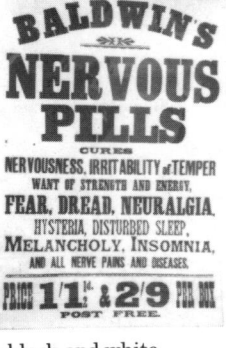

A black and white
advertising poster, c1880,
36 by 24in (91 by 61cm).
$45-70

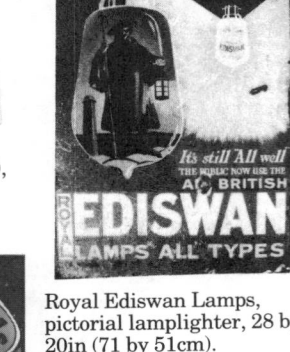

Royal Ediswan Lamps,
pictorial lamplighter, 28 by
20in (71 by 51cm).
$100-150

Mew's Isle of Wight, W B
Mew, Langton & Co Ltd, 40
by 28in (101 by 71cm).
$250-350

Eat Quaker Oats, 42 by
24in (107 by 61cm),
mounted in wood frame.
$60-100

A folio of offset lithographs,
printed by The Sunday
Times, by Alan Cracknell
and others, c1960.
$600-900

The Sunday Times
Christmas Gift Guide

Fry's Chocolate, 30 by 36in
(76 by 92cm), mounted in
wood frame.
$150-250

Walbran Ltd, Leeds, for
High Class Fishing Tackle
of every Kind, 30 by 24in
(76 by 61cm).
$60-100

Puritan Soap, Pure as the
Breeze, 24 by 36in (61 by
91cm), mounted in wood
frame.
$60-100

Fry's pure breakfast Cocoa,
36 by 24in (92 by 61cm),
mounted in wood frame.
$45-70

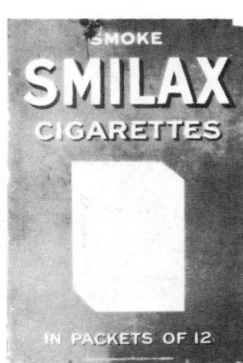

Smoke Smilax Cigarettes, in packets of 12, 36 by 24in (91.5 by 61cm).
$75-150

Lucille Ball, signed in full.
$60-100

Charles Chaplin, signed, on still from 'The Countess from Hong Kong', slight creasing, 7 by 9½in (18 by 24cm).
$150-200

Katharine Hepburn, signed, The Little Minister.
$100-200

Photographs

Abbott and Costello, a portrait photograph, inscribed by subjects, 'To Bernard from your Pal, Lou Costello, Bud Abbott', 10 by 13in (25.5 by 33cm), framed and glazed.
$150-200

Louis Armstrong, signed, slight creasing, 8 by 10in (20 by 25.5cm).
$60-100

Clara Bow, signed, with inscription, creased, 8 by 10in (20 by 25.5cm).
$150-250

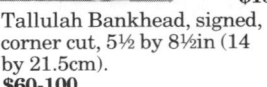

Tallulah Bankhead, signed, corner cut, 5½ by 8½in (14 by 21.5cm).
$60-100

James Cagney, signed, marks to reverse, 5 by 7in (12.5 by 18cm).
$75-150

Charles Chaplin, signed, in white, creased, small hole, adhesion marks to reverse, 8 by 10in (20 by 25.5cm).
$150-250

Alfred Hitchcock, signed, 11 by 14in (28 by 35.5cm).
$300-400

Dorothy Dandridge, a film still, 10 by 8in (25.5 by 20cm).
$45-70

Harry Houdini, signed.
$150-250

A full length portrait photograph of Nancy Astor, by Dorothy Wilding, mounted on tissue, 11½ by 7½in (29 by 19cm), framed and glazed.
$75-150

Charles Boyer, signed, slight staining, 8 by 10in (20 by 25.5cm).
$45-70

Joan Crawford, signed, slight creasing, 8 by 10in (20 by 25.5cm).
$60-100

Jack Holt, signed, slight creasing, 8 by 10in (20 by 25.5cm).
$30-50

Boris Karloff, signed, slight adhesion marks, 5 by 7in (13 to 18cm).
$250-350

Laurel and Hardy, signed, some creasing, 7 by 5in (13 by 18cm).
$250-350

Steve McQueen, with inscription, some creasing, 8 by 10in (20 by 25.5cm).
$150-250

Margaret Rutherford, signed.
$60-100

Disneyalia

Walt Disney, a black and white half length portrait photograph, inscribed, 10 by 8in (25.5 by 20cm).
$45-70

Two original hand paintings on celluloid, from the Walt Disney film Snow White and the Seven Dwarfs, with label of authenticity, 6½ by 9½in (16.5 by 24cm), framed and glazed.
$1,000-1,400

A Walt Disney illustration, signed pen, black ink and watercolour, c1940, 3 by 4in (7.5 by 10cm), contained in an autograph book.
$2,250-3,500

Eight enamel on copper children's bracelet charms, 12 tin and glass charms, other boxed games, and an Army & Navy 'Special Box'.
$75-150

Nine original animated celluloids including Felix the Cat, The Pink Panther, Inspector Clouseau, and others.
$150-200

Scripophily

Greenock Bank Co, Scotland, £1, 1838.
$800-1,200

Royal Bank of Scotland, £1, 1872.
$450-700

Bank of England, £1, 22 July 1814, some foxing.
$450-600

Bank of England, £1, 6 September, 1816.
$450-700

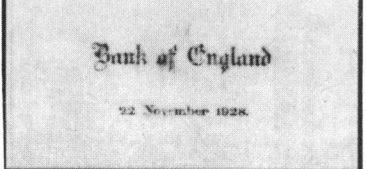

Bank of England, 10/– and £1 Nos. A01 0000 90, in presentation parchment envelope.
$3,000-4,500

Glass

A rock crystal figure of
Quanyin, 10½in (26.5cm).
$1,300-1,800

A Chinese painting on
glass, in moulded ebonised
frame, 19thC, 28½in (72cm)
wide.
$800-1,200

Inros

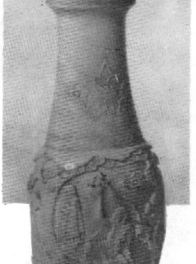

A boxwood three-case inro,
formed as a terrapin, signed
in an oval reserve Chuichi,
late 19thC.
$4,000-5,500

A small roiro two-case inro,
tiny chips, unsigned, 19thC.
$800-1,200

Ivory

A silver mounted ivory
ewer of European form,
damaged, late 19thC, 5½in
(14.5cm).
$750-1,000

A Chinese ivory vase,
mid-19thC, 6in (15cm).
$300-400

An ivory group of a
fisherman, signed, 11in
(28cm).
$700-900

A Chinese carved and
stained ivory table screen,
with carved ivory stand,
and Dog of Fo terminals,
19thC, 11in (28cm).
$450-700

A Japanese aikuchi, Meiji
period, 15in (38cm).
$750-1,000

Jade

A carved yellow jade snuff
bottle.
$1,000-1,400

A celadon jade censer and
domed cover, in box.
$2,250-3,000

Lacquer

A pair of Chinese lacquered
lunch boxes.
$1,000-1,400

A Japanese black and gold
lacquer jardinière, early
19thC, 20½in (52cm) diam.
$3,000-4,500

A Japanese
tortoiseshell and
lacquer cabinet with
silver mounts,
Kodansu, c1880.
$700-900

A Japanese bronze
elephant, cast seal mark,
Meiji period, 28in (71cm)
wide, on carved hardwood
stand.
$4,000-5,500

Metal

A late Ming gilt bronze figure of a Deity, 16th/17thC, 15in (38cm), wood stand.
$1,300-1,800

A pair of Japanese bronze vases, heightened in gilt and silver, 19thC, 12½in (31cm).
$4,000-5,500

A set of Japanese bronze cranes, modelled from originals in Kyoto Temple, 20thC, largest 57in (144.5cm).
$2,250-3,000

A pair of Chinese gilt bronze cranes mounted as candlesticks, 19thC.
$250-350

Netsuke

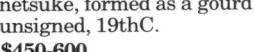

A brass and silver Yatate netsuke, formed as a gourd, unsigned, 19thC.
$450-600

A Shan bronze drum, 26in (66cm) wide, and beater.
$1,300-1,800

A Chinese needle holder with amber drop, early 19thC.
$75-150

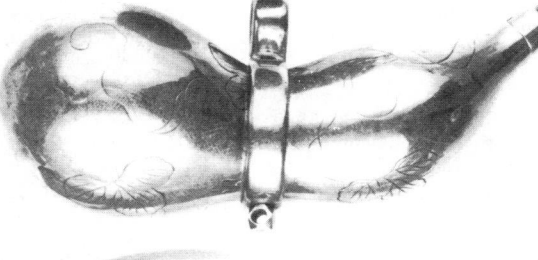

A silver netsuke, modelled as a double gourd with screw top, unsigned, late 19thC.
$450-700

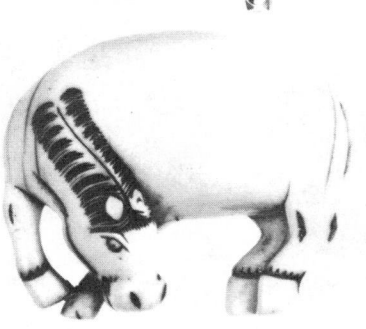

An ivory netsuke of a grazing horse, unsigned, c1800.
$600-900

A gold, silver, red and black lacquered wood netsuke of a dog, with inlaid eyes, crack in tail, unsigned, 19thC.
$450-600

Snuff Bottles

A stained walrus ivory snuff bottle, c1800.
$800-1,200

An ivory netsuke of Hotei, style of Yoshinaga, Kyoto School, unsigned, c1800.
$450-600

Wood

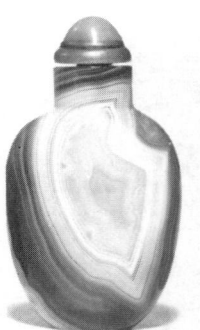

A banded agate snuff bottle, c1800.
$1,500-2,600

A cinnabar covered box, 19thC, 11in (28cm) diam.
$600-900

An early marble figure of Avalokitesvara, Sui/early Tang Dynasty, 11in (28cm).
$4,000-5,500

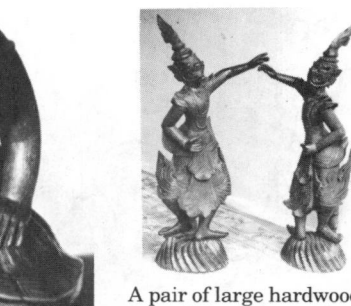

A wood okimono, signed Shinpuken Masakatsu, late 19thC, 3½in (8cm).
$3,000-4,500

A pair of large hardwood carved Eastern temple figures.
$1,000-1,400

Miscellaneous

A sandstone head, damaged ear lobes, Ming Dynasty or later, 11in (28cm), with velvet covered wood plinth.
$3,000-4,500

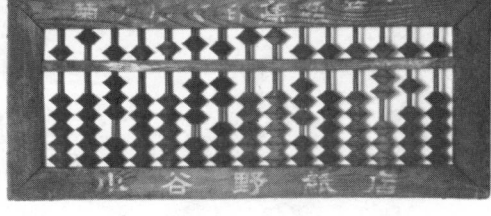

A Japanese shop sign, Kamban, c1880.
$450-700

A Japanese storage bin, with lift off lid, 23in (58cm) diam.
$600-900

Russian

Icons and Russian Works of Art

A Damascan picture easel, inlaid with mother-of-pearl, c1900, 72in (182.5cm).
$450-700

A pair of Damascan wall brackets, inlaid with mother-of-pearl, 19thC, 35in (89cm) high.
$450-700

The Glykophelusa Mother of God, encased in a repoussé and chased silver oklad, foil enriched with seed pearl vestments, multi-coloured pastes and semi-precious stones, the oklad Viatka, 1796, 13 by 11in (33 by 28cm).
$3,000-4,500

The Guardian Angel, surrounded by 6 Chosen Saints, on an olive brown ground, 19thC, 14 by 12in (35.5 by 30.5cm).
$400-500

The Martyr Saint Antipa, on a tan ground, 12 by 10½in (30.5 by 26.5cm).
$600-900

Saint John the Baptist from the Deisis, on a brown ground, c1800, 21 by 17½in (53 by 44cm).
$1,200-1,600

The Iverskaya Mother of God, covered with an engine turned parcel gilt oklad, marked with initials Cyrillic CG, Moscow, 1899, in a wooden kiot, 5 by 4½in (12.5 by 11cm).
$600-900

Papier Mâché
Miscellaneous

A Continental papier mâché box, with gold mounts, c1770.
$800-1,200

A Victorian papier mâché box with hinged lid, mother-of-pearl inlaid, the base stamped 'Jennens & Bettridge', 9½in (24cm).
$150-200

A Victorian papier mâché jewellery cabinet, inlaid with mother-of-pearl, marked J. Bettridge, late Jennens & Bettridge, 19in (48cm).
$1,300-1,800

An early Victorian papier mâché chair, inlaid with mother-of-pearl, signed Jennens & Bettridge.
$600-900

A pair of Regency silver mounted papier mâché coasters, 5½in (14cm).
$1,300-1,800

A collection of 10 papier mâché lobed sweetmeat dishes, decorated with a mother-of-pearl coat of arms, heightened in gilt, 4½in (11cm).
$150-250

A Victorian papier mâché lap top, inlaid with mother-of-pearl heightened in gilt, with fitted interior, 18in (45.5cm).
$1,200-1,600

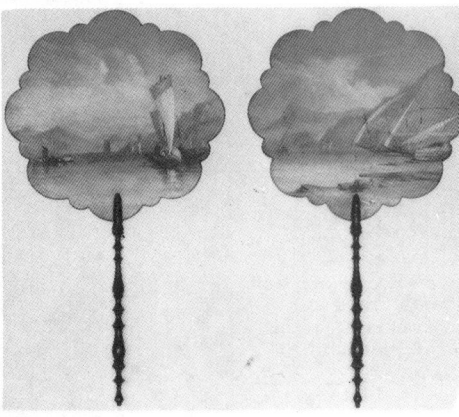

A pair of early Victorian papier mâché fans, signed Jennens & Bettridge, 17½in (44cm) high.
$450-700

A Victorian papier mâché inkstand, fitted with 2 glass ink bottles and a pen tray, inlaid with mother-of-pearl, 10in (25cm) wide.
$150-250

A mid-Victorian black, gilt and mother-of-pearl japanned papier mâché music stand, with detachable rest, on a telescopic brass shaft, 20in (51cm) wide.
$800-1,200

A pair of Victorian papier mâché face screens, 15in (38cm) high.
$250-350

A Regency green and gilt japanned papier mâché tray, with later stand, 32½in (82.5cm).
$1,500-2,600

Pine Furniture
Beds

A pine cot, simulated
bamboo, 28in (71cm) wide.
$300-400

A Georgian rocking crib,
repainted in original style,
c1800, 32in (81cm).
$300-400

Bookcases

A two-piece double arch
door bookcase, c1820.
$800-1,200

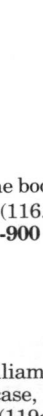
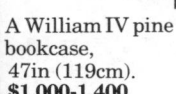

A pine bookcase,
46in (116.5cm).
$600-900

A William IV pine
bookcase,
47in (119cm).
$1,000-1,400

A Welsh pine glazed
bookcase, with 2 bowfront
drawers, 2 cupboards below
with raised panel doors, on
ball feet, c1840, 55in
(139.5cm).
$1,500-2,600

A bookcase, c1780, 43in
(109cm).
$1,000-1,400

A pine bookcase, doors with
coloured glass borders,
c1880, 42in (106.5cm).
$400-500

Chairs

A child's Windsor chair,
c1875.
$150-200

A breakfront bookcase,
made from old timber, 90in
(228cm).
$1,300-1,800

A child's beech high chair,
with new cane seat.
$60-100

A pine high chair which
converts to a play table,
with porcelain beads, 38in
(96.5cm) high.
$250-350

A Yorkshire elm and beech slat back armchair, c1875.
$300-400

A pine armchair.
$150-250

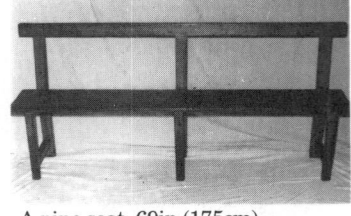

A pine seat, 69in (175cm).
$150-200

An Italian painted pine bench, the seat formed from the lid of a cupboard, late 17thC, 83½in (212cm).
$5,500-7,000

An elm and beech carver chair, c1890.
$150-250

Chests

A pine commode chair, c1850.
$150-250

A pine chest of drawers, with green tiled back and replacement handles, c1860, 34½in (86cm).
$400-500

A pine chest of drawers, with bracket feet, c1820, 36in (91.5cm).
$400-500

A decorative painted folding chair, probably Indian.
$150-200

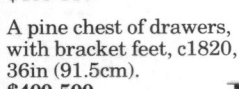

A pine chest of drawers, 42in (106.5cm).
$250-350

A pine chest of drawers, with original handles and escutcheons, c1840, 34½in (86cm).
$250-350

A Victorian pine chest, painted in the traditional style of the North East, c1890, 36in (91cm).
$300-400

A Scottish pine chest of drawers, with bobbin turning at the sides, c1850, 49in (124.5cm).
$250-350

A pine chest of drawers with splash back, 41½in (105cm).
$400-500

A pine chest of drawers, with new handles, 36in (91.5cm).
$600-900

A pine chest of drawers with gallery back, c1865, 42in (106.5cm).
$300-400

A pine chest of drawers, c1890, 33in (84cm).
$250-350

A Victorian chest of drawers, recently decorated in the traditional style of a dairy, c1860.
$400-500

An Edwardian chest of drawers, recently painted in traditional style, the drawers with plywood bottoms, c1910, 33in (84cm).
$300-400

A Victorian chest of drawers, heavily restored paintwork to depict family butcher's shop, 43in (109cm).
$400-500

A miniature chest of drawers, c1880, 14in (35.5cm).
$75-150

A small bedside chest of drawers, depicting an early agricultural event, heavily restored paintwork, 18in (46cm).
$250-350

A large blanket chest, with dovetail joints, c1875.
$150-250

A pine bow front chest of drawers, c1860.
$400-500

A chest of drawers, with original crystal screw handles, recently painted in traditional style, c1840, 40in (101.5cm).
$400-500

A Victorian chest, repainted in the traditional style of the East Coast sea captains, c1885.
$400-500

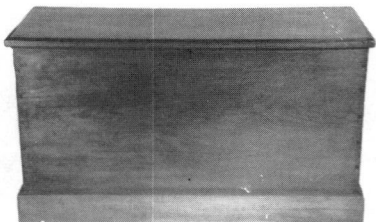

A pine chest, with dovetail joints and original brass handles, c1880, 44in (111.5cm).
$250-350

A pine tool chest, each drawer fitted with compartments lined with cork, original handles, 25in (63.5cm).
$300-400

A specimen chest, c1880, 40in (101.5cm). **$450-700**

A chest of drawers with original paint, c1820, 37in (94cm). **$450-700**

An early Irish mule chest, with original knobs and mock drawer fronts, c1850. **$300-400**

A Victorian bowfront veneered chest of drawers, c1850, recently overpainted in traditional style with East Coast maritime theme, 42in (107cm). **$450-700**

A William and Mary painted pine blanket chest, the hinged top above a case with 6 false drawers above 2 long drawers, on bun feet, New London County, Connecticut, c1730, 41in (104cm) wide. **$10,000-12,000**

A nest of drawers, c1820, 43in (109cm) high. **$450-700**

A Chippendale pine chest of drawers, New England, c1770, 40in (101.5cm) wide. **$1,000-1,500**

A Shaker pine chest of drawers, on shaped bracket feet, traces of red stain, probably Harvard, Massachusetts Community, 43½in (110cm) wide. **$1,500-2,000**

A miniature green painted pine blanket chest, on shaped plank feet, paint restored, American, 19thC, 9½in (24cm) high, with a red painted bench. **$400-500**

A serpentine front chest of drawers with apron, original crystal knobs and mahogany feet, c1860. **$300-400**

A small pine blanket chest, painted in blue, the top centering a rectangular reserve with inset corners, on straight bracket feet, Pennsylvania, late 18thC, 33in (84cm) wide. **$4,000-5,000**

Commodes

Cupboards

A pine hiring chest, c1875,
45in (114cm).
$150-250

A Louis XV Provincial pine
commode, 34in (86cm).
$900-1,300

A pine bow fronted barrel
back corner cupboard, with
carved shelves and a slide,
c1740.
$4,000-5,500

A pine corner cabinet with
astragal glazed doors, 41in
(104cm).
$800-1,200

A pine corner cupboard,
19thC.
$1,500-2,600

A Welsh food cupboard,
18thC, 40in (101.5cm).
$1,500-2,600

A Georgian stripped pine
corner cabinet, 86½in
(220cm) high.
$1,200-1,600

An Irish arched glazed
corner cupboard, c1830.
$1,300-1,800

A Federal painted pine corner
cupboard, in 2 sections, the upper
section with moulded broken
cornice, the lower section with 2
moulded panels centering a
moulded panelled cupboard door,
68½in (174cm) wide.
$1,000-1,500

A pine corner cupboard,
c1860, 46in (116.5cm).
$600-900

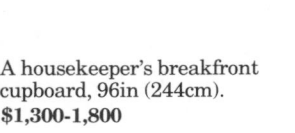

A housekeeper's breakfront
cupboard, 19thC.
$1,500-2,600

A housekeeper's breakfront
cupboard, 96in (244cm).
$1,300-1,800

A pine corner cupboard, c1800, 55½in (139.5cm) high.
$450-700

A hand-stripped satinwood pot cupboard, c1890, 12in (30cm).
$150-200

A German pine cupboard, 35in (89cm).
$800-1,200

A panelled cupboard, c1800, 44in (111.5cm).
$450-600

A Victorian pine linen press, c1800, 49in (124.5cm).
$800-1,200

A narrow pine cupboard with 2 doors, c1840, 22½in (57cm).
$400-500

A pine cupboard and chest of drawers, 26in (66cm) wide.
$800-1,200

A Georgian linen press, 47½in (120cm).
$900-1,300

A pine linen press, c1850, 35½in (90cm).
$600-900

A pine tall cabinet, the panelled door opening to an interior with 3 shelves, traces of green paint, probably New York, late 19thC, 26½in (66cm) wide.
$1,200-1,500

A bowfront corner cupboard, 32in (81cm) high.
$300-400

Penny Lampard

28 High Street
Headcorn, Kent, England
on A274

between Maidstone and Tenterden

Offering over 3,000 sq. ft. of furniture
Open six days a week
Sunday by appointment only

Tel: 011 44 622 890682

Tel: 011 44 622 861377

A Gothic pine food cupboard, 53½in (135cm).
$800-1,200

A fielded panel food cupboard, c1780, 57in (144.5cm).
$1,200-1,600

An Irish food cupboard, 58in (147cm).
$1,000-1,400

An Irish food cupboard, c1850, 54in (137cm).
$1,200-1,600

A fielded panel food cupboard, c1800, 56in (142cm).
$1,200-1,600

A European armoire, repainted, c1880, 42in (106.5cm).
$450-700

A Belgian painted armoire, c1820, 72in (182.5cm).
$1,500-2,600

A Scottish pine press, with panelled sides, c1780, 50in (127cm).
$1,000-1,400

A Victorian pine housemaid's cupboard, c1860, 44in (111.5cm).
$700-900

A Shaker pine cupboard and chest of drawers, with a single raised panelled door opening to an interior with one shelf, on board feet, probably Pleasant Hill Community, Kentucky, mid-19thC, 40in (101.5cm) wide.
$8,000-9,000

A pine step-back cupboard, the moulded cornice above 2 glazed cupboard doors opening to shelves, on straight bracket feet, American, 19thC, 54in (137cm) wide.
$2,000-3,000

A pine cupboard, c1850, 24in (61cm).
$150-200

A pine bedside cabinet, 30in
(76cm) high.
$150-250

A pair of reproduction pine
bedside cabinets, 13½in
(34cm).
$250-350

A pine cupboard, c1840,
21in (53cm).
$250-350

A pine cupboard, c1850,
72½in (183cm).
$450-600

A pine huffer, c1840, 31½in
(79.5cm).
$400-500

A European cabinet, c1860,
32in (81cm).
$400-500

An Austrian pine display
cabinet, c1800.
$800-1,200

A pine game safe with
copper roof, for hanging 16
brace of game birds, 37in
(94cm).
$600-900

A pine clerk's desk on stand,
with double hinged top,
stand not original, c1860,
21in (53cm).
$250-350

A bonheur du jour, with
restored top, c1860.
$300-400

Desks

A bonheur du jour, c1860.
$300-400

A Scottish secretaire,
heavily restored with new
interior, c1850.
$600-900

A Georgian double teller's
desk, with spindle gallery,
c1780.
$450-600

An Irish dresser, c1840, 48in (122cm).
$750-1,000

A pine dresser, 19thC, 60in (152cm).
$600-900

An English pine dresser, c1850, 88in (223.5cm).
$1,500-2,600

An Irish dresser, c1880, 63in (160cm).
$800-1,200

A West Country style dresser, c1830, 36in (91.5cm).
$1,000-1,400

A country pine glazed dresser, with butterfly catches, c1840, 78in (198cm).
$1,000-1,400

An Irish dresser, c1860, 52in (132cm).
$700-900

An Irish dresser, c1860, 52in (132cm).
$700-900

A Scottish spice dresser, with astragal glazed cupboard, c1840, 48in (122cm).
$750-1,000

A pine glazed kitchen dresser/display cupboard, c1800, 51in (129.5cm).
$800-1,200

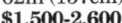
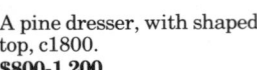

A Welsh pine dresser with 2 glazed cupboards, original handles and hooks, c1790, 62in (157cm).
$1,500-2,600

A pine dresser, with shaped top, c1800.
$800-1,200

A kitchen dresser with blind astragal glazing, c1860, 74in (188cm).
$1,300-1,800

An early Victorian pine dresser base, with original handles, c1840, 58in (147cm).
$800-1,200

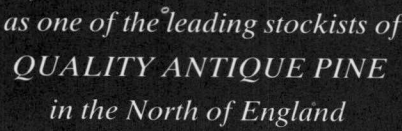

An Irish dresser, c1840,
68in (172.5cm).
$900-1,300

A miniature pine dresser
base, c1840, 25in (63.5cm).
$600-900

A pine free-standing base,
c1860, 46in (116.5cm).
$300-400

Dressing Tables

A pine washstand/dressing
table, c1860, 30in (76cm).
$250-350

A pine base unit, c1870,
60in (152cm).
$450-700

A Cornish dresser, 18thC,
58in (147cm).
$1,500-2,600

A pitch pine dressing table,
c1880, 39in (99cm).
$300-400

An English ash hand
stripped dressing chest,
c1890, 42in (106.5cm).
$400-500

A satinwood hand stripped
dressing chest, c1890, 36in
(91.5cm).
$400-500

Mirrors

A pine dressing mirror,
c1850, 23½in (60cm).
$150-200

A carved pine picture
frame, 30 by 36in (76 by
92cm).
$150-200

Make the most of
Miller's
*CONDITION is absolutely
vital when assessing the
value of an antique.
Damaged pieces on the
whole appreciate much
less than perfect
examples. However a rare,
desirable piece may
command a high price
even when damaged.*

A pine side table, 33in (84cm).
$150-250

An ash and elm tilt-top side table, c1840, 21in (53cm) square.
$100-200

A pine and elm tilt-top pedestal table, c1860, 46in (116.5cm) diam.
$450-700

A French pine oval tilt-top table, 55in (140cm).
$450-600

A pine writing table with a hinged drop leaf, c1820, 36in (92cm).
$150-250

An early pine table, 42in (106.5cm).
$400-500

A pine farmhouse table, c1840, 63in (160cm).
$450-600

A small pine table with bamboo style legs, 21½in (54cm) diam.
$250-350

A pine topped table with carved oak base, 48in (122cm).
$450-600

A small pine base, 24in (61cm).
$150-200

A small table, 24in (61cm).
$45-70

A pine table, 22½in (57cm) high.
$75-150

A Chippendale pine dough table, on block and baluster turned legs joined by block and baluster turned stretchers, with ball feet, 49½in (125cm) long.
$1,000-1,500

Wardrobes

A gentleman's wardrobe, c1740, 165in (419cm).
$1,500-2,600

A pine wardrobe with astragal glazed insets, 48in (122cm).
$800-1,200

An Austrian wardrobe, with original metalwork, c1870.
$600-900

A French Louis XV painted pine bedroom suite, c1905, comprising: wardrobe, 75in (190.5cm), dressing table, 47in (119cm), a pair of chairs, chest of drawers, 50in (127cm), a pair of pot cupboards, 17½in (44cm), and a bed head.
$6,000-9,000

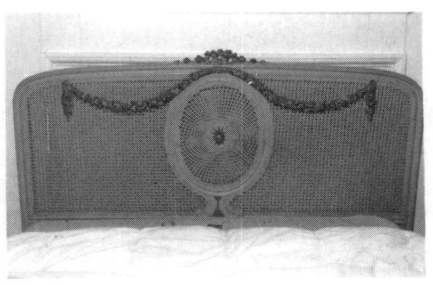

A pine wardrobe, with shelves and hanging space in the upper part, c1850, 57in (144.5cm).
$900-1,300

A pine wardrobe with marked Wedgwood insets, carved top and garland decoration, 46in (116.5cm).
$750-1,000

A pine fielded panelled wardrobe, c1880, 48in (122cm).
$400-500

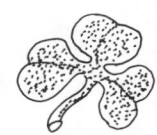
659

Washstands

A single washstand with high splashback, and drawer under the potboard, c1860.
$150-250

A washstand, c1760, 13in (33cm).
$250-350

A bowfront washstand, c1780, 35in (89cm).
$300-400

A pine washstand, c1850, 24in (61cm).
$150-250

A marble topped washstand, c1860, 30in (76cm).
$250-350

A painted pine marble topped washstand, with original paintwork and handles, c1860, 36in (92cm).
$300-400

A pine and satinwood washstand, with blue and white tiled back, c1870, 42in (106.5cm).
$300-400

A Victorian washstand in satin walnut with marble top and tiled upstand, c1875.
$400-500

A pine washstand, 30in (76cm).
$150-250

Miscellaneous

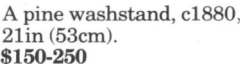

A pine washstand, c1880, 21in (53cm).
$150-250

An early pine box, with original fittings, c1820, 45in (114cm).
$300-400

A fitted pine box, 39in (99cm).
$250-350

A pine panelled coffer, 51½in (130cm).
$300-500

A pine plate rack, 22in (56cm).
$100-150

A pine spice rack, 28in (71cm).
$100-200

A pine box, 21in (53cm).
$60-100

A pine pot rack, 37in (94cm).
$60-100

A Victorian tack box, recently painted in a rich burgundy and depicting an ancient sport, c1880.
$250-350

A pine box, 14½in (36.5cm).
$75-150

A pine towel rail, 26½in (67cm).
$60-100

A pine towel rail, 29½in (75cm) high.
$60-100

A fitted pine wine cellar, c1850, 20in (51cm).
$150-250

Pine shelves, c1870, 37in (94cm).
$150-200

A pine fireplace surround,
52in (132cm) high.
$150-200

A pine panelled fireplace,
c1860.
$250-350

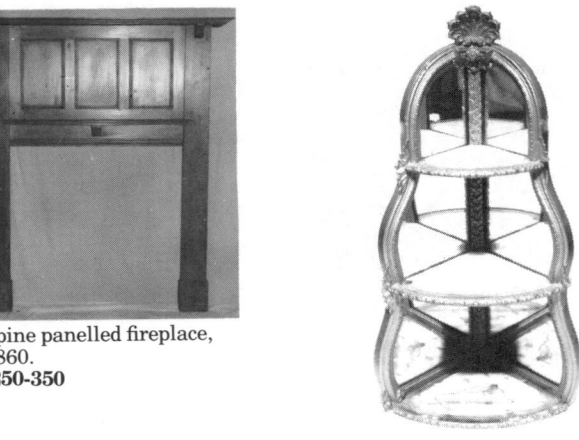

A pine corner bracket with
gilt decoration, c1900, 34in
(86cm) high.
$250-350

A pine standard lamp,
64½in (163cm) high.
$250-350

A French provincial pine
butchers block Usines X
Aubert Dijon, 68in
(172.5cm).
$1,500-2,600

A pair of Italian stripped
pine girandoles, lacking
candle sconces, one with
later plate, 26 by 17½in
(66 by 44cm).
$1,300-1,800

A pine carousel horse, 40in
(101.5cm) high.
$700-900

An Irish 8-day clock in pine,
some restoration to clock
face door.
$1,300-1,800

A pair of Italian stripped
pine girandoles, with
3-branch tôle sconces, 27 by
17½in (69 by 44cm).
$1,500-2,600

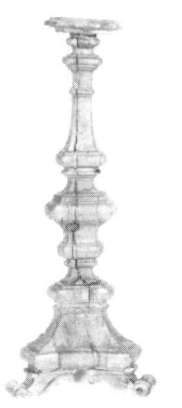

A carved pine torchère, 41in
(104cm) high.
$250-350

A pine frame, 30 by 23½in
(76 by 59.5cm).
$75-150

Kitchenalia

A cast iron pan, 13in (33cm) long.
$15-30

A small enamel saucepan, 4½in (12cm) diam.
$15-30

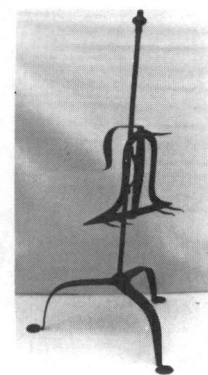

An English wrought iron standing toaster, c1780, 28in (71cm) high.
$250-350

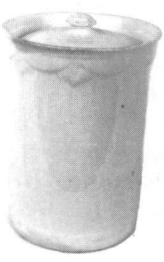

An early white storage jar, 8in (20cm) high.
$25-35

A milk cooler, 11in (28cm) high.
$15-30

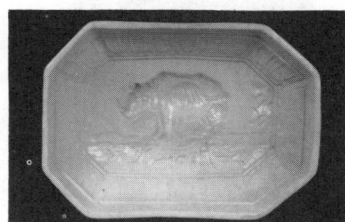

A creamware jelly mould, with rhinoceros imprint, 8 by 6in (20 by 15cm).
$75-150

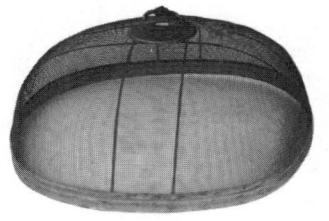

A wire meat cover, 14in (35.5cm) long.
$15-30

A George III fruitwood mutineer, 6in (15cm) high.
$250-350

A mallet.
$30-50

An oak knifebox, 18thC, 8in (20cm) high.
$100-150

A corner wire vegetable rack, 15in (38cm) wide.
$30-50

A Welsh butter press, 8½in (22cm) diam.
$45-70

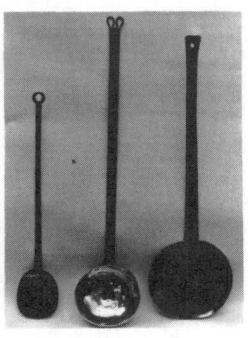

Three English kitchen
tools, c1780.
$100-200 each

A cherrywood egg cup
stand, c1780, 12in (30.5cm)
high.
$900-1,300

A meat cover with porcelain
knob, 10in (25cm) diam.
$15-30

An aluminium plate
warmer, 14in (35.5cm).
$15-30

A Georgian tea cosy, 14in
(35.5cm) high.
$30-50

A cheese board for placing
full truckles, 22in (56cm)
diam.
$75-150

A wooden iron bound
plunger butter churn, early
19thC.
$150-200

A stoneware pestle and
mortar, 6½in (16.5cm).
$30-50

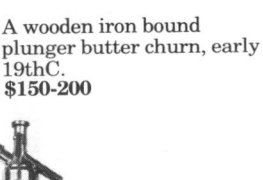

A soda syphon, 14in
(35.5cm) high.
$15-30

A George III oak, brass
mounted coffee grinder, 7in
(18cm) square.
$150-250

A butter dish with carved
wood surround, 8in (20cm)
diam.
$25-35

A painted wooden splint
basket, painted in alternating
red and black design,
surrounded with gilt banding,
probably Pennsylvania,
mid-19thC, 11in (28cm) wide.
$1,000-1,500

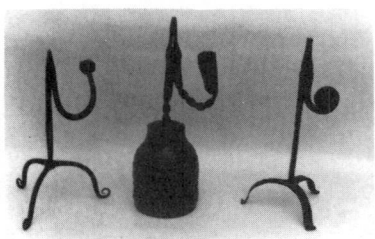

Three English wrought iron rushlights, 18thC, 8in (20cm) high.
$150-250 each

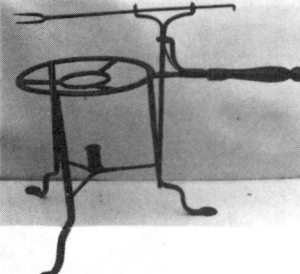

A set of 4 limeware candlesticks, 19thC, 13in (33cm) high.
$1,200-1,600

An English wrought iron trivet/toaster, c1770, 18in (45.5cm) high.
$400-500

A wrought iron griddle, c1760, 15in (38cm) long.
$60-100

A Shaker maple covered oval basket, with bentwood handle, c1850, 14in (35cm) long.
$1,500-2,000

A mangle, Nelson & Co, London, c1910, 30in (76cm) wide.
$150-200

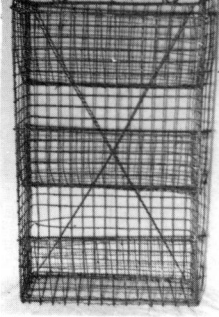

A wire vegetable rack, 16½in (42cm) wide.
$30-50

A boxwood glove powder container, c1840, 5in (12.5cm) high.
$60-100

A French galvanised bottle holder for drying bottles, 40in (102cm) high.
$150-200

An elm mousetrap, 18thC, 10in (25cm) high.
$250-350

An English brass and iron trivet, c1790, 12in (30cm) high.
$150-200

An elm mousetrap, 18thC, 7in (18cm) high.
$250-350

A bottle-carrying basket, 17in (43cm) high.
$25-35

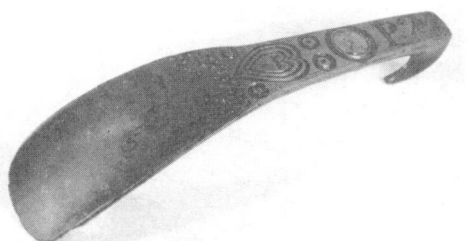

An English boxwood shoe horn, late 17thC, 7in (18cm) long.
$450-700

A candlebox with drawer for flint and steel, 8in (20cm) high.
$150-250

A pair of walnut and brass bellows, c1800, 23in (58.5cm) long.
$250-350

A set of brass letter scales, with weights, on mahogany base.
$150-200

An American burl wood bowl, mid-19thC, 24in (61cm) diam.
$2,000-3,000

An ash bread peel, 18thC, 18in (46cm) high.
$100-150

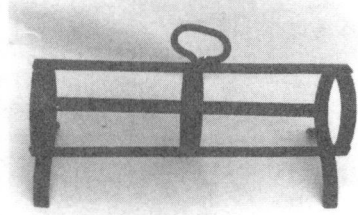

A wrought iron pipe kiln, c1760, 16in (41cm) long.
$150-200

A French pine cheese store, 34½in (87.5cm).
$400-500

A wooden basket.
$30-50

A knife board with polish,
25½in (64.5cm).
$15-30

A treen barrel container,
4in (10cm) high.
$30-50

A washing boiler, 10in
(25cm) high.
$15-30

Agriculture

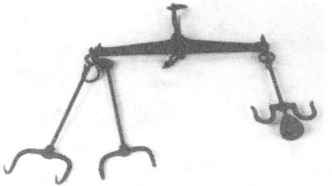

A pair of baker's scales.
$100-150

A watering can with copper
rosette.
$15-30

A pine beer barrel stand,
27in (68cm) long.
$150-200

A pine wheelbarrow, c1860.
$150-250

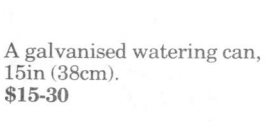

An elm and iron trolley,
c1860, 32in (81cm).
$100-200

A galvanised watering can,
15in (38cm).
$15-30

Tunbridgeware

A Tunbridgeware pencil box, early 19thC, 9in (23cm) wide.
$100-200

Smoking and Snufftaking

A pewter pipe stand, 4½in (11cm) long.
$15-30

A cigar moulder, 1947, 22in (56cm) long.
$15-30

Drinking Vessels

A Scandinavian birchwood goblet and cover, signed and dated 1904, 16in (40.5cm) high.
$450-600

The Dining Room

A Georgian mahogany cheese coaster, 18in (45.5cm) wide.
$300-400

Needlework

A rare lacemaker's 'flash', used by lacemakers to illuminate their work; candlelight is intensified by water in glass flasks, c1800.
$900-1,300

Games & Pastimes

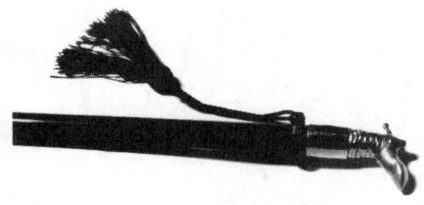

A silver handled walking stick, with rosewood shaft, c1850, 37in (94cm) long.
$450-700

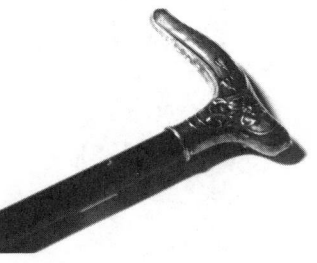

An English Art Nouveau silver handled cane, on an ebonised shaft, c1880, 36in (92cm) long.
$250-350

A Russian cane with silver gilt handle, overlaid with coloured enamels, on a ebonised shaft, c1900.
$1,500-2,600

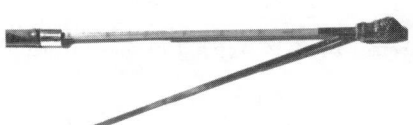

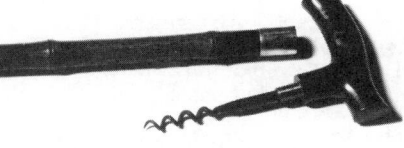

A bamboo walking stick containing a boxwood horse measuring rule, dated UK 1890, 36in (92cm) when closed.
$150-250

A bamboo walking cane containing a corkscrew, with tortoiseshell clutch handle, 36in (92cm) long.
$400-500

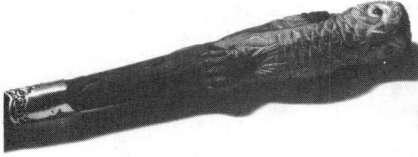

A Victorian carved and painted parrot's head handle cane with gilt collar, c1870.
$150-250

A Victorian cane with a carved wood handle in the form of a perched owl, with silver collared ebonised shaft, 34in (86cm) long.
$300-400

A Continental lady's cane, with rose quartz handle inset with several rock crystal cameos containing insects, horseshoes, birds, etc, with enamel collar and ebonised shaft, c1880.
$900-1,300

A leather hat box, 13in (33cm).
$60-100

A leather Gladstone bag, 15in (38cm) wide.
$45-70

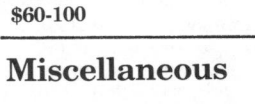

A fitted picnic basket, early 20thC.
$60-100

A medicine ball from a gymnasium, 10in (25cm).
$60-100

Miscellaneous

A game of deck quoits, 16in (40cm) square.
$100-200

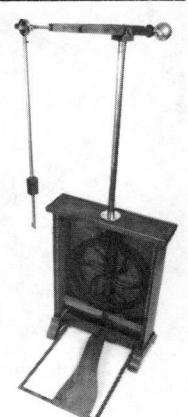

A mahogany church wardens pipe rack, c1760, 15in (38cm) high.
$450-600

A French tattooing machine, 68in (172.5cm) high.
$700-900

A table croquet set, mallets 11½in (29cm) long.
$60-100

In the last 12 months the jewellery world has been rocked to its foundations by the results of the sale of the late Duchess of Windsor's jewels.

The sale was conducted by Nicholas Rayner for Sotheby's, in a huge circus tent which was erected opposite the Hotel Beau Rivage on the shores of Lake Geneva. Over 1,200 potential bidders packed the tent, together with 200 of the world's top press, a team of radio reporters and 17 TV crews on the evenings of the 2nd and 3rd April 1987.

An atmosphere of near hysteria was reached as prices rocketed to over six times the anticipated estimate. A staggering $46,500,000 was realised to benefit the Pasteur Institute in Paris for further research into Aids, Cancer and Retroviruses. The 31 carat McLean diamond was purchased by Japanese business man, Tsuneo Takagi for a record price of nearly $3,000,000 whilst Elizabeth Taylor, bidding by private satellite from her poolside in California, outbid all others for the diamond-set 'Prince of Wales Feathers Clip', for which she paid $525,000.

The London jeweller, Laurence Graff, purchased three of the major lots, including the fabled Emerald Engagement Ring, which was originally made by Cartier's in London, back in the 1930's from a huge emerald which they purchased from the Great Mogul in Baghdad. Believing that there was no-one in the world at that time with sufficient money to purchase the complete stone as a piece of jewellery, they had it cut in two, and it is from half this stone, that the Emerald Engagement Ring was made. The other two lots purchased by Mr Graff were a pair of Canary yellow diamond clips and a matching pair of diamond earrings.

Later in the year the jewels of the late Ingrid Bergman were offered for sale in New York, whilst in France, Brigitte Bardot sold off some of her remaining gems to benefit an animal sanctuary. The Bergman and Bardot items, though exciting, fetched much nearer their current market value, which once again confirms that the enormous variation in prices fetched at auction depends solely upon desirability to people of limitless means who are determined to possess a particular item of jewellery no matter what the cost. Intrinsic value, quality of stones or settings play very little part in these circumstances. It is also interesting to note the large proportion of purchasers paying astronomical sums for items who prefer to remain anonymous.

Jewellery

A miniature painting on ivory in an 18ct gold mount, c1830.
$900-1,300

The Duchess of Windsor's famous flamingo brooch, made by Cartier in Paris, set with rubies, emeralds, sapphires, citrines and diamonds, 1940, sold for **$750,000**

A pearl set brooch of foliate design, on trace link neckchain.
$250-350

A Victorian gold, enamel, diamond and pearl brooch, in case from Bright & Sons, Scarborough.
$450-700

A diamond, enamel and gold brooch/pendant, set with 7 diamonds and 6 pearls, on a chain.
$400-500

PRICE
Prices in jewellery can vary enormously
1. According to age and condition
2. The basic materials from which it is made
3. Whether it is hand made or mass produced
4. The quality of the stones set in the items
5. Whether the item is at present fashionable

The last consideration could be the most important of all, because, although fashions go in cycles, it may be many years before an unfashionable item becomes marketable once again. The only value often in these instances is that of the basic materials from which the item is made, i.e. Scrap Value

A Victorian 15ct gold
brooch set with diamonds.
$750-1,000

A pair of Victorian black
and white banded agate
earrings, set with a star
motif in rose diamonds, and
gold fittings.
$250-350

A diamond 'snowdrop'
brooch, 19thC.
$4,000-5,500

A Battersea enamel, c1780,
set in modern 9ct gold
surround.
$900-1,300

A silver marcasite cameo
brooch, c1930.
$300-400

A Victorian 15ct gold cross
set with 7 matched pyrope
garnets.
$450-600

A pair of amethyst pear
drop earrings, with
diamond set swag mounts
and pendant drop.
$700-900

A Victorian 9ct gold
chain, with
swivel type fastener,
original condition, 60in
(152cm) long.
$700-900

A pair of Victorian gold
earrings, set with opals and
decorated with seed pearls
and enamel.
$450-600

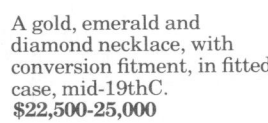

A gold, emerald and
diamond necklace, with
conversion fitment, in fitted
case, mid-19thC.
$22,500-25,000

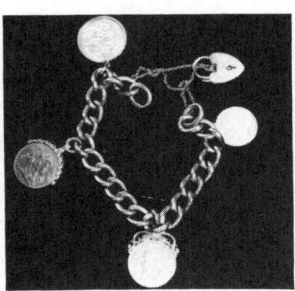

A 9ct gold charm bracelet, with 2 sovereigns 1903 and 1918, a gold one pound piece 1898 and a half sovereign 1897.
$400-500

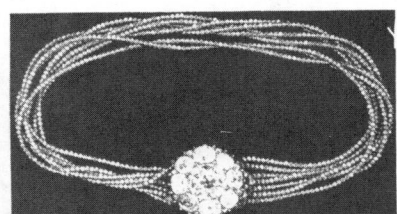

A diamond cluster bracelet, the reverse engraved with script initials, on 7 fine gold back chains.
$5,500-7,000

An Indian ruby and diamond gold bracelet with matching bar brooch, 13.5dwt.
$450-700

A silver link bracelet, set with 'Scotch pebbles'.
$75-150

A Victorian 15ct gold snake link bracelet, set with red garnets cut 'en cabochon'.
$1,300-1,800

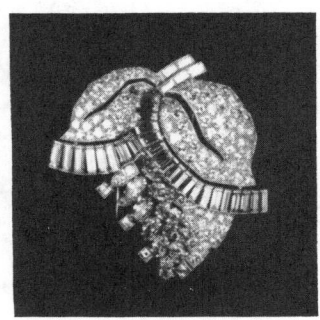

A Cartier rosebud clip brooch, with diamond baguettes.
$13,500-17,500

A diamond star, late 19thC.
$1,500-2,600

A sapphire and diamond panther clip, part of the Duchess of Windsor's collection, by Cartier, Paris, in 1949. The sapphire weighs 152.35 carats. The panther set with 106 sapphires weighing 5 carats and brilliant cut diamonds weighing 4.90 carats. Purchased for **$1,000,000** by the Cartier Museum.

A Victorian 15ct gold and silver brooch, set with rose diamonds, the body enamelled in green.
$1,500-2,600

An 18ct bar brooch, set with rubies, diamonds and split seed pearls.
$400-500

A Victorian pendant and earrings in high ct gold with garnets, c1880.
$2,250-3,500

A 15ct gold pearl set pendant of twin rail septafoil outline with amethyst centre and drop, on trace link neckchain.
$400-500

A Victorian cameo, c1870.
$800-1,200

A copy of Tutankhamun's ring made for an exhibition in Madrid by Dommerech, 18ct gold lapis and turquoise.
$750-1,000

An Edwardian diamond and pearl pendant, in a fitted case from Mappin & Webb Ltd.
$1,500-2,600

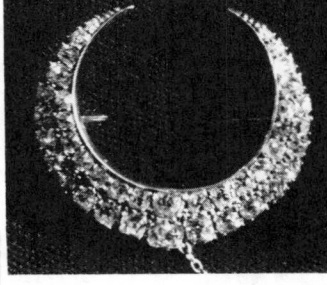

A red amber necklace.
$250-350

CAMEOS

Jewellery set with cameos reached a peak of popularity during the Victorian period, although fine examples of cameos have been around for much longer. Cleopatra was known to have emeralds carved in her own likeness, the stones being obtained from her own emerald mines near the Red Sea in about 2000 BC!

The most valuable cameos are usually of 'Hardstone' – (Sardonyx, cornelian, agate or in rare cases even ruby and other precious stones). But by far the most common is the shell cameo, often originating in Italy and usually carved from the 'Helmet' shell (Cassis Madagascariensis). Good use was made of the three layers of colour to achieve a very pleasing effect. Here again, quality of carving is the criterion as well as intricacy of the setting, when assessing the value. Shell cameos have been imported in their millions over the years, to be made up by the jewellers of Birmingham and London in a great variety of designs and materials including gold, silver, pinchbeck and jet and even on occasions gold plated base metal

A late Victorian crescent brooch, set with a double row of diamonds, with gold and silver settings, c1890.
$4,000-5,500

A Victorian gold, diamond and black and white cameo carved onyx butterfly design brooch.
$750-1,000

A rose diamond and enamel
buckle.
$900-1,300

A pair of bell earrings, held
by birds in gold filigree
work, c1880.
$1,200-1,600

An Edwardian filigree plate
chain link evening purse,
the clasp decorated with
semi-precious stones with
matching fleur-de-lys
pendant to handle.
$100-200

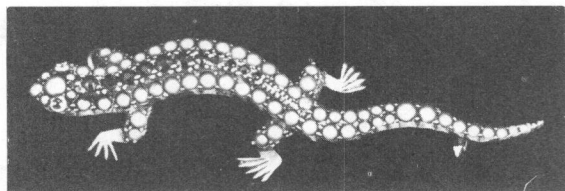

A Victorian ruby and half
pearl lizard brooch.
$450-700

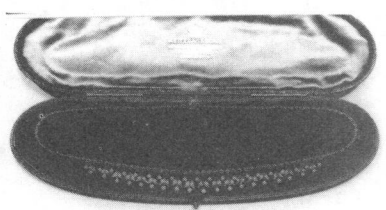

A 15ct gold necklace of split
seed pearls, in original case.
$800-1,200

A pair of Victorian gold and
enamel earrings, set with a
central pearl, c1870.
$900-1,300

A gold, turquoise, coral and
white enamel pendant and
earrings, c1865.
$4,000-5,500

l. A ruby and diamond
pendant/brooch.
$3,000-4,500

r. A diamond spray cocktail
clip.
$3,000-4,500

A turquoise, aquamarine and diamond necklace.
$16,000-21,000

A pair of natural pearl and diamond drop earrings, c1930.
$2,250-3,500

A ruby, diamond and natural baroque seed pearl brooch.
$2,250-3,500

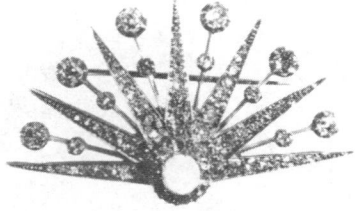

A gold set brooch, centred with an opal and diamond set cluster and rays, converts to an aigrette, in Goldsmiths and Silversmiths Company fitted case.
$1,500-2,600

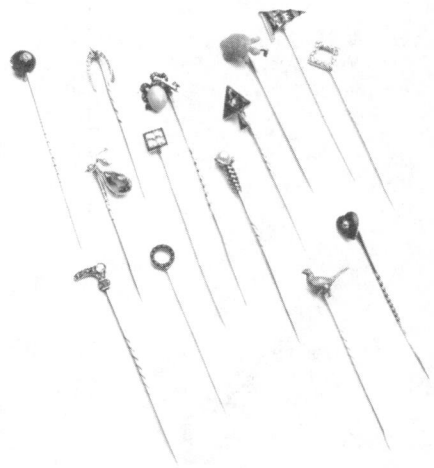

A collection of gem set stick pins.
$150-1,300 each

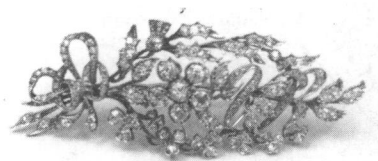

A Victorian diamond set scroll brooch, with initials V.R.
$2,250-3,500

Make the most of Miller's

Price ranges in this book reflect what one should expect to pay for a similar example. When selling one can obviously expect a figure below. This will fluctuate according to a dealer's stock, saleability at a particular time, etc. It is always advisable to approach a reputable specialist dealer or an auction house which has specialist sales.

A 2ct emerald ring, with diamond surround.
$4,000-5,500

A marcasite pendant on silver.
$900-1,300

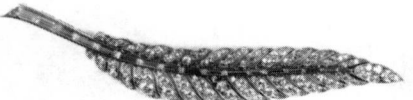

A platinum and diamond
feather brooch, with
baguette cut stones.
$900-1,300

A pair of Victorian hand
carved Whitby jet earrings.
$75-150

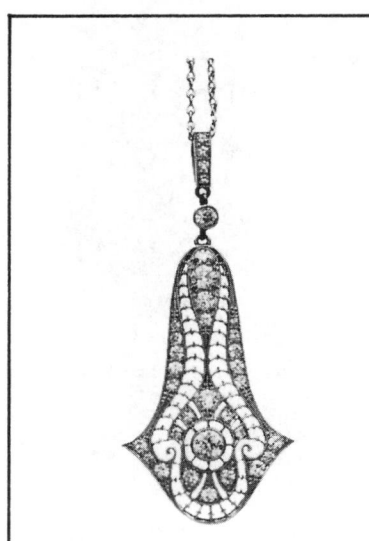

A platinum and diamond
pendant.
$1,300-1,800

An Edwardian pendant/
brooch, the centre set with a
green stone surrounded by
seed pearls, on a fine gold
chain.
$150-250

A rivière necklace of
amethysts, set in 15ct gold,
c1880.
$2,250-3,500

A silver marcasite watch,
c1940.
$150-200

A green hardstone and gold
brooch, in the form of a
fruiting vine, with mat
gold leaves, and cabochon
green hardstones forming
the grapes.
$300-400

CORAL

The coral most commonly
found in Victorian jewellery
is of *Mediterranean* origin. It
is a secretion of Calcium
Carbonate formed by the
Coral Polyp and grows on the
sea bed rather like a forest of
pink, white and *orange*
coloured trees. The smaller
branches of these can be
broken into tiny pieces and
drilled and strung as
necklaces or earrings, but the
most desirable pieces are
heads and cameos from the
trunk of the coral, the latter
often set in the Castellani
style settings of the time.
Fashion dictates the most
desirable colour, and at
the moment it is the most
delicate pink of the *'Angel
Skin'* variety which
commands the highest price.

The greatest concentration of
coral carvers today is around
Naples in Italy where they
have been plying their trade
for many years if not
thousands of years, the only
difference now being that
much of the coral upon which
they work is imported from
Japan.

There also exists *Black Coral*
– this type is found mostly in
the waters off *Hawaii.*

An Edwardian enamelled
gold and gem set pendant.
$750-1,000

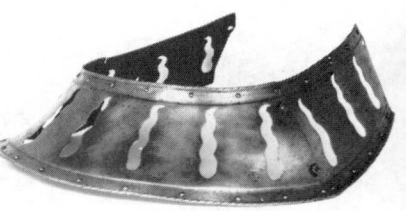

A German bright steel horse's peytral, some internal patching, early 16thC.
$3,000-4,500

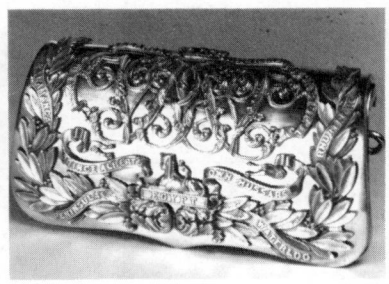

A Victorian officer's full dress pouch, to the 11th, Prince Albert's Own Hussars.
$450-700

A German close helmet, some damage and patching, mid-16thC, 12in (30.5cm).
$5,500-7,000

Cannon

A Spanish cannon, 18thC.
$10,500-14,000

Edged Weapons – Bayonets

An English plug bayonet, with stylised human head finial, minor grip bruising and blade rust, blade 11in (28cm).
$150-250

Daggers

A Scottish silver mounted dirk, inscribed Pillin Manufacturer, Sure Strike, early 19thC, 12in (31cm) long.
$900-1,300

A Nazi Railway Protection Force 1938 pattern officer's dagger, by Eickhorn.
$1,200-1,600

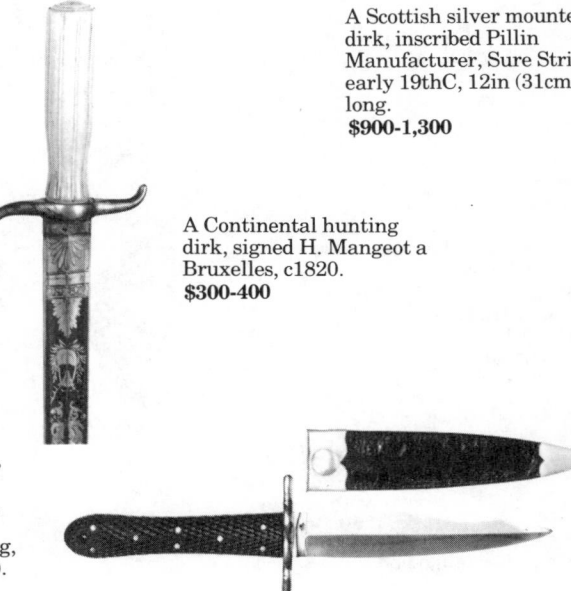

A Continental hunting dirk, signed H. Mangeot a Bruxelles, c1820.
$300-400

An English fighting dirk, made for the American market by S Maw & Son, London, minor rust staining and grip bruising, c1880, blade 5in (12.5cm).
$75-150

A Turkish kindjal, with straight single edged blade and foliate brass inlay, 21½in (55cm) long.
$600-900

Knives

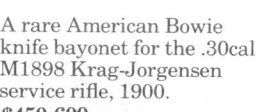

A Mediterranean fighting knife, some pitting, grip cracked, c1800, blade 4in (10cm), in a leather covered sheath.
$100-200

A rare American Bowie knife bayonet for the .30cal M1898 Krag-Jorgensen service rifle, 1900.
$450-600

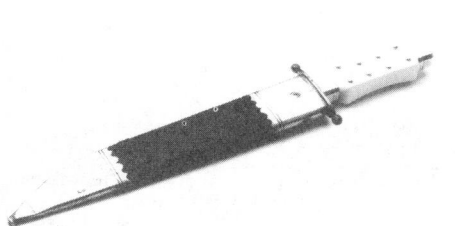

A Bowie knife, by J English & Hubers, Philadelphia, with ivory grip and nickel mounts.
$750-1,000

Swords

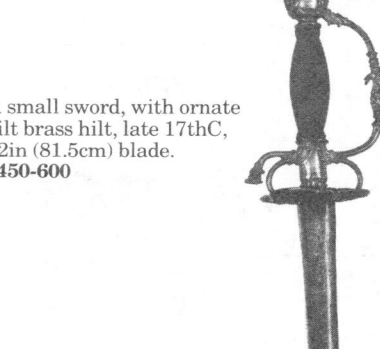

A small sword, with ornate gilt brass hilt, late 17thC, 32in (81.5cm) blade.
$450-600

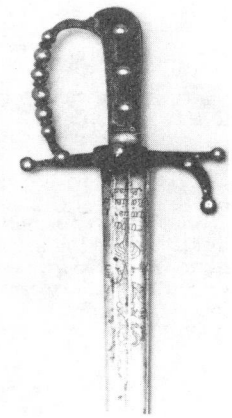

A chiselled steel small sword, probably English, late 17thC, 42in (106.5cm).
$2,250-3,000

An Austrian or German hunting hanger, with inscription 'Vivat Carolus VI Römischer Kayser', early 18thC, 24in (60cm).
$1,300-1,800

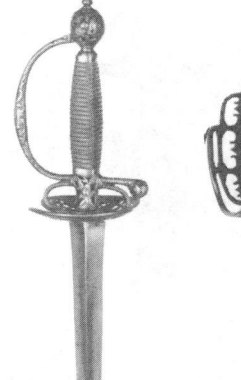

A small sword, the hilt pierced with flags and martial trophies and decorated with scrolling foliage, c1760, 34½in (87cm) blade.
$450-600

A Scottish military basket hilted Cavalry Officer's backsword, marked Andrea Ferara, c1770, 33½in (85cm).
$1,500-2,600

A Spanish Bilboe hilted
broadsword, the iron hilt
with rounded pommel, the
ricasso struck with maker's
name, pitting, c1700, 35½in
(90cm) blade.
$250-350

A rare Swedish Partizan,
model 1697, for Pikemen of
the King's Guard, some
minor pitting, 23in (58.5cm)
head.
$150-250

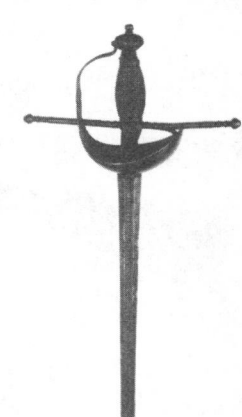

A Spanish rapier, the steel
hilt of Bilboe form with
knucklebow and basket
guard forged as one piece,
guard screw missing.
$300-400

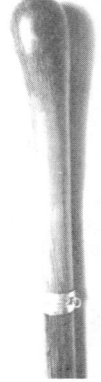

A Victorian sword case,
with fine blue and gilt
blade, English, c1870.
$450-600

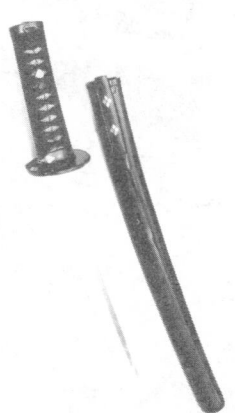

A Japanese short sword
Wakizashi, Koto blade
15thC, mounting from Edo
period, c1800.
$1,200-1,600

Swords – Eastern

An Arabian jambiya, blade
7½in (19.5cm), with part of
its woven belt with silver
buckle.
$750-1,000

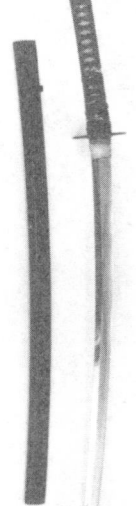

A Japanese sword, with
single edged blade, fully
signed on the tang, 38in
(96.5cm) long.
$1,500-2,600

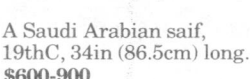

A Saudi Arabian saif,
19thC, 34in (86.5cm) long.
$600-900

A silver and gold mounted
khanjar, 19thC.
$600-900

A Japanese aikuchi, minor
blade pitting, 6in (15cm).
$600-900

Blunderbusses

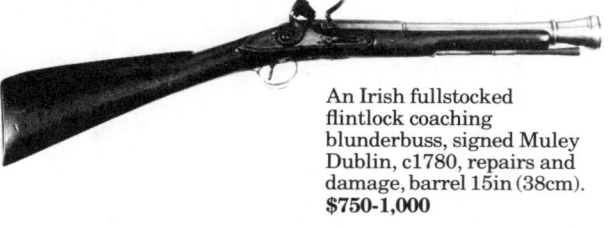

An Irish fullstocked flintlock coaching blunderbuss, signed Muley Dublin, c1780, repairs and damage, barrel 15in (38cm).
$750-1,000

An English fullstocked flintlock coaching musketoon, signed T. Iackson, one breech flat stamped with the maker's mark of a crown over 'T.I' and two crowned 'P' London Proof House marks, c1780, minor pitting, barrel 18in (46cm).
$1,500-2,600

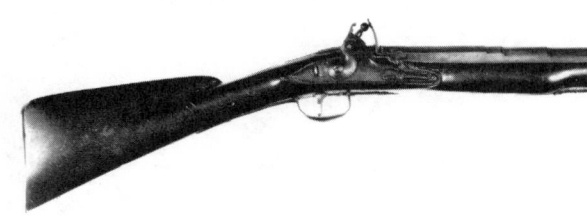

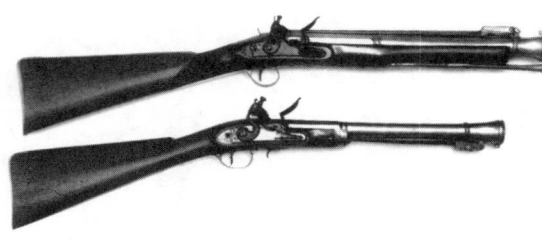

A Branden & Potts blunderbuss with bayonet.
$1,500-2,600

A J Richards blunderbuss with bayonet.
$1,300-1,800

Muskets & Sporting

A Birmingham proved 25 bore, .577 cal, half-stocked percussion sporting rifle, by R Davis, London & Madras, the patchbox cover replaced, 33in (84cm) barrel.
$400-500

A Victorian detached wheel lock for a sporting rifle, in the German style of the late 17thC, some damage to mechanism and wheel linkage, pan missing, 10in (25cm) overall.
$150-250

A rare French 21 bore boxlock percussion double barrelled sporting gun, signed Guillot a Meaux, c1840.
$450-700

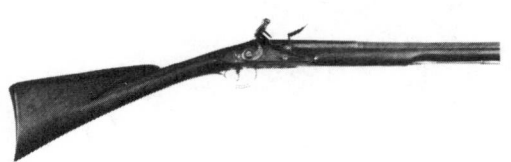

A rare English fullstocked musketoon, by Webb London, damage, c1770, 18in (46cm) barrel.
$1,300-1,800

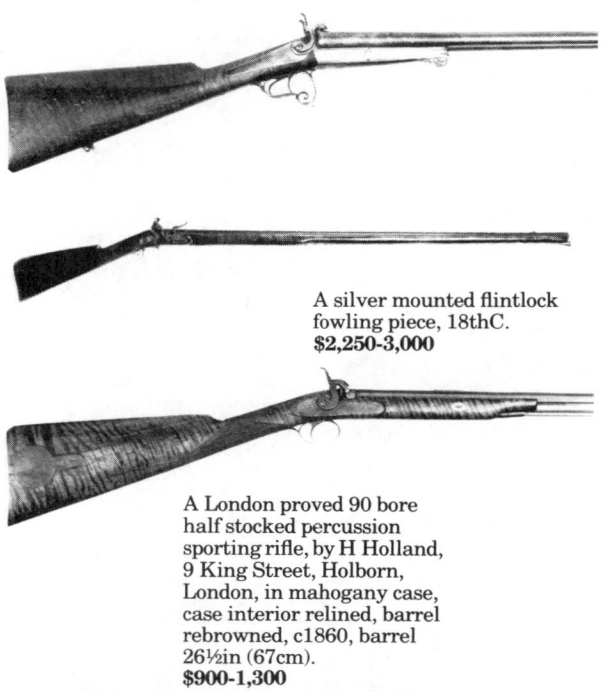

A silver mounted flintlock
fowling piece, 18thC.
$2,250-3,000

A Belgian 16 bore le
Faucheaux type underlever
double barrelled sporting
gun, signed F.P.B. Faure le
Page A Paris, the action
body lockplates and guard
borderline inlaid in gold,
some damage, c1855, barrel
26in (66cm).
$450-600

Powder Flasks

A London proved 90 bore
half stocked percussion
sporting rifle, by H Holland,
9 King Street, Holborn,
London, in mahogany case,
case interior relined, barrel
rebrowned, c1860, barrel
26½in (67cm).
$900-1,300

A Musketeer's powder
flask, probably English,
c1640-60, 10 by 11in (25 by
28cm).
$800-1,200

Rifles

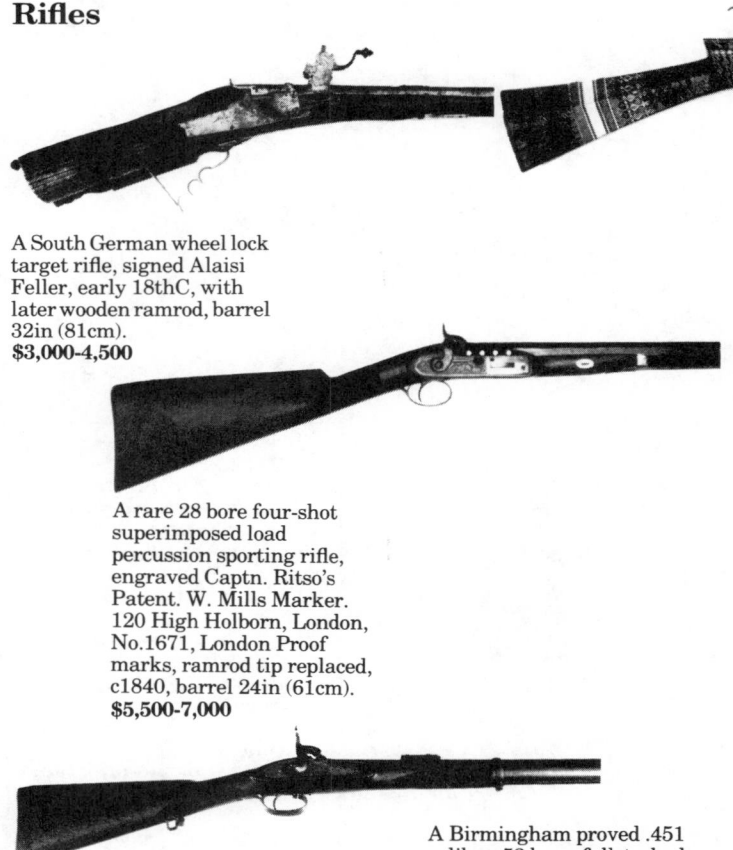

A South German wheel lock
target rifle, signed Alaisi
Feller, early 18thC, with
later wooden ramrod, barrel
32in (81cm).
$3,000-4,500

A Turkish miquelet lock
rifle, late 18thC, and later
bone tipped ramrod, barrel
35in (89cm).
$1,300-1,800

A rare 28 bore four-shot
superimposed load
percussion sporting rifle,
engraved Captn. Ritso's
Patent. W. Mills Marker.
120 High Holborn, London,
No.1671, London Proof
marks, ramrod tip replaced,
c1840, barrel 24in (61cm).
$5,500-7,000

Miller's is a price Guide not a price List

*The price ranges given
reflect the average price a
purchaser should pay for
similar items. Condition,
rarity of design or pattern,
size, colour, provenance,
restoration and many
other factors must be
taken into account when
assessing values.
When buying or selling, it
must always be
remembered that prices
can be greatly affected by
the condition of any piece.
Unless otherwise stated, all
goods shown in Miller's
are of good merchantable
quality, and the valuations
given reflect this fact.
Pieces offered for sale in
exceptionally fine
condition or in poor
condition may reasonably
be expected to be priced
considerably higher or
lower respectively than
the estimates given herein.*

A Birmingham proved .451
calibre, 52 bore, fullstocked
percussion military match
rifle, marked E. Jones,
c1860, barrel 32½in
(82.5cm).
$800-1,200

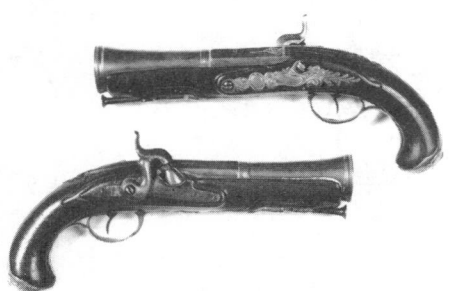

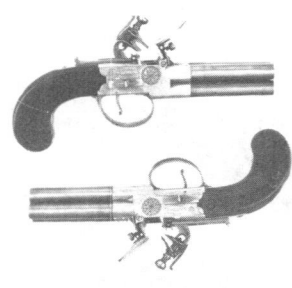

A pair of blunderbuss pistols, with engraved brass flared barrels and relief decorated mounts, 18thC, converted at a later date to percussion mechanism, 11in (28cm) long.
$1,200-1,600

A .41RF Colt No.1 Derringer, serial no. 1940, some damage, c1880.
$300-400

A pair of 80 bore screw barrel tap-action boxlock flintlock 4-barrelled pocket pistols, in early 19thC English style, signed H Nock, London, 3½in (8.5cm) barrels.
$700-900

An English 16 bore fullstocked percussion Officer's pistol, by John Egg, Successor to D Egg, No.1 Pall Mall, London, c1850.
$400-500

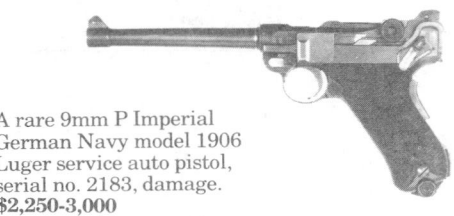

A rare 9mm P Imperial German Navy model 1906 Luger service auto pistol, serial no. 2183, damage.
$2,250-3,000

A Birmingham proved .450CF Pryse type top break extracting 5-shot double action pocket revolver, serial no. 6804, retailed by Wilkinson & Son, 27 Pall Mall, London.
$400-500

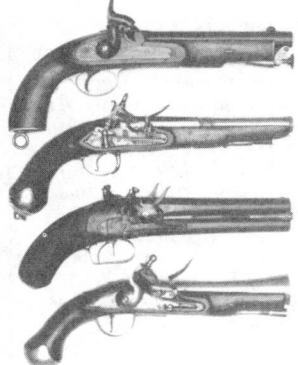

Flintlock pistols, from top:

An EIG pistol.
$600-900

A Spanish miquelet pistol.
$1,500-2,600

A double-barrelled pistol by Tatham.
$2,250-3,000

A blunderbuss pistol by Galton.
$1,300-1,800

A Dixon & Sons common top pistol flask, as cased with pepperbox revolvers, 4in (10cm).
$75-150

Price

Prices vary from auction to auction – from dealer to dealer. The price paid in a dealer's shop will depend on:
1) what he paid for the item
2) what he thinks he can get for it
3) the extent of his knowledge
4) awareness of market trends
It is a mistake to think that you will automatically pay more in a specialist dealer's shop. He is more likely to know the 'right' price for a piece. A general dealer may undercharge but he could also overcharge.

Revolvers

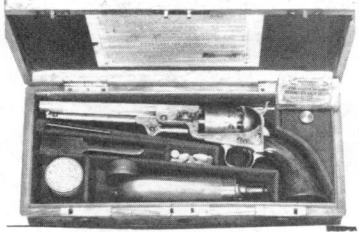

A cased 6-shot London Colt
navy percussion revolver.
$4,000-5,500

A rare 120 bore Adams
Patent Model 1851 5-shot
self-cocking percussion
revolver, serial no. 30,441B,
retailed by H Egg,
1 Piccadilly, London.
$800-1,200

A .44-40 calibre Colt single
action army 6-shot revolver,
Model 1873, Serial No.
235851, stamped Colt
Frontier Six Shooter, 1902.
$800-1,200

A Birmingham proved 72
bore Joseph Cooper type
6-shot self-cocking
percussion pepperbox
revolver, c1855, some
damage, barrel 3in (7.5cm).
$150-250

Medals

An American Indian peace
medallion dated 1853.
$3,000-4,500

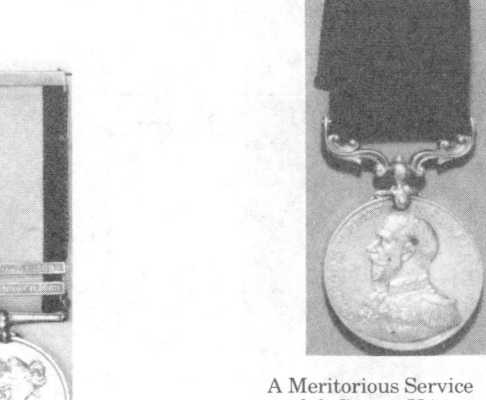

A Meritorious Service
medal, George V issue,
122347, T Jones, CPO
Newhaven War Services.
$150-250

Two clasps, Emerald 13
March 1808, Basque Roads
1809, E Wylde,
Midshipman, edge bruise
and minor contact marks,
with silver riband bar.
$5,500-7,000

A British Waterloo medal to
Will.M. Bemond Private
2nd Life Guards, issued
1816-17, inscribed
Wellington June 1815.
$400-500

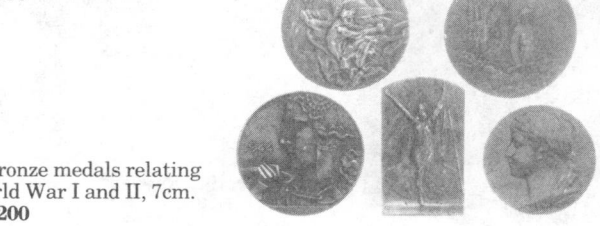

Five bronze medals relating
to World War I and II, 7cm.
$100-200

Militaria

A South African Chief's medal, awarded as a mark of esteem on the occasion of the Royal visit to South Africa by their Majesties King George VI and Queen Elizabeth, 1947, silver, 2½in (6.2cm) high.
$750-1,000

A 3rd Reich Führerstandarte for Hitler's car.
$5,500-7,000

A German 3rd Reich auxiliary cruiser war badge with diamonds.
$6,000-8,000

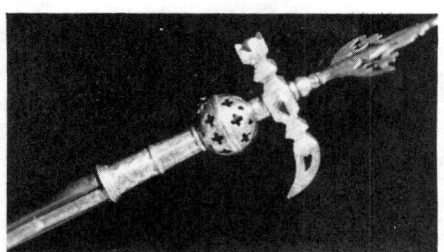

A Continental poleaxe, probably German, as carried by the Provosts of German mercenary companies as a badge of office, c1600, 15in (38cm) head.
$450-600

An Austrian officer's spontoon, late 17thC.
$900-1,300

Helmets

Drums

A Victorian sable busby, 11th Hussars officer.
$700-900

A 1st Battalion Grenadier Guards rope tension side drum, by George Potter & Co, Aldershot, embellished with the Royal Arms, King's Crown, 1914-18, with a cover and a pair of drumsticks.
$750-1,000

A Victorian Yeomanry cavalry helmet, to the Fife Light Horse.
$1,200-1,600

A Hanoverian Raupen helmet, c1840.
$5,500-7,000

DIRECTORY OF INTERNATIONAL AUCTIONEERS

This directory is by no means complete. Any auctioneer who holds frequent sales should contact us for inclusion in the 1989 Edition. Entries must be received by April 1988. There is, of course, no charge for this listing.

America

Acorn Farm Antiques,
15466 Oak Road, Carmel,
IN 46032
Tel: (317) 846-2383

ALA Moanastampt Cain (David H Martin),
1236 Ala Moana Boulevard,
Honolulu, HI 96814

Alabama Auction Room Inc,
2112 Fifth Avenue North,
Birmingham, AL 35203
Tel: (205) 252-4073

B Altman & Co,
34th & Fifth Avenue, New York,
NY 10016
Tel: (212) OR 9 7800 ext 550 & 322

Ames Art Galleries,
8729 Wilshire Boulevard, Beverly Hills, CA 9021
Tel: (213) 655-5611/652-3820

Arnette's Auction Galleries Inc,
310 West Castle Street,
Murfreesboro, TN 37130
Tel: (615) 893-3725

Associated Appraisers Inc,
915 Industrial Bank Building,
Providence, RI 02906
Tel: (401) 331-9391

Atlanta's ABCD Auction Gallery (Clark, Bate and Depew),
1 North Clarendon Avenue,
Antioch, IL 30002
Tel: (312) 294-8264

Bakers Auction,
14100 Paramount Boulevard,
Paramount, CA 90723
Tel: (213) 531-1524

Barridoff Galleries,
242 Middle Street, Portland,
ME 04 101
Tel: (207) 772-5011

C T Bevensee Auction Service,
PO Box 492, Botsford, CT 06404
Tel: (203) 426-6698

Frank H Boos,
1137 S Adams, Birmingham,
MI 48011
Tel: (313) 644-1633

Richard A Bourne Co Inc,
Corporation Street, PO Box 141/A,
Hyannis Port, MA 02647
Tel: (617) 775-0797

Bridges Antiques and Auctions,
Highway 46, PO Box 52A,
Sanford, FL 32771
Tel: (305) 323-2801/322-0095

George C Brilant & Co,
191 King Street, Charleston,
SC 29401

R W Bronstein Corp,
3666 Main Street, Buffalo,
NY 14226
Tel: (716) 835-7666/7408

Brookline Auction Gallery,
Proctor Hill Road, Route 130,
Brookline, NH 03033
Tel: (603) 673-4474/4153

Brzostek's Auction Service,
2052 Lamson Road, Phoenix,
NY 13135
Tel: (315) 678-2542

Buckingham Galleries Ltd,
4350 Dawson Street, San Diego,
CA 92115
Tel: (714) 283-7286

Bushell's Auction,
2006 2nd Avenue, Seattle,
WA 98121
Tel: (206) 622-5833

L Butterfield,
605 W Midland, Bay City,
MI 48706
Tel: (517) 684-3229

Butterfield,
808 N La, Cienega Boulevard, Los Angeles, CA 90069

Butterfield & Butterfield,
1244 Sutter Street, San Francisco,
CA 94109
Tel: (415) 673-1362

California Book Auction Galleries,
358 Golden Gate Avenue, San Francisco, CA 94102
Tel: (415) 775-0424

C B Charles Galleries Inc,
825 Woodward Avenue, Pontiac,
MI 48053
Tel: (313) 338-9023

Chatsworth Auction Rooms,
151 Mamaroneck Avenue,
Mamaroneck, NY 10543

Christie, Manson & Wood International Inc,
502 Park Avenue, New York
Tel: (212) 826-2388 Telex: 620721

Christie's East,
219 East 67th Street, New York,
NY 10021
Tel: (212) 570-4141

Representative Offices:
California:
9350 Wilshire Boulevard, Beverly Hills, CA 902 12
Tel: (213) 275-5534

Florida:
225 Fern Street, West Palm Beach,
FL 33401
Tel: (305) 833-6592

Mid-Atlantic:
638 Morris Avenue, Bryn Mawr,
PA 19010
Tel: (215) 525-5493

Washington:
1422 27th Street NW, Washington,
DC 20007
Tel: (202) 965-2066

Midwest:
46 East Elm Street, Chicago,
IL 60611
Tel: (312) 787-2765

Fred Clark Auctioneer Inc,
PO Box 124, Route 14, Scotland,
CT 06264
Tel: (203) 423-3939/0594

Cockrum Auctions,
2701 North Highway 94,
St Charles, MO 63301
Tel: (314) 723-9511

George Cole, Auctioneers and Appraisers,
14 Green Street, Kingston,
NY 12401
Tel: (914) 338-2367

Coleman Auction Galleries,
525 East 72nd Street, New York,
NY 10021
Tel: (212) 879-1415

Conestoga Auction Company Inc,
PO Box 1, Manheim, PA 17545
Tel: (717) 898-7284

Cook's Auction Gallery,
Route 58, Halifax, MA 02338
Tel: (617) 293-3445/866-3243

Coquina Auction Barn
40 S Atlantic Avenue, Ormond Beach, FL 32074

Danny's Antique Auction Service (Pat Lusardi),
Route 46, Belvidere, NH 07823
Tel: (201) 757-7278

Douglas Galleries,
Route 5, South Deerfield,
MA 01373
Tel: (413) 665-2877

William Doyle,
175 East 87th Street, New York,
NY 10128
Tel: (212) 427-2730

DuMochelle Art Galleries,
409 East Jefferson, Detroit,
MI 48226
Tel: (313) 963-6255

John C Edelmann Galleries Inc,
123 East 77th Street, New York,
NY 10021
Tel: (212) 628-1700/1735

Robert C Eldred Co Inc,
Box 796, East Dennis, MA 02641
Tel: (617) 385-3116/3377

The Fine Arts Company of Philadelphia Inc,
2317 Chestnut Street,
Philadelphia, PA 19103
Tel: (215) 564-3644

Fordem Galleries Inc,
3829 Lorain Avenue, Cleveland,
OH 44113
Tel: (216) 281-3563

George S Foster III,
Route 28, Epsom, NH 03234
Tel: (603) 736-9240

Fred's Auction House,
92 Pleasant Street, Leominster,
MA 01453
Tel: (617) 534-9004

S T Freeman & Co,
1808 Chestnut Street,
Philadelphia, PA 19103
Tel: (215) 563-9275

Col K R French and Co Inc,
166 Bedford Road, Armonk,
NY 10504
Tel: (914) 273-3674

Garth's Auctions Inc,
2690 Stratford Road, Delaware,
OH 43015
Tel: (614) 362-4771/369-5085

Gilbert Auctions,
River Road, Garrison, NY 10524
Tel: (914) 424-3657

Morten M Goldberg,
215 N Rampart Street, New Orleans, LA 70112
Tel: (504) 522-8364

Gramercy Auction Galleries,
52 East 13th Street, New York,
NY 10003
Tel: (212) 477-5656

Grandma's House,
4712 Dudley, Wheatridge,
CO 80033
Tel: (303) 423-3640/534-2847

The William Haber Art Collection Inc,
139-11 Queens Boulevard,
Jamaica, NY 11435
Tel: (212) 739-1000

Charlton Hall Galleries Inc,
930 Gervais Street, Columbia,
SC 29201
Tel: (803) 252-7927/779-5678

Hampton Auction Gallery,
201 Harwick Street, Belvidere,
NH 07823
Tel: (201) 475-2928

Hanzel,
1120 S Michigan Avenue, Chicago,
IL 60605
Tel: (312) 922-6234

Harbor Auction Gallery,
238 Bank Street, New London,
CT 06355
Tel: (203) 443-0868

Harmer's of San Francisco Inc,
49 Geary Street, San Francisco,
CA 94102
Tel: (415) 391-8244

Harris Auction Galleries,
873-875 North Howard Street,
Baltimore, MD 21201
Tel: (301) 728-7040

Hart,
2311 Westheimer, Houston,
TX 77098
Tel: (713) 524-2979/523-7389

Hauswedel & Nolte,
225 West Central Park, New York,
NY 10024
Tel: (212) 787-7245

G Ray Hawkins,
7224 Melrose Avenue, Los Angeles, CA 90046
Tel: (213) 550-1504

Elwood Heller & Son Auctioneer,
151 Main Street, Lebanon,
NJ 08833
Tel: (201) 23 62 195

William F Hill Auction Sales,
Route 16, East Hardwick,
VT 05834
Tel: (802) 472-6308

Leslie Hindman,
215 West Ohio Street, Chicago,
IL 60610
Tel: (312) 670-0010

The House Clinic,
PO Box 13013A, Orlando, Fl 32859
Tel: (305) 859-1770/851-2979

Co Raymond W Huber,
211 North Monroe, Montpelier,
OH 43543

F B Hubley Et Co,
364 Broadway, Cambridge,
MA 02100
Tel: (617) 876-2030

Iroquois Auctions,
Box 66, Broad Street, Port Henry,
NY 12974
Tel: (518) 942-3355

It's About Time,
375 Park Avenue, Glencoe,
IL 60022
Tel: (312) 835-2012

Louis Joseph Auction Gallery (Richard L Ryan),
575 Washington Street, Brookline,
MA 02146
Tel: (617) 277-0740

Julia's Auction Service,
Route 201, Skowhegan Road,
Fairfield, ME 04937
Tel: (207) 453-9725

Sibylle Kaldewey,
225 West Central Park, New York,
NY 10024
Tel: (212) 787-7245

Kelley's Auction Service,
PO Box 125, Woburn, MA 01801
Tel: (617) 272-9167

Kennedy Antique Auction Galleries Inc,
1088 Huff Road, Atlanta,
GA 30318
Tel: (404) 351-4464

Kinzie Galleries Auction Service,
1002 3rd Avenue, Duncansville,
PA 16835
Tel: (814) 695-3479

La Salle,
2083 Union Street, San Francisco,
CA 94123
Tel: (415) 931-9200

L A Landry (Robert Landry),
94 Main Street, Essex, MA 01929
Tel: (603) 744-5811

Jo Anna Larson,
POB 0, Antioch, IL 60002
Tel: (312) 395-0963

Levins Auction Exchange,
414 Camp Street, New Orleans,
LA 70130

Lipton,
1108 Fort Street, Honolulu,
HI 96813
Tel: (808) 533-4320

F S Long & Sons,
3126 East 3rd Street, Dayton,
OH 45403

R L Loveless Associates Inc,
4223 Clover Street, Honeoye Falls,
NY 14472
Tel: (716) 624-1648/1556

Lubin Galleries,
30 West 26th Street, New York,
NY 10010
Tel: (212) 924-3777

Main Auction Galleries,
137 West 4th Street, Cincinnati,
OH 45202
Tel: (513) 621-1280

Maison Auction Co Inc,
128 East Street, Wallingford,
CT 06492
Tel: (203) 269-8007

Joel L Malter & Co Inc,
Suite 518, 16661 Ventura
Boulevard, Encino, CA 91316
Tel: (213) 784-7772/2181

Manhattan Galleries,
1415 Third Avenue, New York,
NY 10028
Tel: (212) 744-2844

Mapes,
1600 West Vestal Parkway,
Vestal, NY 13850
Tel: (607) 754-9193

David W Mapes Inc,
82 Front Street, Binghamton,
NY 13905
Tel: (607) 724-6741/862-9365

Marvin H Newman,
426 South Robertson Boulevard,
Los Angeles, CA 90048
Tel: (213) 273-4840/378-2095

Mechanical Music Center Inc,
25 Kings Highway North, Darien,
CT 06820
Tel: (203) 655-9510

Milwaukee Auction Galleries,
4747 West Bradley Road,
Milwaukee, WI 53223
Tel: (414) 355-5054

Wayne Mock Inc,
Box 37, Tamworth, NH 03886
Tel: (603) 323-8057

William F Moon & Co,
12 Lewis Road, RFD 1, North
Attleboro, MA 02760
Tel: (617) 761-8003

New England Rare Coin Auctions,
89 Devonshire Street, Boston,
MA 02109
Tel: (617) 227-8800

Kurt Niven,
1444 Oak Lawn, Suite 525, Dallas,
TX 75207
Tel: (214) 741-4252

Northgate Gallery,
5520 Highway 153, Chattanooga,
TN 37443
Tel: (615) 842-4177

O'Gallerie Inc,
537 SE Ash Street, Portland,
OR 97214
Tel: (503) 238-0202

Th J Owen & Sons,
1111 East Street NW, Washington,
DC 20004

Palmer Auction Service,
Lucas, KS 67648

Park City Auction Service,
925 Wood Street, Bridgeport,
CT 06604
Tel: (203) 333-5251

Pennypacker Auction Centre,
1540 New Holland Road,
Kenhorst, Reading, PA 19607
Tel: (215) 777-5890/6121

Peyton Place Antiques,
819 Lovett Boulevard, Houston,
TX 77006
Tel: (713) 523-4841

Phillips,
867 Madison Avenue, New York,
NY 10021
Tel: (212) 570-4830

525 East 72nd Street, New York,
NY10021
Tel: (212) 570-4852

Representative Office:
6 Faneuil Hall, Marketplace,
Boston, MA 02109
Tel: (617) 227-6145

Pollack,
2780 NE 183 Street, Miami,
FL 33160
Tel: (305) 931-4476

Quickie Auction House,
Route 3, Osseo, MN 55369
Tel: (612) 428-4378

R & S Estate Liquidations,
Box 205, Newton Center,
MA 02159
Tel: (617) 244-6616

C Gilbert Richards,
Garrison, NY 10524
Tel: (914) 424-3657

Bill Rinaldi Auctions,
Bedell Road, Poughkeepsie,
NY 12601
Tel: (914) 454-9613

Roan Inc,
Box 118, RD 3, Logan Station,
PA 17728
Tel: (717) 494-0170

Rockland Auction Services Inc,
72 Pomona Road, Suffern,
NY 10901
Tel: (914) 354-3914/2723

Rome Auction Gallery (Sandra A
Louis Caropreso),
Route 2, Highway 53, Rome,
GA 30161

Rose Galleries Inc,
1123 West County Road B,
Roseville, MN 55113
Tel: (612) 484-1415

Rosvall Auction Company,
1238 & 1248 South Broadway,
Denver, CO 80210
Tel: (303) 777-2032/722-4028

Sigmund Rothschild,
27 West 67th Street, New York,
NY 10023
Tel: (212) 873-5522

Vince Runowich Auctions,
2312 4th Street North, St
Petersburg, FL 33704
Tel: (813) 895-3548

Safran's Antique Galleries Ltd,
930 Gervais Street, Columbia,
SC 29201
Tel: (803) 252-7927

Sage Auction Gallery,
Route 9A, Chester, CT 06412
Tel: (203) 526-3036

San Antonio Auction Gallery,
5096 Bianco, San Antonio,
TX 78216
Tel: (512) 342-3800

Emory Sanders,
New London, NH 03257
Tel: (603) 526-6326

Sandwich Auction House,
15 Tupper Road, Sandwich,
MA 02563
Tel: (617) 888-1926/5675

San Francisco Auction Gallery,
1217 Sutter Street, San Francisco,
CA 94109
Tel: (415) 441-3800

Schafer Auction Gallery,
82 Bradley Road, Madison,
CT 06443
Tel: (203) 245-4173

Schmidt's Antiques,
5138 West Michigan Avenue,
Ypsilanti, MI 48 197
Tel:.(313) 434-2660

K C Self,
53 Victory Lane, Los Angeles,
CA 95030
Tel: (213) 354-4238

B J Selkirk & Sons,
4166 Olive Street, St Louis,
MO 63108
Tel: (314) 533-1700

Shore Galleries Inc,
3318 West Devon, Lincolnwood,
IL 60659
Tel: (312) 676-2900

Shute's Auction Gallery,
70 Accord Park Drive, Norwell,
MA 02061
Tel: (617) 871-3414/238-0586

Ronald Siefert,
RFD, Buskirk, NY 12028
Tel: (518) 686-9375

Robert A Siegel Auction Galleries
Inc,
120 East 56th Street, New York,
NY 10022
Tel: (212) 753-6421/2/3

Robert W Skinner Inc,
Main Street, Bolton, MA 01740
Tel: (617) 779-5528

585 Boylston Street,
Boston, MA 02116
Tel: (617) 236-1700

C G Sloan & Co,
715 13th Street NW, Washington,
DC 20005
Tel: (202) 628-1468

Branch Office:
403 North Charles Street,
Baltimore, MD 21201
Tel: (301) 547-1177

Sotheby,
101 Newbury Street, Boston,
MA 02116
Tel: (617) 247-2851

Sotheby Park Bernet Inc,
980 Madison Avenue, New York,
NY 10021
Tel: (212) 472-3400

1334 York Avenue, New York,
NY 10021

171 East 84th Street, New York,
NY 10028

Mid-Atlantic:
1630 Locust Street, Philadelphia,
PA 19103
Tel: (215) 735-7886

Washington:
2903 M Street NW, Washington,
DC 20007
Tel: (202) 298-8400

Southeast:
155 Worth Avenue, Palm Beach,
FL 33480
Tel: (305) 658-3555

Midwest:
700 North Michigan Avenue,
Chicago, IL 60611
Tel: (312) 280-0185

Southwest:
Galleria Post Oak,
5015 Westheimer Road, Houston,
TX 77056
Tel: (713) 623-0010

Northwest:
210 Post Street, San Francisco,
CA 94108
Tel: (415) 986-4982

Pacific Area:
Suite 117, 850 West Hind Drive,
Honolulu, Hawaii 96821
Tel: (808) 373-9166

Stack's Rare Coin Auctions,
123 West 57th Street, New York,
NY 10019
Tel: (212) 583-2580

Stalker and Boos Inc,
280 North Woodward Avenue,
Birmingham, MI 48011
Tel: (313) 646-4560

Sterling Auction Gallery,
62 North Second Avenue, Raritan,
NJ 08869
Tel: (201) 685-9565/464-4047

Stremmel Auctions Inc,
2152 Prater Way, Sparks,
NV 89431
Tel: (702) 331-1035

Summit Auction Rooms,
47-49 Summit Avenue, Summit,
NJ 07901

Superior Stamp & Coin Co Inc,
9301 Wiltshire Boulevard,
Beverly Hills, CA 90210
Tel: (213) 272-0851/278-9740

Swann Galleries Inc,
104 East 26th Street, New York,
NY 10021
Tel: (212) 254-4710

Philip Swedler & Son,
850 Grand Avenue, New Haven,
CT 06511
Tel: (203) 624-2202/562-5065

Tait Auction Studio,
1209 Howard Avenue,
Burlingame, CA 94010
Tel: (415) 343-4793

Tepper Galleries,
110 East 25th Street, New York,
NY 10010
Tel: (212) 677-5300/1/2

Louis Trailman Auction Co,
1519 Spruce Street, Philadelphia,
PA 19102
Tel: (215) K1 5 4500

Trend Galleries Inc,
2784 Merrick Road, Bellmore,
NY 11710
Tel: (516) 221-5588

Trosby Auction Galleries,
81 Peachtree Park Drive, Atlanta,
GA 30326
Tel: (404) 351-4400

Valle-McLeod Gallery,
3303 Kirby Drive, Houston,
TX 77098
Tel: (713) 523-8309/8310

The Watnot Auction,
Box 78, Mellenville, NY 12544
Tel: (518) 672-7576

Adam A Wechsler & Son,
905-9 East Street NW,
Washington, DC 20004
Tel: (202) 628-1281

White Plains Auction Rooms,
572 North Broadway, White
Plains, NY 10603
Tel: (914) 428-2255

Henry Willis,
22 Main Street, Marshfield,
MA 02050
Tel: (617) 834 7774

The Wilson Galleries,
PO Box 102, Ford Defiance,
VA 24437
Tel: (703) 885-4292

Helen Winter Associates,
355 Farmington Avenue,
Plainville, CT 06062
Tel: (203) 747-0714/677-0848

Richard Withington Inc,
Hillsboro, NH 03244
Tel: (603) 464-3232

Wolf,
13015 Larchmere Boulevard,
Shaker Heights, OH 44120
Tel: (216) 231-3888

Richard Wolffers Inc,
127 Kearney Street, San
Francisco, CA 94 108
Tel: (415) 781-5127

Young,
56 Market Street, Portsmouth,
NH 03801
Tel: (603) 436-8773

Samuel Yudkin & Associates,
1125 King Street, Alexandria,
VA 22314
Tel: (703) 549-9330

Australia

ASA Stamps Co Pty Ltd,
138-140 Rundle Mall, National
Bank Building, Adelaide, South
Australia 5001
Tel: 223-2951

Associated Auctioneers Pty Ltd,
800-810 Parramatta Road,
Lewisham, New South Wales 2049
Tel: 560-5899

G J Brain Auctioneers Pty Ltd,
122 Harrington Street, Sydney,
New South Wales 2000
Tel: 271701

Bright Slater Pty Ltd,
Box 205 GPO, Lower Ground
Floor, Brisbane Club Building,
Isles Lane, Brisbane, Queensland
4000
Tel: 312415

Christie, Manson & Woods
(Australia) Ltd,
298 New South Head Road, Double
Bay, Sydney, New South Wales
2028
Tel: 326-1422

William S Ellenden Pty Ltd,
67-73 Wentworth Avenue,
Sydney, New South Wales 2000
Tel: 211-4035/211-4477

Bruce Granger Auctions,
10 Hopetoun Street, Huristone
Park, New South Wales 2193
Tel: 559-4767

Johnson Bros Auctioneers & Real
Estate Agents,
328 Main Road, Glenorchy,
Tasmania 7011
Tel: 725166 492909

James A Johnson & Co,
92 Boronia Road, Vermont,
Victoria 3133
Tel: 877-2754/874-3632

Jolly Barry Pty Ltd,
212 Glenmore Road, Paddington,
New South Wales 2021
Tel: 357-4494

James R Lawson Pty Ltd,
236 Castlereagh Street, Sydney,
New South Wales
Tel: 266408

Mason Greene & Associates,
91-101 Leveson Street, North
Melbourne, Victoria 3051
Tel: 329-9911

Mercantile Art Auctions,
317 Pacific Highway, North Sydney,
New South Wales 2060
Tel: 922-3610/922-3608

James R Newall Auctions Pty Ltd,
164 Military Road, Neutral Bay,
New South Wales 2089
Tel: 903023/902587 (Sydney ex)

P L Pickles & Co Pty Ltd
655 Pacific Highway, Killara, New
South Wales 2071
Tel: 498-8069/498-2775

Sotheby Parke Bernet Group Ltd,
115 Collins Street, Melbourne,
Victoria 3000
Tel: (03) 63 39 00

H E Wells & Sons,
326 Rokeby Road, Subiaco, West
Australia
Tel: 3819448/3819040

Young Family Estates Pty Ltd,
229 Camberwell Road, East
Hawthorn, Melbourne 2123
Tel: 821433

New Zealand

Devereaux & Culley Ltd,
200 Dominion Road, Mt Eden,
Auckland
Tel: 687429/687112

Alex Harris Ltd,
PO Box 510, 377 Princes Street,
Dunedin
Tel: 773955/740703

Roger Moat Ltd,
College Hill and Beaumont Street,
Auckland
Tel: 37 1588/37 1686/37 1595

New Zealand Stamp Auctions,
PO Box 3496, Queen and
Wyndham Streets, Auckland
Tel: 375490/375498

Alistair Robb Coin Auctions,
La Aitken Street, Box 3705,
Wellington
Tel: 727-141

Dunbar Sloane Ltd,
32 Waring Taylor Street,
Wellington
Tel: 721-367

Thornton Auctions Ltd,
89 Albert Street, Auckland 1
Tel: 30888 (3 lines)

Daniel J Visser,
109 and 90 Worchester Street,
Christchurch
Tel: 68853/67297

Austria

Christie's,
Ziehrerplatz 4/22, A-1030 Vienna
Tel: (0222) 73 26 44

Belgium

Christie, Manson & Woods
(Belgium) Ltd,
33 Boulevard de Waterloo, B-1000
Brussels
Tel: (02) 512-8765/512-8830

Sotheby Parke Bernet Belgium,
Rue de l'Abbaye 32, 1050 Brussels
Tel: 343 50 07

Canada

A-1 Auctioneer Evaluation
Services Ltd,
PO Box 926, Saint John,
NB E2L 4C3
Tel: (508) 762-0559

Appleton Auctioneers Ltd,
1238 Seymour Street, Vancouver,
BC V6B 3N9
Tel: (604) 685-1715

Ashton Auction Service,
PO Box 500, Ashton, Ontario,
KOA 180
Tel: (613) 257-1575

Canada Book Auctions,
35 Front Street East, Toronto,
Ontario M5E 1B3
Tel: (416) 368-4326

Christie's International Ltd,
Suite 2002, 1055 West Georgia
Street, Vancouver, BC V6E 3P3
Tel: (604) 685-2126

Miller & Johnson Auctioneers Ltd,
2882 Gottingen Street, Halifax,
Nova Scotia B3K 3E2
Tel: (902) 425-3366/425-3606

Phillips Ward-Price Ltd,
76 Davenport Road, Toronto,
Ontario M5R 1H3
Tel: (416) 923-9876

Sotheby Parke Bernet (Canada)
Inc,
156 Front Street, Toronto, Ontario
M5J 2L6
Tel: (416) 596-0300

Representative:
David Brown,
2321 Granville Street, Vancouver,
BC V6H 3G4
Tel: (604) 736-6363

Denmark

Kunsthallens,
Kunstauktioner A/S,
Købmagergade 11 DK 1150
Copenhagen
Tel: (01) 13 85 69

Nellemann & Thomsen,
Neilgade 45, DK-8000 Aarhus
Tel: (06) 12 06 66/12 00 02

France

Ader, Picard, Tajan,
12 rue Favart, 75002 Paris
Tel: 261.80.07

Artus,
15 rue de la Grange-Batelière,
75009 Paris
Tel: 523.12.03

Audap,
32 rue Drouot, 75009 Paris
Tel: 742.78.01

Bondu,
17 rue Drouot, 75009 Paris
Tel: 770.36.16

Boscher, Gossart,
3 rue d'Amboise, 75009 Paris
Tel: 260.87.87

Briest,
15 rue Drouot, 75009 Paris
Tel: 770.66.29

de Cagny,
4 rue Drouot, 75009 Paris
Tel: 246.00.07

Charbonneaux,
134 rue du Faubourg Saint-
Honoré, 75008 Paris
Tel: 359.66.57

Chayette,
10 rue Rossini, 75009 Paris
Tel: 770.38.89

Delaporte, Rieunier,
159 rue Montmartre, 75002 Paris
Tel: 508.41.83

Delorme,
3 rue Penthièvre, 75008 Paris
Tel: 265.57.63

Godeau,
32 rue Drouot, 75009 Paris
Tel: 770.67.68

Gros,
22 rue Drouot, 75009 Paris
Tel: 770.83.04

Langlade,
12 rue Descombes, 75017 Paris
Tel: 227.00.91

Loudmer, Poulain,
73 rue de Faubourg Saint-Honoré,
75008 Paris
Tel: 266.90.01

Maignan,
6 rue de la Michodière, 75002 Paris
Tel: 742.71.52

Maringe,
16 rue de Provence, 75009 Paris
Tel: 770.61.15

Marlio,
7 rue Ernest-Renan, 75015 Paris
Tel: 734.81.13

Paul Martin & Jacques Martin,
3 impasse des Chevau-Legers,
78000 Versailles
Tel: 950.58.08

Bonhams, Baron Foran,
Duc de Saint-Bar, 2 rue Bellanger,
92200 Neuilly sur Seine
Tel: (1) 637-1329

Christie's, Princess Jeanne-Marie
de Broglie,
17 rue de Lille, 75007 Paris
Tel: (331) 261-1247

Sotheby's, Rear Admiral J A
Templeton-Cotill, CB,
3 rue de Miromesnil, 75008 Paris
Tel: (1) 266-4060

Monaco

Sotheby Parke Bernet Group,
PO Box 45, Sporting d'Hiver, Place
du Casino, Monte Carlo
Tel: (93) 30 88 80

Hong Kong

Sotheby Parke Bernet (Hong
Kong) Ltd,
PO Box 83, 705 Lane Crawford
House, 64-70 Queen's Road
Central, Hong Kong
Tel: 22-5454

Italy

Christie's (International) SA,
Palazzo Massimo Lancellotti,
Piazza Navona 114, 00186 Rome
Tel: 6541217

Christie's (Italy) SR1,
9 Via Borgogna, 20144 Milan
Tel: 794712

Finarte SPA,
Piazzetta Bossi 4, 20121 Milan
Tel: 877041

Finarte SPA,
Via delle Quattro, Fontane 20,
Rome
Tel: 463564

Palazzo International delle Aste ed
Esposizioni SPA,
Palazzo Corsini, Il Prato 56,
Florence
Tel: 293000

Sotheby Parke Bernet Italia,
26 Via Gino Capponi, 50121
Florence
Tel: 571410

Sotheby Parke Bernet Italia,
Via Montenapoleone 3, 20121
Milan
Tel: 783907

Sotheby Parke Bernet Italia,
Palazzo Taverna, Via di Monte
Giordano 36, 00186 Rome
Tel: 656 1670/6547400

The Netherlands

Christie, Manson & Woods Ltd,
Rokin 91, 1012 KL Amsterdam
Tel: (020) 23 15 05

Sotheby Mak Van Waay BV,
102 Rokin 1012, KZ Amsterdam
Tel: 24 62 15

Van Dieten Stamp Auctions BV,
2 Tournooiveld, 2511 CX The
Hague
Tel: 70-464312/70-648658

Singapore & Malaysia

Victor & Morris Pte Ltd,
39 Talok Ayer Street, Republic of
Singapore
Tel: 94844

South Africa

Ashbey's Galleries,
43-47 Church Street, Cape Town
8001
Tel: 22-7527

Claremart Auction Centre,
47 Main Road, Claremont, Cape
Town 7700
Tel: 66-8826/66-8804

Ford & Van Niekerk Pty Ltd
156 Main Road, PO Box 8,
Plumstead, Cape Town
Tel: 71-3384

Sotheby Parke Bernet South
Africa Pty Ltd,
Total House, Smit and Rissik
Streets, PO Box 310010,
Braamfontein 2017
Tel: 39-3726

Spain

Juan R Cayon,
41 Fuencarral, Madrid 14
Tel: 221 08 32/221 43 72/222 95 98

Christie's International Ltd,
Casado del Alisal 5, Madrid
Tel: (01) 228-9300

Sotheby Parke Bernet & Co,
Scursal de Espana, Calle del
Prado 18, Madrid 14
Tel: 232-6488/232-6572

Switzerland

Daniel Beney,
Avenue des Mousquines 2,
CH-1005 Lausanne
Tel: (021) 22 28 64

Blanc,
Arcade Hotel Beau-Rivage, Box
84, CH-1001 Lausanne
Tel: (021) 27 32 55/26 86 20

Christie's (International) SA,
8 Place de la Taconnerie, CH-1204
Geneva
Tel: (022) 28 25 44

Steinwiesplatz,
CH-8032 Zurich
Tel: (01) 69 05 05

Auktionshaus Doblaschofsky AG,
Monbijoustrasse 28/30, CH-3001
Berne
Tel: (031) 25 23 72/73/74

Galerie Fischer,
Haldenstrasse 19, CH-6006
Lucerne
Tel: (041) 22 57 72/73

Germann Auktionshaus,
Zeitweg 67, CH-8032 Zurich
Tel: (01) 32 83 58/32 01 12

Haus der Bücher AG,
Baumleingasse 18, CH-4051 Basel
Tel: (061) 23 30 88

Adolph Hess AG,
Haldenstrasse 5, CH-6006 Lucerne
Tel: (041) 22 43 92/22 45 35

Auktionshaus Peter Ineichen,
CF Meyerstrasse 14, CH-8002
Zurich
Tel: (01) 201-3017

Galerie Koller AG,
Ramistrasse 8, CH-8001 Zurich
Tel: (01) 47 50 40

Koller St Gallen,
St Gallen
Tel: (071) 23 42 40

Kornfeld & Co,
Laupenstrasse 49, CH-3008 Berne
Tel: (031) 25 46 73

Phillips Son & Neale SA,
6 Rue de la Cité, CH-1204 Geneva
Tel: (022) 28 68 28

Christian Rosset,
Salle des Ventes, 29 Rue du Rhone,
CH-1204 Geneva
Tel: (022) 28 96 33/34

Schweizerische Gesellschaft der
Freunde von Kunstauktionen,
11 Werdmühlestrasse, CH-8001
Zurich
Tel: (01) 211-4789

Sotheby Parke Bernet AG,
20 Bleicherweg, CH-8022 Zurich
Tel: (01) 202-0011

24 Rue de la Cité, CH-1024 Geneva
Tel: (022) 21 33 77

Dr Erich Steinfels, Auktionen,
Rämistrasse 6, CH-8001 Zurich
Tel: (01) 252-1233 (wine) &
(01) 34 1233 (fine art)

Frank Sternberg,
Bahnhofstrasse 84, CH-8001
Zurich
Tel: (01) 211-7980

Jürg Stucker Gallery Ltd,
Alter Aargauerstalden 30,
CH-3006 Berne
Tel: (031) 44 00 44

Uto Auktions AG,
Lavaterstrasse 11, CH-8027
Zurich
Tel: (01) 202-9444

West Germany

Galerie Gerda Bassenge,
Erdener Strasses 5a, D-1000 West
Berlin 33
Tel: (030) 892 19 32/891 29 09

Kunstauktionen Waltraud Boltz,
Bahnhof Strasse 25-27, D-8580
Bayreuth
Tel: (0921) 206 16

Brandes,
Wolfenbütteler Strasse 12, D-3300
Braunschweig 1
Tel: (0531) 737 32

Gernot Dorau,
Johann-Georg Strasse 2, D-1000
Berlin 31
Tel: (030) 892 61 98

F Dörling,
Neuer Wall 40-41, D-2000
Hamburg 36
Tel: (040) 36 46 70/36 52 82

Roland A Exner,
Kunsthandel-Auktionen,
Am Ihmeufer, D-3000
Hannover 91
Tel: (0511) 44 44 84

Hartung & Karl,
Karolinenplatz 5a, D-8000
Munich 2
Tel: (089) 28 40 34

Hauswedell & Nolte,
Pöseldorfer Weg 1, D-2000
Hamburg 13
Tel: (040) 44 83 66

Karl & Faber,
Amiraplatz 3 (Luitpoldblock),
D-8000 Munich 2
Tel: (089) 22 18 65/66

Graf Klenau Ohg Nachf,
Maximilian Strasse 32, D-8000
Munich 1
Tel: (089) 22 22 81/82

Numismatik Lanz München,
Promenadeplatz 9, D-8000
Munich 2
Tel: (089) 29 90 70

Kunsthaus Lempertz,
Neumarkt 3, D-5000 Cologne 1
Tel: (0221) 21 02 51/52

Stuttgarter Kunstauktionshaus,
Dr Fritz Nagel,
Mörikestrasse 17-19, D-7000
Stuttgart 1
Tel: (0711) 61 33 87/77

Neumeister Münchener
Kunstauktionshaus KG,
Barer Strasse 37, D-8000
Munich 40
Tel: (089) 28 30 11

Petzold KG- Photographica,
Maximilian Strasse 36, D-8900
Augsburg 11
Tel: (0821) 3 37 25

Reiss & Auvermann,
Zum Talblick 2, D-6246
Glashütten im Taunus 1
Tel: (06174) 69 47/48

Gus Schiele Auktions-Galerie,
Ottostrasse 7 (Neuer Kunstblock),
D-8000 Munich 2
Tel: (089) 59 41 92

Galerie,
Paulinen Strasse 47, D-7000
Stuttgart 1
Tel: (0711) 61 63 77

J A Stargardt,
Universitäts Strasse 27, D-3550
Marburg
Tel: (06421) 234 52

Auktionshaus Tietjen & Co,
Spitaler Strasse 30, D-2000
Hamburg 1
Tel: (040) 33 03 68/69

Aachener Auktionshaus, Crott &
Schmelzer,
Pont Strasse 21, Aachen
Tel: (0241) 369 00

Kunstauktionen Rainer
Baumann,
Obere Woerthstrasse 7-11,
Nuremburg
Tel: (0911) 20 48 47

August Bödiger oHG,
Oxford Strasse 4, Bonn
Tel: (0228) 63 69 40

Bolland & Marotz,
Feldören 19, Bremen
Tel: (0421) 32 18 11

Bongartz Gelgen Auktionen,
Münsterplatz 27, Aachen
Tel: (0241) 206 19

Christie's International Ltd,
Düsseldorf:
Alt Pempelfort 11a, D-4000
Düsseldorf
Tel: (0211) 35 05 77

Hamburg:
Wenzelstrasse 21, D-2000
Hamburg 60
Tel: (4940) 279-0866

Munich:
Maximilianstrasse 20, D-8000
Munich 22
Tel: (089) 22 95 39

Württemberg:
Schloss Langenburg, D-7183
Langenburg

Sotheby Parke Bernet GmbH,
Munich:
Odeonsplatz 16, D-8000 Munich 22
Tel: (089) 22 23 75/6

Kunstauktion Jürgen Fischer,
Alexander Strasse 11, Heilbronn
Tel: (07 131) 785 23

Galerie Göbig,
Ritterhaus Strasse 5 (am
Thermalbad ad Nauheim)
Tel: (Frankfurt) (611) 77 40 80

Knut Günther,
Auf der Körmerwiese 19-21,
Frankfurt
Tel: (611) 55 32 92/55 70 22

Antiquitaeten Lothar Heubel,
Odenthaler Strasse 371, Cologne
Tel: (0221) 60 18 25

Hildener Auktionshaus und
Kunstgalerie,
Klusenhof 12, Hilden
Tel: (02103) 602 00

INDEX

696